Kuan-yin

The Chinese Transformation of Avalokiteśvara

THE INSTITUTE FOR ADVANCED STUDIES OF WORLD RELIGIONS

An Institute for Advanced Studies of World Religions book, sponsored by the Columbia University Committee on Asia and the Middle East

IASWR Series

Avatāra: The Humanization of Philosophy Through the Bhagavad Gītā,
Antonio T. de Nicolás (Nicolas Hays, Ltd.)

A Buddhist Leader in Ming China: The Life and Thought of Han-Shan Te-Ch'ing,
by Sung-peng Hsu (The Pennsylvania State University Press)

Buddhist Monastic Discipline: The Sanskrit Prātimokṣa Sūtras of the Mahāsāṃghikas and Mūlasarvāstivādins,
Charles S. Prebish (The Pennsylvania State University Press)

Hua-yen Buddhism: The Jewel Net of Indra,
Francis H. Cook (The Pennsylvania State University Press)

The Holy Teaching of Vimalakīrti: A Mahāyāna Scripture,
translated by Robert A. F. Thurman
(The Pennsylvania State University Press)

The Renewal of Buddhism in China: Chu-hung and the Late Ming Synthesis,
Chün-fang Yü (Columbia University Press)

Scripture of the Lotus Blossom of the Fine Dharma: The Lotus Sūtra,
translated by Leon Hurvitz (Columbia University Press)

Sūtra of the Past Vows of Earth Store Bodhisattva: The Collected Lectures of Tripiṭaka Master Hsüan Hua,
translated by Bhikṣu Heng Ching
(The Buddhist Text Translation Society and the Sino-American Buddhist Association)

The Syncretic Religion of Lin Chao-en,
Judith A. Berling (Columbia University Press)

A Treasury of Mahāyāna Sūtras: Selections from the Mahāratnakūta Sūtra,
translated by The Buddhist Association of the United States,
Garma C. C. Chang, General Editor
(The Pennsylvania State University Press)

觀 *Kuan-yin* 音

THE CHINESE TRANSFORMATION OF AVALOKITEŚVARA

Chün-fang Yü

COLUMBIA UNIVERSITY PRESS

NEW YORK

Columbia University Press
Publishers Since 1893
New York   Chichester, West Sussex

Library of Congress Cataloging-in-Publication Data
Yü, Chün-fang, 1938—
Kuan-yin : the Chinese transformation of Avalokiteśvara / Chün-fang Yü.
p. cm.
Includes bibliographical references and index.
ISBN 0–231–12028–1 (cloth : alk. paper) — ISBN 0–231–12029–X (pbk. : alk. paper)
1. Avalokiteśvara (Buddhist deity) I. Title II. Series. III. Series: Institute for Advanced Studies of World Religions. IASWR series

BQ4710.A8 Y8 2000
294.3′4211—dc21   00–024015

Casebound editions of Columbia University Press books are printed on permanent and durable acid-free paper.

Printed in the United States of America

c 10 9 8 7 6 5 4 3 2 1
p 10 9 8 7 6 5 4 3 2

Credits: Portions of chapters 6 and 10 appeared as "Guanyin: The Chinese Transformation of Avalokiteshvara," in Marsha Weidner, ed., *Latter Days of the Law: Images of Chinese Buddhism, 850–1850* (Lawrence, Kan.: Spencer Museum of Art and the University of Kansas in Association with the University of Hawaii Press, 1994), 151–81.

A section of chapter 8 was used in "The Cult of Kuan-yin in Ming-Ch'ing China: A Case of Confucianization of Buddhism?" in Irene Bloom and Joshua Vogel, eds., *Meeting of the Minds* (New York: Columbia University Press, 1997), 144–74.

An earlier version of chapter 9 appeared as "P'u-t'o Shan: Pilgrimage and the Creation of Chinese Potolaka," in Susan Naquin and Chün-fang Yü, eds., *Pilgrims and Sacred Places in China* (Berkeley: University of California Press, 1992), 190–245.

An earlier version of Appendix A will appear in Susan Mann and Yu-ying Cheng, eds., *Under Confucian Eyes* (Berkeley: University of California Press, forthcoming).

A portion of Appendix B appeared as "Chinese Women Pilgrims' Songs Glorifying Guanyin," in Donald S. Lopez, Jr., ed. (Princeton: Princeton University Press, 1995), 179–80.

To Chi-chen Wang (1911–),
my mother and also my first teacher

獻 給

我的母親——也是我的啟蒙老師

Contents

CONTENTS

Preface

This book has taken me a long time to write. Many individuals, institutions, and funding agencies have helped me in my intellectual and physical journeys in carrying out the research necessary for this book. Before I thank them and acknowledge my indebtedness and gratitude, I would like to say a few words about why I decided to undertake this project in the first place, for this is a question that I have been asked many times over the years. The importance of Kuan-yin in Chinese and indeed East Asian Buddhism is obvious to anyone familiar with these cultures and, with the increasing interest in New Age spirituality since the 1970s, even modern Americans have come to know her name. Despite the great fame of Kuan-yin, however, there have been surprisingly few comprehensive studies on this bodhisattva. Japanese and Western scholarly works have tended to concentrate on certain art historical or textual aspects.

My interest in Kuan-yin comes from my maternal grandmother. Growing up in China during World War II, I moved with my family a great deal, from north to central China, and finally to the western provinces. Like most Chinese families in those years of great turmoil and deprivation, children shared bedrooms with parents and sometimes with grandparents. I always slept in the same room with my maternal grandmother, who was a devout Buddhist. She was usually the first person in the household to get up each morning. After her morning toiletries, her day began with offering incense to the white porcelain statue of Kuan-yin holding a baby, chanting the Great Compassion Dhāraṇī, and reciting her personal prayers. Sometimes she would talk to Kuan-yin about matters worrying her. Kuan-yin was indeed the "Goddess of Mercy" to my grandmother, who regarded her as both savior and confidant. Although my grandmother had not received a formal education, she knew many traditional legends by heart and daily delighted (and frightened) us by telling stories about gods, goddesses, ghosts, and the underworld. It was she who first told me the story of Princess Miao-shan when I was about five. She also introduced me to the living world of miracles when I was eight.

This happened in the predawn hours by the banks of the Yangtze River in Wuhan, after the war had ended. We had been waiting for three months in order to secure seats in a boat that would take us back home. Finally, our chance came and the whole family was camped by the riverbank, waiting to get on board. Suddenly my grandmother insisted that we not board the ship because she had a vision of Kuan-yin standing in the middle of the river and gesturing with her right hand for my grandmother to stay away. My grandmother immediately knew that Kuan-yin was telling her that the ship was not safe. My mother, a product of the May 4th Movement, a college graduate and history teacher, was at first reluctant to listen. But my grandmother was adamant and my mother eventually gave in. Soon after leaving port, the ship ran into mines planted by the retreating Japanese army. It sank. If we had been on board, what chance would we have had of surviving the shipwreck when none of us could swim and the children were so very young (my brother was five and sister two)? This question has haunted me ever since.

In the subsequent years of my life with my grandmother, lasting until I went off to college and her death at about that same time, I came to know Kuan-yin as she knew her. She loved to tell and retell the story of Princess Miao-shan and other miracles of Kuan-yin. I never asked her why she was so devoted to Kuan-yin, because I took it as a matter of course; it seemed to me that everyone worshiped Kuan-yin. But now when I think about it, the circumstances of my grandmother's life put her faith in Kuan-yin in a particularly poignant light. Married on the eve of the Boxer Rebellion (1900) when she was barely eighteen to a widower more than twice her age, she assumed the duties of a matriarch of a large and complex joint family, bore two daughters and then became a widow at the age of thirty. Deprived of her inheritance by her brothers-in-law and the sons of the first wife, she lamented her bitter fate for failing to bear a son. Marriage could not have been a pleasant experience for her. My grandmother's prayer to Kuan-yin for a male heir was eventually answered when my mother gave birth to my younger brother, on whom my grandmother doted.

So, like most Chinese people, my idea of Kuan-yin was basically similar to that of my grandmother. Imagine my surprise when I first came across Avalokiteśvara (the Sanskrit version of Kuan-yin) in my classes at Columbia University. Not only was this bodhisattva most assuredly not a goddess, but there was no mention of Princess Miao-shan anywhere. In fact, there is very little narrative in the scriptures about this bodhisattva. How and why Avalokiteśvara was transformed into Kuan-yin assumed a compelling personal as well as intellectual urgency for me, although I soon realized that I could not easily find the answer to this puzzle. I had to prepare, and learn many things I did not know. Other writings and projects occupied me in the meantime.

My formal study of Kuan-yin began in the summer of 1983, when I went back to China for the first time since my family had left for Taiwan in 1949. Through the graces of Mr. Chao P'u-chu (Zhao Puchu), president of the Chinese Buddhist Association and Professor Jen Chi-yü (Ren Jiyu), director of the Institute of World Religions at the Chinese Academy of Social Sciences (CASS), I was able to visit several major temples and pilgrimage sites that are central to Kuan-yin worship, including P'u-t'o Island, as well as study archival material in major libraries in Beijing. A fellowship from the American Council of Learned Societies in 1985-86 and another grant from the National Science Foundation administered by the Committee on Scholarly Communication with China in 1986-87 made it possible for me to take leave from teaching and carry out fieldwork in China. I want to thank Mr. Chou Shao-liang (Zhou Shaoliang), the Librarian of the Chinese Buddhist Library of Literature and Artifacts, located in Fa-yüan Ssu, who was most generous in making available materials, including those of his own private collection, for my use. Similarly, I want to thank the late Professor Wu Hsiao-ling (Wu Xiaoling) of the Institute of Literature, CASS, a leading authority on popular literature and drama, for generously sharing his personal collection of *pao-chüan* ("precious scrolls") with me. I was privileged to have had many illuminating conversations about Kuan-yin in Chinese drama, novels, and popular literature with him during the winter of 1986. Mr. Li Shi-yü (Li Shiyu), an authority on Chinese popular religion and precious scrolls, was another unfailing source of help and support in my early groping in this area. He also accompanied me during my fieldwork in Hangchow and P'u-t'o in the spring of 1987. Mr. Li taught me what to look for and how to see in the field. He showed me that conducting interviews with pilgrims could be an enjoyable experience by genuinely enjoying it himself. Like Professor Wu, he was equally generous about lending or even giving me materials essential for my research from his own collection. Without their help, I would not have been able to locate, much less read, the dozen precious scrolls about Kuan-yin.

There are two individuals in the United States whom I want to thank in particular for the completion of this project. One is Angela Howard and the other Susan Naquin. I was introduced to Angela by a mutual friend, Professor Wu Pei-yi, in 1985, and have been fortunate to have her as a colleague at Rutgers since 1990. Very early in my research I realized that a knowledge of Kuan-yin's iconography would be crucial to my understanding of the Chinese transformation of this bodhisattva, but unfortunately I had no training in art history. Angela came to my aid at this most critical point. For more than ten years, she has been my teacher and guide in Chinese Buddhist art. In the process, I have learned far more than the iconography of Kuan-yin, but without her help, it would have been impossible to take the first step in this direction. My friendship with Susan Naquin also dated to 1985, when we discovered that we shared a common interest in pilgrimage as a result of our separate researches. We decided to collaborate and organized a conference and later edited the book *Pilgrims and Sacred Sites in China.* Susan has been a constructive critic and a loyal friend over the years. She was always the first one on whom I would try my ideas and test my hypotheses. She has always challenged me to think more precisely and write more clearly. Even more importantly, it was due to her constant encouragement that I succeeded in banishing the tempting idea of giving up when I was periodically overwhelmed by the enormity of the task.

I have benefited from criticisms and comments from colleagues when I presented earlier drafts of several chapters in lectures, symposia, or conferences held at Columbia, Yale, Harvard, Chicago, Stanford, the University of Virginia, the University of Illinois, the University of Texas at Austin, Princeton, the University of Pennsylvania, and the Institute of Modern History of the Academia Sinica, Taipei. The list of acknowledgements is a long one, but I want to thank Patricia Berger, Suzanne Cahill, Robert Campany, Chih-wah Chan, Wm. Theodore deBary, Glen Dudbridge, Patricia Ebrey, Jan Fontein, Charlotte Furth, Robert Gimello, Peter Gregory, Barend ter Haar, Ping-chen Hsiung, Chi-chiang Huang, Matthew Kapstein, Paul Katz, Dorothy Ko, Kuo Li-ying, Lai Swee-fo, Ellen Johnston Laing, Yuet Keung Lo, Marc McWilliams, Victor Mair, Susan Mann, Nagatomi Masatoshi, John McRae, F. W. Mote, Hiroshi Obayashi, Reiko Ohnuma, Daniel Overmyer, Mu-chou Poo, Evelyn Rawski, Paul Schalow, Anna Seidel, Robert Sharf, the Rev. Sheng-yen, Conrad Shirakawer, Daniel Stevensen, Michel Strickmann, K'ang-i Chang Sun, Stephen Teiser, Wang Ch'iu-kuei, Marsha Weidner, Pei-yi Wu, and Anthony Yu for either sharing their own research, pointing out areas for further deliberation, or alerting me to new sources I might not otherwise have known about. Libraries and museums in the United States and abroad have been crucial for this study. I want to thank particularly Nelson Chou and Helena Fu of the East Asian Library at Rutgers, and Martin Heijdra of the Gest Library at Princeton for bibliographical assistance. I am grateful for the courtesy extended to me by responsible individuals at many museums, particularly Roderick Whitfield of the British Museum, Albert Lutz of the Rietburg Museum, Yevgeny Lubo-

Lesnitchenko and Maria Ptchelina of the Hermitage Museum in St. Petersburg, Li Yü-ming of the National Palace Museum in Taipei, Maxwell Hearn of the Metropolitan Museum of Art in New York, Teresa Bartholomew of the Asian Art Museum in San Francisco, Yang Hsiao-neng of the Atkin-Nelson Gallery in Kansas City, Elinor Pearlstein of the Fine Art Institute of Chicago and Jan Stuart of the Freer Gallery.

The writing of the book was supported by two more fellowships, one from the Pacific Cultural Foundation of Taiwan, and the other from the National Endowment for the Humanities, several smaller research grants from the Research Council of Rutgers University, as well as two sabbatical leaves from Rutgers. I have been very fortunate to receive so much assistance and support from all these individuals, institutions, and funding agencies. While taking full responsibility for whatever errors may remain in the book, I hope I have not completely failed to live up to the trust they have placed in me.

I would like to thank Jennifer Crewe, editorial director, and production editor Roy Thomas at Columbia University Press for shepherding the manuscript through to the finished book. Thanks also to Linda Gregonis, who did the copyediting, and to Anne Holmes, who did the glossary-index.

I would like to end on another personal note. My son David has lived with this book for almost half of his young life. Being the only child of a single, busy, academic parent, he was exposed to the tribulations of frequent moves connected with my research. I was therefore surprised and grateful that he chose to go with me to China in 1986 when he was fourteen, rather than stay in the United States. He was my fellow pilgrim as we traveled, following the traces of Kuan-yin. To his constant inquiry, "When are you going to finish the book?" I can now say, "It is done." Without his patience, this project would have been impossible, and without his delightful companionship, this task would have been unimaginable.

Kuan-yin

The Chinese Transformation of Avalokiteśvara

1

Introduction

Kuan-yin (Perceiver of Sounds), or Kuan-shih-yin (Perceiver of the World's Sounds) is the Chinese name for Avalokiteśvara, the Bodhisattva of Compassion, who has been worshiped throughout the Buddhist world. In 1976 C. N. Tay published a long article on Kuan-yin with the subtitle, "The Cult of Half Asia," because he dealt primarily with Chinese scriptural, literary, and historical references. A Chinese saying aptly describes the great popularity of this savior bodhisattva: "Everybody knows how to chant O-mi-t'o-fo [Amitābha], and every household worships Kuan-yin." Under Chinese influence, Japanese, Koreans, and Vietnamese have also used the same names (Kannon or Kanzeon in Japanese, Kwanse'um in Korean and Quan-am in Vietnamese). However, the cult of Avalokiteśvara is, of course, not limited to East Asia, but exists all throughout Asia.

The bodhisattva has also become well known in the United States and Europe, the combined result of feminism and the immigration of Buddhist teachers to the West. Although Buddhism was introduced to the United States in the nineteenth century (Fields 1986), political events in Asia since World War II greatly facilitated the religion's westward movement. When China became Communist in 1949, many Chinese monks escaped to Hong Kong, Taiwan, Singapore, and the United States. Similarly, while most Tibetan lamas escaped to India, some came to the United States when Tibet was occupied by China in 1959. With the end of the Vietnam War in 1975 and the arrival of new immigrants from Vietnam and other Southeast Asian countries since the 1980s, people in America have been exposed to many forms of Buddhism, as well as the different names and identities of the bodhisattva. Avalokiteśvara is present in all these Buddhist traditions. In addition, American feminist scholars have become interested in uncovering a goddess tradition—either in the West prior to the rise of patriarchal Christianity or in the deities of non-Western religious traditions.[1] In the latter case, Kuan-yin, together with Tārā, Kālī, and Durgā, are the favorite candidates for such citations. In light of these recent developments, Tay's claim made about Kuan-yin more than twenty years ago is far too modest.

The contemporary focus on Kuan-yin as a great "goddess" is understandable, for this is how most East Asians see her. I was also first introduced to this deity as such by my maternal grandmother, as I described in the preface. Many blanc de Chine porcelain statues of Kuan-yin made in the seventeenth and eighteenth centuries on display in museums (where many Westerners first encounter the deity) are also decidedly feminine. However, Avalokiteśvara has never been worshiped as a goddess in India, Tibet, Sri Lanka, or Southeast Asia. Nor indeed was Kuan-yin perceived to be feminine by the Chinese at first, for many paintings from Tun-huang dating to the tenth century clearly show him with moustaches.[2] The sexual transformation from the masculine Avalokiteśvara to the feminine Kuan-yin seems to be a unique Chinese phenomenon that deservedly has fascinated many scholars.

Despite my own initial obsession with this riddle, however, I have come to realize that this is not the only, albeit the most interesting, aspect of Avalokiteśvara worthy of our attention. Other characteristics of the bodhisattva are equally intriguing. For instance, why did Avalokiteśvara become so popular in the Buddhist world, whether countries were under the predominant influence of early Buddhism or the Mahāyāna and Vajrayāna Buddhist traditions? Bodhisattvas are beings dedicated to the salvation of everyone; in carrying out this noble task, they choose to become buddhas instead of seeking personal nirvāṇa as arhats do. As such, they form new cultic objects for Mahāyāna and Vajrayāna Buddhists, while the early Buddhists only worship the historical Buddha, and use "bodhisattva" to refer only to the Buddha's previous lives before his final enlightenment. Indeed, the early Buddhist belief in a very limited numbers of bodhisattvas, namely Śākyamuni Buddha in his previous existences and Maitreya, the Future Buddha, and the Mahāyāna belief in many bodhisattvas and the corresponding call for all people to give rise to *bodhicitta* (the thought for enlightenment spurring one onto the path of the bodhisattva) is one of the most significant differences between the two Buddhist traditions. If Avalokiteśvara is worshiped in all the Buddhist countries, what does this do to the received wisdom?

I can think of at least two reasons why the cult of Avalokiteśvara succeeded in taking root in so many countries in Asia. First of all, next to the Buddha,

Avalokiteśvara was one of the few bodhisattvas whose cult enjoyed a continuous popularity in India. From the early centuries of the Common Era until Buddhism disappeared from India in the twelfth century, Avalokiteśvara retained the devotion of the faithful. New texts and new artistic forms developed with time. Because India was the homeland of Buddhism, the prominence of Avalokiteśvara there resulted in his being welcomed and accepted into other Buddhist countries. The second reason for the bodhisattva's success outside of India was related to the very nature of Buddhism as a religion. Just as Buddhism coexisted with Vedic Brahmānism and Hinduism in India, it also did not try to replace the indigenous religions in the host countries where it was introduced. Called Lokeśvara (Lord of the World) in Cambodia, Vietnam, and Java; Lokanātha (Protector of the World) in Burma; Nātha Dēviyō in Sri Lanka; and Chenresi (*spyan-ras-gzigs,* "One Who Sees with Eyes") in Tibet, Avalokiteśvara might not be identified by the same name, but all the South, Southeast, and East Asian Buddhist cultures have known and worshiped this bodhisattva.

Although the bodhisattva is the embodiment of compassion, cultures have made different choices in representing him/her. China and countries having historical and cultural connections with her, such as Japan, Korea, and Vietnam identify Kuan-yin as the exemplar of wisdom for meditators and the "Goddess of Mercy," who is particularly kind to women, while in Sri Lanka, Tibet, and Southeast Asia, Avalokiteśvara has been very much identified with royalty (Boisselier 1965, 1970; Chutiwongs 1984; Holt 1991; Kapstein 1992; Monnika 1996). The deification of kings, creation of talismanic images of deities, and the belief in the images' empowerment of rulers were ideas prevalent in the Southeast Asian continent and archipelago. Stanley J. Tambiah (1982: 5–19) discusses such beliefs and the worship of both Hindu and Buddhist images in the Khmer kingdom of Cambodia, the Champa kingdom of Vietnam, and the kingdoms of Indonesia. For instance, King Bhavavarman II (r. mid-seventh century) of pre-Khmer period Cambodia took Lokeśvara or the Lord of the World as his personal deity and had the image made for worship. In the Champa kingdom of south Vietnam, the Indrapura kings (ca. 875–920 C.E.) were fervent devotees of Avalokiteśvara. King Indravarman II erected a temple in honor of the deity in 875 and named the building Śrī Lakṣmindralokeśvara, blending his own name with that of Avalokiteśvara (Howard 1996a:233).

All the Southeast Asian countries, with the exception of Burma, shared the ideology of the cult of the "divine king" (*devarāja*) in which the ruler was identified with a deity, Hindu or Buddhist. The most famous example is the construction of Angkor Wat, one of the largest stone temples in the world, during the twelfth and thirteenth centuries in Cambodia. The Angkor Wat was regarded as a dwelling place for deities including the divine kings. The pantheon is a mixture of Hindu and Buddhist deities and deified kings, exemplified by the Devarāja. The cult of Lokeśvara reached its zenith under Jayavarman VII (r. 1181–ca. 1218) who built the Bayon temple complex at the center of the royal city Angkor Thom. He made Buddhism the state religion. At the Bayon there are large towers bearing huge faces that are believed to be images of the deified king in the form of Lokeśvara. Not only the king was identified with the bodhisatt-va, but his first wife, Queen Jayavajadevi, might be represented posthumously by a statue usually identified as Tārā, the bodhisattva's attendant (Jessup and Zephir 1997:304; Bunnag 1984:161; Zwalf 1985:176).

bodhisattva [handwritten margin note]

Tara [handwritten margin note]

Similarly, Avalokiteśvara was worshiped as the guardian deity of the country by the Ceylonese rulers since the fifteenth century and the Javanese kings in the pre-Islamic thirteenth to fifteenth centuries. In Tibet, Avalokiteśvara is worshiped as the patron deity of the country, and the most famous ruler, King Srong-bstan sgam-po (d. 649) and the Dalai Lama are believed to be the incarnations of Avalokiteśvara. The Pai people in Yünnan who founded the Nan-chao and Ta-li kingdoms, corresponding to the Chinese T'ang (618–906) and Sung (960–1279) dynasties, held similar beliefs. Known as A-ts'o-yeh Kuan-yin, the bodhisattva was worshiped as the founding father of the country and guardian deity of the ruling house (Yü 1991; Howard 1996a). The Pai shared Avalokiteśvara's royal symbolism with the neighboring countries with whom they had active interaction. Indeed, as represented by later Mahāyāna and Vajrayāna sūtras, Avalokiteśvara is a cosmic figure, creator and savior of all beings and all worlds. The royal symbolism came quite naturally in a context with no pre-existing or competing symbolism.

It is clear that Kuan-yin did not have to become a goddess. Why then in China was the bodhisattva not connected with royalty? Was it because the Chinese royal ideology and symbolism were already established before the introduction of Buddhism and thus did not allow similar developments in China? The Chinese emperor received his legitimation through the Mandate of Heaven, which was first formulated in the Chou dynasty (1122–256 B.C.E.). He was the Son of Heaven and formed a triad with Heaven and Earth. All of these ideas were further refined in the Han dynasty (206 B.C.E.–220 C.E.). The Confucian ideology dominated the Chinese understanding of royalty throughout China's imperial history. Although periodically, individual rulers might use Buddhist ideas to legitimize their rules, their efforts were limited and did not last long. For instance, the Northern Wei emperor Wen-cheng (r. 453–465) had five Buddha caves carved at Yün-kang, each Buddha representing a prior emperor, thus symbolizing his desire to create a theocracy. The female Emperor Wu Tse-t'ien (r. 684–704) claimed to be Maitreya and Emperor Ch'ien-lung (cr. 1736–1765) Mañjuśrī Bodhisattva (Forte 1976; Farquhar 1978). But except for the case of the late nineteenth-century Ch'ing Empress Dowager Tz'u-hsi's dressing up as Kuan-yin for amusement and dramatic effect, I do not know of any ruling emperor who claimed to be the incarnation of Kuan-yin.

The idea of Kuan-yin—a compassionate universal savior who responds to anyone's cry for help regardless of class, gender, or even moral qualifications—was an idea unfamiliar to the Chinese. This was a new deity who not only could bring spiritual enlightenment, but also save one from worldly difficulties and grant one material satisfactions as well as a "good death" and postmortem salvation. No native god or goddess in China prior to the arrival of Kuan-yin possessed all these abilities. Moreover, although there were goddesses in China before the appearance of Kuan-yin, none of them seemed to have enjoyed lasting and continuously active cults. There was thus a religious vacuum in China that Kuan-yin could conveniently and comfortably fill.

In examining the reasons why the Chinese people accepted Buddhism during the Han, Eric Zürcher made the observation that, "In spite of occasional (and surprisingly rare) terminological borrowings from Confucian and Taoist lore, the most striking aspect of Han Buddhism is its novelty. The view that Buddhism was accepted because it, in certain ways, accorded with indigenous traditions must be rejected: Buddhism was attractive not because it sounded familiar, but because it was something basically new" (1991:291). What he says about Han Buddhism as the "exotic alternative" is equally applicable here. Chinese people became attracted to Kuan-yin not because he/she bore any resemblance to any indigenous deity, but precisely because none of them was like him/her. Once Kuan-yin was accepted, however, the bodhisattva, just like Buddhism in general, was perceived and understood in a way molded by Chinese culture. The Chinese transformation of Kuan-yin can be regarded as a case study for the Chinese transformation of Buddhism. A culture may be attracted by the exotic, but it cannot resist changing the strange to the familiar. In a sense, what Edward Said says about one culture's treatment of another is relevant here: "It is perfectly natural for the human mind to resist the assault on it of untreated strangeness; therefore cultures have always inclined to impose complete transformations on other cultures, receiving these other cultures not as they are but as, for the benefit of the receiver, they ought to be" (1978:67).

Buddhism thus supplied the necessary symbols and ideals to the host countries. In accommodating itself to the different religious and cultural traditions in the various Asian countries, new and different forms of Buddhism developed. In the case of Sino-Japanese Buddhism, the creation of T'ien-t'ai (Tendai), Hua-yen (Kegon), Pure Land (Jōdo), and Ch'an (Zen) schools is a prominent example. Although the Chinese based their main teachings and practices on some scriptures translated from Indic languages, the specific emphases and formulations reflected the native modes of thought and cultural values. Scholars of Chinese Buddhism call this process "sinification."[3]

I prefer the terms "transformation" or "domestication" to describe the same phenomenon. This is particularly fitting in the case of Avalokiteśvara, for this bodhisattva underwent many transformations by taking on different identities, assuming different appearances in art, and giving rise to different practices and rituals in a number of Asian countries aside from China. In the process, the bodhisattva became domesticated to serve the interests and needs of the host countries that adopted him/her. I thus use the term "domestication" in the same sense that other scholars do to the process by which Buddhism became adapted in cultural regions other than China.[4] While Avalokiteśvara is a great bodhisattva of universal appeal, he also assumed local characteristics. Similarly, as Kuan-yin came to be worshiped in China, she/he also became linked with specific places and developed local cults. The selective choices made by the host cultural traditions resulted in the bodhisattva's domestication.

I should explain why in this chapter I use both the masculine and feminine pronouns (she/he) when I refer to Kuan-yin. As we shall read in the following chapters, Kuan-yin was perceived as masculine and was so depicted in art prior to and during the T'ang (618–907). However, by the early Sung (960–1279), around the eleventh century, some devotees saw Kuan-yin as a female deity and new forms of feminine Kuan-yin images began to be created by Chinese artists. The feminine transformation of the bodhisattva probably reached its completion during the Yüan (1206–1368). Since the Ming, or the fifteenth century, Kuan-yin has generally been perceived and represented as completely feminine. However, even when Kuan-yin was so presented in literature and art, the orthodox Buddhist clergy has refused to acknowledge Kuan-yin as feminine. Images of Kuan-yin enshrined in Buddhist monasteries, even today, continue to be made according to the iconographic conventions established during the T'ang. One does not see the feminine White-robed Kuan-yin or the Fish-basket Kuan-yin, for instance, worshiped in the monastery as an icon. Iconic images of Kuan-yin in the temples continue to be masculine—or at most asexual—in appearance. Some individual artists of late imperial China also chose to paint Kuan-yin with moustaches, in the same way Kuan-yin was depicted at Tun-huang. For this reason, the inclusive she/he seems to be the best way of referring to Kuan-yin, for even after Kuan-yin became feminized, some people still regarded the bodhisattva as masculine.

In order to provide a comparative and theoretical framework for the cult of Kuan-yin in China, I now discuss what is known about Avalokiteśvara in India, followed by a sketch of the history of Buddhism in China. I then explain the methodology I used in this study and conclude with a brief description of each of the chapters of the book.

Avalokiteśvara in India

Although all Buddhists pay homage to and take refuge in the Three Treasures—Buddha, Dharma, and Saṃgha—they do not understand them the same way. One of the most distinctive features of the Mahāyāna tradition is its call for everyone to give rise to *bodhicitta* (the thought of enlightenment), and achieve enlightenment not just for oneself but for all living beings. This new aspiration is valued more highly than the earlier arhat ideal, which aims at entering nirvāṇa upon attaining enlightenment. The career of a bodhisattva is a very long and arduous one. After making vows, one trains oneself along the bodhisattva path by practicing virtues (with giving at the head of the list), mastering meditation, and penetrating into the wisdom of emptiness (which is understood as everything being devoid of self-nature). Because bodhisattvas vow to save everyone, they remain in the world and are always accessible. But only the bodhisattvas advanced in the path became objects of devotional cults for the faithful. Avalokiteśvara is one of the "celestial" or "cosmic bodhisattvas" called Great Beings (Mahāsattvas, *ta-shih*) of Mahāyāna Buddhism (Snellgrove 1986; Robinson and Johnson 1997; Basham 1981).[5] Like Maitreya and Mañjuśrī, he has reached the elevated tenth stage of the bodhisattva path. Regarded as the perfect embodiment of compassion, he became one of the most popular bodhisattvas in India. Developing alongside devotional Hinduism and competing with it, Mahāyāna sūtras such as the *Karaṇḍavyūha Sūtra,* composed during the fourth to seventh centuries (Winternitz 1927, 2:306–7), used cosmic symbolisms reminiscent of Śiva and Viṣṇu in describing Avalokiteśvara. The bodhisattva was venerated as a supreme deity in his own right.

Art historians and Buddhist scholars do not agree about the exact dates when the cult of Avalokiteśvara appeared in India. For example, both Marie-Therese de Mallmann (1948) and Gregory Schopen (1987) put the beginning of the cult in the fifth century. But Nandana Chutiwongs (1984) suggests that literary and iconic data show that Avalokiteśvara appeared in north and northwest India no later than the second century of the Common Era and by the fifth century he was already widely worshiped there.[6] The uncertainty about the beginning of the cult of Avalokiteśvara in India is a reflection of the ongoing debates about the origin and early history of Mahāyāna Buddhism. It is not clear when the earliest textual references to the bodhisattva appeared. There is a traditional consensus that he was first mentioned in the *Sukhāvatīvyūha Sūtra*, the *Mahāvastu*, the *Cheng-chü kuang-ming ting-i ching*, the *Druma-kinnara-rāja-paripṛcchā Sūtra*, the *Lotus Sūtra*, and the *Heart Sūtra*, all of which have long been believed to have been written before 300 C.E. But the dating of these works is now a subject of debate.[7]

Another factor that has influenced scholars to put the beginning of the cult of Avalokiteśvara no earlier than the fifth century is the lack of devotional narratives datable to an earlier period. As pointed out by Holt,

> In comparison with the massive number of icons found throughout Buddhist Asia and the manifold ways in which this bodhisattva was accorded great spiritual (and temporal) importance within respective Asian cultures historically, it is surprising to find that the amount of religious literature dedicated to the description of Avalokiteśvara is relatively limited. To be sure, many short Sanskrit tracts (now reconstructed from the Tibetan), mainly containing *dhāraṇīs* for the purpose of invoking the power of the bodhisattva to eradicate "sins" or to cure physical diseases, were composed for the benefit of his propitiation. But these texts contain few myths characterizing the bodhisattva's "personality" or "cultic character." The fact that so many images of Avalokiteśvara were created and yet the amount of narrative literature relative to his "character" and "history" is comparatively scant may indicate that while Avalokiteśvara is known to have attracted a number of Mahāyāna monastic devotees, particularly as an object of concentrated meditation, the great popularity of his cult among the laity occurred historically in a period later than the time in which most Mahāyāna literary traditions were becoming fixed. (1991:30)

Schopen uses epigraphical data from a fifth-century northern Indian Buddhist community at Mathurā to show that the emergence of Avalokiteśvara as a cultic figure was connected with "a decided drop in the number of lay donors—particularly women—and a corresponding rise in monk donors, by the sudden appearance of a specific group of monks who called themselves *śākyabhikṣus*, and by the appearance of a very specific and characteristic donative formula" (1987:116). This suggests that Avalokiteśvara was at first primarily worshiped by a special segment of the Saṃgh and only later by the monastic and lay population in general.

But because earlier images of Avalokiteśvara do not have inscriptions, nor do we have contemporary historical accounts describing the religious practices connected with the worship of the bodhisattva, it seems to me that it is difficult to conclude that he was not an object of devotion prior to the fifth century in regions other than Mathurā. For instance, an incomplete triad with Amitābha and Avalokiteśvara to his left was discovered in Taxila in 1961. It has a Kharoṣṭhī inscription. Based on the script of the inscription, John Brough (1982:70) dates the triad to the second century C.E. and suggests the missing figure Mahāsthāmaprāpta. Chutiwongs also points out that archaeological evidence provides strong proof that his images were first created in Gandhāra and Mathurā by the second century C.E. soon after the rise of Mahāyāna and the beginning of the making of Buddhist icons.

Even though the question of when Avalokiteśvara first appeared in Indian cultic life cannot be settled, all evidences confirm that by the fifth century, his presence was well attested by contemporary reports. The Chinese pilgrim Fa-hsien, who traveled to Mathurā in about 400 C.E., reported that the Mahāyāna monks worshiped Avalokiteśvara, together with Prajñā-pāramitā [Perfection of Wisdom] and Mañjuśrī by presenting offerings to their images (Legge 1965:46). By the time Hsüan-tsang traveled in the northwest during the years 630 to 645, the cult was firmly established and he provided eyewitness accounts of Avalokiteśvara images that responded to prayers of devotees from all walks of life, from kings to monastics and ordinary people.[8] As new texts and rituals developed, new Avalokiteśvara images were created in other parts of India. His popularity remained undiminished until the disappearance of Buddhism from its homeland.

I now describe briefly the different types of Avalokiteśvara images in Indian art and the main stages of the cult's development.[9] Such a sketch is necessary, I believe, for two reasons. First, unless we know something about the Indian forms of Avalokiteśvara, it is impossible to judge to what extent the Chinese Kuan-yin was a replica of an existing model or an original creation. The second and more crucial reason is that by such a survey one point will become abundantly clear: none of the Indian forms of the bodhisattva are feminine.

The beginning of the creation of Avalokiteśvara images occurred during the Kuṣāṇa dynasty. Scholars generally attribute the promotion and dissemination of Buddhism to Kaniṣka I, the dynasty's third ruler. The Kuṣāṇas (Kushans) were originally a part of what the Chinese called the Yüeh-chih people and lived in the area of present Kansu province in northwest China. They were forced to emigrate to the west during the Former Han and arrived in Bactria about 135 B.C.E. Under Kaniṣka I, who began his rule probably around 120 C.E. and was a great patron of Buddhism, Buddhist art production and missionary activities received much support. As a result, Buddhism flourished not only in northwest India, but also in the countries along the Silk Road. From there the religion was introduced into China. The early translators of Buddhist scriptures into Chinese were not natives from India proper, but Parthians,

Scythians, Sogdians, and other residents of what the Chinese called the West Regions.

Susan L. and John Huntington (1985) speaks of the popularity of images of Śākyamuni Buddha, Maitreya, and Avalokiteśvara during this period. Avalokiteśvara appears either independently or as a member of a triad. He is often depicted as the "Bearer of the Lotus," Padmapāṇi. For instance, an image from Loriyan Tangai of the Kuṣāṇa period shows him holding a lotus in his left hand. He is dressed in princely garb and wears a turban, a sign of his royal nature. He has a moustache and sits in a posture of "royal ease," with his right leg pendant (Huntington 1985:139). A Buddha triad dated to 152 C.E. has the Buddha flanked by two bodhisattvas, the fierce looking Vajrapāṇi ("Bearer of the Thunderbolt") on his right and the benign Padmapāi on his left.[10] Vajrapāṇi is dressed as an ascetic with a short kilt and an animal skin tied about his shoulder, whereas Padmapāṇi is garbed as an Indic prince, adorned with elaborate jewels and wearing a royal turban (Huntington 1985:154). The choice of these two figures as attendants of the Buddha reveals a fundamental Buddhist understanding of enlightenment. Since the Buddha, the Enlightened One, has both wisdom and compassion, he is attended by the two bodhisattvas who represent these two complimentary and equally necessary qualities. Avalokiteśvara is a symbol of compassion and Vajrapāṇi is a symbol of wisdom. The latter would be replaced by Mañjuśrī, for instance, in Ellora during the seventh century and Ratnagiri in Orissa about the eighth century (Huntington 1985:270, 446).

After the fifth century, Avalokiteśvara images began to change. First, assimilating attributes of Maitreya, he became more ascetic than regal. Second, he increasingly assumed the status of an independent deity. Summarizing the trend, Chutiwongs says,

> He is the most popular Bodhisattva at Elūrā, where his images number 110 in all, about three times as many as those of any other Bodhisattva. One of the favorite themes in the Buddhist art of Mahārāṣṭra is the so-called 'Litany of Avalokiteśvara,' in which the Bodhisattva is portrayed as the Saviour from Perils. Numerous examples illustrating such a theme occur in the late Gupta and Post-Gupta cave-temples at Kānheri, Ajaṇṭā, Elūrā and Auraṅgabād. . . . These scenes are apparently pictorial representations of the prayer addressed to Avalokiteśvara by his devotees, before and during their undertaking difficult journeys. Avalokiteśvara in this aspect was undoubtedly the patron of travelers, merchants and pilgrims. The fact that the population of Western India was famous for its trading activities obviously has some bearing on the outstanding prevalence of this theme in the western part of India.(1984:45)

For the same reason, Kuan-yin as savior from perils as eulogized in the *Lotus Sūtra* was also a favorite subject among the frescoes in Tun-huang, the terminus of the Silk Route.

A Sarnath image of Avalokiteśvara dated to the second half of the fifth century clearly indicates his male gender. Draped in a diaphanous robe, his genital bulge is distinct.[11]

By the end of the Gupta period in the sixth century, Avalokiteśvara appeared to have attained the status of an independent and principal deity who had his own retinue and was worshiped for specific purposes. As Avalokiteśvara became a major cultic icon, he was attended by other bodhisattvas just as the Buddha. For instance, an early to mid-sixth century image of him as protector against ten perils including elephants, lions, and robbers in Cave 90 at Kānheri depicts him as being flanked by two female attendants, Tārā ("Star") on his right and Bhṛkuṭī ("Abundantly Full Hall," meaning "achievement of the fully enlightened mind") on his left (Huntington 1985:264). They represent compassion and wisdom, corresponding to Avalokiteśvara and Vajrapāṇi. The earliest eleven-headed Avalokiteśvara in India dated to the late fifth to early sixth century is also found at Kānheri, at Cave 41 (figure 1.1; Huntington 1985:265). Multi-armed Avalokiteśvara, typical of Tantric Buddhist art, flourished in northeast India during the post-Gupta period. Sometimes possessing two, but other times up to sixteen arms, he carries attributes that often include symbols of other popular Hindu and Buddhist deities:

> The kamaṇḍalu, tridaṇḍa (three-stalked stick), akṣamālā [rosary] and pustaka [scroll and brush] reveal the ascetic side of his personality, and the two last mentioned items underline simultaneously his quality as the Great Teacher and the Master of All Knowledge, equal to the God Brahmā. His third eye, the triśūla [lance and trident], pāśa [noose] and aṅkuśa [hook] associate him with Maheśvara, or the Lord of All Soul (Paśupati). And, the invisible pāśa or noose which binds forever the individual soul (paśu) to its Lord (pati), becomes Avalokiteśvara's infallible noose (amogha-pāśa) of Compassion, with which he draws to him the mortal souls for their deliverance. The ratna [jewel] or cintāmaṇi [wish-fulfilling jewel] symbolizes his manifold and inexhaustible power of giving, and his unfailing answer to prayers, while the daṇḍa or staff of punishment occasionally appears among his attributes as a warning to mischievous souls and evil-doers. Regal elements, which had grown faint in the iconography of Avalokiteśvara after the Kuṣāṇa period, become apparent again in the medieval art of North India in a most striking manner. In a number of his manifestations, he assumes the seated posture typical of kings, the seat of "royal ease" or

Figure 1.1. Eleven-headed Avalokiteśvara in Cave 41, Kānheri, Mahārāṣṭra, India. Ca. Late fifth–early sixth century C.E. *Courtesy of John C. Huntington.*

> mahārājalīlāsana, indicating his supremacy, not only over the spiritual world but also over the material and mundane sphere of glory and fame. His companions increase in number and in significance, extolling even more the sublime position of the central figure. (Chutiwongs 1984:49–50)

Later on, during the Pāla period, from the eighth to the twelfth centuries, esoteric Buddhist iconography provides more evidence of Avalokiteśvara as a cosmic savior. A stele of the late eleventh century from Nalanda, for instance, shows Avalokiteśvara being "attended by Tārā and Sudhanakumāra (Very Rich Prince) to his right, and Bhṛkuṭī and Hayagrīva (Horse-Neck) to his left, while above, all five of the *jina* Buddhas are represented. The animal-headed, skeletal figure at the extreme bottom left of the stele is the *preta* [hungry ghost] Sūcīmukha. . . . This *preta*, whose destiny it is to be insatiably hungry, is being saved by the bodhisattva, who lets him suck the nectar that falls from his hand" (Huntington 1985:392–93).[12] As revealer of saving dhāraṇīs, Avalokiteśvara plays a central role in many Tantric scriptures. Interestingly, a specific figure identified by Huntington as Ṣaḍakṣarī (Six Syllables) Lokeśvara was found in Bihār; it dates to around the late eleventh or twelfth century and represents a personification of the six-syllable mantra, *Oṃ maṇi padme hūṃ* (O Thou with the Jeweled Lotus!), the most popular mantra of Avalokiteśvara (Huntington 1985:394).

The origin of the cult of Avalokiteśvara has long interested scholars. One of the early sūtras important for his cult is the longer version of the *Sukhāvatīvyūha Sūtra*, a text compiled in northwest India around 100 C.E. in which Avalokiteśvara is singled out together with Mahāsthāmaprāpta as the two main attending bodhisattvas of Amitābha Buddha. Like Amitābha, he is described as full of light. This led Mallmann to suggest that the bodhisattva was a solar deity derived from Iranian Zoroastrian sources. Alexander C. Soper has also written on the light symbolism of the Buddha and Maitreya and argued for a close connection between Iranian religious ideas and Kushan art of northwest India (1949–50). He believes that the Gandhāran Buddha bears similarities to Mithra-Helios.[13] According to Mallmann (1948:82), originally similar to Apollo, Mithra, Helios, and Hermes, Avalokiteśvara was then transformed into "a protector of the Buddhist Dharma and a power dispelling the forces of darkness, ignorance, and irreligion." She thought that his cult could be traced to the great Greco-Buddhist king Kaniṣka in the second century in northwest India where the earliest images of the bodhisattva have also been found. Giuseppe Tucci (1948) disagreed. He downplayed the bodhisattva's light symbolism, but emphasized the figure's "compassionate glance." John Holt (1991: 30–39), who summarizes the debates, offers a compromise by suggesting that we should pay equal attention to the light symbolism and the quality of compassion of the bodhisattva.

Instead of looking for the antecedents of Avalokiteśvara outside of the Buddhist traditions, Tucci and other scholars saw them in two earlier *Avalokita Sūtras* contained in the Lokottara Mahāsāṃghika *Mahāvastu.* The title of the texts shares part of the bodhisattva's name and attests the earliest use of the term "*Avalokita*" (look, glance). Both texts glorify Śākyamuni Buddha when he was a bodhisattva. Although scholars do not agree about the dating of these texts, they do share the view that these texts with the emphasis on "survey" and "light" provide inspiration for the conception of Avalokiteśvara.[14] Although the meaning of *avalokita* is clear, the bodhisattva's name is not. As Holt (1991) points out, Buddhologists have not been able to agree on a uniform explanation of the name Avalokiteśvara. Why is it so? "Separately, the Sanskrit terms *avalokita* and *īśvara* are rather clear, meaning "glance" or "look" and "lord," respectively. But when compounded to form *avalokiteśvara,* the name of the bodhisattva has been taken to variously mean "Lord of what we see," "Lord who is seen," "Lord who is seen (from on high)," "Lord who sees," or "Lord who sees (from on high)" (Holt 1991:31). Hsüan-tsang (ca. 596–664), the famous Chinese pilgrim to India, translated Avalokiteśvara as "Kuan-tzu-tsai" (Master Perceiver). But the popularity of this name has always been surpassed by Kuan-yin or Kuan-shih-yin, which results from compounding *Avalokita* and *Īśvara* meaning "He who perceives the sounds of the world."

The creation of Kuan-yin images in China followed quite closely after the translation of Buddhist scriptures, as I shall show in the next chapter. The different stages in the evolution of Avalokiteśvara's iconography in India also occurred in China, but with innovations. Starting with the creation of new iconography such as the Water-moon Kuan-yin (who is androgynous) in the tenth century, Chinese artists increasingly depicted the bodhisattva in a clearly feminine fashion after the Sung (960–1279). Beginning with the Ming (1368–1644), if not earlier, there appeared sets of paintings depicting Kuan-yin in five, thirty-two, or fifty-three forms. There are also the so-called "thirty-three forms of Kuan-yin" in Sino-Japanese Buddhist art since the Kamakura period (1185–1333).[15] These multiple forms of bodhisattva are supposed to be illustrations of the thirty-three manifestations of Kuan-yin in the *Lotus Sūtra,* or the thirty-two in the *Śūraṅgama Sūtra.* But they in fact do not bear much resemblance to the scriptural sources. Aside from the Water-moon (#12) and White-robed (#6) Kuan-yin, celebrated in Chinese art, but not mentioned in any sūtras, three others refer to legends created in China. They are Fish-basket (#10), Clam-dwelling (#25), and Wife of Mr. Ma (#28).[16]

Although we cannot say that the feminization of Kuan-yin was introduced by the artists and artisans, they certainly helped the trend by providing visual aids to people's conceptualization of her. The artists who first painted or sculpted a feminine Kuan-yin must have reflected a contemporary prevailing view of her. In this sense, art is both an index of the changing views of Kuan-yin as well as an agent to promote such a change. Why in China alone did Avalokiteśvara undergo a sex change? This is a question that may never be satisfactorily answered. However, it seems to me that at least two factors are relevant for our consideration. The first has to do with Chinese culture and Chinese religion. The second has to do with the relative scarcity of the "history" of Avalokiteśvara in Buddhist scriptures. Perhaps the very lack of a well-developed myth about the bodhisattva made the creation of new myths in China possible. These myths about Kuan-yin, moreover, were created according to the Chinese views about deities and thus could answer the religious needs of the Chinese people.

From Buddhism in China to Chinese Buddhism: A Short Historical Sketch

In order to understand how Avalokiteśvara was transformed into Kuan-yin, it is necessary to have some knowledge about how Buddhism became indigenized in China. The two processes were intimately connected, for both were examples of domestication. Just as Buddhism was gradually changed from a foreign religion into Chinese Buddhism, the bodhisattva was similarly transformed into the Chinese "Goddess of Mercy." Indeed, the latter process can be used as an excellent case study for the former one.

The introduction of Buddhism into China was carried out by Central Asian, particularly Parthian, and Indian missionary monks who, following the Silk Route used by caravan traders, arrived in China during the second half of the Han dynasty (206 B.C.E.–220 C.E.). By the first century of the Common Era, historical sources record the existence of three Buddhist communities located in P'eng-ch'eng (present-day T'ung-shan, Kiangsu) in the lower Yangtze region, Loyang in central China, and Chiao-chou in present day Vietnam. Buddhism was at first poorly understood. For instance, the Buddha was worshiped together with the Yellow Emperor and the deified Lao Tzu, the two principal gods of religious Taoism. Like them, the Buddha was regarded as a deity who could teach the secrets of immortality.

Art provides another example of how Buddhism was at first grafted onto indigenous beliefs. The Queen Mother of the West was the most important Taoist goddess of the immortality cult. She was the first Chinese deity represented in art. By the first century of the Common Era, the Chinese carved her image on stones or bricks and used them to adorn the tombs of wealthy people. The image would be situated along the upper part of the tomb wall below the ceiling, indicating a heavenly space. When the Chinese began to create the image of the Buddha, they made him resemble the Queen Mother of the West. Images of the Buddha were found on tomb reliefs in Mao-hao and Shih-tzu-wan in Leshan, Szechwan, dated to the late second century. Both the iconography and the location of the Buddha image in the tombs were the same as those of the Queen Mother of the West (Wu Hung 1986; Tang Changshou 1997). The Buddhist teaching of rebirth (*saṃsāra*), a totally unfamiliar concept to the Chinese, proved a greater problem to understanding. The only way the Chinese could make sense of rebirth was by positing that Buddhism taught the continued existence of a soul after death, an idea completely contrary to the teaching of "no-self" (*anātman*), a central tenet of Buddhism.

The energies of early missionaries and their Chinese collaborators were concentrated on the translation of Buddhist scriptures. Depending on the personal backgrounds and interests of the translators, the sūtras chosen for translation could be from early Buddhist or Mahāyāna traditions. In this way, the Chinese were exposed to a whole range of Buddhist literature, from stories of the Buddha's previous lives, to manuals of meditation and the teaching of *śūnyatā*, or the lack of inherent nature of all things, expounded in the *Perfection of Wisdom* sūtras. Names of famous translators of this early period are An Shih-kao (ca. 148–168), Lokakṣema (Chih-lou-chia-ch'en, ca. 168–188), Chih-ch'ien (ca. 220–251) and Dharmarakṣa (233–313). It is interesting to note that with the exception of the *Lotus Sūtra of the True Law* (Cheng-fa-hua ching) translated by Dharmarakṣa in 286, Avalokiteśvara either does not appear at all in the sūtras translated during this early period, or when he does appear, for instance, in the *Vimalakīrti Sūtra* translated by Chih-ch'ien, he plays a very minor role compared to that of Mañjuśrī.

After the fall of the Han, China was divided between the north and the south. It was during these years of disunity and instability that Buddhism started to be established on the Chinese soil. Buddhism in North China, which was ruled by non-Chinese rulers, enjoyed imperial patronage. Buddhist devotion took concrete forms with the large-scale rock sculptures at Yün-kang near Ta-t'ung and Lung-men near Loyang, capitals of the Northern Wei.

Buddhism in the south was characterized by its philosophical speculation and participation by members of aristocratic classes. It was helped by the renewed interest in the thought of Lao Tzu, Chuang Tzu, and the *Book of Changes*. Known as the "Dark Learning" (*hsüan-hsüeh*), it provided the vocabulary and framework to interpret some of the newly introduced Buddhist philosophies. The practice of matching concepts from Buddhism with those of the indigenous traditions was called *ke-yi,* and it became a favorite way of making Buddhist ideas familiar to the educated adherents. Although this was an efficient expediency, it was abandoned when a better understanding of Buddhism was made possible by the masterful translator Kumārajīva (ca. 401–413) who, together with his assistants, produced the definitive translations of most of the important Mahāyāna sūtras.

During the latter Han and the Six Dynasties, or the first six hundred years of the Common Era, the same period when Buddhism was becoming established, momentous changes also were taking place in Taoism, the native religion of China. Because Confucianism became the state ideology during the Han, Buddhism and Taoism had to compete for imperial patronage and lay support. What worked for Buddhism was often eagerly imitated and copied by Taoists and vice versa (Zürcher 1980, 1982). The Taoist religion began as the Way of the Celestial Masters (Cheng-i, Correct Unity) when Lao Tzu, as a god, revealed himself to the first Celestial Master, Chang Tao-ling, in Szechwan. The movement was noted for its parish organization in which both men and women held leadership roles, and moral codes, collective confession, and petitioning rituals to invoke divine powers to cure diseases were used. It was also characterized by the recitations of the *Tao Te Ching,* now interpreted in a new and unconventional way. During the fourth century C.E. two new movements sprang up in the south. The Shang-ch'ing (Upper Clarity) scriptures were revealed to a man named Yang Hsi (330–386?) on Mt. Mao in present day Kiangsu. Gods and spirits appeared to Yang at night from 364 to 370. One of these deities was Lady Wei Hua-ts'un (251–334) who was the main initiator of Yang and the first patriarch of the new movement. She had died thirty years earlier and had held the position of "libation pourer," thus implying her membership in the Way of Celestial Masters (Strickmann 1977). The texts taught individual salvation through the taking of drugs, visualization of the gods, and mystical union with them. The gods were intercessors and mediators, and salvation lay in knowing the "true form" of heavenly places and their inhabitants. The initiated enjoyed an intimate relationship with these divinities who became intercessors. They would deliver to the adept "the keys of celestial kingdoms and nourish him with divine effluvia, sometimes mouth to mouth. The gods descend into the adept and take him up to the skies, hand in hand" (Robinet 1997:121). The texts were written in a poetic and elegant language, appealing to Yang's primarily elite audience.

Another Taoist movement, the Ling-pao (Spiritual Treasure), appeared around 400 C.E., some thirty years after the Shang-ch'ing and in the same county, southwest of Nanking. Like the latter, this movement was also connected with a new corpus of revealed scriptures. But unlike Shang-ch'ing, it borrowed consciously and extensively from Buddhist sūtras and concerned themselves "with bodhisattva-like intensity" with salvation of all beings, not just fellow members (like the Way of the Celestial Masters) or a select few initiates (like the Shang-ch'ing) (Bokenkamp 1997:8).

Readers may wonder why I discuss developments in Taoism in this sketch of Chinese Buddhism. This has to do with my methodology. I firmly believe that we must always examine new developments in one religion while keeping our eyes open for what is going on in others. Chinese religions, like the Chinese people, did not exist in isolated and segregated compartments. They carried on conversations with each other and sometimes quarreled with each other. They borrowed from as well as gave to each other. There are two developments in Taoism that interest me most. First, the transcendent was not sharply demarcated from the immanent. Human beings could become gods and gods human beings. Not only sagely figures such as Lao Tzu were seen as human incarnations of gods, but an obscure person such as Yang Hsi could be designated as the recipient of revelation. Second, they underlined the central importance of texts. A text is indeed, as Robinet puts it, "a token of the bond between gods and men" (1997:44). The texts, moreover, were dictated or revealed by deities for the salvation of their devotees. These two characteristics can be regarded as possible inspirations for the legend of Miao-shan and the indigenous sūtras revealed by Kuan-yin, discussed in chapters 8 and 3 respectively.

When China was reunited under the Sui (581–618), Buddhism also began a new phase. The most noticeable development during the Sui and the succeeding T'ang (618–907) dynasty was the creation of indigenous Chinese Buddhist schools. Some schools, such as T'ien-t'ai and Hua-yen, are known for their philosophical synthesis, while others, such as Pure Land and Ch'an, are noted for their religious practice. None of these Chinese schools had Indian antecedents. They were truly Chinese creations. A school singled out one or a group of scriptures as having the highest authority. Thus, the Hua-yen school regarded the *Hua-yen (Avataṃsaka) Sūtra*, the T'ien-t'ai the *Lotus Sūtra*, and the Pure Land school the so-called three sūtras of Pure Land as their most authoritative scriptures. However, through the hermeneutics of "classification of teachings" (*p'an-chiao*), both T'ien-t'ai and Hua-yen recognized the diverse teachings represented by the entire corpus of Buddhist scriptures by assigning them to different periods in the Buddha's teaching career.

As the Chinese created new schools of Buddhism, the same self-confidence was reflected in their creation of Buddhist art. Kuan-yin increasingly became a favorite choice for artists. Because Kuan-yin is mentioned prominently in the *Lotus Sūtra*, *Hua-yen Sūtra*, and the Pure Land sūtras, the fame of the bodhisattva understandably grew as these schools became important in T'ang

China. The rising popularity of Kuan-yin was reflected in the rock sculptures at the Lung-men caves. From 500 to 530, the first period of intensive rock-cutting, the leading deities portrayed were Śākyamuni and Maitreya, with Amitābha and Kuan-yin playing minor roles. This was reversed in the second period of intensive rock-cutting, between 650 and 710, in the early T'ang dynasty. Tsukamoto compiled a list giving the total number of dated and undated statues at the site: the most popular was Amitābha with 222, followed by Kuan-yin with 197, Śākyamuni, 94, and Maitreya, 62 (Ch'en 1964:171–72). The statues of Kuan-yin in Lung-men, like those of buddhas and other bodhisattvas, appear masculine and sometimes include a thin moustache. Kuan-yin usually carries a lotus (an attribute of the form of Avalokiteśvara known as Padmapāṇi) in one hand and a water bottle in the other.

A great impetus of image making was provided by the translation of esoteric Buddhist sūtras during the T'ang. Esoteric Buddhism put great emphasis on the correct ways of setting up a sacred arena, the creation of the image of the deity according to exact stipulations, and the visualization of the deity so created for worship. Such precise and exact procedures for meditation, called *sādhanas*, are always included in the esoteric scriptures. Another feature of these texts is the inclusion of *dhāraṇīs,* "strings of syllables abbreviated from longer passages or strung together for psychological effect" (Robinson and Johnson 1997:125). The deities who reveal these dhāraṇīs and who are the object of the visualization meditation are always multi-armed. Images of Kuan-yin created in the T'ang and earlier usually were based on scriptural stipulations or Indian and Central Asian models, although there were also individual modifications and innovations.

Chinese Buddhist schools have continued to exist in China up to the present time. Since the Sung (960–1279), however, there has been a pronounced tendency to combine the schools. T'ien-t'ai and Hua-yen were referred to as the Teaching (Chiao) schools. There were movements that combined the Teaching schools with Ch'an (*Ch'an Chiao ho-i*), and Ch'an with Pure Land (*Ch'an Ching ho-i*). This predilection for harmonizing different Buddhist traditions was also represented by a similar movement combining Buddhism with Confucianism and Taoism, commonly known as "Three Teachings in One" (*San-chiao ho-i*). The same tendencies were found among Confucians and Taoists. This trend was promoted by individuals and dynastic governments alike from very early on. For instance, Chang Jung, a scholar-official who lived during the Southern Ch'i (479–502), held the Confucian *Classic of Filial Piety* and the Taoist *Tao Te Ching* in his left hand and the Buddhist *Lotus Sūtra* in his right hand on his death bed (*Nan-ch'i shu*, 41/8b). Individual rulers might shift their support from one religion to another, but it was a common practice for them to advocate the harmonization of all three teachings. The result of such cross-fertilization can be seen in the rise of Ch'an Buddhism in the T'ang, Neo-Confucianism in the Sung, and Ch'uan-chen (Complete Realization) Taoism during the Southern Sung and Yüan (1230–1368) periods.

Monastic Buddhism and Neo-Confucianism were masculine and patriarchal. Despite its rhetoric of nonduality, Ch'an Buddhism did not provide the same opportunities for women practitioners as it did for men. Buddhist doctrine had, after all, always interpreted being female as a consequence of bad karma. One of the most attractive promises of Pure Land Buddhism was that there would be no women in the Western Paradise. Even if a person failed to go to the Pure Land, the merit created in this life would guarantee that one would not be born as a woman in the next. Such beliefs and sentiments did not empower women or take women's religious needs seriously. Nor did they foster respect for feminine symbols or veneration of goddesses. Similarly, Neo-Confucianism was a very male oriented, patriarchal, and hierarchical system of thought. It did not recognize the presence of goddesses, nor provide much support for the intellectual and spiritual strivings of real women. Although its stated program was universal sagehood, its real intended audience was educated men. It did not encourage or promote devotionalism. It did not appreciate religious enthusiasm and emotional fervor. There was thus an imbalance and a deprivation. There was too much yang and not enough yin.

Ch'uan-chen Taoism, on the other hand, both revered the feminine symbol yin and provided opportunities for the religious aspirations of actual women. Founded by Wang Che (1123–1170), the school advocated celibacy and self-transformation by the practice of interior alchemy. Among Wang's chief disciples, the so-called "Seven True Ones," one was Sun Pu-erh (1119–1182), wife of Ma Tuan-yang, the second patriarch. She was also known as Immortal Lady Sun (Sun Hsien-ku). Many women were attracted to the school, and a large number of the poems in Ch'uan-chen works were addressed to women (Tao 1980:57). In the so-called Southern School of the interior alchemy made famous by Po Yü-ch'an (fl. 1209–1224), a similar openness and hospitality to women prevailed. Po wrote approvingly of a woman who became a goddess and praised her highly. The wives of two of his followers were famous practitioners and a number of Po's disciples have women acolytes.[17]

A related phenomenon was the appearance of the cult of the "Eight Immortals" in the Yüan, which was made very popular by the plays written about them in the Yüan and Ming. These semi-mythical personages lived during the T'ang and before. The Complete Realization school regarded two of the "Eight Immortals," Chung-li Ch'üan and Lü Tung-pin, as earlier patriarchs. One of this group is a woman who was known as Immortal Lady Ho (Ho Hsien-ku).

The fame of the Eight Immortals was not limited to Taoism in late imperial China. They have become familiar fixtures in the popular imagination down the ages. One can see them not only in plays and stories, but also in paintings and decorative arts such as porcelain and embroidery.

In this light, the feminization of Kuan-yin and new developments in religious Taoism could be seen as responses to the patriarchal stance of institutional Buddhism and Neo-Confucianism. The latter, for practical purposes, was the state religion of late imperial China. If Neo-Confucianism and organized Buddhism had not lacked feminine symbols and female practitioners, Kuan-yin may not have undergone a sexual transformation. We can look at this together with the two factors I already mentioned. Namely, because China already possessed an ideology of kingship, Kuan-yin did not become connected with the royalty, as Avalokiteśvara did in other Asian countries. And because China did not have a native tradition of universal saviors, Kuan-yin could and did occupy the empty space with amazing success. One of the strengths of Buddhism, it seems to me, is that it always supplied what was lacking in the native traditions. That is why alone among all imported religions, Buddhism could have "gone native" and become accepted as one of the Three Teachings of China.

As Buddhism became domesticated, regional centers with distinctive characteristics developed. This was true not only for the Five Houses of Ch'an, but also the Buddhist art of Tun-huang and Szechwan. The first truly Chinese Kuan-yin image was the Water-moon Kuan-yin, datable to the tenth century. After that, several indigenous forms of Kuan-yin, all feminine, began to appear. At the same time, regional pilgrimage centers devoted to Kuan-yin evolved, together with their local myths and legends about the deity. We can then speak of localization as a further stage in the domestication of both Buddhism and Avalokiteśvara in China.

The Methodology of the Study

I am interested in the long and complicated process by which Avalokiteśvara was transformed into Kuan-yin. I see the sexual transformation of the bodhisattva within the framework of his/her domestication. The latter, in turn, has to be viewed within the larger picture of how Buddhism became Chinese. One fruitful way to begin, I think, is to examine the many media through which Kuan-yin was made known to the Chinese people. The actors who were responsible for managing the media were at the same time creating new messages and images of the bodhisattva.

Scriptures, miracle tales, myths, art, literature, rituals, and pilgrimages are some of the media I discuss in the following chapters. Monks, literati, poets, artists, and common women and men have all contributed to the creation and dissemination of the cult. It is my hope that as we begin to see how the cult of Kuan-yin took root in China, we will no longer simplistically assign it to any neat niche that can be labeled "Buddhist" in contrast to Confucian or Taoist, or "popular" in contrast to "elite." To give one example, I shall demonstrate that the Child-giving Kuan-yin was worshiped not just by "ignorant" women but also by Confucian literati. Moreover, far from being a vulgar Chinese popularization, this understanding of the bodhisattva had a firm scriptural anchor. This study, then, adds further evidence that in studying Chinese religion, the two-tiered model of elite versus popular or the division into the three "isms" is not a viable methodology, a trend that has happily been gaining wider acceptance in the last two decades.

What is my methodology in pursuing this study? I was trained as an intellectual historian and a historian of Chinese Buddhism. For over twenty-five years I have taught college courses on world religions and I identify myself as a historian of religion in terms of my discipline. In my previous work I relied heavily on scriptures, historical documents (Buddhist chronicles and dynastic histories), individual works by Buddhist monks and literati, and monastic and local gazetteers. These are standard tools that I continue to use in this study. But because of the unique nature of this subject, I made a conscious decision in the beginning of the project to utilize additional resources and disciplines. Daniel Overmyer (1998) has advocated recently the method of "THF" (text, history, and fieldwork) as a fruitful way to study Chinese religion. I was forced to adopt this approach independently some years ago when I began this study, using historical and visual texts and engaging in fieldwork. I do not use individual images of Kuan-yin simply as illustrations, but try to understand how the evolution of Kuan-yin's iconography not only reflected but also influenced the changing perceptions of the bodhisattva. I firmly believe that for this study as well as for all studies of Chinese religion, it is absolutely necessary to use both written texts and artistic images. Most of the chapters in the book begin with personal observations about some contemporary aspects of the cult of Kuan-yin before I go into a discussion of their historical origins and developments. These observations are based on my fieldwork notes. Because the cult of Kuan-yin was not just a historical phenomenon, but a prominent feature of contemporary Chinese religion, I feel I am justified in doing so. I have noted the differences between the modern cult and its earlier counterpart whenever necessary. Incidentally, when I use the word "cult" in this book, I follow its first and third senses found in the *Oxford English Dictionary*: "worship, reverential homage" and "devotion or homage . . . esp. as paid by a body of professed adherents or admirers." The word has unfortunately acquired a derogatory connotation in contemporary usage, and to many people it now means what the *Webster's New Universal Unabridged Dictionary* defines as "a religion or sect considered to be false, unorthodox or extremist, with members often living outside of conventional society under the direction of a charismatic leader." This is emphatically not what I mean when I use the term. Here I concur with Robert Campany's use of the term (1993:262–63).[18] Because Kuan-yin is not only an important Buddhist deity and worshiped by Buddhist monastics and lay people, but she is also a major Chinese goddess and venerated by the Chinese people in general and members of sectarian religions in particular, it is necessary to examine popular religious literature, especially the *pao-chüan* or precious scrolls which were first composed by monks and lay leaders in the sixteenth century to propagate Buddhist and sectarian religious messages. In sum, I have used diverse source materials and methodologies in this study. I believe that only by adopting a multidisciplinary approach can one do justice to a topic of such complexity. I will now summarize the contents of each chapter.

In chapter 2 I discuss the scriptural sources for the cult of Kuan-yin. For in the introduction and dissemination of the faith in this bodhisattva, scriptures definitely played an important role. Buddhist sūtras provided the initial inspiration for the cult of Kuan-yin in China and their authority continued to be invoked for its support. I shall discuss important sūtras from both exoteric and esoteric Buddhism to see why and how this bodhisattva is important. But the Chinese did not simply adhere to the scriptural depictions and definitions of Kuan-yin, nor did they strictly follow the scriptural stipulations and directions for worshiping Kuan-yin, for otherwise there would not have been any Chinese transformation. On the other hand, I would argue that many of the changes can still be explained on the basis of some scriptural sources. Even the indigenous scriptures were not created out of thin air, but are elaborations or modifications of some famous sūtras.

It is in examining the innovations and comparing them with the scriptural models that we can begin to trace the sources and the development of the cult of Kuan-yin in China. Following the growing fame of Kuan-yin, Chinese indigenous scriptures were created as early as the fifth century. Many such scriptures have not survived, with only the titles recorded in the Buddhist bibliographical catalogues. But one of them, the *Kuan-shih-yin Sūtra Promoted by King Kao* (Kao Wang Kuan-shih-yin ching), has attained a canonical status. Believing the Age of the Degenerate Law was soon arriving, pious Buddhist leaders chose to have the sūtra carved on sūtra slabs on the hills of Fang-shan in 616 outside of present-day Beijing, together with the *Lotus*, *Vimalakīrti*, *Avataṃsaka*, *Nirvāṇa*, and *Prajñā-pāramitā* sūtras, to preserve them from destruction. It was introduced into the Tripiṭaka collections of the Ming, and has remained the favorite scripture to be printed and distributed for free by the faithful in order to generate merit even in present-day Taiwan. This and other famous and influential indigenous sūtras are discussed in chapter 3.

Although sūtras glorifying Kuan-yin were translated into Chinese quite early on, knowledge about and faith in the bodhisattva did not come from the sūtras alone. Scriptural authority regarding Kuan-yin was made real through testimonials provided by actual persons who experienced the life-saving miracles. At the same time, the kind of miracles handed down to us tended to conform to the ones promised by the sūtras. There is thus a reciprocal and mutually validating relationship between the two types of literature. In chapter 4 I take up miracle tales about Kuan-yin. Known as *kan-ying* (influence-response) or *ling-ying* (efficacious responses), such stories constitute one subgenre of the Buddhist miracle literature. Soon after the translation of the *Lotus Sūtra*, there were already miracle stories about people who invoked the bodhisattva, first by the name Kuang-shih-yin and later, Kuan-shih-yin. Sixty-nine tales were recorded in a collection compiled as early as 501, incorporating two even earlier collections. Although the individuals who reported having experienced the miracles came from all walks of life, it is interesting to note that the compilers of these early tales were literati officials. In the succeeding centuries, more such collections were compiled, providing testimonials to the compassionate actions of this savior. As Robert Campany (1993) argued convincingly, miracle tales played a powerful role in generating and reinforcing the faith in Kuan-yin. As such tales were increasingly gathered into independent anthologies from the T'ang on, other miracle tale collections glorifying the *Lotus Sūtra* include proportionately fewer stories about Kuan-yin (Matoba 1980, 1982, 1984, 1986). This is not surprising, for although the *Lotus Sūtra* provides the most important scriptural basis for the faith in Kuan-yin, as the bodhisattva took root in China, he/she achieved an independent status.

These three chapters provide basic data about Kuan-yin's importance in the translated and indigenous sūtras as well as testimonies about the bodhisattva's saving powers. But how do we know that this information was disseminated in society? Of the many sūtras about Kuan-yin, which ones became well-known? Of the many forms of Kuan-yin, which ones become the objects of cultic worship? In order to form a context for the texts, we have to turn from a study of the scriptural description of the bodhisattva to his/her cultic manifestations. I therefore provide two case studies on the domestication of the scriptural Avalokiteśvara. In chapter 5 I describe the cult of divine monks who were believed to be the incarnations of the Eleven-headed Avalokiteśvara, while in chapters 7 and 8 I describe the cult of the Thousand-handed and Thousand-eyed Avalokiteśvara, who was believed to have manifested as Princess Miao-shan. Pao-chih (425–514), Seng-chieh (627–710) and his contemporary Wan-hui were three monks who were reputed for their thaumaturgical abilities. They were worshiped as manifestations of the Eleven-headed Avalokiteśvara. The frequent reports of Kuan-yin appearing as a monk in visions or dreams to his devotees, the popularity of the Eleven-headed Kuan-yin in art, and the deified monks as human manifestations of Kuan-yin must therefore be examined in relation to each other.

Chapter 7 examines the soteriology and procedure of *Ta-pei Ch'an* (Ritual of Great Compassion Repentance), the ritual of confession centering on the Thousand-handed Avalokiteśvara that was first formulated by the Sung T'ien-t'ai master Chih-li (960–1028) and has continued to be performed up to the present. In chapter 8 I discuss the legend of Princess Miao-shan, who is believed by the Chinese to be the human incarnation of Kuan-yin. I argue that Miao-shan is not just any manifestation of the bodhisattva, but specifically the domesticated Thousand-handed Avalokiteśvara whose cult has enjoyed great popularity in China since the T'ang and was made familiar to the people through art, the chanting of the *Ta-pei Chou* (Great Compassion Dhāraṇī), and the ritual of repentance. I argue that the choice of a woman instead of a monk reflected not only the gender change in art, but also the rise of a new type of organized lay Buddhism in the Sung that claimed equal validity for lay practice and probably provided more opportunities for women to participate in the religion.

Together with the creation of indigenous Chinese sūtras, iconographies, and hagiographies of Kuan-yin, the bodhisattva has also been provided with a Chinese home. The mythological Potalaka mentioned in Buddhist scriptures and traditionally believed to be located in India was transposed onto the island of P'u-t'o, situated off-shore in Chekiang Province. Pilgrimages made this Buddhist inscription of the Chinese landscape a reality. The process of domesticating Avalokiteśvara by locating him/her on Chinese soil is discussed in chapter 9.

While monks and literati played leading roles in the composition and compilation of miracle records, temple gazetteers, ritual texts, and possibly indigenous sūtras glorifying Kuan-yin, other actors and media contributed more conspicuously to the construction of the feminine Kuan-yin. In chapters 6 and 10 I examine the White-robe, South Sea, and Fish-basket, the three indigenous forms of feminine Kuan-yin popular in late imperial China. Art and literature were the media that created and popularized these images. Monks and lay Buddhists promoted the feminine Kuan-yin as a universal savior and ideal for emulation. Although they might have had a special significance for women, I argue that these feminine forms of Kuan-yin were known to both men and women and worshiped in both elite and popular strata of society.

In chapter 11 I discuss a fourth feminine form of Kuan-yin, that of the Venerable Mother. I am interested in the possible sources for this image, her relationship to the Eternal Mother, and the sectarian appropriations of her by examining some important precious scrolls promoting her. These were usually written by anonymous authors, some of them connected with sectarian religions, and were chanted aloud in the accompaniment of music to groups of people, usually women. They present Kuan-yin as the creator and savior of humankind, identical to the Eternal Mother, the Great Goddess who, according to some other sectarian texts, are intimately related to her. I also use the scriptures and liturgical texts of some religious sects, such as the Hsien-t'ien Tao (Way of the Former Heaven) and the Li Chiao (Principle Teaching), which were founded in the sixteenth and seventeenth centuries and are still practiced today, to show the central position of Kuan-yin. In these chapters I also address the relationship between the feminine Kuan-yin and women. What messages do the feminine images of Kuan-yin have for Chinese women? In what ways are women empowered by the feminine Kuan-yin? At the same time, what accommodations has the cult of Kuan-yin made to the Confucian tradition? I thus revisit the initial questions of gender and domestication.

In chapter 12 I review the central themes of the book and reiterate some of my major findings. I conclude by inviting the reader to consider with me the central concern of this project: how the transformation of Kuan-yin can be viewed as a case study of the transformation of Buddhism in China. In what ways have the indigenous Chinese traditions influenced the conceptions and perceptions of Avalokiteśvara, the imported Bodhisattva of Compassion? And in what ways has Kuan-yin, the domesticated "Goddess of Mercy," affected Chinese religion?

When I first decided to undertake the study, I had planned to confine it to the feminine Kuan-yin from the Sung on. However, once I began to grapple with the complicated questions of origins and developments, I was forced to go backward in time as well as venture beyond my own familiar sources and methodologies. Just as I have used art history and literary materials in addition to Buddhological and historical sources, I have also broadened the scope of the study on the cult of Kuan-yin, focusing on some of its key aspects, from the Period of Division, or the third to sixth centuries, to the present. Because I use the various media as the organizing principles in discussing the cult of Kuan-yin, chapters of the book do not follow a strict chronological line. In general, the early chapters deal with the earlier developments of the cult and the later chapters the later developments. For instance, chapters 2, 3, 4, and 5 use materials dating to the Period of Division and the T'ang. Chapters 6, 7, and 8 mostly cover the developments of the cult during the Sung, and chapters 9, 10, and 11 look at trends in the Ming and Ch'ing. There are, however, some unavoidable overlaps. It is not my intention to provide a history of the cult of Kuan-yin in every dynasty. Nor have I tried to describe the cult found in the entire country. In terms of the regions I have mentioned, depending on the subject matter, the early chapters tend to concentrate on the north, while the later chapters are concerned with central and southeastern provinces such as Honan, Kiangsu, and Chekiang, reflecting the geographical shift in the history of Chinese Buddhism in general.

Because of the enormity of the subject matter, I do not claim that I have provided either a chronological or geographical survey of the cult of Kuan-yin in China. Nor do I believe that I have answered all the questions. All I can say is that by posing the kinds of questions about the bodhisattva, using the kinds of methodologies, and examining the types of materials that I have done in this book, I have solved to my own satisfaction the initial puzzle that has fascinated me since my childhood: why is Kuan-yin so popular in China? What does being popular mean in Chinese religion? And how did Kuan-yin achieve this popularity?

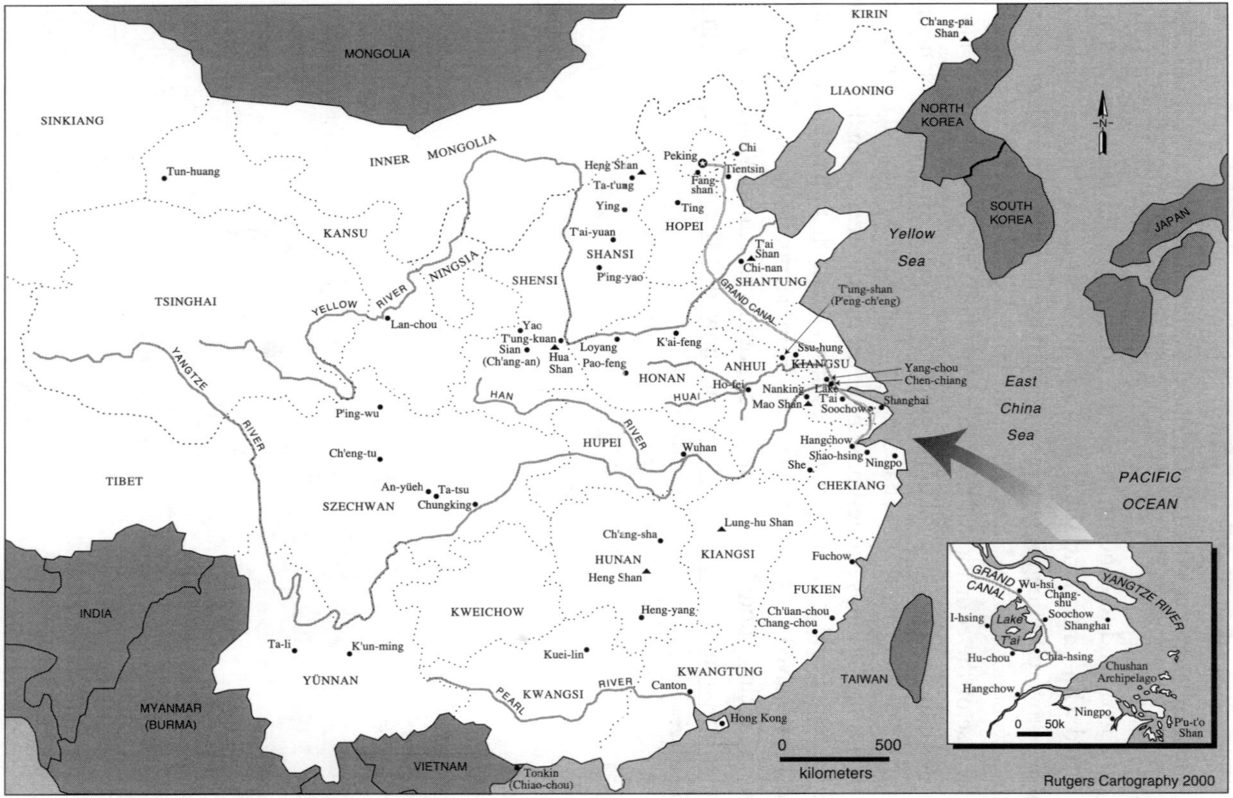

Map 1. Place names.

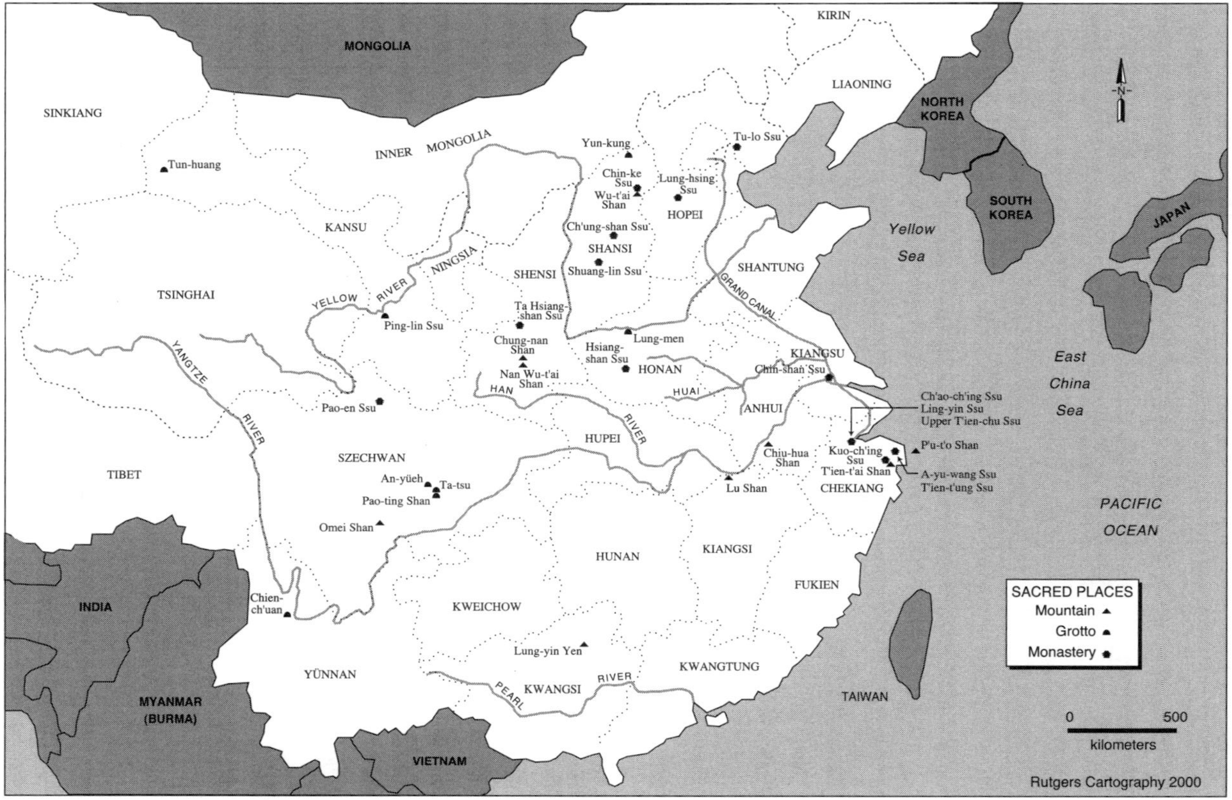

Map 2. Buddhist sites.

2

....

Scriptural Sources for the Cult of Kuan-yin

I begin this study with a review of the Buddhist sūtras that introduced the bodhisattva to China. I do so not because I want to privilege texts over other sources, but for the simple reason that the Chinese would not have known Kuan-yin if there were no Chinese translations of Buddhist scriptures. Sūtras, therefore, constituted the first medium through which the cult of Kuan-yin became formed and then transformed. Yet despite the importance of scriptures, to which the Buddhist elite have traditionally granted the only normative authority, it would be naive to assume that the texts were ever universally studied by the faithful, or that what they describe and prescribe was ever completely followed by believers. In the study of Buddhism in general, but particularly in the present case, one must pay equal attention to the ideal picture found in texts and to the reality of the people's actual practices provided by epigraphical, art historical, ritualistic, and literary data. As Gregory Schopen pointed out, when scholars in Buddhist studies (and religious studies as well) rely solely on canonical texts as their primary and sometimes only source, the result is often distorted, if not downright mistaken (Schopen 1997:1–14). On the other hand, it is only when we know how Kuan-yin was originally presented in the scriptural texts that we can appreciate the extraordinary transformations this bodhisattva has undergone in China. It is only by a careful examination of the gaps between the Chinese Kuan-yin and his/her roots in the scriptural sources that we can come to know the whole story of this bodhisattva.

There are numerous Buddhist scriptures connected with Kuan-yin. Gotō Daiyō, for instance, lists the more than eighty sūtras in which the bodhisattva appears (Gotō 1958:283–88). This is by no means an exhaustive list, for the esoteric sūtras connected with Kuan-yin alone amount to eighty-eight and occupy 506 pages of the Taishō canon (volume 20), the modern edition of the Chinese Buddhist Tripiṭaka printed during 1922–1933 in Japan. When we examine these sūtras, however, it quickly becomes apparent that they do not treat the bodhisattva in the same way.

Avalokiteśvara's roles vary widely, ranging from a walk-on bit player of the attending entourage surrounding Śākyamuni Buddha to the leading star of his own grand dramas of universal salvation. The faces of the bodhisattva in canonical scriptures, just as in art and other mediums, is thus highly multivocal, multivalent, and multifaceted. Four kinds of roles can be discerned. Listed in ascending importance they are (1) a stick figure as a background prop; (2) a close associate and future successor of Amitāyus (Measureless Life) or Amitābha (Measureless Light) Buddha, thus a future buddha; (3) as the revealer of efficacious methods of salvation either through invocation of his name or specific dhāraṇīs at the request of Śākyamuni Buddha, he emerges as a savior and sometimes is identified as a past buddha; and (4) an independent savior. Although roles 2, 3, and 4 are found in China (role 1 understandably never receives much attention), it is really role 4 that has become dominant. The different roles Avalokiteśvara assumes in the scriptures might reflect the increasing importance of his stature. On the other hand, they might also reflect different cultic traditions about the bodhisattva. At least three separate and distinct cults can be identified: that of a compassionate savior not bound to a specific place as represented by the *Lotus Sūtra*, that of the chief helper of Amitābha Buddha found in the Pure Land sūtras, and that of a sage connected with the holy island Potalaka, as seen in the *Avataṃsaka Sūtra*. The three cultic traditions developed independently. In the esoteric scriptures, Avalokiteśvara is usually identified as living on Potalaka.

In the following survey of sūtras, I use a typology based on the ascending importance of his roles, rather than listing them in accordance to their sectarian affiliations in Chinese Buddhism, such as the *Lotus Sūtra* with the T'ien-t'ai, the *Avataṃsaka Sūtra* with the Hua-yen, the *Longer Sukhāvatīvyūha Sūtra* (Wu-liang-shou ching) and the *Sūtra of Visualization on Amitāyus Buddha* (Kuan Wu-liang-shou ching) with the Pure Land, or the *Heart Sūtra* and *Śūraṅgama Sūtra* associated with the Ch'an school. Although such classification provides evidence that Kuan-yin is worshiped in all major schools of Chinese Buddhism, yet there are also some compelling reasons why this is not a good classifying device. This is because while these texts were included in the foundational canons for those schools, Chinese monks, not to mention ordinary lay people, did not study sūtras according to their sectarian affiliations. These and certain esoteric sūtras have enjoyed favor with devotees of Kuan-yin regardless of their orientation, so it is meaningless to adhere to such an artificial distinction. Moreover, as I have argued elsewhere, the tendency of merging or combining different schools has been so strong since the Sung dynasty that we should be careful not to impose strict sectarian distinctions, which are very much associated with the Japanese model, onto the Chinese reality (Yü 1981, 1998).

The typology used here is instead based on the roles and functions of Kuan-yin. It helps us understand why the Chinese have chosen specific scriptures for emphasis as they did, for it was precisely these scriptures that highlighted the central role of Kuan-yin as the savior. While paying attention to the various roles of the bodhisattva, I also follow closely the names the translators gave to Avalokiteśvara as well as his physical appearance as described in these texts.

The Bodhisattva as One of the Buddha's Attending Entourage

One of the earliest scriptures in which the bodhisattva, whose name is given as Kuan-yin, is mentioned is the *Cheng-chü kuang-ming ting-i ching* (Sūtra on the Mental Fixation of Integral Illumination), a sūtra belonging to the Perfection of Wisdom group, translated by the Indo-Scythian Chih-yao in 185. Kuan-yin is the last of thirty attending bodhisattvas who are called "enlightened gentlemen" (*ming-shih,* T 15:451c). This text is one of the earliest Buddhist sūtras translated into Chinese, less than forty years after the coming of the Parthian monk An Shih-kao whose arrival in Loyang in 148 signaled the real beginning of the introduction of Buddhism into China.[1] The translation of many sūtras has been attributed to Lokakṣema, a contemporary of Chih-yao. Paul Harrison (1993), who has made extensive study of Lokakṣema's works, accepts only nine as undisputably done by the translator. A search of these sūtras yields an interesting discovery: Avalokiteśvara does not appear in any of them, not even as a bit player. It is Mañjuśrī and, in some cases, Maitreya, who heads the list of attending bodhisattvas. It is not difficult to understand why Mañjuśrī, but not Avalokiteśvara, is mentioned in these sūtras. They belong primarily to the Perfection of Wisdom literature that extols wisdom, embodied by Mañjuśrī, more than compassion, represented by Avalokiteśvara. Avalokiteśvara is called K'uei-yin (He Who Peeks the Sounds) in the *Ugrapariprcchā Sūtra* (T 12:15b) by the Parthian translator An Hsüan (ca. 180). Similarly, the same name is found in the *Vimalakīrti Sūtra,* which was translated by Chih-ch'ien (ca. 220–252), another Indo-Scythian monk (T 14:519b). In these two sūtras Avalokiteśvara appears together with some fifty other bodhisattvas. He receives a more prominent role when he is singled out together with Ta-shih-chih (Mahāsthāmaprāpta) as one of the two foremost bodhisattvas in Amitābha's Land of Bliss in the sūtras centering on this Mahāyāna Buddha. The revelant passages describing Avalokiteśvara in the Sanskrit version of the *Longer Sukhāvatīvyūha Sūtra* are translated by Luis Gómez:

> One of them is Avalokiteshvara, the bodhisattva mahasattva. The other is called Sthamaprapta. Departing from this, our buddha-field, they were reborn in the Land of Bliss. And all the bodhisattvas who have been born in this buddha-field are endowed with the thirty-two marks of the superior human being, possessing perfect bodies. They are experts in meditation and psychic powers, experts in the analysis by means of discernment. They are skillful, of sharp faculties, in control of their faculties, possessing the faculties of those who have perfect knowledge, their faculties neither depressed nor agitated, having gained higher receptivity, possessing endless and limitless virtue. (1996:97–98)

This sūtra was one of the earliest Mahāyāna scriptures translated into Chinese. It was translated twelve times, out of which five versions have been preserved. Translator attributions of these recensions have long been in dispute (Fujita 1970:13–115). Of the surviving recensions, the earliest was attributed to Lokakṣema. In this version of the sūtra, whose Chinese title is *Fo-shuo Wu-liang ch'ing-ching p'ing-teng chüeh ching* (Sūtra of the Enlightenment of Measureless Purity and Equality Spoken by the Buddha),[2] Avalokiteśvara and Sthāmaprāpta are said always to attend Amitābha and to be able to go to the numerous buddha lands of ten directions at will. It does not emphasize light symbolism, but declares, "When good men or good women meet with a crisis and experience fear, if they take refuge in Avalokiteśvara, none will not receive deliverance." However, *Fo-shuo Wu-liang-shou ching* (Sūtra of the Buddha of Measureless Life Spoken by the Buddha), whose translation has traditionally been attributed to the Sogdian Sanghavarman in 252,[3] does play up the majestic light of the two bodhisattvas, which is said to "shine universally on the three thousand chiliocosms." In 1160 Wang Jih-hsiu, a Pure Land devotee, compiled *Ta O-mi-t'o ching* (The Greater Amitābha Sūtra) using all available Chinese versions of the text, and he placed equal emphasis on Avalokiteśvara's majestic light and salvific power:

> Amitābha Buddha and all the bodhisattvas and śrāvakas (voice-hearers) in his land issue light of various degrees from their crowns. Whereas the śrāvakas send out light of seven *chang* (ten Chinese feet), the bodhisattvas send out light of many myriads of thousands miles. There are two bodhisattvas who are foremost in honor. One is called Kuan-shih-yin and the other Ta-shih-chih who always sit on either side of the Buddha and attend

> to him on state matters. The Buddha and the two bodhisattvas discuss the present and future events of the worlds in the ten directions. When the Buddha wants to send them to other buddha lands, they can immediately go there with their divine feet just as a buddha. They can also come down to this world in their duplicate bodies to assist the Buddha's transforming work. However, although they are here, they are nevertheless not absent from that land. Their wisdom and majestic power are without peer. The light issuing from their crowns illuminates the worlds of a thousand buddhas. If people living in this world, be they men or women, should encounter dangers, crises, fearful events, or troubles with the government, as long as they take refuge in Kuan-shih-yin Bodhisattva with singleness of mind, they will receive deliverance without fail. (T 12:336a)

The interest shown to this sūtra was soon reflected in art. One of the earliest Amitāyus triads dates to the 420s C.E. Sculpted in stucco, it can be found in Ping-lin Ssu Cave 169, which is located in eastern Kansu(*Yung-ch'ing Ping-lin Ssu*, pls. 21, 24). The names of the bodhisattvas are clearly identified in the inscribed cartouches. Kuan-shih-yin is on the left side of Amitāyus and holds a lotus bud in one hand. This clearly indicates the beginning of the Pure Land faith in China. Inspired most likely by Hui-yüan's (344–416) energetic promotion of the Pure Land faith, art began to reflect both the belief in Amitābha/ Amitāyus and Kuan-yin as well as the paradisiacal beauty of the Pure Land itself. A stele excavated from the Wan-fo Monastery in Ch'eng-tu, Szechwan, undated but found together with stelae dating to 523 and 548 C.E., have two headless bodhisattvas (most likely Kuan-yin and Ta-shih-chih, the attendants of Amitābha) depicted on the front side, while the reverse side has Amitābha in the middle, and the Pure Land represented by a garden with canals serving as the pond of rebirth with the blessed swimming among the lotuses. Some fifty years later, the same interest in rebirth in the Pure Land led to the production of similar art in the north. For instance, Cave 2 of the Southern Hsiang-t'ang-shan carved during the Northern Ch'i (550–577) depicted a scene of the Pure Land and rebirth comparable to the Szechwan example (Howard 1996a:16–17, Howard et al. forthcoming; Yüan 1991). The depiction of the Pure Land and the triad would become major themes in Chinese Buddhist art in later periods.

The Bodhisattva as a Future Buddha Succeeding Amitāyus or Amitābha

Several sūtras translated into Chinese quite early have as their main theme the bodhisattva's receiving the prediction of becoming a buddha in the future. Two have not survived, but judging from their titles, their message is similar to that found in *Sūtra of Kuan-shih-yin Bodhisattva's Receiving Prediction* (Kuan-shih-yin P'u-sa shou-chi ching), translated by the Khotanese monk Dharmodgata in 453.[4] Śākyamuni reveals that in the past he was a king living under a buddha whose land was infinitely more splendid than that of Amitābha. The king meditated in the garden and entered a samādhi. Two lotus stems sprang forth from the ground to his left and right and two young boys were born out of a transformation of the lotuses. They were respectively Kuan-yin and Shih-chih. After the nirvāṇa of Amitābha and the end of the Age of True Dharma, Kuan-yin would become a buddha whose name would be Tathāgāthā Universal Light King of Merit Mountain (P'u-kuang Kung-te-shan Wang Ju-lai, T 12:356a-357a). A similar story is found in *Karuṇā-puṇḍarīka Sūtra* (Pei-hua ching) translated by T'an-wu-ch'en in 414–426. In this case, Kuan-shih-yin was the eldest of one thousand sons of a *cakravartin* or world conqueror. He made a bodhisattva vow under Buddha Precious Treasure, who then predicted that Kuan-shih-yin would succeed Amitāyus and be given a similar title as above (Pien-chu I-chieh Kuang-ming Kung-te-shan Wang Ju-lai, T 3:185–86).

The relationship between Amitāyus and the bodhisattva is presented in these sūtras as being that which pertains between a monarch and heir apparent or a father and son. This kind of royal and kinship imagery must have impressed the Chinese very favorably, for the earliest Chinese apocryphal or indigenous scripture entitled *Sūtra of the Original Cause for Kuan-shih-yin Bodhisattva's Rebirth in the Pure Land* (Kuan-shih-yin P'u-sa wang-sheng ching-t'u pen-yüan ching) was indeed built around this theme. Mentioned in a catalogue compiled in 265–316 but without the name of a translator, it identifies the father as Śākyamuni, the mother as Amitābha, and the two sons as Kuan-shih-yin and Ta-shih-chih. Highlighted by the loving mother's tragic early death and the cruel treatment of the young children by the evil stepmother, the story presents a fascinating indigenous understanding of the relationships between the dramatic personae of the Buddhist scriptures. I discuss this text in chapter 3.

Kuan-yin and Kuan-shih-yin, therefore, were names used interchangeably in the earliest translations. Some scholars, including Ting Fu-pao (1874–1952), claimed that Kuan-yin was a contraction of Kuan-shih-yin that was used only beginning in the T'ang in order to avoid the taboo name of Emperor T'ai-tsung (r. 627–49), which was Li Shih-min (Tay 1976:17). This is clearly not the case, for in fact, Kuan-yin already appeared before Kuan-shih-yin, the name made famous by Kumārajīva when he translated the *Lotus Sūtra* in 406. In these early sūtras where the bodhisattva is mentioned, there is no reference to his physical appearance, nor any explanation concerning the meaning of his name. For the latter point, we have to turn to the *Lotus Sūtra*, among others.

The Bodhisattva Assumes the Role of a Savior

One of the central scriptures glorifying the bodhisattva is the *Lotus Sūtra*, which was translated into Chinese six times, of which three versions have survived. Karashima Seishi (1992) has compared the Chinese translations with the Sanskrit and Tibetan versions. The first is *Sūtra of the Lotus of the Correct Law* (Cheng fa-hua ching), translated by Dharmarakṣa, a native of Scythia, in 286. Chapter 23 of that sūtra is entitled "Universal Gateway" (P'u-men) and is devoted to Avalokiteśvara, who is called by the enigmatic name Kuang-shih-yin ("Abhalokaśvara," Sound-Illuminator of the World). This is a savior who delivers people from seven perils, frees them from the three poisons of lust, hatred, and ignorance, and grants infertile women either sons or daughters. The relevant passage concerning the name states:

> The Buddha told the Bodhisattva Inexhaustible Intent, "If sentient beings encounter hundreds, thousands, or millions of difficulties and disasters and their sufferings are unlimited, they will be delivered right away when they hear the name of Kuang-shih-yin and be freed from all pain. That is why he is called Kuang-shih-yin. If someone keeps the name in his heart and falls into a fire which rages through the hills and fields, burning forests, shrubs and houses, the fire will immediately die down when he hears the name of Kuang-shih-yin. If a person enters into a river and becomes frightened because of the swift current, when he calls the name of Kuang-shih-yin and takes refuge in him single-mindedly, the authority and supernatural power of the bodhisattva will protect him from drowning and enable him to reach safety. When a person sails in the ocean with many people to obtain pearls, corals, amber, etc. and the boat carrying the treasure enters a whirlpool and is about to be sunk by a sea monster, if he secretly thinks about the bodhisattva's majestic power and calls his name, then he and his companions will all be saved. [This is followed by the bodhisattva's saving people from the perils of wind, weapons, demons, imprisonment and robbers, all resulting from calling his name.] The realm of Kuang-shih-yin is without limit because it has his authority, supernatural power and merit. Because he is full of illuminating light (*kuang*), he is therefore called Kuang-shih-yin. (T 9:129a)

This earliest surviving version of the *Lotus Sūtra* makes it clear that hearing and calling the name of the bodhisattva are the chief reason the faithful will be saved, and that the bodhisattva is closely associated with light, which is the reason why he is called "Kuang-shih-yin." As John Holt noted in *Buddha in the Crown*, one of the most distinctive features of texts concerning Avalokiteśvara is indeed the strong presence of light symbolism (1991:31–34). But it leaves the connection between the bodhisattva and "sound" unspecified. Honda Yoshihide made a fascinating and convincing argument that the name "Kuang-shih-yin" has the same meaning as "Hsien-yin-sheng" (Manifesting Sound). This is the name of a bodhisattva corresponding to Avalokiteśvara in the *Sūtra of Illuminating Prajñā* (Fang-kuang po-jo ching, T 8:1b), translated by Moksala, a native of Khotan, the center of Central Asian Buddhism, in 291, five years after this sūtra. In both instances, the bodhisattva illuminates or enlightens the world through his voice or sound. The sound that has the power to enlighten is thus a special quality of the bodhisattva, but has nothing to do with the "sound" uttered by the suffering supplicant (Honda 1930:15–17, 27).

The next surviving translation of the sūtra is known as *Sūtra of the Lotus Flower of the Wonderful Law* (Miao-fa lien-hua ching); it was made in 406 by Kumārajīva, the famous translator from Kucha. This sūtra, along with the third version, known as *Sūtra of the Lotus Flower of the Wonderful Law with an Additional Chapter* (T'ien-p'in miao-fa lien-hua ching) translated by Jñānagupta and Dharmagupta in 601 take a different view. These translations have subsequently become the orthodox interpretation of the bodhisattva's name throughout East Asia. Both versions give the name of the bodhisattva as Kuan-shih-yin (Perceiver of the World's Sounds). The "Universal Gateway" is chapter 25 in Kumārajīva's translation and chapter 24 in Jñānagupta and Dharmagupta's version. Originally, neither Kumārajīva's nor Dharmarakṣa's version contained the gāthā section at the end of the chapter. It is found only in the translation made by Jñānagupta and Dharmagupta. Of the three, Kumārajīva's translation has always been the most popular version in China, and therefore the gāthā section was added to his version from the latter. When the Buddha is asked by Bodhisattva Inexhaustible Intent why Kuan-shih-yin is called this name, the Buddha answers, "Good man, suppose there are immeasurable hundreds, thousands, ten thousands, millions of living beings who are undergoing various trials and suffering. If they hear of this bodhisattva Perceiver of the World's Sounds and single-mindedly call his name, *then at once he will perceive the sound of their voices* and they will all gain deliverance from their trials" (Watson 1993:298–99, italics mine). Here the only requirement for a person to be saved is to call the name of the bodhisattva. A crucial sentence that I underlined previously is missing in Dharmarakṣa's translation: the bodhisattva's perceiving or recognizing the sound uttered by those who call his name. The name "Kuan-shih-yin" now makes perfect sense.

Chinese commentators interpreted the name by emphasizing the connection between the bodhisattva's perception or observation and the sounds made by the faithful who called out his name. Seng-chao (374–414), a brilliant disciple of Kumārajīva, wrote in his *Commentary on the Vimalakīrti Sūtra*, "Kumārajīva says that when anyone meets danger, he/she should call the name of and take refuge in the bodhisattva. As the bodhisattva perceives the sound, the person will receive deliverance. He is also named Kuan-shih-nien (Perceiver of the World's Thoughts), or Kuan-tzu-tsai (Master Perceiver)" (HTC 27:350a). It is interesting to note that Kumārajīva knew that the bodhisattva was also called Kuan-tzu-tsai, but used the other name in his translation instead. Chi-tsang (549–629), the founder of the Three-treatise School, wrote a commentary on the *Lotus* and explained the name Kuan-shih-yin this way: "*Kuan* is the wisdom which can perceive and *shih-yin* is the realm which is perceived. When realm and wisdom are mentioned together, we have the name Kuan-shih-yin" (T 34:624c). He also repeated the earlier commentator Fa-yün's (467–529) elaborate four-fold scheme of interpreting the name. In his commentary on the *Lotus*, Fa-yün states, "Kuan-shih-yin may be named four ways. The first is Kuan-shih-yin, which means that he delivers by perceiving the sounds of the world. The second is Kuan-shih-shen [body], which means that he delivers by perceiving the bodily karma of the sentient beings. The third is Kuan-shih-i [intentions], which means that he delivers by perceiving the mental karma of the sentient beings. The fourth is Kuan-shih-yeh [karma], which contains the previous three names. If you ask me why we only use the name Kuan-shih-yin, my answer is that to create karma by speech is easy, but to do good with regard to body and intention is hard. Moreover, in this Sahā world of ours, we usually worship the Buddha with our voices. That is why Kuan-shih-yin becomes the established name" (HTC 42:381a).

The *Sūtra of Visualization on Amitāyus Buddha* (Kuan Wu-liang-shou Fo ching) has always been recognized as one of the three main scriptures of the Pure Land School (together with the *Longer Sukhāvatīvyūha* and the *Shorter Sukhāvatīvyūha* sūtras). There is only one extant Chinese version of the sūtra that was traditionally attributed to Kālayaśas (ca. 424–453), another monk from Central Asia, who was supposed to have translated it in 430. Modern scholarship has called this into question. First of all, Kālayaśas was not listed as the translator in the authoritative catalogue *Ch'u san-tsang chi-chi* (A Compilation of Notices on the Translation of the Tripiṭaka) compiled by Seng-yu (445–518) in 515. He classified the sūtra under those whose translators were unknown. According to Sueki Fumihito (1986a, 1986b), who has studied this issue extensively, there are several different opinions regarding the origin of the sūtra. Although some scholars believe that the sūtra was composed in India (Hayashima 1964; Hirakawa 1984), others believed that it was composed in

Central Asia (Kasugai 1953, Fujita 1985), yet still other scholars believed that it was composed in China (Tsukinowa 1971).

Recently, scholars tend to see the sūtra as a product of several stages. Although the original frame was established in Central Asia, most likely in Qoco (Kao-ch'ang), located in Turfan, the sūtra was compiled with later additions in China (Yamada 1976; Pas 1977). This sūtra offers sixteen topics for visualization, which is the meaning of *kuan*. The tenth topic deals specifically with the visualization of Kuan-shih-yin. The passage instructs the meditator to visualize the bodhisattva's features in such great detail that some scholars have suggested that it might be based on the model of an actual image (Pas 1995:38). The detailed iconographic description, particularly a buddha who is usually taken to be Amitābha on his crown, serves as a standard for later artistic renditions and identification of the bodhisattva. The light symbolism that is already present in the *Lotus* receives even stronger emphasis: "Within the circle of light emanating from his whole body, appear illuminated the various forms and marks of all beings that live in the five paths of existence. On top of his head is a heavenly crown of gems like those fastened (on Indra's head), in which crown there is a transformed Buddha standing, twenty-five yojanas high" (Takakusu 1969:182).

This sūtra is closely related to five other visualization sūtras that originated in Central Asia, probably also Turfan, and were translated into Chinese from the end of the fourth to the middle of the fifth century.[5] All of them teach the practitioner to engage in visualization so that a vision of the buddha or bodhisattva can be created. Mental concentration, not calling of the holy name, is therefore the central focus. The obtaining of the divine vision guarantees the meditator's salvation. The practitioner is told that Amitābha, Kuan-shih-yin and Ta-shih-chih would appear before him at the time of death to welcome him to the Pure Land. *Kuan* in this case is, therefore, better understood as contemplation or visualization than observation, perception, or investigation.

The *Śūraṅgama Sūtra* (Shou leng-yen ching) was traditionally believed to have been translated by Paramiti in 705. This attribution has also been called into question, and modern scholarship regards this sūtra to have been composed in China (Mochizuki 1946). The bodhisattva is called Kuan-shih-yin or Kuan-yin, but it offers a different explanation for the name. It provides yet a third meaning of *kuan*. The bodhisattva begins by describing how he obtained samādhi by meditating on the organ of hearing as instructed by a buddha also named Kuan-shih-yin under whom he studied:

> At first by directing the organ of hearing into the stream of meditation, this organ was detached from its object, and by wiping out (the concept of)

> both sound and stream-entry, both disturbance and stillness became clearly non-existent. Thus advancing step by step both hearing and its object ceased completely, but I did not stop where they ended. When the awareness of this state and this state itself were realized as non-existent, both subject and object merged into the void, the awareness of which became all-embracing. With further elimination of the void and its object both creation and annihilation vanished giving way to the state of Nirvāṇa which then manifested. (Luk 1966:135)

The sound mentioned here is not that made by the faithful who cry out his name, but any sound that, when examined (*kuan*) with penetrating insight, leads to the realization of *śūnyatā*. Although the bodhisattva saves beings from various dangers and grants fourteen kinds of fearlessness in this sūtra, the reason he can do so is different from that given in the *Lotus*. "Since I myself do not meditate on sound but on the meditator, I cause all suffering beings to look into the sound of their voices in order to obtain liberation" (Luk 1966:139).[6] The bodhisattva concludes by once more linking his name to his meditation on hearing: "That Buddha praised my excellent method of perfection and gave me, in the presence of the assembly, the name of Kuan-shih-yin. Because of my all-embracing (absolute function of) hearing, my name is known everywhere" (Luk 1966:142). In the *Śūraṅgama Sūtra*, therefore, *kuan* is understood neither as perceiving and responding to the cries for help uttered by the faithful, nor visualizing the divine visage of the bodhisattva, but as investigating the real nature of sound and realizing it as being void.

Let us continue with our survey of the chronological appearance of the bodhisattva's names. Bodhiruci combined the two names and called the bodhisattva Kuan-shih-tzu-tsai (Master Perceiver of the World) in *Treatise on the Lotus Sūtra* (Fa-hua ching-lun), which he translated in 508. The name Kuan-tzu-tsai was used for the first time in *The Great Prajñā-pāramitā Sūtra* (Ta po-jo p'o-lo mi-to ching), translated by Hsüan-tsang in 663, and the eighty-volume version of *Hua-yen ching* (Avataṃsaka Sūtra), translated by Śikṣānanda in 695–699 (in contrast to the sixty-volume version of the sūtra done by Chüeh-hsien in 420 in which the bodhisattva is called Kuan-shih-yin). K'uei-chi (632–682), Hsüan-tsang's chief disciple, provided an explanation for the name in his *Profound Eulogy on the Heart Sūtra* (Po-jo hsin ching yu-tsan) and, following his own master, condemned the older name Kuan-shih-yin as wrong:

> [The bodhisattva] practiced the six perfections in the past and has now obtained the fruit of perfection. Because he is foremost in observing everything with wisdom, he has now accomplished ten kinds of mastery (*tzu-*

tsai). First, he has mastery over lifespan because he can either prolong or shorten his life. Second, he has mastery over mind, for he is untainted by life and death. Third, he has mastery over wealth, for he can materialize it whenever he so desires and this is the result of his perfection in giving. Fourth, he has mastery over karma, for he only does good deeds and encourages others to do the same. Fifth, he has mastery over life, for he can go wherever he pleases and this is the result of his perfection in discipline. Sixth, he is the master of superior understanding, for he can change into whatever he so pleases and this is the result of his perfection in patience. Seventh, he is a master of vows, for he can establish happily whatever he perceives and this is the result of his perfection in vigor. Eighth, he is a master of supernatural power, for he is fully endowed with paranormal abilities resulting from his perfection in samādhi. Ninth, he is a master of insight, for while following words and sounds he penetrates into the wisdom. Tenth, he has mastery over Dharma, for his understanding always accords with the scriptures and this is the result of his perfection in wisdom. His position is next in line to become a buddha, but his realization is the same as a buddha. There is no obscure place that he does not illuminate. He is thus called Kuan-tzu-tsai (Master Perceiver). If one calls him Kuan-yin, both the word and the meaning are lost. (HTC 41:439a)

Why did translators give this bodhisattva two different names? Despite the criticisms of Hsüan-tsang and K'uei-chi, they continued to favor Kuan-shih-yin or Kuan-yin. There is also no evidence to justify the charge that the earlier translations of this name were mistakes. In fact, these various Chinese names are translations from two different spellings of the bodhisattva's name. Kuan-shih-yin was the translation for Avalokitasvara, whereas Kuan-tzu-tsai was the translation for Avalokiteśvara. Fa-yün, who compiled a dictionary of translated terms, *Fan-i ming-i chi* (Meaning of Buddhist Terms), commented that the two names resulted from two different versions in the imported scriptures (T 54:1062a). In an article published in 1927, Mironov confirmed the observation made by Fa-yün in the fifth century. He studied the Sanskrit fragments of the *Lotus Sūtra* manuscripts brought by Ōtani's expedition from Eastern Turkestan or Sinkiang. "In one of the three sets of fragments which for paleographical reasons may be assigned to the end of the fifth century A.D. he happened to find three fragments of the twenty-fourth chapter, devoted to the praise of Avalokiteśvara. The name of the Bodhisattva is spelt Avalokitasvara. As the name occurs *five times* on an incomplete leaf, the possibility of a clerical error is hardly admissible. The circumstance is especially important, as the Petrovsky MS. of SP. from Kashgar has the usual form Avalokiteśvara. Thus a hereto missing link between the Indian and Chinese traditions seems to have been found. It cannot be doubted that Avalokitasvara was the original form, later supplanted by Avalokiteśvara" (Mironov 1927:243). Building on this discovery, Gotō suggests that Avalokitasvara was used in scriptures coming into China from Kucha such as those translated by Kumārajīva and other Central Asian missionaries, while Avalokiteśvara was found in scriptures originating in India such as those translated by Hsüan-tsang who obtained the texts during his long sojourn there (Gotō 1958:9).

The translators of the Chinese sūtras, therefore, had access to the two different versions of the bodhisattva's name. It is interesting that despite strong objections against the name of Kuan-yin or Kuan-shih-yin voiced by Hsüan-tsang and others, it is this name that all East Asians have come to use in referring to this bodhisattva. Commentators, as I have indicated before, have also come up with fanciful interpretations of the "sound" part of the name.

Before I turn to the esoteric sūtras that present Kuan-yin as a savior who reveals powerful dhāraṇīs, I want to discuss the bodhisattva's appearance in the scriptures discussed so far. With the exception of the *Sūtra of Visualization on Amitāyus Buddha,* which provides detailed instruction about how to visualize the bodhisattva, none of the rest describe his physical appearance. Because of the lack of specification, artisans who made images could not create any distinct iconography for him but followed models introduced from India and Central Asia. A number of fifth-century gilt bronze images of the bodhisattva who was called either Kuang-shih-yin and Kuan-shih-yin in the inscriptions have survived. Many bear the reign era of T'ai-ho (477–499) of the Northern Wei. The earliest of this type found in a collection in the West is represented by the gilt bronze identified as the "Lotus-bearer" and dated 453 from the Freer (figure 2.1; Howard 1993:99). The inscriptions generally express the wish that the dead parents will stay with Kuan-shih-yin forever as found in the inscription of a 470 bronze or that they would be born in Potalaka and be with Kuang-shih-yin as expressed in the inscription of a 498 bronze (Matsubara 1995: I:35, 88). The majority have the bodhisattva standing, with the right hand holding a lotus and the left hand either grasping a scarf or holding a bottle. But sometimes he is also depicted as sitting in a pensive pose with his right hand touching his chin. The so-called "buddha in the crown," one of the most important attributes of Kuan-yin, was never depicted at this time. According to Angela Howard, it was not until the third quarter of the sixth century that this image first appeared. In fact, Kuan-yin was depicted no differently from Maitreya in this early stage.[7]

Matsumoto Eiichi made the same suggestion about the iconographic identity between Kuan-yin and Maitreya and cited an example to prove his point.

Figure 2.1. The "Lotus Bearer," dated 453 C.E. *Courtesy of the Freer Gallery of Art, Washington, D.C.*

As recorded in the *Sung shu* (History of the Sung), fascicle 53, Tai Yung was a skillful sculptor and was asked by his friend Chiang I of Chi-yang (in present-day Shantung Province) during the Yüan-chia era (420–430) to make an image of Kuan-yin. He devoted himself to the task for several years but without success. Then he had a dream in which he was told that the reason he could not succeed was because his friend had no affinity with Kuan-yin and that he should make a Maitreya image instead. Upon waking, he decided to tell Chiang I who in the meantime sent him a letter making the same request because the latter also had the same dream on the same night. Without much alteration he could quickly finish the image successfully.[8] Indeed, the parity of these two bodhisattvas was also attested by the numerous images of them made by the faithful (Matsumoto 1937:8–9).[9]

Although the sūtras do not describe what Kuan-yin looks like, some of them do speak of the various forms or manifestations (*hua-shen*) he can assume. In general, we can distinguish two types of his manifestations. The first is a list of the bodhisattva's manifestations in either superhuman, human, or nonhuman forms in order to carry out his work of salvation based on the spiritual principle of *upāya* (*fang-pien*, skillful means). This is the case found in the *Lotus*, *Śūraṅgama* and *Karaṇḍavyūha* (Ta-sheng chuang-yen pao-wang ching, Sūtra of the Mahāyāna, the Precious King of Adornment), an important esoteric sūtra. The second is represented by esoteric scriptures in which the bodhisattva appears with multiple heads and hands holding various symbolic implements, revealing dhāraṇīs with marvelous efficacy. Another outstanding characteristic about the esoteric sūtras is that they also provide very detailed instruction concerning rules of either carving and casting or painting the image of the bodhisattva.

The *Lotus Sūtra* speaks of the bodhisattva appearing in thirty-three different forms.[10] It states, "Good man, if there are living beings in the land who need someone in the body of a Buddha in order to be saved, Bodhisattva Perceiver of the World's Sounds immediately manifests himself in a Buddha body and preaches the Law for them" (Watson 1993:301). Following the same formulae, the bodhisattva manifests himself in the bodies of a pratyeka-buddha, a voice-hearer, King Brahmā, Śakrā, Self-mastering God [Īśvara], Great Self-mastering God [Maheśvara],[11] a great heavenly general, Vaiśravaṇa, a petty king, a rich man, a householder, a chief minister, a Brahmin, a monk, a nun, a layman believer, a laywoman believer, the wife of a rich man, a householder, a chief minister, or of a Brahmin, a young boy or a young girl, a heavenly being [deva], a dragon, a yakṣa, a gandharva, an asura, a garuḍa, a kiṃnara, a mahoraga, and a vajra-bearing god. Banners from Tun-huang provide some illustrations of these diverse manifestations.[12]

Several points need to be made. First of all, the thirty-three manifestations of the bodhisattva had relevance to a religious universe intelligible only to people living in ancient India. Brahmā, Śakrā, and Śiva were Hindu gods. Vaiśravaṇa, devas, and cakravartin were important deities and ideal types of the Indian spiritual and epistemological universe. Even the nonhuman inhabitants of that cosmos such as the asura, nāga (dragon), and yakṣa were intelligible only to readers brought up in the Indian cultural context. That was why Gotō argued convincingly that the author of this chapter of "Universal Gateway" of the *Lotus Sūtra* must have been consciously addressing an audience familiar with Vedic and Hindu mythologies and beliefs. By making the Buddhist bodhisattva capable of assuming the forms of all the important pre-Buddhist and non-Buddhist deities, Avalokiteśvara was thus elevated above them all (Gotō 1958:294–95).

Moreover, the number thirty-three is meaningful only in the Vedic and Hindu context. It must be related to the Heaven of the Thirty-three Gods, or the heaven of the god Indra, one of the most powerful Vedic deities, where he rules over the thirty-two devas. It is the second of the six heavens of form; its capital is situated on the summit of Mt. Sumeru, which is in the center of the universe. The number therefore has a symbolic, but not literal, meaning (Gotō 1958: 167–68).

Second, the forms Avalokiteśvara assumes in order to preach the Dharma more effectively are generic, but not individualized persons. It does not say that the bodhisattva appears as a king with a specific name, not to mention a biography, but rather as a generic king without any identity. It is more a role than a personality. Third and finally, of the forms Avalokiteśvara assumes, only seven are feminine. I make these points now in order to highlight the contrast with the Chinese thirty-three forms of Kuan-yin that eventually replaced them, some of which will be discussed in later chapters. In the latter case, all the forms with clearly Vedic and Hindu connotations disappeared. The Chinese forms were predominantly feminine, and they often refer either to some historical incidents that happened in China or some legends familiar to a Chinese audience. This was one of several means through which Avalokiteśvara was thereby transformed into Kuan-yin.

Avalokiteśvara's manifestations also feature in the *Śūraṅgama Sūtra* and the *Karaṇḍavyūha Sūtra*. Although almost all of the thirty-two forms mentioned in the *Śūraṅgama Sūtra* correspond to those found in the *Lotus*, a major difference is that the *Śūraṅgama* provides explanations of why the bodhisattva chooses to assume each form. Great care is taken in justifying the appropriateness of each form for each type of the bodhisattva's audience so that the importance of *upāya* is made clear. I cite some relevant passages for illustration:

- If there are living beings who desire to be lords of devas to rule over the realms of the gods, I will appear as Śakrā to teach them the Dharma so that they reach their goals.
- If there are living beings who wish to roam freely in the ten directions, I will appear as Īśvaradeva to teach them the Dharma so that they reach their goals.
- If there are living beings who enjoy discussing well-known sayings and practice pure living, I will appear as a respectable scholar to teach them the Dharma so that they reach their goals.
- If there are living beings who wish to govern cities and towns, I will appear as a magistrate to teach them the Dharma so that they reach their goals.

- If there are women who are eager to study and learn and leave home to observe the precepts, I will appear as a bhikṣuṇī to teach them the Dharma so that they reach their goals.
- If there are women who are keen to fulfil their home duties thereby setting a good example to other families and the whole country, I will appear as a queen, a princess, or a noble lady to teach them the Dharma so that they reach their goals.
- If there are young men who are chaste, I will appear as a celibate youth to teach them the Dharma so that they reach their goals.
- If there are dragons (nāgas) who wish to be freed from bondage in their realms, I will appear as a nāga to teach them the Dharma so that they reach their goals (Luk 1966:136–38).

The thirty-two manifestations of the bodhisattva in the *Śūraṅgama Sūtra* follow closely those in the *Lotus*, with the omission of Vajrapāṇi, and the substitution of Vaiśravaṇa (Heavenly King of the North) with the Four Heavenly Kings. The *Lotus* clearly was the model for the *Śūraṅgama*. Like the *Lotus*, the *Śūraṅgama* promises believers deliverances from various dangers. Sharing a characteristic common to esoteric scriptures glorifying Avalokiteśvara, which I discuss later, the *Śūraṅgama* lists the benefits one by one and calls them the fourteen fearless powers bestowed by the bodhisattva.[13] Building on its hermeneutics of "hearing" and "sound," the sūtra provides a philosophical link between insight into the real nature of everything as void and the resultant psychological state of fearlessness. It is in this way reminiscent of the view put forward in the *Heart Sūtra* where Avalokiteśvara is said to be free from fear because he does not have any "thought-coverings" as a result of having penetrated into the voidness of everything (Conze 1959:163).

The *Śūraṅgama Sūtra* shares another distinctive feature with the esoteric scriptures in that it refers to Avalokiteśvara as having many heads, arms, and eyes:

> When I first realized the hearing mind which was most profound, the Essence of Mind (i.e., the Thatāgata store) disengaged itself from hearing and could no longer be divided by seeing, hearing, feeling and knowing, and so became one pure and clean all-pervading precious Bodhi. This is why I can take on different wonderful forms and master a countless number of esoteric mantras. I can appear with one, three, five, seven, nine, eleven and up to 108, 1,000, 10,000, and 84,000 sovereign (cakra) faces; with two, four, six, eight, ten, twelve, fourteen, sixteen, eighteen, twenty, twenty-four and up to 108, 1,000, 10,000 and 84,000 arms making various gestures

(mudrās); and with two, three, four, nine up to 108, 1,000, 10,000, and 84,000 clean and pure precious eyes, either merciful or wrathful, and in a state either of still imperturbability (dhyāna-samādhi) or of absolute wisdom (prajñā) to save and protect living beings so that they can enjoy great freedom. (Luk 1966:141)

The *Karaṇḍavyūha Sūtra*, translated by T'ien-hsi-tsai into Chinese from a Tibetan version around 1000, has a number of esoteric characteristics as well. It is included in the section on esoteric sūtras in the Taishō canon (T vol. 20). Because this is one of the few sūtras that present Kuan-yin as a universal savior, I shall discuss it in greater detail in the next section. I mention here only that according to this sūtra, the bodhisattva appears in the following twenty forms to save all beings: buddha, bodhisattva, pratyeka-buddha, voice-hearer, Maheśvara, Nārāyana, Śakrā, Brahmā, God of the Sun, God of the Moon, God of Fire, God of Water, God of Wind, nāga, Vināyaka, yakṣa, Vaiśravaṇa, king, minister, father, and mother (T 20:50c-51a). It is interesting to note that compared with the earlier thirty-three or thirty-two manifestations, more Hindu gods are mentioned in this sūtra, which clearly tries to present Avalokiteśvara as the creator of the cosmos as well as a universal savior. Only one of the manifestations, that of a mother, is feminine.

I now turn to the forms of Avalokiteśvara found in the esoteric sūtras glorifying this bodhisattva who teaches saving dhāraṇīs, of which the *Karaṇḍavyūha* can be counted as one example. A word about terminology may be necessary. I use the word "exoteric" to translate the Chinese *hsien* and "esoteric," *mi*, two categories for the classification of Buddhist scriptures used in China and the rest of East Asia. Esoteric Buddhism is also called Tantric Buddhism, whose distinguishing marks are the emphasis placed on the possibility of everyone's achieving Buddhahood in one lifetime and the use of mantra or dhāraṇī, mudrā, maṇḍala, and visualization to obtain both spiritual and worldly benefits. The deities visualized in these *sādhana*s or practices, moreover, are supernatural and supramandane, sporting multiple arms and heads, for instance.

In including several texts translated before the T'ang under the discussion of esoteric or Tantric sūtras, I do not follow the established Japanese scholarship on this topic. Japanese scholars make a distinction between the so-called mixed (*zō*) and pure (*jun*) esoteric Buddhism, reserving the latter for the texts translated in the T'ang by the Tantric master Amoghavajra, specifically those preached by Vairocana, the Dharmakāya Buddha, namely the *Mahāvairocana Sūtra* (Ta-jih ching) and *Tattvasaṃgraha Sūtra* (Chin-kang-ting ching). In contrast, they consider all esoteric scriptures translated before the T'ang and preached by Śākyamuni, the Nirmāṇakāya Buddha, as "mixed," even if these texts share the ritual stipulations and soteriological goals similar to the "pure" ones. There is definitely a sense of hierarchy in the classification, as this sweeping generalization by a Japanese scholar makes clear: "*Zōmitsu* [mixed esoteric Buddhism] followers perform their rituals to obtain secular benefits . . . but *junmitsu* [pure esoteric Buddhism] followers pursue the attainment of Buddhahood. *Zōmitsu* sūtras have little relationship to Buddhist thought in their contents, but *junmitsu* equivalents attempt to harmonize esoteric rituals and Mahāyāna Buddhist thought" (Matsunaga 1979:ii). Because such a hierarchical distinction reflects the sectarian interests of Japanese Shingon Buddhism, which wants to privilege Kūkai's textual transmission, scholars nowadays are careful not to impose it on the historical reality of Chinese Buddhism.[14]

One of the earliest such sūtras is the *Dhāraṇī Sūtra of Invoking Avalokiteśvara Bodhisattva to Dissipate Poison and Harm* (Ch'ing Kuan-shih-yin P'u-sa hsiao-fu tu-hai t'o-lo-ni ching—*Ch'ing Kuan-yin ching* for short) translated by Nan-t'i during the last years of the Eastern Chin dynasty (317–420). The T'ien-t'ai school has always put special emphasis on this sūtra ever since the T'ien-t'ai master Chih-i (538–597) used it as one of the sources for the last of the four forms of samādhis: neither walking nor sitting samādhi (Stevenson 1986:50; Donner and Stevenson 1993:28, 275–80). Although the bodhisattva appears in this sūtra in an ordinary human form and not with multiple heads and arms like other esoteric sūtras, it places the same degree of emphasis on the keeping of the dhāraṇīs as the latter.

The title of this sūtra is explained by the story set forth in the beginning of the scripture. A delegation of Vaiśalī citizens who suffer from all kinds of horrible diseases caused by yakṣas comes to the Buddha with an urgent request for help. The Buddha tells them to invoke Avalokiteśvara by offering him willow branches and pure water. The bodhisattva appears in front of the Buddha and proceeds to teach the people to chant three sets of dhāraṇīs, the last of which, consisting of fifteen phrases, is particularly powerful. Known as the "divine dhāraṇī of six-character phrases" (*liu-tzu chang-chü shen-chou*), chanting it together with the three-fold calling of Avalokiteśvara's name will save people from all kinds of dangers. To cite just a few examples, Avalokiteśvara will guide lost travelers by appearing in the form of a human being and leading them to safety; he will create a well and provide food to save people dying of thirst and hunger. Women who are on the point of death because of difficult childbirths will live; merchants who lose property to robbers will recover it because the latter will have a sudden change of heart. The dhāraṇī not only saves people from sufferings in this world, but will enable them not to be reborn in the realms of hell, hungry ghosts, animals, and asuras. Instead, they will be born in a place where they can see the Buddha and become freed after listening to the Dharma.

Avalokiteśvara is called the "Great Compassionate One" (Ta-pei) in this sūtra and is declared to be the savior who "courses in the five realms of rebirth" to carry out the work of salvation (T 20:36b).

Beginning in the Northern Chou dynasty (556–681), more esoteric scriptures about Avalokiteśvara with new dhāraṇīs were introduced into China. The deity in these scriptures appears not in a regular human form, but in the esoteric forms of many heads and many arms. The first of these new forms of Avalokiteśvara to be introduced to China was the Eleven-headed Avalokiteśvara (Ekadaśamukha, Shih-i-mien). The number eleven represents the cardinal and collateral points, zenith, nadir, and the fixed point of the center, the Indian symbolism of totality. Mallmann (1948) suggests that this assemblage of heads represent the epithet "all-sidedness" (Samantamukha, Ch. P'u-men or "Universal Gateway") given to the bodhisattva by the title of chapter 24 of the Sanskrit version of *Lotus Sūtra* (Strickmann 1996:140). Three sūtras, translated by Yeh-she-ch'üeh-to between 563 and 577, Hsüan-tsang in 659, and Amoghavajra in the eighth century are about this deity. Next, it was Avalokiteśvara holding a lasso (Amoghapāśa, Pu-k'ung-ssu-so), with which he drew to him the suffering beings for their deliverance, who figured in seven sūtras, the earliest of which was translated by She-na-ch'üeh-to in the Sui dynasty (581–618) and the rest by, among others, Hsüan-tsang and Bodhiruci (d. 727) in the T'ang dynasty. Sūtras on the Thousand-handed and Thousand-eyed Avalokiteśvara were translated next; thirteen of these were done during the T'ang. Aside from those by Chih-t'ung (done in 627–649), and Bhagavadharma (done in 650), Hsüan-tsang, Bodhiruci, and the three Tantric masters Śubhākarasiṃha (636–735), Vajrabodhi (670–741), and Amoghavajra also made their translations. A fourth esoteric form of Avalokiteśvara, in which he is holding the wheel of a wish-granting jewel (Cintāmaṇicakra, Ju-i-lun), symbolizing his limitless power of giving and his ever-ready graciousness to answer all prayers, is the subject of yet another nine sūtras, which were translated by I-tsing, Bodhiruci, Śikṣānanda, Vajrabodhi, Amoghavajra, and others, all in the T'ang.

Although these esoteric scriptures are devoted to different forms of Avalokiteśvara, they nevertheless share some common characteristics. The first of these is, of course, the emphasis on the chanting of the dhāraṇīs. Like the *Ch'ing Kuan-yin ching* and the *Karaṇḍavyūha*, they promise unfailing deliverance from all possible disasters and the gaining of worldly benefits and transcendent wisdom. They always categorize the benefits by listing them numerically. They emphasize minute, detailed, and correct procedures: how to make either a three-dimensional image of the deity (*maṇḍala*) or representational imagery painted on white cotton cloth (*pata*) or white wool, how to prepare the ritual arena, how many times one should chant the dhāraṇī, what ritual ingredients one should use in performing the fire offering (*homa*) to the deity, what hand gestures (*mudrā*) to perform and what visualizations of the deity to carry out during the rite. There are also magical recipes for averting specific disasters. Finally, all of the sūtras, with the exception of those translated by Hsüan-tsang, refer to the bodhisattva as Kuan-shih-yin.

Did the sequence in which the esoteric sūtras were translated into Chinese reflect the same sequence in which the various Tantric forms of the bodhisattva appeared in India? One would assume this was the case. But it is difficult to document the evolution. One reason is that not all the Tantric forms enjoyed equal popularity in India and China. For example, although the eleven-headed and thousand-armed Avalokiteśvara figures were very popular in China and a number of images have survived, the same cannot be said about them in India. Another reason why one should be cautious in imposing a rigid temporal sequence in the emergence of these Tantric forms of Avalokiteśvara is their simultaneous presence in some dhāraṇī collections. Michel Strickmann called our attention to two such collections of dhāraṇīs: one being the *Dhāraṇī Miscellany* (T'o-lo-ni tsa-chi) in ten fascicles and the second the *Collections of Dhāraṇī Sūtras* (T'o-lo-ni chi ching) in twelve fascicles. The former does not have the name of a translator, but because it is attached to Seng-yu's catalogue, it has been dated to the first half of the sixth century. The latter is an extract made by the Central Asian monk Atikura in 654 of a much larger work, *The Sūtra of the Great Vajra Bodhimaṇḍa* (Chin-kang ta-tao-ch'ang ching), which was never translated. Strickmann lamented the fact that the dhāraṇī-sūtras had been almost entirely neglected in contemporary Buddhist studies due to their rather unique characteristics: "for the dhāraṇī-sūtras as a group are too diffuse and heterogeneous, not to say too 'magical' to have warranted serious and prolonged attention. As far as the historiographical tradition, because of its main concern with outstanding personalities, it can find little room for discussion of a body of texts that is largely anonymous as well as unabashedly practical in orientation." He termed dhāraṇī-sūtras "efficient texts" because "they were written in view of realization, not philosophical reflection." They "form the basis for rituals and we must envisage them as circulating among persons to whose needs they corresponded, lay persons as well as monks and nuns" (Strickmann 1990:80).

For students interested in the actual rituals of invoking Kuan-yin as well as the real fears and hopes of the devotee engaged in such rituals, these two dhāraṇī collections offer invaluable information. Therefore, I discuss some highlights concerning the cult of Avalokiteśvara in these collections. The *Dhāraṇī Miscellany* contains thirty-seven dhāraṇīs revealed by Avalokiteśvara, scattered in six of the ten fascicles.[15] These dhāraṇīs are supposed to help the reciter eliminate sin, recover from eyesore, stomachache, fever, poison, unconsciousness, leprosy, memory loss, skin diseases, diarrhea, dysentery, fear, madness, swollenness of the body, and possession by ghosts and demons. They can also help one to achieve all one's wishes, including the wish to change one's gender. There are several different ways of invoking the bodhisattva, representing undoubtedly different ritual traditions. One says that the devotee must keep a fast (not eating meat, drinking wine, or taking the five forbidden pungent roots—garlic, the three kinds of onions, and leeks) for seven days. Then one must burn incense made of sandalwood in front of the image while chanting the dhāraṇī 108 times. With a concentrated mind, one calls the name of Avalokiteśvara three times and one's wish will be fulfilled. If one is spiritually advanced, the bodhisattva will appear in one's dream (T 21:607b). Another version provides a somewhat different way of invoking the bodhisattva. It says that the devotee should smear the ground in front of the image of the bodhisattva with fragrant mud, offer incense and flowers day and night to the image, and recite the dhāraṇī 120 times during each of the six periods of the day and night (morning, noon, evening and night, midnight, dawn). Responding to his prayer, Avalokiteśvara will appear in a form suitable to him and fulfill all his desires (T 21:607c).

Although both *sādhana*s mention the worship of the image of the bodhisattva, which clearly serves as the focus of the ritual, they do not describe how the image is to be created nor what it looks like. This is fortunately provided by a third text:

> You should use either pure white wool or fine cotton cloth to paint the image of Avalokiteśvara who is clothed in white and sits on a lotus flower. He holds a lotus in one hand and the other hand holds a water-pot (*kuṇḍikā*). His hair is piled high. From the eighth to the fifteenth day of the month, you should carry out the ritual. Wear new and clean clothes. Purify the ground in front of Avalokiteśvara's image with cow dung and then cover it with fragrant mud. Put raw milk in twelve containers, superior incense in four clay pots, flowers in sixteen jars, and pure water in four large clay pots. Burn black agura incense in sixteen clay lamps. Make a fire with resinous wood and place eight hundred lotus flowers to your side. With a mind full of respect, chant the dhāraṇī. Each time it is chanted, throw one lotus flower into the fire. Make your chanting continuous and your virtuous mind to be uninterrupted. Avalokiteśvara will appear from the east. He issues forth great brilliance which burns on top of the fire. He appears amidst the fire and looks exactly like the painted image. He is clothed in white, his hair is piled high, and he holds a lotus flower and a water-pot. When you see the bodhisattva, do not fear but should know that you will never be born in hell, among animals or hungry ghosts. You shall obtain whatever you wish. (T 21:612b-c)

This is a remarkable passage for a number of reasons. First of all, as pointed out by Strickmann, we have here the earliest description of a Buddhist *homa* or fire sacrifice. Originally the central rite of the ancient Vedic religion, *homa* was clearly non-Buddhist and Buddhist literature frequently refers to it as being practiced by Brahmins and pariah sorcerers. But Buddhists themselves eventually appropriated the *homa* sacrifice and it became a central feature of tantric *sādhanas*. According to Strickmann, the Buddhist *homa*, in its developed version, is essentially a ritual banquet, a fire sacrifice offered to the divinity. The prototypes for the Buddhist *homa* are two parallel rites that appeared earlier: the first consists of throwing mustard grains into the fire to chase away demons and the second consists of burning diverse kinds of incense in front of the icon to make the chosen deity appear (Strickmann 1996:141–42). While the rite just described represents the second type, the first rite of throwing mustard grains into fire is equally represented in the esoteric ritual texts connected with Avalokiteśvara discussed later in this chapter. The second point about the passage worth noting is its insistence on the color white being associated with the bodhisattva. Not only must the material with which the image is to be created be white in color, but the bodhisattva himself is to be painted as being clothed in white.

"The white clad one" (Pāṇḍaravāsinī, Pai-i) could therefore have originally been an epithet for the bodhisattva himself. But it was later turned into a goddess, who, together with Tārā, Bhṛkuṭī, Prajñāpāramitā, Locana, and Uṣṇīṣarāja, surround Avalokiteśvara in the maṇḍala described in chapter 2 of the *Mañjuśrīmulakalpa* (Fundamental Ordinance of Mañjuśrī, Ta-fang-kuang p'u-sa tsang Wen-chu-shih-li ken-pen i-kuei), a text compiled during different times from the early eighth to the tenth century (Przyluski 1923; Macdonald 1962). The Sanskrit original was lost, but it was translated into Chinese by T'ien-hsi-tsai, the same person who translated the *Karaṇḍhavyūha,* which is discussed in the next section. It provides theological justifications for the bodhisattva's transformations into any form, including that of a woman, to convert different types of living beings: "The bodhisattva had not only the possibility of assuming any form, but this means of adaptation to milieu and to circumstances was in fact necessary to convert the different classes of beings. And among these categories (e.g. birds, yakṣas, etc), the woman's form was expressly referred to as a means of 'guiding beings by worldly methods.'"[16] The goddesses accompanying Avalokiteśvara are not so much "consorts," but rather "handmaidens" or "hypostases" of the bodhisattva. David Snellgrove (1987: I,150) argues that unlike the Hindu divinities, Avalokiteśvara is celibate and providing him with a feminine entourage must have been inspired by the contemporary custom of princely figures who appeared thus in real life. This text could have provided a theological basis for the female White-robed Kuan-yin. Other local cults, such as the Brilliant Kings (Ming-wang, vidyarāja) in Yünnan and Szechwan seemed to be based on the same text (Howard 1999).

Avalokiteśvara also occupies a prominent position in the second collection of dhāraṇī-sūtras, the *Collections of Dhāraṇī Sūtras*, composed in the seventh century. The work provides a picture of the Tantric divine hierarchy. The first two fascicles are devoted to Uṣṇīṣa, the next two to Prajñāpāramitā, referred to as "Mother of Buddhas." The next three fascicles (4, 5, and 6) are devoted to Avalokiteśvara, who is represented as having five forms: the eleven-headed, the thousand-armed, Clad-in-white, Amoghapāśa, and horse-headed (Hayagrīva, Ma-t'ou). Fascicles 7, 8 and 9 are consecrated to Vajrapāṇi. Fascicles 10 and 11 are for gods and the last fascicle is on the great celebration of the rite of propitiation and is addressed to the entire divine assembly. Citing Ōmura Seigai as the authority, Strickmann calls this a complete maṇḍala in design and the prototype for the Womb-treasury Maṇḍala (Strickmann 1996:134; Ōmura 1918: 212–55). This collection mentions the eleven-headed Avalokiteśvara together with the thousand-armed and Amoghapāśa Avalokiteśvara, although the individual scriptures dedicated to them were translated into Chinese during different times. It seems that by the middle of the seventh century, when this text was compiled, all the esoteric forms of Avalokiteśvara, with the exception of Cintāmaṇicakra, had already appeared in India. Moreover, they must have been equally popular so that they were included in this collection.

I now turn to a discussion of the individual esoteric sūtras introducing major forms of Kuan-yin. First, let us take a look at the *Sūtra of the Divine Dhāraṇī on the Eleven-headed Avalokiteśvara [Spoken] by the Buddha* (Fo-shuo Shih-i-mien Kuan-shih-yin shen-chou ching) translated by Yeh-she-ch'üeh-to in the latter half of the sixth century. This is the earliest text introducing the first Tantric form of the bodhisattva into China.

The sūtra calls for a daily routine of bathing in the morning (if bathing is impossible, then at least rinsing the mouth and washing both hands), followed by reciting the dhāraṇī 108 times. The result is the gaining of ten rewards in one's present life:

1. not suffering from any disease;
2. constantly being remembered by buddhas of the ten directions;
3. always possessing money, things, clothes, and food sufficiently and without want;
4. being enabled to overcome all enemies;
5. being enabled to cause all sentient beings to give rise to hearts of compassion toward oneself;

6. never being harmed by poison, evil charm, or fever;
7. never being hurt by knife or stake;
8. not being drowned by water;
9. not being burned by fire; and
10. not suffering a sudden death.

On the other hand, the following four compensations will become one's own: (1) seeing innumerable buddhas before one dies; (2) never falling into hell; (3) not being harmed by any animal; and (4) being reborn in the land of the Buddha Amitāyus. If one has committed the four *pārājikas* (deserving expulsion from the monastery) and the five deadly sins (leading to rebirth in the Avīci Hell), by chanting this dhāraṇī but once, all the sins will be extinguished.

It then describes the method of worship. First make an image of the Eleven-headed Avalokiteśvara with white sandalwood. The sūtra gives very specific instructions: The wood must be solid and fine-grained, but not from a withered tree. The length of the image should be one Chinese foot and three inches. It should have eleven heads, the three heads in front having faces of a bodhisattva, the left three heads having angry faces, the right three heads having faces of a bodhisattva but with dog's teeth protruding from the top, the head in the back having a laughing face, and the head topping all the other ten having a buddha face. All the faces look forward and are surrounded by halos. The eleven heads are adorned with flowery crowns, and Amitābha Buddha appears on each of the crowns. Kuan-shih-yin holds a bottle in the left hand with lotus flowers issuing from the opening of the bottle, and the right arm is draped with jeweled bracelets with the hand assuming the fear-not mudrā.

When the image is completed, place it on a high platform facing the west. Scatter the ground with flowers. From day one to day seven, chant the dhāraṇī three periods each day: 108 times in the morning, 108 times at noon and 108 times in the evening. One does not have to offer any food, but from day eight to day thirteen, one should offer food, drink and fruit. Do not put them on regular plates but on servers woven with clean grass. The practitioner kneels on a cushion made of sedge grass facing the statue. On the fourteenth and fifteenth day, make sandalwood fire offerings in front of the image and also place a clean copper container filled with one pint of Sōma oil in front of the practitioner. Then take incense made of the Aguru tree and of a thickness equal to a chopstick, prepare 1008 sections of this kind of incense, each being one inch in length. Starting from the noon of the fifteenth day, the practitioner takes one section of the incense, smears it with Sōma oil, recites the dhāraṇī over it and then throw it into the sandalwood fire. He does so until all of the 1008 sections are finished. He should not eat anything for these two days. On the night of the fifteenth day, Avalokiteśvara enters the place of practice and the sandalwood statue shakes by itself. At that time, the whole earth also shakes. The face of the Buddha sitting on the topmost head of the statue praises the practitioner and promises to grant all his wishes.

The sūtra ends with various recipes to deal with moon eclipses, nightmares, diseases of people and animals, and disturbance caused by ghosts. Here are two examples: place equal amounts of realgar and yellow ocher on leaves, chant the dhāraṇī 1008 times in front of the image of Avalokiteśvara, bathe with warm water mixed with the above. All obstacles, nightmares, and diseases will go away. For getting rid of evil ghosts who have entered one's home, place 108 sticks of incense in front of the image, chant the dhāraṇī once over each stick and throw it into the fire. When all the incense sticks are finished, all evil ghosts will scamper and do not dare to stay (T 20:149b-151b).

The next group of esoteric sūtras introduced into China center on Avalokiteśvara holding a lasso (Amoghapāśa), the earliest of which is the *Dhāraṇī Sūtra of Amoghapāśa* (Pu-k'ung-ssu-so chou ching) translated by She-na-ch'üeh-t'o in the Sui period (581–618). The bodhisattva preaches this sūtra containing the dhāraṇī in his palace in Potalaka. The efficacy of chanting the dhāraṇī is immediate, for if a person fasts for but one day and night while chanting it, he or she will right away recover from a whole host of illnesses such as fever, pain of eye, ear, lip, tongue, gum, heart, belly, knee, back, or waist problems, arthritis, piles, diarrhea, constipation, scabies, ulcers, and epilepsy. The person can also be saved from imprisonment, and be protected against insults, scandals, or being beaten and killed. This is so because the dhāraṇī can reduce the present suffering of a person who has committed serious sins in past lives. Like the sūtra previously discussed, it also provides a list of specific benefits as well as guidelines for the creation of the image. In order to obtain the following results, a person should fast for a day and night on the eighth, fourteenth, or fifteenth day of the month, and recite the dhāraṇī seven times during the day and seven times at night. One should not think of anything else, nor talk to anyone. As a result, the following twenty benefits can be obtained during one's present life:

1. All diseases will not bother you. Even if you should become ill, you will quickly recover because of the power of your good karma.
2. Your body will be supple and your skin will be luscious. People will respect and like you.
3. Your senses will be well guarded.
4. You will get great wealth and obtain whatever you want and no one will be able to rob you of it.

5. Fire cannot burn you.
6. Water cannot sweep you away.
7. Kings cannot oppress you. You will be lucky in whatever endeavor you decide to undertake.
8. Hailstones cannot harm you, nor can evil dragons poison you.
9. You will not suffer from droughts, nor should you fear storms or whirlwinds.
10. If insects endanger your crops, just do this: mix sand with water, read the dhāraṇī seven times over it and put it in the eight corners around your field, making a boundary, then prepare water by chanting the dhāraṇī over it. When you sprinkle the water above and below as well as all over the crop, all harmful insects will be destroyed.
11. You will not be attacked by demons who either suck your energy or make love to you in your dreams.
12. You will be liked by all sentient beings who will always respect you without ceasing.
13. No one will harbor resentment against you.
14. If a bad person should want to harm you, he will not succeed but will depart voluntarily.
15. All curses and magic will disappear by themselves without being able to cause you any harm.
16. You will be the strongest among any crowd.
17. You will be free from any vexation.
18. When you are in a battle, just chant the dhāraṇī with singleness of mind, and all arrows, knives, and staffs will not touch your body.
19. Friendly gods will always protect you.
20. In each rebirth you will not depart from the four Abodes of Brahmā [compassion, pity, sympathetic joy, and equanimity]. (T 20:399c-400a)

The sūtra also promises a "good death," for eight auspicious blessings will be enjoyed by the faithful reciter of the dhāraṇī at the moment of death:

1. On the day of death, Avalokiteśvara will appear in front of you in the form of a monk.
2. Your mind will not be scattered and your body will be comfortable and free from pain.

3. Although you may be sick, you will not be covered by urine, excrement, or other impurities.
4. You will maintain correct mindfulness and will not be confused or disoriented.
5. You will not die lying face down.
6. You will gain eloquence on the day of your death.
7. You will be reborn in any buddha land of your choice.
8. You will always have good friends who do not forsake you. (400a)

The making of the bodhisattva's image is also of central concern to the sūtra, which gives this instruction: Have a piece of white cloth woven, five feet wide and ten feet long. Do not cut it in any way. Do not use glue in making the paint, but mix incense, milk, and colors together. Draw the image of Avalokiteśvara, making him look similar to Śiva. His hair is wound into a topknot and he wears a crown. Black deerskin covers his left shoulder. His body is covered with jeweled necklaces. The painter should keep the eight fasting commandments (not to kill; not to take things not given; not to have sex; not to speak falsely; not to drink wine; not to use cosmetics and personal adornments; not to enjoy dancing or music; and not to sleep on fine beds but on a mat on the ground) and not eat improper food. He should bathe and wear clean clothes. The one who practices the chanting of the dhāraṇī should put the image in a pure place. Cover the ground in front of the image with cow dung. Make the ritual space sixteen feet square. Scatter white flowers on it. Set down eight vases, each containing one peck of water. Place flowers therein. . . . He should fast for three days and three nights (if this is impossible, then at least one day and one night), and bathe after relieving himself. Kneel in front of the image, and chant the dhāraṇī 1008 times. The practitioner will see himself issue forth bright light like a torch in front of the image. He will then become very glad. Avalokiteśvara will appear and grant him whatever he wishes (401c-402a).

Amoghapāśa can also be depicted with a three-dimensional image. The thirty-fascicle version of the sūtra translated by Bodhiruci in the eighth century gives this stipulation: "Use gold or silver to cast the image of Amoghapāśa. It should be eight fingers in length. He has three faces and two arms. The front face is compassionate, the left face showing great anger with bulging eyes and a wide-open mouth, and the right face showing slight anger with knitted eyebrows and closed mouth. His head wears a jeweled crown with a transformed buddha on it. His left hand holds a lasso and his right hand is raised with the palm open. His body is covered with a heavenly garment decorated with necklaces of seven jewels. He sits majestically on a lotus throne" (T 20:252b).

Another group of esoteric texts were introduced after this and they glorify the Thousand-handed and Thousand-eyed Avalokiteśvara. There are thirteen versions all together; all were translated during the T'ang (618–907). The number of translations, some by very famous monks, indicate the fame and popularity of this particular Tantric form of Avalokiteśvara. Maria Dorothea Reis-Habito has made a careful comparison of different versions of the text, concentrating on the one made by Chih-t'ung in 650 and that of Bhagavadharma in 627–649 that were based on two different Sanskrit originals (1993:97–117). The two have some very significant differences. In China, Bhagavadharma's version is the better known, although that of Chih-t'ung provides important information about image making and fascinating miracles resulting from chanting the dhāraṇī not found in the former. Before I come to these latter points, I first provide a synopsis of the sūtra translated by Bhagavadharma, known as *Ch'ien-shou ching* (Sūtra of a Thousand Hands) for short, which is also by far the most important of all the esoteric scriptures in China.

The sūtra is spoken by the Buddha in the palace of Avalokiteśvara located on the island Potalaka. Suddenly there is a great illumination and the three thousand *chiliocosms* turn golden in color, shaking all over while the sun and moon become dull by comparison. Bodhisattva Dhāraṇī King (Tsung-ch'ih-wang) asks the Buddha why this is happening and the Buddha answers that it is because Avalokiteśvara is going to reveal the dhāraṇī. Avalokiteśvara then takes over the center stage. He speaks with the first person pronoun "I" in the sūtra.

> When I practiced under a buddha by the name of Ch'ien-kuang-wang Ching-chu Ju-lai (Thousand-light King Tathāgata of Tranquil Abode) innumerable kalpas ago, the buddha took pity on me and all sentient beings. Touching my forehead with his golden hand, the buddha instructed me to keep this dhāraṇī and work in the future for the benefit of beings living in evil times. I was at that time a bodhisattva of the first stage, but as soon as I heard the dhāraṇī, I advanced right away to the eighth stage of the bodhisattva path. Filled with joy and exaltation, I vowed, "If I am capable of benefiting and comforting all sentient beings in the future, let me be endowed with a thousand hands and a thousand eyes right away." As soon as I made the vow, this happened. So from that epoch long ago, I have kept the dhāraṇī. As a result, I have always been born where there is a buddha. Moreover, I have never undergone birth from a womb, but am always transformed from a lotus. (T 20:1066)

Having explained the origin and efficacy of the dhāraṇī, Avalokiteśvara calls upon anyone who wants to keep this dhāraṇī to give rise to the thought of compassion for all sentient beings by making the following ten vows after him:

> Namaḥ Avalokiteśvara of Great Compassion, may I quickly learn all Dharma.
>
> Namaḥ Avoliketeśvara of Great Compassion, may I speedily obtain the eye of wisdom.
>
> Namaḥ Avalokiteśvara of Great Compassion, may I quickly save all sentient beings.
>
> Namaḥ Avalokiteśvara of Great Compassion, may I speedily obtain skillful means.
>
> Namaḥ Avalokiteśvara of Great Compassion, may I quickly sail on the prajñā boat.
>
> Namaḥ Avalokiteśvara of Great Compassion, may I speedily cross over the ocean of suffering.
>
> Namaḥ Avalokiteśvara of Great Compassion, may I quickly obtain the way of discipline and meditation.
>
> Namaḥ Avalokiteśvara of Great Compassion, may I speedily ascend the nirvāṇa mountain.
>
> Namaḥ Avalokiteśvara of Great Compassion, may I quickly enter the house of non-action.
>
> Namaḥ Avalokiteśvara of Great Compassion, may I speedily achieve the Dharma-Body.
>
> If I face a mountain of knives, may it naturally crumble, if I face a roaring fire, may it naturally burn out, if I face hell, may it naturally disappear, if I face a hungry ghost, may it naturally be satiated, if I face an Asura, may its evil heart naturally become tame and, if I face an animal, may it naturally obtain great wisdom.

After making such vows, one should sincerely call the name of Avalokiteśvara as well as the name of Amitābha Buddha, who is Avalokiteśvara's original teacher. If anyone recites the dhāraṇī, should he fall into an evil realm of rebirth, or not be born into one of the buddha lands, or not attain unlimited samādhi and eloquence, or not get all the wishes he desires in the present life and, in the case of a woman, if she detests the female body and wants to be born a man in her next life, Avalokiteśvara promises that all these [wishes] will come true. Otherwise he will not achieve complete, perfect enlightenment.

If anyone steals or damages the Saṃgha's property, by reciting this dhāraṇī, the sin will be forgiven. Anyone who has committed the five sins and ten evil deeds, who slanders the Dharma and corrupts monastic discipline, or who destroys temples and steals monks' possessions, is freed from the guilt by chanting this dhāraṇī. But if one has doubts about the efficacy of the dhāraṇī, then the consequences of even a slight mistake will not disappear, how much more a sin so serious?

The keeping of the dhāraṇī will result in fifteen kinds of good rebirth and the avoidance of fifteen kinds of evil deaths. The fifteen kinds of evil deaths from which one is saved are: (1) from hunger and suffering; (2) from being imprisoned by cangue and beaten with staffs; (3) at the hands of one's enemies; (4) from fighting on the battlefield; (5) by being mauled by wolves or other vicious animals; (6) by being attacked by poisonous snakes and scorpions; (7) by drowning or being burnt by fire; (8) by poison; (9) by witchcraft; (10) from madness; (11) by falling from a tree or a cliff; (12) from an enemies' curse; (13) by being killed by heretic gods and demonic ghosts; (14) from chronic and lingering illnesses; (15) by suicide. The fifteen kinds of good rebirths one enjoys are: (1) always being ruled by a virtuous king wherever one is born; (2) always to be born in a good country; (3) always living in a peaceful time; (4) always meeting with good friends; (5) always born without any physical defects; (6) but with a pure and ripe heart for truth; (7) not breaking any precepts; (8) having harmonious and virtuous family members; (9) fully endowed with money and food; (10) always respected and taken care of by others; (11) never getting robbed; (12) always having one's desire fulfilled; (13) always being protected by nāgas, devas, and virtuous gods; (14) can see the Buddha and listen to the Dharma in the place of birth; (15) can understand and penetrate the correct Dharma.

The dhāraṇī consisting of 84 phrases is then revealed.[17]

> All the assembled reach different levels of realization. Some attain the fruit of stream-entrant, once-returner, nonreturner, or arhat. Others attain the first, second, third, fourth, fifth, all the way to the tenth stage of the bodhisattva path. Unlimited numbers of sentient beings give rise to the bodhicitta.
>
> In keeping the dhāraṇī, one should stay in a clean room, purify oneself by bathing, and put on clean clothes. Hang a banner on which an image of the bodhisattva is depicted, light a lamp, offer flowers, delicacies, and food, and concentrate one's thoughts without allowing them to wander. One can expect that Sunlight and Moonlight Bodhisattvas as well as many gods and immortals come to bear witness. Avalokiteśvara will look after the practitioner with his thousand eyes and protect him with the thousand hands. As a result, one will understand all worldly classics, including the Vedas and all heterodox philosophies thoroughly. By chanting the dhāraṇī, one will be able to cure 84,000 kinds of illnesses and order gods and ghosts to subdue

Māra and heterodox teachers. If a person who either studies the sūtra or practices meditation in the wilderness is bothered by evil spirits and cannot concentrate, just by chanting this dhāraṇī once, they will be bound and subdued by it. If anyone gives rise to the thought of compassion for sentient beings and decides to keep the dhāraṇī as taught, Avalokiteśvara will order nāgas, benevolent gods, and deva-guardians of the secrets of Vairocana always to follow and surround him without leaving his side. They will protect him as if he were their eyes or their very life. (T 20:106b-108b)

This sūtra, like all esoteric sūtras, shows great interest in ritual matters. As part of the *sādhana* or ritual requirement, detailed instructions on constructing a sacred space are provided: recite the dhāraṇī twenty-one times over a knife. Use the knife to demarcate the boundary on the ground. Or one can recite the dhāraṇī twenty-one times over pure water and pour it on all four sides to create a boundary. Or one may use white mustard seed. Recite the dhāraṇī twenty-one times and then scatter the seeds on all four sides. Alternatively, one can also create a boundary through visualization. Or recite the dhāraṇī twenty-one times over clean ashes or five-colored twine. Either of these methods can serve to create markings for the space's boundary (T 20:109b).

The correct keeping of the spell, as we have seen, leads to spiritual and mundane benefits. The sūtra also offers many recipes to deal with various problems or to attain specific goals. To get a sense what they are like, here are a few samples. If one wants to order a ghost around, get a skull from the wild, wash and clean it. Set up a sacred area in front of the image of the Thousand-handed and Thousand-eyed One, worship it with flowers, incense, food, and drink. Do so for seven days, and the ghost will appear and do whatever it is ordered. If a woman suffers from a difficult childbirth, recite the dhāraṇī twenty-one times over sesame oil, rub it in her belly button and her vagina and the baby will come out easily. If someone has a phobia about being in the dark and is afraid to go out at night, make a necklace with white threads, recite the dhāraṇī twenty-one times and tie it with twenty-one knots. When this is worn on the neck, fear will vanish (T 20:110b-c). The sūtra ends by identifying the names of the forty mudrās of Avalokiteśvara and the benefits they bestow on the worshiper (T 20:111a-b).

This sūtra only provides the names of the forty mudrās and the specific benefits they bestow, but no illustrations. They are, however, found in the version translated by Amoghavajra (T [1064]20:117a–119b). Because either the entire set of these mudrās or some of them were visible on the images of Kuan-yin created in the T'ang and Sung dynasties, I think a knowledge of them should be useful and I therefore translate them as follows.[18]

1. If you desire wealth and want to have many jewels, then you should make the *cintamaṇi mudrā* while holding the jewel of wish-fulfillment in your hand.[19]
2. If you seek safety from various worries, then make the *pāśa mudrā* with the hand holding the lasso.
3. If you want to be free from diseases of the belly, then make the *pātra mudrā* with the hand holding a precious begging bowl in your hand.
4. If you want to subdue all ghosts and goblins, then make the *khadra mudrā* while holding a sword in your hand.
5. If you want to subdue heavenly demons and heretics, then make the three-pronged *vajra mudrā.*
6. If you want to subdue your enemies, then make the one-pronged *vajra mudrā.*
7. If you want to be forever free from fear and worry, then make the *abhaya mudrā,* which bestows fearlessness.
8. If you want to regain your eyesight, then make the *sūryamaṇi mudrā* holding the sun with a crow inside in your hand.
9. If you seek to remain cool in the face of fear, then make the *candramaṇi mudrā* holding the moon with a tree and hare inside in your hand.
10. If you desire an official position, then make the *dhanur mudrā* of holding a precious bow.
11. If you want to meet good friends on the path early on, then make the *bana mudrā* of holding a precious arrow.
12. If you want to get rid of various illnesses, then make the willow branch *mudrā.*
13. If you want to get rid of evil obstructions, then make the *camari mudrā* of holding a white flywhisk.
14. If you want to maintain harmonious relationships among the family members, then make *the kalaśa mudrā* of holding a water bottle.
15. If you want to keep tigers, wolves and other vicious animals away, then make the *bohai mudrā* of holding a placard.
16. If you want to be always free from governmental oppression, then make the *parasu mudrā* of holding a hatchet.
17. If you want to have good male and female servants, then make the jade ring *mudrā.*

18. If you want to obtain all kinds of merits, then make the *puṇḍarīka mudrā* of holding a white lotus.
19. If you want to be reborn in the pure lands of the ten directions, then make the *utpala mudrā* of holding a blue lotus.
20. If you want to obtain great wisdom, then make the *darpana mudrā* of holding a precious mirror.
21. If you want to see buddhas of the ten directions face to face, then make the purple lotus *mudrā.*
22. If you want to obtain treasures hidden underground, then make the casket *mudrā.*
23. If you want to accomplish the way of immortality, then make the five-colored cloud *mudrā.*
24. If you want to be born in Brahmā heaven, then make the *kuṇḍī mudrā.*
25. If you want to be born in any of the various heavenly palaces, then make the *padma* (red lotus) *mudrā.*
26. If you want to avoid robbers, then make the *kunta mudrā* of holding a precious javelin.
27. If you want to call and command good gods, then make the *śaṅkha mudrā* of holding a precious couch.
28. If you want to call and command ghosts, then make the *munda* (skull) *mudrā.*
29. If you want to have buddhas of the ten directions to come quickly to touch you and give you predictions, then make the *akṣamālā* (rosary) *mudrā.*
30. If you want to obtain a wondrous voice for speaking in Sanskrit, then make the *ghaṇtā* (bell) *mudrā.*
31. If you want to have great eloquence, then make the *mudrā* (seal) *mudrā.*
32. If you want always to be protected by dragon kings, then make *ankusa mudrā* of holding an iron hook.
33. If you want to protect all living beings with compassion, then make the *daṇḍa mudrā* of holding a monk's staff.
34. If you want all living beings to respect and love you, then make the *añjali mudrā* with two palms touching.
35. If you want to be near the buddhas in every rebirth, then make the transformation buddha *mudrā.*

36. If you want to be born in the palace of the buddha but not in a womb in all future rebirths, then make the transformation palace *mudrā.*
37. If you want to be erudite, then make the *sūtra mudrā.*
38. If you want to achieve the nonretrogressing bodhicitta with this body and retain it until you become a buddha, then make the *cakravartī-cakra mudrā* of holding a golden wheel.
39. If you want to quickly receive predictions from buddhas of the ten directions through having your head touched by them, then make the *mudrā* of the emanated Uṣṇīṣa-Buddha (or Buddha in the crown).
40. If you want to have a good vegetable, fruit and grain harvest, then make the *āmalaka mudrā* of holding grapes. (T 20:111a-b)

Bhagavadharma's version does not provide rules for the making of the bodhisattva's image, but other versions do. Let us look at the translations by Chih-t'ung, Bodhiruci, and Su-p'o-lo. Chih-t'ung's version is entitled *Ch'ien-yen ch'ien-pi Kuan-shih-yin P'u-sa t'o-lo-ni shen-chou ching* (Sūtra of the Divine Dhāraṇī of the Thousand-eyed and Thousand-armed Avalokiteśvara) and consists of two fascicles. In a long preface, the story of the sūtra's transmission is related in great detail, and provides very interesting information on the importance of image making.

> The Thousand-eyed and Thousand-handed Bodhisattva is the transformative manifestation of Avalokiteśvara performing miraculous feats of subduing demons. Earlier, during the Wu-te era (618–626), a monk from central India by the name of Ch'ü-t'o-t'i-p'o came to the capital with an image done on fine wool together with a sūtra on how to build a maṇḍala and how to form mudrās, but emperor Kao-tsu was not impressed, so the monk left in disappointment. Then in the Chen-kuan era (627–649) a monk from north India presented the Sanskrit text of *The Dhāraṇī of the Thousand-eyed and Thousand-armed One* and Emperor T'ai-tsung ordered Chih-t'ung of the Ta-tsung-ch'ih Ssu to translate it together with the Indian monk. . . . Another Indian monk arrived from the West and presented a sūtra to Chih-t'ung who translated it as well. It was not different from the first one except in lacking the section on the basic mantra (*shen-chou*). Hui-lin, abbot of the Ch'eng-chin Ssu of Chang-chou (present-day Wu-chin, Kiangsu) knew a Brahmin monk from Northern India named Su-chia-shih who practiced this *sādhana* and prayed faithfully day and night forming mudrās before the maṇḍala which had been set up according to the rules. Hui-lin often asked him about the procedures and wrote them down. He

> asked a lay devotee named Li T'ai-yi who knew Sanskrit and was also learned in Confucian and Taoist classics to go over the text. In the year Shen-kung (697) a wise man arrived from the capital and brought the second sūtra translated by Chih-t'ung, the one lacking the basic mantra, and Hui-lin added to it in order to make it complete. Ta-mo-chan-t'o was a Brahmin monk originally from Udayana who knew dhāraṇīs well. The emperor often asked him to translate. He painted a portrait of the Thousand-armed Bodhisattva and presented the sūtra to the emperor, who ordered palace women to embroider the portrait of the bodhisattva and artists to paint it in order to disseminate it throughout the country. (T 20:83b-c; Reis-Habito 1993:103–7)

Chih-t'ung's text gives the rules for creating Avalokiteśvara's image. It says that according to the Sanskrit sūtra, the image should be painted on a piece of white wool. It should be ten elbows in width, which is equivalent to sixteen Chinese feet. The length should be twenty elbows, which is equivalent to thirty-two feet. The bodhisattva's body should be golden in color, like sandalwood. The face should have three eyes and on the palm of each one of the thousand hands there should also be an eye. One should not mix the paint with glue but use milk and colors only. The bodhisattva wears a seven-jeweled crown and his body is covered with necklaces. There is another text that says that because there is no fine white wool in this country, it is all right just to use a piece of white silk. The bodhisattva should be five feet in height and have two arms. There is no need to paint a thousand eyes and a thousand arms. But be sure to add a third eye on the forehead of the bodhisattva. Anyone who wants to practice this *sādhana* must first of all make a painting according to rules. The artisan must observe the eight fasting commandments. Each time he goes to the restroom he must take a bath. After the image is completed, both the artisan and the dhāraṇī practitioner should confess their transgressions in front of the image for fear that they may have erred. Install the image in the mandala, prepare offerings and perform the ritual for twenty-one days. The Thousand-eyed and Thousand-armed Avalokiteśvara will definitely issue forth great light brighter than the sun and moon. This will happen unless the worshiper is insincere (T 20:93c-94a).

The sūtra explains why Avalokiteśvara has such an unusual appearance: during the time of Vipaśyin Buddha (the first of the seven buddhas of the past), the bodhisattva manifested this form in order to subdue demons, when a buddha emerged from each of his thousand eyes, and a *cakravartin* (wheel-turning universal monarch) from each of his thousand arms. He was thus foremost as a destroyer of demons.[20] It also relates several stories to show the miraculous power of the dhāraṇī. As we shall see in chapter 3, these miracle tales were copied verbatim in a set of Chinese indigenous sūtras that have been circulated since the T'ang. The first story tells how formerly a plague raged in Kashmir and the afflicted would die within a day or two. When a Brahmin carried out the ritual as described in the sūtra, the plague immediately disappeared because the demon who caused it was forced to leave the country. Another story tells about an elder living in Vārāṇaśī who had only one son, who was predicted to die at sixteen. When he was fifteen, a Brahmin came to the door begging for food. He saw the elder and his wife looking worried and sad. Their faces were haggard and had no luster. When he asked them the reason and was told the cause, he told the elder not to worry because he had a way to make the son live a long life. So the Brahmin performed the ritual for one day and one night, at the end of which King Yama came to tell him that although the boy should live only to be sixteen, and thus had only one more year to live, because of this good causation, he would now live until eighty years old. When the elder and his wife learned this, they were overjoyed and sold everything and donated it to the Three Treasures. Thus it is clear that the divine efficacy of this ritual is inconceivable.

Like the other esoteric sūtras previously discussed, the dhāraṇī can be used in specific ways as a recipe to dispel difficulties and obtain benefits. For instance, when a woman is having a difficult childbirth, recite the dhāraṇī twenty-one times over ghee and feed it to her, and she will assuredly have an easy delivery and give birth to a good-looking boy or girl who will be blessed through life, well loved and respected by everyone. If one suffers pain in the eye, then have a dhāraṇī master recite the dhāraṇī of the Thousand-eye mudrā twenty-one times and seal the patient's eye with the mudrā and the eye will recover from the affliction (T 20:87a).

Two other versions of the sūtra provide very useful information about the iconography of the Thousand-armed Avalokiteśvara and the creation of his image. Both make it abundantly clear that the mudrās discussed earlier were attributes of the Bodhisattva. We read as follows in Bodhiruci's version: The bodhisattva wears a flowery crown on his head that has a transformed buddha. There are eighteen arms frontally, two arms with folded palms held before the heart, and each of the fourteen hands holds a one-pronged vajra, a three-pronged vajra, a sūtra, a seal, a monk's staff, a jewel, a wheel, a blooming lotus, a lasso, a willow branch, a rosary, a bottle, a hand bestowing sweet dews, a hand bestowing fearlessness, and finally, two hands are held in front of the belly button with the right hand on top of the left, both palms up. The remaining 982 hands also hold various implements or form mudrās as stipulated by the sūtra (T 20:101b).

The last version of the Thousand-armed Avalokiteśvara sūtra I discuss is entitled *Sūtra of the Secret Method [Spoken] by Master Perceiver Bodhisattva Who Has a Thousand Luminous Eyes* (Ch'ien-kuang-yen Kuan-tzu-tsai P'u-sa mi-mi-fa ching), translated by Su-p'o-lo. It is not recorded in any catalogue, the version contained in the modern Taishō Tripiṭaka being a Japanese copy dated 1125 (T 20:126c). It was probably translated or composed in the T'ang, for the name of the bodhisattva, Kuan-tzu-tsai (Master Perceiver), began to be used only with Hsüan-tsang. This explains the reason why Avalokiteśvara is described as having "a Thousand Luminous Eyes," because he illuminates living beings with these many eyes (T 20:125a). The author of the sūtra is familiar with the Bodhisattva's forty mudrās, but divides them into five categories, namely those of Thatāgata, Vajra, Maṇi (Wish-fulfilling Jewel), Lotus, and Karma (Enterprise). Each category contains eight mudrās. The Tathāgata group dispels difficulties and the mudrās are: transformation buddha, lasso, fear-not, white fly whisk, placard, hatchet, lancelet, and willow branch. The Vajra group subdues and its mudrās are three-pronged vajra, one-pronged vajra, sword, palace, wheel, begging bowl, sun, and moon. The Maṇi group brings benefits and its mudrās are wish-fulfilling jewel, bow, sūtra, white lotus, blue lotus, bell, purple lotus, and grapes. The Lotus group makes people love and respect you. Its mudrās include: folded palms, mirror, seal, jade ring, kalaśa bottle, kuṇḍī bottle, red lotus, and monk's staff. Finally, the Karma group is for enticement and command. Its mudrās include hook, buddha on the crown, rosary, couch, arrow, casket, skull, and five-colored cloud (T 20:120a).

Depending on what one wishes to achieve or obtain, the sūtra instructs the person to make an image of the bodhisattva with the appropriate attribute, form the specific mudrā and recite a corresponding mantra. For example, if one wants to be rid of illnesses, one should practice the method of obtaining medicine from the willow branch. The bodhisattva in this case holds a willow branch in the right hand, while the left hand is placed on his left breast with the palm showing. When the painting is completed, the supplicant forms the mudrā with his right arm bent and the fingers of the right hand spread [imitating the willow branch?] He then recites the mantra and massages his body all over.

Another point setting this sūtra apart from others is its exalted view of Avalokiteśvara. Śākyamuni Buddha is represented here as declaring that Avalokiteśvara already attained Buddhahood long before him with the title of Bright True Dharma (Cheng-fa-ming) and as a buddha he instructed Śākyamuni, who labored as an ascetic until the latter could eventually become the Buddha. We shall see the same theme appear in an indigenous Chinese sūtra, the *Sūtra of Kuan-shih-yin's Samādhi* (Kuan-shih-yin san-mei ching) discussed in the next chapter. The glorification of Avalokiteśvara does not end here. He is credited with the ability of teaching the buddhas of the ten directions. This is the case because Avalokiteśvara is in fact the Dharmakāya (*fa-shen*), literally "Body of the Dharma," who emanates twenty-five bodhisattvas, each having eleven heads, forty hands, and an equal number of eyes on the hands. The "thousand hands" are no longer the hands of just one Avalokiteśvara, but the twenty-five emanated Avalokiteśvara who are empowered to go to the twenty-five realms of existence to conquer evil and save beings.[21] This indicates that this sūtra properly belongs to the following section, for it shares the same theme with the *Karaṇḍavyūha Sūtra*, which also presents Avalokiteśvara as the universal savior.

Of all the Thousand-eyed and Thousand-handed Avalokiteśvara sūtras, the one translated by Bhagavardharma has become the best known in China through the ages. As Reis-Habito points out, this is the only version that contains the sections on the ten great vows and the blessing of the fifteen kinds of good deaths as well as protection from fifteen kinds of bad deaths. The dhāraṇī's concrete power over death and the comprehensiveness of the bodhisattva's vows could be the reasons for this particular sūtra's greater attraction. In this case, its very lack of complicated instructions on image making or rules for visualization might have contributed to its democratic appeal for ordinary people. Surviving Tun-huang manuscripts dated to the eighth century testify to its popularity. Some of the copies are excerpts of the ten great vows and are called *Invocation of the Great Compassionate One* (*Ta-pei ch'i-ch'ing*). Simple forms of repentance ritual consisted of recitation of the vows and the dhāraṇī seemed to have been practiced already at that time (Reis-Habito 1993:121–32). Because of the great popularity enjoyed by this sūtra, Ta-pei became identified specifically with the Thousand-eyed and Thousand-handed Avalokiteśvara from the T'ang period on, though previously it is an epithet used in other sūtras to describe Avalokiteśvara in general. Through the ritual of repentance called *Ta-pei Ch'an* created by the Sung T'ien-t'ai master Chih-li (960–1028), who used Bhagavadharma's version as his source, the text and its mantra, known familiarly as the *Great Compassion Dhāraṇī* (*Ta-pei Chou*), became even more famous (this is discussed in chapter 7). Around the same time, during the eleventh to twelfth century, the exotic Tantric bodhisattva of a thousand hands and eyes also became domesticated and transformed into Princess Miao-shan (discussed in chapter 8).

No banner, fresco, or other depictions of the thousand-armed Avalokiteśvara found at Tun-huang can be dated earlier than the ninth century. Using copies of the text found among the Tun-huang documents as evidence, however, Reis-Habito suggests that the cult of Ta-pei took root there soon after Bhagavadharma translated the scripture in the mid-seventh century. She thinks that the reason for this was because of its proximity to Khotan, an important oasis on the Southern Silk Road in present day Sinkiang and the place where Bhagavadharma translated the sūtra. She further argues that Khotan was probably the center for the cult of Avalokiteśvara. Indeed, this can be substantiated not only by the observations made by pilgrim-travelers, but also by the transmission of sūtras. Fa-hsien reached Khotan in 475 and there obtained the *Avalokiteśvara's Dhāraṇī Sūtra of Eliminating Sins* (Kuan-shih-yin mieh-tsui t'o-lo-ni ching, no longer extant). Hsüan-tsang traveled through Khotan in 640 and observed the religious fervor of the ruler and also among the people. As for sūtras originating in Khotan, it was the Khotanese monk Dharmodgata who translated the *Sūtra of Avalokiteśvara Receiving the Prediction.* Kumārajīva's *Lotus* also originated in Khotan. Chü-ch'ü Ching-sheng (d. 464), a cousin of Chü-ch'ü Meng-hsün (r. 401–433), the king of the Northern Liang who ruled Tun-huang and promoted the circulation of the "Universal Gateway" chapter as an independent sūtra distinct from the *Lotus*, studied Mahāyāna Buddhism in Khotan, and translated the *Visualization on Avalokiteśvara Sūtra* (no longer extant) that he obtained from Turfan. Finally, the eighty fascicle version of the *Hua-yen Sūtra* translated by Śikṣānanda in 695 also originated in Khotan (Reis-Habito 1993:124).

The last sūtras centering on new Tantric forms of Avalokiteśvara are those about Cintāmaṇīcakra (Ju-i-lun). Again, there are nine translations, all done during the T'ang, thus making this Tantric form of the bodhisattva contemporaneous with the Thousand-eyed and Thousand-handed Avalokiteśvara in terms of their temporal introduction into China. The version done by Bodhiruci, entitled *Dhāraṇī Sūtra of Cintāmaṇīcakra* (Ju-i-lun t'o-lo-ni ching) explains the meaning of the name by having Avalokiteśvara tell Śākyamuni that the dhāraṇī is like the wish-fulfilling maṇi jewel, which can satisfy all the desires of living beings. When Avalokiteśvara reveals this dhāraṇī, all the demons' palaces shake and the gates of the hells open, releasing living beings from suffering and enabling them to achieve rebirth in the heavens (T 20:188b-189a). The devotee is told to go to a clean room, and sit cross-legged facing the east day and night. He should visualize the bodhisattva, who is as bright as the newly risen sun, sitting on a lotus throne. Facing this mental image, he chants the dhāraṇī 1,080 times without interruption during the six periods. The result of this concentrated practice is that Avalokiteśvara will appear to the devotee during his dream and tell him, "Good man, do not fear. I will grant you anything you wish." One will then see Amitābha or the Pure Land, or the seven-jeweled palace on Potalaka, the home of the bodhisattva (T 20:189b-c).

The sūtra, like those just discussed, promises many worldly benefits, but unlike them, it prescribes different numbers of recitations for people of different social status. During the six periods, a king should recite the dhāraṇī 1,080 times; a queen or a royal concubine, 900; a prince, 800; a princess, 700; a minister, 600; a Brahmin, 500; a kṣatriya, 400; a vaiśya, 300; a śūdra, 200; a monk, 108; a layman, 106; a laywoman, 103; a boy, 100; and a girl, 90 (T 20:190a).

Compared with the exoteric sūtras discussed earlier, several characteristics of the esoteric sūtras stand out in sharp contrast. No matter to which form of Avalokiteśvara the esoteric sūtras are dedicated, they all emphasize (1) the importance of creating the image in the stipulated fashion, which always includes a detailed description of the Bodhisattva's physical appearance, that is, holding a lotus and a bottle in his hands, covered with jeweled necklaces, and so on as an aid to visualization; (2) the exact number of times the dhāraṇī must be chanted, be it 21, 108, 1,008 or 1,080 times; (3) when the *sādhanas* are performed correctly, Avalokiteśvara will appear to the devotee in a vision either as a monk or in a form as imagined by the practitioner; and (4) the concrete benefits that are both mundane and spiritual resulting from such cultic practices.

I have devoted considerable space to a description of these esoteric scriptures centering on Avalokiteśvara because, with the possible exception of *Ch'ing Kuan-yin ching* and the *Ch'ien-shou ching*, they are not very well known. Most students of Chinese Buddhism, including myself prior to my study of Kuan-yin, usually stay away from the esoteric scriptures, regarding them as a bit too specialized. As a result, there is a gap in the current scholarship on Chinese esoteric Buddhism. Although a huge body of such scriptures exists, the majority of them having been translated in the T'ang and Sung periods, with the exception of Strickmann, few scholars have used them as sources for the reconstruction of the kind of religious beliefs and practices they presented to their contemporary audiences in China. Even a cursory summary such as the one I have provided might be helpful to provide a concrete sense of this type of literature.

The second reason for going into some detail about the promises Avalokiteśvara makes to the faithful is that such scriptures create a new identity of this deity not found in the earlier exoteric scriptures. Although the *Lotus Sūtra*, the *Śūraṅgama Sūtra*, and the Pure Land *Visualization Sūtra*—the three most important scriptures promoting faith in Kuan-yin since the Six Dynasties—promise similar worldly benefits as well as salvation from evil rebirths to those vouchsafed by the esoteric texts, in them Kuan-yin is subordinated to Śākyamuni and Amitābha respectively. In the esoteric scriptures, on the other hand, Avalokiteśvara increasingly assumed an independent role as a universal savior. As a response to the development of the cults of Śiva and Viṣṇu in Hinduism, the esoteric Avalokiteśvara exhibits similar omnipotence and omniscience. The process reached its culmination in the *Karaṇḍavyūha Sūtra*. As we shall soon see, the bodhisattva is declared to be the creator of the universe, including even Śiva himself.

The Bodhisattva as Universal Savior

The *Karaṇḍavyūha Sūtra* is a very important scripture for the cult of Avalokiteśvara because it is one of the very few sūtras in which a mythological account about the life of this bodhisattva is given. Holt provides a succinct summary of this sūtra, some parts of which I shall quote next. He puts the date of the text anywhere from the fourth to the seventh century of the Common Era. The Sanskrit version that he uses may not be identical with the one the Chinese translation was based on, for there seem to be a number of differences.

> Once while Gautama the Buddha was performing a meditation at the Jetavana monastery in the midst of his disciples and an attendant heavenly throng, a meditation aimed at the "purification of everything," bright golden rays began to appear, lighting up the entire monastery and the surrounding countryside. Viskambhu, amazed and filled with great joy, asked the Buddha about the source of these glorious rays of light. The Buddha responded by saying that they came from Ārya Avalokiteśvara, who was preaching the *dharma* of *nirvāṇa* to all the suffering denizens of the tortuous Avīci Hell (dominated by a woeful lake of fire). To an incredulous Viskambhu, he continued: as a result of Avalokiteśvara's preaching of the dharma, the lake of fire in the Avīci Hell was cooled and turned into a refreshing lotus pond and the sufferings of all of its inhabitants were thereby overcome. This miracle was then reported to Yama, Lord of Hell, who wondered what deity this might be. Recognizing Avalokiteśvara, Yama praised his virtues with a long eulogy.
>
> Anxious for Avalokiteśvara's arrival in the human abode, Viskambhu eagerly asked the Buddha when he might be expected in this realm. The Buddha replied that Avalokiteśvara had then proceeded to visit *pretaloka,* where the suffering "departed" in the form of hungry and thirsty ghosts heard his sermon on dharma in the form of the AGKs [*Avalokiteśvara-Guṇa-Karaṇḍavyūha*]. Like the "rain of *dharma,*" water flowed from each of his pores to assuage their miserable conditions. The *pretas* were thus disabused of their belief in the permanent self, which had led them to commit karmic actions of greed resulting in their unfavorable rebirths. They were all thus transformed into bodhisattvas to dwell in the world of Amitābha's paradisiacal buddha field, Sukhāvati.

> The Buddha then proceeded to tell that once, long ago, when he was incarnated as a merchant during the time of the Buddha Vipaśyin, he had heard that former buddha enumerate the many qualities of Bodhisattva Avalokiteśvara. The bodhisattva originally had appeared from a shot of light emanating from the primordial self-existent buddha of the cosmos, who was engaged in his perpetual, deep meditation. From Avalokiteśvara's body (that of a mahāpuruśa), the world as we know it was created: the sun and the moon from his eyes, Maheśvara from his brow, Brahmā and the other gods from his shoulders, Sarasvatī from his teeth, the wind from his mouth, the earth from his feet, and Varuṇa from his stomach. (Holt 1991:47–48)

What comes after this passage in the Chinese translation makes the intention of the writer abundantly clear—to claim Avalokiteśvara's supremacy over Śiva.

> At that time the Bodhisattva Kuan-tzu-tsai (Master Perceiver) told Maheśvara saying, "In the future when the world enters the Age of Degenerate Law, people attached to wrong views will all say that you are the lord of the universe from the beginningless beginning and that you have created all beings." At that time, sentient beings, having lost the way of enlightenment, they will become confused by their ignorance and make the following statement:
>
> *The great body of emptiness,*
> *makes the great earth your seat.*
> *The world as well as all sentient beings,*
> *are all evolved from this body. (T 20:49c)*

The next section is the story of Avalokiteśvara's previous incarnation as a divine horse named Balāha who saved the prince Sinhala, who was the previous incarnation of Gautama Buddha. I turn again to Holt's summation.

> After Sinhala led a crew of 500 other merchants on a seagoing venture in search of precious jewels, his ship was taken by storm and wrecked off the coast of the island of Tāmradvīpa (Lanka). By the grace of the lord to whom Sinhala was devoted, the 500 shipwrecked sailors safely reached the shores of the island, where they were warmly embraced by troops of celestial nymphs. In reality, the nymphs were *rākṣis* plotting to devour the captain and his men. The "nymphs" feigned shared distress with the merchants, seduced them, and begged them to become their husbands. One night after Sinhala had spent the evening in the arms of his beautiful nymph, the lamp

> in his room began to laugh. Sinhala asked the lamp the reason for the laughter, and the lamp replied by telling him that a previous group of shipwrecked merchants had been similarly treated by the nymphs but ultimately had been imprisoned and eventually devoured, for the beautiful nymphs in reality were vicious *rākṣis* in disguise. The light warned Sinhala that he and his comrades were in imminent danger and that there was only one possible means by which they could be saved. The lighted lamp told Sinhala that on the seashore there stood a white-winged horse named Balāha ready to take him and his 500 comrades away to safety, but that no one should open his eyes until he had safely landed on the further shore. Alarmed by the light's revelation, Sinhala quickly assembled his fellow merchants and instructed them in the advice that had been given. They then scurried down to the shore and mounted the waiting Balāha, who thereupon rose majestically into the sky. The *rākṣis,* seeing that their prey was escaping, called out in loud lamentations. The merchants, all except Sinhala, were touched with both pity and desire, opened their eyes to look back, and dropped back down into the ocean, where they were immediately devoured. Sinhala alone escaped and, after landing on the shore, went back to his father's house in Sinhakalpa. (Holt 1991:49)

The story in the Chinese version ends with a happy family reunion. It does not have the gruesome denouement in which the prince's former "wife," a bewitching *rākṣi,* followed him back to the palace, managed to seduce the father who married her and made her the new queen. She then got all the *rākṣis* to come to the kingdom and eventually devoured the king and his family. The prince finally made the people see the truth. They proclaimed him the new king, who succeeded in banishing the *rākṣis* to the forest and restored peace in the country (Holt 1991:49–50).

The last long section of the sūtra in the Chinese version is the revelation of and chorus of praise to the "six-character" dhāraṇī *Oṃ maṇi padme hūṃ* (O Thou with the Jeweled Lotus!). The Buddha declares that this dhāraṇī is the "subtle and wondrous original mind" of Avalokiteśvara. The dhāraṇī is a wish-fulfilling jewel, but so far nobody knows about it. If one should come to know the dhāraṇī, not only oneself, but one's ancestors of seven generations back, will all achieve salvation. That is not all. The benefit of the dhāraṇī even extends to strangers who come into contact with the dhāraṇī-keeper or the tape worms living inside his body.

> The worms living inside the body of the person who holds this dhāraṇī are destined to reach the stage of a non-retrogressing bodhisattva. If the

> person carries the dhāraṇī on his body or wears it on his head, from anyone who sees him, it is like seeing a stūpa containing a relic or seeing a Tathāgata. . . . When a person chants this dhāraṇī as instructed, he attains unlimited eloquence and develops the heart of great compassion. . . . When the breath of such a person touches someone else, the latter will develop a heart of compassion and, leaving anger and other poisons behind, achieve the stage of a non-retrogressing bodhisattva, and speedily realize *anuttara-samyak-saṃbodhi* [complete unexcelled enlightenment]. If a person wearing or carrying this dhāraṇī should touch someone else's body with his hand, the person so touched will also speedily attain the status of a bodhisattva. (T 20:59b-c)

Most of the last volume of the sūtra is similarly devoted to the wonders of the six-syllable dhāraṇī (T 20:59c-64a). The bodhisattva as the creator of the universe might be the inspiration for the beautiful images of "Lokeśvara with Radiating Arms" created in the Angkor period during the late twelfth and early thirteenth century. Three of them (cat. 96, 97, 98) were included in the exhibition "Sculpture of Angkor and Ancient Cambodia: Millennium of Glory" held at the National Gallery in Washington, D.C., in 1997. The catalogue notes that the cult of Avalokiteśvara enjoyed unprecedented popularity during the reign of Jayavarman VII when these images were made. The bodhisattva has one head and eight arms. "His body, cosmic in aspect, is covered almost entirely with miniature images of the Buddha, as if they issued from every pore of his skin" (Jessup and Zephir 1997:314).

One measure of the popular reception of a scripture is provided by the depiction of its themes in art. The "Universal Gateway" chapter of the *Lotus Sūtra* is a well-known example. According to *Record of the Lotus Sūtra* (Fa-hua chuan-chi), Chü-ch'ü Meng-hsün was credited with the promotion of this chapter as an independent scripture. The king was a Buddhist devotee. He suffered from illness and was told to chant the chapter, for "Kuan-yin has a special affinity with people of this land." He did so and recovered from his illness. From then on, this chapter, known as *Kuan-shih-yin ching* (Kuan-shih-yin Sūtra), started to circulate as an independent scripture (T 51:52c). Among the scriptures recovered from the caves of Tun-huang, the British Museum alone has 1,048 copies of the *Lotus,* and almost 200 copies of the *Kuan-yin Sūtra* are in collections outside of China (Murase 1971:41).

A recent study provides a more complete accounting. According to Fang Kuang-ch'ang, 2,000 copies of the *Lotus Sūtra* are held at the Beijing Library, and when those held in Japan, England, France, and Russia are added together, he estimates that there are more than 5,000 extant copies of the sūtra. While a few could be dated to before the Sui dynasty (581–618), the majority were copied during the Sui and T'ang, indicating the growing popularity of Kuan-yin during this time. Many contain dedicatory inscriptions explaining why the copy was made. Fang provides several examples, all dated to the seventh century, which express wishes for the safety and prosperity of the country and the royal family, the hope to recover from one's illness, or the desire for the welfare of one's family, and relatives. Thirty-five copies of the sūtra, moreover, in the form of individual books, were made in court during the Kao-tsung reign of the T'ang period, dated 671 (1997:215–19). Among documents recovered from Cave 16 (sealed around 1035) in Tun-huang, there are "sūtra lectures" (*chiang-ching-wen*). These were delivered by monks as part of religious services for lay people known as "popular lectures" (*su-chiang*). They are expositions in prose and poetry on Buddhist sūtras. One of these is the "Sūtra Lectures on the *Lotus*." The worship of Kuan-yin is its central theme. Written probably in the T'ang period, it declares that "the blessings from worshiping Kuan-yin are the most superior." The Buddha is made to announce, "If a good man or woman can keep and recite the name of Kuan-shih-yin Bodhisattva, worship and make offerings to him for one day, the person's merit will be the same as making offerings to 62 billion bodhisattvas" (Wang et al. 1957:II.502, 515).

Miyeko Murase has gathered evidence for the popularity of Kuan-yin in other artistic media preserved in Tun-huang. Among the frescoes in the existing 492 caves in Tun-huang, more than 28 are illustrations of the "Universal Gateway" chapter. Wall paintings depicting Kuan-yin saving beings from perils range over a period of about four hundred years, from the early seventh to the eleventh century. Cave 45, which is dated to the eighth century, for instance, contains a wall painting of Kuan-yin with as many as thirty-five transformations (Miyeko Murase 1971:65). Kuan-yin was depicted on silk or paper during a short period of one hundred years, from the ninth to the tenth century. Hand-written copies of the *Kuan-yin Sūtra* with illustrations were also made during the same period. One book held at the British Museum has been dated to the early tenth century because it was executed with a pen instead of a brush (figure 2.2). "The choice of scenes and depiction of stories in this book bear a strong resemblance to the Kuan-yin paintings on the walls of Tun-huang cave-temples and on the hanging scrolls found at that site. This suggests that models or pattern books were used by local artists who perhaps formed an atelier where the use of such models maintained the tradition for a long time" (Murase 1971:43). During the Northern Sung, printed small books or hand-scrolls of the *Lotus Sūtra* with illustrations began to appear, and these seem to have replaced large wall paintings and hanging banners. Murase suggests that these "portable Lotus pictures" now became personal property of the devout

Buddhists. These books were so popular that they were mass produced. She further notes that there was a sudden increase of their production in the Yüan, and that this continued to rise in later periods (66–67).

Another indication of Kuan-yin's independent status as a savior and not simply an attendant of a buddha is that he begins to be depicted as the central figure in devotional icons. The earliest evidence for this new trend is a dated (548) stele found in the Ten-thousand Buddha Monastery (Wan-fo Ssu) in Szechwan and kept in the Provincial Szechwan Museum (figure 2.3). It was modeled after an earlier stele (523) that shows Śākyamuni Buddha being attended by four bodhisattvas, with four monks and two heavenly kings by his two sides, and a group of lively entertainers, musicians, and dancers under him. The Kuan-yin stele, donated by a monk, has the same format, except the four attending bodhisattvas are manifestations of Kuan-yin as well. Kuan-yin is clearly treated as the central iconic figure, comparable to the Buddha (Yuan 1991:27–32). A 538 stele showing Kuan-yin flanked by two attendants from the

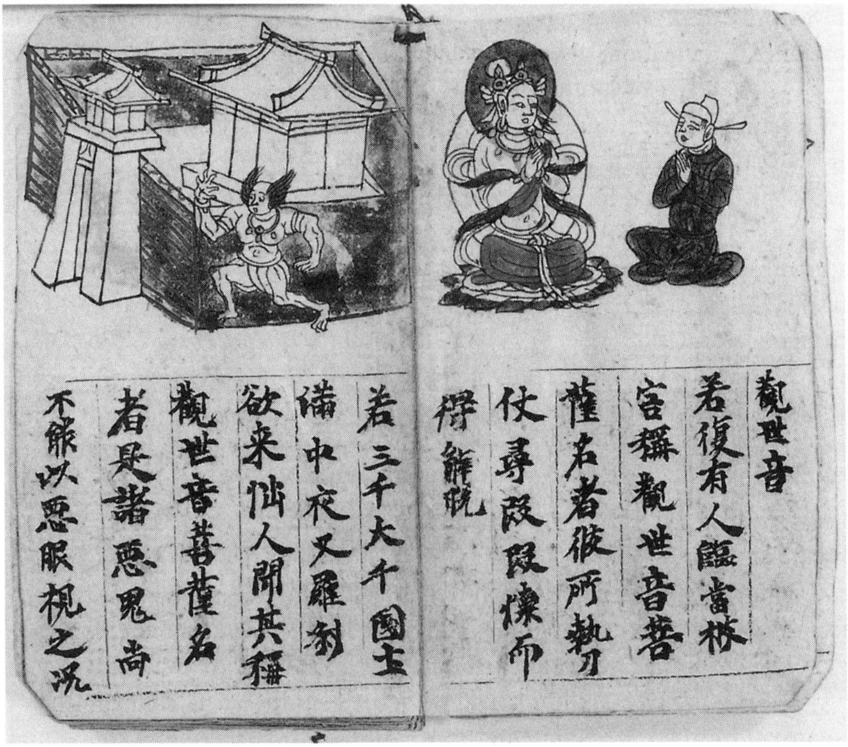

Figure 2.2. Illustrated "Kuan-yin Sūtra" from Tun-huang, dated early tenth century. *Courtesy of the British Museum.*

Indianapolis Museum is a simpler example. Although these were created for public worship and housed in temples, smaller ones might be made specifically for private devotional use. A gilt bronze Kuan-yin shrine dated 599 kept at the Nelson-Atkins Museum of Art is similar in showing Kuan-yin at the center, flanked by two bodhisattvas and two monks (figure 2.4). Because of its small size (8 1/2 inches), it was most likely intended to have been enshrined at the home of the devotee for private worship, as the miracle stories that I examine in chapter 4 would indicate. The equivalence between the Buddha and Kuan-yin was further implied by the architectural layout of monasteries in the Sung. According to T. Griffith Foulk, "Another common arrangement featured sets of five hundred and/or sixteen arhats arrayed behind a central figure of the bodhisattva Kuan-yin or the 'crowned Śākyamuni' (*pao-kuan* Shih-chia). The central figure was flanked by images of Shan-ts'ai T'ung-tzu (Sudhana) and Yüeh-kai Chang-che [Elder Yüeh-kai]" (Foulk 1993:170). The presence of Shan-t'sai, who appears in the *Avataṃsaka Sūtra* (Hua-yen ching) attests to the importance of this sūtra. Elder Yüeh-kai, incidentally, is the person who leads a delegation of five hundred people to ask the Buddha for help when his country is ravaged by pestilence as related in the *Ch'ing Kuan-yin ching* (T 20:34c). His presence in Sung monasteries was a tangible measure of the sūtra's popularity.

The attraction of Avalokiteśvara as a cosmic god as depicted in the esoteric sūtras must be very great. In fact, we can find evidence of positive responses to this new idea in new iconographies of this deity. From the T'ang on, Kuan-yin was depicted as holding a willow branch and a water bottle instead of holding a lotus and a water bottle as in the earlier iconography of the bodhisattva. Inspired by the Indian prototype, Kuan-yin was at first depicted as the "lotus bearer." The earliest example of this is the gilt bronze Kuan-yin image dated 453 from the Freer Gallery (figure 2.1). But due to the influence of the *Ch'ing Kuan-yin ching* and other Tantric sūtras, the lotus was replaced by the willow. For while the former stipulates the offering of the willow branch and water bottle to Avalokiteśvara as the ritual prerequisite to invoking him for assistance, willow branch is mentioned specifically as an effective cure for disease in the sūtras featuring the Thousand-armed Avalokiteśvara (T 20:88a; 122b). A hand holding a willow branch is of course one of the forty mudrās as well. Chinese artists increasingly began to depict Avalokiteśvara as holding a willow branch from the T'ang period on. For instance, a dated (703) triad from the Ch'i-pao-t'ai (Terrace of the Seven Treasures) held at Tokyo National Museum (figure 2.5) shows Kuan-yin holding a willow branch, and a late T'ang painting of Kuan-yin from the Rijksmuseum of Amsterdam (figure 2.6) also shows him holding a willow branch in his right hand and a bottle of ambrosia in his left hand, surrounded by the eight perils from the *Lotus Sūtra*. In the Ming and

Figure 2.3. Stele of the Five Kuan-yins from the Wan-fo Ssu, Szechwan, dated 548 C.E.
Courtesy of Angela F. Howard.

Ch'ing, after Kuan-yin had been feminized, even when she was shown not holding anything in her hand, the willow branch would still be depicted as emerging from the water bottle, which might be shown sitting beside her.

Another indication of the willow branch and pure water as established attributes of Kuan-yin is provided by the *gāthā* in her praise sung during the celebrations of her "birthday," which are held on the nineteenth day of the second month, the sixth month, and the ninth month. Included in the *Ch'an-men jih-sung* (Daily Liturgies of the Ch'an School), a text published in 1834 that con-

Figure 2.4. Kuan-yin, dated 599. *Courtesy of the Nelson-Atkins Museum of Art.*

tains materials dated to earlier periods, the "Celebratory Rite for Bodhisattva Kuan-shih-yin's Holy Birthday" (Kuan-shih-yin P'u-sa sheng-tan chu-yi) fuses elements from the *Lotus Sūtra*, and the *Ch'ien-shou ching*. It calls for the chanting of Kuan-yin's name three times, followed by the chanting of the Great Compassion Dhāraṇī seven times. Then the following gāthā is to be sung accompanied by music:

The Bodhisattva is the Perfectly Penetrating One. Born in the forest of seven jewels, her true form has a thousand hands and a thousand eyes. She sits in the Potalaka Palace. Sprinkling sweet dew with a willow branch, she nourishes the entire Dharma Realm universally. Displaying her supernatural powers and riding on thousand layers of ocean waves, she arrives in full splendor in this place of truth.

Figure 2.5. Amitābha triad from the Terrace of the Seven Treasures, dated 703.
Courtesy of the Tokyo National Museum.

The grace of the wondrous Kuan-yin Bodhisattva is hard to repay,
Her purity and splendor are the result of spiritual cultivation carried out in many kalpas.
Thirty-two different manifestations are found in many worlds.
She has been transforming beings in Jambudvīpa for innumerable kalpas.
The sweet dew in the bottle is constantly sprinkled everywhere,
The willow branch in her hand has been there for numberless autumns.
A thousand prayers rising from a thousand places are all answered.

Figure 2.6. Kuan-yin holding a willow branch, late T'ang (618–907). *Courtesy of the Rijksmuseum, Amsterdam.*

She has always been a boat transporting people from the ocean of suffering.
(Fo-chiao chao-mu k'e-sung, 90–92)

One more example of how the Tantric sūtras might have provided the source for the Chinese iconography of Kuan-yin is attested by the presence of the Dragon Princess (Lung-nü) as the bodhisattva's attendant. Both the sūtras celebrating Amoghapāśa and the Thousand-armed Avalokiteśvara mention the bodhisattva's visit to the palace of the Dragon King at the bottom of the ocean in order to teach the inhabitants there his salvific dhāraṇī. In gratitude, the Dragon Princess offers the bodhisattva a priceless pearl (T 20:88b; 252b). Many popular precious scroll (*pao-chüan*) texts written in the late imperial times make the Dragon Princess' offering a pearl to Kuan-yin a key point in their plot (to be discussed in chapter 10).

In Chinese paintings and sculptures of Kuan-yin after the T'ang, the bodhisattva is attended by a pair, a boy and a girl. The boy is usually taken to be Sudhana, the pilgrim from the *Avataṃsaka Sūtra,* and the girl the Dragon Princess. However, one sūtra describing how to perform the ritual of worshiping the Thousand-handed Avalokiteśvara, the *Ch'ien-shou Kuan-yin tsao tz'u-ti fa i-kuei* (Rules for the Sequential Setting up of Thousand-handed Avalokiteśvara), translated by Śubhakarasiṃha (636–735), might provide the earliest inspiration for this iconography. The text begins by describing how the image of the bodhisattva should look: he is golden in color. He sits cross-legged on a large lotus throne that has thirty-two petals, each of which contains many small petals. They are adorned with innumerable maṇi pearls. The bodhisattva is accompanied by three groups of attendants: the eight great bodhisattvas, a retinue of twenty-eight, and in front of him, "a heavenly girl with childlike eyes (*t'ung-mu t'ien-nü*) holding lovely flowers and a seven-year-old boy holding a sūtra" (T 20:138). The text gives the names, their mantras and detailed iconographical descriptions of the twenty-eight retinues of Avalokiteśvara.[22] We cannot say for sure that this and other scriptures provided the direct sources for the iconographical elements of Kuan-yin images in later periods, for the artisans were usually anonymous, or even in the cases where we know their names, they did not tell us where they got their ideas. Yet it is safe to say that the Chinese artisans did not create the images without following some rules, though very often they might not always have followed them faithfully, but made individual choices and modifications. In some cases, instead of following some scriptural models, the Chinese artisans might have copied the images or paintings of the bodhisattva brought to China by missionary monks. To what extent the foreign models faithfully followed the scriptural stipulation is another open question.

It is possible, fortunately, to compare the scriptural models with some actual executions. The discrepancy is often quite striking. The sizes, media, and attributes of the images rarely adhere faithfully to the scriptural regulation. Of all the surviving esoteric forms of Avalokiteśvara, the eleven-headed one is most numerous. Donald Wood (1985) described all the extant images in China and Japan. Seven extant reliefs of the Eleven-headed Avalokiteśvara from the Ch'i-pao-t'ai, completed in 703 under Empress Wu (ca. 624–705), are now kept in different museums of the world.[23] The one in the Tokyo National Museum (figure 2.7) shows the deity having ten small heads placed in three superimposed tiers above the main head as if attached to a headdress.

Among the caves of Tun-huang, there are many examples of the Tantric Kuan-yin. According to the statistics compiled by Henrik Sørensen, the Eleven-headed Avalokiteśvara is most popular, for more than one hundred of this deity are represented by both banner-paintings and murals. This is followed by the Thousand-handed Avalokiteśvara, Cintāmaṇicakra and finally Amoghapāśa, who are depicted in over forty, thirty-nine, and six respectively (Sørensen 1991–1992:302–5). Cave 334 contains a drawing of a seated Eleven-headed Avalokiteśvara with two arms dated prior to 642, while Cave 321 has a standing six-armed eleven-headed Avalokiteśvara, the lowest left hand holding a bottle, the lowest right hand a willow, dated to the reign of Empress Wu (*Chung-kuo shih-k'e Tun-huang Mo-kao-k'u*, III:82, 55).[24] He is the principal figure, flanked by Mañjuśrī and Samanthabhadra in Cave IX of T'ien-lung Shan, created about the same time (Lee and Ho 1959:136). Other fine examples are found in Japan, such as the image in Hōryūji created in the eighth century in the T'ang style. Amoghapāśa and Cintāmaṇicakra Avalokiteśvara were also represented in art after those sūtras were translated in the T'ang. Of all the esoteric forms of Avalokiteśvara introduced into China, however, it is the Thousand-handed and Thousand-eyed Avalokiteśvara who became most popular in China. Why this was so will be explored in later chapters.

It is clear from this survey that there is a rich source from both exoteric and esoteric scriptures that can serve as models for artists to depict the various forms Avalokiteśvara assumes to help sentient beings. Indeed, many images and drawings of this bodhisattva have been created using such scriptural sources as their basis. Public icons in monasteries continue to be of this kind. But when we look at the sets of Kuan-yin paintings, be they five, thirty-two, or fifty-three, made by artists in late imperial period intended for private devotional viewing, no discernable connection with scriptural sources is present. They were indigenous creations by Chinese artists who showed unrestrained freedom in their imagery of a Kuan-yin who looked remarkably like a beautiful Chinese lady. Similarly, the same pattern is discernable in the use of Buddhist

Figure 2.7. Eleven-headed Kuan-yin, dated 703. *Courtesy of Tokyo National Museum.*

texts. While sūtras are chanted in liturgical settings in monasteries, indigenous scriptures are often used for private purposes. As discussed in the next chapter, indigenous sūtras were created on the basis of canonical scriptures such as the *Lotus* and the *Ch'ien-shou ching*, reflecting their popularity and prestige. When we examine the contents of the indigenous sūtras, however, they astonish us by their bold imagination and their frank "native" appearances.

Of the multiple sets depicting Kuan-yin, the one with five forms probably was the earliest. Such a set painted by Ting Yün-p'eng (1547–ca.1628) is kept at Nelson-Atkins Museum in Kansas City (figure 2.8). All five are feminine. The

Figure 2.8.

Figure 2.8. Five forms of Kuan-yin, c. 1579–1580, by Ting Yün-p'eng (1547–c. 1621).
Courtesy of the Nelson-Atkins Museum of Art.

majority of the thirty-two forms and the fifty-three forms are also feminine. At least four sets of thirty-two forms of Kuan-yin are extant. One set painted by Hsing Tz'u-ching, a woman painter living during the fifteenth to the sixteenth century in the Ming periods is kept at the Palace Museum in Taipei. A set attributed to Tu Chin of the mid-fifteenth century is at the Tokyo National Museum. Another set with only twenty-eight images remaining of the original thirty-two, attributed to Ting Yün-p'eng (1547–ca.1621), is kept at Anhui Provincial Museum, and the fourth set, painted by the daughter of the famous painter Ch'ou Ying (1494–ca.1552) is kept by a private collector in the United States (Laing 1988:70–72). The drawings in the four sets are identical, all are done in the *pai-miao* line-drawing style, but the gāthās appended to them are sometimes different. For instance, one of the forms shows Kuan-yin sitting on a mythological lion-like animal called *hou,*[25] an iconography not found prior to the Ming. Although the image in the sets by Tin Chin and Ting Yün-p'eng is the same as that in the Palace Museum set painted by Hsing Tz'u-ching (figure 2.9), as well as the set in Anhui Provincial Museum, the gāthās are different.

A set of the fifty-three forms of Kuan-yin compiled and printed with a preface by Hu Ying-lin (1551–1602), a historian with a strong interest in the Kuan-yin lore, has been reprinted in several modern editions. All thirty-two forms are repeated here, but many new ones are also added. Forty-two of the fifty-three are definitely feminine, and eleven are masculine including Kuan-yin appearing in the forms of buddhas, monks, ministers, and so on, drawing inspiration from the *Lotus* and *Śūraṅgama* sūtras. The number fifty-three refers to the fifty-three visits the young pilgrim Sudhana makes in search of truth as described in the *Avataṃsaka Sūtra*, another text providing scriptural basis for the cult of Kuan-yin in China. The forty-fascicle version of the sūtra translated by Prajñā in 798 is particularly important. It is a translation of the *Gandavyūha*, the section of the sūtra that describes Sudhana's pilgrimage. Kuan-yin is the twenty-eighth "good friend on the path" (*shan chih-shih*) Sudhana visits for instruction. Sitting on a diamond boulder in a clearing amidst a luxuriant wooded area, Kuan-yin, who is referred to in the sūtra as the "brave and virile great hero" (*yung-meng ta-chang-fu*), preaches the Dharma to him.

In the *Avataṃsaka*, Kuan-yin is credited with the power to save people from similar perils as those mentioned in the *Lotus*. When one calls on the name of Kuan-yin, one can go without fear into a forest infested with bandits and wild beasts. One is freed from fetters and chains, and one is saved from drowning in the raging ocean. When thrown onto burning coals, on calling Kuan-yin's name, one is not killed, for the flames will become lotus sprouts in a lake. By the late T'ang, artists liked to combine the depictions of Kuan-yin in these two sūtras. This is quite a common theme among the tenth century frescoes at Tun-

Figure 2.9. Kuan-yin riding on a *hou* (from Hsing Tz'u-ching's Thirty-two Forms of Kuan-yin), dated to the sixteenth century. *Courtesy of the National Palace Museum, Taiwan.*

huang (Fontein 1967:78) and among wood-block illustrations of Buddhist scriptures printed in the Sung and later. Such a wood-block print dated 1432 (figure 2.10) shows Kuan-yin appearing as a minister from the *Lotus* on the upper half and Sudhana paying homage to Kuan-yin from the *Gandavyūha* in the lower half. It is interesting to note that Kuan-yin in both renderings looks decidedly feminine.

The artists who painted these multiple sets of Kuan-yin figures seem to favor certain feminine forms that they would use repeatedly. I discuss these feminine images of Kuan-yin in chapters 6 and 10. They depicted the bodhisattva this way because the male Avalokiteśvara had become completely transformed into the feminine Kuan-yin in late imperial China. When did this astonishing change take place? How did this happen and who was responsible

Figure 2.10. Illustrated sūtra combining the *Lotus* and the *Hua-yen*, dated 1432. *Courtesy of Chou Shao-liang (Zhou Shaoliang).*

for this change? And ultimately, why? These are the issues I deal with in the rest of this book. Artistic depictions of Kuan-yin are one of the important sources for tracing this process of transformation. How an artist chose to depict Kuan-yin was to some extent dictated by the contemporary conceptions of the bodhisattva, though there was always room for innovation. But at the same time, how Kuan-yin was represented in art could also mold the viewer's conception of him/her. There is a circularity between the medium, its source, and its influence. This is not limited to the medium of art, but applies equally to other media involved in the construction and dissemination of the Chinese cult of Kuan-yin.

In this chapter I have discussed the scriptures important for the belief in Kuan-yin. In order really to understand their impact, one must study the connection between the texts and the Chinese context: were the texts actually read, studied and followed? Who did so, monastics or lay people or both? And perhaps even more importantly, how do we know that these texts were indeed well known in China? These are difficult questions; the following chapters are, in a sense, different attempts to come up with some answers from a variety of angles. Art, miracle stories, indigenous scriptures, precious scrolls, and so on can tell us much about the Chinese reception, assimilation and modification of the sūtra texts. In concluding this chapter and anticipating the following ones, I would suggest that the Chinese definitely did not accept all the sūtras passively or equally. Certain scriptures, such as the *Lotus* and the *Ch'ien-shou ching* quickly became the favorites, while some of the others were kept on the reading lists of learned clerics and educated lay devotees, but remained marginal to or even neglected by the people at large. In the case of Tantric sūtras, because the elaborate and demanding ritual of meditation made enormous demands on the practitioner's time and concentration, it was restricted to a select group (some texts were explicitly addressed to men only) and thus rarely if ever practiced by the general populace at all. The requirement of image making in accordance with strict rules would again restrict its practice to a person of some means. Both would then limit the Tantric *sādhana*s to an elite group that would be primarily monastic and male. Their emphasis on image making and the chanting of dhāraṇīs did, however, have a lasting impact on the practice of Chinese Buddhism and the development of the cult of Kuan-yin. We see people from all walks of life express their faith in the bodhisattva through chanting of a sūtra (most commonly the "Universal Gateway" chapter of the *Lotus Sūtra*) or dhāraṇī (most commonly the "Great Compassion Dhāraṇī"), and having an image of Kuan-yin made for the benefit of their family members or themselves. Most frequently, it was by calling Kuan-yin's name, which was the most democratic method of religious supplication, since it was not restricted to any class, status, or gender, that the Chinese faithful tried to contact Kuan-yin in order to gain worldly benefits as well as salvation.

3

Indigenous Chinese Scriptures and the Cult of Kuan-yin

In the summer of 1986, while doing research at the Palace Museum in Taipei, I found two hand-copied Buddhist scriptures that I had not seen before. The first one was copied by the famous Ming painter Tung Ch'i-ch'ang (1555–1636) in 1558 and was kept in the palace of Emperor Ch'ien-lung; it bears the seals of Emperors Ch'ien-lung and Chia-ch'ing. Its title is *Pai-i Ta-pei wu-yin-hsin t'o-lo-ni* (Five Mudrā Dhāraṇī of the Great Compassionate White-robed One). It contains the names of Śākyamuni Buddha, Amitābha Buddha, Kuan-yin, and White-robed Kuan-yin; a dhāraṇī consisting of thirteen phrases; and a short testimonial penned by Tung himself that reads, "This should be given to a person who desires to have an heir for continuous chanting. Due to the merit of this magical spell, a son of wisdom and blessedness will be born to one. May the power of the Buddha Dharma be without end." The second set of scriptures consists of three short fascicles and their names are: *Fo-ting-hsin Kuan-shih-yin P'u-sa ta t'o-lo-ni ching* (Kuan-shih-yin Bodhisattva's Great Dhāraṇī Sūtra of the Buddha's Essence), *Fo-ting-hsin Kuan-shih-yin P'u-sa liao-ping chiu-ch'an fang ta t'o-lo-ni ching* (Bodhisattva Kuan-shih-yin's Great Dhāraṇī Sūtra, A Recipe for Curing Diseases and Safeguarding Childbirth Issuing from the Buddha's Essence), and *Fo-ting-hsin Kuan-shih-yin P'u-sa chiu-nan shen-yen ta t'o-lo-ni ching* (Bodhisattva Kuan-shih-yin's Great Dhāraṇī Sūtra Saving One from Disasters and Leading to Divine Manifestations Issuing from the Buddha's Essence). This set of scriptures was written in gold ink on indigo paper, also during the Ming. According to the description under the first title, they were translated anonymously during the T'ang, and the Ming copy was supposed to have been based on a Yüan copy written in 1337 that is kept in the collection of

Chung-ts'ui Palace. The frontispiece depicts the Water-moon Kuan-yin sitting on a rock being worshiped by Sudhana and the Dragon King with the Dragon Princess offering pearls (figure 3. 1). None of these is found in any existing canon of Buddhist scriptures.

Four months later, in the winter of 1986, I came across the same scriptures among the holdings of rare books in the Chinese Buddhist Artifact Collection and Library, located at Fa-yüan Ssu, Beijing. There were other titles among the hundred woodblock print copies of scriptures I read there, for instance, the "Universal Gateway" chapter of the *Lotus Sūtra*, and the *Kao Wang Kuan-shih-yin ching* (King Kao's Kuan-shih-yin Sūtra), but copies of the above-mentioned two scriptures constituted the majority. They were all printed in the Ming. While the earliest was dated 1428, most of the rest were printed in the Wan-li era, roughly during the 1600s. These pamphlets all followed the same format: on the frontispiece was a portrait of the White-robed Kuan-yin sitting on a rock. She was attended on either side by Sudhana and the Dragon Princess. There are bamboos behind her, a white parrot hovering on her upper right side, and a vase with willow branches standing by her right side (figure 3.2). Some-

Figure 3.1. Frontispiece of the *Fo-ting-hsin t'o-lo-ni ching*, dated to the Ming (1368–1662). *Courtesy of the National Palace Museum, Taiwan.*

times she holds a baby on her lap (figure 3.3). This tableau clearly consists of iconography of Nan-hai (the South Sea or Potalaka), Pai-i (White-robe) Kuan-yin, and Sung-tzu (Child-giving) Kuan-yin, three major feminine images of Kuan-yin that emerged during and after the Sung (which I discuss in chapters 6 and 10). At the back of each pamphlet, a portrait of Wei-t'o is followed by a tablet-like plaque stating the name, place, reason, and date the sūtra was printed for free distribution. After this, there usually are appended miracle stories that happened in the past or more recently to people who chanted the sūtra. None of the stories predate the T'ang, while those that happened in the Yüan and Ming predominate. In cases where the miracles happened to the donor or his friends and relatives, great care was taken to provide specific details that make them read like first-person testimonials. Like the books and pamphlets left in temples for free distribution today in Taiwan, the quality of the paper and print varies a great deal depending on the status and economic means of the donor. Excellent quality of both printing and paper can be seen from a copy of the *Five Mudrā Dhāraṇī of the Great Compassionate White-robed One*, the same scripture hand copied by Tung Ch'i-ch'ang, which was printed in 1611 and donated by Princess Jui-an, the younger sister of the Wan-li emperor.[1]

These are the so-called apocryphal sūtras (*i-ching*, "suspicious scriptures" or *wei-ching* "spurious scriptures"). In the course of studying the cult of Kuan-yin in China, I have subsequently come across other such sūtras promoting the faith in Kuan-yin. Why did the Chinese put their faith in them? Since there were already a great number of "canonical" Buddhist sūtras advocating Kuan-yin, why was there a need for the "apocryphal" scriptures? What are the similarities and differences between genuine versus the forged scriptures? What roles did the latter play in the establishment and spread of the Kuan-yin cult? As we ponder these questions, it becomes clear that we should examine the criteria that have traditionally been used in distinguishing the genuine from forged scriptures and see if there are objective and verifiable standards used throughout. Situated at the vantage point of modern Buddhological scholarship that enables us to have a clearer understanding of the developmental history of the entire corpus of Buddhist scriptures, perhaps it is necessary to reevaluate the traditional distinction just mentioned. Indeed, during the past three decades there has been a trend to revise earlier attitudes. Beginning in the 1970s Makita Tairyō (1970, 1976) has in his various studies alerted us to the positive value of these texts. Instead of dismissing them as "forgeries," he regards them as valuable documents revealing contemporary understandings of Buddhism. In recent years, his interpretation has been adopted by scholars such as Michel Strickmann, Antonio Forte, Robert Buswell, Matthew Kapstein, Li-ying Kuo, and Stephen Teiser. Studying similar apocryphal scriptures in other Buddhist

Figure 3.2. Frontispiece of the *Fo-shuo Kuan-shih-yin chiu-k'u ching,* printed and donated by Imperial Concubine Cheng in 1573–1615. *Courtesy of Chung-kuo wen-wu t'u-shu-kuan, Fa-yüan Ssu, Beijing.*

traditions, they also see these scriptures as creative attempts to synthesize Buddhist teachings and adapt them to the native cultural milieu (Strickmann 1990; Forte 1990; Buswell 1989, 1990; Kapstein 1989; Kuo 1998; Teiser 1988, 1994).

The terms "suspicious" or "spurious" scriptures were first used by compilers of Chinese Buddhist bibliographical catalogues (*ching-lu*). Let us now review briefly the traditional views about these scriptures and the criteria used in so designating them.

Buddhist Catalogues and Attitudes Regarding Indigenous Scriptures

Compiling bibliographical catalogues of Buddhist scriptures were major undertakings for Chinese exegetes. Up until the eighteenth century, there were

Figure 3.3. Frontispiece of the *Pai-i Ta-pei wu-yin-hsin t'o-lo-ni ching*, dated 1603. *Courtesy of Chung-kuo wen-wu t'u-shu-kuan, Fa-yüan Ssu, Beijing.*

seventy-six such catalogues; some of those are no longer extant. The majority, fifty-nine catalogues or 78 percent of the total, were compiled in the T'ang and earlier (Tokuno 1990:31). The earliest catalogue was made by Tao-an (314–385) who compiled the *Comprehensive Catalogue of Scriptures* (Tsung-li chung-ching mu-lu) in 374. This catalogue is no longer extant, but the section on suspicious scriptures (*i-ching lu*) was copied by Seng-yu (445–518), who in 515 compiled the *A Compilation of Notices on the Translation of the Tripiṭaka* (Ch'u-san-tsang chi-chi). Tao-an used the term "non-Buddhist scriptures (*fei Fo-ching*)" to refer to twenty-six texts listed in the record. Thus we know that forged sūtras had appeared as early as the fourth century. Tao-an was distressed by the indiscriminate mixture of the genuine with the false and regarded the latter as despicable.

Seng-yu, the compiler of the earliest extant catalogue, was the first scholar to use three criteria to distinguish a forgery from a genuine scripture, namely, its meaning and phraseology were "shallow and coarse"; it did not come from the "foreign region" and lastly, it was not translated by a "western guest" (T 55:39a). While the first criterion was subjective and used only by him, the next two were accepted by all later compilers as objective standards.

Of all the later catalogues, Chih-sheng's (668–740) *K'ai-yüan shih-chiao lu* (Record of Śākyamuni's Teachings, Compiled in the K'ai-yüan Era), which appeared in 730, had the most long lasting consequence. According to the *Fo-tsu t'ung-chi* (Record of the Lineage of the Buddhas and the Patriarchs) compiled in 1260, the scriptures that he regarded as authentic were accepted into the official canon (T 49:374c). Especially after the canon started to be printed, from around 971–983 and onward, Chih-sheng's catalogue became even more influential. Except for those sūtras that were translated after his time, only the ones accepted as authentic were printed in subsequent collections. As a result, even if a sūtra was questionable in its origin, if it was vouchsafed by Chih-sheng, it could remain in the canon of East Asian Buddhism. Those branded as suspicious or spurious were cast outside the canon. Unless they were copied by hand or printed separately by others, which was true for only a small minority, many were lost and forgotten (Tokuno 1990:53). In regard to indigenous scriptures centering on Kuan-yin alone, we find as many as thirteen no longer extant titles listed in the catalogues.[2] Two sūtras that were judged to be spurious, the *Sūtra of Kuan-shih-yin's Samādhi* and *King Kao's Kuan-shih-yin Sūtra*, have come down to us. The scriptures I saw in Taipei and Beijing are not listed in any catalogue. Yet from historical records of various kinds, we know that they were very popular in China already during the T'ang. Therefore, although the authors of bibliographical catalogues all took upon themselves the task of protecting the True Law, they could not prevent either the creation of indigenous scriptures or, ultimately, their dissemination. Thus, from the time of Tao-an to that of Chih-sheng, during three hundred fifty years, the number of indigenous sūtras recorded in ten catalogues increased from 26 titles in 30 fascicles to 406 titles in 1074 fascicles (Makita 1976:25–27).

One reason catalogues could not stem the growth of indigenous scriptures was, perhaps, because they often differed among themselves as to what was and was not a "spurious scripture." Let me cite just two examples. The first is the celebrated case of Ni-tzu (her dharma name was Seng-fa), the daughter of Chiang Mi-ch'u, the erudite scholar at the National University who lived at the end of the Northern Ch'i. She started to produce sūtras in 499, when she was nine, and eventually authored twenty-one scriptures. Following Tao-an, Seng-yu classified them as forged sūtras because, "sitting quietly with closed eyes, she recited these texts fluently as if she knew them from previous lives [*su-hsi*]. She sometimes said that she went up to heaven, but other times that she received them through revelation" (T 55:40b). Fei Ch'ang-fang retold the same stories in *Li-tai san-pao chi* (Record of the Three Treasures throughout Successive Generations; compiled in 597), but regarded them as legitimate scriptures precisely because she knew them from previous lives (T 49:97a; Tokuno 1990:38, 45).

Another example is the celebrated *King Kao's Kuan-shih-yin Sūtra*, which is discussed in the next section. Its name appears for the first time in Tao-hsüan's *Ta T'ang nei-tien lu* (The Record of Buddhist Scriptures of the Great T'ang), compiled in 664, under the section on miracles relating to sūtras of different periods. He stressed in this section the miraculous responses resulting from chanting sūtras. He put this indigenous scripture, which he called *Chiu-sheng Kuan-shih-yin ching* (Kuan-shih-yin Sūtra Which Saves Lives), right there with *Lotus Sūtra*, *Nirvāṇa Sūtra*, and *Hua-yen Sūtra* (T 55:339a). The compiler of the *Ta Chou k'an-ting chung-ching mu-lu* (Catalogue of Sūtras, Authorized in the Great Chou), compiled in 695, shared the same attitude. Thirty-five years later, however, this scripture was listed under spurious scriptures in *K'ai-yüan shih-chiao lu* by Chih-sheng. He reasoned that, because this scripture was revealed in a dream and was not translated, it was no different from those produced by Seng-fa (Ni-tzu) and should similarly be declared to be a forgery (T 55:675a).

Compilers of catalogues, therefore, did not always agree among themselves as to what was a genuine or a forged scripture. But two criteria were generally upheld. First, the scripture had to be composed outside of China and then brought into China. Thus, the existence of a Sanskrit or some Central Asian original of the scripture constituted a strong proof of its authenticity. This alone was not sufficient, however, for how do we know that the original in a foreign language was not itself a forgery? The participation of a foreign master in the translation of the scripture was a necessary second criterion, for only a foreign master could establish a sūtra's real status in its land of origin. For this reason, the presence of a foreign master symbolized the orthodoxy of the scripture. Even if many of the foreign missionaries did not have a good command of Chinese and could not have been the real translators of the sūtras, many translations were attributed to them (Forte 1990:243). But as Hayashiya Tomojiro pointed out as early as forty years ago, of the 1,700 extant sūtras translated from Indic languages, 400, or one fourth of the translations in the Taishō Tripiṭaka, were wrongly attributed (Strickmann 1990:79).

For all these reasons, scholars have come to question the appropriateness of continuing to use the term *wei-ching*. For instance, Makita suggested using instead "scriptures composed by the Chinese people." These texts represent beliefs of the common people and can serve as valuable material in helping us understand how the Chinese people came to accept and absorb Buddhism

(Makita 1976:104). Tokuno (1990:62) suggested using "indigenous scriptures." Strickmann, on the other hand, wanted to use the expression "original Chinese scriptures," and argued forcefully on their behalf:

> [I]n terms of "authenticity" there is little to choose between a sūtra written in fourth-century Kashmir and one composed in fourth-century Ch'ang-an. With reference to the Buddha whose authority they claim, both are equally apocryphal; with regard to the religious conditions of their own time and place, they may both be of exceeding interest. Indeed, the importance of Chinese apocryphal sūtras may be proportionate to their distance from their nominal source. They offer a wide view of the acculturation and synthesis of Indian Buddhist elements on foreign soil. (1990:78)

These "revisionist" views concerning *wei-ching* may be linked with a more comprehensive understanding of the complete process in the creation of both the Southern and the Northern, exoteric as well as esoteric Buddhist canons. The Buddha did not write any scripture. The Pāli canon, the body of authoritative texts for the Theravāda Buddhists, was based on oral transmission traced back to the Buddha and formulated only during the second century B.C.E., some three hundred years after the Buddha's death. The Buddha taught the Dharma, but the Dharma was not exhaustively revealed by the Buddha. For there were other buddhas before the appearance of Śākyamuni Buddha, and he will be followed by another. Yet all buddhas reveal the Dharma. In fact, not only other buddhas, even the great disciples and bodhisattvas could reveal the Dharma when inspired by the Buddha. For the Dharma of Buddhism is found in the truths spoken by the Buddha, but not in his words and sounds (Davidson 1990:294, 316). For this reason, all Mahāyāna sūtras, which of course appeared long after Śākyamuni's nirvāṇa, can be regarded as Buddha's teaching. Moreover, in the Tibetan Nyingmapa school there is the Treasure (*gTer ma*) tradition. For many years and even today, new "treasure texts" have been discovered and they are accepted as genuine. In the words of a contemporary Nyingma scholar, "Hundreds of Tertons, the Discoverers of Dharma Treasures, have found thousands of volumes of scripture and sacred objects hidden in earth, water, sky, mountains, rocks and mind. By practicing these teachings, many of their followers have reached the state of full enlightenment, Buddhahood. Various schools of Buddhism in Tibet have Termas but the Nyingma school has the richest tradition" (Tulku Thondup Rinpoche 1986:13).

The Chinese tradition was well prepared for the reception of these kinds of texts, which in some ways resemble the Confucian apocrypha. According to Jack Dull, the reign of the usurper Wang Mang (9–23 C.E.) was a turning point in the rise of the Confucian apocrypha. Emperor Kuang-wu, who restored the

Han and established the Later Han dynasty (25–220 C.E.), was an enthusiastic promoter of these texts and decreed in 56 C.E. that all Confucians should be familiar with them. The Confucian apocryphal texts are known by many different names, but the most common ones are *ch'an* (prognostication) and *wei* (woof or transverse threads of a fabric, thus the counterpart or completion of the classic, which is literally the warp or lengthwise threads of a fabric). The advocates of these texts, who belonged to the New Text (Chin-wen) School, claimed that the apocrypha were either delivered by fabulous animals such as dragons or birds to future rulers or written by Confucius in order to explain the hidden meanings of the classics (Dull 1966: 479). Scholars of the Old Text (Ku-wen) School regarded these texts as forgeries manufactured by "vulgar Confucians" (*su-ru*) for political purposes. With the eventual triumph of the Old Text School, the apocrypha were proscribed in 217 C.E. But this did not stop people from either consulting the existing ones or even creating new ones. After the Han, at least ten more proscriptions were decreed in the next one thousand years. But these did not seem to have much effect. For by the time they were first proscribed at the end of the Han, parts of these texts were already securely attached to the classics in the form of commentary material. Therefore, "the texts continued in their fragmentary form as an essential part of the Confucian tradition" (Dull 1966:498).

At the end of his study, Dull calls for an investigation of the influence of Confucian apocrypha on the development of Taoism and Buddhism. "Both Taoism and Buddhism were strongly influenced by New Text Confucianism in general and specifically by the apocrypha, especially in the post-Han period. Religious or popular Taoism drew heavily on ideas from the apocrypha and Buddhism seems to have availed itself of these ideas both indirectly from Taoism and directly from the apocrypha themselves" (Dull 1966:443). I concur with his view. In the next chapter, I discuss the central importance of *kan-ying* (stimulus and response) in the worldview of Yin-yang Confucianism, which is profusely expressed in the Confucian apocrypha. This clearly exerted influence on the creation of Buddhist miracle tales. For now, I suggest that Chinese acceptance of the Confucian apocryphal texts surely predisposed them to regard the revealed Taoist texts as well as the Buddhist indigenous scriptures under discussion with tolerance and openness.

Makita divided indigenous Chinese scriptures into six categories: (1) those promoting the interests of the ruling authority, (2) those criticizing policies of the same, (3) those trying to reconcile Buddhism with Chinese traditional thought or comparing the two, (4) those proselytizing a specific faith, (5) those linked with particular persons' names, and (6) those promising cures, blessings and other "superstitions" (1976:40). He then classified indigenous scriptures advocating the Kuan-yin faith under categories 4 and 5. As I show later, however, some texts can just as easily be put under categories 1 and 6. In fact, Kuan-yin was a favorite hero/heroine in indigenous Chinese sūtras. As I argue in the next section, I think these texts played a very important role in the indigenization and domestication of this great Buddhist deity.

Some Important Indigenous Scriptures Celebrating Kuan-yin

Sūtra of the Bodhisattva Kuan-shih-yin [Who Explains] the Conditions to Be Born in the Pure Land *(Kuan-shih-yin P'u-sa wang-sheng ching-t'u pen-yüan ching)*

The extant version of this sūtra does not give a name for the translator, although Seng-yu stated that T'an-wu-chieh translated it in about 421 C.E. when the latter traveled in the Western Regions (T 55:12a-b). Diana Paul has translated the entire text and provided some commentaries. She points out that there is no recension in either Sanskrit or Tibetan and it is probably a Chinese rather than Indian composition (Paul 1985:264). It is difficult to come up with an exact dating of the text. The lack of any external documentation of the text, either of its use or its being mentioned in a datable work, leaves the aforementioned catalogue entry the only clue as to its dubious pedigree. So I choose to discuss this as the first indigenous sūtra not so much because of its antiquity, but rather on account of several of its characteristics, which are typical of indigenous sūtras as a whole.

The sūtra bears eloquent testimony to the popularity of the Pure Land faith. It also emphasizes the idea that Kuan-yin is destined to be a future buddha, for he is bound to only one more rebirth before Buddhahood (*i-sheng pu-ch'u*). Both themes are found in the *Sūtra of Kuan-shih-yin Bodhisattva's Receiving the Prediction* translated by Dharmodgata in 453, as I mentioned in the previous chapter. Although the present text does not offer any new theological innovation, it is anything but uninventive in creating a story about Kuan-yin's family life and spiritual journey.

Let me first summarize the sūtra. It opens with Śākyamuni on top of Vulture Peak surrounded by an assemblage of human and nonhuman listeners. A brilliant light suddenly radiates in front of the Buddha, illuminating southern India and gradually reaching other lands. At the same time, within this brilliant light, a verse is being recited:

Endowed with great compassion and the doors to liberation,
I eternally dwell on Mt. Potalaka in this world.

Observing the world during the six periods of day and night,
My original vows give rise to benefits for all.

Astonished by this miraculous display of light and sound, the assembly asks each other for an explanation, and finally a great bodhisattva by the name of Dhāraṇīśvara-rajā (Tsung-chih Tzu-tsai) asks the Buddha, who gives an explanation:

> From the west, beyond Buddha lands more numerous than twenty thousand times the sands of the Ganges, there is a world called the "Pure Land." In this land living beings do not have any suffering. They only experience happiness of all kinds. In this kingdom there is a Buddha named Amitābha. The holy ones of the Three Vehicles completely fill his land. There is one Bodhisattva named Kuan-shih-yin who is bound to only one more rebirth [before Buddhahood]. For a long time during which various habits are cultivated, Kuan-yin accomplishes the practice of compassion. Kuan-yin would like to come to this land now to reveal the fundamental causes for birth in the Pure Land. Displaying this brilliant light which illuminates the entire world, Kuan-yin will come here soon. You should ask Kuan-yin about the cause for this verse. (Paul 1985:268)

Kuan-yin, accompanied by an assembly of one hundred thousand great bodhisattvas, arrives to pay homage to the Buddha. He then occupies the center stage and tells Dhāraṇīśvara-rajā a dramatic and poignant story about his past. Countless eons ago in a country called Manivati in southern India, there lived a wealthy Brahmin and his wife. They did not have any children, which was a source of great sorrow. So they prayed to the gods, and in a short time the wife became pregnant and gave birth to a boy. Three years later, she gave birth to another boy. Both were handsome, and the father was ecstatic. He called in a fortuneteller to examine the two sons. What the fortuneteller saw, unfortunately, was disaster. After much hesitation, he told the parents reluctantly, "These children, although they are handsome, will separate from their parents shortly. The older son I will call Early Separating (Tsao-li). His younger brother I will call Quickly Separating (Su-li)." Sure enough, the prediction came true and the mother became mortally ill when the two brothers were respectively seven and five years old.

After saying her good-bye to her husband and sons, she passed away. The father at first did not want to marry again. But he eventually married another Brahmin's daughter who was reputed to be virtuous at heart. Soon a worldwide famine devastated the land and the father decided to go north to a mountain called Daṇḍaka to gather fruits. The journey would take seven days. When he did not return after fourteen days,[3] the wife became worried. She was afraid that if her husband did not return, she would not be able to care for the two children. And even if he came back with the fruits, he might not give her any because of his love for his own sons. She therefore decided to do away with her stepsons. She hired a boatman and took them to the "isolated island shore," promising them that they would find food there. Pretending to prepare food on board, she told the children to go ashore to find fruits and vegetables. But once they were gone, she sailed back home secretly without them. When the boys discovered that they were abandoned, they cried pitifully day and night. Then the older boy, Early Separating, remembering what their natural mother told them before her death, said, "I must awaken to the thought of supreme, perfect enlightenment, become accomplished in the great compassion of the Bodhisattva, and open the doors to enlightenment. First I must save others and then later I will become a Buddha. For those who have no parents, I will appear and serve as their parents. For those who have no eminent teacher, I will appear as their eminent teacher. For those who are poor, then I will appear as their benefactor. For kings and ministers of state, merchants, householders, rulers, and Brahmans, for the four assemblies and the eight groups [of living beings], for all the various kinds of beings, there is none for whom I will not appear. I vow that I will always remain on this island. In all lands, in all directions, I will bestow peace and happiness. I will become[4] the mountains, rivers, land, and vegetation, five grains, and the sweet fruits to enable the living beings to receive and make use of them, rapidly leaving the life-death cycle. I vow that I will be born where my mother is and will not separate from where my father is. In this way I profess one hundred vows to the end of my life" (Paul 1985:272–73).

When the father returned from his fruit-gathering trip, he immediately asked for his sons. The stepmother told a lie, saying that they were out searching for food. He then asked his friend, who told him the truth. The father went to the isolated island in the South Sea searching for them, but all he could find were white bones heaped up in one spot and clothing scattered on the seashore. Realizing that his beloved sons had died, he gathered their clothing and bones, wept and made a vow: "I vow that I will save all evil living beings and realize Buddhahood. I will become the great land, the water, fire, and wind, the vegetation, and forests in order to support all living beings. I will become the five grains to increase the nourishment of others. As a god or human or spirit, in all worthy or unworthy shapes and forms, there is no land where I will not appear." Saying this, he makes five hundred vows.

Kuan-yin then reveals the identities of the key figures of this drama. The father was no other than Śākyamuni Buddha, the mother Amitābha Buddha, the older brother, Early Separating, was Kuan-shih-yin himself and the younger brother, Quickly Separating, was Mahāsthāmaprāpta. The good friend was Dhāraṇīśvara-rajā, the mountain Daṇḍaka was Vulture Peak, and the isolated island was Mt. Potalaka. Kuan-yin makes a special point of saying that he will always remain on that island. He will preach on top of a huge diamond-shaped rock and stay in a seven-jeweled palace, where he will call the names of his parents. He is dependent upon this thought to be born in the Pure Land and to attain the bodhisattva stage of irreversibility.

The sūtra ends with Śākyamuni Buddha praising Kuan-yin and declaring that the conditions for being born in Pure Land are exactly as Kuan-yin says. The Buddha says further,

> I and Amitābha each convert from the beginning to the end of time. Take the case of the mother and father who have one very young child who falls down to the bottom of a well. His father goes down to the bottom of the well to look for his child and to place him on the shore. His mother is on the shore and embraces and cares for him. The close relatives help the mother care for him together with the assistance of friends. The child does not return to the mud in the well. I am like the compassionate father. The five kinds of lowly living beings are like the bottom of the well. Amitābha is like the compassionate mother who waits at the side which is like the Pure Land. Kuan-yin Bodhisattva is like the friend who has realized irreversibility and does not return [to earlier stages of Bodhisattvahood]. You ought to know that by entering this world in the middle of the five lowly [kinds of living beings], by teaching and changing the deluded and ignorant living beings in the six evil destinies, you cause them to be born in the Pure Land. Amitābha draws you out and does not abandon you. Kuan-yin and Mahāsthāmaprāpta protect and cause the irreversibility and nonreturnability of all [Bodhisattvas and others] who depend upon past conditions for professing their vows. (Paul 1985:275–76)

This sūtra is remarkable for several reasons. First of all, unlike all the "canonical" scriptures discussed in chapter 2, this provides a continuous narrative about Kuan-yin's family background and career. He is related not only to Amitābha Buddha as the Pure Land Sūtras claim, but also to Śākyamuni Buddha. The two buddhas are his parents and the other major bodhisattva of the Pure Land tradition, Mahāsthāmaprāpta, his younger brother. This construction of a family affiliation between the buddhas and bodhisattvas is the second distinguishing feature of the text. The writer was reluctant to leave Śākyamuni Buddha, the founder of the religion as well as the revealer of the *Lotus Sūtra*, out of the picture. The solution was to turn the two buddhas into husband and wife. This is the only text that presents Amitābha Buddha as feminine. Third, although the text puts the rebirth in the Pure Land as the highest goal, the writer was clearly familiar with other currents of thought found in different scriptural traditions. For instance, the statement that Kuan-yin would appear as a parent for those who have no parents or a teacher for those who have no teacher, and so on can come right out of the "Universal Gateway" chapter of the *Lotus Sūtra*. Similarly, Kuan-yin's vow of becoming mountains, rivers, land, the vegetation, five grains, and sweet fruits so that all sentient beings could receive and make use of them is very reminiscent of the same selfless generosity found in *Karaṇḍavyūha Sūtra*.

The eclectic openness to diverse strands of thought is a common characteristic of indigenous sūtras. Finally, writers of indigenous sūtras all aimed to package foreign ideas in a familiar form. What images are better known in Chinese culture than those of the evil stepmother and a child falling into the well? Stepmothers were so universally believed to be evil and untrustworthy that Han funerary monuments depicted the exceptionally righteous stepmothers, such as the Righteous Stepmother of Ch'i, for public admiration (Wu Hung 1989:264–66, 1995:204–5). In his famous *Family Instructions for the Yen Clan* (Yen shih chia-hsün), the sixth-century scholar Yen Chih-t'ui announced, "The second wife is certain to mistreat the son of the previous wife" (Teng 1968:13). As for the images of a child and a well, any Chinese reader who is familiar with *Mencius* (IIA:6) will undoubtedly respond to them while reading this passage of the text.

Kuan-yin Samādhi Sūtra Spoken by the Buddha
(Fo-shuo Kuan-yin san-mei ching)

This sūtra was first mentioned in the catalogue *Chung-ching mu-lu* in 594. Except for two fragments recovered from Tun-huang, the only complete manuscript copy, made during the Nara period (710–784), is kept in Kyoto National Museum. This has been studied by Makita Tairyō (1976:212–46). Recently, Harumi Hirano Ziegler (1994) translated this sūtra into English and wrote a master's thesis on it. She made the intriguing suggestion that this indigenous scripture was composed by Chih-i (538–579), the T'ien-t'ai master, sometime between 560 and 568. His main purpose was to make meditation practices more accessible to people of all social classes by taking advantage of the popularity of the cult of Kuan-yin. Other characteristics of the sūtra stand out. It elevates Kuan-yin to a supreme position. He is declared to be a buddha in the past known as True Dharma Light under whom Śākyamuni studied as an ascetic disciple. Kuan-yin grants the wishes of all who carry out this seven-day meditation. It is true that the name of the sūtra was first mentioned in Chih-i's *Kuan-yin hsüan-i* (Profound Meanings of the Kuan-yin Sūtra), written sometime after 593. It is also true that Chih-i and the T'ien-t'ai tradition in general promoted faith in Kuan-yin. Moreover, not only Chih-i, but other Buddhist masters belonging either to his circle or his tradition refer to the past status of Kuan-yin as a buddha, as well as Śākyamuni's tutelage under him.[5] Finally, the emphasis on meditation as the royal path to enlightenment as well as for the elimination of sins as shown by this scripture is a typical T'ien-t'ai concern, as we shall see in chapter 7. For all these reasons, even though Ziegler does not conclusively state that Chih-i was definitely the writer, circumstantial evidence certainly makes his candidacy a persuasive one. But even if he was not the real author, Chih-i and others showed real tolerance toward indigenous scriptures by citing the text. Their attitude is something of which students of Chinese Buddhism should take note in evaluating indigenous scripture.

I now summarize the sūtra and quote some passages from Ziegler's English translation. When it opens, Śākyamuni is in samādhi and remains silent for a long time without speaking. Perplexed, Ānanada asks the Buddha for an explanation, and he then tells the assembled disciples, "I observe that the three realms are empty, without existence, and also without stability. Moreover there is no reality in existence and also no permanence. All dharmas are void and tranquil. They exist because of causes and conditions. If [causes and conditions] aggregate, then [all dharmas] are produced. [These] can be spoken and also cannot be spoken" (Ziegler 1994:103).

Kuan-yin alone responds to this lecture on *śūnyatā* and gives his own discourse on it. The Buddha tells Ānanada, "This sūtra is named the *Avalokiteśvarasamādhi-sūtra*. When I was a bodhisattva in the past, I constantly saw that a buddha of the past recited this sūtra. Now I have become a buddha and I also am reciting it, without ever stopping. I have now attained buddhahood as the good result of [reciting] this Sūtra" (104). Here Śākyamuni acknowledges the recitation of this sūtra as the cause for his enlightenment. Later in the sūtra, he picks up this theme again and makes the supremacy of Kuan-yin more explicit. "I recall that Avalokiteśvara Bodhisattva became a buddha before I did. His epithets were the Right Dharma Light Tathāgata. . . . At that time I was a disciple cultivating ascetic practices under that buddha. I held fast to this sūtra and recited it without ceasing for seven days and seven nights. Moreover I never thought of eating nor of the five desires. Accordingly I saw that a multitudinous number of all the buddhas of the ten directions stood in front of me. With this I became awakened to the path and now I have attained buddhahood. My epithet is Śākyamuni. I hold fast to this sūtra and still recite it just as I used to" (115).

The heart of the scripture is the description of its meditation method and the accompanying visions the meditator will experience during the seven days:

> If you desire to practice [the teaching of] this sūtra, you should clean the inside of the house, hang banners and canopies, scatter flowers, burn incense, sit upright for seven days and seven nights, and recite this *Avalokiteśvarasamādhi-sūtra* without giving rise to extraneous thoughts. At that time Avalokiteśvara Bodhisattva will manifest himself. His form is a purplish gold color. He is one *chang* and two *ch'ih* tall (about twelve feet). On the back of his head he has a halo, the color of which is similar to that of white silver. Holding a lotus flower he manifests himself in front of that person. During the seven days there is a miracle [every day]. On the first day, [Avalokiteśvara] reveals *candana* (sandalwood) and *kunduruka* and has practitioners smell them. On the second day, he reveals a big bright light in the middle of the night; practitioners are able to see it and their minds are greatly delighted. On the third day, he reveals a lotus flower which is as large as a wheel; that flower is flourishing and looks like the color of white silver. On the fourth day, he reveals a heavenly being who is one *chang* tall (about ten feet). [The heavenly being] puts on a heavenly garment and appears in front of his people. After the practitioners see him, they enjoy it together and discuss about all dharmas. On the fifth day, [Avalokiteśvara] manifests himself and witnesses [the practitioners'] own attainment of samādhi. [The practitioners] see their own infinite transmigrations in the past. On the sixth day, [Avalokiteśvara] further reveals a heavenly palace which is made out of miscellaneous jewels of five colors. There are four bodhisattvas who sit upright expounding the Dharma. After the practitioners see this, their minds gradually brighten, and they clearly see the ten directions. Then they are greatly delighted and wholeheartedly respect the Dharma. On the seventh day, Avalokiteśvara Bodhisattva manifests himself. His light is radiant, brighter than the sun. After the practitioners see him, their minds wildly pulsate. Avalokiteśvara Bodhisattva raises his left hand and pats the practitioners' heads. They attain security and stability in their mind (106–7).

Not only the buddha land of Amitābha in the west, but four other buddha lands in the east, north, zenith, and nadir become visible to the meditator through Kuan-yin's power. The benefits resulting from reciting the sūtra in this fashion include the six supernatural powers, attaining of wisdom, and remission of sins. The sūtra then teaches a dhāraṇī (111), which is also recommended for recitation. It then continues with more specific promises of good rewards. Some of these are identical to those found in the "Universal Gateway" chapter of the *Lotus Sūtra*, with the curious omission of obtaining children of one's desire, and other esoteric scriptures discussed in chapter 2. It therefore promises a good life and an end to transmigration, rebirth in a buddha land, not being reborn in the evil paths of hell, hungry ghosts, animals, and asuras, not be born with a female body, and the guarantees that "when Maitreya appears in the world he will become the primate of the three assemblies" (121). A final claim of the scripture for being a gospel of universal salvation occurs near the end of the text when Kuan-yin declares that through the recitation of the sūtra, even the five types of people who are barred from attaining buddhahood can do so.[6]

Like the *Karaṇḍavyūha* mentioned in chapter 2, the sūtra promises deliverance and enlightenment not only to the practitioners, but even to those who listen to it and remember it. "If people listen to this *Avalokiteśvarasamādhi-sūtra*, [even] the blind will receive enlightenment. If there are sentient beings who can listen to this sūtra and remember it without forgetting, they will not fall into the Avīci hell for five kalpas" (104). It forewarns that there will be people who "will not believe in this sūtra, and say to each other, 'This sūtra is not spoken by the Buddha, but spoken by demons.' They will talk to each other, and burn this sūtra, and they will vie with others in destroying [this sūtra]" (116).

Like the others discussed in this chapter, this indigenous sūtra is synthetic in nature. Although it contains some novel tenets, the most revolutionary one being that Śākyamuni was a student under Kuan-yin when the latter was a tathāgata, it is possible to trace its main components to "orthodox" scriptures. The combination of the teaching of *śūnyatā* with the format of a seven-day meditation regimen, for instance, are already emphasized in the *Samādhi Sūtra of Direct Encounter with the Buddhas of the Present* (Pratyutpanna-Buddha-saṃmukhā-vasthita-samādhi Sūtra, Pan-chou san-mei ching), one of the earliest sūtras translated by Lokakṣema during the second century (Harrison 1990). This sūtra teaches a method of realizing the Mahāyāna fundamental insight of "emptiness" through a rigorous training in the contemplation of the Buddha. It is generally considered to be one of the seminal scriptures in the *nien-fo* (contemplation of the Buddha) tradition in China. The sūtra speaks of *nien-fo san-mei,* which is defined

> as a form of mental concentration that enables the devotee to behold all the Buddhas "as if they were presently standing before his eyes." The sūtra states that the devotee should spend from one day and one night up to seven days and nights contemplating the Buddha, at the end of which Amitābha Buddha will appear to him in a dream, if not when he is awake. . . . According to the *Pan-chou san-mei ching*, Buddha contemplation is a two-step process beginning with the visual or mental contemplation of the Buddha Amitābha

> and leading to the realization of the nonduality between the Buddha Amitābha (the object of contemplation), and the mind of the contemplator. The key factor in the transition to the second step lies in the experience of *samādhi*. The intense contemplation of Amitābha leads to the coalescence of the meditating subject and the object of meditation. Once *samādhi* is reached, the devotee awakens to the reality of emptiness whereby he sees everything nondualistically—without discrimination between subject and object. (Yü 1981:49–50)

This sūtra exerted a great deal of influence in the Six Dynasties. Hui-yüan (344–416) and Chih-i, among others, followed the teaching of the sūtra. Except for the fact that this indigenous sūtra substitutes Kuan-yin for Amitābha, the basic ideas of the *Pan-chou san-mei ching* are clearly discernable. At the same time, the influence of the *Lotus* and esoteric sūtras such as the *Dhāraṇī Miscellany* are also very much present. Instead of stressing visualization of Kuan-yin, it is the recitation of the sūtra and the dhāraṇī that receives primary attention. The author takes different ideas from diverse sources and then repackages them—a trait that occurs over and over again in indigenous scriptures. The text, just as the miracle stories analyzed in the next chapter, is very detailed in describing the visions of Kuan-yin resulting from meditation practices. It specifies the bright light, the purplish gold body of the bodhisattva, his height, and his touching the devotee with his hand. All these details are reported by individuals who experienced Kuan-yin's miraculous responses. Did they influence each other? Were they both influenced by oral traditions about Kuan-yin? Indigenous scriptures and miracle tales are two powerful media promoting and transmitting the cult of Kuan-yin in China. As I argue later in this chapter, they existed in the same religious milieu and carried the same proselytizing agenda. It is therefore not surprising that they should also share the same beliefs and vocabulary.

King Kao's Kuan-shih-yin Sūtra *(Kao Wang Kuan-shih-yin ching)*

Of all indigenous scriptures promoting faith in Kuan-yin, this is the most famous. Not only has it received much scholarly attention (Makita 1970, 1976; Kiriya 1990), it is also one of the favorite texts chosen by the faithful to be printed and distributed for free down the ages until today. Its popularity among the faithful, who have spent money to have it preserved and propagated through art, is also attested. For instance, on a votive stele kept in the Asian Art Museum in San Francisco supposedly made during the Northern Ch'i (550–577), the text of this sūtra is inscribed on the lower half and Kuan-yin is shown being attended by Ānanada and Kāśyapa, with two bodhisattvas and two heavenly kings on the upper half (figure 3.4).[7] This scripture was first mentioned by Tao-hsüan's *Ta T'ang nei-tien lu* (The Record of Buddhist Scriptures of the Great Tang), compiled in 664. There are five extant versions: there is the one carved in Lei-yin Cave about 616 and another in Number 3 Cave (with slabs dated 665 and 669) in Fang-shan, near Beijing, the third being the text originally discovered in Turfan and now preserved in the Deguchi Collection in Japan. This has been extensively studied by Makita, who dates it to around the eighth century. The fourth is the one recovered at Tun-huang and the fifth the one found in the Taishō Tripiṭaka. The latter two have not been dated (Kiriya 1990:10).

The scripture bears different titles. For instance, it is identified as *Fo-shuo Kuan-shih-yin ching* (Kuan-shih-yin Sūtra Spoken by the Buddha) and *Ta-wang Kuan-shih-yin ching* (Great King's Kuan-shih-yin Sūtra) on the slab in Lei-yin Cave. It also went by the names of *Chiu-sheng Kuan-shih-yin ching* (Sūtra of Kuan-shih-yin Who Saves Lives) and *Hsiao Kuan-shih-yin ching* (Small Kuan-shih-yin Sūtra). The Japanese version goes by the name of *Kuan-shih-yin che-tao ch'u-tsui ching* (Sūtra of Kuan-shih-yin's Breaking the Knife and Eliminating Sin). Earlier versions of the text consist of no more than a list of names of buddhas and the promise of secular benefits obtained by worshiping Kuan-yin. But the later it got, the more verbose the text became and it eventually came to contain confessions, prayers, and the names of various buddhas and dhāraṇīs. The central idea of the scripture was based on the belief propagated in many translated Mahāyāna sūtras and well established by the sixth century: namely, sins could be expiated by calling the Buddha's names, reciting a sūtra or chanting a dhāraṇī. Just as the *Lotus* advises the faithful to call on the name of Kuan-yin, other sūtras of Buddha's names (*Fo-ming ching*) encourage the practice of repentance and confession of one's sins through the recitation of lists of buddha's names (Shioiri 1964).

The origin of this scripture lies with the story about a person being saved from imprisonment and impending execution by chanting this very sūtra revealed by Kuan-yin. The miracle moved "King Kao," who pardoned the prisoner and spread the sūtra. But who was this unfortunate prisoner and who was this King Kao? Buddhist chronicles and secular histories suggest three different candidates for the hero of the story: Wang Hsüan-mo (388–468), Lu Ching-yü (d. 542), and Sun Ching-te, who also lived in the sixth century. King Kao, on the other hand, could be no other than Kao Huan (496–547), the powerful prime minister of the Eastern Wei and the titular founder of the Northern Ch'i.

Of the three persons named here, Lu had the most intimate connection with Kao Huan. Makita provides a detailed description of their long and complicated relationship. Lu came from a distinguished family. A native of Hopei, his uncle was enfeoffed in 528 as an earl, but Lu nevertheless lived a very strict and simple life. He was friendly with Buddhist clerics and wrote prefaces to

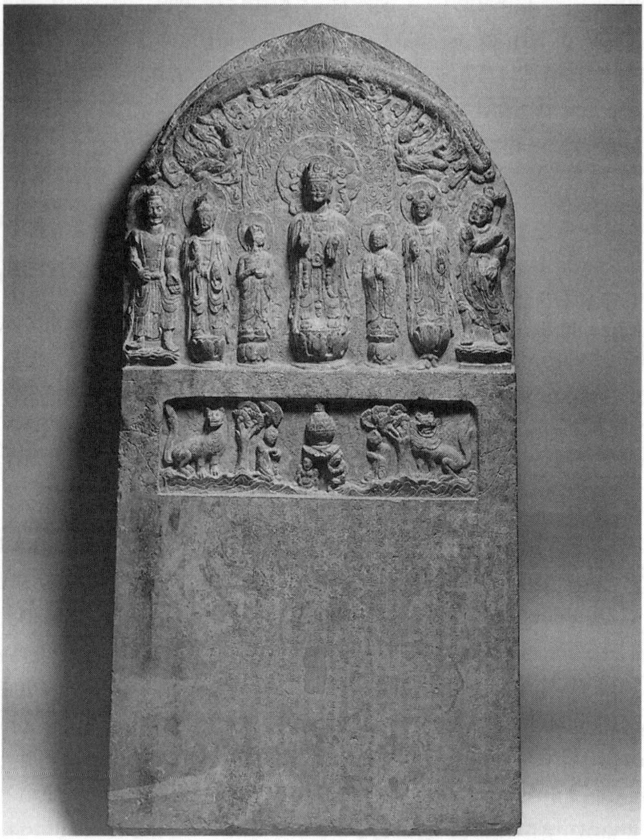

Figure 3.4. Buddhist votive stele with the *King Kao's Kuan-yin Sutra,* made during the Northern Ch'i (550–577). *Courtesy of the Asian Art Museum, San Francisco.*

translated scriptures. After Kao Huan set up Hsiao-ching as emperor and moved the capital to Yeh in present Hopei, thus precipitating the separation of the Eastern from the Western Wei, he took Lu and a number of other literati to the new capital. Though Kao Huan was the prime minister in name, his real power was still greater. Lu's cousins rebelled against Kao in late 537 and were crushed ten months later. Lu was implicated in this failed coup and was put in prison to await sentencing. In his biography currently found in the *Pei shih* (History of the Northern Dynasties), it says, "When Ching-yü was incarcerated in the prison of Chin-yang, he recited the sūtra with single-mindedness. The shackles suddenly fell off by themselves. At that time another person was sentenced to death, but because he dreamt of a monk teaching him a sūtra and he silently chanted it a thousand times after waking up, the knife broke by itself at the time of execution. When the ruler heard about this, he pardoned the prisoner. The sūtra became disseminated and was known as *King Kao's Kuan-shih-yin Sūtra*" (Makita 1970:161–66).

The author of the *Pei shih* based his biography of Lu on a lost one originally contained in the *Wei shu* (History of Wei) by Wei Shou. Wei was a close friend of Lu and therefore a reliable source. But the account actually contains two separate miracle tales, one about Lu and the other about an anonymous prisoner. Lu was said to have chanted a Buddhist sūtra whose name was not identified. Since Lu was reputed to be both a Confucian scholar and a Buddhist devotee, he was certainly familiar with Buddhist scriptures and did not have to be taught by someone else. However, the other condemned convict was supposed to have been taught a sūtra by a monk in his dream who could be no other than Kuan-yin, since the bodhisattva is often so described in dhāraṇī sūtras such as the one revealed by the Thousand-armed Avalokiteśvara, translated by Chih-t'ung. When he chanted it a thousand times, the executioner's knife broke and he was pardoned. As we shall see, the circumstances and details resemble very closely those of Sun Ching-te. As a historical account, this record found in the *Pei shih* is quite vague and unsatisfactory. The stories of Lu and the anonymous convict are telescoped together. It implies that the sūtra Lu chanted was the same one revealed by the monk in the convict's dream. But we are not given any evidence that this was indeed the case. And who was King Kao? This is also unclear. Lu was hired by Kao Huan to tutor his sons upon release. Two of the sons later became emperors of the Northern Ch'i. It is rather ironic that the sūtra became identified with Lu's persecutor, who later became his benefactor. There is no question that the most likely candidate for King Kao must be Kao Huan. The reason why this indigenous scripture survived while many others did not could be due to its promotion by a powerful ruler.

But there were two other persons whose miraculous escapes from death were connected with the origin of the scripture. Wang Hsüan-mo's story happened earlier than Lu's. Like Lu, however, Wang also was not often mentioned in Buddhist chronicles, leaving Sun Ching-te alone to be the "revealer" of the sūtra. Wang's biography is found in the *Sung shu* (History of Sung, fascicle 76) written in 487 by Shen Yüeh. Wang served as a general during the northern campaign in 450, but was sentenced to die because he was blamed for the defeat. While in prison, he dreamt of someone teaching him to chant the "Kuan-yin Sūtra" a thousand times to avoid death. He did so upon waking. When he chanted one thousand times, the order to pardon him suddenly arrived. It is noteworthy that the sūtra he was told to chant is simply called "Kuan-yin Sūtra" and no mention is made of "Kao Wang."

"Kuan-yin Sūtra" was a popular name for the "Universal Gateway" chapter of the *Lotus Sūtra* ever since the third century. When Dharmarakṣa's *Sūtra of the Lotus of the Correct Law*, the earliest translation of the *Lotus Sūtra*, appeared in 286, this chapter probably already existed separately. As we have read in the last chapter, the independent circulation of this chapter received a strong boost as a result of its promotion by the Northern Liang ruler Chü-ch'ü Meng-hsün (r. 401–433) whose faith in it was influenced by T'an-wu-ch'en (385–433).[8] Kūmarajīva had completed his translation of the *Lotus* by 406, and it was the "Universal Gateway" chapter from this version that the faithful referred to as the "Kuan-yin Sūtra." We know this was the case from the story of Wang found in *T'ai-p'ing yü-lan* (Collection for Imperial Viewing of the T'ai-p'ing Era, fascicle 654) and *T'ai-p'ing kuang-chi* (Extended Record of the T'ai-p'ing Era, fascicle 111), both completed in 983. The relevant passages from the latter read: "[Wang] dreamt of a person telling him that if he recites the *Kuan-yin Sūtra* a thousand times, he can escape from this disaster. Wang answered that he might lose his life at any moment, how could he find enough time to do that? The person then taught him to chant ten sentences which are: 'Kuan-shih-yin, Adoration of the Buddha, there is a cause linking me with the Buddha, there is a condition linking me with the Buddha, Buddha and Dharma are mutually linked; eternity, bliss, true-self, and purity; I call Kuan-shih-yin in the morning, I call Kuan-shih-yin in the evening, each call comes from the mind, Buddha-invocation is not separate from the mind.' When Wang woke up, he chanted it a thousand times. When he was about to be executed, General Shen Ch'ing-chih remonstrated with the throne and Wang was pardoned."

The reason why Wang at first thought he could not do as the person in the dream told him was because he took the "Kuan-yin Sūtra" to be the "Universal Gateway" chapter and it was indeed too long. The ten sentences, on the other hand, were sufficiently succinct to be chanted many times easily. Although they were not identified here as *King Kao's Kuan-shih-yin Sūtra*, they were indeed so identified later by Chih-p'an who wrote the *Fo-tsu t'ung-chi* in 1269. Referring to these ten sentences, Chih-p'an wrote,

> The sūtra has only ten sentences. It was no other than the one transmitted to Wang Hsüan-mo of the Sung dynasty (424–479) and the one recited by Sung Ching-te which is being printed today in the marketplace. But people in later generations have expanded it capriciously so that its phraseology has become vulgar and uneven, causing knowledgeable people to doubt its authenticity. In our dynasty, during the Chia-yu era (1056–63) Lung Hsüeh-mei's wife lost her eyesight. She was advised to pray at the Upper T'ien-chu Monastery. One night she dreamt that a person in white taught her to chant the "Kuan-yin Sūtra in Ten Sentences." She chanted it without ceasing and

> recovered her sight in both eyes. Mr. Chao of Ch'ing-hsien wrote about it and published it. Kuan-yin taught this extremely succinct text to save people from great danger, and from those ancient times until now there have been three miraculous responses. Do we dare not to believe it? (T 49:357c)

Although the first six phrases are found in existing recensions of *King Kao's Kuan-yin ching*, the last four are missing. But it has been suggested, as Chih-p'an does here, that this sūtra of ten phrases might indeed be the original form of this indigenous scripture (Kiriya 1990:15–16).[9] What is interesting is that Chih-p'an not only did not condemn it as a spurious text, he actually encouraged his contemporaries to have faith in it by citing the miracles that happened to two persons living in the remote past as well as one person living much closer to him in historical times. Moreover, as time changed, the revealer of the sūtra also changed from a monk to a woman in white. Starting in the tenth century, Kuan-yin increasingly became known as the White-robed One, and the Upper T'ien-chu Monastery in Hangchow has been a cult center for her (discussed in chapters 6). It makes sense that Mrs. Lung received a dream from Kuan-yin after she prayed at the temple. Kuan-yin saved Wang and Sun from prison and death, but saved Mrs. Lung from blindness. We can detect a characteristic that may be generalized for all indigenous scriptures. Not only does *King Kao's Kuan-shih-yin ching* lack a fixed format and exact wording, its "legitimacy" also has to be updated by constantly referring to verifiable miracles that happened to real persons at specific times and places. In this way, indigenous scriptures, like records of miracle tales, placed Kuan-yin firmly on Chinese soil by closely linking the salvific deeds of the bodhisattva with the suffering lives of the Chinese people.

Chih-p'an mentioned this indigenous scripture under three different titles (*King Kao's Sūtra*, *Sūtra of Ten Phrases*, and *Sūtra of Relieving Suffering*) at nine different places in fascicles 36, 38, 52, and 53 of *Fo-tsu t'ung-chi*. The above-mentioned three persons served as the protagonists in these miraculous stories. This inclusive attitude was already found in the *T'ai-p'ing kuang-chi,* which recorded the stories of Lu Ching-yü (fascicle 102) and Sun Ching-te (fascicle 111). Unlike Lu and Wang, Sun was neither a scholar nor a general. He was called a *mu-shih* (conscripted gentleman), a low-level common soldier. His story was first reported by Tao-hsüan in the *Hsü kao-seng chuan* (Continuation of the Biographies of Eminent Monks, fascicle 29), which all later accounts follow:

> Formerly, during the T'ien-p'ing era (534–537) of Yüan Wei dynasty, a common soldier from Ting-chou [in present-day Hopei] named Sun Ching-te had an image of Kuan-yin cast which he enshrined in his room at the bar-

racks. When he returned at the end of the year, he often worshiped it. Later he was implicated by robbers and put in prison in the capital. Because he could not stand the torture, he confessed to crimes he did not commit. He was sentenced to die. The night before he was to be executed, he felt very contrite and cried. He made a vow to himself, saying: "It must be due to my past sins that I am accused falsely. Now that I have paid off my karmic debt, I wish to suffer for the pains of all sentient beings." Soon after that he fell into a sleep-like state and dreamt a monk who taught him to chant the *Sūtra of Kuan-yin Who Saves Lives*. There are buddhas' names in it. He was instructed to chant it a thousand times and then he could avoid death. Upon waking up, he chanted the sūtra transmitted to him in the dream and did not make any mistakes. He chanted only a hundred times by daybreak. While he was led through the streets, he continued to chant it as he walked. He completed the one thousandth time just when he was about to be executed. When the executioner tried to behead him, the knife broke into three sections. He had to change knives three times, but Sun was still unhurt. Surprised, they reported this to Prime Minister Kao Huan and asked him to pardon Sun. Kao ordered the sūtra copied and spread throughout the world. This is then what is called *King Kao's Kuan-yin Sūtra* today. When Sun was released, he went back to his barracks and saw three cuts made by a knife on the neck of the Kuan-yin image. (T 50:692c-693a)

Tao-hsüan was so impressed by this story that he repeated it in three other chronicles, the *Shih-chia fang-chih* (Buddhist Gazetteer, T 51:972b) compiled in 650, the *Chi shen-chou san-pao kan-t'ung lu* (Record of the Miraculous Responses of the Three Treasures in China, T 52:420a, 427a) compiled in 664, and the *Nei-tien lu* (Record of Buddhist Classics and Allusions, T 53:339a) compiled the same year. In none of these accounts did he mention the names of Wang or Lu. Probably due to his influence, other Buddhist chronicles such as the *Fa-yüan chu-lin* (Forest of Gems from the Garden of Buddhism) of 668, *Fo-tsu li-tai t'ung-tsai* (A Comprehensive Record of the Buddhas and Patriarchs in Successive Generations) of 1333, and *Shih-shih chi-ku lüeh* (Brief Compilation of Buddhist History) of 1354 also only mentioned the name of Sun (Kiriya 1990:44–49). It is probably safe to say that Tao-hsüan was responsible for making Sun the hero of this mythic tradition. Sun's story was more dramatic than those of Lu or Wang and had the advantage of glorifying both the image and the sūtra as conduits of Kuan-yin's grace. Therefore, by the thirteenth century, if not earlier, Sun became exclusively and inseparably connected with this indigenous scripture.

The ideological basis as well as the method of religious practice as revealed by this scripture are entirely based on those of the "Universal Gateway" chapter of the *Lotus Sūtra*. If the latter were not already widely known in society, it would have been difficult for the former to become famous so quickly. Indigenous scriptures are ultimately dependent on the fame of the "orthodox" sūtras for their acceptance. As we shall read in the next chapter, soon after the first translation of the *Lotus Sūtra* in 286, there were miracle stories of people who invoked the bodhisattva with this particular name, Kuang-shih-yin, following Dharmarakṣa's usage. After Kumārajīva made a new translation of the *Lotus* in which the name of the bodhisattva was rendered Kuan-shih-yin, within one hundred years, Lu Kao (459–523) compiled in 501 a collection of stories using Kuan-shih-yin as the bodhisattva's name. In the meantime, his contemporaries Liu I-ch'ing (403–444) and Wang Yen also compiled miracle tale collections that contained a number of stories about Kuan-yin (Makita 1970:168; Kiriya 1990:21–22). There was abundant proof that as a result of the popularity of the "Universal Gateway" chapter, Kuan-yin had become widely worshiped by people during the Six Dynasties.

It is not hard to understand the reason for the "Universal Gateway" chapter's popularity. It promises that whoever invokes the bodhisattva's name with a sincere mind will be saved from seven perils (fire, water, wind or rākṣasa, knives, ghosts, shackles and enemies) and three poisons (greed, ignorance, and anger), as well as having two wishes (for a son and a daughter). Moreover, such concrete and practical benefits could be attained not by demanding intellectual knowledge or meditation but by invocation—one of the most egalitarian and democratic practices. No wonder its appeal was universal. When we examine the sixty-nine miracle stories contained in Lu Kao's *More Records of Kuan-shih-yin's Responsive Manifestations*, eight correspond to the peril of knives, twenty-two correspond to the peril of shackles, and fourteen correspond to the peril of enemies. They represent more than half of the entire book. After the gāthā section was added to the chapter in the Sui translation, made in 601, the seven perils were further elaborated into twelve perils, among them "being sentenced to die by the ruler, yet the knife will break in sections" and "being put in prison and having hands and feet shackled in chains, yet one is released from such confinement," perils number 4 and 6, respectively. They were the ones Sun Ching-te, Wang Hsüan-mo, and Lu Ching-yü experienced. Indeed, some entries from the collection of miracle stories were almost identical to the experiences of the three men. Like our sūtra, these miracle stories were also meticulous in providing the names of the persons who experienced them. In order to prove that the author did not fabricate the stories, he was careful to cite the sources for such stories. Moreover, 1,000 times was also the required number of times for the chanting to take effect.

It has often been uncritically assumed that Buddhist monks are the protectors of orthodoxy and only vulgar people fabricated indigenous sūtras. This was a stance the compilers of Buddhist bibliographical catalogues liked to take, but the actual situation was much more complicated. As we noted earlier, neither Tao-hsüan nor Chih-p'an questioned the authenticity of the present sūtra. In fact, they played a role in promoting its fame. Another telling example is provided by the choice of this scripture for carving at Fang-shan. Kiriya (1990) has called attention to the interesting fact that this text was carved twice in two different caves there. The first cave, Lei-yin Cave, dated 616, was one of the eight earliest carved by Ching-wan, the monk who started the project at Fang-shan. There are 146 slabs of stone on which nineteen sūtras are carved. Of this total, seventy-six slabs are sūtras belonging to the Lotus tradition, occupying a little more than half of the total number of stone slabs. *King Kao's Sūtra* is one of these. The other slabs record the texts from the *Vimalakīrti*, *Hua-yen*, *Nirvāṇa*, *Prajñāpāramitā*, and *Śrimala* Sūtras, all "orthodox" Mahāyāna scriptures (Kiriya 1990:28, 64). Therefore, when Ching-wan was convinced that the Latter Age of the Dharma was upon him and wanted to preserve Buddhist sūtras for future generations, he included this "spurious sūtra" among his choices. As Tao-hsüan and Chih-p'an did before him, he did not discriminate against it on account of its dubious origin. This could be taken as an evidence that the scripture must have been very popular in the early seventh century. The fact that it originated in Hopei, the home of Eastern Wei and Northern Ch'i where Kao Huan and his family held sway might also account for its inclusion at Fang-shan. Political patronage definitely played a role in the creation and dissemination of indigenous scriptures.

Two Sets of Dhārahi Sūtras Popular Since the T'ang

In discussing the five recensions of *King Kao's Sūtra,* we noted that two of them, the Tun-huang text and the one included in the Taishō Tripiṭaka, both contain dhāraṇīs. The indigenous sūtras glorifying Kuan-yin discussed in this section also emphasize the centrality of the dhāraṇī. Dhāraṇīs are indispensable elements of Tantric Buddhist sūtras. The Esoteric school in China was established by three masters in the T'ang, Shan-wu-wei or Śubhakarasiṃha (636–735), Chin-kang-chih or Vajrabodhi (670–741), and Pu-k'ung or Amoghavajra (705–774) who translated a great number of Tantric scriptures and established rules for Tantric rituals. Among the three, Amoghavajra's influence was the greatest. He received patronage under three emperors, Hsüan-tsung, Su-tsung, and T'ai-tsung. Like all Tantric practitioners, he stressed the importance of chanting and keeping dhāraṇīs. For instance, he offered Su-tsung a dhāraṇī he translated in 758 with the request that the emperor should wear it on different parts of his body. This was undoubtedly the dhāraṇī known as *Ta-sui-ch'iu t'o-lo-ni* (Dhāraṇī of Great Wish-fulfillment), a woodblock copy of which has been recovered from Cave 17 of Tun-huang. Dated the twenty-fifth day of the sixth month in the fifth year of T'ai-p'ing hsing-kuo (980) of the Northern Sung, it depicts Ta-sui-ch'iu, a Tantric form of Kuan-yin, sitting inside a large circle. He carries implements and weapons in eight arms. Sanskrit syllables of the dhāraṇī are written inside the circle and underneath there is the Chinese text promising the benefits resulting from chanting the dhāraṇī. The names of the donor as well as the carver are also visible in the cartouches (Whitfield and Farrer 1990:106–7). In 762 on T'ai-tsung's birthday, Amoghavajra offered him another dhāraṇī, which he had translated. Again, he promised that all desires could be fulfilled by chanting this dhāraṇī. T'ai-tsung ordered monks and nuns in the realm to memorize it by heart within one month and then chant it twenty-one times every day. At the beginning of each new year they were to report to the emperor the total numbers of times they had chanted it in the previous year. He also ordered dhāraṇī pillars erected all over the country with this dhāraṇī carved on them (Ch'en 1964:325–26).

In the last chapter, I discussed many important esoteric sūtras that promote the chanting of dhāraṇīs. All these could have served as models, or at least inspirations, for the authors of the indigenous dhāraṇī dūtras discussed here. In the esoteric sūtras, however, the chanting of dhāraṇīs is always carried out in a prescribed ritual format: it has to be done in front of a Kuan-yin image and as an integral part of more elaborate purification, fast, fire sacrifice, or other Tantric rite. This is where our present dhāraṇī sūtras differ, for the chanting of dhāraṇīs seems to be the only requirement.

Unlike the previous three indigenous scriptures whose titles are found in sūtra catalogues, all the texts discussed in this section are not mentioned in any catalogue. The first set of dhāraṇī sūtras in three fascicles were supposed to have been translated during the T'ang. This claim is probably not too far-fetched. Indeed, among the manuscripts brought back from the famous sealed Cave 17 of Tun-huang by Paul Pelliot in 1907, there are hand-written copies of this very sūtra made during the early part of the eleventh century (P 3916).[10] Another indication of its popularity during the eleventh century is provided by the accidental discovery in 1974 of two hand-written copies of the text, which were hidden together with other sūtras inside the main Śākyamuni image housed in the fourth level of a wooden pagoda in Ying County, Shansi. Known as Śākyamuni Pagoda of the Buddha Palace Monastery, the structure was erected in 1056 under the Liao.[11] The frontispiece of a woodblock printed copy of this same sūtra dated 1102 has been published in Cheng Chen-t'o's *Selections from Ancient Chinese Woodblock Prints* (figure 3.5). Aside from the hand-written version found in Taipei and the woodblock printed versions found in Beijing, other printed copies are also kept at the Sackler Museum at Harvard University and the Indianapolis Museum of Art (figure 3.6). It is apparent that this indigenous sūtra enjoyed considerable popularity since at least the eleventh century.

The first text opens with Kuan-yin addressing the Buddha, "I will teach the suffering sentient beings the *sādhana* of the 'great unobstructed sovereign dhāraṇī of the five wisdom mudrās' (*wu-ai tzu-tsai wu-chih-hsin yin ta t'o-lo-ni fa*),[12] which can protect one from all disasters, save one from all suffering, and satisfy all one's desires. Once heard, the dhāraṇī will wipe away all sins: sins of pride against the Three Treasures, teachers, and parents; sin of killing beings incurred at weddings of one's children or the first month celebration after the birth of a child. Even though such sins will normally lead one to be born in the Avīci Hell, if one has someone copy the dhāraṇī and then chants it every day in front of a buddha image, offering incense and flowers, one can avoid such a sad fate. The benefit of performing this *sādhana* is even greater, for at the moment of death, you will see bodhisattvas from the ten directions come forward to welcome you. They will touch your head with their golden arms and say to you, 'Good man (or good woman), when you are born in the Pure Land, we will protect you as if you were our own eyes and cherish you forever.' "

The sūtra has a special message for women: All women who detest their female bodies and desire to be reborn as men should have someone write this dhāraṇī for them and enshrine this in front of a Buddha image. "Worship it with flowers every day without interruption and when you die, you will be born in the Western Paradise instantly and effortlessly, as a he-man flexes his arms. You will find yourself sitting on a lotus, surrounded by thousands of dancing girls who will always entertain you."

The text promises to offer protection against loss of money, bad dreams, and chronic illnesses. Secret Trace Vajrapāla (Chin-kang mi-chi) will safeguard the devotee's residence from demons. The practitioner is finally assured a vision of Kuan-yin if he or she retires to a quiet place and chants the dhāraṇī with eyes closed from one to seven times. When that happens, one will also see the Buddha and enjoy the blessings of a wheel-turning monarch (*cakravartin*).

Of the set of three short texts, only the first fascicle contains a dhāraṇī. About half of the phrases in the dhāraṇī are identical to those of the *Ch'ien-shou ching*. This can not be a coincidence, but must have resulted from conscious copying. If an exhaustive search were attempted, it would not be surprising if we could find the rest of the dhāraṇī in some other dhāraṇī collections.

The second fascicle is a talisman against difficulties in childbirth. At the

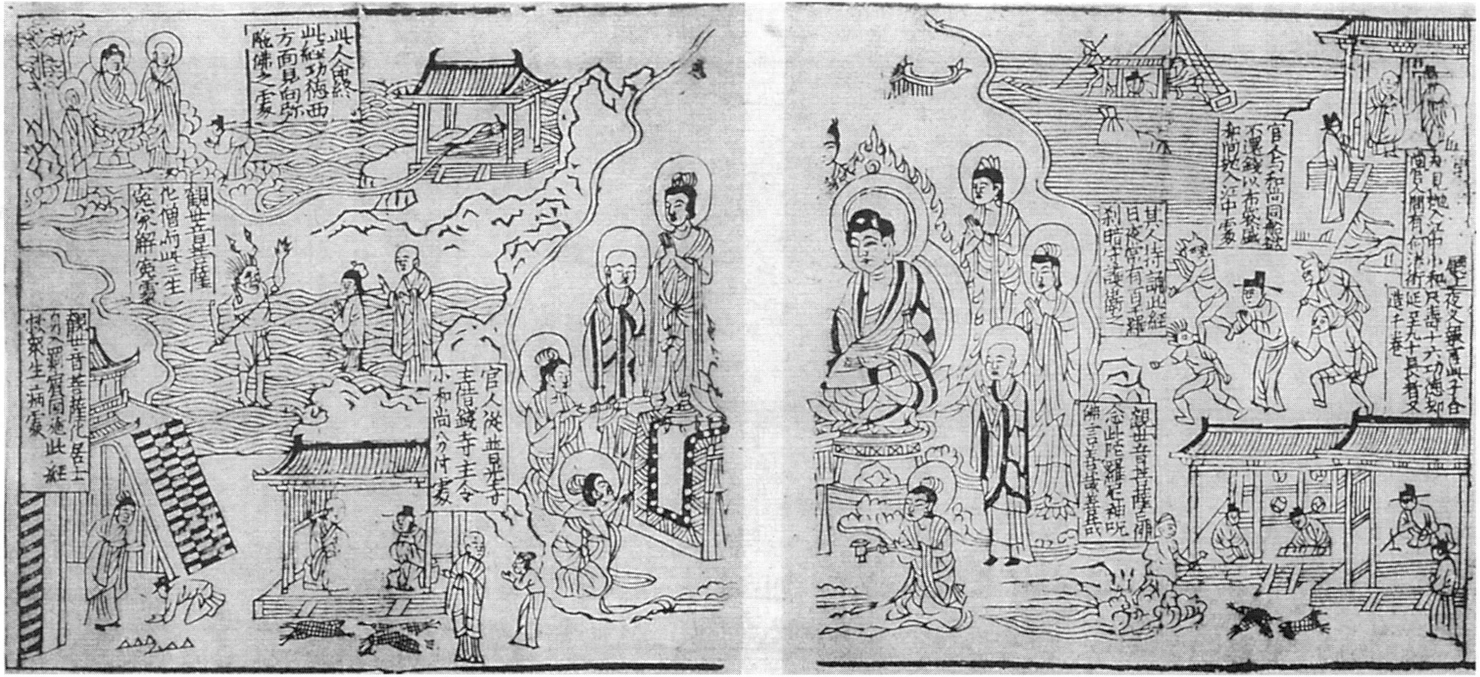

Figure 3.5. Illustration of the *Fo-ting-hsin t'o-lo-ni ching* printed in 1102. From Cheng Chen-t'o's *Chung-kuo ku-tai mu-k'e hsüan-chi*, vol. 1.

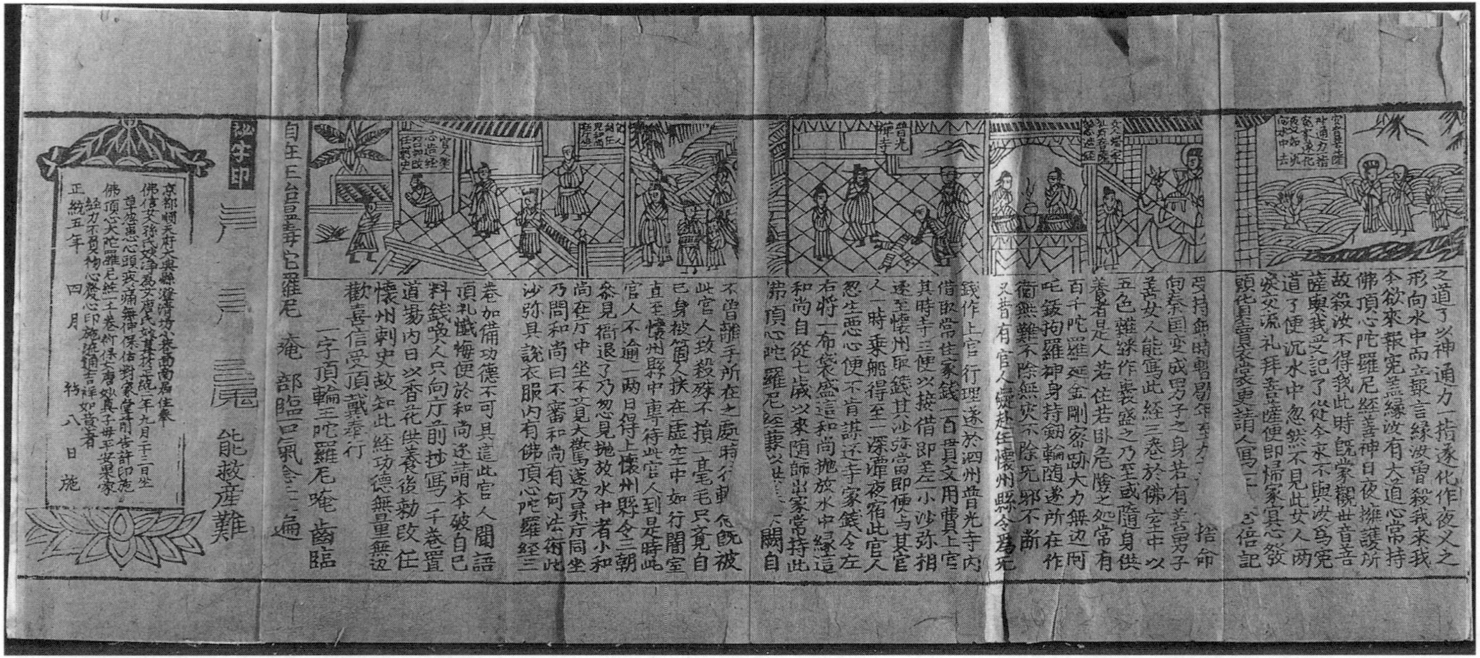

Figure 3.6. Illustrated *Fo-ting-hsin t'o-lo-ni ching* with dedicatory plaque dated 1440. *Courtesy of the Indianapolis Museum of Art.*

time of delivery, if a woman is plagued by demons who cause her great pain, she should immediately have someone write the dhāraṇī and the "secret character seal" in vermilion ink and swallow it (the ashes?) with incense water; then she will give birth to a wise boy or a beautiful girl right away. If the placenta does not become separated and is going to cause damage to the baby so that either the baby dies in place of the mother or vice versa, or both baby and mother would die, the pregnant woman should follow the above procedure. This will cause the dead baby to abort; it should be thrown into a river right away. Pregnant women are warned not to eat dog meat, eels, or birds. They should invoke the name of Pao-yüeh Chih-yen Kuang-yin Tzu-tsai-wang Fo (Sovereign Master Buddha of Precious Moon and the Light and Sound of Wisdom Peak), a buddha who is singled out for emphasis in the *Five Mudrā Dhāraṇī of the Great Compassionate White-robed Kuan-yin,* to be discussed later.

Aside from childbirth, the sūtra also offers advice on the art of dying. When one's relative is about to die, gather some pure earth from the western direction, mix it with the ashes from the burnt dhāraṇī and put this on top of the dying person's chest. Then wrap the person up with cloth. Due to the power of this dhāraṇī, the dead will go to the Pure Land in the west right away, without going through the forty-nine days of intermediate existence.

There is a strong hint that these indigenous scriptures posed a challenge to orthodox Buddhist beliefs and practices. He who copies this set of three scriptures is declared to have the equal amount of merit equal to having the entire Buddhist canon printed. One is also advised to cast buddha images in purplish burnished gold as offerings to these scriptures. We are reminded here of the claim that *King Kao's Kuan-yin Sūtra* was superior to the "Universal Gateway" chapter. A similar example is found in the *Sūtra of Kuan-shih-yin's Samādhi as Spoken by the Buddha*. As we read above, Śākyamuni declared in this indigenous sūtra that he had been a disciple studying under Kuan-yin who was a buddha with the name Tathāgata Bright True Dharma. Śākyamuni became enlightened only after he chanted this scripture for seven days and nights.

The third fascicle is the longest and also the most Chinese in flavor. In its structure and style, it reads almost like a transformation text (*pien-wen*) or precious scroll (*pao-chüan*). In a manner reminiscent of the beginning of the *Ch'ing Kuan-shih-yin ching*, it opens with a horrible disaster scene. People were dying of a plague epidemic in Kashmir. Once infected, they would die within one or at the most two days. Kuan-yin appeared as a layman wearing a white garment who went to each house to cure people and instructed them to copy these three volumes of scripture and worship them with devotion. When people did this, the epidemic immediately moved to other countries. The rest of the text tells three miracle stories, all designed to show Kuan-yin's efficacious manifestations (*shen-yen*).

The first story is about an elder living in Vārāṇasī. This is identical to the miracle story found in Chih-t'ung's *Sūtra of the Divine Dhāraṇī of the Thousand-eyed and Thousand-armed Avalokiteśvara* discussed in chapter 2. The writer of the indigenous sūtra copied the latter's plot but added another section linking the story to itself. The elder was very rich but had only one son. When the boy was fifteen, he suddenly became ill and no doctor could cure him. An elder from the neighborhood paid the father a visit, and seeing how depressed the latter was, asked about the cause. When informed, the elder instructed the father to have these three volumes copied on white silk and to hang this facing the buddha image. The father should burn incense in front of the scripture and the son's life would be prolonged. The father followed the instruction and even before the copying was finished, the son indeed completely recovered. Lord Yama was moved by this miracle to send a demon messenger to the father, saying, "Your son was destined to live sixteen years and he is fifteen now. He was originally supposed to live only one more year. But because a good friend taught you to copy these three volumes of scriptures, his life has now been extended to ninety years. So I am here to report this good news." The parents were overjoyed. They opened their storage room and sold gold and pearls in order to make a thousand more copies.

The second miracle story was about a woman whose nationality was unspecified. She kept this dhāraṇī and made offerings to the scriptures every day. Three incarnations ago she had once used poison and killed someone. This person wanted to revenge his death in this life. So he entered her womb as her son and, hugging her heart and liver, caused her great pain in childbirth and tried to kill her. After birth, the boy, who was comely and obedient, lived to be two years old and then suddenly died. Stricken with grief, she cried with loud lamentation and threw the boy's corpse into the river. This same sequence of events, beginning with the boy's birth, happened three times in a row. The third time this happened, it proved too much for her to bear. Standing by the river for a long time, she cried piteously and could not bring herself to give up her son's corpse. Kuan-yin appeared in the form of a monk and said to the woman, "Do not cry, Woman, for this is not your child, but your enemy whom you killed three life times ago. He has tried to kill you three times, but because you keep the dhāraṇī sūtra, he could not harm you. If you want to see the true form of your enemy, then look in the direction my finger is pointing." So saying, Kuan-yin used his divine power and pointed at the dead child who, turning into a fierce yakṣa, stood above the water and said to the woman that he had indeed tried to revenge his death but could not because she was protected by many good gods day and night on account of the dhāraṇī sūtra. Now that he had been exposed by the bodhisattva, he would no longer try to get even with her. The yakṣa then sank into the river and disappeared. The woman was greatly shaken up and thanked Kuan-yin profusely. After she returned home, she sold her clothes and asked someone to make a thousand copies of the scripture. She worshiped it without interruption and lived to be ninety-seven years of age. After death she became reincarnated as a man in the "Country of Ch'in" (China).

This story reflects the Chinese belief about the "demon child," namely that "certain infants are not ordinary children but evil spirits sent to cause the parents grief, perhaps as retribution for sins they have committed" (Ebrey 1993:175). Several stories in the *Record of the Listener* (I-chien chih) by Hung Mai (1123–1202) quoted by Ebrey make it clear that such a belief was common in the Sung. The demon child either causes difficult childbirths by grasping the mother's intestines, or after birth, dies in infancy and thus brings grief to the mother. Both details are found in our miracle story.

The last miracle related by the text happened in China, and includes identifiable place names. A literati-official was appointed as the county magistrate in Huan-chou (present-day Jui-yang, Honan). He had no money to make the trip, so he borrowed 100 strings of cash from P'u-kuang Monastery in Ssu-chou. The abbot sent a novice to accompany him to his destination in order to get the money back. They traveled together in the same boat. By nightfall, the official was suddenly seized with an evil thought. Because he did not want to pay the money back, he ordered his servants to put the novice in a bag and dumped him in the river. But the novice had kept this dhāraṇī sūtra since he was seven and always carried it on his person. Unharmed, he felt as if he was being supported by someone in midair and carried through a dark room. He arrived safely in Huai-chou. Two days later the official also arrived. When he saw the novice standing in the hall of the county government office, he was frightened speechless. The novice explained that he was protected by the three volumes of scripture that he had hidden inside his robe. The official repented and used his own salary to have a thousand copies made from the novice's original sūtra. He installed them in a temple and worshiped them with incense and flowers. Eventually this official was promoted to be the governor of the region.

The miracle stories contained in the last volume sound suspiciously like testimonials to the efficacy of the dhāraṇī sūtra that were only later incorporated into the indigenous scripture itself. For obviously, if the story of the novice from P'u-kuang Monastery were part of the sūtra's so-called volume 3, he could not have been carrying the "three volumes," one of which contained the story of how he had been saved. It is, however, highly significant that he was identified as a novice from this monastery, for this was established by Seng-chieh (d. 710) of the T'ang who was believed to be an incarnation of Eleven-headed Kuan-yin (discussed in chapter 5). P'u-kuang Monastery, which was better known as P'u-kuang-wang Monastery, of Ssu-chou (present-day Ssu-hung, Kiangsu), was an important cultic center for Kuan-yin worship.

Now let us turn to the *Dhāraṇī Sūtra of Five Mudrās of the Great Compassionate White-Robed Kuan-yin*. A copy of this was made by Tung Ch'i-ch'ang, and other woodblock-printed copies from the Ming have survived. The text is rather short. In order to give the reader a sense of the scripture, I provide a translation of the entire scripture, using the version printed in 1609:

The mantra that purifies the karma of the mouth: An-hsiu-li, hsin-li, mo-ho-hsiu-li, hsiu-hsiu-li, suo-p'o-ho [svāhā].

The mantra that pacifies the earth: Nan-wu-san-man-to, mo-to-nan, an-tu-lu-tu-lu-ti-wei, suo-po-ho.

The sūtra-opening gāthā:

The subtle and wondrous dharma of utmost profundity
Is difficult to encounter during millions, nay, billions of kalpas.
Now that I have heard it [with my own ears], I will take it securely to heart
And hope I can understand the true meaning of the Tathāgata.
Invocation:
Bowing my head to the Great Compassionate One, Po-lu-chieh-ti
Practicing meditation focused on the sense of hearing, [the bodhisattva] entered samādhi
Raising the sound of the tide of the ocean,
Responding to the needs of the world.
No matter what one wishes to obtain
[she] will unfailingly grant its fulfillment.
Homage to the Original Teacher Śākyamuni Buddha
Homage to the Original Teacher Amitābha Buddha
Homage to the Pao-yüeh Chih-yen Kuang-yin Tzu-tsai-wang Fo (Sovereign Master Buddha of Precious Moon and the Light and Sound of Wisdom Peak)
Homage to Great Compassionate Kuan-shih-yin Bodhisattva
Homage to White-robed Kuan-shih-yin Bodhisattva
Front mudrā, back mudrā, mudrā of subduing demons, mind mudrā, body mudrā.

Dhāraṇī. I now recite the divine mantra. I beseech the Compassionate One to descend and protect my thoughts. Here then is the mantra:

Nan-wu-ho-la-ta-na, shao-la-yeh-yeh, nan-wu-a-li-yeh, po-lu-chieh-ti, shao-po-la-yeh, p'u-ti-sa-to-po-yeh, mo-ho-chieh-lu-ni-chia-yeh, an-to-li, to-li, tu-to-li, tu-tu-to-li, suo-p'o-ho.

When you ask someone else to chant the dhāraṇī, the effect is the same as when you chant it yourself.

According to Toshio Ebine (1986), the earliest documentary evidence for this short dhāraṇī sūtra is a stele rubbing bearing the date 1082. A white-robed Kuan-yin holding a baby is carved on the stele and there is an inscription containing this scripture penned by Ch'in Kuan (1049–1100). The stele rubbing was published in a 1981 art book, *Famous Paintings of Kuan-yin's Precious Images in Successive Dynasties*, and a 1986 article by Toshio Ebine (1986; see figure 3.7). Unfortunately, neither provides any information about its provenance. From the penmanship of the inscription and the iconography, I doubt that this was carved in the Sung. A Ming or even Ch'ing dynasty date is more likely.

This indigenous scripture presents the White-robed Kuan-yin as a fertility goddess. She is really no other than the so-called "Child-giving Kuan-yin" (Sung-tzu Kuan-yin), a maternal figure holding a baby boy in her arms. Many porcelain figurines known as Te-hua ware that were made in Fukien during the Ch'ing from the seventeenth century onward have been preserved (figure 3.8). Nicknamed "the Goddess of Mercy" by missionaries and foreign visitors to China, this form of Kuan-yin has usually been regarded as an example of folk religious art. Not attested in the textual and iconographic canons, Child-giving Kuan-yin has so far received very little scholarly attention. By contrast, the White-robed Kuan-yin (Pai-i Kuan-yin), a favorite subject of literati and Ch'an painters since the Sung, has been regarded to be a typical example of the so-called "Zen painting." Representing the teaching of emptiness of the *Heart Sūtra* and symbolizing the serenity of Ch'an meditative states, the White-robed Kuan-yin has been a fitting icon for meditators within the walls of monasteries and beyond. It is no wonder that so many specimens have been preserved in Japanese temples, like the one by Mu-ch'i located at Daitokuji in Kyoto.

If we had to choose two extreme examples of Kuan-yin—one popular and mundane, the other elite and spiritual—they would have to be the Child-giving Kuan-yin and the White-robed Kuan-yin. However, the two images of Kuan-yin were not as different as they at first appeared to be. White-robed Kuan-yin was as much a great meditator as a great fertility goddess. Therefore, the Child-giving Kuan-yin was a variant of the White-robed Kuan-yin, representing another facet of her. As a fertility goddess, she was worshiped as much by the literati as by the ordinary womenfolk. Moreover, the cult of White-robed Kuan-yin as granter of sons received its scriptural authority as much from a

Figure 3.7. Stele of the White-robed Kuan-yin with inscribed text attributed to Ch'in Kuan (1049–1100). From *Li-tai Kuan-yin pao-hsiang ming-hua,* vol. 2, no. 144.

Figure 3.8. Te-hua blanc de Chine Kuan-yin, seventeenth century. *Courtesy of the Rijksmuseum, Amsterdam.*

number of indigenous scriptures, including the one under discussion, as from the *Lotus Sūtra*. Finally, it was through the promotion of literati beneficiaries who received sons by chanting these indigenous scriptures that the White-robed Kuan-yin emerged as the Giver of Sons. The creation of this indigenous sūtra was a testimony to the popularity of the White-robed Kuan-yin, the earliest Chinese feminine form of Avalokiteśvara, whose cult appeared around the tenth century.

Leaving discussion of the iconography of White-robed Kuan-yin to chapter 6, I want to focus here on the religious belief in this deity as revealed in this indigenous sūtra. For the author of the *Dhāraṇī Sūtra of Five Mudrās of the Great Compassionate White-robed One*, she was primarily a fertility goddess. Many testimonials written by literati either about the miraculous births of their own sons or those of their friends were attached as appendixes to this scripture, serving as evidence for the statement I am about to make. They were printed between the end of the sūtra text and the dedicatory plaque identifying the donor who sponsored the current copy of the text. Although a few of these stories found their way into standard collections of miracle tales, the majority did not. Anthologies and collected essays of literati, moreover, did not, as a rule, include this kind of information, which was of a highly intimate and autobiographical nature. Therefore, save for the accidental preservation of these testimonials, we would never have known this aspect of the religious lives of the literati in late imperial China.

Among the miracle stories collected in the thirty-five copies of this sūtra that I studied at the Library of Fa-yüan Ssu in Beijing, the earliest dates mentioned fall into the eleventh century, some during the Yüan, but an overwhelming number dating to the Ming. A survey shows the following types of donors: degree holders (provincial and metropolitan), magistrates, prefects, account keepers of the Confucian schools, investigating censors, drafters in the secretariat, directors of the ministry of justice, and, among the military, commissioners-in-chief and assistant commanders. Consorts of imperial princesses and other members of the imperial family also figured prominently. As for geographical distribution, there does not appear to have been any particular pattern, although central and north China (the capital and its environs) were mentioned more often than the extreme south or other border regions.

The miracle heading all the testimonials in most copies of the scripture was supposed to have taken place in the T'ang. This also served as an explanation for the origin of this text, which was simply called the "White-robed Kuan-yin Sūtra."

> During the T'ang dynasty there was a gentry-scholar who lived in Heng-yang (in modern Hunan province). He was quite advanced in age but still

> had no heir. In his effort to secure a son, he went everywhere and prayed for divine help. One day he suddenly met an old monk who gave him the *Pai-i Kuan-yin ching* (The White-robed Kuan-yin Sūtra). The monk told him that this sūtra was taught by the Buddha and whoever chanted it would obtain the fulfillment of all his heart's desires. If he wanted to have a son, he would be able to receive a son of great wisdom and the baby would be born miraculously wrapped in a white caul (*pai-i ch'ung-pao*).[13] After this, he and his wife chanted the scripture with sincerity. In several years they had three sons who were all born in the same manner described by the monk. When the prefect of Heng-yang heard this, he paid for the printing and distributing of the scripture in order to secure a son. In less than one year, a son was born to the prefect. (HTC 134:969)

In some other versions, more details were provided. For instance, a Mr. Chiang who was the district magistrate of Wu-yang (in present-day Shantung) had a relative who served as the prefect in Heng-yang and had personally witnessed this miracle. Using this scripture, the relative and his wife prayed for a son and succeeded. He then passed this scripture to Mr. Chiang and told the latter to chant the dhāraṇī. This is how the scripture became known (nos. 285, 291). In either case, it was through the promotion of literati-officials among their own circles that this particular dhāraṇī sūtra became popular.

The next clearly identifiable time when we find this sūtra mentioned in connection with a cult of the White-robed Kuan-yin identified as a giver of children is during the Yüan dynasty, in the thirteenth century. Again, as before, it was circulated among friends of similar background. Interestingly, this time the south, possibly Kwangtung, was where the text originated. According to one testimony, Wang Yü, a native of Nanking, was over forty but still had no son. In 1265 he went to visit his friend Ma Ch'ao and saw a copy of this sūtra in front of the latter's family altar. Ma then told him that in the spring of 1260 when the army had returned from the south, one among the captured southerners who had stayed in his house had left behind this scripture. After Wang took it home, he chanted it without interruption every day. On the night of the fourteenth in the fourth month, 1267, his wife, née Liu, dreamt of a person in white who, wearing a golden crown and accompanied by a boy, said to her, "I am delivering a holy slave to you." Liu accepted the boy and upon waking up the next morning, she gave birth to a baby boy who was handsome and wrapped in a white caul. They named him Holy Monk Slave (Sheng-seng Nu).

Even from these two cases, it is clear that the crucial proof of the efficacy of this dhāraṇī sūtra is the manner of the baby's appearance at birth. In fact, the phrase *pai-i ch'ung-pao*, which I have translated as "doubly wrapped in a white caul," appeared with regular consistency in all the testimonials. Fortunately, two stories make this enigmatic expression clear and prove my initial intuitive hunch to have been correct. The first story concerned Ch'ao Yung-hsien, the left secretariat of the heir apparent (5a), who was a native of Ch'ang-shu, Kiangsu. His wife was very devoted to this sūtra. On the sixteenth of the seventh month in 1586, a baby girl was born with a cloth as white as snow covering her head, face, chest, and back. When the midwife lifted it, her eyes and eyebrows could then be seen. He had several sons already, but only this daughter possessed the miraculous sign of the "white cloth." That is why the story was recorded and handed down (no. 291).

The second reference occurs in a story related to an early Ch'ing devotee whose son, when born, "had a caul which was white all over" (*pao-i chieh pai*) (*Kuan-shih-yin P'u-sa ling-kan-lu*: 56a-b). Playing on the pun *pai-i*, such a sign indicated to the believer that the baby was a gift from the White-robed Kuan-yin herself. This belief may have served as the basis for a curious Japanese painting made by Kano Hōgai in 1888 entitled *Kannon, Compassionate Mother*, which is nicknamed *Kannon with Bubble* (figure 3.9). Although Kuan-yin has a moustache in the painting, the bodhisattva is wearing a white robe. A baby enveloped in a balloon is looking up at Kuan-yin, who is pouring the sweet dew into the bubble and seems to be sending the baby down to earth. This is a good illustration of how the baby acquired the epithet *Pai-i ch'ung-pao* as indicated in the miracle stories. Unfortunately, I have not come across any similar paintings in China. I also do not know if the Japanese understood this painting in this way.[14]

One copy of the scripture dated 1614 contains a helpful description of how to chant the dhāraṇī as a postscript. Entitled "Rules for Chanting the Sūtra," it reads: Each morning, purify the mouth and body. Burn incense and do devotions. First chant the three mantras from the beginning of the sūtra. Each should be chanted three times. Next, chant the "gāthā of opening the sūtra" one time. After that, kneel down and chant the *White-robe Sūtra* 7, 11, 51, or 108 times. Once you decide on a specific number, always stick to it and do not vary or skip your practice. If you go out, chant silently in your mind, which is also allowed. Each time you chant, you can pray for a son, for general blessings, or for long life depending on what you wish and dedicate the merit of the sūtra chanting to this end. If for any reason you cannot chant yourself, you can also ask someone else do it for you. Do not seek quick results. The more devout you are and the longer you keep at it, the more certain it is that an efficacious response will come your way. Chanting the dhāraṇīs 5,084 times constitutes one *tsang* (canon). This satisfies one great dedication of merit. You can then start again to pray for another blessing (no. 299).

Figure 3.9. *Kannon, Compassionate Mother* (*Kannon with Bubble*), dated 1888, by Kano Hōgai.
Courtesy of the Freer Gallery of Art, Washington, D.C.

Aside from faithful chanting of the dhāraṇī sūtra, the good deeds required to repay Kuan-yin's gift of heirs were always in the form of spending money to have copies of the scripture printed and distributed free of charge. The most common numbers cited were either 500 or 1,000 copies, while the maximum was 5,084, which was again called one canon (*tsang*).[15] One testimonial provided a fund of useful information about the religious activities of some of the literati in connection with keeping the dhāraṇī. Ting Hsüan, a native of Yi-pin in Nan-yang prefecture (present-day Honan Province), was fifty and still had no heir. He printed this sūtra and distributed it for free. He also made an image of Kuan-yin by melting down 1,000 *catties* (one *catty* equals 1 1/3 pounds) of iron and gilding these with gold. It stood sixteen *ch'ih* (Chinese feet) high and was kept in the southern park of the city. It happened that Hsin Ch'ien, the grand commandant, in order to get a son, had built a shrine dedicated to the White-robed Kuan-yin in the north of the city. So this image was moved to the temple. The government official bought several *mu* (6.6 *mu* equals one acre) of good land, and the income from this was intended to be used for incense and candles in order to keep the temple in operation for future generations. Soon after this, Ting dreamt of a woman who gave him a white carp. In the morning, a son was born who was wrapped in a white caul. This was the fourth of the twelfth month, 1583.

When the image was first removed from the southern park, the groundskeeper had a dream in which Kuan-yin appeared to be unhappy. When he told Ting about the dream, Ting had another image made just like the one before. He also invited a mendicant monk to stay and watch over the image. An old man in white came to him in a dream as if to give him approval. The next day, while he was talking with a visitor about this dream, someone happened to come along with woodblock plates of this sūtra, asking for a buyer. He obtained them and printed a thousand copies for distribution. He also found a good artist to draw several hundred copies of the White-robed Kuan-yin to be distributed to believers for free. In the fourth month of 1586 he had another son. Hsin Ch'ien, the temple builder, by then had also had a son and a daughter (no. 291).

In this remarkably detailed testimonial, we can get a glimpse into the mechanism through which a cult of the White-robed Kuan-yin as the bestower of heirs might have started in various locations in China. Sale of woodblock plates of the scripture, printing of the text, painting of the White-robed Kuan-yin image, casting of the same image, and building of temples dedicated to her all went hand in hand. The promoters of the cult, just like the protagonists in indigenous scriptures and collections of miracle tales, were often men of means and influence. The cult was quite independent of monastic backing. One chanted the scripture in the privacy of one's home and it did not require any

Figure 3.10. Cast-iron Child-giving Kuan-yin, probably seventeenth century. *Courtesy of Reitburg Museum, Zurich.*

ritual that had to be performed by monks. The monk mentioned in the previous story served as a caretaker of the image in the donor's private cloister. Life-sized statues of the White-robed Kuan-yin as Giver of Sons holding a baby boy such as the ones held at the Rietburg Museum (figure 3.10 a-b) might have been enshrined in the cloisters dedicated to her. Others, such as the gilt-bronze image from the Asian Art Museum of San Francisco (figure 3.11), because of its small size, might have been made for private devotions and worshiped at home. For people of lesser means, crude woodblock print posters (figure 3.12 a-b) could have served the same purpose.

But did Buddhist specialists really play no role in the creation of this and other indigenous scriptures? I suspect the story about the monk in the T'ang giving the text of the *White-robe Sūtra* to the gentry-scholar in Heng-yang was

Figure 3.11. Gilt bronze Child-giving Kuan-yin, late seventeenth–early eighteenth century. *Courtesy of the Asian Art Museum, San Francisco.*

(a)

(b)

Figure 3.12. The White-robed, Child-giving Kuan-yin, probably eighteenth century: a. *Courtesy of the Hermitage Museum, St. Petersburg; b. Courtesy of the Taiwan Museum of History, Taipei.*

not entirely apocryphal. In fact, monks are often mentioned as revealers of one text or another in other collections of miracle stories connected with Kuan-yin, as in the case of *King Kao's Kuan-yin Sūtra*. Might it be the case that monks created indigenous scriptures and literati devotees promoted them? If this really was so, then the traditional dichotomy between these two groups, just like that between the elite and popular, would then have to be reexamined.

Although they were not translations from Sanskrit originals, indigenous scriptures were, at least the ones that I have been discussing, really not forgeries. They contained elements from identifiable Mahāyāna sūtras. This was discovered by Yüan Huang (1533–1606), the literatus who also promoted morality books. He probably did more than anyone else to popularize the chanting of the *White-robe Sūtra*. He did not have a son until he was forty. He started to chant this scripture and had a son in 1580. When he compiled a collection of texts to help people in obtaining heirs, entitled *Chi-ssu chen-ch'üan* (True Instructions on Praying for an Heir), he put this text at the very beginning. He also correctly identified the dhāraṇī as the same one contained in the *Kuan-tzu-tsai P'u-sa sui-hsin t'o-lo-ni ching* (Master Perceiver Bodhisattva's Dhāraṇī Sūtra Conforming to One's Wishes), which was translated by Chih-t'ung in the T'ang. The same dhāraṇī was relied upon by the famous Tripiṭaka Master Hsüan-tsang in crossing the perilous desert on his way to India in the seventh century. The dhāraṇī, according to Huang, was therefore a translation from Sanskrit and was contained in the Buddhist canon, even though the scripture as it now stood could not be found there.

Ch'ü Ju-chi (1548–1610) and his friend Yen Tao-ch'e, two scholars responsible for the compilation of an important Ch'an chronicle, the *Record of Pointing at the Moon* (Chih-yüeh lu), were also faithful chanters of this dhāraṇī. Ch'ü Ju-chi wrote a postscript to the sūtra that appeared at the end of the 1607 text. He described how he and a group of friends chanted it for the sake of securing sons, what religious experiences he had, and why he wanted to promote this sūtra. Although the text is rather long, it is translated here in its entirety, for it provides a rare glimpse of the private religious life of a highly educated literatus in late imperial times. It also offers important information about the networks of literati worshipers of Kuan-yin.

> I began to chant this dhāraṇī in the second month of 1580 together with my friends Li P'o-shu and Yen Tao-ch'e. Soon afterwards Li had a son and three years later Yen also had a son. I alone failed to experience a divine response. I often blamed myself for my deep karmic obstructions, for I could not match the two gentlemen in their piety. Then one evening in the third month of 1583 I dreamt that I entered a shrine and a monk said to me, "In

chanting the dhāraṇī, there is one buddha's name you have not chanted. If you chant it, you shall have a son." Upon waking up, I could not understand what he meant by the missing buddha's name, for I had always chanted the various names of Kuan-yin on the different festival days of her manifestation. In the winter of 1585 I traveled north and was stuck at a government post-house because the river was frozen. On the twelfth day of the twelfth month I entered a small temple and saw this sūtra by the side of the *hou* animal mount on which Kuan-yin sat. It had been donated by Wang Chi-shan, a judicial clerk. When I opened it to read and saw the name of Sovereign Master Buddha of Precious Moon and the Light and Sound of Wisdom Peak, a name of which I had never heard up until that time, I had a sudden realization. I knelt down and kowtowed to the seat. I started to chant the name of the buddha upon returning and after only three days, a son was born. It accorded perfectly with my dream.

In 1586 I went to the capital and Hsü Wen-ch'ing, Yü Tsung-pu, and other friends were all chanting the dhāraṇī in order to obtain sons. Yü's wife, furthermore, became pregnant after she had a strange dream. So we discussed plans to print this sūtra and promote its circulation. I had earlier consulted the catalogues of the Northern and Southern Tripiṭakas [two collections of Buddhist scriptures compiled in the Ming] but did not find it listed in either one. I thought this must be a true elixir of life secretly transmitted by foreign monks. Later Yüan Huang told me that this was actually the same dhāraṇī as the "Dhāraṇī Conforming to One's Heart's Desire," two versions of which were included in the Tripiṭaka. When I learned about this, I rushed to Lung-hua Monastery to check the Tripiṭaka kept in the library. Although there were some variations in the sequence of sentences and the exact wordings of the mantra between the text found in the Tripiṭaka and that of the popular printed version, the efficacy of chanting the dhāraṇī was universally guaranteed. I could not help but feel deeply moved by the wonder of Kuan-yin's universal responsiveness and the divinity of the faithful chanters' sincere minds. The text in the Tripiṭaka did not just promise sons, but the fulfillment of many other desires in accordance with the wishes of sentient beings. According to the instructions given in the sūtra contained in the Tripiṭaka, this dhāraṇī should be revealed only to those who are in possession of great compassion. If given to the wrong person, disastrous results will happen, for bad karma caused by hatred might be created if the person used the dhāraṇī to subdue enemies or avenge past wrongs. Taking this warning to heart, my friend Hsü and myself decided that instead of reprinting the version found in the Tripiṭaka, we would print the dhāraṇī alone together with the stories about obtaining sons included in the popular versions of this text, which were in circulation. After fasting and bathing, Hsü wrote out the sūtra and gave it to an engraver to make the woodblock plates for printing.

The term "dhāraṇī" means to keep all virtues completely. The extended meaning of the term then is thus the keeping of all virtues. For this reason, the merit of keeping the dhāraṇī is indeed limitless. With this, Kuan-yin teaches people to do good. Therefore if the practitioner does good, when he chants the words of the dhāraṇī, blessings as numerous as the sands of the Ganges will instantly come to him. But if he does not dedicate himself to goodness, he will lose touch with the basis of the dhāraṇī. Even if he chants it, the benefit will be slight. I cannot claim to have realized this ideal, but I am willing to work hard toward it together with fellow practitioners. The conventional view of the world says that ordinary people are totally different from sages and that an ordinary person cannot be transformed into a holy person. Because he narrows his potentiality in this way, he cannot keep the dhāraṇī. On the other hand, if a person falls into the other extreme of nihilism and thinks that in emptiness there is no law of causality, he also cannot keep the dhāraṇī because of his recklessness. When one realizes that the common man and the sage possess the same mind and there is not the slightest difference at all, one has departed from the conventional view. When one realizes that this One Mind can manifest as either ordinary or saintly and this is due to the clear working of the law of causality, one has then departed from the nihilistic view. Departing from these two erroneous views and following the One Mind in teaching the world, one can then chant the dhāraṇī. Like pumping on the bellows for wind or striking the flint for fire, the effect will be unfailingly efficacious.

As Ch'ü Ju-chi tells it, because he did not at first invoke the name of Pao-yüeh Chih-yen Kuang-yin Tzu-tsai-wang Tathāgata whose identity was unknown to him, he could not obtain a son sooner. Who is this buddha? As we saw earlier, he also appears in another indigenous scripture. He is not a fictitious buddha. On the contrary, he is one of the seven buddhas of healing mentioned in the *Sūtra of the Merit of the Original Vows Made by the Seven Medicine Buddhas of Lapis-Lazuli Light* (Yao-shih liu-li-kuang ch'i-fo pen-yüan kung-te ching). The reason he was singled out for veneration might be because the third vow made by this buddha in this sūtra was to protect pregnant women in child-birth.

Although indigenous scriptures used elements of Buddhist scriptural traditions, they must also find an expression conforming to Chinese cultural tastes and sensibilities in order to broaden their appeal, as in the case of Kuan-yin iconography. In the final analysis, the creation of indigenous scriptures, just like the creation of distinctively Chinese forms of Kuan-yin such as the Water-moon and White-robe, and a sacred landscape anchoring the major Buddhist deities on native soil such as the four great pilgrimage sites of China (discussed in chapters 6 and 9) were all necessary steps of transforming and domesticating Buddhism. In order to do so, emperors (and empresses) and commoners, monks and the literati, elite and ordinary folks all seem to have contributed their efforts.

Two Indigenous Scriptures Attributed to Ming Empresses

The authorship and dates of the indigenous scriptures just discussed are very difficult, if not impossible, to establish. It is not hard to understand why. Because creators of these scriptures would like them to pass as genuine ones, it is no wonder that they tried to cloak their origins in mystery. It is for this reason that the two indigenous scriptures attributed to the two Ming empresses who claimed to have received them in dreams are of considerable interest, for they can shed some light on the circumstances surrounding the creation of indigenous sūtras. The accounts providing the background information also underscore the close relationship between royal patronage and indigenous scriptures.

The first sūtra is entitled *Ta Ming Jen-hsiao Huang-hou meng-kan Fo shuo ti-i hsi-yu ta kung-te ching* (Sūtra of the Great Merit of Foremost Rarity Spoken by the Buddha Received by the Empress Jen-hsiao of the Great Ming in A Dream). The sūtra was introduced into the canon compiled in the Ming (HTC 1). Empress Jen-hsiao (1361–1407) was the wife of the Yung-lo emperor. Her family name was Hsü and she was reputed to be a patroness of literature, having been credited with the authorship of *Ku-chin lieh-nü chuan* (Biographies of Exemplary Women from Ancient Times to Today). She also sponsored the compilation of *Nei hsün* (Instructions for the Inner Quarters) and *Ch'üan-shan shu* (Exhortations). Mayumi Yoshida (1998) has convincingly demonstrated that the empress used the compilation of these didactic materials to legitimate the rule of her husband, the Yung-lo emperor. There was good reason for Yung-lo wanting to appear as an upholder of morality, for he deposed his nephew, the Emperor Hui who was the designated heir to the first Ming ruler, T'ai-tsu, and declared himself the emperor in 1403, only three years into Emperor Hui's reign. The empress referred to this political change and in fact credited her husband's success to the protection provided by this revealed sūtra.

In a long preface dated 1403, the year her husband became the emperor, she explained the origin of this sūtra. She related that one night in the first month of the thirty-first year of Hung-wu (1398), she was reading sūtras in her room after burning incense and meditating. Suddenly a purplish gold light filled the whole room and as if in a dream she saw Kuan-yin appear in the Tantric form of a thousand hands and a thousand eyes, known as Ta-pei, from within the light. She rose to greet the bodhisattva, who led her on a journey. Standing on a lotus of a thousand petals and holding a rosary of seven jewels in her hand, Kuan-yin walked ahead of her. They traveled through colored clouds, crossed the bridge named "Wisdom" and arrived at a holy realm marked by a gate on which there was a placard with the words "The First Bodhimaṇḍa of the Vulture's Peak" written on it in gold letters. After passing through the gate, she saw that the roads were paved with gold, lapis lazuli, coral, amber, and other precious jewels. There were exotic plants and rare birds who intoned Buddhist chants. Young maidens and youths paraded and made offerings to the Buddha and other holy beings. She was astonished by the wondrous scene and wondered what merit she had accumulated in her previous lives that enabled her to be blessed with this vision.

As if reading her thoughts, Kuan-yin smiled and told the empress that this was the place where Buddha preached the Dharma. No one in all the eons had ever had the opportunity to come here. But because the empress had achieved enlightenment in her former existence, she had been given the privilege to receive the *Sūtra of the Great Merit of Foremost Rarity*, because she would soon face a great disaster. This sūtra excelled all other sūtras and could save one from all calamities. If a person would recite it diligently and sincerely for one year, he or she would obtain the fruit of a stream-entrant, for two years, that of a once-returner, for three years, that of a nonreturner, for four years, that of an arhat, for five years, that of a bodhisattva, and for six years, that of a buddha. Kuan-yin then sprinkled her head with sweet dewy water, which cleared her mind completely. After this, Kuan-yin handed her a scripture that turned out to be none other than this very sūtra. After reading it once, she could understand its general meaning. The second time left her with total understanding, and after the third time she achieved perfect recall. Kuan-yin told her that they would meet ten years later. Just as the empress was going to say something else, she was awakened from the dream by the voices of the palace ladies. She immediately got hold of paper and brush and wrote down every word and every dhāraṇī of the sūtra as revealed to her. During the four years of trouble, which she referred to as the nonexistent years of Hung-wu 32–35 instead of Chien-wen 1–4 (1399–1402) of Emperor Hui, she recited the sūtra everyday and could feel no fear. Now that peace had descended once more on the realm, she did not want to keep the wonderful sūtra for her private benefit, but wanted to share it with everyone by having it printed and distributed widely.

The sūtra is in two fascicles. The first fascicle is the shorter of the two, running four printed pages. It talks about the nature of mind and nature, echoing the views of Mahāyāna sūtras such as *Śūraṅgama Sūtra* or *Sūtra of Perfect Enlightenment* (Yüan-chüeh ching), two popular scriptures favored by Ch'an monks and the literati in late imperial period. In answer to Śāriputra's questions about how one can know the true nature of mind and nature, and how can one understand emptiness, the Buddha told the assembly, "You should give rise to the mind of purity while dwelling nowhere. Because you obtain purity as a result of seeing reality as it is, that is why it is called 'of foremost rarity.' If you want to know the mind and nature of the Buddha, you should know that this mind and nature is not something that I have alone, but is possessed by all sentient beings. But the self-nature is fundamentally rooted in random thought; that is why the selfsame mind starts to discriminate. For this reason people become deluded about the eternally abiding true Mind and lose the pure nature of true emptiness" (HTC I:696).

The second fascicle is twice as long, and dhāraṇīs spoken by various bodhisattvas occupy six printed pages. Clearly, they are the central message of the sūtra. The reader is urged to chant the sūtra and dhāraṇīs. The chanting will protect the faithful from all worries and suffering. It will save the person from fire, water, robbers, poison, and wild animals. It will help dead ancestors of one's nine generations back to achieve deliverance. It will bring intelligent sons to him who has no heir. It will prevent a person from going to Avīci Hell. Finally, "If a good man or a good woman recites even one sentence, one gāthā, or one dhāraṇī of this sūtra, he or she will obtain blessings and virtues unmeasurable" (HTC I: 693). The sources for these ideas are easily found in *Ch'ing Kuan-yin ching*, *Ch'ien-shou ching*, *Karaṇḍavyūha Sūtra,* and other orthodox Mahāyāna scriptures.

Whether sūtras received in a dream should be considered authoritative was debated among early bibliographical cataloguers. We referred earlier to the different views held by Seng-yu and Fei Ch'ang-fang concerning the twenty-one scriptures Ni-tzu received in her dreams. But in the eyes of Empress Hsü as well as her contemporaries, this question obviously never arose, for otherwise her sūtra would not have been introduced into the canon. The sūtra possessed a unique feature, namely, it already existed in the buddha land. Kuan-yin handed it to her in the dream, but did not dictate the words to her as was the case with *King Kao's Sūtra*. This might have been influenced by the Treasure tradition of Tibetan Buddhism. Emperor Yung-lo was in fact a great patron of Tibetan Buddhism. He inherited this practice from the Yüan dynasty. His motivations for bestowing honors on lamas probably came both from religious faith and from political considerations. T'ai-tsu bestowed the title National

Preceptor (Kuo-shih) on four imperial preceptors of the Yüan dynasty. The Yung-lo emperor increased both the prestige as well as the real power of the Tibetan lamas. During his reign, there were five kings (Wang), four Dharma-kings (Fa-wang), two "sons of the Buddha of the Western Heaven" (Hsi-t'ien Fo-tzu), nine "Great National Teachers Consecrated by Sprinkling" (Kuan-ting Ta-kuo-shih), and eighteen "National Teachers Consecrated by Sprinkling" (Kuan-ting Kuo-shih) (*Ming shih*:331). The five kings were not just religious titles of honor, but they were given fiefs, and were in fact no different from secular rulers. Tibetan Buddhist influence at court must have been considerable and it would have been easy for Empress Hsü to have some idea about the Tibetan views on revealed scriptures.

The Treasure (*gTer ma*) tradition in Tibet has been represented primarily by the Nyingmapa lineage. It can be traced to the eleventh century and is intimately connected with Padmasaṁbhava, the "Precious Guru" who introduced Buddhism to Tibet in the eighth century. Treasure texts are discovered and encoded by certain individuals, identified as "treasure discoverers." They are believed to be chosen by Padmasaṁbhava, who hid the Treasure texts for future discovery many centuries ago. There are two principal types of revelatory treasures: "The 'Earth Treasure' (*sa-gter*) are actual objects, not only texts but also ritual artifacts, professed to have been retrieved from a physical place: the ground, the side of a mountain, or the inside of a statue or architectural structure, such as a column. The other kind of Treasure are the 'Mental Treasures' (*dgongs-gter*), which are said to have been hidden in the discoverer's memory; these are accessed in visionary experience" (Gyatso 1998:147). Although I suspect that the Tibetan Treasure tradition might have some influence on the creation of indigenous Chinese scriptures in the Ming period, the direction was not necessarily one way. Janet Gyatso, who has studied the Treasure tradition extensively, points out there are analogues in and possible actual influence from early Taoist legends about the Ling-pao scriptures in the Taoist tradition. Just as famed texts found by Treasure discoverers were written in ḍākinī script, celestial officials had texts written in a celestial script and hidden in a casket, later retrieved by a Taoist adept (Bokenkamp 1986). Indeed, as I indicated in chapter 1, not only the Ling-pao, but the Way of Celestial Masters as well as the Shang-ch'ing traditions all boasted of scriptural corpus dictated or revealed by gods and spirits for the benefit of the faithful. While it is difficult to locate the exact points of contact between Taoist revealed scriptures, Tibetan Treasure texts, and indigenous Chinese sūtras, it is important that we bear in mind that there must have been a close relationship among them.

The second indigenous scripture created in the Ming was revealed to Empress Dowager Li, the mother of Emperor Wan-li, also in a dream. The title of this sūtra is *Fo shuo Ta-tz'u-chih-sheng Chiu-lien P'u-sa hua-shen tu-shih tsun-ching* (Exalted Sūtra Spoken by the Buddha on the Incarnation of the Great Compassionate and Supreme Holy Nine-lotus Bodhisattva to Save the World). The extant version of the sūtra was printed by her son, the emperor, in 1616, two years after her death. According to the dedicatory plaque printed at the end of the text, he had one *tsang* or 5,084 copies made to honor her. Parallel to this, there was also an extant Taoist sūtra whose title also contained the curious sobriquet "Nine-lotus," printed in the same year by the emperor (Chou 1985: 310).[16] Both Empress Dowager Li and her son promoted a cult of the Nine-lotus Bodhisattva, and she was identified as an incarnation of the bodhisattva.

The Empress Dowager's dream was preceded by the sudden appearance of auspicious lotuses in bloom in her palace on the seventh day of the seventh month in 1586. Two days later, on the ninth day, other unusual lotuses bloomed in the palace. Emperor Wan-li was greatly pleased and instructed eunuchs to invite officials to view the flowers and write poems about them. The next year she received the scripture in a dream. In order to commemorate this event, Wan-li erected a stele with an image of "the Holy Nine-lotus Mother" inscribed on the front and "Poems on Auspicious Lotuses" on the back at Tz'u-shou Ssu located at Peking, the capital. The eulogy says that because of the queen mother's benevolence and compassion, Heaven has been moved to send down auspicious lotuses.

To commemorate this lucky event and preserve its memory for future generations, an image of the "Great Being" [Kuan-yin] is thereby inscribed on stone. By putting the image of his mother, who was called the "Holy Nine-lotus Mother," on the front and a eulogy dedicated to Kuan-yin on the back of the stele, the emperor cleverly indicated that his own mother was the Nine-lotus Bodhisattva who was in turn an incarnation of Kuan-yin. Two more stelae were erected later, one, in 1589, at Sheng-an Ssu and another, in 1594, at Tz'u-en Ssu. Rubbings from all three stelae have survived. In the 1587 stele, for instance, the bodhisattva was depicted exactly as the White-robed Kuan-yin who, sitting leisurely on a balcony, looks at the pond below from which nine large lotuses, two white and seven red, rise in bloom. Behind her, luxurious bamboos fill the background; a white parrot sits prominently on the branches. On her right, a vase containing willow branches sits on a lotus pedestal. In the lower left corner, the boy pilgrim Sudhana (the 1592 stele alone also shows both Sudhana and the Dragon Princess, who stands in the lower right corner) worships her with folded hands (figure 3.13). The stele's adoption of this iconography was clearly not by accident, for this was how Kuan-yin was most familiarly depicted in the sixteenth century. Through this device, the promoters of the cult of the Nine-lotus Bodhisattva wanted to make sure that people would have no trouble realizing that the queen mother was a bodhisattva who was in turn the feminine White-robed Kuan-yin. It has been reported that there was once a scroll enshrined at Ch'ang-ch'un Ssu, built in 1618, on which a tablet with the name of the Nine-lotus Bodhisattva was paired with a tablet with the title of Empress Dowager Li, implying that the two were the same (Li and Naquin 1988:161). Not only was the bodhisattva enshrined at temples in the capital, her traces were also found on Mt. T'ai. The 1802 edition of the *T'ai-shan chih* (Gazetteer of Mt. T'ai), quoting passages from Ku Yen-wu's essay, said, "The front hall in the Palace of Pi-hsia Yüan-chün enshrines her. Empress Dowager Wan-shou chung-tsun hsiao-ting [Li] was the Nine-lotus Bodhisattva. She was worshiped in a hall behind that of Yüan-chün" (10:28b).

The sūtra begins with a dialogue between the Buddha and Kuan-yin who, grieved by the sufferings of mankind brought about by their own ignorance and evil deeds, asks the Buddha for succor. Buddha, in reply, makes a prediction about the appearance of the Nine-lotus Bodhisattva, who will bring peace and happiness to the world. Using identical language to that traditionally applied to the Western Paradise, Buddha describes the kingdom ruled by this bodhisattva. The sūtra ends by urging people to chant the sūtra diligently, and especially the dhāraṇī revealed therein. Without spelling it out in detail, the scripture nevertheless implies a close relationship between Kuan-yin and Nine-lotus Bodhisattva who, in turn, is made to point to Empress Dowager Li. The bodhisattva is described as intimately connected with lotus flowers in nine ways: they issue forth from her heart, they are realized by her nature, seen by her eyes, heard by her ears, smelled by her nose, spat out by her mouth, grown from the top of her head, sat on by her body, and stepped upon by her feet (thus the "nine lotuses").

As for the source of the term "Nine-lotus," there is no exact equivalent in Buddhist scriptures. Because there is much Pure Land coloration in the text, however, it could be derived from the "nine grades of rebirth" (*chiu-p'in wang-sheng*). Expressions such as "nine grades of lotus flowers" (*chiu-p'in lien-hua*) and "nine grades of lotus platforms" (*chiu-p'in lien-t'ai*) are often used in Buddhist literature.

As discussed in chapter 11, during the late Ming, sectarian *pao-chüan* or "precious scrolls" very frequently used the term "nine-lotus." It appears on the title of an early text known as *Huang-chi chin-tan chiu-lien ch'eng-hsin kuei-chen huan-hsiang pao-chüan* (Precious Scroll of the Imperial Ultimate Golden Cinnabar Nine Lotuses of Correct Faith which Lead Us Back to Our Original Home by Taking Refuge in the Truth). We do not know when it was first written, but 1523 was the date when it was first printed.[17] Like many other White Lotus sectarian texts, it worships the Venerable Mother (Wu-sheng Lao-mu)

Figure 3.13. Stele of the "Nine-Lotus Bodhisattva," dated 1587. *Courtesy of Chou Shao-liang (Zhou Shaoliang).*

as the supreme deity. Human history is divided into three kalpas, each under one buddha: the Lamp-lighting Buddha, Śākyamuni Buddha, and Maitreya Buddha. Nine-lotus symbolizes the highest realm where the saved ones will attend the Dragon Flower Assembly (Lung-hua Hui) and become reunited with the Mother who is the creator. "Nine-lotus" and similar ideologies are also found in the *Yao-shih pen-yüan pao-chüan* (Precious Scroll of the Original Vow of Medicine Buddha) of 1543 and the *Hsiao-shih chieh-hsü lien-tsung pao-chüan* (Precious Scroll on a Brief Commentary Concerning the Reception and Continuity of the Lotus School) of 1659 (Li and Naquin 1988:151, 161). In the sectarian tradition of White Lotus scriptures, there was in fact a general term, "Nine-lotus sūtra," for there was more than one text bearing this name (Ma and Han 1992:612). So this was obviously a favorite term among the sectarians. Empress Dowager Li was a patroness of the Pao-Ming Ssu, which, under the charismatic leadership of the nun Kuei-yüan, was a headquarters for White Lotus followers (discussed in chapter 11). She could very well have come across this term through her association with the nun. The precedence of Empress Hsü's scripture with its emphasis on dhāraṇīs was a second obvious source.

I started this chapter with questions about the relationships between indigenous sūtras and genuine sūtras and the roles that indigenous sūtras played in the acceptance of Buddhism or the faith in Kuan-yin in China. We have examined the cases of several such scriptures. Some are well known, while others are very obscure. It is now time to make some general remarks in conclusion.

First, although indigenous sūtras were written in China, they nevertheless were based on orthodox Buddhist sūtras. In religious thought and method of practice, there is congruence between the two. While *Lotus*, Pure Land, and Tantric traditions provided the main ideological underpinnings, invocation of the name and chanting of dhāraṇīs were taken as infallible routes to a fruitful spiritual life. *King Kao's Sūtra* was firmly based on the *Lotus Sūtra* and the dhāraṇī sūtras, mainly the *Chi'en-shou ching*, from which specific dhāraṇīs have been lifted. Creation did not thus mean fabrication. The authors of indigenous sūtras usually engaged in some innovative "repackaging." This may be called their conservative nature.

Second, although indigenous sūtras were conservative, they could at the same time show creativity and independence. *King Kao's Sūtra*, for instance, was much more succinct than the "Universal Gateway" chapter of the *Lotus*. Other indigenous sūtras attempted to make religious practice more accessible and palatable. In so doing, they sometimes adopted a critical stance toward orthodoxy and posed a challenge to it.

Third, by insisting on linking the origins of indigenous sūtras to the miraculous experiences of real persons in history, they deliberately particularized, localized, and individualized the universal truths of Buddhism and thereby grounded them on Chinese soil. Truths then were no longer preached by the Buddha in the remote past in far-away India, but are revealed by Kuan-yin in the ever present here and now. Certainly, in the establishment and development of the cult of Kuan-yin in China, indigenous scriptures played an important role. Like miracle tale collections, pilgrimages, and iconography, indigenous scriptures also served as an indispensable medium in transforming this originally universal bodhisattva into the most beloved Chinese Buddhist deity.

4

Miracle Tales and the Domestication of Kuan-yin

Anyone who visits a temple in Taiwan, Hong Kong, or even Mainland China can find posters, pamphlets, brochures and books on the side tables or stacked on bookshelves along the walls of the main hall. They are printed by lay devotees and are placed there for visitors to browse through or take home for later reading. Among the pious literature distributed for free in this fashion, there are many canonical or indigenous scriptures, the latter being represented by *King Kao's Kuan-yin Sūtra*. Among canonical works, the *Diamond Sūtra*, the *Heart Sūtra*, and the *O-mi-t'o ching* (Shorter Sukhāvatīvyūha Sūtra) are very popular, but the "Universal Gateway" chapter of the *Lotus Sūtra* is by far the favorite. Among the many books distributed are also stories about Kuan-yin's miraculous responses. This is one of the best ways for a true believer to spread the Dharma and to create merit for him or herself at the same time.

The compilation of such stories about Kuan-yin's salvific deeds is not, of course, a modern phenomenon, but contemporary stories, like their ancient counterparts, are characterized by their specificity. When we examine the modern stories, they attract our attention by their ability to address our current concerns. The persons experiencing the events and the place and time of the events are usually carefully noted, just as in the past. Today Kuan-yin saves devotees from cancer and car accident rather than imprisonment and shipwreck. As times change, people begin to have new problems and new fears instead of their old ones. Kuan-yin is nevertheless still always ready and capable of rendering help.

In thus updating and upgrading the bodhisattva's competence, the stories contribute to the continuing faith of people in this savior. I argue that this has been the role played by the miracle stories all along. It is through such stories that the Chinese people form a personal connection with Kuan-yin. The stories concretize the knowledge about Kuan-yin provided by the scriptures and make the sculpted and painted images of Kuan-yin come to life. Miracle tales teach people about Kuan-yin and validate what the scriptures claim the bodhisattva can do. They also bear a close relationship to the cult of icons. Experiences of miracles often lead to the creation of icons or, conversely, the worship of Kuan-yin images facilitates the experiences. Finally, how a person experiencing such a miracle sees Kuan-yin in a vision can often be predetermined by the existing iconography of the bodhisattva or, in another direction, lead to the creation of new forms of the bodhisattva. There is a circularity among Kuan-yin, the devotee, and the icon.

When I interviewed pilgrims on P'u-t'o Island in March 1987, I asked if they knew of any stories about Kuan-yin's response either to their own prayer or somebody else's. Invariably the reply was affirmative. For example, a young woman of twenty-four came with her mother, a retired nurse of forty-nine, from Shanghai to fulfill a vow (*huan-yüan*). Two years earlier, the mother had developed cancer of the intestines. When she was operated on, the cancer was very advanced and had spread. So the doctor sewed her up and predicted that she would die soon. The mother prayed to Kuan-yin for a whole year and vowed that if she should survive, she would come to P'u-t'o to give thanks. Two years had passed and she was well, so the mother and daughter traveled to the island.

Another pilgrim I interviewed was a fifty-year-old fisherman from Ningpo, who had come to P'u-t'o six times. He told me that originally he did not believe in Buddhism. But in 1977, his left little finger was bitten by a snake and the whole arm became paralyzed. He went to Shanghai and Beijing for a cure but had no success after spending 4,000 *yüan* (the exchange rate was $1 to 3 *yüan*). His mother then accompanied him to pray to Kuan-yin at the Buddha's Peak (a nickname for Hui-chi Monastery, situated on the highest point of the island). One month later he had a dream in which he received a shot. It was so piercingly painful that he jumped up in his sleep and woke his wife. Soon after he could move his left arm. Believing that Kuan-yin had saved him, he came in 1979, the first year P'u-t'o was reopened to the public after the Cultural Revolution. He went up to the Buddha's Peak following the Pilgrim's Path (an uphill path leading from Fa-yü Monastery to Hui-chi Monastery), bowing every three steps to show his thankfulness.

He also told me about a miracle that happened to eight fishermen whom he met. Their boat went out with three other boats three years before I met him. There was a big storm and the other boats capsized, drowning more than forty people. They followed a light that appeared in front of them, and reached P'u-t'o safely. When they embarked, the light also disappeared. They started coming every year on the nineteenth day of the sixth month (one of the three holy days of Kuan-yin, the day Kuan-yin achieved enlightenment), making one full prostration after walking every three steps along the Pilgrim's Path.

Miracle Tales and the Theory of *Kan-ying*

I have called these stories "miracle tales," for they share a common feature with miracles as understood in the Western religious traditions. According to the *Encyclopaedia Britannica*, a miracle is "an extraordinary and astonishing happening that is attributed to the presence and action of an ultimate or divine power" (*Micropaedia* VI:927c). What happened to the individuals whose stories I have retold would undoubtedly have been viewed by them as nothing but extraordinary and astonishing. They would also attribute them to the divine power of Kuan-yin. The Chinese word for such stories, however, is *ling-kan*, "efficacious response," or *ling-ying*, "efficacious response," or *ying-yen*, "evidential manifestation." All these expressions are derived from a world view that believes that everything is interrelated and interdependent. This belief is called *kan-ying*, which literally means "stimulus and response," or "sympathetic resonance." John Henderson, referring to it as "cosmic resonance," says, "According to this theory, things of the same category but in different cosmic realms were supposed to affect one another by virtue of a mutual sympathy, to resonate like properly attuned pitch-pipes" (1984:20). The relationship between the devotees and Kuan-yin is built on the theory of *kan-ying*: their prayer and calling of Kuan-yin's name aloud is the initiating stimulus or trigger that, when it is sincere and desperate enough, is answered by Kuan-yin's response. Kuan-yin does not act gratuitously. Human suppliants are linked to Kuan-yin through sincerity (*cheng*), for it is through sincerity that the mechanism of stimulus and response is set into motion. Although Avalokiteśvara was already known in India as the savior from perils, and Buddhist scriptures proclaim this as a central message, the Chinese compilers of miracle tales nevertheless understood the miraculous workings through this indigenous epistemological lens, just as the persons who experienced the events did.

In order for us to understand why the Chinese see Kuan-yin in this way, it may be helpful to discuss briefly the Chinese views of the universe prior to the introduction of Buddhism into China. The world in which human beings live is called, in Chinese, "Heaven and Earth" (*t'ien-ti*). Unlike most other religions, Chinese religion does not have a creator god. On the contrary, as seen in the

Book of Changes (*I-ching*), one of the basic Confucian classics and a divinatory handbook of great antiquity, Heaven and Earth is the origin of everything in the universe, including human beings. This creating and sustaining force, otherwise known as Tao or the Way, is seen as good, and the highest goal of human life is to live in conformity to it. There is no God transcendent and separate from the world and there is no heaven outside of the universe to which human beings would want to go for refuge. The *Book of Changes* contains sixty-four hexagrams that are made up of eight trigrams. The first and second trigrams, known as *ch'ien* and *k'un*, represent the two prime principles of yang and yin, which constitute the Tao, as well as Heaven and Earth, which are the physical representations of these principles.

Although these ideas are datable to the Chou (1111–249 B.C.E.), they received further refinement during the Han dynasty (206 B.C.E–220 C.E.), particularly from Tung Chung-shu (c. 179–c. 104 B.C.E.) and his contemporaries. According to them, all living and nonliving things in the universe are constituted out of *ch'i*, which has been translated as vital force, material force, or life force. *Ch'i* refers to yin and yang and the five phases of wood, fire, earth, metal, and water, which evolve from the interaction of the two. This is the worldview shared by all Chinese religions. Such a worldview has been described as "organic, vitalistic, and holistic" and the universe is seen as "a dynamic, ongoing process of continual transformation" (Tu 1989:72). Because humans share the same substance with the universe, there is the possibility for communication between us and our environment. This belief is implied by the concepts of Mandate of Heaven (*t'ien-ming*) and stimulus and response (*kan-ying*).

The Mandate of Heaven was originally used by the Chou founders to justify their rebellion against the previous Shang dynasty. According to them, the last two Shang rulers lost their mandate because they were deficient in virtue. The mandate went to the Chou founders because they were virtuous. Heaven not only gave and took away its mandate, it also sent blessings or warnings before it did so. Thus the Chinese believed in omens and portents, taking them to mean Heaven's responses to the behavior of mankind. Tung Chung-shu, the architect of Han Confucianism, was a firm believer of such ideas. He said, "When a great ruler is about to arise, auspicious omens first appear; when a ruler is about to be destroyed, there are baleful ones beforehand. Things indeed summon each other, like to like, a dragon bringing rain, a fan driving away heat, the place where an army has been being thick with thorns. Things, whether lovely or repulsive, all have an origin" (Needham 1956:282). The Han Chinese interest in observing natural phenomena was related to the ruler's intense obsession with omens. Systematic notation of spots on the sun began in 28 B.C.E. and the first seismograph in the world was invented in 132 C.E. in order to pinpoint earthquakes, which were regarded as signs of disorder in nature. Tung Chung-shu's views influenced greatly the Confucians of the New Text School and writers of the Confucian apocrypha who made *kan-ying* an article of faith during the first and second centuries of the Common Era.

Writing on the relationship between Chinese Buddhism and the cosmology of sympathetic resonance, Robert Sharf observes, "From the time of the Han, dynastic histories typically included a chapter entitled 'five phases' which recorded occurrences of 'unusual phenomena' or 'wonders' (*kuai*) including earthquakes, avalanches, feather-rain, and the birth of two-headed chickens. The principle of *kan-ying* was invoked to explain moral retribution, ritual efficacy, natural and astronomical cycles, political upheavals, and so on. It should not, therefore, be surprising to discover that *kan-ying* also influenced the Chinese understanding of Buddhist cosmology and practice" (1991:187). Indeed, during the Six Dynasties (220–589) when the earliest miracle stories about Kuan-yin were compiled, the dynastic histories contain treatises with names such as the "Treatise on Numinous Proofs" ("Ling-cheng chih" in the *Wei shu*), the "Treatise on Auspicious Tallies" ("Fu-jui chih" in the *Sung shu*), and the "Treatise on Auspicious Omens" ("Hsiang-jui chih" in the *Nan Ch'i shu*). For the writers of these treatises as well as the Confucian apocryphal texts in which the miraculous also abound, *kan-ying* was a fact of life that was validated by such unusual happenings in the world. I would argue that the fascination with the strange and anomalous that led to the production of the genre called *chih-kuai*, or what Robert Campany calls "strange writings," literature during the Six Dynasties was related to this. The compilation of miracle tales, which can be regarded as a subgenre of this literature and frequently shares data with it, is the application of the native *kan-ying* theory to Buddhist soteriology.

The philosophical explanation for the mutual influence between nature and humans was explained by Tung Chung-shu thus, "Heaven possesses yin and yang and man also possesses yin and yang. When the universe's material force of yin arises, man's material force of yin arises in response. Conversely, when man's material force of yang arises, that of the universe also arises in response" (Chan 1963:283–4). This provides the foundation for the Chinese belief in the correspondence between microcosm and macrocosm: a person is a small universe replicating the greater universe without.

The Confucian tradition identified the Mandate of Heaven with the innate goodness of human nature which was first emphasized by Mencius (c. 372–289 B.C.E.). Human nature is good because it is bestowed by the Way, and according to the *Book of Changes*, "What issues from the Way is good and that which realizes it is the individual nature" (Chan 1963:266). To follow our inborn moral nature and cultivate it to its fullest potential should be the goal of humankind.

In the Confucian tradition, the spiritual force fueling this self-transformation and self-realization is called "sincerity" (*ch'eng*) or "humanity" (*jen*). Sincerity is the main theme in the *Doctrine of the Mean* (*Chung-yung*), a chapter in the Confucian classic the *Book of Rites* (*Li-chi*). When a person fully develops his or her nature through sincerity, he or she forms a trinity with Heaven and Earth. It is safe to say that this was the ultimate goal for Chinese who were educated in the literati tradition. But even for those who were not necessarily so educated, such as women and commoners, who also featured in the miracle stories, the belief in the cosmic power of sincerity was universal. The only difference is that this same spiritual force was directed toward making a contact with Kuan-yin, instead of one's own sagehood.

The belief in sympathetic resonance formed the ideological base of the accounts of filial sons (*Hsiao-tzu chuan*), a subject studied by Keith Knapp. According to him, these accounts started to be written during the Later Han, around the second century, and became very popular during the Six Dynasties (Knapp 1996:100). Many of these accounts contain miraculous responses from Heaven called forth by the filial sons' sincerity, which was expressed through their perfect filial piety. Some of these stories were illustrated in tombs and offering shrines. For instance, of the fifteen piety stories illustrated on the walls of Wu Liang Shrine, which was completed in 151 C.E., six are miracle stories (Knapp 1996:150). Some of the Confucian miracle stories about filial sons could have served as models for the Buddhist miracle stories discussed later.

Buddhist biographers and theologians shared the same fascination with the idea of sympathetic resonance. Miracle stories were collected by both monks and lay people. Popular miracle tale collections served as sources for monastic biographies. Hui-chiao (497–554) wrote the *Biographies of Eminent Monks* (Kao-seng chuan), the earliest surviving work of the genre, and devoted one section to wonder-working monks. He was familiar with contemporary miracle tale collections and drew material from them. He mentioned *Hsüan-yen chi* (Records in Proclamation of Manifestations) and *Ming-hsiang chi* (Signs from the Unseen Realm) by title and used twenty stories from them in his work. He also stated that he had used the *Yu-ming lu* (Records of the Hidden and Visible Worlds) by Liu I-ch'ing (403–444), who was also the author of the *Hsüan-yen chi,* which is also known as the *Ming-yen chi* (Records of Manifesting the Unseen Realm), the *Kan-ying chuan* (Records of Responses to Stimuli) by Wang Yen-hsiu (fl. 465–471), the *Cheng-ying chuan* (Accounts of Verified Responses) by Chu Chün-t'ai (fifth century), and the *Sou-shen lu* (Records of Searching for Spirits) by T'ao Yüan-ming (365–424) (T 50:418b-c). Tao-hsüan (596–667), the Vinaya master and the author of the *Continued Biographies of Eminent Monks* (Hsü kao-seng chuan), was a great believer and promoter of miracles. He wrote the *Records of Spiritual Resonance Associated with the Three Treasures in China* (Chi shen-chou san-pao kan-t'ung lu) in which he compiled miracles wrought by relics, stūpas, images, sūtras, and divine monks. He was also the author of the *Records of Spiritual Resonance of the Vinaya Master Tao-hsüan* (Tao-hsüan lü-shih kan-t'ung lu) in which he recorded a series of interviews he conducted with spirits. He used the term *kan-t'ung* in these two works and in the biographies to refer to the supernatural events. Tsan-ning (919–1001), the compiler of the massive *Biographies of Eminent Monks Compiled in the Sung* (Sung kao-seng chuan), followed his usage and used this term to title the section on monks who experienced miraculous responses with this term. As pointed out by John Kieschnick, the expression *kan-t'ung* comes from the "Great Treatise" of the *Book of Changes*: "When stimulated, it penetrates." Tao-hsüan and Tsan-ning saw no conflict between the indigenous idea of spiritual or sympathetic resonance and the Buddhist idea of karma. Rather, they were seen as complementary to each other (Kieschnick 1997:101).

As the cult of Kuan-yin spread in China, there was growing scholastic debate concerning the workings of *kan-ying* (Fukushima 1979:36–49). Since in real life there were plenty of cases in which people were not always successful in eliciting Kuan-yin's response, theological explanations then became necessary. According to Chi-tsang (549–623), the bodhisattva both affects and responds. The T'ien-t'ai school uses the image of water and moon to describe the "wonder of affect and response," one of the thirty wonders concerning the invocation of Buddhas. The relationship between the sentient beings and the Buddha is compared to that between water and moon in the *Miao-fa lien-hua ching hsüan-i* (Mysterious Meanings of the Lotus Sūtra): "Water does not rise, nor does the moon descend. Yet in a single instant, the one moon is manifested in manifold [bodies] of water. [Similarly] Buddhas do not come and sentient beings do not go. The power of the good roots of compassion should be perceived in this way" (T 33:697c). Robert Sharf summarizes the discussion thus, "The power of beings to affect a response in the Buddha is identified with the power of the impetus or *chi*, the source of which lies in the karmic accumulation of good deeds. In later exegetical work in China and Japan, the image of the moon on the water becomes the standard illustration of the workings of *kan-ying*" (1991:223).[1]

According to Mahāyāna Buddhism, all sentient beings are endowed with buddha nature. There is no essential difference separating buddhas and bodhisattvas from ordinary people, the only distinction being that buddhas and bodhisattvas are those who are enlightened whereas ordinary people have not achieved the same realization about the nature of reality. In this regard, there is congruence between Buddhist ontology and the indigenous Chinese one. Just as humankind can form a trinity with Heaven and Earth, they can also become buddhas through the experience of enlightenment. Sincerity and good karma are hereby equally emphasized and skillfully harmonized.

Miracle Tales about Kuan-yin

In 1970 Makita Tairyō published an edited and annotated edition of the three earliest Chinese collections of miracle tales about Kuan-yin (which I shall refer to as the first, second, and third collection for short). He used a Japanese hand-copied manuscript made during the Kamakura (1185–1333) period and kept in a Tendai temple, the Seirenji in Kyoto, as the basis of the edition. They are:

1. *Kuang-shih-yin ying-yen chi* (A Record of Kuang-shih-yin's Responsive Manifestations), written from memory by Fu Liang (374–426), based on an earlier work with the same title and written by Hsieh Fu before 399 but lost in that year due to war. It has seven stories.
2. *Hsü Kuang-shih-yin ying-yen chi* (Continued Records of Kuang-shih-yin's Responsive Manifestations), written by Chang Yen in mid-fifth century. It has ten stories.
3. *Hsi Kuan-shih-yin ying-yen chi* (More Records of Kuan-shih-yin's Responsive Manifestations), compiled by Lu Kao in 501. It has sixty-nine stories.

Although these collections were once well known and famous Buddhist monks referred to them by name, they did not survive as independent works in China.[2]

Individual stories were adopted and incorporated into biographies of eminent monks and encyclopedic collections such as the seventh century Buddhist work *Fa-yüan chu-lin* or the tenth century *T'ai-p'ing kuang-chi*. The discovery of this Japanese copy of these lost works and Makita's careful study of them provide us with valuable information about the earliest evidence for the cult of Kuan-yin in China. Donald Gjertson is the first Western scholar to emphasize the value of Buddhist miracle tales, including the ones contained in these collections, because they "were concerned not with intricacies of doctrine or subtleties of speculation, but with the mechanics of popular faith" (1989:xii). Robert Campany has translated a number of stories from the collections and made sophisticated theoretical analyses of them (1991, 1993, 1996a, 1996b). I agree with his suggestion that the initial success of the bodhisattva among the

Chinese faithful was his "newness". Not only was it the first time in Chinese religion that a deity manifested himself as a "strikingly immediate, concretely salvific, unfailingly responsive presence," but also because he was exotic and unfamiliar. The miracle tales that were compiled from eyewitness oral accounts reported by the faithful would in turn inspire and instill faith in the bodhisattva among potential readers and listeners. It is through the circular spiral consisting of confirmed devotees, miracle tales and future converts that Kuan-yin was domesticated (1993:256–68).

Before I begin to discuss the stories, let me first say something about the sources I use. Because of their unique value arising from their being the oldest accounts, I use these three earliest collections as my main sources in discussing miracle tales about Kuan-yin. Other relevant materials include some seventy stories from the three biographies of eminent monks and other monastic chronicles. Although these sources are dated and cover tales that happened before the tenth century, three other miracle tale collections were compiled much later. The first is the *Kuan-shih-yin ching-chou chih-yen chi* (Record of Manifestations [Resulting] from Recitation of Kuan-shih-yin Sūtras and Mantras) compiled by the layman Chou K'e-fu in 1659. The second is the *Kuan-yin tz'u-lin chi* (Compassionate Grove of Kuan-yin) compiled by the monk Hung-tsan in 1668, and finally the *Kuan-shih-yin ling-kan lu* (Record of Kuan-shih-yin Bodhisattva's Efficacious Responses) published in 1929 by an anonymous author. Although all three contain stories that happened a long time ago, and some are actually taken from earlier collections, more stories in the later collections happened after the tenth century, particularly in the Ming and Ch'ing period. It is curious that no collections compiled prior to the seventeenth century have survived as independent works. Chou K'e-fu, Hung-tsan, and the anonymous compiler often mentioned the titles of some miracle tale collections as their sources, but these are no longer extant. As we reach the twentieth century, compilation and publication of miracle stories became very popular, particularly in the 1910s and 1920s. During my research in various locations in China and Taiwan, I came across half a dozen such compilations that were published either in Peking or Shanghai with donations by the faithful. I chose the last one mentioned mainly because it is most extensive in its coverage. In the following discussion, when I refer to early collections, I mean the tales edited by Makita Tairyō, and when I refer to later collections, I mean the collections compiled by Chou K'e-fu, Hung-tsan, and the one published in 1929 in Shanghai.

I discuss how the miracle tale collections served as a medium for the domestication of Kuan-yin in this chapter by focusing on several questions. First of all, who were the compilers? Do choices differ when made by monks and lay persons? What role did the literati play in promoting belief in Kuan-yin? Second, to whom does Kuan-yin appear and how does the bodhisattva appear: in dreams or in broad daylight? as a male or a female? monk or lay person? From what dangers does Kuan-yin rescue the believer and what benefits does the bodhisattva bestow? Third, what is the connection between icons, visions, and the changing iconography of Kuan-yin? Fourth, how are the collections organized? Are the individual stories simply listed one after another without any clear organizational principle? Are they categorized to fit a scriptural paradigm, thereby serving to provide evidential proof for the truth of the sūtras? And finally, compared to the early collections, do the later collections show marked departures reflecting historical changes effected both by new developments within the cult and the new anxieties and hopes of believers? Although it may not always be possible to answer all the questions fully, I would like to have the reader keep them in mind as we wade through this rich and fascinating material.

Three Earliest Collections

Let us begin with the three earliest collections of miracle stories about Kuan-yin. All three compilers came from the gentry-literati class. Because they wrote prefaces for the collections and their biographies are found in standard dynastic histories, it is fairly easy to place them socially and spiritually. Fu Liang (374–426), the compiler of the first collection, served as an official under both the Eastern Chin and Sung dynasties, reaching the position of president of the Department of the Affairs of State under the Sung. He came from an influential gentry family and was well known as a scholar of classics (*Sung shu* 43; *Nan-shih* 15). He related in the preface that his father Fu Yüan was given a copy of an earlier collection containing more than ten tales compiled by Hsieh Fu. In 399 he escaped from K'uai-chi (present-day Shao-hsing, Chekiang) when Sun En attacked the city. When he returned, he could no longer find the volume. He then wrote down seven stories from memory. Hsieh Fu, the original writer of the lost collection, was a recluse, living in the mountains for more than ten years. He was once offered an official position but refused to accept it (*Chin shu* 94). He, Fu Yüan and Hsi Ch'ao (336–377), the author of *Feng-fa-yao* (Essentials of the Dharma), were Buddhist devotees and close personal friends. Thus, Fu Liang, the compiler of the earliest surviving miracle tale collection, was introduced to Buddhism by his father.

Chang Yen, the compiler of the second collection, served as the grand secretary in the Secretariat of the Heir Apparent under the Sung. He came from an aristocratic background, descending from Chang Liang of the Han, and is mentioned in the biography of his father Chang Mao-tu (*Sung shu* 53). He also came from a Buddhist family. He was friendly with Pei-tu, a monk famous for his magical powers active in the capital of Chien-kang (present-day Nanking). His nephew Chang Jung (444–497) wrote a work on the Vinaya that was included in the Buddhist polemical and apologetic work, *Hung-ming chi* (Collection in Propagating and Illuminating Buddhism). In the preface to his collection, he mentioned that when he read Fu Liang's accounts, he was greatly moved. Inspired, he gathered together what he had heard and wrote the stories down in order to pass them on to those who share the same delight in such tales.

Lu Kao (459–532), the author of the third collection, was related to Chang Yen, who was the first cousin of his maternal grandfather. Like Chang, he also came from an influential gentry family and had believed in Buddhism since his youth. He served as an adjunct in the service of the director of instruction under the Southern Ch'i as well as an official in the Liang (*Liang shu* 26; *Nan-shih* 48). In the dated preface (501) to his collection, he mentions the first two collections by their authors and titles and provides a genealogy of this literature by tracing it to Hsieh. He refers to his effort as a "continuation," thus its title.

Clearly these three collections were produced by authors belonging to a distinctive social stratum. The authors were educated Buddhist laymen from distinguished gentry families. They all lived in the Wu area, in present-day Kiangsu and Chekiang. They moved in the same circles and were familiar with each other's work. The most striking feature shared by these stories is the name used for the bodhisattva: Kuang-shih-yin. This is the name used in all the seventeen stories contained in the first and second collections. Four stories out of sixty-nine in the third collection also use this name, while the rest use the more familiar name of Kuan-shih-yin. When we recall that the earliest translation of the *Lotus Sūtra* made by Dharmarakṣa in 286 refers to the bodhisattva by this name in the "Universal Gateway" chapter, the reason for their choice makes sense. Being educated Buddhist laymen, they undoubtedly were familiar with the translation and thus followed its usage. By the time the third collection was compiled, however, Kūmarajīva's translation was already available and the bodhisattva was called Kuang-shih-yin in this new translation. The miracle stories can thus tell us about the changing popularity of the two versions of the sūtra. They also give us an amazing proof of how quickly the "good news" about the bodhisattva's grace proclaimed by the *Lotus* found willing ears and believing hearts in China. The first such story, recounted in the first collection and translated later in this chapter, was dated to the Yüan-k'ang era (291–299). Less than fifteen years after the sūtra was translated into Chinese in Ch'ang-an, the bodhisattva's presence was already known in Loyang. In this particular case the protagonist was said to have an ancestry that hailed from the Western Regions, which probably refers to India, based on his surname of Chu. Although he might have known the bodhisattva prior to his move to Loyang, however, it did not necessarily mean that he became a convert to Kuan-yin outside of China. In fact, when we consider the early date of these stories (mostly the fifth century), it is quite surprising that only six out of the eighty-six stories in these three collections are about non-Chinese.

Some information about the protagonists of these eighty-six stories might be useful. Twenty-eight stories are about monks and fifty-eight are about ordinary people. Among the former, although a few, such as Chu Fa-i and Chu Fa-ch'un, were quite famous clerics, the majority were common monks whose names were not found in any monastic biographies. As for the latter, we find officials, generals, bureaucrats, and literati, but more often the hero of the story was an ordinary person, including petty officers, soldiers, peddlers, fishermen, hunters, prisoners, criminals, robbers, and starving vagrants. Women, particularly old women and widows, also made their appearances. Clearly, neither monks nor elite laymen dominated these stories. Although it may be true that foreign monks first introduced the belief in Kuan-yin to the Chinese, the cult certainly was not confined within the monastic circle but penetrated into all social strata.

The geographical spread of the cult revealed by the stories is also illuminating. Although three stories took place in a foreign country, three in an unidentified place and thirty took place in the south, fifty stories took place in the north, which was under alien rulers. Faith in Kuan-yin clearly had a strong appeal to people living in the north. This was probably because the north experienced more wars and social upheavals and life was more precarious. And because Buddhism in the north was more devotional and oriented to practice, in contrast to gentry Buddhism in the south, which emphasized philosophy, the simple piety advocated by the *Lotus Sūtra* might have had a stronger appeal there. We recall that *King Kao's Kuan-yin Sūtra* originated in the north as well. Surviving images of Kuan-yin excavated in the north also testify to the central importance of the deity. Most of the images of Kuan-yin created during the Northern Wei to the Northern Ch'i, in the fifth and sixth centuries, were independent icons. Some devotees even regarded Kuan-yin as another Buddha. For instance, an image found in Lung-men carried an inscription dated the fourth year of Cheng-kuang (523) of the Northern Wei. The devotee who had it made called the deity "Kuan-yin Buddha" in the dedication (Sun 1996:211–14).

The first and second collections share a commonality, which sets them apart from the third collection. The stories do not follow any organizational principles. They are not grouped together either geographically or historically. There is no specific theme running from one story to the next either, except that they all have to do with the protagonist's desperate need for help and Kuan-yin's speedy aid when called upon. In the initial period of Kuan-yin worship represented here, the bodhisattva is shown to be able to appear anywhere and everywhere. One does not have to pray to him in a temple or in front of his image. Nor does one have to perform any prescribed ritual in order to receive divine aid. Although the compilers were knowledgeable Buddhist laymen, they were more interested in making known the marvelous efficacy of this new universal savior, rather than educating their readers by linking the stories to any scriptures. The third collection groups the stories according to the deliverances promised and performed by Kuan-yin in the "Universal Gateway" chapter of the *Lotus Sūtra* and the *Ch'ing Kuan-yin ching*, which was probably translated by 420 C.E.—barely eighty years before Lu compiled his collection. He first narrated the forty-five stories, arranging them according to the dangers his protagonist faces by using the categories found in the "Universal Gateway" chapter: three stories about fire, six about water, one about running into rakṣasas, eight about execution, twenty-two about imprisonment, fourteen about robbers, and one about seeking the birth of a son. Then he narrated another fourteen stories illustrating the four types of dangers mentioned in the *Ch'ing Kuan-yin ching*: five stories about finding the way after being lost, four about returning to one's native place, three about recovering from serious illnesses, and two about remaining unharmed after encountering ferocious animals. After telling the first three stories, he says, "The above three stories [confirm] what the 'Universal Gateway' says, 'if you enter the fire, fire cannot burn you.'" Or, he may say, "The above four stories [confirm] what the *Ch'ing Kuan-yin ching* says about returning to one's native place."

Here I have translated the seven stories from the first collection, compiled early in the fifth century by Fu Liang, and use them as a framework to discuss some important issues common to these and related tales.

First Story: Escape from Fire

The first story is about a miraculous escape from fire:

> Chu Ch'ang-shu's ancestors were originally from the Western Regions. They had accumulated much property over generations and were very wealthy. During the Yüan-k'ang era [291–299] of the Chin, he moved to Loyang. He was a devout believer in the Buddha and particularly loved to recite the *Kuang-shih-yin Sūtra*. One day his neighbor's house caught fire. His own house was made of thatch and was situated downwind. He thought to himself that because the fire was so near, even if they could manage to save some possessions, it would not be very much. Remembering what the *Kuang-shih-yin Sūtra* says, "If one encounters fire, one should call [the bod-

hisattva]" single-mindedly,[3] he told his family members not to try to carry things out of the house nor to try to put out the fire with water, but just to chant the sūtra with sincerity. The fire soon consumed the neighbor's house. When it reached the fence outside his own house, the wind suddenly turned back and the fire then stopped. Everyone took this to be an efficacious response. But there were four or five juvenile delinquents living in the neighborhood who scoffed at it, saying that because the wind happened to change direction, there was nothing miraculous about it. They decided to wait for a warm, dry night, and then they would burn the house. If it still did not burn, only then would they agree it was a miracle. Sometime later the weather did indeed become very dry and hot and the wind was also blowing hard. The youths secretly got hold of some torches and threw them onto the roof. They did this three times and each time the torches died out. They became very frightened and ran home. The next morning they came to Ch'ang-shu's house and told him what had happened the previous night. They begged him for forgiveness. He said to them, "I have no divine power. I just called on Kuang-shih-yin and meditated on him. It must be the protection given by his majestic efficacy. You should repent and believe in him." Everyone in the neighborhood marveled with amazement about this.[4]

This is the only story among the seven that credits the chanting of the *Kuang-shih-yin Sūtra* (the "Universal Gateway" chapter) as the reason why Chu Ch'ang-shu was spared from the fire. All the other stories, as we shall see, emphasize the calling of the bodhisattva's name. But even in this case, the triggering impetus for the bodhisattva's intervention lies in the devotee's oral chanting as well as mental concentration on him (*sung-nien*), as is made clear in his statement to the young troublemakers. We come across the word *nien* very often in the miracle stories. This is for a very good reason, as we read in the last chapter, for *nien* has the dual meanings of vocal invocation and mental meditation at the same time.

Accounts of filial sons, on which this Buddhist miracle story might be modeled, contain similar miracles in which a filial son is saved from imminent danger of certain death by natural disasters. For instance, in two second century stories about filial sons, a fire miraculously stops due to a supernatural response to a man's sincere piety (Knapp 1996:179). They moved Heaven with their filiality, just as Chu moved Kuan-yin with his sincere faith. The accounts of filial sons were written by the literati to inculcate filial piety among the readers. Writers of miracle stories about Kuan-yin, as we read previously, were also literati who wanted to introduce their readers to Kuan-yin and instill in them an abiding faith in this new deity. It is more than likely that the writers of these

Kuan-yin stories were familiar with accounts of filial sons. They shared the same indigenous belief in sympathetic resonance with the authors of the accounts. They also used the same literary format in telling the stories. Sometimes, as in this story, a filial miracle story could be adapted to serve Buddhist ends. Because their readers were familiar with the stories from the accounts of filial sons, they would be responsive to miracle stories about Kuan-yin.

Story Two: A Monk's New Voice

This story is about a monk receiving a new voice:

> Monk Po Fa-chiao, a native of Chung-shan (present-day Ting County, Hopei), was a diligent and devout person. He wanted to recite sūtras but lacked the voice. He was very unhappy about it. He told his fellow monks, "Kuang-shih-yin can help a person fulfill his wishes in this very life. I will now pray to him with singleness of mind. If my sincerity is weak and cannot move the bodhisattva, my previous sins from bad karma will not be eliminated. I would rather die than live a long life but without a good voice." After saying that he refused to eat and concentrated his mind with utmost sincerity. After three or four days he became weak and his disciples asked him to give up, saying, "One's voice, like other endowments, is determined and cannot be changed in one life. You should cherish your health in order to practice religion." But he told them not to disturb him because his determination was unshakable. After five or six days he became even weaker and could only breathe. His companions were greatly worried, fearing that he was going to die. On the morning of the seventh day, however, he suddenly opened his eyes and looked happy. He told the disciples that he had received a good response. He asked for water to wash and uttered three gāthās. His voice was so loud that it could be heard two to three *li* away. The villagers were all startled and wondered what strange voice was coming from the temple. When they came to inquire, they realized that this was no other than the voice of the monk. He recited half a million words after this. His voice sounded like a bell and showed no sign of weakness. People at that time all realized that he was a person who had achieved the realization of the Way. He was still alive at the end of Shih Hu's reign [r. 334–349, the third emperor of the Latter Chao], when he was over ninety years of age.

This story introduces a theme not identified with the perils mentioned in the sūtras. This was a case of a healthy person living a normal life who did not face any life-threatening danger. Moreover, according to the theory of karma, one's physical endowments, like one's lifespan and other circumstances, are predetermined and cannot be altered. However, because he wanted to chant the sūtras with a beautiful voice, which he did not have, he was willing to die in order to get it. He was motivated by a sincere desire to glorify Buddhism, and Kuan-yin granted him his wish. Here is an impressive example of how the indigenous ideas of sincerity and sympathetic resonance influenced the Buddhist idea of karma.

It also bears a striking similarity to the even more dramatic story of Gunabhadra found in the *Biographies of Eminent Monks*. Gunabhadra arrived in Canton in 435 after a dangerous journey from Ceylon during which the wind suddenly stopped and the boat was marooned in the ocean. He asked his fellow passengers to concentrate on the buddhas of the ten directions and call on Kuan-yin. He himself secretly chanted a dhāraṇī sūtra, repented to the bodhisattva and worshiped him. The wind rose up and rain began to fall. Then the boat could continue to sail. After he arrived in China, he was well received. But because he could not speak Chinese, he had to rely on translators. When he was asked to give lectures on the *Hua-yen Sūtra* by the prime minister, he felt very ashamed because he himself could not speak the language. That same night, he performed a repentance rite and begged Kuan-yin for help. He then dreamt of a person in white who carried a sword in one hand and a man's head in the other. The person asked Gunabhadra why he was worried. When told the reason, he told Gunabhadra not to worry. He cut off Gunabhadra's head and put the head he was holding on the latter instead. The next morning when Gunabhadra woke up, he could speak Chinese perfectly (T 50:344b).

Similar stories, though much less spectacular than this one, that tell about other monks who gained wisdom or eloquence are found in other monastic collections. Because a monk's reputation was closely related to his ability to either chant sūtras or give lectures on sūtras, it is understandable that a good voice and an ability to explain Buddhist doctrines would be highly prized qualities in a monk. In the *Biographies of Promoters of the Lotus Sūtra* (Hung-tsan fa-hua chuan), there is the story about the monk Shih Fa-ch'eng (562–640), who was committed to the constant chanting of the *Lotus Sūtra* as his vocation. At one time, however, he was exhausted both physically and mentally and felt that he had to give up his practice. So he carried out a ritual program of worshiping Kuan-yin and prayed for protection. When he finished the twenty-one day rite, he suddenly saw a giant in white standing in front of the Buddha image. The giant gave him some medicine and asked him to swallow it. After that he became doubly vigorous in body and mind. He could then recite the sūtra without stopping (T 8:37b). The T'ien-t'ai master Tsun-shih (963–1032), who wrote a ritual manual based on the *Ch'ing Kuan-yin ching* and was a great promoter of repentance rites, a subject discussed further in chapter 7, also figured prominently in the miracle tale tradition. According to the *Fo-tsu t'ung-chi* compiled by Chih-p'an around 1260, he was born as a result of his mother having prayed to Kuan-yin for a son. She dreamt of a beautiful woman who gave her a pearl to swallow. When he was seven months old, he could already call the name of Kuan-yin by following his mother's example. Later in life, he achieved great renown in Chekiang for his extreme austerities. Once when he became ill, he saw Kuan-yin touching him,[5] pulling out several worms from his mouth as drops of sweet dew poured from the bodhisattva's fingertips into his mouth. He recovered and his physical shape also changed. The crown of his head grew more than an inch, his hands came down to below his knees, his voice became as loud as a booming bell, and his skin was as fair as white jade (T 49:207b).

The Dharma master by the name of Hui-tsai (997–1083) lived slightly later than Tsun-shih. He was said to be confused and dull by nature. He chanted the Great Compassion Dhāraṇī all his life and hoped to be able to understand Buddhist teachings. One night he suddenly dreamt of an Indian monk who was several meters in height. The monk took off his robe and put it on Hui-tsai, saying, "Hui-tsai, remember me all your life!" The next day when he attended the lecture, he immediately understood what was being said. He achieved a thorough enlightenment (T 49:215b-c).

In the collections of miracle tales compiled in late imperial China, "gaining wisdom" (*te-hui*) constituted a separate category. Not only monks and nuns, but also ordinary men and women were encouraged to call on Kuan-yin to improve their intellectual abilities. Sheng-yen, a contemporary Ch'an master teaching in Taipei and New York, delights in telling his audiences about how slow-witted he was when he worked as a young novice in Kiangsu. He did not understand the lectures, nor could he learn how to chant. His master told him to do continuous prostrations in front of the Kuan-yin image, chant Kuan-yin's holy name, and concentrate on the bodhisattva with single-mindedness. He did so faithfully for six months and one day he suddenly understood everything. When I did my fieldwork in Hangchow and P'u-t'o in 1987, I came across a number of young people who were hoping to pass the examinations to enter high schools or colleges. When asked why they had come to P'u-t'o, they answered that they hoped Kuan-yin would grant them intelligence.

Story Three: Deliverance from Being Killed

This story is about deliverance from being killed, or in the vocabulary of the "Universal Gateway," from being threatened by a knife:

After Shih Hu died, Jan Min (d. 352) persecuted non-Chinese.[6] Even Chinese who physically resembled barbarians were killed. At that time there were three non-Chinese monks in the capital Yeh (in present-day Hopei) who knew that they were going to die. So among themselves they figured out a way to escape their predicament. They said to each other that Kuang-shih-yin could save people from perils. So they decided to take refuge in the bodhisattva and recite a sūtra together to beg him for help. They did so day and night without stop. Several days later, soldiers came to the temple to get them. They surrounded the temple and three came in carrying knives in their hands, intending to kill the monks. One monk was hiding behind the wall of the lecture hall, which was behind a thicket of trees. When the soldier came and thrust out the knife to kill the monk, the knife struck a tree trunk. It became crooked like a hook and could not be taken out. The next person came forward to kill him. But his knife broke into two pieces, one piece flying to the sky and the other coming back at him. When the last person saw this strange happening, he became frightened and dared not go forward. He threw down his knife and asked, "What divine skill do you have that you cannot be harmed by knives?" To which the monk replied, "I have none. It is just because I heard that the government is killing non-Chinese. I feared that I could not escape so I had no choice but to turn my thoughts to Kuang-shih-yin. This must be divine protection." The men hurried back and reported this to Min, who pardoned the three monks. The monk Tao-i heard this story himself at Yeh.

This and the following story introduce us to the violent world of the fourth and fifth centuries, in which a person could become imprisoned, sentenced to execution, or summarily killed for no other reason than that he happened to be in the wrong place or on the wrong side of a conflict. Although there are only two stories of this nature in the first collection, they increased enormously in the third collection, which includes eight stories about execution and twenty-two about imprisonment. They provide a vivid sociological and psychological template of that period. In fact, a number of later stories bear a striking resemblance to the story that gave rise to the indigenous sūtra *King Kao's Kuan-yin Sūtra* discussed in chapter 3.

Story Four: Release from Shackles

To Chuan was a native of Ho-nei [present-day Ju-yang, Honan]. During the years 345 to 356 he served as an official under Kao Ch'ang, the governor of Ping-chou [present-day Shansi], who was feuding with Lü Hu, the governor of I-chou [present-day Hopei]. To was captured by the Lü faction and thrown into prison, together with six or seven compatriots. They were shackled securely together and were soon to be executed. Monk Chih Tao-shan was in Lü's camp and he had known To previously. When he heard that the latter was in prison, he came to visit and talked to him through the door. To then told the monk that his life was in danger and asked if there was any way that he could be saved. The monk answered that no human method would be of any use but Kuang-shih-yin could save people from danger. If he could concentrate and beg the bodhisattva sincerely, he would quickly receive a response. To had heard about Kuang-shih-yin, so after this conversation, he started to follow the monk's advice. For three days and nights he took refuge in the bodhisattva with utmost sincerity. He felt the shackles beginning to loosen and when he tried to shake them, suddenly they fell away from his body. He prayed to the bodhisattva, "My own shackles have now become loosened by themselves due to your compassionate protection. But I still have several companions and cannot bear to escape by myself. You, Kuang-shih-yin, save all universally. Please also free them." After the prayer he touched the others, and each one also became free of the shackles, as if someone had cut them loose. So they opened the prison door and left. Even when they walked among the guards, no one noticed them. They scaled the city gate and escaped. About that time day was dawning. After they walked four or five *li* they did not dare to go any further, because it was daylight. So they hid among tall grasses and fell asleep. Soldiers were sent out to search for them. They burned bushes and trampled on the grass and searched for them everywhere. But only this small area of land where they were hiding did not get searched. They escaped and arrived home safely. They became firm believers in Buddhism and showed extraordinary faith and reverence. The monk Tao-shan later came south and told Hsieh Fu [the original compiler of the collection] about this.

This story bears a striking similarity to a second century story about a man named Wei Tan. As recounted by Knapp, Wei was captured by hungry bandits together with several tens of other people. One of the bandits admired Wei's generous and respectful demeanor. He secretly loosened Wei's bindings and told Wei to run away. But Wei would not leave without the others and this so impressed the bandits that they let everyone go (Knapp 1996:180–81). Like the first story of Chu Ch'ang-shu, this could have been a Buddhist adaptation of a Confucian filial miraculous account to glory Kuan-yin. This story is also interesting on two other accounts. First of all, it was a monk, Tao-shan, who told To Chuan to concentrate his thoughts on Kuang-shih-yin to ask for deliverance, and who later related the story to Hsieh Fu, who then wrote it down. This was not an isolated incident, but was replicated in other stories. Though not exclusively, monks were often the agents who promoted faith in Kuan-yin and instructed people about the correct method of showing faith in Kuan-yin. Second, all the tales in the first collection emphasize that mental concentration on, sometimes accompanied by invocation of, the bodhisattva with great sincerity was the key to deliverance.

Except for the first story about Chu Ch'ang-shu, there was no mention about chanting the *Kuan-yin ching*, nor any specification of how many times one must call the name of the bodhisattva before a miracle occurs. This would change in the stories compiled in the third collection. Not only the recitation of the *Kuan-yin Sūtra* is mentioned more frequently, but a specific number, most frequently one thousand times, as in the case of *King Kao's Kuan-yin Sūtra*, was necessary to trigger a divine response from Kuan-yin. For instance, four stories (27, 34, 35, and 36) specify chanting the sūtra one thousand times, whereas the three others variously specify three hundred (no. 37) and ten thousand times (no. 62), and one story (no. 67) calls for the invocation of the bodhisattva's name one thousand times. The interest in such ritual exactitude probably reflected influences of the various *sādhana* instructions included in the esoteric scriptures discussed in chapter 2. As we read earlier, they usually specify a specific number of times for the chanting of the dhāraṇī, be it 21, 108, 1008, or 1080 times, before it becomes effective.

Similarly, I would suggest that "the person in white" who mysteriously appeared in the dreams of Gunabhadra and Fa-ch'eng after they performed rites of repentance might be the esoteric Kuan-yin, who is often described as being clothed in white in the same *sādhanas*. At the same time, it is also important to keep in mind that the term "white-clad" (*pai-i*) can also have other less esoteric connotations. It can be understood to mean a lay person, in contrast to a monk, who wears black robes. The Chinese followed the Indian usage of referring to a lay person as one who wears white clothes. A famous example for such usage is the layman Vimalakīrti, who is the protagonist of the sūtra named after him. That sūtra has been one of the favorites among the monks and gentry Buddhists since its translation in the third century, and would thus have been familiar to the compilers and readers of the miracle tales. Finally, in contrast to the color yellow, which symbolizes Taoism in the popular mind, the color white would also indicate that the deity is not a Taoist one.[7] The origin of the term is obscure and cannot be pinpointed to any specific source. Perhaps different individuals might have different understandings in accordance with their backgrounds and levels of education. However, the different connotations of *pai-i* would all refer to Kuan-yin who, being a bodhisattva, is neither monk nor, of course, Taoist. In the early period, the white-clothed person who appeared in these tales was unmistakably male, but he would be replaced by the feminine White-robed Kuan-yin in later miracle tale collections.

Stories Five and Six: The Peril of Water

The next two stories are about deliverance from being drowned or what the *Lotus Sūtra* calls the "peril of the water."

> The river south of Shih-feng [present-day T'ien-t'ai, Chekiang] has many currents and its banks are steep. It is very winding and also full of rocks. Even during the daytime it is very fearsome to travel on it. Lu Shu is originally from Kwangsi and is now living in Shih-feng. He told me that his father once traveled on the river. When he was some ten *li* from home, it got dark and the weather suddenly became stormy. The sky became as dark as black lacquer and he could not tell whether he was heading east or west. He thought for sure he would be shipwrecked and drowned. He turned his mind to Kuang-shi-yin. He called the bodhisattva's name and also meditated on him. After a short time, the light of a fire appeared on the shore, as if someone held a torch. It shone on the river making everything very clear. He could thus return home. The fire was always guiding the boat, about ten steps ahead of it. Lu Shu was friendly with Hsi Ch'ao and the latter told me the story.

Hsi Ch'ao, as we recall, was a friend of the compiler's father and a noted scholar of Buddhism. It is a characteristic of all miracle tales that the writer always notes the source of his story whenever possible. If the writer heard the story from somebody, he would provide the person's identity. Even in later compendia, it is usual for the compilers to cite the written sources from which a particular story originated. The chain of transmission guarantees the authenticity of the story.

> Hsü Jung was a native of Lang-ya [present-day Tung-hai, Kiangsu] and often went to Tung-yang [in present-day Shantung]. Once when he returned by way of Ting-shan [present-day Hang County, Chekiang], the boat was sucked into a whirlpool and floundered in the waves because the boatmen were unfamiliar with the river. He had nothing else to do but call Kuang-shih-yin with a concentrated heart. Instantly the boat was lifted up, as if by several dozen men. After the boat emerged from the whirlpool, it could sail

smoothly. Then it got dark and a storm arose. They lost their direction and the waves became more turbulent. Jung continued to chant the sūtra. After a while they saw a fire on top of the mountain. Turning the boat around they followed it and thus arrived at port safely. Once they disembarked, the light also disappeared. All the passengers were surprised, doubting it could be a fire made by human beings. Next day they asked the local people about the fire on the mountain. But the local people were surprised to hear about it, saying, "With such a big storm yesterday, how could there have been a fire? We did not see any." It then became clear that it must have been a divine light. Later Jung became the protector-general of K'uai-chi and told Hsieh Liang himself about this story. There was a monk by the name of Chih Tao-yün who traveled on the same boat with him, and also saw this miracle. He told me the same thing as that which was related by Jung.

Story Seven: A Miraculous Cure

The last story in the first collection is about a miraculous cure performed by Kuan-yin on the monk Fa-i (307–380). Curing diseases is one of the new promises found in the *Ch'ing Kuan-yin ching*, but not in the "Universal Gateway" chapter of the *Lotus Sūtra*. In the third collection, three stories are about people being cured by the bodhisattva and are offered as validation of the *Ch'ing kuan-yin ching*. Tale number 67, the only dated one, relates that in 446 a monk called Hui-sheng living in present-day Kiangsu became deaf and dumb as a result of illness. Thinking that there was no medicine capable of curing him, he turned his heart to Kuan-shih-yin totally and called the bodhisattva's name a thousand times. As soon as he finished the last invocation, he recovered the use of his eyes and ears. Since the sūtra had only been translated recently, by interpreting these stories in this light, the compiler Lu Kao shows us the speed with which a new sūtra became known among the faithful, particularly those who were educated. By contrast, what happened to Fa-i was interpreted by Fu Liang differently. Fu chose to see it as a confirmation of the ability of the bodhisattva to appear in different forms, one being that of a monk, as announced in the "Universal Gateway." It may also indicate that knowledge of the *Ch'ing Kuan-yin ching* was probably not yet available to him.

> Monk Fa-i lived in the mountains and loved to study. He became ill but continued to work hard, and the illness got worse. He sincerely called on Kuang-shih-yin. Several days went by like this. One day he took a nap during the daytime and dreamt a monk came to visit him in order to cure him. He cut open Fa-i's chest and stomach and washed his intestines, which were all

knotted together and looked very dirty. After washing them, the monk stuffed them back into the body and told Fa-i, "Your illness is now cured." Upon waking up he felt relieved of any illness and returned to his former self. He lived on Mt. Pao in Shih-ning [in present-day Chekiang] in 372 and my father used to visit him. He liked to tell this story and my father always felt great respect toward him. The sūtra says that the bodhisattva can appear in the form of a monk. I believe that what Fa-i dreamt was a confirmation of this.

Visions of Kuan-yin in the Early Miracle Tales

Although all the tales in the three early collections affirm unfailing deliverance from different kinds of perils effected by the bodhisattva, very few report the devotees' actual seeing their savior. In most cases, we are simply told that the devotee called Kuan-yin's name with the utmost concentration and sincerity, and in response a miracle occurred. The devotee clearly felt the presence of Kuan-yin and credited him with the deliverance. But she or he could not tell what the bodhisattva looked like. It is thus very fortunate for us that several tales do report visions of Kuan-yin. They provide important clues as to how Kuan-yin was conceived by the faithful in this early period.

The story about Fa-i (no. 7) says that Kuan-yin appeared in his dream as a monk. In fact, when the bodhisattva did appear to his devotees in human form, he usually appeared as a monk. Two stories (nos. 7, 9) in the second collection and four stories in the third collection (nos. 21, 23, 24, and 62) identify Kuan-yin as a monk. While Kuan-yin appears to the protagonists of the first five stories in their dreams and saves them from imprisonment, he interacts with the devotees in a waking state in the last one. The story relates how in 462 when P'eng-ch'eng (present-day T'ung-shan, Kiangsu) fell, a man by the name of Han Mu-chih fled, and in the confusion lost his son, who was kidnapped. Being a pious Buddhist, Han vowed to chant the *Kuang-shih-yin Sūtra* ten thousand times in hopes of getting his son back. He also invited monks to his home for a vegetarian feast whenever he finished one thousand recitations. But there was no response, even after he had recited the sūtra six or seven thousand times. He interpreted this as a lack of sincerity on his part. So he redoubled his efforts and began to recite the sūtra day and night, without keeping track of the number. In the meantime, his son was sold as a slave to someone in I-chou (in present-day Szechwan). One day when the son was laboring alone in the field, he suddenly saw a monk, who came to him and asked if he was Han Mu-chih's son. Surprised, he answered yes. The monk then asked him if he would like to see his father again. To which the son again answered yes, asking how was that possible? The monk replied that because the father had been most persistent in pressing him, he had now decided to bring the son home. The monk then told the boy to hold tight onto the corner of his cassock. When the son did so, he felt he was being lifted and carried off by someone. Soon they arrived outside the door of the father's new residence, which the son did not recognize. The monk stayed outside but ordered the boy to go in and see if anyone was at home. When the son went inside, he saw his father sitting there reciting the sūtra. The father and son were overjoyed at seeing each other. When the son told the father the holy personage who had brought him home was outside, the father rushed out to thank him. But the monk was nowhere to be seen.

In one of the stories (#21), not only did the bodhisattva appear as a monk to a Mr. Hsia in his dream and free him from imprisonment in 411, but also told him that he was Kuan-shih-yin. However, because Hsia was apparently ignorant of Buddhism, he thought that "Kuan-shih-yin" was the name of a real monk. Only when he asked some monks whom he met after his successful escape where he could find a monk by the name of Kuan-shih-yin was he told that it was the bodhisattva. He then had a golden image made and wore it around his neck, became a vegetarian, and converted to Buddhism. In these stories that identify Kuan-yin as a monk, no description is provided about his physical characteristics. We are not told how old he was or what he looked like. Only in one instance (tale no. 9 of the second collection), is he described as smiling, standing eight Chinese feet (*ch'ih*) tall. However, a story found in Tao-hsüan's *Continued Biographies of Eminent Monks* describes Kuan-yin and includes a telling detail that hints at the close link between the existing iconography and visionary experiences.

> When the monk Hung-man was still living in the secular world, he suffered from paralysis of both his feet when he was fifteen. He constantly chanted the *Kuan-shih-yin Sūtra* for three years. One day he suddenly saw a monk holding a water bottle standing in front of him. When he asked the monk, "Where are you from?" The monk answered, "Because you constantly call me, that is why I have come." Man then bowed down and asked, "What evil karma did your disciple accumulate from previous lives that I should suffer this paralysis?" The monk answered, "Because in your past life you captured and bound living beings, that is why you are now reaping these evil consequences. Close your eyes and I shall cure you." When he did as instructed, he felt a nail of six or seven inches being pulled from each of his knees. By the time he opened his eyes to thank the monk, the latter was gone. He got up and could walk normally as before. He then realized that the monk was Kuan-yin and he vowed never to get married (T 50:663a).

As I have mentioned in previous chapters, Indian and Chinese images of Kuan-yin usually show him holding a water bottle (*kuṇḍikā*, *ts'o-p'ing*). Just as existing iconography might predispose how a devotee saw Kuan-yin in his vision, scriptural description of the bodhisattva could have played a similar role. As noted in chapter 2, Kuan-yin is connected strongly with light symbolism in the scriptures. It is therefore not surprising that next to seeing Kuan-yin as a monk, the bodhisattva was most frequently experienced as a brilliant light. Thus, tale number 5 in the second collection tells us that the monk Tao-t'ai dreamt of someone telling him that he would die at forty-two. When he reached that age, he became seriously ill. He donated all his possessions in order to seek a blessing. A friend told him that according to the sūtra [the *Kuang-shih-yin ching*], to call the name of Kuang-shih-yin once would equal the merit resulting from making offerings to sixty-two billion bodhisattvas. Therefore he should turn his heart to Kuang-shih-yin with sincerity and he would be able to increase his lifespan despite the unfortunate dream prediction. Tao-t'ai believed him and concentrated his mind on the bodhisattva day and night for four days. On the fourth night he was sitting on the bed, which was shielded by a curtain. He suddenly saw Kuang-shih-yin come in from outside. The bodhisattva, whose legs and feet were covered with golden light, said to him, "Are you calling me?" But when he pushed aside the curtain, he could not see anyone. Covered with perspiration, he felt refreshed and his illness went away. He told this story to people when he was already forty-four years old. Tales number 19 and 61 in the third collection also report the bodhisattva appearing as bathed in shining light. Tale number 19 is about a man by the name of K'ai Hu who was imprisoned and sentenced to die. He recited the *Kuan-shih-yin Sūtra* with a concentrated mind for three days and nights. Then in the middle of the third night, he saw the bodhisattva sending out brilliant light. The shackles broke by themselves and the jail door, illuminated by the light, opened to let him out. The light shone in front of him leading the way. After more than twenty *li* the light disappeared, but by then he had reached safety.

Tale number 61 tells the miraculous experience of a man by the name of Pan Tao-hsiu who became a soldier in 410 when he was in his twenties. But he got separated from the army, became lost, and was sold as a slave. Wandering far from home, he constantly thought of Kuan-shih-yin and hoped to see the bodhisattva in his dreams. One day he found himself alone on a mountain, and he suddenly saw the true form of Kuang-shih-yin [notice the bodhisattva being called by both names in this story] radiating a light that was so brilliant that the entire mountain turned golden in color. He hastily bowed and prostrated in front of the bodhisattva. When the light disappeared, he found himself back in his native village. Following familiar roads, he returned to his home, to the great amazement of everyone.

When Pan was said to have seen the bodhisattva in his "true form" (*chen-hsing*), what does it mean? What was the true form of Kuan-yin? The story leaves it unexplained, but I would suggest that it refers to the form of the bodhisattva as depicted in contemporary iconography.[8] Images of Kuan-yin often figure in the miracle tales. They were worshiped as icons. They were created to give thanks to the bodhisattva after the devotee was saved from danger. Sculpted images stood in as substitutes to receive the blows from the executioner's knife on behalf of the worshiper. Sometimes they were carried on the body or worn in the hair by devotees as talismans. But they also influenced the contents of the devotees' visionary experiences, which, in turn, sometimes led to the creation of new iconography.

Icons, Miracles, and Iconography

Buddhist art, like all religious art, is intimately connected with the spiritual lives of the faithful. Sculpted and painted images of Kuan-yin are first and foremost icons, although they can, of course, be appreciated as beautiful objects of art. I first discuss the close relationship between the devotees and icons of Kuan-yin revealed in some early miracle tales and then link the new forms of Kuan-yin appearing in devotees' visions of the bodhisattva as contained in some later tales to the development of new iconographic representations. Art and miracle tales served as effective media for the domestication and transformation of Kuan-yin. As the foreign Avalokiteśvara increasingly became intertwined with the lives of Chinese men and women, the bodhisattva was gradually changed into the Chinese Kuan-yin.

Let us recall the story of Sun Ching-te, the hero of the origin myth of the famous indigenous *King Kao's Kuan-yin Sūtra*. As related by Tao-hsüan and translated in the previous chapter, Sun worshiped an icon of Kuan-yin that he kept in his room. When he managed to finish chanting the sūtra that had been revealed to him in a dream one thousand times prior to his beheading, the executioner's knife broke into three sections. Although the executioner changed the knife three times, the same thing happened. When Sun was pardoned and returned to his room, he saw three cuts made by a knife on the neck of the Kuan-yin image. The implication is clearly that the icon bore the blows of the knife, thus sparing Sun. This was supposed to have happened to Sun between 534 and 537 C.E.

Two stories in the third collection report identical happenings. Tale number 13, which is dated, describes a miracle that happened more than one hundred and fifty years earlier than Sun's. It tells the story of someone from P'eng-ch'eng who, between 376 and 395, was wrongly accused of being a robber and sentenced to die. He worshiped Kuan-yin and always wore a golden image of the bodhisattva inside his hair knotted behind his neck. When he was led out to be killed, he concentrated his thoughts even more firmly on Kuan-yin. When the executioner's knife struck his neck, there was a metallic sound and the knife broke. Although another knife was substituted three times, no harm could be done to him. Everyone was astonished and he was questioned by the official in charge. He answered that he had no special magic, except that he worshiped Kuan-yin and wore his image on his neck. When they loosened his hair and examined the image, there were three cuts on its neck. Tale number 14 is very similar, except that it is about someone living in Szechwan who wore the icon hidden inside a portable sandalwood shrine. He was caught in hand-to-hand combat and struck on his neck. He heard a metallic sound but did not feel any pain. When he had escaped from the ensuing melee, he took out the portable shrine, which looked intact. But when he opened it and looked at the icon, he saw that it bore several cuts, clearly made by the enemy's knife.

Instead of going to a temple to worship Kuan-yin, these early devotees carried the icons on their bodies as talismans. Since they were worn inside the hair, or on top of the crown (as we read in the following story), they must have been small and light. Indeed, a number of tiny gilt bronze images of Kuan-yin, some measuring only two centimeters or so, have survived and can be seen in museums. Art historians usually take them to be votive images made by humble people who could not afford larger ones. When we view them in the light of such miracle tales, we might speculate that they were small because they were intended to be used as personal talismans. Icons were also sometimes created for such devotional use as a result of miraculous deliverance. For instance, Tale number 17 tells the story of Nan-kung Tzu-ao who lived in Shensi during the fourth century. His native city was sacked and many residents were killed. Knowing that he was going to die, Tzu-ao put all his faith in Kuan-yin. When his turn came to be executed, for some reason the executioners suddenly became too tired to raise their hands. Surprised, the official asked him what he could do. Without knowing why, he answered that he was good at making saddles and was thus pardoned. When he returned home, he had a small Kuan-yin icon made. He put it inside a sandalwood portable shrine and always wore it on the top of his head.

A very interesting story about a Buddhist devotee and his personal icon of Kuan-yin has been preserved. In the preface to *Signs from the Unseen Realm*, a work familiar to Lu Kao, the compiler of the third collection, Wang Yen related his own intimate relationship with a votive icon of Kuan-yin first given to him by his refuge master when Wang was living in Chiao-chih (present-day Vietnam) as a child. He described it as having been finely made, resembling the ones created in the Yüan-chia era (424–453). Although he was very young, he and his younger brother diligently worshiped it. Later when they returned to the capital, the family home had to be renovated and there was no proper place to keep the image. So it was taken to a temple for temporary safekeeping. At that time, however, ordinary people were engaged in making coins privately and many gilt bronze images got stolen and melted down because of this. Several months after the icon was sent to the temple, he was sleeping during the daytime and had a dream in which he saw the icon by his side. Curious about the dream, he decided to go to the temple and take the icon home, although it was already getting dark. That same evening, more than ten images were forcibly removed from the temple by robbers. After that the icon shone brightly at night, illuminating the ground around it for about a three-foot radius. This happened in the fall of 463.

In 471 he moved to Wu-yi (in present-day Anhui) and befriended a monk from the Monastery of Many Treasures located in the capital. He asked the monk to keep the Kuan-yin image in that temple temporarily. Several years went by and he did not think of the image. But in 478 he met the monk again and was reminded by the latter that the image was still in the temple. When he went to the capital, he visited the abbot of the temple and asked for the image kept there. But the abbot told him that no such image was there. He was very disappointed and felt great sadness over losing the image. That same night he had a dream in which a man told him that the image was indeed still in the temple but the abbot had forgotten about it. Still in a dream, the man took him back to the temple and opened the door to the main hall. He saw clearly the image belonging to him nestled among many small images in the eastern section of the hall. The next morning he went back to the temple and told the abbot about his dream. When the abbot led him to the hall and opened it, they found the image in the eastern section of the hall. He took it back. That was the thirteenth day of the seventh month of 479. Wang Yen concludes this amazing story by saying that he had worshiped it ever since (Lu Hsün 1973:563–64).

The kind of relationship Wang Yen had with his personal icon may be difficult for a modern reader to appreciate, though not his contemporaries, as he shared it with them in the preface. Twice he found a safe home for it in a temple so that it would not be disturbed by the rebuilding of his home or the uncertainties of travel. From the matter-of-fact way Wang Yen relates the story, Buddhist images were apparently either donated to temples or put there for temporary residence by the faithful in the fifth century, just as some are today. The icon sent him warnings or directions through dreams. He regarded the icon as the embodiment of the bodhisattva. Their relationship covered a period of some twenty years. When a devotee enjoyed such an intimate rapport with the icon, it is then possible to imagine that when he had a vision of Kuan-yin either in a dream or in a waking state, he would be most likely see the bodhisattva in the form depicted by contemporary iconography.

During the second half of the fifth century, Kuan-yin became a favorite subject for gilt bronzes. The earliest surviving gilt bronze Kuan-yin outside China, inscribed with the date "the 30th year of Yüan-chia" (453) is at the Freer Gallery of Art in Washington, D.C. The bodhisattva holds a lotus in his right hand and a bottle in his left hand. He is bejeweled, with a *dhoti* draped from waist to knees, a cape covering his shoulders and forming an X in front of his body, and a long billowing stole contouring the figure as if being blown by winds (figure 2.1; Howard et al. forthcoming). Might the icon worshiped and beloved by Wang Yen be something similar to this?

Although visions and images of Kuan-yin feature prominently in the miracle tales as we have seen, specific identification between the appearances of the bodhisattva and the forms of the images is surprisingly scarce. Could it be that the linkage was so obvious that the compilers did not think it necessary to mention it? Aside from the case of Pan Tao-hsiu who was said to have seen the "true form" of the bodhisattva as depicted in the contemporary iconography just related, I have come across only one other case making a similar specification. This is the story of the monk Hsüan-chi (639–706) found in the *Biographies of Promoters of the Lotus Sūtra*. His extraordinary visionary experiences all resulted from recitation of the *Lotus Sūtra*.

> When he first began to recite the *Lotus Sūtra* and had completed 2,000 recitations, he dreamt of entering a large hall. The hall was surrounded by golden mountains on its four walls. Light shone brightly. There were niches in all the mountains and enshrined in all the niches was Kuan-yin. He prostrated and circumambulated and was full of emotion. He then saw a crystal vase containing a relic. When he tried to take it, he suddenly woke up. When he finished chanting the sūtra 5,000 times, he was at rest in the daytime but suddenly fell into a trance in which he saw several hundred sandalwood niches all enshrining Kuan-yin. He touched the niches with his hands and they came toward him. He also saw innumerable golden pearls flowing downward from the sky. They were brilliant and lovely. When he opened his mouth and swallowed them, he felt joy all over. After a duration of about two meals, he woke up and had no sense of hunger. From then on he was full of ease in mind and body and became even more diligent in his efforts. He recited the sūtra five times every twenty-four hours. When he finished chanting it 9,000 times, a strange bird suddenly flew in from outside and

alighted to rest on his bosom. After staying there seven days and nights, it flew away. Then he dreamt of a person of seven or eight *ch'ih* in height. His appearance was comely and dignified, looking the same way as the usual images. From the waist down, the bodhisattva was beautifully adorned with colorful ornaments. Hsüan-chi prostrated himself with happiness and addressed Kuan-yin Bodhisattva by name. He approached and touched the feet of Kuan-yin, calling him the Great Compassionate One. Kuan-yin touched the crown of his head several times and then lifted up his hands. Hsüan-chi drank the milk [flowing from the finger-tips of Kuan-yin ?]. He woke with a start (T 50:46c-47a).

In the three separate visions of Kuan-yin described here, images of the bodhisattva appear in the first two, while in the last one Kuan-yin appears in person. In his dream the monk saw a multitudes of Kuan-yin images enshrined within niches. To enclose Buddhist images within niches was very common in the sculpture complexes at Yün-kang, Lung-men, and elsewhere. It was such a common practice that these kinds of images were called "images in niches" (*k'an-hsiang*) in Szechwan. The mention of niches on mountains could refer to such cliff sculptures in these places. When Kuan-yin finally appeared in his dream, he could immediately recognize the bodhisattva because Kuan-yin looked exactly like the images popular at that time. Kuan-yin was usually depicted as beautifully adorned with jewels and ornate surface ornaments in Northern Chou and Sui sculptures, such as the specimen located at the Museum of Fine Arts in Boston (figure 4.1). Moreover, because the statues were often taller than a real person, the height of eight *ch'ih* (feet) would be a rather accurate measure. What Hsüan-chi reported seeing in his trance could thus be an accurate description of a contemporary Kuan-yin statue. We can take this as an example of how a person's familiarity with contemporary iconography could predispose him to see the bodhisattva in a certain way in his visionary experiences. There were also indications that what a person saw in a vision provided the basis for how Kuan-yin was depicted iconographically. For instance, Wang Yen included a story about a man named Kuo Hsüan-chih in his *Record of the Unseen Realm*. Kuo, a native of T'ai-yüan, was imprisoned in 408. He prayed to Kuan-shih-yin and had a vision of the bodhisattva that night. He was later pardoned and released. He then "painted an image of the bodhisattva based on what he had seen and established a shrine for religious practice" (Lu Hsün 1973:601).

In the pre-tenth-century miracle stories examined here, when Kuan-yin appeared in person in the devotees' dreams, he appeared either as a monk, a person wearing white,[9] a person about eight Chinese feet (*ch'ih*) in height, or a

Figure 4.1. Gilt bronze Kuan-yin, dated c. 580. *Courtesy of the Museum of Fine Arts, Boston (Francis Bartlett Fund).*

person bearing close resemblance to an image. None was feminine. However, when we examine the miracle tales in later collections, we find a striking new change. Although the bodhisattva continued to appear in the forms just mentioned, Kuan-yin increasingly also appears as a woman. Starting in the tenth century, we begin to read tales in which Kuan-yin appeared as a woman in white, then a woman carrying a fish-basket, and finally in the Ch'ing, increasingly as an old woman. These forms correspond to the White-robed Kuan-yin, Fish-basket Kuan-yin, and Old Mother Kuan-yin. They are indigenous forms of the bodhisattva created after the tenth century. As we shall see in later chapters, these new and feminine forms of Kuan-yin did not follow scriptural traditions, but were indebted to indigenous sūtras, legends, and miracle tales. It cannot be coincidental that Kuan-yin appeared in feminine forms in tales from the tenth century onward just as the bodhisattva was also depicted visually in a similar way. Although I cannot offer specific evidence, I would like to suggest that the early feminine forms of Kuan-yin might have been created based on someone's vision. He could either have painted the image himself, like Kuo did, or have a painter do it following his own description. But once a feminine image of Kuan-yin became available, more people would naturally come to see the bodhisattva in this way, whether in their dreams or in their conceptions.

The earliest example of the White-robed Kuan-yin with a clearly feminine appearance occurs in the two images of the bodhisattva gracing the entrance to the Yen-hsia Grotto in Hangchow, which Angela Howard dates to the 940s (figure 4.2; Howard 1985:11). The rulers of the Wu Yüeh Kingdom were great patrons of the Kuan-yin cult. According to the *Gazetteer of Upper T'ien-chu Monastery* (Hang-chou Shang T'ien-chu chih), before Ch'ien Liu (851–932), the founder of the Wu Yüeh Kingdom, came to power, he dreamt of a woman in white who promised to protect him and his descendants if he was compassionate and did not kill like the others. She told him that he could find her on Mt. T'ien-chu in Hangchow twenty years later. After he became king, he dreamt of the same woman, who asked for a place to stay. In return she would agree to be the patron deity of his kingdom. When he discovered that only one monastery on Mt. T'ien-chu housed an image of White-robed Kuan-yin, he gave his patronage to it and established it as the T'ien-chu K'an-ching Yüan (Cloister for Reading Scriptures at T'ien-chu), the former name for Upper T'ien-chu Monastery, which became one of the most important pilgrimage centers for Kuan-yin worship (STCC 1980:31).

The monastery underwent a major revival in 939 under the monk Tao-i who discovered a piece of marvelous wood lying in the stream from which a bright light shone. He took the wood to the local artisan K'ung to carve an

Figure 4.2. The White-robed Kuan-yin at the Yen-hsia Grotto, Hangchow, dated to the 940s. *Courtesy of Angela F. Howard.*

image of Kuan-yin. But when K'ung cut the wood open, he found a "spontaneously formed" image of Kuan-yin inside the wood. Attracted by its beauty, he decided to keep it for himself and carved another one for Tao-i. However, forewarned by a person in white in his dream, Tao-i succeeded in getting back this miraculous image (STCC 1980:29). Although we are not told what the image looked like, we can assume that it was a feminine looking, White-robed Kuan-yin. Not only did the bodhisattva appear in such a form in Ch'ien Liu's dream, she also manifested as a woman wearing a white garment in a story connected with the Sung statesman Tseng Kung-liang (990–1078). In 1042, Tseng returned to his native home in Ch'üan-chou to attend his mother's funeral. A monk by the name of Yüan-ta was a fellow passenger in his boat. When they arrived in Hangchow, they decided to go to the Upper T'ien-chu Monastery to worship Kuan-yin. As they entered the temple, they were greeted by a woman wearing a white garment who told them, "When Mr. Tseng is fifty-seven years old, you will serve in the secretariat-chancellery and the reverend elder will also receive the title of a great master." After saying this, she disappeared. When the predicted time arrived, Tseng was indeed appointed a grand councilor and the monk was also given the title of great master because of his friendship with Tseng (T 49:411c).

I have cited these examples in order to show the connection between the new iconography of the White-robed Kuan-yin and the gender change of the "person in white." The iconography of White-robed Kuan-yin was probably derived from the Water-moon Kuan-yin, which was the first indigenous iconography created in China. Although there are a number of similarities between these two types of iconography, which will be dealt with in chapter 6, Water-moon Kuan-yin is nevertheless masculine or asexual, whereas the White-robed Kuan-yin is distinctively feminine. It is very puzzling that in all the miracle accounts I have perused, I have not come across any reference to a vision of the Water-moon Kuan-yin. Could it be that because the figure of a "white-clad person" had already become such a fixed topos in the miracle tale genre by the tenth century that the new iconography of Water-moon Kuan-yin was seen through this lens? And as reports of people seeing the lady in white became disseminated, was the Water-moon Kuan-yin transformed into the White-robed Kuan-yin? In chapter 6 I discuss more fully the origins of the Water-moon Kuan-yin, which I hypothesize as being connected with Buddhist philosophy and ritual. I will also deal at greater length there with the relationship between specific miracle tales about feminine Kuan-yin and the various types of feminine Kuan-yin images such as the Fish-basket and Old Mother in chapters 10 and 11. Now I turn to the later miracle tale collections to focus on their characteristics.

Distinctive Characteristics of Later Miracle Tale Collections

All the three later miracle tale collections begin with excerpts from sūtras glorifying Kuan-yin. I think this arrangement serves two purposes. First, the compilers want the reader to see the sūtras and miracle tales as integrally related to each other. The teachings of the sūtras illuminate the miracles, and the miracles in turn validate the scriptural teachings. Second, the collection is supposed to function as a self-contained anthology that instructs and enlightens the reader about the salvific nature and record of Kuan-yin. Even if the reader has no prior exposure to Buddhism, the compilers hope to instill in the reader a basic understanding and, more importantly, an incipient faith in the bodhisattva after he or she reads the selected sūtra excerpts and stories. The collections were compiled for pedagogical and proselytizing purposes. By examining the sūtras selected for inclusion in the collections, we can get a sense about what constituted a Kuan-yin catechism for the compilers.

Chou K'e-fu, who compiled the *Manifestations [Resulting] from Recitation of Kuan-shih-yin Sūtras and Mantras* in 1659, was a layman. He stated in his preface that he had already compiled collections of miracle tales resulting from the recitation of the *Diamond Sūtra*, the *Pure Land Sūtras*, the *Lotus Sūtra*, and the *Hua-yen Sūtra*. He dedicated himself to this task because he believed that the merit from making a donation of the Dharma (*fa-shih*) was measureless. Undoubtedly because he had already compiled separate miracle tale collections for the other sūtras, in this collection he included only the *Sūtra of Great Compassion Dhāraṇī* (the *Ch'ien-shou ching*) translated by Amoghavajra, the indigenous sūtra *Dhāraṇī Sūtra of the Five Mudrās of the Great Compassionate White-robed One* discussed in chapter 3, a eulogy for Kuan-yin written by the Sung Ch'an master Ta-hui (1088–1163), and two short critical essays dispelling common misunderstandings about Kuan-yin written by the Ming Pure Land master Chu-hung (1535–1615). He included 118 miracle stories arranged chronologically, covering the periods from the Chin to the Ch'ing periods. Seventy persons involved in these miracle stories had lived before the Sung, and forty-eight after. Of these people, twenty-seven were monks, consisting of about one quarter of the total. Among the laypeople, he included four emperors: Emperor Wen of the Sung (r. 424–453), Wen-tsung of the T'ang (r. 826–840), Emperor Li (r. 961–975) of the Southern T'ang, and Emperor Yung-lo (r. 1402–1424) of the Ming period. Twelve women were also listed; one was the legendary Ma-lang-fu or Wife of Mr. Ma, but no nuns were included. Other protagonists of miracle stories were statesmen Fan Chung-yen and Shih Hao of the Sung, as well as an anonymous Ming-era cripple from Shantung.

By contrast, the *Compassionate Grove of Kuan-yin,* compiled by the monk Hung-tsan in 1668, devotes more space to monks. Of the 150 stories, 81 are about monastics (including 5 nuns), and the rest about laypeople. He includes seventy-one people who lived before the Sung and eighty-four who lived after, thus giving equal weight to more recent times. The sūtra excerpts chosen for inclusion at the beginning of the collection are also more extensive and scholastic. They are: Chih-i's commentary on the "Universal Gateway" chapter included in his *Mysterious Meaning of Kuan-yin* (Kuan-yin hsüan-i), the *Karuṇāpuṇḍarīka Sūtra*, the *Sūtra of Kuan-shih-yin Bodhisattva's Receiving Prediction*, the *Sūtra of Great Compassion Dhāraṇī*, the "Universal Gateway" chapter, the *Śūraṅgama Sūtra*, the *Hua-yen Sūtra*, the *Visualization of the Buddha Amitāyus Sūtra*, the *Eleven-headed Divine Dhāraṇī Heart Sūtra*, *Karaṇḍavyūha Sūtra*, and finally, the *Ch'ing Kuan-yin ching*. Like Chou, Hung-tsan also included five tales about pious emperors, although his choices were not identical to Chou's. Hung-tsan used stories of Wen-tsung of the T'ang, and Sung rulers Jen-tsung (r. 1022–1063), Ying-tsung (r. 1063–1066), Hsiao-tsung (r. 1162–1188), and Li-tsung (r. 1225–1264). The intense interest in noting Buddhist sympathies among the rulers and literati-officials is a characteristic of Buddhist chronicles such as the *Fo-tsu t'ung-chi*, the *Li-tai fo-tsu t'ung-tsai*, the *Shih-shih chi-ku lüeh* (Brief Compilation of Buddhist History) and the *Shih-shih chi-ku lüeh hsü-chi* (Continuation of the Brief Compilation of Buddhist History) among others. In fact, these served as some of the original sources for the two compilers, who also used monks' biographies, earlier miracle tale collections, and other secular sources.

Because these two collections were compiled by two contemporaries who were a lay Buddhist and a monk respectively, I thought it would be interesting to compare the stories they selected and see if there are significant differences because of their status. Except for the fact that the monk compiler included more sūtras and more monastics, however, I could not find any other striking differences. In fact, there are a number of common features shared by these two collections. First of all, both include the story of Sun Ching-te, the man who received the indigenous *King Kao's Kuan-yin Sūtra*. In addition to Sun, Chou included the story of Lu Ching-yü, and Hung-tsan the story of Wang Hsüan-mo. As described in chapter 3, Lu and Wang were originally identified as the recipients of the revealed sūtra. There is therefore no discernable difference in the compilers' attitudes toward this famous indigenous scripture.

Second, each compiler included the story of Ma-lang-fu (Wife of Mr. Ma) who, also known as Kuan-yin with a fish-basket (Yü-lan Kuan-yin), is one of the most famous feminine manifestations of the bodhisattva. Both relate the story of a beautiful woman fish-seller who came to Shensi in 817. Attracted by her beauty, many young men proposed to marry her. She said that she would marry the man who could memorize the "Universal Gateway" chapter in one night. The next morning twenty men passed the test. She told them that since she could marry only one of them, she had to increase the difficulty. This time she would marry the man who could memorize the *Diamond Sūtra* in one night. The next day, ten people passed the test. Again she had to raise the requirement and asked them to memorize the entire *Lotus Sūtra* in three days. This time only the young man by the name of Ma succeeded. On their wedding day, however, she took ill and as soon as the wedding ceremony was completed, she died and her body immediately started to rot. After she was buried, a foreign monk came to pay her respects and told Ma and the townspeople that she was actually the bodhisattva. Ma-lang-fu was called Fish-basket Kuan-yin in later periods, as we shall read in chapter 10. She would become a favorite subject for paintings and poems written by Ch'an monks, not to mention her appearance in plays, novels, and precious scrolls. More relevant to our concern with the close connection between miracle tales and iconography, she would be canonized as one of the thirty-three forms of Kuan-yin in Sino-Japanese art after the Sung. Although it is sometimes the case that orthodox Buddhist monks refused to recognize the fact that Kuan-yin could appear as a woman, such as Chu-hung's criticism of the legend of Princess Miao-shan as a creation of "vulgar monks" (discussed in chapter 8), this is not the case here. Hung-tsan the monk and Chou K'e-fu the layman apparently shared the same view, that Kuan-yin had indeed manifested as this clever and beautiful fish-seller.

Third, both collections include stories of emperors who either experienced the bodhisattva's efficacious responses or served as protectors of the faith. Interestingly, all of the stories have something to do with Kuan-yin icons. Because I have emphasized the role icons played in the miracle tales and suggested that there was a dialectic relationship between the two media, it will be interesting to examine some of these stories for further proof of my argument.

The story about Emperor Wen-tsung of the T'ang is included in both collections as well as in the Buddhist chronicles *Fo-tsu t'ung-chi*, *Li-tai fo-tsu t'ung-tsai*, and *Shih-shih chi-ku lüeh*. The emperor loved to eat clams and his officials stationed along the coastal areas would regularly send clams as tribute, adding to the burdens of the fishermen. One day in 831 the chef, as usual, was preparing clams for the emperor. But on that occasion the clam was an extraordinarily large one and no matter how he tried, he could not open it. The emperor was informed of this strange event. When he offered incense and prayed to it, the clam opened by itself, revealing a fine image of the bodhisattva inside. The emperor had it enshrined within a sandalwood case lined with damask and sent it to Hsing-shan Monastery for the monks to worship. He asked the court officials for an explanation of this miracle. They suggested sending for the Ch'an master Wei-cheng of Mt. Chung-nan near Ch'ang-an.[10]

Wei-cheng told the emperor that no response was without a cause and the miracle was inspired by the emperor's believing heart. He then told the emperor about the scriptural teaching that the bodhisattva would appear in a form in accordance with the need of the devotee in order to teach him. The emperor asked, "I have now seen the form of the bodhisattva, but I have not heard the teaching." To which the Ch'an master asked, "When you witnessed this, did you think it was usual or unusual? Did you believe or not believe?" The emperor answered that it was unusual but that he had believed and the master said, "Now you have already heard the teaching." Satisfied, the emperor ordered Kuan-yin images to be set up in all the temples in the realm (*Kuan-yin tz'u-lin chi* 478).

A story similar to this one is found in the *Ku-chin t'u-shu chi-ch'eng* (Synthesis of Books and Illustrations of Ancient and Modern Times) except that it happened to Emperor Wen of the Sui (r. 581–604). As a result of the miracle, the emperor stopped eating clams (497:36a). In the *I-chien chih* (Record of the Listener), written by the Sung writer Hung Mai, we find yet another version of the same story. This time it happened to a man by the name of Yü Chi of Li-shui (in present-day Kiangsu). During the Hsüan-ho era (1119–1125) he was traveling on the Huai River, an area that produced a lot of clams. Whenever the boatmen bought the clams for food, he would pay them and then release the clams into the water. One day the boatmen obtained a heavy basketful of clams and were going to cook them. Yü tried to redeem them with twice the purchase price but was refused. When the clams were put into the pot, suddenly a big noise came out of the pot and shortly thereafter, a bright light followed. The boatmen were greatly frightened. When they looked carefully, they saw a huge opened clam, revealing an image of Kuan-yin within the shell. The bodhisattva was surrounded by two bamboo plants, which looked alive. The crown, clothes, necklaces, and bamboo leaves were formed of fine pearls. He instructed the boatmen to repent of their sins and call on Buddha's name. He took the shells back home with him (I:293).

Of the different versions of the story, it seems to me that the last one is probably the most plausible. It is highly unlikely that the story originated with Emperor Wen-tsung. For as Stanley Weinstein tells us, Wen-tsung was hostile toward Buddhism and promulgated an edict to purge the Saṃgha in 835, four years after his supposed conversion as suggested by the story (1987:111). The historicity of the story is not the point under discussion, however. I am more interested in pointing out the link between miracle tales and the iconographic renderings of Kuan-yin. Just as the Fish-basket Kuan-yin is traceable to the story about Mr. Ma's wife, this story is the origin myth for the "Clam-dwelling" Kuan-yin, another one of the thirty-three forms of the bodhisattva popular in China and Japan.

Hung-tsan included two more stories about emperors and Kuan-yin icons, copying almost verbatim from the *Fo-tsu t'ung-chi*, as he did with the story just cited. Emperor Jen-tsung wore a jade crown on which there was an image of Kuan-yin. In 1023 his attendants asked him to wear something else because it was very heavy. He declined, saying, "All the officials who bow to me are men of talent and virtue. I really do not dare to receive their veneration. But because of the hierarchical distinction between the ruler and subjects, there is no way around it. However, when I wear this crown, they are worshiping the bodhisattva instead of me" (*Kuan-yin tz'u-lin chi* 490). This story reminds us of devotees wearing Kuan-yin icons either on the head or behind the neck in the earlier collections. It also reminds us of the iconographical convention of depicting Kuan-yin with Amitābha in his crown, which must have been very familiar to people living in the Sung. The last story is about Li-tsung, who in 1241 dreamt of Kuan-yin sitting among bamboos and rocks. He ordered a stele carved of the image together with a eulogy written by himself. He added the adjective "of broad and extensive efficacious responses" (Kuang-ta Ling-kan) to the title of Kuan-yin.[11] The stone stele was bestowed on the Upper T'ien-chu Monastery in Hangchow (*Kuan-yin tz'u-lin chi* 490–491). By the thirteenth century, the new iconography of Kuan-yin sitting among natural surroundings of rocks and bamboo groves was well established, the earliest prototype being the Water-moon Kuan-yin created in the tenth century. This is another example of how the prevailing Kuan-yin iconography could have predisposed how the emperor saw the bodhisattva in his dream. On the other hand, an image made of Kuan-yin in such a fashion by order of the emperor would undoubtedly lend prestige to that iconography and promote its popularity.

I want to turn now to the last miracle tale collection, published in 1929. This is a huge work compared to the ones discussed so far. Consisting of two volumes of 234 and 167 tales each, it has 401 tales altogether. In contrast to the previous collections, it includes more stories that took place after the Sung, particularly in the Ming and Ch'ing period, those from the T'ang and before occupying only one sixth of the total. It also includes far more stories about laypeople, only fifty-two being monastics (four nuns). This could be because the anonymous compiler was a layperson himself.[12] Like Chou K'e-fu, the lay Buddhist compiler we discussed before, the present compiler also included an indigenous sūtra, the *Kuan-shih-yin san-mei ching* (Sūtra of Kuan-shih-yin's Samādhi), in his scriptural excerpts at the beginning of his work. The other sūtras included are: the *Karuṇāpuṇḍarīka Sūtra*, the *Śūraṅgama Sūtra*, the *Lotus Sūtra*, the *Hua-yen Sūtra*, the *Great Compassion Dhāraṇī Sūtra*, and the "Six-character Mantra" (*Oṃ maṇi padme hūṃ*) from the *Karaṇḍavyūha Sūtra*.

The collection follows a thematic format. The compiler arranges the stories into ten categories, with each category being further subdivided into more minute and specific divisions. While we can discern a rough chronological order, there is, however, considerable skipping through dynasties from one part of the collection to another. In this regard, it differs from the two previous Ch'ing collections, which followed a strict chronological order, modeled undoubtedly upon the Buddhist chronicles and lives of eminent monks. In linking groups of stories to either perils avoided or blessings granted, the compiler wants to validate and verify the scriptural teachings about Kuan-yin. Although much more voluminous than the collection of Lu Kao compiled in 501, the modern collection does share the same organizational principles.

The miracle tales are recorded under thirty-one categories, which are subsumed under ten general categories.

I. Relief from various diseases, 49 stories
   - A. eye diseases, 8 stories
   - B. foot diseases, 6 stories
   - C. throat diseases, 2 stories
   - D. leprosy, 3 stories
   - E. possession, 3 stories
   - F. skin diseases, 5 stories
   - G. stomach and intestinal diseases, 6 stories
   - H. fever, 2 stories
   - I. epilepsy, 1 story
   - J. madness, 1 story
   - K. smallpox, 12 stories

II. Rescue from water and fire, 42 stories
   - A. water, 33 stories
   - B. fire, 9 stories

III. Rescue from imprisonment and other dangers, 55 stories
   - A. from prison, 19 stories
   - B. from other dangers, 36 stories

IV. Obtaining sons and blessings, 58 stories
   - A. obtaining sons, 42 stories
   - B. obtaining other blessings, 16 stories

V. Obtaining wisdom, lengthening lifespan, and resurrection, 30 stories

- A. obtaining wisdom, 8 stories
- B. extension of lifespan, 4 stories
- C. resurrection from death, 18 stories

VI. Reward of filial piety and good rebirth, 30 stories

- A. parents' recovery due to children's filial piety, 7 stories
- B. rebirth in Pure Land, 19 stories
- C. rebirth in heaven, 3 stories
- D. nonretrogression, 1 story

VII. Karmic retribution, 43 stories

- A. immediate karmic retribution in life, 8 stories
- B. meeting King Yama, 1 story
- C. making manifest evil karma, 23 stories
- D. rewarding repentance, 11 stories

VIII. Manifesting divine presence through marvels, 54 stories

- A. by transformations, 7 stories (examples including Wife of Mr. Ma and the clam)
- B. by efficacious anomalies, 23 stories
- C. by supernormal powers, 6 stories
- D. by subduing demons, 18 stories

IX. Manifesting divine presence through overcoming natural disasters, 10 stories

- A. drought, 3 stories
- B. rainfall, 6 stories
- C. driving away locusts, 1 story

X. Manifesting divine presence through light, visions, protection, and instruction, 20 stories

- A. light, 7 stories
- B. visions, 14 stories
- C. protections, 5 stories
- D. quelling rebellions, 3 stories
- E. instruction, 1 story

When we compare the kinds of miracles recorded in this collection with those in the earlier collections, several differences immediately become noticeable. First, while some miracles were never or seldom mentioned in the earlier collections, they become very prominent in this one. One example is praying to Kuan-yin for sons. Although the "Universal Gateway" chapter proclaims that Kuan-yin can enable couples to have sons or daughters, this is not at all an important theme in the early miracle tale collections. As we have seen, the dangers of imprisonment and execution or the perils of drowning and fire are more frequent themes. Only Lu Kao included one story of someone named T'ai who prayed to have a son. He vowed to the monks that only if the son were to be born on the eighth day of the fourth month (birthday of the Buddha), would he consider it to be an auspicious response. A son was indeed born to him on that day and he named it Kuan-shih-yin (No. 55). The two Ch'ing collections, not surprisingly, include more stories about obtaining sons. There are twelve in Chou's collection and thirteen in Hung-tsan's, with three identical stories included in both. Interesting, while Chou only included one story about a monk being born as a result of his mother's prayer to Kuan-yin, Hung-tsan included seven stories of monks born in this fashion, again reflecting his obvious interest in monastics. In the modern collection, forty-two stories are about obtaining sons, by far the most numerous single subcategory among them all. Could this be a reflection of the increasing anxiety about maintaining the lineage structure after the Sung? Could this also be a response to the newly available indigenous sūtras helping people to achieve this goal? Many of these stories make specific reference to the *White-robed Kuan-yin Sūtra* (a simplified title for the *Five Mudrā Dhāraṇī of the Great Compassionate White-robed One Sūtra* discussed in chapter 3). Some of them also stated explicitly that when the baby was born, he was "doubly wrapped in white caul" (*pai-i ch'ung-pao*), a sure sign that this was a gift from the White-robed Kuan-yin. Incidentally, this alerts us to the fact that miracle tales and indigenous scriptures shared the same intellectual and religious discourses. Like the relationship between miracle tales and iconography, there was also the same dialectical and reinforcing relationship between these two media.

Instead of simply being less frequent, some types of miracles included here are not found in earlier collections at all. This again reflects social, technological, and moral changes. I have in mind two examples. One is the increased awareness of and interest in the different types of diseases from which Kuan-yin could save the devotees. Therefore, instead of simply noting that the bodhisattva saved one from illness, we are told the specific kinds of diseases. While none appeared in any of the previous collections, twelve cases of smallpox are found in this one, all of which happened during the Ch'ing. Might the increased attention to the variety of diseases be a reflection of the sophistication of medical knowledge made available through the writing and publication of medical texts in late imperial times? It was not coincidental that smallpox was singled out as a disease from which Kuan-yin could rescue one in these later miracle stories; it was a major disease that caused great concern (Leung 1987; Chang 1996). Knowledge of this disease became available only in the Sung period. According to Charlott Furth, "Sometime in the Sung, physicians had begun to distinguish the symptoms of smallpox from those of other fevers and rashes of childhood and to write about smallpox as a separate medical discipline" (1999:180). Another example is provided by the stories about filial sons, daughters, or daughters-in-law who secretly cut off a piece of flesh from their thighs or arms and serve it as medicine to cure their hopelessly ill parents or parents-in-law. This practice, known as "curing parents by cutting the thigh" (*ke-ku liao-chin*), became quite widespread in the Ming and Ch'ing periods. I discuss it extensively in chapter 8 and argue that we can take this as a case illustrating how Confucian values transformed the cult of Kuan-yin. The inclusion of stories with this theme clearly reflects this new religious practice in late imperial China.

In sum, miracle tales about Kuan-yin are an important and enduring genre in Chinese Buddhism that began in the fifth and sixth centuries and are still being produced and collected today. Miracle tales served as a powerful medium for transforming and domesticating Kuan-yin. Because the stories relate real people's encounters with the bodhisattva in specific times and places and under critical circumstances, Kuan-yin was no longer the mythical figure mentioned in the sūtras, but rather became what Robert Campany calls a "real presence."

I believe that images and paintings of Kuan-yin have played a decisive role in shaping the devotees' visions of the bodhisattva. At the same time, I argue that artistic creations should also be seen in the context of ritual and religious devotion. They were intended to serve as icons. I am particularly interested in tracing the changing visions of Kuan-yin contained in the tales, for I believe that they provide us with important clues to the bodhisattva's new identities in China. While Kuan-yin never appeared as a woman in the early tales, we do find that the bodhisattva appears in several feminine forms in stories after the Sung. This is not surprising, for it was during the same period that feminine forms of Kuan-yin were created by artists. This helps to confirm the intimate connection between art and religious experience. It is perhaps appropriate to repeat what Hu Ying-lin (1551–1602), scholar and bibliophile, had to say on this subject. In the preface to a collection of fifty-three forms of Kuan-yin together with eulogies, entitled *Kuan-yin Ta-shih tz'u-jung wu-shih-san hsien-hsiang tsan* (Eulogies to the Fifty-three Compassionate Manifestations of the Great Being Kuan-yin) that he compiled, he first pointed out that all statues and paintings of Kuan-yin made in his time depicted the bodhisattva as a woman. He then said that all bodhisattvas, not only Kuan-yin but also Mañjuśrī and Samanthabhadra, were dignified and good-looking. But to have Kuan-yin wearing women's clothing was something that had not been done before. He cited examples from earlier miracle tales (some we have examined) to show that Kuan-yin always appeared in the form of a monk. He also cited the famous Sung work, *The Catalogue of Paintings Compiled in the Hsüan-ho Era* (Hsüan-ho hua-p'u), to show that all the renowned T'ang and Sung painters did not depict Kuan-yin as being dressed in women's clothing. He then offered two explanations for Kuan-yin's sexual transformation. First, because of the scriptural teaching about Kuan-yin's manifestations and because Kuan-yin was most frequently worshiped by women, somehow most of the manifestations gradually took on feminine forms. Second and more to the point, "because all the Kuan-yin images nowadays are in the form of a woman, people no longer dream of the bodhisattva as a man. Since people no longer see Kuan-yin appear in a male form in their dreams, they come to think that the bodhisattva is really a woman. But dreams are produced by the mind and verified by the eye. Since the bodhisattva seen by the eye and thought of by the mind is not male, Kuan-yin naturally manifests herself as a female in dreams" (Hu Ying-lin 1980:1a,2a).

Miracle tales about Kuan-yin provide strong evidence for my thesis that Kuan-yin has been worshiped in China by both monastics and laymen and women. In fact, the cult cuts across all social classes. As we have seen, miracle tale collections were compiled by both monks and literati. The collections included stories about people from diverse walks of life who, for a brief moment, experienced a salvific encounter with Kuan-yin, and their lives were subsequently transformed in a profound way. Buddhist sūtras glorifying Kuan-yin received verification from such tales. Scriptural teachings were no longer doctrinal and abstract, but became practical and concrete through the living testimonies of real men and women. At the same time, through their tales about their dreams or visions of Kuan-yin, the devotees helped to make the bodhisattva take on increasingly Chinese manifestations. Avalokiteśvara was in the process transformed and domesticated.

5

Divine Monks and the Domestication of Kuan-yin

As we have read in previous chapters, when Kuan-yin appeared in the dreams and visions of devotees prior to and during the T'ang, he most frequently took the guise of a monk. Even after Kuan-yin's sexual transformation beginning in the Sung, it is still possible for one to encounter the monk's form in miracle stories, although much less frequently, proving the staying power of this early image. Because Buddhism was first introduced into China by foreign missionary monks and the cult of Kuan-yin in China was first promoted by monks, it is only natural that the Chinese people would associate buddhas and bodhisattvas with the monastic community and monks, both foreign and native. Kuan-yin did not, however, only occasionally visit his devotees as a monk. The Chinese rather quickly came to regard certain monks as incarnations of the bodhisattva.

By the eighth century, two monks, Pao-chih (425–514) and Seng-chieh (d. 710) were worshiped as manifestations of the Eleven-headed Kuan-yin. Ennin (793–864), the Japanese pilgrim who visited China from 838 to 847, noted the widespread popularity of the cult of Seng-chieh, who was painted on temple frescoes, represented with statues, and worshiped in special halls dedicated to him in monasteries. Ennin was given a portrait of Seng-chieh as well as a sandalwood shrine containing images of Pao-chih, Seng-chieh, and that of a third monk, Wan-hui, who was a contemporary of Seng-chieh and also believed to be a manifestation of Kuan-yin, as souvenirs (Makita 1984:35). In chapter 8 we shall meet another incarnation of Kuan-yin, Princess Miao-shan, who was regarded by the believers in the twelfth century to be the manifestation of the Thousand-handed and Thousand-eyed Kuan-yin. It is interesting that in some four hundred years, not only the gender and status of the bodhisattva's incarnations changed, but also the bodhisattva's own identity. In one way, the change clearly reflected the changing popularity of the two Tantric forms of the bodhisattva. While the Eleven-headed Kuan-yin enjoyed great popularity in the T'ang, the Thousand-handed and Thousand-eyed Kuan-yin became so in the Sung.

In this chapter, I discuss briefly the lives and careers of Pao-chih and Seng-chieh. Although separated by two centuries and set apart by some important differences in their respective teachings and actions, they do nevertheless share one significant characteristic in common: both monks were thaumaturges. This is, of course, a category that all three Buddhist biographies have recognized. Hui-chiao (497–554), the first to compile the biographies of 257 Chinese monks, put the section on "Divine Wonders" (*shen-i*), which recorded the lives of thaumaturges, after the translators and exegetes, but before the meditators, elucidators of the Vinaya, those who sacrificed themselves, chanters of scriptures, benefactors, hymnodists, and proselytizers. Tao-hsüan (596–667) and Tsan-ning (919–1001) wrote two sequels, covering monks who had lived since Hui-chiao's time and collecting 485 and more than 500 biographies apiece. Although the categories and sequencing were changed, the section on monks who worked wonders is found in both. Now called "Spiritual Resonance" (*kan-t'ung*), it is placed after the translators, exegetes, meditators, elucidators of the Vinaya, defenders of the Dharma, but before those who sacrificed themselves, chanters of scripture, benefactors, and those who have miscellaneous talents.

The secure position the thaumaturges held in the biographies of eminent monks was clearly related to the Chinese fascination with the marvelous and their respect for those who worked wonders. The latter, in turn, was nurtured by the legends about the immortals that had been created by the Chinese indigenous tradition, independent from Buddhism and long before its introduction. Indeed, there is much commonality between the Buddhist wonder-working thaumaturges and the Taoist immortals. Mu-chou Poo compared the contents of *Shen-hsien chuan* (Biographies of the Immortals), commonly attributed to Ko Hung (280–340), one of the greatest Taoists, and Hui-chiao's *Kao-seng chuan* (Biographies of Eminent Monks) and found that "the stories about the immortals and the eminent monks reflected a common mentality: a psychological need for an easy way to salvation; an attempt to control supernatural forces; and urge for solutions to some earthly problems concerning life and death" (1995:172).

Pao-chih and Seng-chieh, moreover, were thaumaturges of a special sort. They were eccentrics noted for their unconventional and startling behavior. In some ways, they anticipated later eccentric figures such as Han-shan and Shih-te, commonly believed to be enlightened Ch'an masters, or divine monks such as the "Cloth-bag Monk" (Pu-tai Ho-shang) and Chi-kung (Master Chi) or Crazy Chi (Chi Tien), who were regarded as incarnations of Maitreya and the "Living Buddha" respectively. Not only did they not represent the values and norms stressed by monastic Buddhism, but by their transgressive life-styles, they posed a challenge to it. Why were such "anti-exemplary" figures celebrated? What does it say about Chinese Buddhism and Chinese religion? Studying Chinese vernacular novels of late imperial times, Meir Shahar finds that the novels constituted an important medium for the transmission of gods' cults. What is surprising to him, however, are the gods depicted in these works: "Most deities as they appear in vernacular novels can be characterized as belonging to one of three groups: women, martial figures, and eccentrics, and all three groups occupied a marginal or problematic position in the usually accepted conception of society" (Shahar 1996:198). Shahar suggests that "the Chinese supernatural, as mirrored in vernacular fiction, was to a large extent an upside-down image of society's official ideology," and like the carnival, the Chinese pantheon "could function as a safety valve and also offer symbolic resources for revolt" (203, 205). Pao-chih and Seng-chieh were eccentrics and Miao-shan was a woman, yet they were believed to be the incarnations of Kuan-yin. Were they chosen as living embodiments of the divine as a relief from orthodoxy and a protest against the established religious authority, be it Buddhist or Confucian?

As I show later in this chapter and in chapter 8, Pao-chih, Seng-chieh and Miao-shan represent alternative ideals and, by doing so, offer compelling challenges to the "official ideology." In attributing new functions to them, however, they were eventually made to uphold the very tradition they criticized. For instance, Pao-chih was credited with the institution of the *Liang-huang ch'an* (Emperor Liang's Penance) and *shui-lu fa-hui* (Dharma Assembly of Water and Land), two very important Buddhist rituals serving the Chinese ancestor cult since the Sung. Seng-chieh was worshiped as the god of the Hui River and invoked by fishermen, sailors, and travelers for a safe journey. Miao-shan, on the other hand, became a symbol of utmost filiality and might have inspired the practice of *ke-ku*, the cult of self-mutilation for the benefit of a dying parent. It is therefore never a simple matter to separate what they originally might have meant to their contemporaries and what the tradition made them mean in later periods. Unless we know more than we do about the entire career of a god or a saint, it is very difficult to give a final verdict. But the sad truth is that we still know far too little about these eccentric "gods." Aside from Meir Shahar's study on Crazy Chi and Makita Tairyō's on Pao-chi and Seng-chieh from which I draw heavily, there has not been any in-depth investigation of these extraordinary and fascinating divine monks.

Although I call them "divine monks" (*shen-seng*), following Chinese convention, they are, for practical purposes, "saints." In fact, the portable sandalwood shrine containing the images of Pao-chih, Seng-chieh, and Wan-hui that Ennin brought back from China was said to contain the "images of three saints" (*san sheng-hsiang*). Until Reginald Ray's book appeared (1994), Buddhist saints had not received serious scholarly attention in either the Indian or the Chinese tradition. It is indeed ironic that this has been the case since, as Ray puts it, "one cannot examine any piece of Buddhist evidence without coming across one or another of these figures, typically associated as they are with the important texts, places, events, lineages, teachings, practices, schools, and movements of Indian Buddhism. The Buddhist saints, at least within the traditional perspective, are an unfailing source of illumination and creativity, and whatever is good may ultimately be traced to them" (1994:3). Ray faults the so-called "two-tiered model" of Buddhism, first advocated by the Theravāda tradition and then eagerly embraced by Western Buddhologists for this long neglect. For according to this view, Buddhism consists of two tiers: monastics and lay Buddhists who pursued different paths and held different values. The cult of the saints, according to this typology, was a manifestation of popular Buddhism (21). He suggests that we should instead adopt a "threefold" model: settled monastics, forest yogis, and householder believers. Saints came out of the forest renunciant tradition (433–447). Although the divine monks such as Pao-chih and Seng-chieh cannot be said to be "forest dwellers," for they actively interacted with emperors, frequented the capital and the palace, or founded temples, they and others like them do seem to differ from regular settled monks. They resembled, in a striking way, the mahāsiddhas (great adepts) of the Vajrayāna tradition. Although they were monks, they did not live within the confines of the monastic grounds or under the constraints of Vinaya rules. Outwardly transgressive and even scandalous, they were, nevertheless, true practitioners of Buddhism and had achieved enlightenment. Such figures, whose numbers are considerable, do seem to warrant a separate category in the scholarship on Chinese Buddhism, which has also long adopted the "two-tiered model."

Pao-chih (425–514)

The earliest account of Pao-chih's life is found in the tomb inscription ("Chih Fa-shih mu-chih-ming") written by Lu Ch'ui (470–526) by order of Emperor Wu of Liang. Lu was born forty-five years after Pao-chih and outlived the latter by twelve years. Hui-chiao, who was born twenty-seven years later than Lu and died twenty-eight years after the latter's death, mentioned the tomb inscription in his biography of Pao-chih, which is included in the *Biography of Eminent Monks* (T 50:394a-395a). The three people, then, were near contemporaries.

Lu Ch'ui was a native of Wu prefecture (present-day Wu county in Kiangsu). He was noted for his erudition and photographic memory. It had been reported that when he was young, he could recite anything after reading it but once. One time he borrowed from someone the *Han shu* (History of the Han Dynasty) and misplaced the four fascicles on the five phases ("Wu-hsing chih"). Based on his memory, he wrote out the missing parts and they turned out to be correct (*Liang shu* 27). He was also a writer of Buddhist essays. Around that time, Fan Chen (ca. 450–515) created a great stir with his essay *Shen-mieh lun* ("On the Extinction of the Soul"), proving that the Buddhist theory of karma and rebirth was untenable. Emperor Wu of Liang, a pious Buddhist, wrote an essay of rebuttal. At the invitation of the monk Fa-yün, sixty-two famous gentry Buddhists joined the battle to defend Buddhism. Lu Ch'ui was one of them who refuted Fan (*Hung-ming chi* 10). Makita estimates that Lu wrote the tomb inscription for Pao-chih when he was forty-five years old (1984:58).

Because it is an inscription on a tomb tablet, Lu's essay is quite short. But some essential points, which were repeated by Hui-chiao, are worth noting. This is what Lu said: except for Pao-chih's surname, which was Chu, very little is known about his early life. In the beginning of the T'ai-shih era (465–471) of the Sung, he began to appear near Mt. Chung and was active in the capital. He looked about fifty or sixty years old at that time and did not show any sign of being different from ordinary people, but around the time when the dynasty changed from Sung to Ch'i [479], he began to show some "efficacious traces" (*ling-chi*). For instance, he let his hair grow long and walked bare-footed. He carried a mirror and pincers at the end of his monk's staff. He sometimes begged for wine and meat, but sometimes went without eating for several days. He could predict the future and read others' minds. He was capable of appearing in several places at the same time. He died in 514 in the buddha hall inside the Hua-lin Garden within the palace. Prior to his death, he moved the image of the temple guardian outdoors and told the other monks that "the bodhisattva is leaving." After that he passed away without any illness within a fortnight (*CLFCC* fascicle 1, in CKFSC 3:368–69).

By contrast, Hui-chiao's biography of Pao-chih is long and detailed. Like Lu Ch'ui, Hui-chiao was also impressed by Pao-chih's eccentric behavior, uncanny ability to predict future events through cryptic expressions, and multiplication of himself. According to Hui-chiao, "At the beginning of the T'ai-shih reign

(465–471) of the Sung (420–479), he suddenly became eccentric and strange: he kept no fixed place of residence, had no regularity in his eating and drinking, and his hair grew several inches longer. He often freely roamed the streets and alleys, clutching a monk's staff from the point of which dangled a pair of scissors and a mirror, and sometimes also a strip or two of silk. During the Chien-yüan reign (479–482) of the Ch'i (479–502), signs of his strangeness were increasingly to be seen. He would not eat for several days, yet he had no appearance of being undernourished. When he spoke with others, his sayings at first seemed incomprehensible but later all were found to be effectual and verified. At times he expressed himself in poetry, and his words were as prophetic accountings" (Berkowitz 1995:582).

Although Pao-chih was friendly with individual monks, he did not live in any one temple permanently. Instead, he wandered around, sometimes staying in the houses of his lay patrons, other times staying temporarily in one temple or another. Emperor Wu of Liang also encouraged him to come and go freely in the palace. Both reported his drinking wine and eating meat or fish, things a monk was forbidden to do. Yet at least in the case of his eating fish, the implication is that he did not really eat it, for the fish was seen later still swimming: "Also at that time [Chih] approached someone and asked for minced raw fish. The man undertook to prepare this for him and went to find some [live fish]. When he had his fill, he [Chih] left. When [the man] turned his gaze back to the basin, the fish was alive and swimming as before" (Berkowitz 1995:582–83).

The biographers did not explain what the implements he carried on his monk's staff meant. They were probably connected with his prophetic function. Mirrors were used to ward off evil and divine the future. But they were usually used by shamans and Taoist priests, and less commonly by monks. The significance of scissors, pieces of cloth, or pincers, is more obscure. In contrast, later accounts either changed some of the things he carried on the staff, or provided new readings for their symbolism.[1]

We learn from Hui-chiao's biography that Pao-chih was knowledgeable about Buddhist scripture and proficient in meditation. That is why he could comment on Fa-yün's lecture on the *Lotus Sūtra*, and engage with Emperor Wu in a Ch'an style encounter dialogue when the latter was troubled by spiritual unrest. But he also proved his qualifications as a traditional Buddhist thaumaturgy by securing rain. What is most striking about the accounts of his contemporaries, however, is that they do not link him with the creation of the Buddhist rituals, nor do they regard him as a manifestation of Kuan-yin. For although he had foreknowledge of his death, showed his "true presence" or signs of a bodhisattva to the Ch'en family, and even referred to himself as "the bodhisattva," neither he nor his contemporaries clearly identified him as Kuan-yin.

Even though Pao-chih was a charismatic thaumaturge, he was not unique. There were probably many others before and after him.[2] His immortality in Chinese Buddhism was certainly connected with the great patronage shown him by Emperor Wu of Liang and, later, Emperor T'ai-tsu of the Ming. When he died, Emperor Wu gave him a lavish funeral, spending 200,000 cash and building a temple at his tomb on a hill at the foot of Mt. Chung. The temple, known as Pao-kung Yüan during the T'ang, became the predecessor of the great Ling-ku Temple in the Ming. T'ai-tsu, the first emperor of the Ming, rebuilt the temple at the Chung-shan Park in Nanking in 1381 in order to utilize the good geomantic location of Pao-chih's tomb, near which the temple had originally stood. The Ming emperor himself was buried on the site of the original temple. Emperor Wu of the Liang had portraits of Pao-chih made and circulated in the country. During the T'ang, he was depicted and eulogized on the famous Stele of the Three Incomparables (*San-chüeh pei*), so named because it brought together the works of the greatest painter of portraits, the greatest poet, and the most outstanding calligrapher. The stele shows the portrait of Pao-chih painted by Wu Tao-tzu (c. 685–758), with a eulogy by Li Po (701–762), and engraved in the calligraphy of Yen Chen-ch'ing (709–785). Although the original stele is no longer extant, a Ming replica is kept in the garden of the Yang-chou Historical Museum and a Ch'ing copy is held at Pao-chih's shrine at the Ling-ku Temple. The Ming stele also bears the twelve poems known as "Songs of the Twelve Temporal Divisions [of the Day]" attributed to Pao-chih, written by the famous Yüan calligrapher Chao Meng-fu (Berkowitz 1995:579–80).

Makita has traced the evolution of Pao-chih's hagiography as constructed by later biographers. In the *Nan shih* (History of the Southern Dynasties), written in the seventh century, a different character with the same pronunciation was chosen for the *pao* in his name. Pao-chih now means "Precious Insignia" instead of the earlier "Preservation of Insignia." This has been the name used by all later writers and is the name by which he is known today. The *Nan shih* also adds more details to the picture of Pao-chih's prophetic prescience by stating that he wore three cloth hats (one on top of each other) when he was summoned by Emperor Wu of Ch'i, implying that there would be three imperial funerals soon. A cloth hat was traditionally worn at funerals. The emperor, his heir apparent, and another prince all died within two years, thus bearing out his prophecy by innuendo. The hat he wore came to be known as "Master Chih's hat" (*Chih-kung mao*) and was prescribed as the proper attire for monks attending funerals. Tao-ch'eng even described how to sew the hat in his *Shih-shih yao-lan* (Essential Readings for Buddhists), which he compiled in 1019. Pao-chih was shown wearing the same hat in a fresco located in Cave 147A at Tun-huang in a picture published by Pelliot in *Touen-Houang* VI (Makita 1984:64).

By the T'ang, Pao-chih was not only regarded to be the manifestation of Kuan-yin, but he was also enshrined as such in Chinese temples visited by Japanese monk pilgrims. The earliest eyewitness report is provided by the monk Kaimei from the Daian Temple, whose biography is found in a record compiled in 1251. Kaimei was in China from 770 to 780 C.E. and made a pilgrimage to Nanking in order to pay his respects to Pao-chih. He visited the shrine of Master Chih and obtained an image of Master Chih as the Eleven-headed Kuan-shih-yin Bodhisattva. When he returned to Japan, he had it enshrined in the middle hall of the South Pagoda Cloister of the Daian Temple for worship. So images of Pao-chih were made in China both for domestic veneration and to be given to Japanese pilgrims as gifts. According to descriptions provided by visitors who saw it in the twelfth century, this was a wooden statue about three Chinese feet (*ch'ih*) tall. It showed Pao-chih tearing his face with hands and thus revealing the form of the bodhisattva. The statue that Kaimei brought back to Japan had long disappeared. But a replica made in the eighteenth century measuring a little over five *ch'ih* is kept in the Saiō Temple in Kyoto (Makita 1984:76).

The strange action of Pao-chih tearing his own face depicted in the image refers to a celebrated story that first appeared in the *Fo-tsu t'ung chi,* compiled by Chih-p'an about 1260. By then, the hagiography of Pao-chih had reached its completion. The story is found in two places under two different rulers. In 482 Emperor Kao of the Ch'i dynasty summoned Pao-chih to the capital. The monk suddenly tore off his face and became "twelve-faced" Kuan-yin. But instead of being impressed, the emperor was annoyed by this, taking it to be a trick to tantalize the masses (T 50:346c). He performed this miracle again in front of Emperor Wu of the Liang dynasty. This happened in 503. The emperor ordered the famous painter Chang Seng-yao (c.480–post 549) to make a portrait of Pao-chih who, again, tore his face with his fingers and revealed Kuan-yin with twelve faces. He constantly changed moods and appearances, fierce in one moment and kind in another, making Chang unable to paint him (348b). The story must have become very popular in the south, for although there is no known iconography of Tantric Kuan-yin with "twelve" heads, Ch'ien Liu, the King of Wu Yüeh, had a devotional wood-block print of the Twelve-headed Kuan-yin made and mass produced in the tenth century (discussed in chapter 6). A copy of this drawing has survived. It shows the main face of the bodhisattva flanked by two other heads on either side and topped by nine smaller heads (figure 6.3). One painting located at the Boston Museum of Fine Arts shows a lohan (arhat) wearing a mask of multiheaded Kuan-yin. This was originally part of the group known as the "Five Hundred Lohans" painted by the Ningpo artisan Chang Chi-ch'ang about 1178 and kept at the Daitokuji in

Kyoto. We see in the foreground a painter holding a brush and his friend holding a piece of paper on which a half-finished portrait is barely discernible (figure 5.1). This must be none other than Chang Seng-yao, the same artist who could not complete Pao-chih's portrait.

Although the *Fo-tsu t'ung-chi* states that these incidents happened in 482 and 503, they are clearly apocryphal. The earliest translation of the Eleven-headed Kuan-yin sūtra, that by Yeh-she-ch'üeh-t'o, did not appear until 570, some seventy years after the reported portrait session with Chang. As Makita rightly observes, this story most likely arose during the last quarter of the eighth century, during 745–770, after Amoghavajra translated the sūtra setting forth the rules for reciting the Eleven-headed Kuan-yin sūtra and when Tantric Buddhism was enjoying its height of popularity (78). As for the portrait of Pao-chih, despite Hui-chiao's statement that Emperor Wu of Liang distributed it all over the land, the first literary record of such a painting was the one done by Fan Ch'iung during the reign of Wen-tsung (r. 827–840) mentioned in Mi Fu's *Hua shih* (History of Paintings), completed around 1103. During the latter part of the T'ang, Pao-chih became a popular subject chosen for temple murals (72). Ennin visited the Li-ch'uan Temple on Mt. Ch'ang-pai in Shantung on his way to Mt. Wu-t'ai in 840. He stated matter-of-factly that Pao-chih was the incarnation (*hua-shen*, "transformation body") of the Eleven-headed Kuan-yin. He reported that according to local legend, Pao-chih manifested himself and entered nirvāṇa there. Moreover, his flesh body (*jou-shen*) had once been there, but after it disappeared, a statue was enshrined in the "Glazed Hall" (Liu-li Tien), so called because all the pillars, doors, and steps were made of green stones. There was a well to the west of the temple that was originally filled with fragrant water. Anyone who drank of it would be cured of diseases. After Pao-chih died, the well also dried up. But it was still shown to pilgrims. Seijin, who came to China more than two hundred and thirty years after Ennin, also reported about his veneration of Pao-chih's image enshrined in the Ch'i-jung Yüan, a temple south of the famous T'ai-p'ing hsing-kuo Ssu in K'ai-feng in 1072. He described the image representing Pao-chih as being thin and black, with his arm uplifted showing his hand from underneath the sleeve (76–77). A sculpture of Pao-chih stands on the cliff of the number 2 niche on Shih-chuan Shan, Ta-tsu, Szechwan. The inscription on the top of the niche states that it was carved in 1083 and records that Emperor Wu of Liang once asked Pao-chih if there was a medicine that would enable one to retain the human body forever.[3] According to *Szechwan t'ung-chih* (General Gazetteer of Szechwan) compiled during the Yung-cheng era (1723–1735), Pao-chih died in the Pei Chih-kung Ssu in Chien-ch'uan (present-day Chien-ke) of Szechwan (46). Thus, as his cult developed, it was no longer confined to Nanking, but spread to Shan-

Figure 5.1. Lohan manifesting himself as the Eleven-headed Kuan-yin, dated ca. 1178 by Chang Chi-ch'ang. *Courtesy of the Museum of Fine Arts, Boston (Denman Waldo Ross Collection).*

tung, Honan, and Szechwan, among other places. Moreover, as with the case of Li-ch'uan Ssu in Shantung visited by Ennin, a temple in Szechwan also claimed to be the place where the saint passed away.

Pao-chih's connection with Buddhist rituals is also a product of hagiography. *Fo-tsu t'ung-chi* describes how the Water-Land Ritual began under the Emperor of Liang. In the eleventh month of the year 503 the emperor had a dream in which a divine monk (*shen-seng*) asked him to perform a great "Water-Land Feast" (*shui-lu ta-chai*) in order to universally save the dead who were suffering in the six realms of rebirth and experiencing the four ways of being born (from eggs, embryos, moisture, and self-transformation). Upon waking, the emperor read the Buddhist canon extensively and took three years to compile a ritual manual. He then held the service at the Chin-shan Temple and ordered the monk Seng-yu to officiate at it. Many efficacious responses resulted from it (T 50:348c). As one can clearly see, there is no mention of Pao-chih's role in the creation of the ritual here at all. An even earlier Sung text, the *Ching-te ch'uan-teng lu* (Transmission of the Lamp Compiled in the Ching-te Era) completed in 1004 also did not mention the ritual in its biography of Pao-chih, although it retained many miraculous stories about him.

Pao-chih has been credited not only with the creation of the Water-Land ritual, but also with the "Emperor of Liang's Confession" from at least the Ming on. These are two of the most popular Buddhist mortuary rituals and they are still widely performed today. Because the rituals consist of chanting sūtras (*ching*) and performing penances (*ch'an*), they are called *ching-ch'an* for short. The service ends with offering food to the dead (*shih-shih*). According to Buddhism, due to the evil karma people commit while alive, they become hungry ghosts after death. As such, they perpetually suffer from hunger and thirst. Only food and drink offered by monks at properly performed rituals can relieve their suffering. Although no one wants to believe that his dead family members have become hungry ghosts, there is always a possibility that this might be the case. And even if it is not so, the sponsoring of such rites will unfailingly generate a great deal of merit, which can be transferred to the dead relatives to help them receiving a good rebirth. It can also bring blessing to oneself in the present life in the form of health, wealth, and long life. For this reason, these rites have always been very popular in China. The performance of such rituals brought income to the temples. In this century, income from such services became a major source of the monks' livelihood. Of all the Buddhist mortuary rites, the Water-Land Assembly is the most elaborate, lasting for seven days. Holmes Welch, who calls the ritual "plenary mass," describes it as "the *tour de force* among rites for the dead . . . very large, very long, and very expensive" (1967:160). In 1934, a prominent Buddhist monk, Fa-fang (1904–1951), commented sadly on the prominence of ritualism in Chinese monasteries: "In every temple of China, although the placard on the main gate says it is such-and-such Meditation Hall, inside the Meditation Hall one realizes that it has been changed into the Hall for Chanting Sūtras and Reciting Penances (*ching-ch'an t'ang*) or the Inner Altar of the Water-Land (*shui-lu nei-t'an*). As for the monks living there, even though they call themselves Ch'an monks, they are simply monks specializing in chanting sūtras and reciting penances" (Makita 1984: 213).

The origin of the Water-Land rite is still unclear. But according to Makita's research, it probably dates from the late T'ang, becoming popular during the Sung when it was performed for the imperial ancestors and the wife of Su Shih (1037–1101) in Ch'eng-tu, Szechwan. It was conducted for the ruling families of the Yüan and the Ming. By the late Ming, it had become so popular that Chu-hung felt the need to revise the text of the rules for the ceremony (Makita 1984:221–23; Teiser 1988:108; Yü 1981:148, 299–300). The full title of the revised text is *Fa-chieh sheng-fan shui-lu sheng-hui hsiu-chai i-kuei* (Ritual Rules for Conducting the Solemn Assembly of Water and Land for Saints and Mortals of the Dharma Realm). It is so named because the Water-Land ritual is an elaborate and all-inclusive banquet to which the souls of all dead sentient beings are invited. When we examine the lists of invited "guests," we get an excellent picture of the Chinese vision of the other world. Not only buddhas and bodhisattvas, but also Taoist gods, popular deities of mountains and rivers, the God of Mt. T'ai and the other gods of the infernal courts, as well as the gods of earth, grains, wind, and rain are included. The invited souls from the realm of the dead represent all social classes. They include not only emperors and ministers, but also Confucian scholars, merchants, farmers, artisans, and soldiers, and Buddhist and Taoist clergy. As the name of the ritual indicates, all people who have died on land and in the water will receive spiritual succor and material sustenance. Thus, even suicides, women who died in childbirth, and aborted fetuses are invited to attend. Water-Land scrolls depicting the invited spirits mentioned in the manual text were made and they would be hung along the temple walls when the ritual was performed. Some Ming specimens have survived. An intact set consisting of 139 scrolls made for the "Water-Land Hall" of Pao-ning Temple in Shansi has been published (*Pao-ning Ssu Ming-tai shui-lu hua* 1988). They have been dated to 1460 based on the style and information found in the colophons. A finer set dated to 1454, unfortunately, has been separated, with thirty-four in the Musée Guimet and two in the Cleveland Museum of Art (Weidner 1994:282).

In the postscript, Chu-hung explains the reason why he decided to revise the manual text. The origin myth of the ritual also receives some new twists. He begins by saying that according to tradition, the ritual text of Water and Land was first created by Emperor Wu of Liang. General Pai Ch'i of the Chin once buried 400,000 people alive in the third century B.C.E. Because of the enormity of his sin, he was consigned to hell for eternity with no hope of relief. He visited Emperor Wu in a dream and asked for help. The emperor consulted Master Chih and others for a way to save him. Chih told the emperor that there was a ritual text in the Buddhist canon. After the text was put together, the emperor prayed for a sign. The whole hall lighted up with brilliance, and he took this as a sign that the text met divine approval. This is how the ritual came to be handed down. But during Chu-hung's own time, the manual used at Chin-shan Temple had become confused, the officiating monks often did what they liked, and different ways of conducting the rite became the norm. He was also much distressed by the lack of uniformity in the paintings hung in the inner and outer altars when the ritual was performed. He therefore decided to use the version written by Chih-p'an as the basis for the ritual. He liked Chih-p'an's text because it was concise and simple. But because the text was only available in Ssu-ming (present-day Ningpo, Chekiang), he had it printed after verifying and revising it so that it could be circulated widely (*YCFH* 19, 6:13b–14a).

Chih-p'an, the author of the manual text kept at Ssu-ming, was the same monk who wrote the *Fo-tsu t'ung-chi*. Since he was the compiler of the ritual manual, it is no wonder that we do not read of his mentioning Pao-chih as the creator of the Water and Land ritual. Ou-i Chih-hsü (1599–1655), a younger contemporary of Chu-hung, provided some additional information about the evolution of the ritual. Significantly, he mentioned that the ritual was not performed during the Sui. According to him, during the Hsien-heng era (670–673) of the T'ang, Master Tao-ying of the Fa-hai Ssu in Ch'ang-an had a dream in which the God of Mt. T'ai came to ask him to preach the Dharma. After this, when he was sitting alone in the abbot's quarters, a strange-looking man appeared and told Tao-ying that he had previously seen the monk at the palace of the God of Mt. T'ai. He then informed the master of the Water and Land rite, which could universally benefit the dead. The text, which was originally compiled by Emperor Wu of Liang, was now kept by a monk named I-chi of the Ta-chüeh Ssu in Kiangsu. He begged the master to go and get it so that he could perform the ritual. Tao-ying agreed to the request. He obtained the text as predicted and conducted the ritual. The strange-looking man again appeared, accompanied by several dozen people, to thank him. It turned out that he was the ghost of King Chuang-hsiang (r. 249–247 B.C.E.) of the Chin dynasty, and his followers were all violent generals who served under him. They were all condemned to suffer in hell. Formerly when Emperor Wu performed the ritual, all the evil officials under King Chou of the Shang dynasty were released, while they themselves had also enjoyed some temporary relief. But because their "cases" were not resolved, they could not be finally released. But now due to the power of the ritual performed by Tao-ying, they would be reborn as human beings. From then on, Tao-ying constantly performed the ritual.

During the Hsien-chung era (1265–1274) of the Southern Sung, Chih-p'an wrote a new manual and had twenty-six Water-Land paintings made to be hung during the ritual. Since that time, the ritual had been continuously performed in the Yüan and Ming. When Ou-i visited Chin-shan Temple in 1646, he asked to see the manual used there and found it very confusing. This was because successive abbots since the Yüan had made many changes in order to make the rite more dramatic and lively. It came to be known as the "Northern Water and Land." By contrast, the ritual based on Chih-p'an's manual was known as the "Southern Water and Land." Ou-i praised Chu-hung for choosing the latter as the basis for his revision. According to Ou-i's testimony, the regulation of the revised ritual was very strict. Only nine persons were allowed to be inside the inner altar: the officiating monk, the sponsor of the ritual, two monks chanting the text, and five monks taking care of incense and candles. Everyone else had to stay outside the curtain if they wanted to watch. Whenever the person in the inner altar left it, before he could reenter, he had to purify himself by taking a bath and changing into a clean set of clothes (*Ling-feng Ou-i Ta-shih tsung lun* 7, 4:12a-13b, quoted by Makita 1984:226).

The biography of Pao-chih contained in the gazetteer of Ling-ku Temple (*Chin-ling fan-ch'a chih*, fascicle 3) compiled at the end of the Ming also credits Pao-chih as originator of the "Emperor Liang's Confessional," a penance ritual popular since the Sung. The story goes like this: Several months after the emperor's wife, Ms. Hao, died, a large python suddenly appeared in the palace one day and started to speak to the emperor. It identified itself as the dead Ms. Hao. Because she was jealous while alive and cruel in her treatment of the other members of the imperial harem, she was turned into a python. She suffered constant pain. Not only was she unable to eat or drink, but there was no place where she could seek shelter. On top of all this, she was constantly being gnawed by insects. Because the emperor loved her in the past, it had now come to seek his help. After saying this, the python crept away. The emperor called all the learned monks together the next day and asked what was to be done. Pao-chih answered that the only way was to perform a ritual of penance and confess one's sins. So a text for the penance was compiled consisting of ten fascicles and a ritual of confession was performed for the sake of the dead concubine. After that, one day the palace was filled with a strange fragrance. When the emperor looked up, he saw a heavenly figure (*t'ien-jen*) of great beauty who told him that she had been transformed from the form of a python. Because of the merit of the ritual, she had now been reborn in the Tuṣita Heaven (CKFSC 3:378–89).

It seems to me that these popular Buddhist rituals were attributed to Pao-chih because of his close relationship with Emperor Wu of Liang. Since the latter was the greatest Buddhist ruler in Chinese history, his prestige was conveniently utilized to promote these rituals. But because the emperor was a layman, Pao-chih had to be made into his teacher and guide. In fact, conversations between Emperor Wu and Pao-chih have been taken by a number of apocryphal writings for their setting. There is, for instance, a work called "Emperor Wu of Liang Asks Master Chih" (*Liang Wu wen Chih-kung*) among the Tun-huang manuscripts. This undoubtedly was inspired by the story about the emperor seeking spiritual advice from Pao-chih, first reported by Hui-chiao. In the *Transmission of the Lamp* (fascicle 29), thirty-six poems are attributed to Pao-chih. Ten poems praise the Great Vehicle, twelve poems are on the twelve divisions of the day, and fourteen poems discuss the fourteen kinds of nonduality. The poems on the "twelve divisions of the day" must again refer to Pao-chih's answer to the emperor's question about the way to deal with his insomnia due to his spiritual unrest, as reported in Hui-chiao's biography. They are typical Ch'an gāthās, however, and, as Makita rightly observes, clearly written by later authors (1984:70). Early this century, a popular novella entitled *Wu Ti wen Chih-kung Chang-lao yin-kuo ching* (Sūtra of Emperor Wu's Asking Master Elder Chih about Causes and Consequences) was published in 1910 in Fukien. Makita has examined it and finds it full of references to events happening in the Ming and Ch'ing, particularly concerning monastic abuses. He suggests that the author was attempting to criticize the Saṃgha, using Pao-chih as a mouthpiece. But the work begins with the story about the emperor and the large python (Makita 1984:84), giving evidence for the enduring fame of this origin myth.

In the centuries after Pao-chih's death, some myths built him up as a specialist on Buddhist rituals and a scholar of Buddhist scriptures, while others exaggerated his eccentricity. The tenth century *T'ai-p'ing kuang-chi* (fascicle 90), for instance, records a story about him not found in Hui-chiao's biography: "He was fond of using urine to wash his hair, and someone among the common monks secretly jeered and scoffed. Now Chih equally knew that many of the monks had not forsaken wine and meat, and that the one who had ridiculed him drank wine and ate pork intestines. Chih of a sudden said to him, 'You scoff at me for using piss to wash my head, but why is it that you eat bags full of shit?'" (Berkowitz 1995:579).

The two faces of Pao-chih, the codifier of rituals and the monastic rebel, do not seem to have much to do with each other. We may also wonder what does the image (or images) of the divine monk have to do with Kuan-yin. On the surface, not very much. But on a deeper level, perhaps a great deal. Buddhist mortuary rituals are conducted for the benefit of the living and the dead. They aim for the universal salvation of all sentient beings. Kuan-yin, as we already know well, is the bodhisattva of compassion par excellence. Chapter 2 introduced us to the role of Kuan-yin as revealer of dhāraṇīs and *sādhana*s in many Tantric sūtras, including those of the Eleven-headed Kuan-yin. The correct knowledge of the rules provided in the *sādhana*s and the exact execution of them are essential for making one's wishes come true. Kuan-yin himself is often the teacher. The Water and Land Rite and the Emperor Wu's Confessional are of course Chinese creations, but they incorporate Tantric elements. What better way to domesticate Kuan-yin than by making a Chinese monk his incarnation who can then teach rituals perfectly suited to the Chinese cultural context?

As for the image of the rebel, Pao-chih has his female counterparts in Miao-shan, Mr. Ma's Wife, and the Woman of Yen-chou, figures we shall meet in chapters 8 and 10. All of them break away from social conventions in order to teach a spiritual lesson. They compel people to question the superficial values of society so that they can find true realization. In this regard, these figures are good representatives of the bodhisattva. They are excellent teachers of *fang-pien* (skillful means), one of the cardinal virtues of Mahāyāna Buddhism.

Pao-chih was not only seen as a rebel and an incarnation of the Eleven-headed Kuan-yin, but as a savior to people facing disasters at the end of the kalpa in his own right. This last point is highlighted in a popular religious tract known variously as the *Wu-kung ching* (Sūtra of the Five Masters), or *Chuan-t'ien-tu ching* (Sūtra of the Heaven-turning Daigram), which has been studied by a Taiwanese scholar (K'e 1983, 1987, 1988). It was first created at the end of the T'ang period to lend legitimacy to a popular uprising led by a commoner, Ch'iu Fu, in eastern Chekiang. Although the rebellion lasted for only eight months in 859 and 860, rebel leaders in later times seemed to continue using the text to bolster their claims. This text was singled out for destruction in the Sung and Ming periods, for instance, in 1124, 1418, and 1474. Even official prohibitions have apparently failed to end its circulation. During the Taiwanese anti-Japanese uprising of 1915, the leader Yü Ch'ing-fang used this same text to motivate his followers. Copies of this text are still being printed and distributed for free as one of the morality books.

The text is composed in a mixture of prose and rhymed verses consisting of either seven or five characters. It is thus similar to the T'ang transformation texts. Kuan-yin predicts that wars and pestilence will descend on the land and cause great devastation. The five masters who are called "bodhisattvas" and are understood to be manifestations of Kuan-yin are headed by Pao-chih. In order to save people from the impending disaster, Kuan-yin together with these five write out eighty-one spells (*fu*) on top of Mt. T'ien-t'ai. When faced with war or pestilence, one should carry these spells for protection. The text contains many predictions for the future, all worded in enigmatic riddles, chief among which is the coming of a messiah-like king who will save the suffering people.

As K'e points out, the fact that Pao-chih was famous for his penchant of making riddle-like predictions and his reputed connection with Kuan-yin is most likely the reason why he became the protagonist of this text. That he could be turned into a revealer of saving spells in a popular religious tract created in eastern Chekiang in the ninth century gives us further evidence for the national fame of not only Pao-chih, the divine monk, but also Kuan-yin, of whom he was an incarnation.

Seng-chieh (617–710)

If Pao-chih remains a divine monk and saint even after his hagiographic transformation, Seng-chieh, the other incarnation of Kuan-yin, succeeds in becoming a god. The main difference between the two is that Seng-chieh was the founder of a temple that eventually became a holy site and the center of his cult. This temple was the P'u-kuang-wang Ssu (Temple of the Universal Light King) located in Lin-huai of Ssu-chou (present-day Ssu-hung, Kiangsu). We have encountered the name of this temple in chapter 3. The third fascicle of an indigenous sūtra probably composed during the T'ang tells the miracle story of how a magistrate borrowed some money from the P'u-kuang-wang Temple, how he tried to drown the young novice from the temple who accompanied him on the trip, and how the latter escaped danger because he was carrying the dhāraṇī sūtra on his body as a talisman. The miracle story testified to the fame of that temple and served, in turn, to broadcast its name and make it even more famous.

Like the case of Pao-chih, one can also trace the transformation of Seng-chieh from a charismatic monk into a divinity. According to Makita Tairyō (1984:28–34), the earliest account about him is the stele inscription about the temple written by Li I (673–742), a younger contemporary of Seng-chieh (*Wen-yüan ying-hua*, fascicle 858). Entitled "Stele of the Great T'ang Universal Light King Temple in Lin-huai County of Ssu-chou" ("Ta-T'ang Ssu-chou Lin-huai hsien P'u-kuang-wang Ssu pei"), the essay is elegant and flowery. It presents Seng-chieh as an eminent monk characterized by his compassion for the common people. But there is nothing strange or eccentric about him. It says that Seng-chieh was a foreigner, hailing from a country in Central Asia. In 661 he came to Lin-huai by the Huai River, and feeling pity for the suffering of the people, decided to build a temple in honor of P'u-chao-wang (Universally Shining King) Buddha. Since that time, men and women near and far, as well as all the boatmen sailing up and down the Huai River, all came to venerate him. They would come to the temple and pray to the Buddha for safety. When they met the master and were impressed by his exalted conduct, they were willing to make donations that further beautified the temple.

Emperor Chung-tsung (r. 684–710) invited him to the palace chapel and asked him to give lectures on the Dharma. The emperor bestowed a placard on the temple. He also had the original name of the temple, P'u-chao-wang, changed to P'u-kuang-wang in order to avoid the taboo character *chao*, which was utilized in one epithet of Empress Wu Tse-t'ien. Seng-chieh died while sitting in meditation on the second day of the third month in 710 in the Chien-fu Temple in Ch'ang-an. The emperor served the master as a disciple and wrapped the master's body with lacquered cloth to preserve it. He gave special permission to seven disciples of the master to be ordained, provided them with three hundred bolts of silk, and gave orders that the funeral party be escorted all the way back to Ssu-chou at government expense. Three days later, they returned to P'u-kuang-wang Temple and buried him. When the faithful came to the tomb to confess their sins, they would be protected against danger and obtain blessings thereafter. Many miraculous responses became widely known and the devotees of the master became numerous.

Seng-chieh appears in this earliest record as an extraordinarily charismatic monk. His close relationship with Emperor Chung-tsung, like that between Pao-chih and Emperor Wu, is also very striking. There is, however, no mention about his being a manifestation of Kuan-yin. Although his fame was directly connected with the temple he founded, we are not told why he chose to build the temple in that particular place, nor why he chose to venerate this particular buddha as the main icon.

More details are provided by later records, which also answer some of these questions. The *T'ai-p'ing kuang-chi* (fascicle 96), compiled some two hundred years after the stele, provides us with several important new pieces of information. Seng-chieh came to Lin-huai with the clear intention of building a temple. When he dug up the ground he found a stele with the name of Hsiang-chi Ssu [of the Ch'i dynasty] and a gilt bronze buddha image with the name "P'u-chao-wang" inscribed on it. That was why he built the temple with this name on that very spot. He was invited to court by Emperor Chung-tsung in 708, honored with the highest title of "National Preceptor" (Kuo-shih).

Several things mark Seng-chieh as an eccentric thaumaturge. He was said to have been able to cure people of their chronic diseases with the water in which he had washed his feet. One time when the emperor remarked that for several months there had been no rain in the capital, and that he was worried about a drought, Seng-chieh began to sprinkle water from a bottle. Soon, to the emperor's great delight, clouds gathered and there was a great downpour. Perhaps the most amazing thing about Seng-chieh is that he was said to have a hole on the top of his head. He normally would plug up the hole with cotton. But when he was alone in his room at night, he would take out the cotton and a wonderful incense smell would emerge from the hole and fill the entire room with vapor. In the morning, the incense fragrance would return to the hole, which he would then stuff tight with cotton again.

When he died, the emperor was going to erect a stūpa and bury him in Chien-fu Ssu, the temple where he died. But a strong wind suddenly blew and a terrible stink from his corpse filled the air of Ch'ang-an. When the emperor asked for an explanation for this strange omen, an official told him that because the master was from Lin-huai, this was probably a sign that he wanted to return there. As soon as the emperor silently agreed, the stink evaporated and was replaced by a wondrous fragrance. Later the emperor asked master Wan-hui, "What kind of personage was the great master Seng-chieh?" To which Wan-hui answered, "He was the transformation body of Kuan-yin (*Kuan-yin hua-shen*). It is just as the 'Universal Gateway' of the *Lotus Sūtra* says, 'If a person can only be converted by a monk or a nun, then [Kuan-yin] will appear as one of these to convert him.' What I mean is exactly this." Earlier, when the master first came to Ch'ang-an, Wan-hui treated him with great respect. The master patted him on the head, saying, "Why are you tarrying here so long, youngster? It is time to go!" After Seng-chieh died, within a few months, Wan-hui also passed away (*T'ai-p'ing kuang-chi* 1961, vol. 2:638).

Tsan-ning's *Sung Kao-seng chuan*, which was finished in 988, not too long after the *T'ai-p'ing kuang-chi*, contains a much longer biography (fascicle 18, T 50:822a-823a). This can be seen as the third stage in the creation of Seng-chieh's hagiography. First, Seng-chieh is identified not just as a manifestation of Kuan-yin, but specifically the manifestation of the Eleven-headed Kuan-yin: "He once slept in the house of Ho Pa. Suddenly his body increased in size and grew more than three *ch'ih* wider and longer than his bed. All were amazed. He next took the form of the Eleven-headed Kuan-yin." The Ho family was so impressed that they donated their house to be converted into the temple. When the foundation was dug, it was discovered that the ancient Hsiang-chi Temple once stood on the same site. This was how the P'u-kuang-wang Temple came to be built. Second, Seng-chieh also emerges as an even greater thaumaturge here. He once cured the imperial son-in-law with the water from the bottle he carried. The water bottle was identified as *ts'ao-kuan* (*kuṇḍikā*), which, as shown in chapter 2, was an attribute of Kuan-yin's iconography. After this his fame as a healer spread. When he was asked to cure someone, he would sometimes brush them with a willow branch (another attribute of Kuan-yin's iconography), while sometimes he ordered them to wash the stone lions who guarded the palace gate, sometimes he threw his water bottle at them, or he simply asked them to confess their sins. Like Pao-chih, he could foretell future events and appear at different places simultaneously. Third, he became a guardian deity of Ssu-chou. Even after he died in 710, he continued to protect the region. In 821, he sang a song at midnight in front of Prefect Su's bedroom. The song went, "South of the Huai River and north of the Huai River, there will be blessings from today. From the east to the west, nothing will fail to ripen." Subsequently, in that year, only Lin-huai enjoyed a good harvest.

In 866 Ssu-chou was attacked by the followers of a renegade rebel soldier. The city was surrounded by them. Seng-chieh manifested himself on top of the stūpa and the enemy all fell asleep. When the soldiers within the city sallied forth and made a surprise attack, the siege was lifted. This miracle was reported to the court and he was given the title "Great Master of Verified Sainthood" (Cheng-sheng Ta-shih). He saved the city two more times, in 888 and 890, by manifesting himself and frightening away the attackers. Then in 894 he appeared in a dream to the prefect T'ai Meng and told the latter, "Coldness and the southeast is without defense." T'ai did not understand what it meant, so he burned quilted robes and sent them to Seng-chieh as an offering, thinking perhaps that the master was cold in the other world. One night, in the middle of the twelfth month, enemy soldiers climbed over the city gate without T'ai's knowledge. He then dreamt of a monk who touched his heart with his staff. T'ai felt a coldness penetrating to his bones. When he woke up with a start, he ordered bugles sounded. The attackers were startled and ran away, and the ringleader was captured. Only then did T'ai understand the significance of the earlier dream.

Seng-chieh often appeared on top of the stūpa as a young monk. People throughout the entire prefecture had faith in him. Those who prayed for wind (for sailing boats) would get wind and those who prayed for sons would get sons. If he was seen smiling, this was a good omen and if he was not smiling, it was a bad omen. When Shih-tsung of the Latter Chou attacked Ssu-chou in 957, Seng-chieh told everyone in their dreams that they should not take the enemy lightly. As a result of this warning, the prefect decided not to fight back but surrendered. The entire prefecture of Ssu-chou thus did not suffer any loss of life. Tsan-ning concludes by saying that in his days wherever a new temple was constructed, a true likeness of Seng-chieh was always installed. The identification tag beside the images would read "Monk Seng-chieh, the Great Saint" (Ta-sheng Seng-chieh Ho-shang). When people prayed to him, whatever they wished to obtain, he would satisfy them.

By the early Sung, Seng-chieh had clearly been transformed from an eminent monk to a divine one. He was regarded not only as the incarnation of the Eleven-headed Kuan-yin, but also the local patron deity of Ssu-chou. Like Kuan-yin, he responded to people's prayers and saved his devotees from diseases, the ravages of wars, and drought. He bestowed sons on them, wind for smooth sailing and bountiful harvests. The *Ching-te ch'uan-teng lu* (Transmission of the Lamp) adds another detail to highlight Seng-chieh's connection with Kuan-yin by stating that "he carried a willow branch in his hand and mingled with the monastics and lay people in the Wu [Kiangsu and Chekiang] and Ch'u [Kiangsi, Hupei and Anhui] regions" (1968:157). P'u-kuang-wang Temple, in the meantime, also became a pilgrimage center and generated popular religious fervor and even fanatic enthusiasm. According to the *Sung shih* (History of the Sung Dynasty), during the reign of T'ai-tsung (960–976), the stūpa of Seng-chieh shone during the daytime, and as a result, several thousand people immolated themselves by burning off fingers, lighting incense sticks on their heads or cutting off their arms. Officials had no way of stopping them (*T'ai-tsung shih-lu* 27). Under the year 1015, the *Fo-tsu t'ung-chi* records that there was a drought in the ninth month. Monk Chih-wu of Ssu-chou was invited to the capital to pray for rain. Once when he prayed for rain in Ssu-chou, he was successful and cut off one arm afterwards. He now vowed that he would cut off the other arm if it rained within seven days. Five days later, it rained, and he cut off the arm. The emperor dispatched messengers to bring medicine to him, but he said it was all right. When people looked at him, to their great amazement, the place where the arm was severed showed no blood. The prefect and commoners all had the same dream in which Seng-chieh told them that Chih-wu was one of the five hundred lohans (arhats) who had come to the earth to save people (T 49:405b). As we shall read more in chapters 7 and 8, religious zeal represented by self-immolation and suicide seemed to be a common phenomenon in medieval China. Although this incident fits the general pattern of religious practices at that time, it also tells us the great attraction of the saint and the site.

Japanese monk pilgrims provided vivid eyewitness accounts of the enormous popularity of Seng-chieh's cult in the late T'ang and Sung dynasties. They saw his images enshrined in temples, portraits painted on temple walls, and special halls called "Seng-chieh Halls" dedicated to his worship in the temple compounds. The cult was not limited to Ssu-chou, but had spread to other parts of China. Instead of being just a god of the Huai River, he was also worshiped by people who had to navigate other rivers and the Chinese coastlines. For instance, Ennin visited K'ai-yüan Temple in Teng-chou (in present-day Shantung) in 840 and reported seeing frescoes of the Western Paradise and Potalaka Pure Land painted on the north wall of the Seng-chieh Hall, located in the western corridor of the temple. Makita rightly takes this as another indication of Seng-chieh's being identified with Kuan-yin, because the latter is intimately connected with Potalaka and the Western Paradise (Makita 1984:35).

Seijin reported that in 1072 when he landed in China, he visited the "Hall of the Great Master of Ssu-chou" on top of Mt. Tung-ju (in Ningpo) and saw several wooden images of Seng-chieh enshrined there. He was told that travelers and sailors always came here to pray for safety on the water. Wooden images of Seng-chieh were particularly worshiped as possessing talismanic power. He was presented an embroidered portrait of Seng-chieh by the boat owner and told that all those who came from or went to Japan must worship it for a blessing. When he visited the Kuo-ch'ing Temple on Mt. T'ien-t'ai, he saw the image of Seng-chieh enshrined in the Penance Hall of the great T'ien-t'ai master Chih-i together with images of Chih-i himself, and the Sixteen Lohans. When he sailed along the Huai River to go to Lin-huai, he was given a copy of the "Biography of the Great Master of Ssu-chou" by the boat owner, further indicating Seng-chieh's popularity among sailors. Seijin also provides information about the presence of Seng-chieh's cult in K'ai-feng, the capital. He mentions in particular what he saw in Fu-sheng Ch'an-yüan. In the east hall the image of Seng-chieh was surrounded by sūtras, and in the Relic Stūpa, the central image of Śākyamuni Buddha was flanked by the image of Maitreya on the east and that of Seng-chieh on the west (Makita 1984:37–38).

Seng-chieh was, of course, not popular only among the common people. The famous T'ang poet Li Po wrote a poem called "Song of Seng-chieh" ("Seng-chieh ko") in which he spoke of the master's discussion with him regarding the "three carts" (*san-ch'e*, a reference to the *Lotus Sūtra*).[4] In 982 Seng-chieh's stūpa was enlarged and rebuilt with thirteen levels. After Chen-tsung bestowed on him the title P'u-chao Ming-chüeh Ta-shih (Great Master of Universal Shining Bright Enlightenment) in 1013 (*Fo-tsu t'ung-chi* 44, T 49:405a), he became even more popular among the gentry and literati. Huang T'ing-chien visited his stūpa in Ssu-chou and wrote an essay to set forth his vows in 1084, and Su Tung-p'o prayed for rain in front of the same stūpa in 1092 (Makita 1984:42). Like the case of P'u-t'o discussed later in chapter 9, the success of the P'u-kuang-wang Temple as a pilgrimage center was intimately connected with its strategic geographic location. Lin-huai, the city where the temple was located, sits at the point where the Huai and Pien Rivers join. It has been a major stop along the transportation route between the north and south since the T'ang. Particularly during the Northern Sung when K'ai-feng was the capital of the nation, the location of Lin-huai was even more critical. Once a traveler crossed the river at Kua-chou, anyone going to the capital from the southeast must also pass through Yang-chou, Ssu-chou, Lin-huai, and Ch'en-liu before reaching his destination. This was the route whether one traveled by land or water. Lin-huai therefore became an unavoidable stop and Seng-chieh, the divine monk of the P'u-kuang-wang Temple, naturally came to be worshiped as a guardian deity by travelers, boat owners, and sailors who must pass under his watching eyes (Hsü 1995:6).

Records of paintings also testify to the existence of Seng-chieh Halls and the worship of his images in the tenth century in Szechwan and Chekiang.[5] A sculpture of Seng-chieh clothed in monastic robes and sitting on a high dais is found in Niche No. 177 in Pei-shan, Ta-tsu, Szechwan.[6] The sculpture is dated to the Northern Sung. A painting of a monk with the same clothing and posture is depicted on the southern wall outside of Cave 72 at Tun-huang. The cartouche identifies him as "Monk Ssu-chou, the Saint" (Sheng-che Ssu-chou Ho-shang) (*Chung-kuo mei-shu ch'uan-chi,* 12:49). Because Seng-chieh is usually depicted very similarly to the bodhisattva Ti-tsang, the two are often confused. In a long and detailed article, Françoise Wang-Toutain (1994) argues why a Tun-huang banner painted during the ninth to the tenth century held at the Bibliothèque Nationale in Paris (Pelliot chinois 4070), which has long been identified as Ti-tsang, is in fact a depiction of Seng-chieh. One suspects that there might be other misidentified examples and as our knowledge about this divine monk and his cult increases, we may be able to find more paintings and images of Seng-chieh.

The earliest dated image of Seng-chieh that has survived in China is a gilt wooden statue of him excavated from the base of a stūpa in the Hsien-yen Temple in Jui-an, Chekiang. Hsü Ping-fang summarizes the discovery made in late 1966 and early 1967. The stūpa was erected in 1043. The 15-cm tall statue is inside a relic box with the year 1042 inscribed on the bottom. Within the box, three groups of other dated objects are found together with the statue: two silver bottles dated 1033, a relic bottle dated 1035 and two silver images of deities dated 1037. The image of Seng-chieh bears the names of a man and his wife, who state that they had the image of the "buddha" (*fo*) made for the benefit of their third son. Hsü estimates that although it is not dated, it must have been made before 1043, when the stūpa was erected. Images of Seng-chieh have also been discovered in five other places; all were created during the eleventh and the twelfth centuries.[7]

From this evidence, it would seem that Seng-chieh was widely worshiped in different parts of China. His traces are found as far away as Tun-huang and Szechwan, but also occur closer to the places in which he was active while still alive, such as Kiangsu, Chekiang, and Honan. Makita made a preliminary plotting of the catchment area of Seng-chieh's cult by compiling a list of temples dedicated to him. Most of them were established between the tenth to the thirteenth centuries, although a few were established as late as the seventeenth and even the nineteenth centuries and located in Kiangsu, Chekiang, Hunan, Fukien, Kwangtung, and Taiwan. Most of them bore names containing "Ssu-chou," indicating their desire of being linked with the "Great Saint of Ssu-chou." The cult of Seng-chieh was strongest in port cities located either along the inland rivers or the coastal regions of Chekiang and Fukien (Makita 1984:38–42). This is because from the Sung on, he was increasingly seen as a god who could not only protect sailors but actually control the water.

The new function of Seng-chieh as a god of water control became noticeable for the first time in some entries in the *Fo-tsu t'ung-chi* (fascicle 46). The Huai River was notorious for its flooding. In the summer of 974, the floods entered Ssu-chou and destroyed people's homes, and in 1001 the water level reached the top of the city gate. During the twelfth century, the Huai River flooded for two years (1118 and 1119) in a row and Ssu-chou again suffered much damage. The second flood inundated the capital. It was so serious that freshwater turtles and sea turtles were seen in the courtyard and rooms of the palace. Several thousand workers labored to fight the flood. The Taoist priest Lin Ling-su worked his spells for several days but without success. Seng-chieh appeared in the palace, suspended in mid-air and flanked by his disciples Hui-an and Mu-ch'a. The emperor burned incense and worshiped him. Soon the master was seen going up (ascending) the city gate and reciting secret spells. Ten thousand people saw a being wearing a white headdress kneeling in front of him as if receiving precepts and instructions. This was the dragon king. The flood soon ended and the emperor bestowed on him the title Great Saint of Ssu-chou (T 49:421c).[8]

Among the manuscripts brought back to England from Tun-huang by Stein, there is a curious text entitled *Seng-chieh Ho-shang yü ju nieh-p'an shuo liu-tu ching* (Sūtra Spoken by the Monk Seng-chieh on the Six Perfections Before His Entering Nirvāṇa). According to Makita, this was an indigenous sūtra popular in Tun-huang, written sometime before the eleventh century when the cave library was closed. The sūtra speaks of a deluge and of all sentient beings turning into aquatic creatures. In view of the perpetual worries people had about the real flooding of the Huai River and the great popularity of the cult of Seng-chieh about this time, it could very well have been composed by someone wishing to promote Seng-chieh in his new role as the god of water control (Makita 1984:44). I translate the entire sūtra here:

> I want to tell the good men and good women of Jambudvīpa: Since I was born in Jambudvīpa, I have been teaching and transforming sentient beings, acting like a great compassionate father to them. I have been trans-

migrating in the world for beginningless kalpas and I have divided my body into ten thousand billion manifestations in order to save sentient beings. Because people in Jambudvīpa do not believe in Buddhism and create much evil karma, I cannot bear to watch. I have therefore decided to enter nirvāṇa and leave my relics and images all over Jambudvīpa in order to transform sentient beings. When the Counterfeit Dharma is completed in the world and the True Dharma prospers again, I shall descend to earth together with Maitreya Buddha. We shall sit together in the transformed city [*hua-ch'eng*] and save those people who have a good affinity [*shan-yüan*] with me.

My original home is in the Eastern Sea. It is a pure land formed by the causes of my previous lives. Because people were stupid, obstinate, and difficult to change, and because they did not believe in Buddhism and created much evil karma, I left my original home and went to the west to teach beings. I was called Śākyamuni Buddha. The East Sea was turned into a great ocean by five hundred poisonous dragons and all sentient beings were submerged in the ocean and changed into sea turtles, fresh water turtles, fish, and water lizards. Later I arrived here from the barbarian country in the west and was born in Jambudvīpa in order to save those who have seeds of the Buddha nature and thus have a good affinity with me. But I see that the people in Jambudvīpa are evil and violent. They kill and eat each other. There is no way they can be transformed. I therefore desire to enter into nirvāṇa and leave my relics and bones in Ssu-chou. If there are good men or good women who are kind in heart and filial, they ought to worship my images and keep a perpetual vegetarian diet. They should also recite my name. They are scattered in various places over Jambudvīpa. I pity those who must suffer from wars and conflicts in this evil world. I feel sorry that all kinds of difficulties and troubles oppress them. I will come back to this country together with Maitreya. Stepping on the ocean, I will make the water dry up. I will then order devas, dragon spirits, and the eight groups of holy beings to create a transformed city in the middle of the Eastern Sea. The walls will be made of gold and silver, the earth will be paved with lapis lazuli, and the palaces will be constructed with the seven jewels.

I will teach Buddhism and transmit only this sūtra. Disciples practicing the six perfections (*liu-tu*) will take refuge in me. The transformed city will be protected from the evils of Jambudvīpa, and shall be eternally peaceful and secure. Food and clothes will come to them naturally. They will perpetually live in bliss. Demons and heretics cannot come to harm them because the city is separated from them by the "weak water" (*jo-shui*).[9] I shall save six kinds of people, those who practice the six perfections.

The first perfection refers to those who respect their parents and the Three Treasures. The second perfection refers to those who do not kill. The third perfection refers to those who do not drink wine and eat meat. The fourth perfection refers to those who do not steal but have a good heart and treat everyone equally. The fifth perfection refers to those who practice *t'ou-t'o* (*dhūta*) and austerities, who delight in building bridges and performing various good deeds. The sixth perfection refers to those who pity the poor and take care of the sick, give away food and clothes, and show charity to the destitute. I will dispatch a hundred young boys to conduct these good people who practice the six perfections onto precious boats. They shall sail through the water without being drowned and reach my transformed city safely.

If a person is not one of my disciples practicing the six perfections, he or she will not give rise to a believing heart when he or she sees this sūtra but will blaspheme the True Dharma. You should know that such a person created the roots of evil in previous lives and is now reaping their evil retribution. The person will be killed by robbers, thieves, soldiers, or plague. Or he or she will be drowned by water or burned to death by fire. Or he or she will catch an epidemic or languish in jail. Evil people all suffer unlimited pain and stay in hell after death with no hope of release. For ten thousand kalpas they will not receive rebirth as human beings again.

Good men and good women, copy this sūtra and cherish it with sincerity. If you encounter the water or fire at the end of the kalpa when the black wind darkens the sky, I will send out limitless light to shine on you. Those who have created the affinity will come to the Buddha country and enter into the transformed city. All shall receive release.

Nan-wu Seng-chieh (Adoration of Seng-chieh)
Nan-wu seng-chin-t'o
Sha-ho-ta-t'o-chih-ta-yeh-an
Pa-le-she
Suo-p'o-ho (Svāhā) (T 85:1063b-1064a).

This is a remarkable document. It presents Seng-chieh no longer as a saint and divine monk, but as a buddha. He is called the "compassionate father," an epithet often applied to Kuan-yin. He has the power to save people from all difficulties, just like Kuan-yin. But unlike the indigenous sūtra *Kuan-yin san-mei ching,* which depicts Kuan-yin as the teacher of Śākyamuni Buddha, this text claims that Śākyamuni is one of Seng-chieh's many manifestations. It promises his second coming in the future: he will descend together with Maitreya, the future Buddha, and create a paradise on earth. This transformed city, however, is not simply a Buddhist pure land, but also a Taoist land of the immortals. It is separated from the profane world and accessible only to the chosen faithful. The clever substitution of its version of the "six perfections" for the traditional Buddhist ones is interesting and clearly reflects its interest in a more lay-orientated ethics. But even more telling is its vision of the future paradise. When Seng-chieh appears on earth again, he will dry up the ocean and do away forever with the threat of any more floods.

The final transformation of Seng-chieh into a purely Chinese god of water occurred with the popular legend of his victory over the water demoness, Water Mother (Shui-mu). A play with the title "Great Saint of Ssu-chou Subduing the Water Mother" ("Ssu-chou Ta-sheng hsiang Shui-mu") had already appeared in the Yüan period. A play with the same title is also found among the catalogues of Ming dramas. The Peking opera "Ssu-chou City" ("Ssu-chou ch'eng"), which is also known as "Presenting the Gift of a Pearl at the Rainbow Bridge" ("Hung-ch'iao seng-chu") is still being performed today. Makita summarizes the plot of the play:

> A water demoness lives under the Rainbow Bridge not far from Ssu-chou. She rules over her kind and calls herself Granny Water Mother. One day she transforms herself into a human being and goes to town. She meets a handsome young man who is the son of the prefect of Ssu-chou. She immediately falls in love with him. He is on his way to take the civil service examinations in the north. She uses her skill and lures him to her underwater residence. Although he already knows that she is a water demoness, he goes. When he sees the "water-repellent pearl" (*pi-shui chu*) on her collar, he makes her drunk and taking the pearl, flees. After she wakes up from her stupor, she becomes very angry and, creating wind and waves, decides to drown the city of Ssu-chou. Kuan-yin feels pity for the plight of the people of Ssu-chou and, calling heavenly gods and soldiers together, comes down to do battle with her. But the water demoness is fierce and does not capitulate. Kuan-yin then changes into an old woman selling noodles. She waits by the side of the road for the demoness. When the latter becomes hungry after doing much battle, she accepts the noodles from the old woman to satisfy her hunger. All of a sudden, the noodles turn into iron chains inside her stomach. They chain her innards together. The Water Mother has no choice but to surrender. (*Hsi k'ao* 21, quoted by Makita 1984:49)

We do not know how the play went in Yüan and Ming times, for only the title has been handed down. But this later version has certainly superimposed the image of Seng-chieh on that of the feminine Kuan-yin. As we shall read in chapter 11, a new guise of Kuan-yin in the late imperial times was that of an old woman. Known as Venerable Mother Kuan-yin, she is ubiquitous in novels and plays, but also in precious scrolls created by and for both sectarian new religions and lay Buddhists. Seng-chieh, the earlier manifestation of the Eleven-headed Kuan-yin, is here absorbed into the Venerable Mother Kuan-yin.

In this chapter we have examined the careers of two divine monks and stages of their hagiographical transformation into incarnations of Kuan-yin. Pao-chih and Seng-chieh enjoyed imperial patronage and popular veneration. Their cults once received official support and gained wide geographical distribution. Yet after the Sung it is probably fair to say that the image of a monk as a manifestation of Kuan-yin has increasingly been replaced by feminine images, chief among which is Princess Miao-shan. This change is also discernable in miracle tales, iconography, and visions of pilgrims and devotees. The memory of Pao-chih and Seng-chieh as eccentric thaumaturges was undoubtedly revived and reinforced by the legends of others like them, such as the Cloth-bag Monk or Crazy Chi. Today, however, Pao-chih is remembered chiefly as the originator of Buddhist rituals and Seng-chieh the god of water control.

But they also served the purpose of domesticating the Eleven-headed Kuan-yin, an imported foreign deity. As the popularity of the Eleven-headed Kuan-yin was replaced by the Thousand-handed Kuan-yin after the T'ang, not a real monk, but a legendary princess would serve the same function. Chapters 7 and 8 will try to indicate how that was done. Before we turn to Princess Miao-shan, however, the first feminine manifestation of Kuan-yin with a Chinese identity, we must try to find out when the bodhisattva was no longer perceived only as a male monk, but also as a feminine figure. For it is only when people came to accept this new way to envision Kuan-yin that a legend such as Princess Miao-shan could become possible. In the next chapter, I offer evidence to show that the feminine transformation of Kuan-yin occurred during the tenth century. I argue that this process can be seen most clearly in the emergence of new iconographies that, unlike scriptures and monastic chronicles, provide unambiguous clues to the bodhisattva's gender.

6

Indigenous Iconographies and the Domestication of Kuan-yin

In the previous chapters I examined several different media that served both to promote the popularity of Kuan-yin in China and to domesticate this foreign bodhisattva. Indigenous sūtras, miracle tales, myths, and legends of divine monks as incarnations of Kuan-yin have all contributed to the process. I have also stressed the intimate and dialectical relationship between visions, media, and iconography.

Art has been one of the most powerful and effective media through which the Chinese people have come to know Kuan-yin. It is also through art that one can most clearly detect the bodhisattva's gradual, yet undeniable sexual transformation. As we have seen, Buddhist scriptures always present the bodhisattva as either masculine or asexual. Kuan-yin usually appears as a monk not only in early miracle stories and in the dreams and visions of the faithful, but wonder-working monks such as Pao-chih and Seng-chieh are also incarnated as the bodhisattva. The statues of Kuan-yin in Yün-kang, Lung-men, and Tun-huang, as well as Kuan-yin images painted on the frescoes and banners of Tun-huang, like those of the buddhas and bodhisattvas, appear masculine, sometimes wearing a thin moustache that clearly indicates his masculine gender.

But the deity underwent a profound and startling transformation beginning sometime during the tenth century, and by the sixteenth century, Kuan-yin had become not only completely Chinese but also the most beloved "Goddess of Mercy," a nickname coined by the Jesuit missionaries who were much impressed by the similarities between her iconography and that of the Madonna. Of all the imported Buddhist deities, Kuan-yin is the only one who has succeeded in becoming a genuine Chinese goddess. So much so that many Chinese, if they are not familiar with Buddhism, are not even aware of her Buddhist origin.

In this chapter I discuss the earliest feminine form of Kuan-yin, the White-robed Kuan-yin, found in Chinese art. Since no similar (or different) feminine forms of Avalokiteśvara are found in Indian, Central Asian, Southeast Asian, or Tibetan artistic traditions, this is a truly Chinese creation. I discuss some later feminine forms of Kuan-yin, also genuine Chinese creations, in chapters 10 and 11. I would, however, see them in the larger context of the creation of indigenous and regional Kuan-yin images in Buddhist art in China, for I see the feminization of the bodhisattva as closely connected with his/her regional cults, both being important processes in the Chinese domestication of Avalokiteśvara.

I first cite four examples to show how people in different parts of China saw and depicted Kuan-yin. Limited by available surviving evidence, I have chosen Tun-huang in Kansu, Hangchow in Chekiang, Ta-tsu in Szechwan, and Ta-li in Yünnan. However, I believe that these were not isolated cases. Other places might have other local traditions that we may come to know if new evidence comes to light. I then discuss the philosophical and ritualistic origins of the Water-moon (Shui-yüeh) Kuan-yin, the earliest dated example of the indigenous Chinese form of the deity. Extensively studied by art historians, this iconography is often cited as an example of the "secularization" of Kuan-yin. I argue, however, that the image not only symbolizes the highest and most profound insights of Buddhism, but was treated as a religious icon and used in a ritualistic setting. Finally, I discuss the White-robe (Pai-i), perhaps the most celebrated Chinese form of Kuan-yin. I will demonstrate its close connection with the Water-moon Kuan-yin on one hand, and with the Child-giving (Sung-tzu) Kuan-yin on the other. I offer compelling evidence to prove that these three do not represent mutually exclusive typologies. By examining the iconographies side by side with texts (miracle stories and indigenous scriptures), it is possible to arrive at new and more accurate interpretations. This proves once more that a methodology combining the visual and the written materials can often yield rewarding discoveries.

Forms and Names of Kuan-yin in Regional Buddhist Art

A large number of silk banners portraying buddhas and bodhisattvas were created by pious donors in Tun-huang. They often have cartouches next to the deities identifying who they are. They also carry inscriptions stating the names of the donors, when the painting was made, and for what reason. Kuan-yin is a favorite subject depicted on these banners. Among the Stein Collection of Tun-huang paintings held at the British Museum, Kuan-yin also appears often. In these paintings, Kuan-yin is identified by names on the cartouches attached to the side of the images. For instance, a painting dated 864 portrays four images of Kuan-yin on the upper register (figure 6.1). He is called, from right to left, Ta-pei Chiu-k'u Kuan-shih-yin P'u-sa (Great Compassionate Kuan-shih-yin Bodhisattva Who Saves [One from] Suffering), Ta-sheng (Great Sage) Chiu-k'u Kuan-shih-yin P'u-sa, Ta-pei Shih-i-mien (Great Compassionate Eleven-faced) Kuan-shih-yin P'u-sa, and Ta-sheng Ju-i-lun (Great Sage Wish-fulfilling Wheel) Kuan-shih-yin P'u-sa. Except for the positions of the hands (the first and third have the left hand up and the right hand down, while the second and fourth are the reverse), they all look alike. Although the last two are esoteric Kuan-yin, they do not have multiple heads or hands. These images of Kuan-yin are local creations that did not follow any rules set down in the *sādhanas*.

Kuan-yin is also called Yen-shou-ming Chiu-k'u Kuan-shih-yin P'u-sa (Kuan-shih-yin Bodhisattva Who Prolongs Life and Saves [One] from Suffering). But the favorite name is Ta-tz'u Ta-pei Chiu-k'u Kuan-shih-yin P'u-sa (Great Merciful and Compassionate Kuan-shih-yin Bodhisattva Who Saves [One] from Suffering). Kuan-yin is addressed as such by Chang Yu-ch'eng, a minor official, who commissioned a painting dated 945 on behalf of his dead parents, wet nurse, and younger brother with the hope that they would be reborn in the Pure Land (figure 6.2). The painting is described by Arthur Waley: Kuan-yin carries a flask in the right hand, while the left hand is raised, with thumb and first finger pressed together holding a willow sprig (1931:26). The big cartouche to the right of the bodhisattva contains a poem setting forth his pious hope:

All things born are unstable as a lightning-flash,
They perish as soon as their karma is exhausted, for they have no permanence.
But the compassionate Kuan-yin rescues creatures of every sort.
In love how deep and tender he builds a bridge (to salvation)!
Spending the fleeting wealth of this world I have made his true image,
The beams of his light flashing and glinting in the splendor of a colored-painting.
My only prayer is that the dead may be reborn in the Pure Land.
That, escaping the pain of the Three Ways, they may mount to Paradise.
(Waley 1931:27)[1]

The concern for a good death and rebirth was indeed foremost in the minds of the donors. It is in Tun-huang that Kuan-yin appears as the "Guide of Souls"

Figure 6.1. Four images of Kuan-yin from Tun-huang, dated 864. From right to left, the images are Ta-pei Chiu-k'u Kuan-shih-yin P'u-sa (Great Compassionate Kuan-shih-yin Bodhisattva Who Saves [One from] Suffering), Ta-sheng (Great Sage) Chiu-k'u Kuan-shih-yin P'u-sa, Ta-pei Shih-i-mien (Great Compassionate Eleven-faced) Kuan-shih-yin P'u-sa, and Ta-sheng Ju-i-lun (Great Sage Wish-fulfilling Wheel) Kuan-shih-yin P'u-sa. *Courtesy of the British Museum.*

Figure 6.2. Kuan-yin, dated 945. *Courtesy of the British Museum.*

(*yin-lu p'u-[sa]*) painted in the late T'ang and early Sung, from the late ninth to early tenth century. Two paintings are in the British Museum and four in the Pelliot Collection in Paris (Vandier-Nicholas et al. 1974, 1976, vol. 15: nos. 130–33). They depict Kuan-yin carrying a censer in one hand and a banner in the other, followed by a small figure representing the aristocratic-looking lady donor on her way to the Pure Land (Whitfield and Farrer 1990:38, 41–42).

The art of Tun-huang has been studied by art historians for nearly a century. Because of the wealth of the material recovered from the site and stored in several major museums around the world, it is possible for scholars to study it abroad as well as on-site. The fame of Tun-huang is well deserved. Nowadays, when people talk of Chinese Buddhist art, they immediately mention Tun-huang and consider its art to be the standard. It is, therefore, perhaps strange that I mention the examples of Kuan-yin from Tun-huang under the section on regional art. I do so in order to contrast those paintings with examples from other regions, where Kuan-yin was called by different names and was depicted in different ways. These did not follow the Tun-huang models, but represented local traditions. In a similar way, perhaps the Tun-huang artists who painted those votive banners were doing the same thing.

Ch'ien Shu (929–988) was the last ruler of the Wu Yüeh Kingdom based in Hangchow and, like his ancestor Ch'ien Liu, a great patron of Buddhism. Following Emperor Aśoka's example, he made 84,000 miniature reliquary pagodas. Dated 955, they were cast in bronze and sometimes gilded. Some of them were brought back to Japan by pilgrims. Others were made of iron, like those found in 1956 among the ruins of the Myriad Buddhas Pagoda in Chin-hua, Chekiang, a site that dates to 965 C.E. Ch'ien Shu also had 84,000 dhāraṇī-sūtras printed, which were placed inside the stūpas. One of these sūtras, bearing a date of 956, is in the collection of the King of Sweden (Howard 1985; Edgren 1972, 1989; Chang 1978).

The emperor also sponsored the printing of 20,000 copies of the twenty-four manifestations of Kuan-yin by using a silkscreen process. A Japanese copy based on the Chinese original has survived. Formerly in the possession of Kōzanji, it is now in the Hisabara Library of Kyoto Imperial University (Soper 1948:41). The Taishō Tripiṭaka includes a reproduction in volume 6 of its *Zuzōbu* (Diagrams and Paintings) section (figure 6.3). The cartouche on the top center provides the name for the print: "Kuan-yin Who Manifests in Response" (Yin-hsien Kuan-yin). It depicts a central image of Kuan-yin with six arms and twelve-heads, is flanked by twenty-four manifestations on both sides. Aside from the two uppermost human figures on the right and left hand, who are identified as Perceiving Master (Kuan-tzu-tsai) and Water-moon Kuan-yin respectively, the rest are not human and are entirely local creations. They, just like the main image of the twelve-headed Kuan-yin, are not based on any scriptures. We can discover their identities by reading the inscription on the lower register:

> The Twelve-headed Kuan-yin Appears in Twenty-four Manifestations in Response [to Prayers].
>
> The first is the manifestation as the Perceiving Master, the second is the manifestation as a precious light, the third is the manifestation as a precious pavilion, the fourth is the manifestation as auspicious grass, the fifth is the manifestation as a golden drum, the sixth is the manifestation as the hand of the Buddha, the seventh is the manifestation as a golden dragon, the eighth is the manifestation as a lion, the ninth is the manifestation as a golden temple bell, the tenth is the manifestation as a golden elephant, the eleventh is the manifestation as a golden bridge, the twelfth is the manifestation as a precious hand bell, the thirteenth is the manifestation as the moon in the water, the fourteenth is the manifestation as a precious stūpa, the fifteenth is the manifestation as a golden phoenix, the sixteenth is the manifestation as a golden well covering, the seventeenth is the manifestation as the foot of the Buddha, the eighteenth is the manifestation as a golden turtle, the nineteenth is the manifestation as an auspicious cloud, the twentieth is the manifestation as a precious jewel, the twenty-first is the manifestation as a golden sparrow, the twenty-second is the manifestation as a stone buddha image, the twenty-third is the manifestation as a golden lotus and the twenty-fourth is the manifestation as a golden wheel.

All the nonhuman manifestations contain the adjective "golden," recalling the light symbolism connected with Kuan-yin that is so much emphasized in the sūtras. Although the twelve-headed Kuan-yin and the nonhuman forms of Kuan-yin are not attested to in scriptures, they apparently represented local beliefs. A book about Hangchow customs compiled in the Ch'ing dynasty makes reference to the twelve-headed Kuan-yin as well as some other forms not mentioned in the tenth century devotional print (*Wu-lin feng-su chi*, 53b).[2]

Let us quickly look at two other examples in the southwest part of China. The first is in Ta-tsu, Szechwan, where Kuan-yin is prominently represented at several Buddhist sculptural sites. Very often Kuan-yin does not appear alone, but as a group of thirteen or of ten images. In Shih-men Shan, for instance, Niche 6 contains a triad of the "Three Holy Ones of the West" (Amitābha flanked by Kuan-yin and Ta-shih-chih). Ten images of Kuan-yin stand on either side. There are eight inscriptions that all bear the date of 1141. On the left wall, the five Kuan-yin images are identified as Pure Vase, Precious Basket,

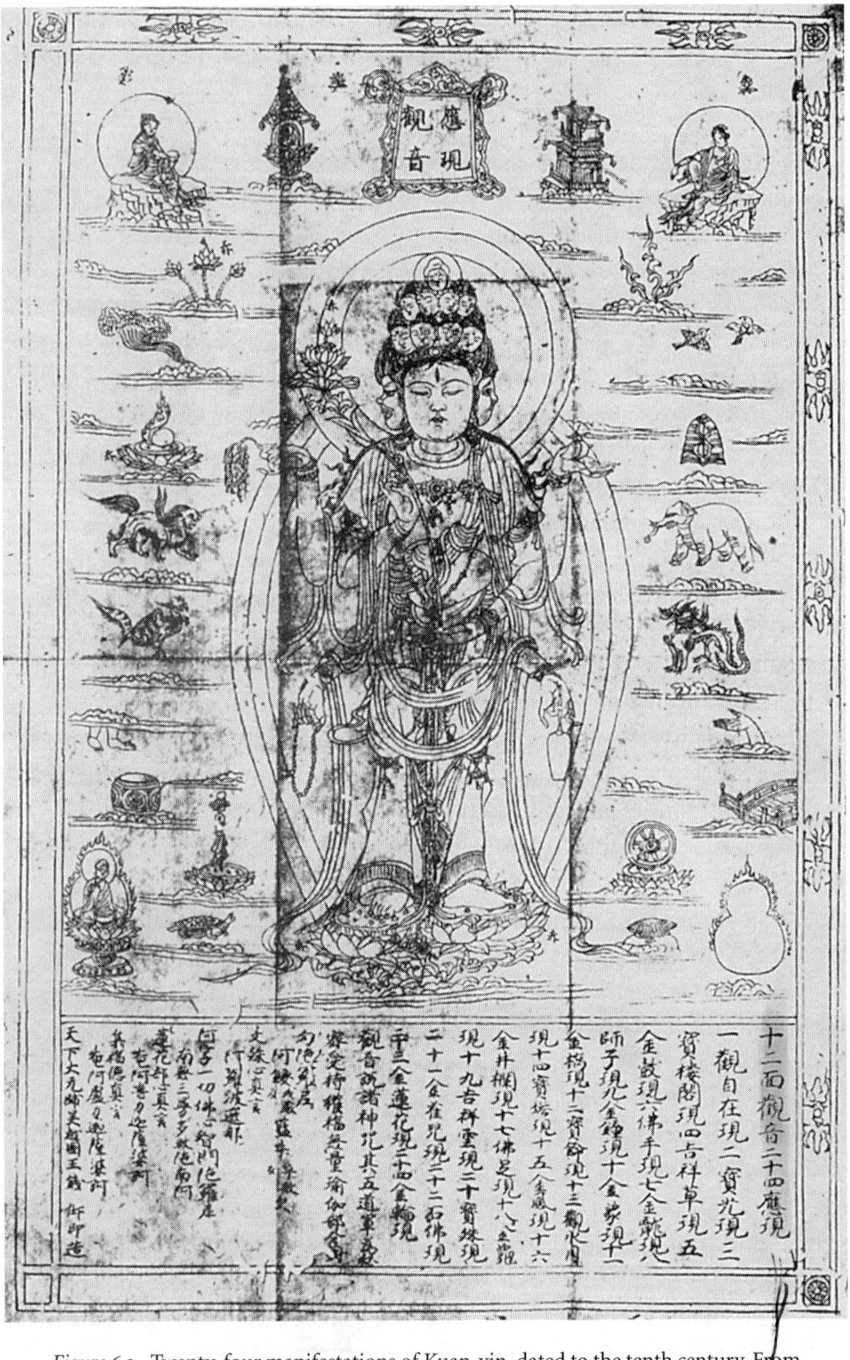

Figure 6.3. Twenty-four manifestations of Kuan-yin, dated to the tenth century. From *Zuzōbu,* vol. 6 of the Taishō Tripiṭaka.

此处不是
十一面观音
而是十二面观音

Precious Sūtra, Precious Fan, and Willow Branch, for they carry these as implements. The five on the right wall are identified as Precious Jewel, Precious Mirror, Lotus Hand, Wish-fulfilling Wheel, and Rosary Hand (*Ta-tsu shih-k'e yen-chiu* 544).

In Pei Shan, Szechwan, Niche 180, which bears an inscription dated 1116, contains a main Kuan-yin image attended by six manifestations on either side, making thirteen images of Kuan-yin all together. Not counting those that are eroded, six images carrying different implements can be seen. On the left side of the main image, there is a Kuan-yin holding a basket and another one holding a seal, while on the right side, starting from the inside (east) and moving outward (west), the four images of Kuan-yin respectively hold a willow branch raised in the right hand, a maṇi-pearl in the left hand, a maṇi-pearl in both hands, and a rosary in both hands (408).

Finally, the same theme was depicted in Niche 4 of Miao-kao Shan, which has no dated inscription. It contains the triad of Amitābha, Kuan-yin and Ta-shih-chih in the center and ten Kuan-yin images carrying a wish-fulfilling pearl, rosary, round mirror, begging bowl, lasso, pure vase, lotus, and so on (557). Most of the implements held by Kuan-yin, with the exception of the basket, are mentioned in the esoteric *Ch'ien-shou ching* dedicated to the Thousand-handed Kuan-yin, which I discussed in chapter 2. The innovation made by the local artisans was to separate them from the original group of forty mūdras and depict instead a nonesoteric, two-handed and one-headed Kuan-yin carrying one of the implements. This is not unusual, for as Angela Howard has commented on other examples of the Thousand-handed Kuan-yin also from Szechwan, "In none of the figures does the artistic visualization perfectly correspond to the textual requirements. It is possible that the carvers developed their own interpretation and took liberties with the texts, a theory supported by the observation that the numerous images of this type found in Sichuan are by no means uniform" (1990:52).

Our second and last example of regional art can be found in Yünnan, where artists depicted the bodhisattva in similarly innovative ways. I refer to the twenty-two images of Kuan-yin included in the famous *Long Roll of Buddhist Images* painted by Chang Sheng-wen in 1173–76 that is located at the National Palace Museum in Taipei (Chapin and Soper 1970–71; Li 1982:106–12). Some of them are identified by name in the cartouches. Four images refer to the founding myth of the Nan-chao Kingdom, which relates how a wonder-working old monk who is an incarnation of Kuan-yin arrives to save the local people from the rākṣasas and leaves an image known as A-ts'o-yeh (Ajaya [All Victorious]) Kuan-yin behind for people to worship. "Kuan-yin as a foreign monk" (frame 58) and "Kingdom-establishing Kuan-yin" (frame 86) represent the old monk, whereas "True-form Kuan-shih-yin" (frame 99) and "I-ch'ang Kuan-shih-yin" (frame 100) represent the A-ts'o-yeh Kuan-yin, better known by the nickname "Luck of Yünnan," given to it by Chapin.

Some names of Kuan-yin are familiar to us, for instance, the Chiu-k'u (Saving [One] from Suffering) Kuan-yin (frame 101), Ta-pei Kuan-shih-yin (frame 102), and Eleven-headed Kuan-shih-yin (frame 103). On the other hand, several others have names not attested elsewhere. There is the P'u-men-p'in ("Universal Gateway" chapter) Kuan-shih-yin who is surrounded by six smaller figures who rescue devotees from perils. They are identified as "Kuan-shih-yin Who Protects One from Bad Karmic Retribution," "Kuan-shih-yin Who Removes Dangers from Elephants," "Kuan-shih-yin Who Removes Dangers from Water," "Kuan-shih-yin Who Removes Dangers from Fire," "Kuan-shih-yin Who Subdues Ghosts and Evil Spirits," and "Kuan-shih-yin Who Removes Dangers from Beasts" (frames 88–90). There is "Kuan-shih-yin Who Saves [One] from Suffering by Seeking Out Voices" (*hsün-sheng chiu-k'u*, frame 91). Reflecting the fame of Mt. P'u-t'o, there is not only "Mt. Potalaka Kuan-yin" (P'u-t'o-lo Shan, frame 97) but also "Kuan-shih-yin of the Desolate Ocean Coast" (*ku-chüeh hai-an*, frame 98). Although it is unusual to see the "Universal Gateway" chapter of the *Lotus Sūtra* and the perils mentioned therein hypostasized, it is at least possible to know where these images come from, but this is not the case with the three-faced and six armed Kuan-yin who is called "Essence of White Water (*pai-shui-ching*) Kuan-yin" (frame 92; figure 6.4).

I mention these examples from different parts of China to make one point. As the cult of Kuan-yin took root in China, the bodhisattva's converts were ready to perceive and present Kuan-yin in new ways more congenial to the Chinese audience. Kuan-yin was not only portrayed in new ways, but also given new epithets and names. The faithful wrote indigenous sūtras and formulated new rituals to glorify and worship Kuan-yin. They told stories about Kuan-yin's miraculous responses and divine incarnations. It is only natural that they also created new and indigenous iconographic representations. I suspect that the Water-moon, White-robe, and other feminine forms of Kuan-yin were originally also local creations. The reason these depictions became popular and achieved a pan-China status while most of the other local manifestations either remained local or were gradually forgotten deserves more research. My hypothesis is that they did not remain simply as art forms, but were enhanced by rituals and religious practices. Once these new forms of Kuan-yin became entrenched in the existential and psychological lives of the faithful, other genres and media such as indigenous sūtras, secular literature such as novels and dramas, and *pao-chüan* further propagated and disseminated them to an ever-widening audience until all Chinese people came to know them.

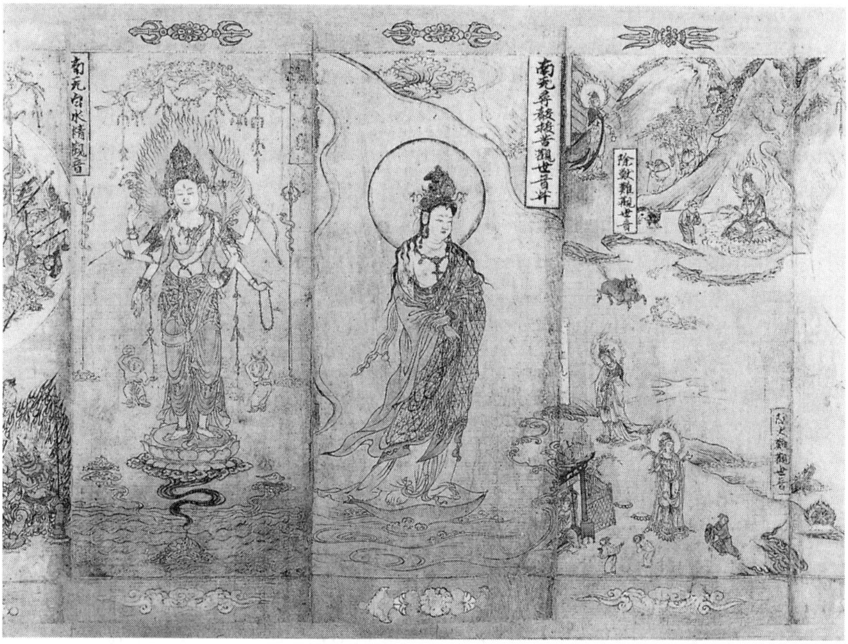

Figure 6.4. "Long Roll of Buddhist Images" painted by Chang Sheng-wen in 1173–76. *Courtesy of National Palace Museum, Taiwan.*

The Water-moon Kuan-yin

It is in Tun-huang that one first comes across the "Water-moon" Kuan-yin, a type much favored by Ch'an and literati painters since the Sung dynasty (Chang 1971; Wang 1987). Like the White-robed Kuan-yin, this form has no uncontested scriptural foundation. The only evidence for the existence of a sūtra bearing this name of the bodhisattva comes from Tun-huang. A sūtra with the title *Fo-shuo Shui-yüeh-kuang Kuan-yin P'u-sa ching* (Moonlight in Water Kuan-yin Bodhisattva Sūtra Spoken by the Buddha) is one of the ten on three scrolls copied by an unidentified scribe in Tun-huang, commissioned by a local official named Chai Feng-ta (fl. 902–966) in the year 958 (Shih 1987:34–37). The ten sūtras were copied to commemorate the ten feast days for the benefit of his dead wife, née Ma.[3] This particular sūtra was copied for the second seventh day.

Although a few sūtras chosen to be copied are considered canonical, such as the *Heart Sūtra*, the majority are indigenous sūtras including the *Shih-wang Ching* (Scripture on the Ten Kings) and the *Yü-lan-p'en ching* (Scripture on the Yü-lan Bowls) (Teiser 1994:107–16). The sūtra is rather short, consisting of only seventeen lines with each line having seventeen characters. The main portion of the sūtra contains the ten great vows followed by the six wishes that the mountain of knives, raging fires, hellish beings, hungry ghosts, asuras, and animals would all be eliminated or pacified. They are excerpts from the *Ch'ien-shou ching* and are identical to the text called "Invocation of the Great Compassionate One" (*Ta-pei ch'i-ch'ing*). As I mentioned in chapter 2, evidence of copying this portion of the sūtra as well as a primitive form of repentance ritual centering around the recitation of it was already attested in Tun-huang in the eighth century. But what does this have to do with the Moonlight in Water Kuan-yin? The beginning and ending portions of the text may contain a clue:

> At the time when monks, nuns, laymen, laywomen, young boys and maidens, all sentient beings, and various people want to practice and recite the Sūtra with the name of "Great Holy Kuan-yin of the Moonlight in Water" (Ta-sheng Kuan-yin Shui-yüeh-kuang P'u-sa), you ought to give rise to the heart of compassion and following me, make these vows. . . .
>
> After you have finished making these vows, then with a mind of utmost sincerity, chant the Extensive, Perfect, Unobstructed Compassionate Heart Dhāraṇī of the Great Merciful and Great Compassionate Perceiving Master Bodhisattva Mahāsattva with the wish that all sufferings in the Dharma Realm will be eliminated and that all sentient beings will achieve enlightenment regarding the Way.

These passages make it clear that the "Shui-yüeh-kuang" Kuan-yin is intimately connected with the vows of and the Great Compassion Dhāraṇī revealed by the Thousand-handed Kuan-yin. Was the name a local variant of "Shui-yüeh?" Most likely. Moreover, Water-moon Kuan-yin might be taken as a variant name for Thousand-handed Kuan-yin, for there was a close relationship between these two forms of Kuan-yin in the art of Tun-huang. Indeed it was in Tun-huang that the earliest dated Water-moon Kuan-yin, painted in 943, was found. This is a silk banner located at the Musée Guimet. A cartouche identifying the figure as "Water-moon Kuan-yin Bodhisattva" appears on the right side of the lower register of a larger painting of the Thousand-armed Kuan-yin. Holding a willow branch in the right hand and a water bottle in the left, the bodhisattva sits on a rock surrounded by water in a relaxed manner known as "royal ease." Lotus flowers grow from the water in abundance, and the bodhisattva rests his left foot on one of them. There are also luxuriant bamboo groves behind him. The surroundings suggest that it is Potalaka, the sacred island home of Kuan-yin. Although Potalaka was believed to be situated somewhere in the ocean south of India, by this time it had been identified by the Chinese with P'u-t'o Island, offshore from Chekiang Province. The most distinctive feature of this new iconography is undoubtedly the large nimbus resembling a full moon that envelops the bodhisattva.

Water-moon Kuan-yin was a popular subject for Tun-huang painters. The complete catalogue of 1982 listing the contents of the caves at Tun-huang identified fifteen wall paintings of the Water-moon Kuan-yin, six were done in the tenth century, and the others from the eleventh to thirteenth century. Recently, scholars have gathered more examples, amounting to more than thirty in all (Wang 1987:32).[4] The genesis of this iconography can probably be dated to the eighth and ninth century, and there is no doubt that painters played a decisive role in the creation of this image. Chang Yen-yüan, for instance, mentioned in his *Li-tai ming-hua chi* (Record of Famous Paintings in Successive Dynasties, preface 847) that Chou Fang (740–800) was the first to paint a Water-moon Kuan-yin in the Sheng-kuang Monastery in Ch'ang-an. The bodhisattva was encircled by a full moon and surrounded by a bamboo grove. The painting has not survived, but it could have served as the prototype for later painters and sculptors, who made this new type of Kuan-yin popular in Tun-huang and Szechwan. Both the *I-chou ming-hua lu* (Famous Paintings of I-chou, preface 1006) and the *Hsüan-ho hua-pu* (Catalogue of Paintings Compiled in the Hsüan-ho Era, preface 1120) record that several famous painters dealt with the Water-moon Kuan-yin image. It was also the basis for the White-robed Kuan-yin, another Chinese form of the bodhisattva that became increasingly popular during and after the Sung (Matsumoto 1926:207, 1937:350).

Although no known scripture or visualization instruction connects Kuan-yin with the moon and water, these icons clearly symbolize the empty and illusory nature of worldly phenomena. They are used in this sense in a number of Buddhist sūtras, treatises, and writings by Buddhist monks and laymen. For instance, in the *Druma-kinnara-rāja-paripṛcchā Sūtra* (Ta-shu-chin-na-lo Wang so-wen ching; Sūtra Answering the Questions of King Druma-Kinnara) translated by Kumārajīva, it states, "You should understand well that everything is empty, markless, and without desire. You should understand that all dharmas are like illusions, flames, the moon in the water, or images in dreams and reflections in mirrors" (T 15:367c). The *Ta-chih-tu lun* (Commentary on the Great Prajñā-pāramitā Sūtra), translated also by Kumārajīva, says, "One may search for it [the phenomenon] everywhere but cannot obtain it. Like illusions or echoes, all phenomena are like the moon in the water. As soon as one sees it, it disappears" (T 25:277c). The same idea is found in the *Chin kuan-ming ching* (Sūtra of the Golden Light) translated by Tan-wu-ch'en (d. 433): "The body of the voice-hearer is like empty space. It is like the illusion of flame and the sound of an echo. Or like the moon in the water. The nature of all sentient beings is like what one sees in a dream" (T 16:335). The *Hua-yen Sūtra* declares that all sentient beings are empty and quiescent in their nature, and all dharmas are without true substance. In describing all dharmas as being without a master, they are compared to illusions, flames, the moon in the water, or images in dream and mirror. One is led to illumination this way. The *Ta-sheng pen-sheng hsin-ti kuan ching* (Sūtra on Observing the Mahāyāna Mind Ground of Original Birth) translated by Prjañā Tripiṭaka in 790, contrasts those who have left home, called "home-leaving bodhisattvas" with those who stay at home, called "householder bodhisattvas":

> *When the bodhisattvas who have left the household observe those who are still living at home,*
> *The latter are like storms which do not last long.*
> *Or like those who delusively become attached to the moon in the water.*
> *They take this for real because of their discrimination and deliberation.*
> *There is originally no moon in the water,*
> *The moon is seen because of the pure water, which serves as the cause.*
> *All dharmas are temporary because they are born of causes.*
> *But the foolish regard them to be the self due to their delusion and calculation (T 3:309b).*

The metaphor is eventually included in a list of ten that are used to help a meditator achieve insight into the truth of *śūnyatā* or the insubstantial nature of everything. The *Ta-po-jo p'o-lo-mi-to ching* (Great Prajñā-pāramitā Sūtra) translated by Hsüan-tsang, for instance, says, "Observe all dharmas as illusions, flames, dreams, the moon in the water, echoes, flowers in the sky, images reflected in mirror, shadows made by light, magical creations, or the gandharvas' city [a mirage city]." A similar list is used in Tantric sūtras as well. For instance, the *Ta-jih ching* (The Great Sun Sūtra) translated by Śubhakarasiṃha in the early eighth century, says, "Bodhisattvas who want to practice the bodhisattva path must cultivate themselves by profoundly observing the ten phrases of causality. Only then will they achieve realization through their thorough proficiency in the True Word. What are the ten? Dharmas are like illusions, flames of fire, dream, shadows, cities of the gandharvas, echoes, the moon in the water, bubbles, flowers in the sky, or wheels traced by fire" (T 18:3c). In Buddhist scholastic literature, the moon in the water is thus eventually listed as one of ten metaphors illustrating that everything in this world is empty in their true nature and without any real substance, because it is dependent on other causes.

The ten metaphors may vary, but the moon in the water is always included in the list.[5]

Since this is a metaphor found frequently in Buddhist scriptures, it is not surprising that Buddhist monks and laymen also liked to use it in their writings and sermons. In chapter 4 we read how Chih-i uses water and the moon in *Fa-hua hsüan-i* to describe the relationship between the Buddha and sentient beings. He returns to the image in explicating the three bodies of the Buddha: "The absolute and the real is the true body, what meditates on and understand it is the reward body and the miraculous body extends this understanding to all its workings. True body is like the void. When responding to the visible objects, it reveals itself just like the water reflecting the moon. The reward body is the celestial moon. Buddhahood (the true body) is like the void, meditation and understanding strengthen and glorify it. The understanding is like the celestial moon while meditation is like the moon in the water [literally, water-moon]" (T 33:745b).

The Buddhist master Yung-chia Hsüan-chüeh (665–713) writes this couplet in his *Song of Enlightenment* (Cheng-tao ko), "To see the image in a mirror is not difficult. How can one grasp the moon in the water?" He also writes, "One moon reveals universally all water, and all water universally contains one moon." In a less poetic and more scholastic mode, he explains the uniquely Mahāyāna teaching that not only the person or self is empty, but also the dharmas, including the five aggregates: "The first is the wisdom of knowing the emptiness of the person. It refers to the wisdom that there is no self in the aggregates, nor is self the aggregates. It is like the hair of a turtle or the horn of a hare. The second is the wisdom of knowing the emptiness of the dharmas. It refers to the wisdom that all dharmas including the aggregates are not real because they rely on causes. They are like the moon in the water or a reflection in the mirror" (*HTC* 111:399). Ch'an monks in the T'ang also used this metaphor in their sermons. For instance, the famous Ch'an master Shih-t'ou Hsi-ch'ien (700–790) used the metaphor in his sermon:

> My teaching is transmitted from the Buddhas of the past. No matter whether it is through meditative samādhi or vigorous effort, you must reach the same realization as that of the Buddha. Know that the Mind is the Buddha and the Mind and the Buddha are the same as sentient beings. Enlightenment and vexations are the same in essence, although they differ in name. All of you should know that your spiritual essence is neither eternal nor impermanent. Your nature is neither pure nor dirty. It is quiescent and perfect. It is possessed by the worldly as well as the sages. It functions

everywhere and has nothing to do with mind, the senses, or consciousness. The three worlds and six paths of rebirth are all manifested by this same Mind. Are there birth and death for the moon in the water or the reflection in the mirror? You must know that you already have everything within you (T 14:609a-b).

We read in the *Fo-tsu t'ung-chi* that the Ch'an master Shih-li was invited by the Emperor Shun-tsung in 805 to the inner court and was asked, "How can sentient beings in this world see into their natures and thereby achieve Buddhahood?" To which he answered, "The Buddhadharma is like the moon in the water. The moon can be seen but cannot be obtained." The emperor was said to be greatly pleased (T 49:380b).

The moon on the water was not just a favorite metaphor used by learned Buddhist clerics and Ch'an masters. The same metaphor was also used by both Li Po (701–762) and Po Chü-i (772–846), the famous T'ang poets. Li wrote a eulogy on the portrait of Master Chih, the divine monk Pao-chih:

The moon in the water cannot be obtained.
His mind is like empty space which is silent, limitless, and without a master.
He walks alone and has no companions (Li T'ai-pai ch'üan-chi *28*).

Po expresses the same sentiment in a eulogy to a painting of the Water-moon Kuan-yin:

Appearing above the pure and translucent water,
Emerging from the vacuous white light,
Once the image is seen by the viewer,
Ten thousand causes and conditions all become empty.
Disciple Chü-i takes refuge with utmost sincerity.
Be my teacher eternally, from life to life and kalpa to kalpa (Wen-yüan ying-hua *783*).

Although the moon and water, or the reflection of the moon in water, were familiar Buddhist metaphors for the transitory and insubstantial nature of things in the world, there is no scriptural basis for linking Kuan-yin with these metaphors. It is here that we can see the bold creativity of Chinese artists, for they took these Buddhist ideas and expressed them through the traditional medium of Chinese painting. Commenting on the many wooden sculptures of Kuan-yin sitting leisurely, with one leg pendant and the other leg raised, in the posture known as "royal ease" (*rājalila, ju-i-tso*), which the Water-moon Kuan-yin also typically assumes, Derek Gillman suggests that this could be copied from imported models carried by Buddhist travelers during the T'ang and Sung. Examples of such images are found among Buddhist sculptures made in Sri Lanka during the eighth to the tenth centuries. This posture can ultimately be traced to Hindu art, which uses it widely in depicting gods and goddesses (Gillman 1983). But even if the posture might be based on a foreign model, the artists put it in an unmistakably Chinese setting. Yamamoto Yōko convincingly argued that the iconography of Water-moon Kuan-yin should be viewed as a Chinese creation of Kuan-yin based on indigenous concepts of sages, retired gentlemen and immortals, but not Indian prototypes. Bamboo (later on replaced by pine) and waterfalls are typical features of Chinese landscapes, but have no relationship to India. Similarly, the relaxed pose of Kuan-yin either leaning against a rock or tree or clasping a knee derives from earlier secular paintings depicting retirement and nobility, but cannot be traced to Buddhist scriptural descriptions. In fact, it was already used in depicting scholars with Taoist leanings as in the brick relief decor of a Nanking tomb (ca. 400) discovered in 1960. More examples of this kind are available, several High T'ang, that date to about the time when this form of Kuan-yin image was created (Yamamoto 1989:28–37).

The emphasis on the Chinese landscape connection is important, but I would like to stress even more the ritual function of the Water-moon Kuan-yin. While it is true that some of the Water-moon Kuan-yins from Tun-huang, like the one located at Musée Guimet, are relaxed and present themselves in a three quarter view, others, like the one dated 968 from the Freer Gallery (figure 6.5), however, is shown frontally, "in an extremely hieratic pose, with no hint of the informality that characterizes the four earlier versions. The hieratic arrangement was to become even more apparent in later representations" (Lawton 1973:90). This frontal pose, together with "the canopy, the nimbus with its central colored strip, and the throne" led Cornelius Chang to emphasize the "iconic" aspects of the painting (Chang 1971:47). Recently, Pan Liang-wen (1996) has stressed the need to examine the iconography in the context of religious ritual. I favor this approach, which I believe will provide a key to unlock the secrets of its origin.

The paintings of Water-moon Kuan-yin, just as gilt bronze images, were created as icons to be worshiped. The most convincing evidence for this is the presence of an altar table filled with offerings in many of the paintings. The bodhisattva is invoked in the cartouche in the Freer painting, for instance, with "Homage to Great Compassionate Water-moon Kuan-yin Bodhisattva Who Saves [One] from Suffering." He holds a willow sprig in the right hand and a bottle of ambrosia in the other. He is attended by two bodhisattvas who hold trays of flowers as offerings. In the lower register, four people kneel in atten-

Figure 6.5. Water-moon Kuan-yin, dated 968. *Courtesy of the Freer Gallery of Art, Washington, D. C.*

dance on either side of the central inscription. Although both the long inscription and the four cartouches identifying the donors and beneficiaries are badly defaced, it is still possible to make out that they are members of the Yin family. The two women on the left are the mother and wife (smaller figure) and the woman on the right beside the man is his concubine. The reason for having this painting made on the fifteenth day of the fifth month, 968 is the wish for a safe childbirth.

We are more fortunate with the Guimét Kuan-yin, for the inscription is in much better shape. The donor was an official named Ma Ch'ien-chin. He explained why he had the painting made on the thirteenth day of the seventh month in 943: In early fall when the moon was full, he remembered his dead mother whose spiritual traces were difficult to discern. Longing for her, he asked a skillful artisan to paint the Thousand-handed Kuan-yin and the artisan's apprentice to paint the Water-moon Kuan-yin. He prayed to Kuan-yin to save the people and protect the country. He wished that all those who gaze on the painting be moved to goodness and not be reborn in hell but achieve enlightenment.

Anecdotal accounts testify to the devotional use of the Water-moon Kuan-yins as icons. In a catalogue of paintings of the Sung, *Sheng-ch'ao ming-hua ping* (Comments on the Famous Paintings of the Sacred Dynasty), written by Liu Tao-ch'ung in the first half of the eleventh century, we find a story about the painter Wu Tsung-yüan (d. 1053): A certain Mr. Kao in the capital had a habit of collecting paintings. For ten years he prostrated himself in front of a painting in his courtyard. Wishing to obtain a scroll painting of the Water-moon Kuan-yin, he asked Wu Tsung-yüan, who agreed to make it. After three years, Wu completed it. By the time Wu brought it to Kao, Kao had already passed away. Wu burned the painting and went away weeping (Chang 1971:85).

Water-moon Kuan-yin was invoked by the faithful for a good rebirth, safe childbirth, and enlightenment. Although these were traditional benefits the bodhisattva was believed to bestow on the worshiper, the ninth-century form of the icon was new. Japanese monk pilgrims noticed the popularity of this new icon and began to transport it back home. Jōgyō brought one home in 839 and commented, "The Great Compassionate One manifests in ten thousand forms and, observing the sentient beings, eliminates suffering and bestows happiness. That is why he shows himself in images and portraits in order to make people have faith. Now in China people believe that he is the cause that can eliminate disasters and produce blessings in the world. Since this form is not known in our country, I have brought it back" (T 55:1050a). Engyō, who went to China with him, also brought back a Water-moon Kuan-yin. They, like the Chinese they encountered at that time, clearly regarded the Water-moon Kuan-yin as a manifestation of the Thousand-handed Kuan-yin. Surely, that must have been the reason why the two were painted together in Tun-huang. This is another case of the Chinese domestication of the Tantric Thousand-handed Kuan-yin. Just as the unknown author used the euhemerization model of Chinese deities in creating the legend of Miao-shan (to be discussed in chapter 8), artists also used Chinese landscape idioms in creating the Water-moon Kuan-yin. Both were successful attempts at making the imported bodhisattva Chinese.

The Water-moon Kuan-yin was not only painted, but also incised on mirrors. The Japanese monk-pilgrim Chōnin brought four such mirrors, made in 985, back to Japan in 988. One of these was found inside the body of the Buddha image in Seiryōji together with a list of all the objects. "It is of bronze with much tin content, about 5" in diameter and rather thin. A figure of Kuan-yin seated on a rock over a lotus pool and near a bamboo grove is engraved into the reverse side of the mirror in a rather stylized manner reminiscent of the woodblock prints" (Henderson and Hurvitz 1956:33). Yamamoto notes that there is a bird hovering to the right of Kuan-yin. She takes it to be the blue bird accompanying the Queen Mother of the West and regards it as another example of how Taoism and popular religion might have influenced the creation of the Water-moon Kuan-yin (Yamamoto 1989:33). Since the bird is always present in the iconography of the Kuan-yin of the South Sea (see chapter 10), and the bird is always identified as a white parrot, I think the bird inscribed on the mirror would more likely be the earliest example of the parrot.

The function of such mirrors might be similar to a later example. An incised relief of the Water-moon Kuan-yin kept at the Freer Gallery (figure 6.6) with two dated inscriptions that appear below the deity contains the spell from the indigenous scripture *King Kao's Kuan-yin Sūtra* discussed in chapter 3. The first inscription was written by a man named Chao Hung from T'ien-shui, in present-day Kansu on the Ch'ing-ming festival in 1095. He states that he lost his father when young and regarded the Buddha as his only refuge. He claims that this is a copy of a painting done by the famous T'ang painter Wu Tao-tzu. He had this stele made in order to promote a wider worship of Kuan-yin and hopes that all those who chant the sacred spell from the scripture would be spared the pain of losing a parent in childhood. The second inscription, appearing in smaller script to the right of the image, was written by Hsü K'ai-hsi, also from T'ien-shui, in 1663. He described how the stone slab with the incised Kuan-yin image was discovered by a farmer, who gave it to his daughter to be used as a washboard. But it shone brilliantly and the family gilded it with gold, treating it as an heirloom. When Hsü was serving as a magistrate, he learned about it and went to the village to investigate. He then had it moved to Pao-ning Ssu for safekeeping.[6]

Figure 6.6. Water-moon kuan-yin stele, dated 1096. *Courtesy of the Freer Gallery of Art, Washington, D.C.*

Shinkaku (1117–1180) included two drawings of the Water-moon Kuan-yin in his *Besson zakki* (Miscellaneous Notes on Other Icons [besides the Buddha]). No. 86 in Vol. 3 of the *Zuzōbu* section of the Taishō Tripiṭaka is based on a Chinese original. It shows the bodhisattva sitting on top of a fantastic rock resembling some arrangements in Chinese rock gardens. Three luxuriant bamboos stand in the background. The inscription on the upper left corner bears a Japanese date, corresponding to the ninth day of the eleventh month of 1088. It states that this painting was originally commissioned by a faithful devotee named Ch'en Cheng-tsung from Ch'uan-chou of the country of Sung (China) on behalf of his son for the latter's safety. It was offered to a temple for perpetual worship. The other drawing, No. 87, is based on a Korean original made during the Koryŏ dynasty (918–1392; Wang 1987:32). It shows the bodhisattva sitting on top of a very rugged rocky mountain. He looks down upon a male worshiper dressed in Korean fashion who holds a hand censer in both his hands. On the upper left, a palace floats in the clouds. Like paintings from Tun-huang, this drawing clearly shows that the bodhisattva is being worshiped.

Shinkaku also copied the "Method of Worshiping the Water-moon Master Perceiver" (*Shui-yüeh Kuan-tzu-tsai kung-yang fa*) to go with the two drawings. If one has any doubt that the Water-moon Kuan-yin was understood by the faithful to be no different from the Thousand-handed Kuan-yin, this should remove it completely. Let us read some relevant passages:

> Recite the mantra facing the image. All your desires will be fulfilled in a short time. If you want to have food and clothing, stay in an uninhabited place, choose either a pure place or an ordinary place, burn incense and prepare flowers to worship the Great Compassionate Worthy One (Ta-pei Tsun-che). All your sins will be dissolved. Your worldly and otherworldly desires will be accomplished.
>
> If you are destined to go to hell because you have broken the precepts, recite the mantra three hundred thousand times. All your sins will be dissolved. You will be reborn in the Western Paradise and see Amitābha Buddha. If all your desires cannot be fulfilled, I vow that I will not attain the unsurpassable Way of the Buddha. You should know that based on my great compassionate vow I will guide those who break the precepts to the West. (T *Zuzōbu* 3:209b-c)

Water-moon Kuan-yin was a frequent subject painted by Tangut artists in Hsi-hsia as well. They followed the Chinese model, but added some local coloring. Among the paintings recovered from Khara Khoto, situated northeast of Tun-huang, and held at the Hermitage Museum, a painting of the Water-moon Kuan-yin dated to the twelfth century provides important evidence that the deity might be worshiped specifically in order to achieve rebirth in the Pure Land (figure 6.7). Like the figures at Tun-huang, the bodhisattva is shown as sitting in the pose of royal ease. He does not hold any implement in his hands. The willow branch is planted inside a bottle placed by his side. Two robust bamboos are in the background. But what catches our attention are an old man and a young boy in the painting. Maria Rudova explains who they are. "The dead man, standing on a cloud in the bottom left corner of the painting, was without question a Tangut. . . . In the bottom right corner, is a group of Tanguts playing musical instruments at the grave site. Music played a role in state ceremonials and religious rituals in the Tangut Empire and therefore provides a fitting accompaniment to the solemn moment when the soul of the righteous man stands at the 'Gate of Paradise.' . . . At the top right, the dead man is shown again, now reborn as a boy, reaching out his hands in prayer to the deity" (Rudova 1993:91, 198).[7] She based her interpretation on related paintings produced in the same time and place. For instance, a painting dated to the late twelfth century and labeled "Greeting the Soul of the Righteous Man on the Way to the Pure Land of Amitābha" (figure 6.8) explicitly illustrates this theme.[8] It shows the worshiper in the lower left corner praying to the Three Holy Ones of the Pure Land with folded hands. A naked boy, enveloped by the ray of light sent out by Amitābha Buddha, is on the point of stepping onto the lotus pedestal held by Kuan-yin and Ta-shih-chih. The Water-moon Kuan-yin assumed the role of "Guide of Souls" in Hsi-hsia.

Like the Water-moon Kuan-yin, the White-robed Kuan-yin was also worshiped in rituals and was depicted with a boy who could either be Sudhana or the reborn donor. Henrik Sørenson describes a painting dated to the Five Dynasties now kept in the Palace Museum in Beijing.[9] It shows the White-robed Kuan-yin seated in the "royal ease" posture on an ornate throne. The robe is drawn partly over the head to cover the crown. "In his right hand he holds the characteristic willow branch and in the left hand he holds the vase containing the nectar. . . . In the right side of the painting is a male worshiper kneeling on a mat. In the air above the worshiper hangs suspended a double-vajra resting on a lotus-throne on a multicolored cloud, and above the double-vajra, slightly to the left is another cloud, in which sits an infant, possibly a boy, who holds a small tray of offerings with his right hand" (Sørenson 1991–92:308–9). The boy riding on the cloud, like the example from Khara Khoto, could be either Sudhana or the reborn worshiper.

In contrast, a painting recovered from Martuk, situated northwest of Tunhuang and kept at the West Berlin State Museum, unmistakably links the White-robed Kuan-yin with the Pure Land tradition. Published in the exhibition catalogue, the painting is dated to ninth to tenth century. The White-robed Kuan-yin is one of six small figures surrounding the main Kuan-yin image in the *tangka*. "At left center, clad in a white robe with a white cloth draped over a tall headdress, sits one of Avalokiteśvara's Chinese embodiments, the so-called Pai-i (white-robed) Kuan-yin or the Sung-tzu (child-bestowing) Kuan-yin. This figure holds his right hand aloft, pointing with the index finger to a child borne on the palm of the left hand" (Laing 1982: 212). The catalogue caption implies that the White-robed Kuan-yin depicted here is holding a baby to be bestowed on the worshiper, like the Child-giving Kuan-yin does in late imperial times. Seen in the light of the examples from Khara Khoto that shared the same religious and cultural milieu, the infant is more likely to be the reborn worshiper than a baby bestowed on the worshiper. However, if Kuan-yin can enable a devotee to be reborn in the Western Paradise as a baby boy, why can he/she not enable a baby boy to be born into the household of the worshiper? Why not indeed, especially since such a promise is already made by the *Lotus*

Figure 6.7. Kuan-yin, "Moon in Water," dated to the twelfth century. *Courtesy of the Hermitage Museum, St. Petersburg.*

Figure 6.8. "Greeting the Soul of the Righteous Man on the Way to the Pure Land of Amitābha," twelfth century. *Courtesy of the Hermitage Museum, St. Petersburg.*

Sūtra? The transition from the White-robed Kuan-yin into the Child-giving Kuan-yin was a logical one.

The White-robed Kuan-yin

Art historians have long noted the similarity between the Water-moon Kuan-yin and the White-robed Kuan-yin (Matsumoto 1926). There are, however, some distinctive differences between the two. First of all, the Water-moon Kuan-yin, like the more traditional images of the bodhisattva, was perceived as masculine. That is why he was sometimes depicted with a moustache, like the image of him in the Freer Gallery (figure 6.5). A story reported by Sun Kuang-hsien (900–968) in *Pei-meng so-yen* (Trivial Talks about Northern Dreams) provides anecdotal evidence for the male gender of the Water-moon Kuan-yin. Chiang Ning was a *chin-shih* during the Hsien-t'ung era (860–874), and he had a reputation for being very handsome. Whenever he visited someone, his host would consider it auspicious. He was given the nickname "Water-moon Kuan-yin" (Wang 1987:31).

The White-robed Kuan-yin, on the other hand, looks decidedly feminine. In fact, not only Kuan-yin, but bodhisattvas in general have looked rather feminine since the T'ang. The Sung monk Tao-ch'eng commented on the appearances of Buddhist images in *Shih-shih yao-lan* (Essential Readings in Buddhism), "The Buddhist images made during the Sung and Ch'i have thick lips and prominent noses. Their eyes are long and their cheeks full, making them appear heroic and manly. Since the T'ang, they have been drawn with fine strokes which make them look beautiful and effeminate, very much like courtesans. That is why nowadays people praise courtesans as bodhisattvas" (T 54:257). Art historians have noted that during the T'ang, the faces of bodhisattvas, including that of Kuan-yin, became round with layered chins, while the body of the images became supple in a natural sway. The trend could have been influenced by the contemporary standard of ideal beauty, which emphasized fullness of face and body. Tuan Ch'eng-shih (d. 863) in the *Ssu-t'a chi* (Record of Temples and Stūpas), describes that Han Kan (active 742–755) had painted Indra, Brahmā, and apsaras on the walls of Pao-yin Ssu using Lord Ch'i's "sing-song girls" as his models (Liu 1983:40). Alexander Soper cited the story about Ch'u Yen (ca. 784) being cured by the bodhisattva who had "destroyer-of-cities" (*ch'ing-ch'eng*) features as a reference to the latter's feminine looks and regarded this as a stage in the gradual transformation of Kuan-yin into a female deity (1960:25).

The second distinguishing characteristic of the White-robed Kuan-yin is of course the fact that the deity wears a white robe that sometimes covers the head as well, serving as a veil. It is the presence of this white garment that led many scholars to trace the origin of the iconography to Tantric sources. Citing H. Maspero, Kenneth Ch'en explains that the popular female Child-giving Kuan-yin (Sung-tzu Kuan-yin) originates in the White-robed Kuan-yin (Pāṇḍaravāsinī, "clad in white"), a figure introduced from Tibet. The popular religion in China then "appropriated" this imagery, completely misunderstanding its original meaning. I cite what he says about this complicated process.

> Through the T'ang and early Sung Dynasties it appears that Kuan-yin was still looked upon as a male figure. The paintings recovered from Tun-huang

> give the best evidence of this, for in these representations Kuan-yin is frequently portrayed with a moustache. . . . During the T'ang Dynasty a new element which brought a change in the form of the bodhisattva entered the picture. This was the introduction in a Tantric sūtra in the eighth century of the concept of a female Kuan-yin clad in white, and from the tenth century on, the painters began to paint this figure, which was called Pai-i Kuan-yin. The French Sinologist H. Maspero has provided what appears to be a reasonable explanation of this change. Mahāyāna Buddhism has always conceived of enlightenment as the conjunction of wisdom and compassion. In Tantric Buddhism these two are symbolized by the male and female. With the introduction of the female element all the buddhas and bodhisattvas are provided with female consorts. Thus the female consort of Avalokiteśvara in Tibetan Buddhism was called the White Tārā (in Sanskrit, Pāṇḍaravāsinī), meaning "clad in white." The Chinese Pai-i Kuan-yin is a literal translation of this term. This Kuan-yin clad in white, introduced into China from Tibet, was soon appropriated from Buddhism by the popular religion in China, and a new figure, Sung-tzu Kuan-yin (Kuan-yin, giver of children), was developed. In this popular form so little remains of the deity Pāṇḍaravāsinī that the connection between the two is not easily apparent. However, Maspero thinks there is a connection. In Tantric Buddhism Pāṇḍaravāsinī belongs to the mandala or cosmogram entitled Garbhakośadhātu, the World of the Womb-treasury. What probably happened was that the Chinese popular religion interpreted this symbolical expression of the womb world literally, and Pāṇḍaravāsinī was converted into the "giver of children." This evolution was entirely in the realm of popular religion, and did not penetrate into Buddhism itself (Ch'en 1964:341–42).

This explanation is not only textually and historically incorrect, but betrays a blatant bias against Chinese "popular religion" based on pure speculation devoid of any concrete evidence. Recently Rolf A. Stein disagreed with the preceding interpretation and convincingly showed that Pai-i (Pāṇḍaravāsinī) should not be confused with the White Tārā.[10] In the Tantric sūtras translated in the T'ang dealing with the "mothers" or female counterparts of buddhas (*fomu*), Pai-i is mentioned together with Tārā, but is distinct from the latter. She is the mother of the lotus clan whose head is Avalokiteśvara. Three other female deities in the Womb-treasury Maṇḍala are also clad in white and can thus be called Pai-i. White is the symbol for the mind of enlightenment, which gives birth to all buddhas and bodhisattvas. That is why the female deities of the lotus clan who are housed in the court of Kuan-yin are all white in color, for they are the "mothers" of buddhas and bodhisattvas (Stein 1986:27–37). The Chinese have thus always kept a clear distinction between White-robed Kuan-yin and Tārā, whose name is transliterated as To-luo. As Stein pointed out, however, Avalokiteśvara is described as clad in white in the ritual *sādhanas* connected with the chanting of dhāraṇīs in a number of esoteric texts, the earliest of which was translated in the first half of the sixth century, the *Dhāraṇī Miscellany* (T'o-lo-ni tsa-chi) in ten fascicles. It contains thirty-seven dhāraṇīs revealed by Avalokiteśvara as well as instructions for the making of his image and rituals of visualization and invocation. As I pointed out in chapter 2, not only the female handmaidens of Avalokiteśvara are described as being "white-clad," but the bodhisattva himself is frequently identified as wearing white garments in the esoteric sūtras translated during the T'ang period. Moreover, the rules about image-making also insist on using white material, be it wool or cloth, for painting the image of Avalokiteśvara. Clearly, the color white has a special significance in these scriptures. However, if we read carefully the descriptions of the White-clad One in these texts, they bear no resemblance to the Chinese White-robed Kuan-yin.

In the Womb-treasury Maṇḍala, four female attendants of Avalokiteśvara in his court all have names containing the word "white" as well. The rituals and artistic depictions of the two maṇḍalas once existed during the T'ang, for it was from China that Kūkai (774–835) obtained the original models, which have been preserved in Japan. But no extant maṇḍalas have survived in China and there is also no evidence that the cultic practices connected with them were ever very popular in China. Representing secret rites open only to elite, male, monastic practitioners who had received initiations, the knowledge of them was naturally restricted to a small number of people. Where did Maspero find the evidence that the Womb-treasury Maṇḍala was so well known among the common Chinese people that they could ignorantly "misinterpret" its meaning?

My theory of the origin of the White-robed Kuan-yin and her connection with the Child-giving Kuan-yin is entirely different. As I discussed in chapter 3, I believe that they are really the same deity with different names. Even if the name "Pai-i" came from esoteric scriptures, the sexual transformation and subsequent popularity were due to and facilitated by indigenous scriptures, miracle stories, and art. The most one can say about the relationship between the latter and Buddhist canonical literature is this: the origin of the White-robed Kuan-yin might be derived from the Tantric sūtras, but the actual creation of the iconography was entirely an indigenous one. Just as the Water-moon Kuan-yin is a Chinese creation based on Mahāyāna and Tantric ideals yet expressed through the medium of landscape painting, the White-robed Kuan-yin is also a Chinese creation. The privileging of the white color might be derived from the Tantric tradition. But the actual iconography of the White-robed Kuan-yin is almost no different from that of the Water-moon Kuan-yin. Monks and lay people, elite and commoners, men and women played their parts in the construction and dissemination of her cult. The White-robed Kuan-yin, as a symbol of enlightenment, was a favorite subject for the so-called Zen paintings created by Ch'an monks during the Sung and Yüan periods. And literati in the Ming, not just the wives, would fervently pray to her, as the fertility goddess, for heirs.

Both the Water-moon and the White-robed Kuan-yin are included in the thirty-three forms of Kuan-yin in Sino-Japanese art. Cornelius Chang suggests that the two might be interchangeable. Because out of the thirty-three forms of Kuan-yin, fourteen of them have names that are simply descriptive, such as "sūtra carrying" (no. 3), "hands joined with palm touching" (no. 29), and so on. Since this is the case, the Kuan-yin who is seated in the water-moon setting of Potalaka Mountain in a white robe may be named by either of the descriptive names (Chang 1971:117). The difficulty of differentiating the two is illustrated by the Water-moon Kuan-yin of the Nelson-Atkins Museum (figure 6.9). Although this Southern Sung painting is identified as Water-moon because of the typical moon-like halo enveloping the bodhisattva, Kuan-yin nevertheless wears the head-covering white robe and looks decidedly feminine. Matsumoto Eiichi remarked long ago that painters drew the White-robed Kuan-yin the same way as the Water-moon Kuan-yin. According to him, another reason for the confusion might be attributed to the technique of drawing. All Kuan-yin paintings from the Sung on were executed in ink and remained white because painters favored monochrome ink drawing under the influence of Ch'an (Matsumoto 1926:212–13). The only way to tell the two forms of Kuan-yin apart is to look for the head-covering white robe.

The inspiration for this distinctive piece of clothing might come from two sources, one accounting for its color, the other its style. As for the color white, aside from the Tantric connection mentioned previously, we should also keep in mind that in Buddhist scriptures, "clad in white (*pai-i*)" refers to a layman instead of a monk, following the Indian tradition. As I mentioned in chapter 4, Vimalakīrti, the famous layman bodhisattva, is called "clad in white." In many miracle stories, as we recall, a person clad in white (*pai-i jen*) often appears. I also suggested that this represented a lay person instead of a monk. Although the person's gender is unspecified in the early stories, the mysterious visitor is increasingly identified as a woman from the tenth century on. The style of the clothing, on the other hand, has been traced to contemporary women's clothing in the Sung. A handscroll titled the "Knicknack Peddler" painted by Li Sung (active circa 1190–1264) in 1211 depicts ordinary city life of the common people

Figure 6.9. Water-moon Kuan-yin, Southern Sung (1127–1279). *Courtesy of the Nelson-Atkins Museum of Art.*

at that time.[11] It shows women wearing veils over their heads, very much like that seen on the White-robed Kuan-yin. Chen-tzu Liu takes this as evidence for the formulation of the unique clothing style of the White-robed Kuan-yin. Since the robe functions as a counterpart of the clothing of common people, it reinforces the identification to Kuan-yin as a commoner. She is not a remote deity, but is accessible to the people (Liu 1983:12).

Let us leave off speculating about the origins of the White-robed Kuan-yin for now and move on to examine her popularity in plastic arts, painting, and other artistic media that has been unsurpassed since the tenth century. Ku Yen-wu (1613–1682), the Ch'ing scholar of philological research and evidential learning, observed, "Among the deities who enjoy the offerings of incense in the temples and monasteries under heaven, none can compete with Kuan-yin. The Great Being has many forms of transformation. But people in the world mostly worship that of the White-robed One. According to the *Liao shih* (History of the Liao Dynasty, [907–1125]), White-robed Kuan-yin lives on Mt. Ch'ang-pai [Perpetually White Mountain, in present-day Jilin province], which is more than a thousand *li* southeast of Mt. Leng [Cold Mountain]. On that mountain, birds and beasts are all white, and no one dares to harm them. Thus we know that White-robed Kuan-yin has been worshiped for a very long time" (*Ku-chung sui-p'i*). Other sources, some of which I discuss later, also point to the tenth century as the beginning of the cult of the White-robed Kuan-yin. Even if she was originally introduced into China through Tantric ritual texts, her eventual success in China was due to a group of indigenous scriptures which promote her as a goddess capable of granting children, the ones we have examined in chapter 3. Her iconography was sinicized and eventually, like Miao-shan, she was also provided with a very Chinese biography in her own precious scroll, the *Miao-ying pao-chüan*.

Several White-robed Kuan-yin paintings were attributed to the T'ang artist Wu Tao-tzu and as a genre, this type of painting has sometimes been connected with the Sung painter Li Kung-lin (ca. 1049–1106) and the *pai-miao* line-drawing technique favored by his school (Cahill 1982:8; Lee 1980:84). Although the attribution to Wu Tao-tzu is not always reliable, dated sculptures of White-robed Kuan-yin in Szechwan go back to the tenth century. The inscription beside Kuan-yin in the Pei-shan Cave Temple in Ta-tsu, Szechwan, for instance, stated that the White-robed Kuan-yin was carved in 936.[12] Two White-robed Kuan-yin statues stand on either side at the entrance to the Yen-hsia Grotto at the western side of the West Lake in Hangchow (figure 4.2). Angela Howard dates them to the early 940s, for they are similar to the group of sculptures at Mt. Chiang-t'ai near Tz'u-yün Cave built by the Ch'ien royal family of the Wu Yüeh Kingdom in 942 (1985:11).

Another source identifying the rise of White-robed Kuan-yin in the tenth century lies with the founding myths of monasteries and convents dedicated to her. For instance, as I related in chapter 4, the establishment of the Upper T'ien-chu Monastery was connected with Ch'ien Liu's dream of a woman in white who promised to protect him and his descendants if he was compassionate. She told him that he could find her on Mt. T'ien-chu in Hangchow twenty years thereafter. After he became king, he dreamt of the same woman, who asked for a place to stay, and in return she would agree to be the patron deity of his kingdom. When he discovered that only one monastery on Mt. T'ien-chu housed an image of White-robed Kuan-yin, he gave it patronage and established it as the T'ien-chu k'an-ching-Yüan, the former name for the Monastery of Upper T'ien-chu, which became one of the most important pilgrimage centers for Kuan-yin worship.

Similar stories accounted for the founding of other temples. Several temples were erected in the tenth century in Chekiang and their founding myths were all connected with images of the White-robed Kuan-yin. For instance, three temples in Hangchow became enlarged from *an* (shrine) to *yüan* (cloisters) as a result of their White-robed Kuan-yin images. Kuan-yin fa-chi Yüan (Cloister of Kuan-yin's Dharma Salvation) was first built in the T'ien-fu era (936–947). It was burned down during the Ch'in-yen era (1127–30). But when a monk saw a divine light one night and found an image of the White-robed Kuan-yin among the rubbles, the temple was restored. Pao-yen Yüan (Cloister of the Precious Cliff) was first built in 967 when a resident of the province gave his house as its site. In the Cheng-ho era (1111–17) the abbot dreamt of a heavenly being wearing white clothing and he gave the temple over to Kuan-yin worship exclusively, intuitively taking the white-clad person to be the White-robed Kuan-yin. Jui-hsiang Yüan (Cloister of the Auspicious Images) was built in 1187 as a result of the monk Ming-tsu's dream of Kuan-yin in white (HCLAC 81).

The Pai-i kuang-jen Yüan (Cloister of the White Robe's Broad Benevolence), commonly known as Pai-i Kuan-yin Yüan, in Ningpo, was first built in 930. Due to the repeated reports of the image's efficacy, it received increased support in 935 and an imperial plaque in 1064. The image was carved from a wooden pillar that would issue white light, silhouetting the outline of Kuan-yin's form. Ch'ien I, the military commissioner, witnessed the miracle and sponsored the making of the image (YYSMC 16:15a-b).

A stele with an incised drawing of Kuan-yin on the upper half and an inscription recording the miracle that led to its enshrinement in the Shou-sheng Yüan (Cloister of Longevity and Holiness) in Chiang-yin, Kiangsu, has survived (figure 6.10). The standing bodhisattva holds a willow branch in her right hand, and her uplifted left hand holds the vase of nectar. She wears a flowing robe, but her head is crowned by an elaborate headdress, not covered by the cape connected with the robe. A large halo in the shape of the moon encircles her head. This image is clearly the Water-moon Kuan-yin, although from the accompanying text it is meant to represent the White-robed Kuan-yin. The stele was carved in 1123 after the official Wang Hsiao-chieh visited the temple and was told the history of the image by the abbot Mi-yüan on the twenty-second day of the second month of that year. However, the story was about an event that had taken place a hundred years before, in 1023. Wang wrote the text at the request of the abbot. Entitled, "Record of the Efficacious and Responsive Kuan-yin of Shou-sheng Cloister of Chiang-yin Who Flowed in From the Sea," it says:

> The Bodhisattva [the image] flowed into Chiang-yin from the sea in the fifth month of 1023. Passengers on a boat met the bodhisattva in the river, who followed the boat shining bright lights. The boatman tried to push it away with the oars. He did so three times, yet three times it followed the boat continuing to shine. When it reached a shallow bend near the river bank, it stopped. On the same night a person wearing white garments appeared to a resident by the name of Wu Hsin in a dream and asked him to donate his right arm. Wu said that he could not bear to part with his right arm, but he would be happy to obey any other command. The white-clad person then told him that he should go to the shopkeeper Li and ask for the sandalwood Li kept in his house to make the arm. Wu waited until the next morning to start his amazing search. But when he heard from the townspeople that a Kuan-yin image measuring about ten *ch'ih* had flowed in from the sea and was resting by the river bank, he went over to take a look. He saw that the bodhisattva indeed did not have a right arm. He then told the assembled onlookers about his dream in which the bodhisattva had asked for the arm and expressed his determination to comply with the request. He then went to the shopkeeper Li and indeed obtained the sandalwood, which was about five *ch'ih* in length. With that he had the right arm made for the bodhisattva. The townspeople welcomed the image and installed it at Shou-sheng. It received widespread worship. Many efficacious responses have been reported after people prayed to it.

The White-robed Kuan-yin's presence was prominent in miracle tales dated to this time. A story similar to this one is found among those about Kuan-yin collected by Hung Mai (1123–1202) in the *Tales of the Listener*. An old village woman suffered from an arm ache that did not seem to improve even after she consulted with doctors. One night she dreamt of a woman in white who told

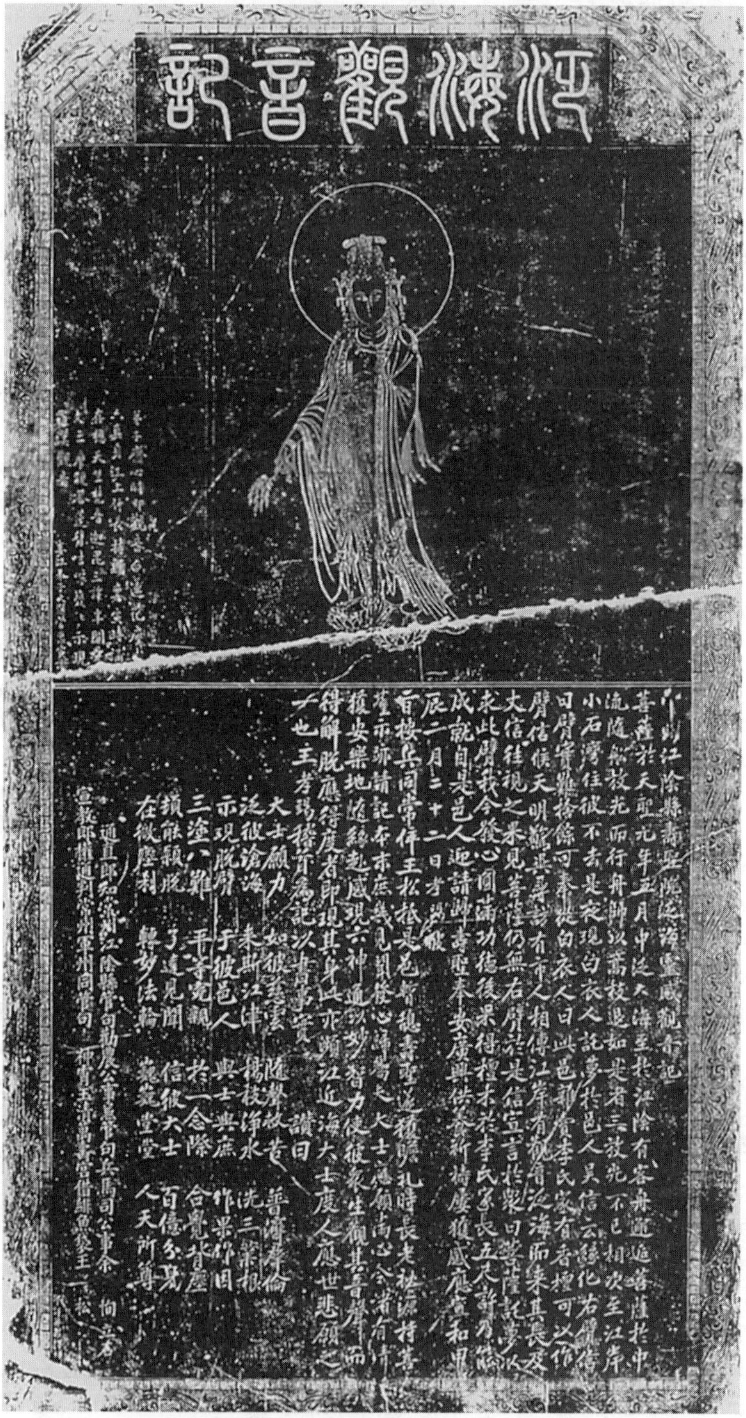

Figure 6.10. "Kuan-yin Who Floats over from the Sea," dated 1124. From *Pei-ching T'u-shu-kuan tsang Chung-kuo li-tai shih-k'e t'o-pen hui-pien* (1991:146).

her, "I also suffer from the same problem. If you would cure my arm, I will do the same for you." When asked where she lived, she said in the western corridor of Ch'ung-ning Monastery in Hu-chou (in Chekiang). The next day the woman went into the city and told her dream to the monk Chung-tao who was in charge of the western dormitory of the monastery. He immediately realized that the person in the dream must be Kuan-yin, for he had an image of the White-robed Kuan-yin in his room and during a renovation project, the arm of the image had accidentally been damaged. He led the woman into the room and she paid obeisance to the image who indeed had a damaged arm. She paid workers to repair the image. When Kuan-yin's arm was restored, the woman also recovered from her arm ache. Hung Mai was told this story by Wu Chieh, a native of Hu-chou (*I chien chih* 1:88).

Not only divine images of Kuan-yin came to be identified with the person in white, but visions of the bodhisattva also increasingly appeared in this form. Although the work is no longer extant, we are told that one collection of miracle tales resulted from a miraculous cure received by the compiler from the White-robed Kuan-yin. Vice minister Pien Chih-pai traveled from the capital to Ling-ch'uan (in present-day Kiangsi) in 1079 and fell ill due to heat stroke. He dreamt of a person in white who sprinkled water on him from head to toe. He felt great coolness and, upon waking, recovered completely. He made a vow to proclaim Kuan-yin's compassion and extensively plant the roots of faith in the people. He combed through records of the past and present, gathered all the miracles attesting to Kuan-yin's efficacious manifestations, and wrote a book entitled *Kuan-yin kan-ying chi* (Collections of Kuan-yin's Miraculous Responses) in four fascicles. The woodblocks were kept at Upper T'ien-chu Monastery (T 49:419c).

These examples can serve as an episodic history of the increasing popularity of the cult of the White-robed Kuan-yin that occurred after the tenth century. There could very well be a link between this cult and Pāṇḍaravāsinī of the Tantric texts. But if this is the case, we have no clear evidence. For the Chinese White-robed Kuan-yin shows no connection with Tantric rituals. Except for the mantras, there is also nothing esoteric about these texts glorifying this deity. She seems to have developed quite independently of Tārā and other Tantric deities, even if she originally had some relationship with them. I am convinced that her cult was due to a group of indigenous texts that present her primarily as the goddess with child-granting efficacy. In this capacity, the White-robed Kuan-yin is a fertility goddess who nevertheless is devoid of sexuality. She gives children to others, but she is never a mother. To borrow a distinction from Karen Horney (1931), she is thus a figure of motherliness, but not motherhood.

These indigenous texts are generically called *Pai-i Kuan-yin ching* (or *chou*) (Sūtra [or Spell] of White-robed Kuan-yin). They are very short, but invariably contain spells or mantras. The chanting and memorization of these texts is believed to be unfailingly efficacious. The most famous among them is the *Pai-i Kuan-yin (or Ta-shih) shen-chou* (The Divine Spell of White-robed Kuan-yin or the Great Being), copies of which are still being widely printed and distributed free of charge by the faithful up the present day. This text was already in use in the eleventh century.[13] Another popular text, *Kuan-yin shih-chü ching* (Kuan-yin Sūtra in Ten Phrases), was sometimes combined with the former and known by several different names, such as *Kuan-yin meng-shou (transmitted in dream) ching*, *Kuan-yin pao-sheng (preserving life) ching*, or *Kuan-yin chiu-sheng (saving life) ching*. This text can also be dated to the eleventh century.[14] Both texts were supposed to be transmitted by the White-robed Kuan-yin to her devotees. While the chanting of these texts is believed to bring relief from all kinds of suffering to the devotee, they are not specifically concerned with fertility. The power to grant children, particularly sons, is attributed to another text: the *Dhāraṇī Sūtra of the Five Mūdras of the Great Compassionate White-robed One*. This is the indigenous sūtra discussed in chapter 3. The White-robed Kuan-yin was turned into the Child-giving (Sung-tzu) Kuan-yin.

I have noted the great popularity this sūtra enjoyed among the literati in the late Ming. Based on the many testimonials written by her grateful devotees, the White-robed Kuan-yin was clearly viewed as a compassionate giver of male heirs. Several characteristics of the miracle accounts appended to the scripture are noteworthy. First, although some of the events were dated to the eleventh, twelfth and thirteenth centuries, the majority seem to be concentrated in the Ming, and especially in the late Ming. Thus, it appears that it was during the years 1400 to 1600 that the cult of the White-robed Kuan-yin as the giver of heirs became firmly established in China.

Second, the wood-block print of Kuan-yin forming the frontispiece of the text usually depicts her holding a baby boy on her lap. This is the classical iconography of Child-giving Kuan-yin (figure 3.8), represented most frequently by the blanc de Chine porcelain and ivory figures produced in Fukien since the sixteenth century. The most celebrated Te-hua porcelain figures were made by a late Ming potter named Ho Chao-tsung who produced many Kuan-yin images in the late sixteenth and early seventeenth centuries (Donnelly 1969, Fong 1990). The resemblance between the iconography of Child-giving Kuan-yin and the Madonna and Child has been widely noted. It is interesting to note that this particular iconography of the Virgin became popular in parts of Europe during the same two centuries.[15] Fukien, like Kuantung, was a coastal province that was visited by Christian missionaries as early as the thirteenth century and, again, on a larger scale, beginning in the sixteenth century. Between the sixteenth and the eighteenth centuries, Spanish conquistadors and missionaries brought sculpture from both Spain and northern Europe to China and the Philippines. They also commissioned Chinese craftsmen to carve Christian images, most frequently the Virgin with the Child. The artisans were Fukienese, coming predominantly from Chang-chou, Fuchow, and Ch'uan-chou, the same cities that produced the image of Child-giving Kuan-yin. Since the same artistic communities produced these religious images, it is not surprising that the Madonnas looked somewhat Chinese, and the Kuan-yins looked almost "Gothic" (Watson 1984:41). The power to grant children is mentioned as one of the many powers of Kuan-yin in the "Universal Gateway" chapter of the *Lotus Sūtra*. Prior to the Ming, however, the depiction of Kuan-yin, even in feminine forms, never included a male child held either in her arms or placed on her lap. The religious basis for this iconography came from Buddhist scriptures, but its artistic rendering might have been influenced by the iconography of the Virgin.

Third, the miracle accounts provided the names and birthplaces of the donors. Donors coming from She County and Hui-chou (in present-day Anhui province) predominated. This is understandable, for Hui-chou merchants were noted for their wealth. The cult was not restricted to this region, but Hui-chou appears to have been over-represented because more of its natives could afford to print the text. An interesting fact is that among the personal names provided for the wives of the donors, seventeen contained the character *miao*, as in Miao-shan.[16] This character *miao*, incidentally, also appeared as part of the names of women donors who commissioned the Kuan-yin statues in Szechwan in the tenth century, as I discuss in chapter 8. Their names clearly have a relationship to the name of Miao-shan.

Miao-ying pao-chüan is a text devoted to the biography of the White-robed Kuan-yin. As the title of this precious scroll indicates, the heroine's name was Miao-ying. The copy I read at the Chekiang Provincial Library was printed by Yao Wen-hai Bookstore in Shanghai, without any date. Fu Hsi-hua reported that there were four editions in existence, the earliest one dated 1860. The text was also known as *Pai-i pao-chüan* (Precious Scroll of White-robed Kuan-yin) or *Pai-i cheng-ch'eng pao-chüan* (Precious Scroll of the White-robed Kuan-yin's Realization of Enlightenment). The story shows obvious debt to *Hsiang-shan pao-chüan*, but also shares some common thematic features with the other popular precious scrolls discussed later.

The story took place in Loyang during the reign of T'ai-tsung (r. 976–996) of the Sung. Mr. Hsü was forty years old when his only daughter Miao-ying was born. She began to keep a vegetarian diet at age seven and when she got older, spent her time chanting the *Lotus Sūtra*. The parents were looking forward to having a son-in-law when she announced that she did not want to get married. Echoing Miao-shan's sentiment, Miao-ying told her parents that marriage and children would increase one's karmic burden and tie one to more suffering. But her parents secretly betrothed her to Wang Ch'eng-tsu, the only son of a local gentry family and made plans with Wang's family to carry out the wedding celebration. The adults tricked her into going out to view the display at the Lantern Festival. Once out, she was abducted by two hundred men sent by the Wang family, who had been waiting in ambush for her. She prayed to Heaven and moved the Buddha (called "Ling-shan Chiao-chu," the Teaching Master of Vulture Peak) who dispatched Heavenly Kings, Guardians, Thunder, Wind, and Rain deities to create a hurricane and, in the confusion, spirit Miao-ying to White Cloud Mountain (Pai-yün Shan).

When the storm subsided, they discovered that she had mysteriously disappeared, leaving behind a copy of the *Lotus Sūtra* near the doorway. Her parents charged Wang with murder. He was imprisoned and subjected to torture. Unable to bear it, he made a false confession to the murder charge. Because of this tragedy, Wang came to realize the capriciousness of life and began to chant the name of the Buddha in prison. He also vowed to become a Buddhist devotee if he were released and allowed to go home. When the emperor celebrated his sixtieth birthday, he declared a general amnesty and commuted Wang's sentence to military exile to a remote place. Accompanied by two jailers, Wang made the journey. But one night when they were in the mountains, they heard the sound of a wooden fish being struck. They eventually found Miao-ying, who had been practicing cultivation there all this time. After she told Wang what happened, he decided to become her disciple and also practice Buddhism. She administered the three refuges and gave him the five precepts. When the two jailers returned home to spread the news, the parents of the couple, the governor, and eighteen other people all decided to go to her whom they called the "Great Immortal" (Ta-hsien), the same title given to Miao-shan. The party listened to her sermons and chanted the Buddha's name together. Finally in one unspecified year, on the third day of the first month, she "ascended to heaven in broad daylight, and became the White-robed Great Being Who Saves Beings from Sorrow and Suffering [Pai-i Ta-shih Chiu-k'u Chiu-nan]."

There is another precious scroll that features the White-robed Kuan-yin as the Giver of Children, who is called the Venerable Mother (Lao-mu). I discuss this in chapter 11, which introduces the bodhisattva in this new guise.

I have noted that the iconography of the White-robed Kuan-yin resembles closely that of the Water-moon Kuan-yin. Using dated specimens of the two as the basis, the two images seem to appear at the same time, although literary sources indicate that the Water-moon was created earlier. Interestingly, despite the popularity of the cult of Water-moon Kuan-yin in T'ang China as reported by Japanese monk-pilgrims, there is little evidence that it continued in later times. No miracle stories, precious scrolls, pilgrimage sites, or popular religious prints are dedicated to the Water-moon manifestation.

The White-robed Kuan-yin, on the other hand, has been ubiquitous. She has not only incorporated the Water-moon form of Kuan-yin, but evolved into a new form—the Child-giving. As P'u-t'o became a famous pilgrimage site in the Ming, the White-robed Kuan-yin was also identified as the Kuan-yin of the South Sea, to be discussed in chapter 10. This is indicated by two hymns addressed to her that may be found in the Bibliothéque Nationale in Paris (Chinois 5865). Neither is dated, but because they are attached to *King Kao's Kuan-yin Sūtra*, copies of which circulated widely in the Ming, these hymns might have been composed during that time. The first is entitled, "The Manifestation of Kuan-yin" ("Kuan-yin shih-hsien"), and it reads:

> With a mind of utmost sincerity, I take refuge in and worship the Holy Master Perceiver (Kuan-tzu-tsai) who is the Bright Ruler of the True Law of P'u-t'o Island, situated by the isolated seashore. Her hair is as purplish black as distant hills, her lips are of gorgeous vermilion red, her cheeks are like morning cloud, and her eyebrows are curved like the new crescent moon. . . . She wears a white garment and sits on a green lotus. Responding to the cries for help from people trapped in danger, she is like a moon appearing in the ninth empyrean or a star reflected in myriad bodies of water. Adoration to the White-robed Master Perceiver Bodhisattva.

The second hymn is intriguingly entitled, "Worship the Stūpa and Pray for Heirs from the White-robed One" ("Pai-i ch'iu-ssu ta li"), and it reads:

> With a mind of utmost sincerity, I take refuge in Kuan-yin who is on P'u-t'o Island emerging from the ocean. Three purple bamboos keep her company and one willow branch flutters over the dusty world. A parrot carrying flowers comes to make offerings, and the Dragon Princess offers her a priceless pearl. She steps on a lotus of one thousand petals and holds a willow branch to save sentient beings. To the One of Great Compassion, Great Vows, Great Holiness, and Great Mercy, I pay obeisance to the *Pai-i ch'ung-pao* (doubly clothed in white).

As discussed in chapter 3, the phrase *Pai-i ch'ung-pao* appears often in the miracle tales attached to the indigenous sūtra glorifying the White-robed Kuan-yin as Giver of Sons. It refers to the baby's still being enclosed in the whitish membrane called a caul, thus "doubly clothed in white." It implies that he is a gift from the White-robed Kuan-yin. It is interesting that in this hymn the phrase itself became hypostasized and so is addressed as a deity in itself.

In this chapter we have seen how the elusive and mysterious figure of the "person in white" who visited the faithful in their visions and dreams reported in miracle stories and monastic chronicles became represented by the distinctive White-robed Kuan-yin, the first clearly feminine forms of the bodhisattva created by Chinese artists. I argued that the creation of new iconographies of Kuan-yin in China was connected with the regional character of Chinese Buddhism and Buddhist art. The new icons were also closely connected with Buddhist theology, ritual, and devotion. In fact, the Water-moon Kuan-yin, an indigenous iconography that appeared before the White-robed Kuan-yin and served as a prototype for the latter, was a good example for both the points I made. The White-robed Kuan-yin gave rise to a cult of fertility in late imperial period. With her own indigenous scriptures, rituals, and miracle stories, she came to be known colloquially as the "Child-giving" Kuan-yin. Feminization of Avalokiteśvara in China was thus inseparable from the domestication and regionalization of the bodhisattva.

With the creation of the White-robed Kuan-yin in the tenth century, Avalokiteśvara took on a feminine and Chinese appearance. In time, other new feminine forms of Kuan-yin: the Fish-basket (or Wife of Mr. Ma), the South Sea, and Old Mother also made their appearances in other regions before they achieved national fame like the Water-moon and White-robed Kuan-yin earlier. We shall take up their stories in chapters 10 and 11. In the meantime, I want to concentrate on another case study of domestication. In the next two chapters, we will see how the famous Thousand-handed Avalokiteśvara celebrated in the esoteric scripture, *Ch'ien-shou ching*, became domesticated first by a ritual, and then by a myth.

7

The Ritual of Great Compassion Repentance and the Domestication of the Thousand-handed and Thousand-eyed Kuan-yin in the Sung

In January 1996, while I was in Taipei, I attended a "Ta-pei ch'an fa-hui" (Dharma Gathering for Great Compassion Repentance) held at Nung-ch'an Temple, the home temple of Ch'an master Sheng-yen. Perhaps because it was a Friday afternoon, the majority of the people who came, around five hundred, were women. They ranged from teens to early sixties, some came with their young children. Although men were clearly in the minority (less than a hundred), they seemed to be more uniform in age; most were in their twenties to forties. They appeared to be college students and professional men. The service lasted about two hours, from two until four o'clock. According to the schedule, which listed activities for both Nung-ch'an Temple and its downtown subtemple, An-ho Fen-yüan, this service is performed twice a month on average in both places. To accommodate the faithful, they often vary the time, sometimes holding it in the afternoon and other times in the evening. They also change the day of the week, alternating between weekdays and weekends. When I asked Sheng-yen why this ritual is performed so often, he answered, "It is because the Chinese people have an affinity (*yu-yüan*) with Kuan-yin." The popularity of this ritual is, of course, not limited to his temple. Temples in Taiwan, Hong Kong, mainland China, and overseas Chinese communities perform it regularly and often.

Led by an officiating monk known as "master of repentance" (*ch'an-chu*) and his assistants, the congregation recited selected passages from the *Ch'ien-shou ch'ien-yen kuang-ta yüan-man wu-ai Ta-pei-shin t'o-lo-ni ching* (The Vast, Perfect, Unobstructed Dhāraṇī Sūtra of the Great Compassionate Heart [Taught by] the Thousand-handed and Thousand-eyed One), known as *Ch'ien-shou ching* for short, a sūtra translated by Bhagavadharma in 650–660 (discussed briefly in chapter 2). The service was a well-choreographed and moving experience. Sonorous chanting was interspersed with singing in lilting cadences. There were constant and vigorous physical movements for the ensuing two hours. The congregation stood, bowed, prostrated, and knelt on both knees for periods sometimes up to ten minutes each. The highlights were the recitation of the dhāraṇī—known as the "Great Compassion Dhāraṇī" (*Ta-pei Chou*)—twenty-one times and the confession of sins.

The ritual as performed in Taiwan and elsewhere follows a text dated to the Ch'ing (1644–1912), which in turn was based on a much longer and more complex one, known as *Ch'ien-shou-yen Ta-pei hsin-chou hsing-fa* (Ritual Procedure for Performing the Great Compassionate Heart Dhāraṇī of the Thousand Hands and Eyes), first created by Chih-li (960–1028).[1] Kamata Shigeo (1973) observed the same ritual performed in Hong Kong in 1973, and it followed the same sequence. Prior to the Sung, before Chih-li created this ritual for repentance, the dhāraṇī was already very popular and people from all walks of life chanted it for different purposes. But often it seemed to have served as no more than a magical spell. It was Chih-li who provided a ritual setting for the chanting of the dhāraṇī, along with a soteriological and institutional grounding. From then on, one must go to a Buddhist monastery and participate in the repentance ritual performed under the direction of monks in order to secure the spiritual as well as material benefits the dhāraṇī is believed to render unfailingly. It is therefore no wonder that the ritual manual, revised in the Ch'ing and still in use today, lists the name of Chih-li right there with those of other bodhisattvas and buddhas for veneration.

Compared with Chih-li's original text, the present ritual manual is greatly simplified. It begins with three invocations of the Great Compassionate Kuan-yin Bodhisattva, which is followed by a gāthā of incense offering. The congregation then reads a passage explaining the reason for performing the ritual, quoted directly from Chih-li's manual. Notice that Kuan-yin is declared to be a Buddha of the past.

> Namaḥ Tathāgata Bright True Dharma (Cheng-fa-ming Ju-lai) of the past who is Bodhisattva Kuan-shih-yin of the present. Having achieved wondrous merits and being possessed of great compassion and mercy, the bodhisattva manifests a thousand hands and eyes in one body. Observing and illuminating the Dharmadhātu and protecting sentient beings, he causes all to develop the broad and vast mind of truth. He teaches all to chant the perfect divine dhāraṇī so that we can depart forever from the evil paths of rebirth and be born in front of the Buddha. Grave sins deserving punishment in Avīci Hell and painful chronic diseases with no cure can both be

eliminated. Samādhi, eloquence, and all wishes of the present life can be obtained. Decidedly and without a doubt, we can all be made to arrive at the land of the buddha. No amount of praise can exhaust the awesome divine power. I therefore prostrate to the Bodhisattva with single-minded sincerity.

This is followed by prostrations to Śākyamuni Buddha, Amitābha Buddha, Tathāgata Bright True Dharma, Great Compassion Dhāraṇī, the Thousand-handed and Thousand-eyed Avalokiteśvara, Mahāsthāmaprāpta, Maitreya, Mañjuśrī, Samanthabhadra, and many other bodhisattvas as well as to Mahākaśyapa and many arhats. The congregation kneels and prostrates after each title is called out. The name of Chih-li is invoked in this context, just before prostrations are made to the Four Heavenly Kings, gods of oceans, rivers, ponds and swamps, gods of trees and herbs, the earth and the mountains, palaces and houses, and so on. After the prostrations, key passages of the *Ch'ien-shou ching* are recited aloud.

The sūtra says:

> If a monk, nun, layman, laywoman, young man, or young girl wants to keep and recite the dhāraṇī, you must give rise to the heart of compassion toward all sentient beings and make the following vows after me:
>
> Namaḥ Avalokiteśvara of Great Compassion, may I quickly learn everything about the Dharma.
>
> Namaḥ Avalokiteśvara of Great Compassion, may I speedily obtain the eye of wisdom.
>
> Namaḥ Avalokiteśvara of Great Compassion, may I quickly save all sentient beings.
>
> Namaḥ Avalokiteśvara of Great Compassion, may I speedily obtain skill-in-means.
>
> Namaḥ Avalokiteśvara of Great Compassion, may I quickly sail on the *prajñā* boat.
>
> Namaḥ Avalokiteśvara of Great Compassion, may I speedily cross over the ocean of suffering.
>
> Namaḥ Avalokiteśvara of Great Compassion, may I quickly obtain the way of discipline and meditation.
>
> Namaḥ Avalokiteśvara of Great Compassion, may I speedily ascend the nirvāṇa mountain.
>
> Namaḥ Avalokiteśvara of Great Compassion, may I quickly enter the house of non-action.
>
> Namaḥ Avalokiteśvara of Great Compassion, may I speedily achieve the Dharma-Body.

If I face a mountain of knives, may it naturally crumble; if I face a roaring fire, may it naturally burn out; if I face hell, may it naturally disappear; if I face a hungry ghost, may it naturally be satiated; if I face an asura, may its evil heart naturally become tame; and if I face an animal, may it naturally obtain great wisdom.

The congregation calls the name of Avalokiteśvara ten times and Amitābha Buddha ten times. This is followed by another sūtra passage in which Avalokiteśvara declares to the Buddha: "If anyone recites the dhāraṇī, should he fall into the three evil realm of rebirth, or not being born into one of the buddha lands, or not attaining unlimited samādhi and eloquence, or not getting all his wishes and desires in the present life, I will not achieve complete, perfect enlightenment. If one does not obtain all that one wishes for in the present life, the dhāraṇī is not called the Great Compassionate Heart Dhāraṇī." This is then followed by collective chanting of the dhāraṇī, repeated twenty-one times.

After the recitation of the dhāraṇī, the congregation kneels and makes the following confession, reading aloud part of the text first composed by Chih-li.

Disciple So and So makes confession with a mind of utmost sincerity. All sentient beings including myself have this One Mind which is originally endowed with thousands of dharmas. It has miraculous power and is illuminated with wisdom. Our mind is equal to the mind of the Buddha above and the same as that of all sentient beings below. But because this tranquil brightness has been obscured by beginningless ignorance, it becomes confused when coming into contact with things and gets attached to them. Consequently, thoughts about self and others arise, thus differentiating the dharmas of equality. Attachments and views are the bases, while body and mouth serve as causes. I have committed all possible sins in my many existences. I have done the ten evil deeds [of killing, stealing, adultery, lying, double-tongue, coarse language, filthy language, covetousness, anger, and perverted views] and five deadly sins [of patricide, matricide, killing an arhat, shedding the blood of a Buddha, destroying the harmony of the Saṃgha]. I have slandered the Dharma and other people, broken the precepts and fasts, destroyed stūpas and temples, stolen monks' possessions, polluted the pure life of a monk and embezzled food and property belonging to the Saṃgha. Such unlimited and innumerable sins have not been confessed to the thousand buddhas who have appeared in the world. When I finish this life, I am bound to be born in the three evil realms of rebirth and suffer multitudes of pain. Moreover, in my present life, I will be tor-

> tured by many troubles. Either painful diseases will hunt me or other worries will pressure me. I cannot cultivate the way because of such obstructions. Now I have encountered the perfect and divine Great Compassion Dhāraṇī, which can quickly destroy all these sinful obstructions, that is why I today recite it with utmost sincerity and take refuge in Kuan-shih-yin Bodhisattva and the great masters of the ten directions, giving rise to the thought for enlightenment, and practicing the action of the True Word [the Great compassion Dhāraṇī]. Together with all sentient beings, I reveal all the sins I have committed and beg for their eventual destruction through my confession. I beseech the Great Compassionate Kuan-shih-yin Bodhisattva to protect us with his/her thousand hands, and illuminate us with thousand eyes so that both internal and external obstructions will be extinguished, vows benefiting the self and others can be fulfilled, original knowledge will be revealed, demons and heretics will be subdued, and the threefold karmas [of speech, body and mind] can be diligently advanced. By cultivating the cause of rebirth in the Pure Land, I am determined to be reborn in Amitābha Buddha's world of Supreme Bliss when I give up my present body and will not go to any other realm of rebirth.

The congregation takes refuge in the Three Treasures after making the confession. The rite concludes by giving praise to Śākyamuni Buddha, Amitābha Buddha, Ch'ien-kuang-wang ching-chu Buddha, Great Compassion Dhāraṇī, Thousand-handed and Thousand-eyed Kuan-shih-yin Bodhisattva, Mahāsthāmaprāpta Bodhisattva and Dhāraṇī King (Tsung-ch'ih-wang) Bohisattva.

While following closely the proceedings of the service and trying to keep pace with the frequent changes in the ritual actions, I could not help but notice that a great number of containers filled with water were lined up along the wall behind the altar. They were plastic bottles of various sizes brought there by participants who would take them home after the service. I was told by someone that the water, thus charged with the power of the service, became "Great Compassion Water" (*Ta-pei shui*), and would have curative effects. Such belief can be traced back to the Sung and earlier. Since the Ch'ing, the chanting of the Great Compassion Dhāraṇī, together with that of the *Heart Sūtra*, has been a part of the morning and evening services of Chinese temples. The performance of the Great Compassion Repentance ritual described here is also an indispensable segment of the liturgy celebrating Kuan-yin's "birthday," carried out on the three holy days (the nineteenth day of the second, sixth, and ninth lunar months). The popularity of this dhāraṇī, as well as the sūtra from which it comes, is also evidenced by their ubiquitous presence in pamphlets published by the faithful and donated to temples for free circulation.

The Great Compassion Dhāraṇī is undoubtedly one of the most effective mediums promoting the cult of Kuan-yin. Many miracles resulting from chanting it have come down to us dating to the T'ang and Sung. It is intriguing to ask, however, how and why this particular dhāraṇī and this particular sūtra have achieved such a lasting success? After all, as described in chapter 2, this is only one of many such dhāraṇīs promulgated by the many esoteric sūtras glorifying Kuan-yin. Although another sūtra, the *Ch'ing Kuan-yin ching* achieved an earlier fame due to the promotion of the T'ien-t'ai patriarch Chih-i (538–597), its popularity did not continue after the Sung. The three sets of dhāraṇīs contained in the *Ch'ing Kuan-yin ching* do not seem to have found as great a following among monks, not to mention the common people, as the Great Compassion Dhāraṇī, even before the Sung period. Consequently, although there was a repentance ritual based on the sūtra formulated by Tsun-shih (963–1032), a contemporary and close associate of Chih-li, the ritual has not come down to the present day.[2]

I suggest that the Sung-era creation of the Great Compassion Repentance by Chih-li was most likely influenced by the popular use of this dhāraṇī since the T'ang period. The rite, once created, served in turn as another important vehicle in promoting this particular dhāraṇī and this particular sūtra. The main reason the repentance could achieve this effect was ultimately because it provided a Chinese ritual context for the worshiping of this originally very foreign Tantric deity. For Chih-li, like Tsun-shih, was a T'ien-t'ai master and, in creating their respective ritual manuals, they followed faithfully the T'ien-t'ai model for performing repentance rituals. This model was first set down in Chih-i's *Fa-hua ch'an-i* (Rites for the Lotus Samādhi Repentance) and subsequently elaborated by another T'ien-t'ai patriarch Chan-jan (711–82), who provided a ten-part sequence for all repentance rituals in his *Fa-hua san-mei hsing-shih yün-hsiang pu-chu-i* (Supplementary Rite of Meditation in Performing the Lotus Samādhi) (Kamata 1973:283; Stevenson 1987:475–76). In subsuming the recitation of the dhāraṇī under the philosophical and ritual framework formulated by the T'ien-t'ai tradition, Chih-li domesticated this esoteric rite.

In this chapter, I first offer some evidence for the increasing popularity of the Great Compassion Dhāraṇī from the T'ang to the Sung, then suggest the reasons for the Sung interest in esoteric scriptures, and finally provide an analysis of Chih-li's repentance ritual. I hope to prove that the T'ien-t'ai repentance ritual created by Chih-li played a major role in the domestication of the esoteric dhāraṇī, which in turn contributed to the transformation of the Thousand-handed and Thousand-eyed Avalokiteśvara into the Chinese Ta-pei Kuan-yin. The popularity of the dhāraṇī and the repentance ritual, centering around the collective recitation of the dhāraṇī contributed to a universal knowledge of the Thousand-handed Kuan-yin in the Sung. The fame of this particular form of Kuan-yin, as I shall argue in chapter 8, led in turn to the creation of the legend of Princess Miao-shan, who was the Chinese incarnation of the bodhisattva.

As I mentioned in chapter 2, the first esoteric sūtra, *Ch'ing Kuan-yin ching*, was a favorite among the T'ien-t'ai monks. The T'ien-t'ai master Chih-i singled this sūtra out for emphasis and used it as one of the sources for the last of the four forms of samādhis: neither walking nor sitting samādhi (Stevenson 1986: 50; Donner and Stevenson 1993:275–80). Tsun-shih, a T'ien-t'ai master living in the same period as Chih-li, wrote a ritual manual entitled *Ch'ing Kuan-shih-yin P'u-sa hsiao-fu tu-hai t'o-lo-ni san-mei i* (Samādhi Rite for the Dhāraṇī Sūtra of Invoking Avalokiteśvara Bodhisattva to Dissipate Poison and Harm). This was based on a much shorter text, the "Ch'ing Kuan-shih-yin ch'an-fa" (Repentance Method of Invoking Avalokiteśvara), which is included in the *Kuo-ch'ing pai-lu* (One Hundred Items about Kuo-ch'ing [Temple]), compiled by Kuan-ting in 605. The rite lasts forty-nine days. Avalokiteśvara is called the "Great Compassionate One" (Ta-pei) in this sūtra and is declared to be the savior who "courses in the five realms of rebirth" to carry out the work of salvation (T 20:36b).

Different versions of the sūtras on the Thousand-handed and Thousand-eyed Avalokiteśvara were all translated in the T'ang period. The ones made by Bhagavadharma and the Tantric master Amoghavajra have been most popular. Chih-li used the sūtra translated by Bhagavadharma as the basis for creating his repentance ritual. Just as the Great Compassion Repentance ritual performed today selectively retains parts of Chih-li's original manual, Chih-li also quoted the sūtra very selectively, retaining certain passages but eliminating whole chunks of others in his ritual manual. More importantly, by creating a rite similar to that of the T'ien-t'ai Lotus Samādhi Repentance, he thoroughly transformed this esoteric text into a document expressing a distinctively T'ien-t'ai religiosity.

Chih-li began his repentance manual by quoting the opening section of the sūtra, setting the scene for Kuan-yin's revelation of the dhāraṇī. The sūtra is spoken by the Buddha in the palace of Avalokiteśvara located on the island of Potalaka. Having explained the origin and efficacy of the dhāraṇī, Avalokiteśvara calls upon anyone who wants to keep this dhāraṇī to give rise to the thought of compassion for all sentient beings by making ten vows after him. These are the ten vows that Chih-li included in his manual. They are retained in the repentance rite performed in Taiwan that I described earlier.

Chih-li's text includes the next section from the sūtra: "If anyone steals or damages the Saṃgha's property, by reciting this dhāraṇī, the sin will be forgiven. Anyone who has committed the five deadly sins and ten evil deeds, who slanders the Dharma and corrupts monastic discipline, or who destroys temples and steals monks' possessions, is freed from all guilt by chanting this dhāraṇī. But if one has doubts about the efficacy of the dhāraṇī, then the consequences of even a slight mistake will not disappear, how much more so a serious sin?" Chih-li used this passage as the basis for his text of confession, but he did not copy the wording exactly. He also omitted the next sūtra passage, which lists the benefits resulting from chanting the dhāraṇī.

Chih-li's text then picks up the next several passages from the sūtra: first the dhāraṇī consisting of eighty-four phrases and then the passage beginning with "After Avalokiteśvara reveals the dhāraṇī, the earth shakes in six ways, flowers rain down from heaven, the buddhas of the ten directions are happy, but demons and heretics are frightened. All the assembled reach different levels of realization. Some attain the fruit of a stream-entrant, once-returner, non-returner or arhat. Others attain the first, second, third, fourth, fifth and all the way up to the tenth stage of the bodhisattva path. Unlimited number of sentient beings give rise to *bodhicitta.*" Brahmā then asks Avalokiteśvara to describe the "marks and characteristics" (*hsing-chuang hsiang-mao*) of this dhāraṇī. Avalokiteśvara replies that it is the great heart of compassion and pity (*ta tz'u-pei hsin*), which is further equated with nine types of heart: the heart of equanimity (*p'ing-teng hsin*), the unconditioned heart (*wu-wei hsin*), the heart of nonattachment (*wu jan-cho hsin*), the heart of contemplating all things as empty (*k'ung-kuan hsin*), the heart of reverence (*kung-ching hsin*), the heart of humility (*pi-hsia hsin*), the heart of nonconfusion (*wu tsa-luan hsin*), the heart of nondiscrimination (*wu chien-ch'ü hsin*) and the heart of unexcelled perfect enlightenment (*wu-shang p'u-t'i hsin*).

Chih-li's text omits the next paragraph of the sūtra, which describes the miraculous protections resulting from chanting the dhāraṇī. But he retained the sūtra's passage on how to set up the sacred ritual space. The sūtra gives many recipes to deal with various problems or to attain specific goals, none of which was included in Chih-li's text. Here as before, Chih-li consistently omitted any reference to the magical and the miraculous.

Of all the esoteric forms of Avalokiteśvara introduced into China, it is the Thousand-handed and Thousand-eyed Avalokiteśvara who became most popular in China. This was widely attested to by the production of images, keeping of the Great Compassion Dhāraṇī by monks and lay people, resulting in miracles, copying of the *Ch'ien-shou ching*, and recitation of key passages such as the "ten vows" and the dhāraṇī in a ritual setting, leading to Chih-li's formulation of the repentance ritual in the Sung.

The Thousand-handed and Thousand-eyed Avalokiteśvara Becomes Ta-pei Kuan-yin

Although the adjectives "rescuer from suffering" (*chiu-k'u*) and "Great Compassionate and Great Merciful" (*ta-tz'u ta-pei*) were applied to the name of Kuan-yin in earlier periods, after the introduction of the *Ch'ien-shou ching* in the T'ang, "Great Compassionate One" (Ta-pei) became identified exclusively with the Thousand-handed and Thousand-eyed Avalokiteśvara. This was due to the quick success his cult achieved in T'ang China. Although this deity was a latecomer among the Tantric forms of Avalokiteśvara introduced into China, because of the promotion of his cult by the three Tantric masters (Śubhakarasiṃha, Vajrabodhi, and Amoghavajra all made translations of the scripture) and the patronage at court, the Thousand-handed and Thousand-eyed Avalokiteśvara could overtake and eventually absorb the fame of other Tantric forms of the bodhisattva. In her dissertation and published articles, Maria Reis-Habito has compared the various Chinese translations of the esoteric scriptures glorifying the Thousand-armed Avalokiteśvara, explained why Bhagavaddharma's version eventually achieved a virtual monopoly, traced the increasing faith in the dhāraṇī among monks and lay people, and attributed the motivation in performing the rite of Great Compassion Repentance to the Confucian virtue of filial piety. While post-Sung sources that she primarily used in advancing her last point might indeed show a strong link between the repentance rite and the cult of the dead, the same cannot be said for the Sung and earlier periods.[3] As I shall show later in this chapter, Chih-li clearly saw the rite in a much broader and wider context of moral reform and spiritual renewal.

In a long and authoritative study, Kobayashi Taichirō (1983) has traced the development of the cult of Ta-pei in the T'ang. Drawing from a wide and diverse range of sources including monk's biographies, epigraphical inscriptions, records of paintings (most of which unfortunately have not survived), and poetry and popular tales, he provides a vivid account of the rising popularity of this newly imported deity. From the evidence of artistic creation expressed in images and paintings, the new cult of Ta-pei was centered in the capital of Ch'ang-an, but also spread to Szechwan. Artistic renderings of the bodhisattva followed closely after each new translations.[4]

Kobayashi regards the end of the T'ang and Five Dynasties periods as a "golden age" for the faith in Ta-pei and sees the religious zeal of three monks as typical examples (1983:85). Recitation of the dhāraṇī, the creation of images, and physical mutilation as an offering to the bodhisattva were characteristic ways of showing their devotion. These three monks exemplified these practices.

Their biographies are found in the *Sung kao-seng chuan*. Chih-hsüan (809–881) was a native of Mei-chou, Szechwan. He was known for his broad knowledge of Buddhism, particularly the Pure Land scriptures. Li Shang-yin and other literate figures admired him. But when he was asked to give lectures in the capital, because of his heavy accent, he could not be understood. He returned to his native place and went to Mt. Elephant Ear (Hsiang-erh Shan)—a cultic center for the Ta-pei faith—and recited the Great Compassion Dhāraṇī. One night he dreamt that a divine monk cut off his tongue and replaced it with a new one. The next morning he woke up speaking perfect Ch'ang-an dialect (T 50:763c).

The second monk, Shen-chih (819–886), a contemporary to the first, started keeping the dhāraṇī when he was twelve. After entering the Saṃgha at the age of twenty, he traveled all over the southeast and cured all kinds of diseases with the Great Compassion water. Many people flocked to him, and he was given the nickname "Monk Ta-pei." In 847–859 he went to the capital and cured the prime minister Pei Hsiu's daughter, who was possessed by ghosts, by chanting the dhāraṇī over her for seven days (T 50:869c).

The third monk, Tao-chou (863–941) was a musician, well known for his beautiful voice in singing Buddhist chants. Motivated by his devotion to Ta-pei, he used his own blood and painted a standing image of the bodhisattva. In 882 when the rebels under Huang Ch'ao occupied Ch'ang-an, he cut off his left forearm (from wrist to elbow) and burnt it as an offering to Kuan-yin, praying for peace. He also cut off his left ear while praying for rain on behalf of some villagers. As a result of his faith, when he died at the age of seventy-eight, his body did not decay. He looked as if he were in a meditative trance. The body was preserved with lacquer and mummified (T 50:859b).

As the efficacy of the dhāraṇī became known, dhāraṇī pillars on which the Great Compassion Dhāraṇī was inscribed began to be erected. The earliest was built by monk Hung-wei in Wo-lung Temple in the capital in 871. Tun-huang manuscripts reveal other evidence about this cult. An abbreviated version of the *Ch'ien-shou ching*, consisting of only the ten vows of Kuan-yin and the dhāraṇī, was circulated. Known as *Ta-pei ch'i-ch'ing* (Invocation of the Great Compassionate One), it was probably recited in a liturgical setting. This was also often copied together with another dhāraṇī, the *Tsun-sheng t'o-lo-ni ching* (The Honored and Victorious Dhāraṇī Sūtra). For instance, two copies made by the monk Hui-lüan contained the two texts. One (S 4378) was made in 899 at the Ta-pei Temple in Hupei, ending with the note, "may the reader preserve it for spiritual merit," while another copy (S 2566) had the dedicatory note, "may the merit be shared by all sentient beings, so that they will all attain Buddhahood." Hui-lüan copied the same text for nineteen years. Filled with faith in Kuan-yin, he traveled from Hupei to Tun-huang and took the dissemination of the dhāraṇī to be his mission. By the end of the T'ang, both the sūtra text and the dhāraṇī were circulated among the monks and the laity. Copies were made either as pious offerings or commissioned by the faithful for religious merit (Reis-Habito 1993:127–32).

During the T'ang, miraculous responses from reciting the Ta-pei Dhāraṇī also appeared in collections of short tales. *Kuang-i chi* (The Great Book of Marvels) has five stories about Kuan-yin including one on the efficacy of the Ta-pei Dhāraṇī. Dudbridge summarizes it in the following. Since the hero was not a monk, it shows that ordinary people also were aware of the power of the dhāraṇī and knew how to chant it.

> Li Hsin recites a *mantra* of Kuan-yin of the Thousand Arms and Eyes. This gives him the power to exorcise a malaria demon. While he is away travelling, his sister sickens, dies, then revives. She explains that beings tormenting her in the graveyard recognized whose sister she was and feared his vengeance. So she is restored just before Li returns home (Dudbridge 1995:182).

The power of the dhāraṇī to exorcise ghosts is one of the many benefits promised by the sūtra. In fact, as I shall show presently, most miracle tales about the dhāraṇī in the Sung were about its power of exorcism. Not only did ordinary people know how to chant the dhāraṇī, some of them could also cultivate the power to turn water into a healing elixir, as did the monk Shen-chih mentioned previously. Several miracle tales contained in the 1929 collection discussed in chapter 4 are about the power of the Great Compassion Dhāraṇī. Except for the first, which was about a monk in the T'ang, all others occurred in the Sung. The monk Chih-i was a native of Ch'ang-sha and his surname was Wu. He originally served as a soldier and loved to hunt. One day he caught a white tortoise, cooked and ate it. Soon boils broke out all over his body. His eyebrows, beard, fingers, and toes all fell off. He was in pure agony and near death. He could not keep his job and became a wandering beggar. While he was begging in An-nan (present-day Vietnam), a monk saw him and took pity on him. The monk said, "You should repent and chant the Great Compassion Dhāraṇī which I will teach you. If you are diligent in doing so, you will receive a good reward." He listened to the advice and chanted the dhāraṇī with singleness of mind. Gradually he recovered from his boils, and his fingers also grew back. He then shaved off his hair and became a monk (*Kuan-shih-yin P'u-sa ling-kang lu* I:11).

The next story is about someone who combines dhāraṇī recitation with Pure Land devotion. Chang Kang was a scholar in the Sung. He made a vow in front of a Buddha image that he would recite the Great Compassion Dhāraṇī 100,000 times in order to achieve rebirth in the Pure Land. When he was sixty, he became ill. He recited the Buddha's name with singleness of mind. Gathering his family together, he said, "The Pure Land of the West is right here and the Amitābha Buddha is sitting on the lotus flower. My grandson Weng-erh (who died when he was three) is worshiping the Buddha, kneeling on golden ground." After this he died while chanting Buddha's name (II:8).

The Great Compassion water features in this story: Miss Wu, the wife of Lü Hung, vice director of the Ministry of Justice, was devoted to Kuan-yin and often experienced miraculous responses to her devotions. She kept several dozen bottles filled with water in a clean chamber. She would recite the dhāraṇī while holding a willow branch in her hand. She saw Kuan-yin send light into the bottles. Those who were sick frequently recovered after drinking the water. The dhāraṇī water would keep a long time without becoming spoiled. It would not freeze even in winter. People called her Madame Kuan-yin (Kuan-yin Yüan-chün). Her two maids were also Pure Land practitioners. One of them was particularly austere. Sometimes she would not eat anything for a whole month, drinking only one cup of the dhāraṇī water each day (II:8).

Barend J. ter Haar (1992) noted the prevalence of the recitation of spells, sūtras and deities' names in the stories collected by Hung Mai (1123–1202) in his *Record of the Listener,* compiled in 1198. He found forty-nine stories about chanting spells and twelve about chanting the names of deities. Of these, the Great Compassion Dhāraṇī was recited eleven times, and Kuan-yin's name seven times. The spell is used seven times to vanquish evil ghosts and twice to heal; the name is used five times to heal. Kuan-yin appears in two cases as a monk, holding a staff and water bottle in one story (III:1318), and without any description of his appearance in the other (III:1441); he also appears in two cases as white-clothed old woman (I:88,89), while in the other cases information is not provided on Kuan-yin's gender. As for the people who practiced these religious activities, out of sixty-one cases, thirty-four involved laymen and twenty-five involved religious specialists such as monks, priests, shamans, and the like. The identities of the remaining two cases were not determined (ter Haar 1992:19–20).

By the Sung, knowledge about the power of the Great Compassion Dhāraṇī to subdue demons and cure diseases appeared to be quite widespread. Although sometimes monks served as transmitters, the practice of chanting the dhāraṇī was definitely not limited to them. People from different walks of life, both men and women, seemed to be chanting it on a regular basis. That was why they could automatically turn to it for help when their lives were threatened. Other beliefs connected with the dhāraṇī, for instance, the efficacy of Ta-pei water to cure diseases, or rebirth in the Pure Land through chanting the dhāraṇī also became pervasive. There was no evidence, however, that anyone was doing any of the Tantric *sādhanas* or using any of the Tantric recipes mentioned in the *Ch'ien-shou ching* to achieve spiritual goals or solve their problems in life. The dhāraṇī took on an independent existence apart from the sūtra. People might have faith in the dhāraṇī as a powerful spell against evils, but they probably would not be aware of its link with Kuan-yin. It was Chih-li who, by creating the repentance ritual, embedded the dhāraṇī in a spiritual context and supplied a lasting linkage between the dhāraṇī, Kuan-yin's ten vows of universal salvation, and the salutary effects of true repentance. In the same process, by formulating the ritual on the basis of T'ien-t'ai soteriology, Chih-li coopted the esoteric rite. He provided a distinctive T'ien-t'ai framework for the chanting of the dhāraṇī. The Thousand-handed and Thousand-eyed Avalokiteśvara was transformed into Ta-pei Kuan-yin.

Chih-li's *Ritual Procedure for Performing the Great Compassion Repentance*

According to Maria Reis-Habito, the first clear reference to the recitation of the Great Compassion Dhāraṇī as an act of repentance was found in the record of the daily religious practice of Ch'an master Chih-chüeh, better known as Yung-ming Yen-shou (904–976). In the *Record of Self-cultivation of Ch'an Master Chih-chüeh* (Chih-chüeh Ch'an-shih tzu-hsing lu), compiled by Wen-ch'ung, he listed the 108 acts his master performed every day. Article 9 of this record says to "Recite the Great Compassion Dhāraṇī of the Thousand-handed and Thousand-eyed Kuan-yin six times every day, in order to repent for the sins of all sentient beings in the Dharma Realm, which they commit with their six senses." Article 70 also refers to the dhāraṇī: "In the evening, light incense for all sentient beings of the ten directions and recite the Prajñā Dhāraṇī [dhāraṇī in the *Heart Sūtra*] and the Great Compassion Dhāraṇī. Pray for them to understand their own minds to be as perfect and clear as Prajñā" (HTC 111:155b, 161a; Reis-Habito 1991:43–44). These references are very interesting, for they serve as important evidence that Yen-shou was a believer in the keeping of the Great Compassion Dhāraṇī, and that he used it in a context of universal repentance. Since he must have been very well known to Chih-li, being active in the same geographical region and still alive when the latter was a teenager, it is entirely plausible that Yen-shou's example inspired Chih-li's devotion to and enthusiasm for the dhāraṇī.

But Yen-shou did not create a ritual format for the recitation of the dhāraṇī.

This was done by Chih-li. What might have been his motivation for imposing a T'ien-t'ai framework on *Ch'ien-shou ching*, an esoteric scripture? Although I have not found any explicit statement on this issue made by Chih-li, I would like to suggest a possible explanation based on what we know about the court's attitude toward Buddhism at that time. Chih-li lived during a time of extensive governmental sponsorship of new sūtra translations. T'ai-tsung set up three halls to do translation in the T'ai-ping hsing-kuo Temple in 980, and two years later formally established a bureau for translating Buddhist sūtras. He thereby renewed the T'ang precedent of governmental sponsorship for Buddhist translation projects, which had declined since 810. Until the translation bureau was disbanded in 1082, for just over one hundred years, translation activity was in full swing, producing 259 sūtras consisting of 727 volumes, second only to the T'ang record. T'ien-hsi-tsai, who translated the *Karaṇḍavyūha* (a sūtra that elevated Kuan-yin to the status of cosmic creator that we discussed in chapter 2), was one of a number of foreign monks involved in translation projects.

T'ai-tsung also sent Chinese monks to the Western Regions to search for the Dharma. There were frequent contacts between Sung China and India during the last four decades of the tenth and the first half of the eleventh centuries (Jan 1967:135; Huang 1990, 1995). Jan Yun-hua pointed out that many of the newly translated sūtras were esoteric. The choice of this type of scripture and the imperial favors bestowed on T'ien-hsi-tsai and other Tantric missionaries seems to have given rise to some opposition among the Chinese monks. The Hua-yen, Fa-hsiang, and Vinaya schools had been favored at court since the T'ang, and in order to protect their traditional interests, monks belonging to these schools could not have looked upon this new development with enthusiasm (Jan 1967:136–38;140–42). Tsan-ning (919–1001), the author of the *Sung kao-seng chuan* and the Vinaya scholar who witnessed these developments, might have been obliquely showing his partisan stance when he lamented the lack of talent among the later Tantric teachers (his contemporaries) in his biography of Amoghavajra (Tsao 1990:149–51).

> [Tsan-ning's] Comment: Concerning the transmission of the teaching, China regards Vajrabodhi as the founding patriarch, Amoghavajra as the second patriarch and Hui-lang as the third patriarch. After them we can expect that there would have been changes for better or worse. Lately, many subsidiary branches have appeared, yet all claim to have received the great teaching of Yü-chia [Tantrism]. Although there are many Tantric teachers, why is it that few have exhibited any efficacious power? Perhaps this is like [the ancient legend which spoke of] the flying animals called *yü-chia* giving birth to dragons, dragons giving birth to phoenixes and then after some

> time, phoenixes giving birth to common birds. Can we hope to avoid change? (T 50:714a; Tso, 149)

Although T'ien-t'ai and Ch'an were not yet very popular at court in the beginning of the Northern Sung and thus were not as threatened by the imperial favor shown to Tantrism, it may not be coincidental that Chih-li and his dharma brother Tsun-shih wrote or expanded repentance rituals based on esoteric scriptures glorifying Kuan-yin. By providing a T'ien-t'ai ritual framework for these Tantric rites, they did not try to compete with Tantrism but rather domesticated it. But at the same time, by anchoring some of the Tantric practices, such as the chanting of dhāraṇīs, in a completely Chinese Buddhist setting, they contributed to the survival of Tantrism in China. For, as pointed out by scholars, despite imperial patronage of Tantrism in the T'ang and early Sung dynasties, this did not penetrate into Chinese society at large. It did not receive real support from either the Chinese elite or the common people (Chou 1944–45:246; Jan 1967:142). Therefore, if Tsun-shih and Chih-li had not incorporated some Tantric elements into the rituals they created, Tantric practices might have entirely disappeared from Chinese Buddhism. But what is important for us to realize is that they did not preserve Tantrism as Tantrism, but rather domesticated it by combining it with T'ien-t'ai doctrinal teaching and meditative practice (*chiao-kuan*).

Chih-li, the Master of Repentance

Chih-li, like his contemporary Tsun-shih, was indeed a firm believer in doctrinal teachings and meditative practices. He was a native of Chekiang, the center of T'ien-tai Buddhism in the Sung. The two monks were good friends and their lives shared a number of similarities. Chih-li's secular surname was Chin, and his family lived in Ssu-ming (present-day Ningpo). His father did not have an heir and, together with his wife, prayed to Buddha for help. He then dreamt of an Indian monk who presented him with a boy, saying, "This is Lo-hou-lo [Rāhula], the son of the Buddha." His wife became pregnant soon after this dream. When Chih-li was born, he was given this name. Chih-li lost his mother at seven and cried uncontrollably. He asked his father to allow him to become a monk. He was ordained at the age of fifteen, and at first studied the Vinaya. But in 979, when he was twenty, he began to study T'ien-tai doctrine and practice with Pao-yün. Although he became a monk, his ties with his father apparently remained strong. His father had a dream the following year about him. In the dream, Chih-li knelt in front of his teacher Pao-yün who poured water from a bottle into his mouth. From then on, Chih-li's understanding of the Perfect and Sudden Teaching of the T'ien-t'ai school became complete. From the age of twenty-two onward, he often lectured in place of his teacher.

In 984 Tsun-shih came from Mt. T'ien-t'ai to study under Pao-yün. Chih-li regarded him as a true friend and treated Tsun-shih like his own brother. In 1000 a great drought threatened the whole prefecture. Chih-li and Tsun-shih performed the Golden Light Repentance, (a ritual based on the *Sūtra of the Golden Light,* Chin-kuang-ming ching, Suvarṇa-prabhāsa Sūtra) in order to pray for rain.[5] He vowed to offer his hand to the Buddha if it did not rain within three days. It rained before the time was up. The prefect Su Chi (987–1035) was so impressed that he wrote about this miracle and had it inscribed on stone for posterity (Getz 1994:67). In 1016, when he was fifty-seven, Chih-li made a vow that he would perform the Lotus Repentance for three years and then immolate himself at its completion as an offering to the wonderful sūtra and in the hope of going to the Pure Land. Early in 1017 he called his disciples together and said to them, "Some people would sacrifice their bodies for half a gāthā or burn themselves to death for the sake of one sentence [of the *Lotus Sūtra*]. This is because the heart of a sage should be devoted to the Dharma. I want to sacrifice my life and offer my body in order to wake up those who are lazy and indolent" (*Ssu-ming chiao-hsing lu* 1, T 46:858a). He made a pact with ten other monks to carry out this three-year project. But when his plan to commit suicide became known, many people including Tsun-shih, the Han-lin scholar Yang I, the governor Li I-keng, and the imperial son-in-law Li Tsun-hsü, all begged him to desist. Eventually, he and the ten monks agreed. When they finished the Lotus Repentance, they performed the Great Compassion Repentance for three years instead of committing self-immolation as originally planned. Even though Chih-li was prevented from carrying out his vow, he was said to have burned off three fingers as an offering to the Buddha (T 46:858c).

Chih-li's readiness to sacrifice his hand to avert drought and later to immolate himself to glorify the *Lotus Sūtra* was clearly not an isolated example, but emblematic of a type of religiosity prevalent at that time. Tsun-shih was equally determined in carrying out these kinds of austere practices. Religious suicide by fire and self-mutilation as a prevalent way of showing one's devotion in medieval China have long fascinated scholars (Gernet 1960; Jan 1965). Although monks before them had immolated themselves or sacrificed body parts to show their devotion to the *Lotus,* in the case of Chih-li and Tsun-shih, their willingness to sacrifice themselves was not only a manifestation of their religious devotion, but was also motivated by their desire to benefit the people. This is, of course, the classical way a bodhisattva behaves, as exemplified by the many *Jātaka* and *Avadāna* stories. An example close in time and geographical location is provided by the supreme deeds of self-sacrifice carried out by Liu Pen-tsun ("Liu, the Original Honored One" 844–907), who was promoted as the fifth patriarch of the Tantric school by Chao Chih-feng (1159–1249?).

Under Chao's evangelical efforts, depictions of Liu's extreme acts of self-sacrifice were carved on the cliffs in three locations in Szechwan. In Vairocana Cave of An-yüeh and two places on Mt. Pao-ting in Great Buddha Creek,[6] Ta-tsu, depictions of Liu's self-mutilations, together with inscriptions, have survived. Known as "Pictures of Ten Smeltings" (*Shih-lien T'u*), they show Liu on the point of burning off his left index finger in 886, lighting incense on his left foot in 937, gouging out his right eye and cutting off his left ear in 939, and on four different occasions in 940, placing a lighted candle on his heart and a bundle of five incense sticks on his head, amputating his left arm, and wrapping his penis with waxed cloth and torching it for a day and a night; and finally, in 941, placing lighted incense sticks on both knees.[7] Liu undertook all these mortification of the flesh with the avowed purpose of helping people, whose names were sometimes identified (*Ta-tsu shih-k'e yen-chiu*, 169–74; 490–92). Although there is no way of knowing if Liu was known to Chih-li and Tsun-shih, or of historically verifying Liu's activities, the tradition linking self-mutilation to benevolent concern for the welfare of society is still very interesting and represents a new model of Buddhist religiosity, beginning with the Sung period.

As we can see from the above, Chih-li, like his friend Tsun-shih, who was known as the "Master of Repentance," was a great devotee of T'ien-t'ai rites of penitence. From 999 on, he spent all his time either performing repentance or giving lectures and never left his temple. He performed the twenty-one-day Lotus Repentance five times, the seven-day *Golden Light* Repentance twenty times, the seven-day Amitābha Repentance fifty times, the forty-nine-day *Ch'ing Kuan-yin* repentance eight times, and the twenty-one-day Great Compassion Repentance ten times. This was in addition to the three-year marathon Lotus Repentance and the three-year continuous Great Compassion Repentance mentioned previously.[8]

Chih-li's intense interest in ritual, including his creation of the Great Compassion Repentance, must be understood in light of his philosophical position in the Home-Mountain/Off-Mountain (Shan-chia/Shan-wai) controversy that was going on in the Sung T'ien-t'ai school. Chih-li was the spokesman for the Home-Mountain camp. For him, the famous dictum of "three thousand realms in one instant of thought" was a reality. True Mind is no different from poisons and purity is no different from pollution, for they are all contained in each person. Unlike the Off-Mountain camp of his T'ien-t'ai compatriots and Ch'an adherents, who emphasized the illusory nature of ignorance, Chih-li regarded evil and impurity as very real and felt that they must be dealt with. Repentance ritual practice was therefore very important for him. For although poison, just as wisdom, cannot be dissipated in the ultimate sense, yet through practice, one can change the configuration. As we shall see in the Great Compassion Repentance formulated by Chih-li, although one cannot remove evil, by repenting and identifying with Kuan-yin through discernment (*kuan*), one can deactivate evil and activate wisdom, which are both contained within oneself from the beginning. Thus, by ritually "playing" Kuan-yin, one can eventually hope really to act as the bodhisattva.

In 1021 when Chih-li was sixty-two, he was asked by the emperor to perform the Lotus Repentance for three days and nights in order to pray for the prosperity of the country. At the request of the head eunuch of the inner court, Yü Yüan-ch'ing, he wrote "Essentials for the Cultivation of [the Lotus Samādhi] Repentance" ("Hsiu-ch'an yao-chih"). He explained the significance of the ten-part ritual sequence of the Lotus Samādhi. Since his own Great Compassion Repentance was modeled upon this rite, what Chih-li said is of great help to our understanding of his views on penitential rites in general. This is, therefore, a very important document. He first listed the ten parts of the Lotus Repentance rite: (1) adorning and purifying the ritual sanctuary, (2) purifying the person, (3) offering of the three deeds, (4) inviting the Three Treasures, (5) praising the Three Treasures, (6) venerating the Three Treasures, (7) repentance of the six sense faculties, together with the other four kinds of repentance [imploring the Buddha, sympathetic celebration of merits, dedication or transference of merits and the profession of vows], (8) circumambulation [of the altar], (9) recitation of the sūtra, and (10) seated meditation and correct contemplation of ultimate reality (*cheng-kuan shih-hsiang*) (T 46:868a-870b). While he followed the traditional sequence set down by Chih-i, he combined seated meditation and contemplation of ultimate reality into one step because of his firm belief in subjecting all phenomenal rites to the discernment of principle.

Chih-li began his essay by talking about the meaning and methods of repentance and commenting on each segment of the ritual. The longest discussion centered on sections (7) and (10). Following the T'ien-t'ai schema, Chih-li distinguished between three kinds of repentance: repentance by ritual action (*tso-fa ch'an*), repentance by obtaining a mental form of a buddha or bodhisattva (*chü-hsiang ch'an*), and repentance by contemplating the unborn (*wu-sheng ch'an*). The first type of repentance refers to performing activities of body and speech according to strict regulations and procedures. The second type of repentance refers to mental visualization with a concentrated mind until visions of a buddha or bodhisattva arise. Finally, the last type of repentance, which is the most important, is explained by Chih-li in these words:

> You should understand that your own mind is originally empty and neither sin nor blessing has a master. When you observe the true form of karma and see the original source of sins, you realize that the Dharma Realm (Dharmadhātu) is perfectly integrated and that true suchness is pure and clear. Although there are three methods, they are carried out simultaneously. One may relax in regard to the former, but should never omit the latter. The unborn is the most important, while visualization is less so. This is because the teaching of wondrous discernment is the chief among all the Mahāyāna teachings. The destruction of sins is like the example of grasses and trees withering when the earth is ploughed over. The manifestation of virtue is like the example of myriad forms being exhaustively revealed when the river is illuminated. One should use this discernment of principle (*li-kuan*) to guide the performance of phenomenal rites (*shih-i*). Then each bow and each circumambulation will eliminate the sins of many kalpas, and the offering of each lamp and each drop of water will create blessings as great as the emptiness of space. So when you orally confess the transgressions created by the six senses, you should mentally perform the three kinds of repentance. When your mind is thus focused, only then are you able to carry out the rite of Lotus Samādhi (HTC 100:905a).[9]

Chih-li provided more extensive explanations about confession and the contemplation of ultimate reality, the seventh and the tenth segments of the ritual. I quote the relevant passages.

> When you first practice repentance, it is called the exposure of sins. Why is this so? Just like the roots of grasses and trees wither when exposed, but grow luxuriant when covered, similarly, the roots of goodness should be covered so that all kinds of goodness can grow, but the roots of evil should be exposed, so that all kinds of evil may die. The ten mind-states that follow the stream and go against the stream (*ni-shun shih-hsin*) lead to the two destinies of delusion and enlightenment. When one is deluded about reality and creates evil, the ten mind-states follow saṃsāra and go against nirvāṇa. Starting with beginningless ignorance, desire and wrong views arise, eventually leading one to the status of an *icchantika.*[10] Discarding the belief in cause and effect, one wallows in saṃsāra and has no hope for release. But now that you have met with the rare opportunity provided by the Three Treasures, as soon as you give rise to the one thought of correct faith, you can rectify the past and cultivate for the future by giving rise to the ten mind-states which go against saṃsāra but follow nirvāṇa.[11] Beginning with a deep faith in the law of cause and effect, you will arrive at the perfect realization

> that the nature of mind is originally quiescent. Each of the previous ten mind-states will then be overturned and destroyed. If you do not understand the former ten minds, you do not know why sin is created. If you do not know the latter ten minds, you are unable to practice repentance. To put what I have said in a nutshell: the character of all sins is no different from the character of ultimate reality. The ten evil deeds, five perversions, four *parajikas* [killing, stealing, carnality, lying about spiritual attainment] and eight heterodox practices [contrary to the eightfold noble path] are all the dharma doors of the poison of principle (*li-tu*) as well as original functions of the polluted nature (*hsing-jan*). The person who achieves this realization is called the one who carries out repentance (*neng-ch'an*). It is also called that which is being discerned (*so-kuan*). Delusion and wisdom are originally nondual. Principles and phenomena are ultimately one. When that which obstructs and that which is obstructed are both brought to an end, and that which confesses and that which is confessed are both forgotten, you are doing nothing although you practice diligently everyday. This is truly repentance without any characteristic of sin (*wu-tsui-hsiang ch'an-hui*). It is also called the repentance of great adornment (*ta-chuang-yen ch'an-hui*) and the supreme foremost repentance (*tsui-shang ti-i ch'an-hui*). You should take this discernment of the unborn principle as the lord and the performance of phenomenal rites as coordinating conditions (T 46:869a-b).

Chih-li called the tenth and last part of the Lotus Samādhi Repentance "method of seated meditation and correct contemplation of ultimate reality" and regarded it as the goal of the entire ritual. He referred to this part as "cultivation proper" (*cheng-hsiu*) because the practitioner exclusively concentrates on the discernment of principle, whereas up until this point, although principle was also involved (so that one's mind became concentrated as a result of identifying phenomenon with principle), phenomenal cultivation (*shih-hsiu*) was definitely the practitioner's immediate concern. How then does one carry out discernment? This is the "door of discernment" (*kuan-men*) according to Chih-li:

> It is to abandon the external for the internal, to seek for the mind and to ignore forms. Do not look for any other dharma and regard it as the condition for cultivation. Just observe [and discern] this present thought which you have right now. The most subtle and fleeting thought is precisely the most important. Why should you discard this delusive thought and look for True Suchness? You should observe this one thought as truly limitless in its virtue and everlasting in its essential nature. All the buddhas of the ten

directions, all sentient beings, past, present, and future, empty space and all the lands are entirely contained in it without exception. It is like a pearl in Indra's Net or a wave in a huge ocean. The wave has no other essence but is formed by the entire ocean. Since the ocean has no limit, the wave is similarly without boundary. Although one pearl is tiny, it reflects all other pearls. The reflections of all the other pearls are contained in this one pearl. Therefore, many pearls are not many, and one pearl is not few. This one thought you have right now is also the same. Its nature penetrates the three worlds and its essence spreads in the ten directions. Nothing is not contained in it and nothing is not produced by it. . . . You should now observe [the truth] that all dharmas are no other than the One Mind, and the One Mind is no other than all dharmas. Do not think that the One Mind produces all dharmas, nor that the One Mind contains all dharmas. Do not set up any dichotomy between prior and posterior, or subject and object. Although we speak of various dharmas, their nature and characteristics are originally empty. Although we speak of One Mind, sages and ordinary people are clearly differentiated. To destroy is to establish. It is neither existent nor non-existent. You should forget both the external world and internal discernment, and cut off the opposition between the two. Because it cannot be described with words nor conceptualized in thought, if one is forced to give it a name, I would call it the inconceivable wondrous discernment. This discernment can not only destroy the outermost limit of all sins, but also reveal the deepest source of principle (T 46:870a-b).

The Manual of the Great Compassion Repentance

Let us now look at Chih-li's Great Compassion Repentance manual in some detail. In the preface Chih-li stated that although he could recite the Great Dhāraṇī by heart since the time he was a child, he did not know the method of keeping it (*ch'ih-fa*). Later, after he began to practice T'ien-tai meditation, when he examined the sūtra text [*Ch'ien-shou ching*], he found that it could serve the dual purposes of gaining wisdom through contemplation (*kuan-hui*) and, at the same time, satisfying the requirement of phenomenal ritual performance (*shih-i*). So he wrote this manual primarily for his own personal use. According to Chih-i's four kinds of samādhi, this would fall under the last category, the neither walking nor sitting samādhi, or *sui-tzu-i* (maintaining awareness of mind wherever it is directed) samādhi. The ritual is to be carried out in twenty-one days and consists of ten parts: (1) sanctify the place of practice; (2) purify the three activities [of mouth, body and mind]; (3) create a ritual space; (4) make offerings; (5) invite the Three Treasures and various gods; (6) praise and prayer; (7) prostrations; (8) making vows and chanting the dhāraṇī; (9) confession and repentance; and (10) practicing discernment. Chih-li used the Lotus Samādhi as the model. When we compare this sequence of ten steps with that of the Lotus Samādhi, however, we find that Chih-li substituted circumambulation and recitation of the *Lotus Sūtra* with prostration, and making vows and chanting the dhāraṇī.

As we saw before, Chih-i distinguished among three forms of repentance: by actions, by contemplation of the forms of a buddha or bodhisattva and by the contemplation of the unborn. Chih-li's manual draws on elements from all these three types of repentance. I now translate selected passages from Chih-li's manual for performing the repentance ritual so that we can have a better idea about this ritual as envisioned by him. Unless I indicate otherwise, these are Chih-li's own words.

1. The sūtra says, "One should stay in a clean room, hang banners, light lamps, and offer incense, flowers, food, and drink." The *Ch'ing Kuan-yin i* (Ritual of Inviting Kuan-yin) recorded in the *Pai-lu* (Hundred items of Kuo-ch'ing Monastery) says, "One should decorate the place of practice by smearing the ground with fragrant earth and hanging banners and canopies. Place an image of the Buddha facing south and an image of Kuan-yin facing east." For this ritual, one should set down an image of the Thousand-handed and Thousand-eyed Avalokiteśvara, or one with forty hands. If neither is available, then a six-armed or four-armed image. Lacking even these, you can use any image of Kuan-yin. If you do not have any image of Kuan-yin, it is all right to use an image of Śākyamuni Buddha or P'u-hsien (Samantabhadra) Bodhisattva. The ten practitioners should sit on the ground facing west. If the earth is wet or sloping, then you can use a low platform to sit on. You should make offerings every day, to the best of your ability. If this is impossible, you must at least do your best on the first day. The session should last twenty-one days. Do not shorten it.

2. Purify the three activities. Both the Sūtra and the *Lotus Samādhi* call for bathing, wearing of clean robes and keeping the body and mind controlled. Even if you are not dirty, you must take a bath each day. For the entire period, do not engage in small talk, social pleasantries, or greetings; do not think about worldly affairs even for a second, but always conduct your mind according to the instruction found in the Sūtra. When you have to relieve yourself or drink and eat, keep the same state of mind without losing it to distraction. Return to the place of practice as soon as you are done with your business. Do not linger behind using it as an excuse. In essence, be clear

about what is permitted and what is prohibited in bodily action, when to be silent and when to express yourself in speech, and how to stop and how to contemplate in thought.

3. On the first day of the session, before making formal prostrations, all the practitioners must create a ritual arena within which they will practice. The boundary of such arena can be demarcated with knives, water, white mustard seeds, visualization, clean ash, or five-colored threads, over which the dhāraṇī must be chanted twenty-one times, as stipulated in the Sūtra.

4. After having thus created the ritual space, stand in front of the Thousand-eyed image and think this way: There is no difference in body and mind between the Three Treasures as well as the sentient beings in the Dharmadhātu and myself. All the buddhas are enlightened, whereas all sentient beings are still deluded. I worship the Three Treasures in order to clear away the obstructions created by delusion for the sake of sentient beings. With these thoughts, everyone kneels down. The penance master offers incense, and then chants a gāthā:

May this incense cloud pervade the ten directions.

Each and every land of the Buddha is adorned with unlimited incense.

May all beings enter into the bodhisattva way, and obtain the fragrance of the Tathāgata.

5. While kneeling down and offering incense, the practitioners think thus, "Although the Three Treasures have been freed from obstructions and attained purity, because of their compassion for sentient beings, they will come to remove suffering and bestow happiness if they are invited with sincerity." Starting with the invocatory formula, "With one mind, we respectfully invite Śākyamuni Buddha, our original teacher," the list of invited guests includes Amitābha Buddha, Ch'ien-kuang-wang-ching-chu Buddha, Tathāgata Bright True Dharma [Kuan-yin], the Great Compassion Dhāraṇī, and all the bodhisattvas and gods mentioned in the *Ch'ien-shou ching*.

6. There is no gāthā of praise in the sūtra. The following one is created for this occasion.

Namaḥ Tathāgata Bright True Dharma who is Kuan-shih-yin Bodhisattva present here in front of us.

Having accomplished wondrous merits and full of great compassion,

You manifest a thousand hands and eyes in one body.

Illuminating the Dharmadhātu and safeguarding sentient beings,

You cause them to develop the broad and vast mind of truth.

Teaching them to keep the perfect and divine Dhāraṇī,

You make them depart forever from evil realms of birth and come to be born in front of the Buddha.

You deliver us from sins deserving punishment in Avīci hell, and chronic painful diseases that no doctor can cure.

You grant us without fail samādhi, eloquence, and all other wishes of this life.

You enable us to quickly master the three vehicles, and ascend the stage of Buddhahood.

Because your august power cannot be adequately praised,

I therefore prostrate to you and take refuge in you with a sincere and concentrated mind.

In offering praise to Kuan-yin with the gāthā, you should be most sincere, and in praying for yourself, use your wisdom and accord with reality. However, you should not ask for the lengthening of your life. Your mind should always be directed toward benefiting sentient beings. Only when you are concentrated and sincere will you receive a response. Never treat this matter carelessly.

7. Since the substance of the Three Treasures is unconditional compassion and they always want to save all sentient beings, you should believe that they are already present in the ritual space even though you cannot see them with your naked eyes. So you should offer them incense, prostrate yourself fully with head touching the ground, and pay obeisance to them. When you come across any mention of the Great Compassion Dhāraṇī and Kuan-yin, you should prostrate three times. But you need not do so when the various gods, ghosts and spirits are mentioned.

The next section on making vows and keeping the dhāraṇī is the longest. Chih-li explained its practice exclusively from the T'ien-t'ai doctrinal perspective. This is followed by a section on confession and repentance. The ritual ends with the person leaving the ritual space, withdrawing to the meditation platform to carry out the practice of discernment.

When we study Chih-li's instructions for conducting the Great Compassion Repentance contained in the manual, it is clear that he not only used the structure of the Lotus Samādhi but also its ritual content as his model. As I pointed out before, although he substituted the recitation of the Great Compassion Dhāraṇī for that of the *Lotus Sūtra*, his interpretive framework for the ritual was nevertheless firmly grounded in the T'ien-t'ai dual emphasis on doctrinal understanding and contemplative practice. As had Chih-i and Chan-jan before him, Chih-li insisted on coordinating between ritual action and discernment of principle, as well as on the threefold repentance all rituals were designed to accomplish. Like the "Invocation of the Great Compassionate One" and other hand-copied excerpts of the *Ch'ien-shou ching* found in Tun-huang, Chih-li's manual emphasized the making of the ten great vows and the recitation of the dhāraṇī as central themes of the scripture. However, he thoroughly subjected these vows to an original interpretation using sophisticated and highly complex T'ien-t'ai hermeneutic categories. The vows were thus no longer simply the aspirations of a naive devotee, but doors through which the profound ten modes of discernment could be practiced.

Similarly, by providing a T'ien-t'ai exegesis on the "nine types of heart" that were said to be the "marks and characteristics" of the dhāraṇī, he made the contemplation of them the climax of the entire rite, when each practitioner would withdraw to carry out solitary meditation. In this way he likewise transformed the dhāraṇī from a magical spell into a gateway for enlightenment. Since, according to Chih-li, the one thought the practitioner has right now is no different from reality, which includes buddhas and sentient beings, truth and poison, then what one thinks becomes crucially important. Following Chih-li's logic one step further, if one thinks of Kuan-yin and repents one's sins, it is like saying that the nature of poison and the nature of wisdom are always parts of oneself; as the force of the latter increases, that of the former naturally decreases. Because "Kuan-yin is our original nature," as Chih-li put it, it is entirely understandable why this repentance ritual can be used as a powerful mechanism for our spiritual transformation. It is also understandable why Chih-li chose to create a new repentance ritual based on the *Ch'ien-shou ching*. Since the sūtra and particularly the dhāraṇī were already very popular in the Sung, and since Kuan-yin had already been worshiped in China for over six hundred years, what would make more sense than to take the familiar dhāraṇī and beloved bodhisattva and make them the means for our salvation and enlightenment? But in doing so, he also successfully domesticated this original esoteric scripture.

As Chih-li made clear in the manual, the Great Compassion Repentance was good for everybody, whether monastic or lay, elite or popular. Although he emphasized the importance of contemplation and discernment, he was accommodating to those who could not do it. As long as one had faith and chanted the dhāraṇī with sincerity, he assured one that it was possible to overcome difficulties in this life and to achieve rebirth in the Pure Land, as well as to attain spiritual development, including experiencing visions of the bodhisattva.

From the available evidence, it is clear that the Great Compassion Dhāraṇī was very popular during Chih-li's time. Tsun-shih was known to be a strong believer in the dhāraṇī. For instance, when he built the Golden Light Repentance Hall of the Lower T'ien-chu Temple in Hangchow, he would chant the dhāraṇī seven times before each pillar was erected and each brick laid.[12] Two more cases from the *Fo-tsu t'ung-chi* provide some information about the popularity of the dhāraṇī and the repentance ritual during the early Sung. Hui-ts'ai (997–1083), a disciple of Tsun-shih, was a devotee of the dhāraṇī. When he was a young man, he was not intelligent and could not understand Buddhism. So he chanted the Great Compassion Dhāraṇī, always praying that he would be able to master the T'ien-t'ai teaching. He then dreamt of an Indian monk measuring many yards in height, telling him, "Hui-ts'ai, remember me all your life!" The monk then took off his cassock and put it on him. When Hui-ts'ai attended the lecture the next morning, he understood everything he heard and reached a thorough breakthrough. In his later years, he lived near Lei-feng Tower in Hangchow and chanted the Great Compassion Dhāraṇī 108 times every day, and the name of Amitābha Buddha day and night, while standing on one leg (T 49:215b-c).

As for the repentance ritual, there was the case of Hui-chou, a contemporary of Chih-li, who, together with ten fellow monks, carried out a three-year Great Compassion Repentance in the early years of T'ien-sheng (1023–1032). Since Chih-li completed his own three-year marathon performance of the same ritual in 1020, it is highly likely that Chih-li inspired Hui-chou to follow his example. Hui-chou also performed a three-year repentance ritual centering on Samantabhadra with fourteen colleagues. At the start of the ritual, he made a vow in front of the image saying that if he was successful in the practice, he would immolate himself as an offering. He indeed did so, sitting serenely amidst the fire built from wood contributed by the faithful, both monastic and lay (T 49:216b).

Was the Great Compassion Repentance performed regularly and the recitation of the Great Compassion Dhāraṇī a part of the daily liturgy in the Sung as it is today? The earliest surviving monastic code, the *Ch'an-yüan ch'ing-kuei* (Ch'an-yüan Code) compiled by Ch'ang-lu Tsung-tse in 1103 does not say so. The only reference to Ta-pei Kuan-yin is question number 21, "Can you be like the Bodhisattva of One Thousand Arms and Eyes?," one of the "One Hundred and Twenty Questions" included in *chüan* 8 of the *Code* that a serious Ch'an practitioner was supposed to examine himself with everyday (Yü 1989:101). It probably refers to the need for aspiring to live up to the standards set by the model of the bodhisattva.[13]

The recitation of the dhāraṇī on special occasions was greatly emphasized by the *Ch'ih-hsiu Pai-chang ch'ing-kuei* (Pure Rules of Pai-chang, Compiled by Imperial Order), first compiled by Te-hui (1142–1204) and published in a revised edition in 1338 under the Yüan dynasty. The dhāraṇī "is to be recited during memorial rituals for the patriarchs of the Ch'an school, and for the founders of temples, during the ritual for the well-being of the emperor, which in Japan is still being performed by the Sōtō School on the fifteenth day of each month, during the ritual of praying for rain, and during all funerary rites for monks and abbots. This code advises the assembly of lay believers present to participate in the recitation of the dhāraṇī, which clearly shows that knowledge of its use was not limited to the members of the ordained sangha, but was also common knowledge among the laity" (Reis-Habito 1993:310). The same applied to T'ien-t'ai monasteries, for according to the *Tseng-hsiu chiao-yüan ch'ing-kuei* (Expanded and Revised Pure Rules for Teaching Cloisters), which was written by Tzu-ch'ing in 1347, the chanting of the Great Compassion Dhāraṇī was also to be done on those occasions. Moreover, it contains a section on the "method of performing the Great Compassion Repentance," which stipulates how the ritual is to be performed on the twentieth day of the fourth month (HTC 101:751a). The progression from using the dhāraṇī on special occasions to its inclusion in daily liturgy in the Ch'ing as evidenced by the *Daily Liturgy of the Ch'an Tradition* was a gradual but logical one. Similarly, the performance of the Great Compassion Repentance also underwent a parallel evolution from infrequent to regular occurrences.

As the popularity of the dhāraṇī and the repentance ritual based on it spread during the Sung, references to Ta-pei Kuan-yin started to appear in other contexts. The *Pi-yen lu* (Blue Cliff Record), the famous Sung *kung-an* collection compiled by Hsüeh-t'ou Ch'ung-hsien (980–1052), contains such a reference. Case 89 asks, "What use does the Ta-pei Bodhisattva make of all those hands and eyes?" Case 54 of the *Ts'ung-jung lu* (Record of Leisure), another famous *kung-an* collection compiled by Wan-sung Hsing-hsiu (1156–1236 or 1166–1246), also uses the same question as its theme (T 48:261a-c).

The many hands of Kuan-yin, with an equal number of eyes looking out from the palms, also fascinated artists and poets in the Sung. Ta-pei paintings, such as the one from the National Palace Museum in Taiwan (figure 7.1) and statues were indeed very popular during the Sung. Although neither Su Shun-ch'in (1008–1048) nor Su Tung-p'o (1036–1101) actually saw the statues made of iron in K'ai-feng, the Northern Sung capital, and another made of red sandalwood in Ch'eng-tu, they both wrote about them. Su Tung-p'o wrote:

> If I ask someone to wield an axe in his left hand and hold a knife in his right, to count the flying geese with his eyes and to time the rolling drums with his ears, nodding to bystanders with his head and ascending the steps of the stairs with his feet, even a wizard would be at his wit's end; not to speak of holding various objects with a thousand hands, and seeing different things with a thousand eyes. But when I sit in *dhyāna* with all thoughts hushed, in a state of consciousness with the clarity of a great bright mirror, there rise before me a jumble of men, ghosts, birds, and beasts, and within me a tangle of forms, sounds, aromas, and flavors. Without one thought arising, I am all-responsive, and proper in all responses. Thus without actually extending

Figure 7.1. The Thousand-handed Kuan-yin, by an anonymous Sung painter. *Courtesy of the National Palace Museum, Taiwan.*

a thousand hands and moving a thousand eyes, the truth is the same (Tay 1976:100–101).

But the growing popularity of the ritual was purchased at a price. As I indicated at the beginning of the chapter, the ritual performed today is a much shortened and simplified version of Chih-li's original. It emphasizes the chanting of the dhāraṇī and portions of the sūtra, including the vows, but the part on the discernment of principle is entirely eliminated. Together with the shift to practicality and efficiency, the motivations for performing this ritual have undoubtedly also undergone changes. Instead of being the vehicle for personal spiritual renewal and enlightenment as Chih-li originally designed, the ritual could now be used as a means to bring about all kinds of benefits, including a filial child's hope for a dead parent's good rebirth. On second thought, however, such a development may not have been a regrettable one. As seen previously, Chih-li affirmed phenomenal ritual action and the central importance of the one present thought. Who is to say that even without a period set aside for meditation, someone participating in the ritual, be they monastic or lay, might not be momentarily transformed into Kuan-yin by single-mindedly thinking about and identifying with the bodhisattva? That we can entertain such a hope is ultimately due to Chih-li's achievement. By creating the Great Compassion Repentance ritual, he made it possible for Chinese from all walks of life to form such a karmic affinity with Ta-pei Kuan-yin, the domesticated Thousand-handed and Thousand-eyed Avalokiteśvara.

The domestication of the Thousand-handed Avalokiteśvara reached its completion with the legend of Princess Miao-shan, which was created by a monk and promoted by a literati-official. The earliest version of the legend was written by Chiang Chih-ch'i, the prefect of Ju-chou, Honan, where the Ta-pei Pagoda of Hsiang-shan (Fragrant Mountain) Temple stood, based on what the abbot told him. The pagoda housed an image of Ta-pei Kuan-yin that was believed to be the "true body" of the bodhisattva, who had once lived there on earth as Princess Miao-shan. The stele recording this story was first carved in 1100 and then recarved in 1308. It still stands in the temple today. By the thirteenth century, the story was already so well known that Wan-sung Hsing-hsiu, the Ch'an master who was mentioned previously, could refer to it in his dharma talks (T 48:261c).[14] With the birth and self-sacrifice of Princess Miao-shan, Ta-pei Kuan-yin became anchored to a concrete place in China. The bodhisattva literally became incarnated as a filial Chinese daughter. This moves us from scripture and ritual to the development of local Kuan-yin cults, which is the subject to be treated in the next two chapters.

8

Princess Miao-shan and the Feminization of Kuan-yin

When I was a young girl growing up in China, I spent many evenings after dinner listening to the stories my maternal grandmother loved to tell. They were stories about loyal ministers and righteous officials, filial sons and chaste widows, fox ladies, female ghosts, and people who died, were given a tour of hell and returned to life. The story that made the most lasting impression on me was the story of Princess Miao-shan (Wonderful Goodness). Many years later, in 1987, when I traveled in different parts of China visiting pilgrimage sites and interviewing pilgrims, I would always ask the people I met if they knew any stories about Kuan-yin. They would often tell me about miracles that happened either to themselves or to people they knew. But most frequently, they would tell me the story of Princess Miao-shan. With very minor variations, they repeated the same story my grandmother had told me in my childhood, which goes like this:

> Miao-shan was the third daughter of King Miao-chuang (Wonderful Adornment). She was by nature drawn to Buddhism, keeping a vegetarian diet, reading scriptures by day, and meditating at night from an early age. The king had no sons and hoped to choose an heir from among his sons-in-law. When Miao-shan reached the marriageable age, however, she refused to get married, unlike her two elder sisters, who had both obediently married the men chosen by their father. The king was greatly angered by her refusal and punished her harshly in different ways. She was first confined to the back garden and subjected to hard labor. When, with the aid of gods, she completed the tasks, she was allowed to go to the White Sparrow Nunnery

> to undergo further trials in the hope of discouraging her from pursuing the religious path. She persevered, and the king burned down the nunnery, killed the five hundred nuns, and had Miao-shan executed for her unfilial behavior. While her body was safeguarded by a mountain spirit, Miao-shan's soul toured hell and saved beings there by preaching to them. She returned to the world, went to Hsiang-shan, meditated for nine years, and achieved enlightenment. By this time, the king had become seriously ill with a mysterious disease that resisted all medical treatment. Miao-shan, disguised as a mendicant monk, came to the palace and told the dying king that there was only one remedy that could save him: a medicine concocted with the eyes and hands of someone who had never felt anger. She further told the astonished king where to find such a person. When the king's messengers arrived, Miao-shan willingly offered her eyes and hands. The father recovered after taking the medicine and came to Hsiang-shan with the royal party on a pilgrimage to offer thanks to his savior. He recognized the eyeless and handless ascetic as no other than his own daughter. Overwhelmed with remorse, he and the rest of the royal family all converted to Buddhism. Miao-shan was transformed into her true form, that of the Thousand-eyed and Thousand-armed Kuan-yin. After the apotheosis, Miao-shan passed away and a pagoda was erected to house her relics.

As we read in chapter 2, Avalokiteśvara, like all great bodhisattvas in Mahāyāna Buddhism, cannot be said to possess any gender characteristics, although in India, Southeast Asia, Tibet, and China up to the T'ang, the deity is usually depicted as a handsome and princely young man. From the time of the Five Dynasties, however, Kuan-yin began to undergo a process of feminization. By the Ming this process reached completion, and Kuan-yin became a completely sinicized goddess. The feminine transformation of Kuan-yin is, of course, not entirely a Chinese innovation, but has a firm scriptural basis. According to the "Universal Gateway" chapter of the *Lotus Sūtra*, Kuan-yin can appear in as many as thirty-three different forms in order to save different types of people. Among these forms, seven are feminine: nun, lay woman, wife of an elder, householder, official, Brahmin, and girl (Hurvitz 1976:314–15).

In the *Śuraṅgama Sūtra*, a sūtra particularly popular since the Sung, Kuan-yin appears in thirty-two forms, of which six are feminine: nun, laywoman, queen, princess, noble lady, and virgin maiden (Luk 1966:137–38). But in China Kuan-yin did not simply appear as such an undefined woman. In fact, a key factor in the successful indigenization and feminization of this Buddhist deity in China is that through various myths and legends the Chinese managed to transform Avalokiteśvara, the ahistorical bodhisattva who transcended temporal and spatial limitations as depicted in the Mahāyāna scriptures, into Kuan-yin, who, known by different Chinese names, led lives in clearly definable times and locations on the soil of China. Only in this way could Kuan-yin conform to the model of Chinese deities. For in China, not only were popular gods such as Kuan-ti and Crazy Chi or the goddess Ma-tsu real people who once lived in specific times and places, but, as Derk Bodde suggested years ago, through the process of "euhemerization," even mythical figures were turned into historical cultural heroes who were venerated as the founding fathers of Chinese civilization (1961:367–408). Unlike ancient Greece, where human heroes were turned into Olympian gods, in China, gods were depicted as real human beings. As studies by Valerie Hansen (1990) and Kenneth Dean (1993) have demonstrated, many new deities whose cults began during the Sung were once ordinary men and women who became deified after death. And if the god or goddess was not originally a human being, as, for instance, in the case of Wen-ch'ang, there were, starting in the Sung, concerted efforts toward personification designed to turn him or her into a human being (Kleeman 1993, 1994). In the case of Kuan-yin, the same process occurred in reverse. Kuan-yin had to become Miao-shan, a living woman, so that she could be worshiped as a Chinese goddess. As Julian Pas remarks, the "human" character of Chinese deities is one of the most distinctive features of Chinese religion: "like human beings, the gods have birthdays, families, careers, titles, temperaments, and authority" (Pas 1991:130).

Although bodhisattvas, including Kuan-yin, are not given birthdays in the Buddhist sūtras (for, unlike Śākyamuni, they are not historical personages), in China, the nineteenth day of the second month (the day Princess Miao-shan was born) became known as Kuan-yin's birthday. The celebration of Kuan-yin's birthday was first listed in the "monthly calendar" section of the *Pure Rules of Huan-chu* (Huan-chu ch'ing-kuei), the monastic code created by the Ch'an Master Chung-feng Ming-pen in 1317 for his own temple, Huan-chu An. He stipulated that offerings of flowers, candles, incense, tea, fruits, and delicacies should be made and prayers (*shu*) be read aloud, just as on the day commemorating the Buddha's nirvāṇa (HTC 111:974a). Like the birthdays of all Chinese deities, this day has been the most important festival for her devotees. This serves as a powerful example of the Chinese transformation of Kuan-yin. A similar example may be found in the identification, over time, of the island P'u-t'o, located off the shore of Chekiang Province, with the mythical Potalaka, the transtemporal and transspatial realm mentioned in the *Hua-yen Sūtra* and other esoteric sūtras. When this originally desolate and obscure island became established as a national and international pilgrimage center, it also gave rise to the cult of Nan-hai Kuan-yin (Kuan-yin of the South Sea, discussed in chapters 9 and 10).

Of the various feminine manifestations Kuan-yin assumed in China, by far the most familiar was the chaste and filial daughter represented by Princess Miao-shan. As Glen Dudbridge (1978) has demonstrated, the core of the legend can be traced to the stele inscription entitled *Ta-pei P'u-sa chuan* (Biography of the Bodhisattva of Great Compassion), composed by Chiang Chih-ch'i (1031–1104), who came to Ju-chou, Honan, as its new prefect in 1099. He became friends with Huai-chou, the abbot of Hsiang-shan Monastery, situated on a mountain two hundred *li* south of Mount Sung and a few miles to the southeast of Pao-feng County, in Ju-chou, Honan. Attached to the monastery was the Ta-pei Pagoda, which housed an image of the Thousand-handed and Thousand-eyed Kuan-yin.

The term Ta-pei, as we read in the last chapter, refers to this iconography specifically. In the T'ang, following the introduction of esoteric forms of Kuan-yin, images of this type became very popular. A divine origin was claimed for many of these images, that is, that they were created by the bodhisattva personally. Li Chien (1059–1109), the author of *Hua-p'in* (On Paintings), described this image at Hsiang-shan Monastery as having been "made in person by a human manifestation of Ta-pei." He compared it to two other Ta-pei Kuan-yin images he had seen, one done by the famous painter Fan Ch'iung during the Ta-chung era (847–859), an image less than a foot in length and with thirty-six arms, and another housed in the T'ien-hsien Monastery in Tung-ching, Hsiang-yang (in present-day Hupei), which was also made "by a human manifestation of Ta-pei." T'ien-hsien Ssu was a nunnery. In the Wu-te era (618–628), when the nuns wanted to have an image of Ta-pei Kuan-yin painted on the wall of the main hall, they sought a good artist. A couple with a young girl came to answer the call, and the girl who did the painting was apparently a manifestation of Kuan-yin (Dudbridge 1978:16; Stein 1986:46; Tsukamoto 1955:269). A painting of the Ta-pei Kuan-yin with forty-two arms located at the Palace Museum in Taipei is attributed to Fan Ch'iung with an inscription saying that he painted this in 850 at the Sheng-hsing Ssu of Ch'eng-tu, Szechwan (figure 8.1).

The case of Hsiang-shan was unique, however, for Kuan-yin not only created an image but lived an embodied life there. As Dudbridge convincingly argues, the cult began through joint promotion on the parts of a local official and the abbot of the temple in 1100, a pattern, as we shall see in chapter 9, often found in the creation of other pilgrimage centers as well. Based on what the abbot told him, Chiang wrote the account, which was penned by the famous calligrapher Ts'ai Ching (1046–1126) and inscribed on a stele in 1100. By the early twelfth century, Hsiang-shan had apparently become a flourishing pilgrimage center.

Chiang did not stay in Ju-chou long. Less than three years after his transfer

Figure 8.1. The Thousand-handed Kuan-yin, painted by Fan Ch'iung in 850 C.E. *Courtesy of the National Palace Museum, Taiwan.*

there, Chiang was reassigned and served as the prefect of Hangchow between November 1102 and October 1103. It is highly likely, as Dudbridge argues, that Chiang brought this story from Honan to Hangchow. In the Upper T'ien-chu Monastery, another pilgrimage center for Kuan-yin worship, there once stood a two-stone stele that might have read "Life of the All-Compassionate One, re-erected" (the first half of the stele was destroyed; it does not survive among extant rubbings). The stele, erected in 1104, repeated the story of Kuan-yin who was Princess Miao-shan (Dudbridge 1982:591–93). As described in chapter 6, the Upper T'ien-chu Monastery was already an important Kuan-yin pilgrimage center in the tenth century, more than a century before Chiang's arrival. This story was probably not known in Hangchow, but once it reached there, it became closely connected with the Upper T'ien-chu, for the popular version of the legend as elaborated in the later *Hsiang-shan pao-chüan* (The Precious Scroll of Hsiang-shan) was supposedly revealed to P'u-ming, a monk of the temple. This story took deep root at the Upper T'ien-chu, perhaps because the Kuan-yin worshiped there was already understood to be feminine. Hsiang-shan declined after K'ai-feng fell to the Chin and Hangchow became the capital of the Southern Sung in 1138. The Upper T'ien-chu Monastery in Hangchow then became the undisputed national pilgrimage center for Kuan-yin worship until P'u-t'o emerged as a serious competitor in later centuries.

Although the legend of Miao-shan was already known in the Sung, it was further elaborated and developed in several different genres during the Ming and the Ch'ing. In the Ming novel *The Complete Story of Kuan-yin of the South Sea* (Nan-hai Kuan-yin ch'üan chuan), the Ming *ch'uan-ch'i* drama *Story of Hsiang-shan* (Hsiang-shan chi) that in turn served as the basis for the Peking opera *Great Hsiang-shan* (Ta Hsiang-shan), and the Ch'ing sectarian text *True Scripture of Kuan-yin's Original Vow of Universal Salvation* (Kuan-yin chi-tu pen-yüan chen-ching). All these works were, in turn, based on the *Precious Scroll of Hsiang-shan.* The earliest surviving edition was from the Ch'ien-lung era, with a preface dated 1773. The text bore yet another preface, which was dated 1103 and written by a monk named P'u-ming of Upper T'ien-chu Monastery; he cannot be otherwise identified.[1] Even if the preface was spurious, the *pao-chüan* was clearly written by the Ming, for it was already referred to by this title in the 1550s.

The great fascination the Chinese people, particularly women, have felt toward this story is itself very interesting for students of Chinese religion. As we have seen in chapter 4, the telling, recording, and retelling of miracle tales about Kuan-yin is one of the most persistent characteristics of the cult of Kuan-yin. The story of Miao-shan is of course a miracle tale, but with two major differences. Whereas Kuan-yin only appeared briefly in visions and dreams in all the other miracle tales, the bodhisattva is supposed to have lived an embodied life as a real woman in this one. Another difference is that in contrast to most of the other miracle tales examined previously which validated in one way or another Kuan-yin's salvific powers promised by the sūtras (chiefly the *Lotus*), the story of Miao-shan offers a "biography" of the Thousand-handed Kuan-yin. The highlight of the story is the transformation of the eyeless and handless young girl into the Thousand-eyed and Thousand-handed Bodhisattva. As we read in the previous chapter, this esoteric form of Kuan-yin, known as Ta-pei (The Great Compassionate One), which was already popular in the T'ang, became even more so in the Sung, having been promoted by new iconography and ritual. The birth of the legend of Miao-shan during this time is another indication for the popularity of the cult of Ta-pei.

In this chapter, I compare the earliest version of the story preserved on a stele with the later version found in the *Precious Scroll of Hsiang-shan* and other texts based on it. In discussing the evolution of the legend, I am interested in several questions: Why did the bodhisattva turn into a woman? Why was the princess given the name Miao-shan? Why did Miao-shan choose to offer her organs in order to save her father? Are there precedents for such behavior in the Buddhist and Chinese traditions? Did Miao-shan bear any resemblance to Taoist women saints? If so, how? And finally, what did the story mean to Chinese women? Did Miao-shan serve as a source of empowerment for them?

The Earliest Version of the Story Recorded on a Stele

Glen Dudbridge (1978) has meticulously traced the origin and evolution of the legend of Princess Miao-shan. The earliest literary source was the stele inscription written by Chiang Chih-ch'i based on a text shown to him by Huai-chou, the abbot of Hsiang-shan Monastery. The transmission of the text was complicated. The abbot claimed that a pilgrim monk from Mt. Chung-nan, outside of Ch'ang-an, in Shensi, brought it when he visited Hsiang-shan Temple. The anonymous pilgrim, in turn, claimed that the original author was the famous Vinaya master Tao-hsüan (596–667), also of Mt. Chung-nan, who learned the story from a divine spirit. Chiang commented on the crudeness of the language and agreed to rewrite the story at the request of Huai-chou in May of 1100. Later in the year, it was copied by the prime minister and calligrapher Ts'ai Ching and carved on a stele. As I stated earlier, when Chiang was transferred to Hangchow, he took the story there and a stele with the same tale was erected at the Upper T'ien-chu Monastery four years later. Although the legend claimed to have a miraculous and hoary origin, its dissemination in the early twelfth century, as Dudbridge convincingly argued, was closely tied to the rising fame of Hsiang-shan Monastery as an important regional pilgrimage center. The choice of Tao-hsüan as the source of the story was also appropriate. As we read in chapters 3 and 4, Tao-hsüan was indeed a firm believer and promoter of miracle tales. Not only did he help to promulgate the story of Sun Ching-te being the recipient of the indigenous sūtra *King Kao's Kuan-yin Sūtra*, he himself also compiled a miracle tale collection, the *Record of the Miraculous Responses of the Three Treasures in China.*

But more related to the subject under discussion, he also wrote a work called the *Record of Spiritual Resonance of the Vinaya Master Tao-hsüan*, in which he asked spirits or divine beings (*t'ien-jen*) a series of questions concerning the origins of miraculous images, relics and sites in China. The story of Miao-shan was supposedly related to Tao-hsüan by a divine spirit (*t'ien-shen*), very much in the manner of the latter work. Whoever the real author of the story was, whether it was really the monk I-ch'ang, a disciple of Tao-hsüan, as claimed by the stele, or in fact the abbot Huai-chou himself, he must have been familiar with this work and that was why he attributed the origin of the story of Miao-shan to Tao-hsüan.

Inspired by Dudbridge's research, Lai Swee-fo (1980) began to investigate the fate of the stele. He first tracked down the three extant rubbings of the Hangchow stele in existing collections, and pointed out that they contained only the second half of the story. He also proved that "Kuan-shih-yin P'u-sa chuan lüeh" ("An Abridged Biography of Bodhisattva Kuan-shih-yin") written by Kuan Tao-sheng (1262–1319), wife of the famous painter and calligrapher Chao Meng-fu (1254–1322), in 1306, which has survived in stele collections, was based on the stele text. But because the local gazetteer *Pao-feng hsien-chih* did not record the text of the Hsiang-shan stele, and the extant three rubbings of the Upper T'ien-chu stele only recorded its latter half, the fate of the original stele and its entire content have long been a mystery. Dudbridge (1982) theorized that the rubbing from Hangchow was from the second of two original stelae, and the first slab was either destroyed or lost. He also did not know if the Hsiang-shan stele still existed.

The mystery has now been resolved. In 1993 Lai Swee-fo made a trip to Hsiang-shan Monastery and saw the 1308 re-erected stele with the inscription originally composed by Chiang Chih-ch'i. The stele is very tall and wide (2.22 meters in height and 1.46 in width) because the text is very long, containing over 3,000 characters. The top portion was damaged during the Cultural Revolution and later repaired, thus resulting in the loss of about ten characters in each line. The second half of the stele corresponds exactly with what has been preserved from the Upper T'ien-chu stele. Lai explained why the first half of the text, running twenty-four lines, was not handed down. Because the slab is so wide, in fact twice the width of a normal stele, it would have required two separate pieces of paper to make the rubbing. It was most likely that the rubbing from the first half of the stele got misplaced or lost early on and thus has remained unknown to scholars until now (Lai 1993).

Dudbridge (1982) had earlier translated the second half of the stele. He also compared the story found in two later sources. The first is the *Lung-hsing Fo-chiao pien-nien t'ung-lun*, a chronicle of Buddhist history in China from 64 to 957 C.E. written by Tsu-hsiu, a monk of Lung-hsing fu (the present-day Nan-ch'ang), in the year 1164; and the second is the *Chin-kang k'e-i*, a vernacular annotation of commentaries on the *Diamond Sūtra* compiled by Chüeh-lien with a preface dated 1551. With the discovery of the entire stele of Hsiang-shan, we can now say with some confidence that both Tsu-hsiu and Chüeh-lien had knowledge of Chiang's inscription, for at times they used identical phrases to those of the stele in various places within their own works, which are much shorter and less detailed. The biography written in 1100 can safely be regarded as the origin of all later compositions.

The significance of the legend as told by Chiang's inscription cannot be overemphasized. By identifying the pan-Buddhist bodhisattva Kuan-yin as Princess Miao-shan, a real woman living and dying in Honan, it transformed the mythical bodhisattva, who was originally not bound to any place. In the meantime, it also transformed Hsiang-shan, a real place in central China, into a holy site. Once the story appeared, as Dudbridge has shown, it was made ever more popular by drama, novels, and most importantly, the *Precious Scroll of Hsiang-shan* from the Ming on. Eventually, Chinese of all social strata and both sexes, mainly through this story, came to know Kuan-yin as this strong-willed yet filial girl who refused to get married.

The stele bears the title "Life of the Great Compassionate One (Ta-pei)"[2] Appendix A contains the entire translation.

Analysis of the Story

The Gender and Name of the Heroine

Several points of this earliest version of the legend of Miao-shan immediately catch our attention. I first take up the gender and name of Miao-shan. The story identifies Kuan-yin with a young girl in a straightforward and matter-of-fact manner. Although some sūtras declare that the bodhisattva can manifest in the form of a woman, previous incarnations of Kuan-yin were all monks. Were there indications prior to 1100 that Kuan-yin appeared as a woman? When did Kuan-yin appear as a woman and how early did the name Kuan-yin become connected with femininity in historical records?

Fortunately, Chinese scholars engaged in evidential scholarship have been very interested in tracing the beginnings of Kuan-yin's gender change. Two Ch'ing scholars, Chao I (1727–1814) and Yü Cheng-hsieh (1775–1850) found several references to either Kuan-yin appearing as a woman to save someone, or to real women being addressed as Kuan-yin. In the first instance, they cite the case from *Fa-yüan chu-lin* of Kuan-yin appearing as a woman in 479 to P'eng Tzu-chiao in prison and loosening him from his shackles (T 53:484c). They cite another case from the histories of the Northern Ch'i (*Pei Ch'i shu* 33:7b) and the Northern and Southern Dynasties (*Pei shih* 90:5b; *Nan shih* 12:9a) compiled earlier of Kuan-yin appearing as a woman to heal the dissolute and emaciated Northern Ch'i emperor Wu-cheng (r. 561–565). As for the examples of real women being addressed as Kuan-yin, the last empress of the Ch'en, née Shen, became a Buddhist nun and received the religious name "Kuan-yin" in 617. Finally they cite the case of Yang Hsiu-lieh's (fl. 737) referring to a nun with great spiritual penetration in his eulogy for her as someone whom people of the time called Kuan-yin (*Chü'an T'ang wen* 396:20a; Chao 34:739; Yü 15:571). The examples they cited, isolated and at times misconstrued,[3] were supposed to prove that as early as the fifth century Kuan-yin had already manifested in a female form, thus refuting the Ming scholar Hu Ying-lin, who claimed that the gender change happened only in the Yüan.

Kuan-yin was used as a name of respect not only for nuns, but apparently also for a Taoist woman saint. Wang Feng-hsien (ca. 835–885) was an important Taoist woman saint whose life is recorded by the late T'ang Taoist master Tu Kuang-t'ing (850–933) in a collection of hagiographical accounts of female Taoist holy women entitled "A Record of the Assembled Transcendants of the Fortified Walled City (*Yung ch'eng chi hsien lu*)," completed around 910.[4] After she embarked on her religious practice, "she did not eat for a year or more. Her flesh and muscles were rich and lustrous, as clean as ice or snow. With a cicada-shaped head and a rounded neck, she seemed made of luminous matter, and had bright pupils. Her appearance was like that of a heavenly person. She was brilliant and perceptive in knowledge and argument. People south of the Yangze River called her Kuan-yin" (Tu 1976, 38:30344b).

Another intriguing question is why the princess is called Miao-shan. Dudbridge tells us that it is a name or epithet in a variety of Buddhist contexts, sometimes as the name of a bodhisattva, Miao-shan P'u-sa (T 16:154a; T 25:443b; 53:283a; 54:1077b). In fact, there is a passage in the *History of the Sui* (Sui shu 69:1608) in which Wang Shao addressed Emperor Kao-tsu in 602, referring to the recently dead Empress Wen-hsien as Miao-shan P'u-sa and implying that she had ascended to heaven (Dudbridge 1978:78). Because of this auspicious connotation, we also find at times that Miao-shan was used for the name of a nun. For instance, the empress of Sung Emperor T'ai-tsung (r. 976–996) had a nurse by the name of Hu Hsi-sheng who was hired by her father Li Ch'u-yün (914–960). After her father passed away, the nurse became a nun and was active in the capital. Emperor T'ai-tsung gave her the name Miao-shan and a rich family by the name of Yüan donated their house for her to build a temple. T'ai-tsung bestowed a plaque for the temple naming it Ch'an Hall of Wonderful Enlightenment, made it a public monastery, and appointed Miao-shan to head it. It was renamed Monastery for National Protection under Jen-tsung (r. 1023–1063), and a stūpa was constructed as requested by Miao-shan.

When the Ta-an Stūpa was completed in 1028, the emperor asked Hsia Sung (984–1050), a Confucian scholar-official, to write a long inscription celebrating the event, in which the two abbesses Miao-shan and her disciple Tao-chien were praised for their leadership in its construction (Huang 1995:106). The project took twenty years and the imperial family members and officials all supported it. Since the monastery and the stele stood in the capital of K'ai-feng, it must have been very well known to the contemporary people. A famous nun by the name not of Miao-shan, but Miao-yin (the name of one of the two sisters of Miao-shan in the legend), was reported by the Japanese monk Seijin who made a pilgrimage to Mt. Wu-t'ai during the years 1068–1077. He reported the wealth and fame of a T'ien-t'ai nun by the name Fa-kuei who was the abbess of the Ch'ung-te Cloister. She received a purple robe and the honorable title "Great Master Miao-yin" from the emperor (Seijin 200, 251). Both these nuns, with the names of Miao-shan and Miao-yin, lived less than a hundred years before Chiang wrote the stele. The names of recent or contemporary famous religious women might also have served as an inspiration, and these two cases should be kept in mind.

But when we ask why these two nuns were given these names, the question is simply pushed further back. Both Miao-shan and Miao-yin may indeed have their ultimate origin in Buddhist scriptures. Dudbridge has shown that the names of almost all the main characters of the Miao-shan legend come from the *Lotus Sūtra*. For instance, chapter 27 features a king by the name of Miao-chuang-yen (Wonderful Adornment) and his queen Ching-te (Pure Virtue). These could be the sources for King Chuang (or Miao-chuang in later versions) and Queen Pao-te (Precious Virtue). The king in the sūtra, just like the king in our story, is hostile toward Buddhism. He is converted by his two pious sons, who are then reborn as two bodhisattvas named Medicine King (Yao-wang) and Medicine Superior (Yao-shang)—the former, in turn, being the hero of chapter 23 of the *Lotus Sūtra*, in which he burns off his arms worshiping the relics of the Buddha housed in stūpas.

As for the names of Miao-shan's two elder sisters, Miao-yen (Wonderful Appearance) and Miao-yin (Wonderful Sound), they also have authentic scriptural pedigrees. While Miao-yen is the name of an eight-year-old novice who preaches the Dharma to the queen and the five hundred court ladies in the palace of King Aśoka after resisting the queen's motherly embrace (T 53:159bc), Miao-yin is the hero of chapter 24 of the *Lotus Sūtra*. Like Kuan-yin in chapter 25, the celebrated "Universal Gateway" chapter, Miao-yin is also a universal savior who can appear in as many as thirty-two different forms in order to preach the Dharma and save sentient beings. Perhaps even more relevant to our story, the sūtra declares: "And for the sake of those who are in the women's quarters of the royal palace, he changes himself into a woman's form and preaches this sūtra" (Watson 1993:295). After tracing the individual constituent elements of the legend to their scriptural sources, Dudbridge rightly concludes,

> [W]e can infer a "melting-pot" process of composition, in which themes and names from the *Lotus* and certain other traditions come together with the firm data of a local situation to form a new synthetic story. In this new creation the name of spiritual career of King Śubhavyūha [Miao-chuang-yen] remain essentially intact, and the other names and themes are grouped around him, surrendering some of their original distinctive identity. The work has been neatly done. By borrowing Miao-yin from the *Lotus*, and Miao-yen and Miao-shan from elsewhere, the author has contrived a "Chinese" family group which shares (though with spurious philology) the family name "Miao." By causing the bodhisattva to sacrifice arms *and* eyes, he makes possible her final transfiguration in the form of the Ta-pei image for which Hsiang-shan was known. (Dudbridge 1978:78–79).

The author of the legend of Miao-shan had indeed correctly singled out the central characters and major themes of the *Lotus Sūtra* for his Chinese audience. During the Sung, woodblock printing of the *Lotus Sūtra* was very popular. One copy, carved around 1160 (sixty years after the Hsiang-shan stele), is located in the Arthur M. Sackler Museum. On the lower left corner of the frontispiece there is a printed inscription with the title, "Preface to the Propagation and Transmission of the Lotus Sūtra of the Wonderful Dharma," narrated by Tao-hsüan. It consists of eight lines made up of four characters each:

Medicine King and Medicine Superior
King Miao-chuang-yen
Three carts take one out of the burning house

The Bodhisattva Never Disparaging
Miao-yin comes east
P'u-hsien comes east
Medicine-king burns arms
Kuan-yin secretly responds.[5]

This succinct synopsis of the *Lotus* tells us vividly what a knowledgeable Buddhist monk considers to be the highlights of the sūtra. They are also, not surprisingly, what the legend of Miao-shan selects from the sūtra. The legend, like the indigenous scriptures examined in chapter 3, combines central elements of Buddhist scriptures with new and local concerns. While Dudbridge calls it a "melting-pot," I call it repackaging—putting old wine in new bottles.

Although we now know that the key elements of the legend can be traced to Buddhist scriptures, we are still left with a major question: Why did the author change the gender of the filial and pious child who converted the heretical king to Buddhism? Why was it a daughter instead of two sons as in the original story? One also wonders why the author did not simply retain the name of Miao-yin instead of using the name Miao-shan, which is not found in the *Lotus*. We have seen that Miao-shan was used as a name for bodhisattvas and nuns. But Miao-shan never became a nun. In fact, she had harsh words to say about Hui-chen, the abbess of the White Sparrow Nunnery and its residents. Although she was not a nun, she lived a rigorously religious life, starting with keeping a vegetarian diet and studying and preaching the Dharma when young, up to and including meditating and functioning as a Buddhist master in her mature age (the *pao-chüan* version is even more pronounced). When we consider the status and career of Miao-shan, we are immediately struck by the similarity between our heroine and the lifestyles and activities of participants in a new lay Buddhist movement who called themselves, "People of the Way," which began to appear in historical documents from the twelfth century on. In the meantime, new feminine forms of Kuan-yin also began to be created before and during this time. I believe that it is only when we take into consideration the dual emergence of feminine forms of Kuan-yin in art and this new lay Buddhist religious movement in the Sung that we can understand why it was a young girl instead of a monk who became the incarnation of Kuan-yin in this particular legend.

Before we look at the new religious movement identified as the White Lotus movement in scholarship, let us first review what is known about lay Buddhism. The Buddhist community or Saṃgha, one of the Three Treasures, consists of monks, nuns, laymen, and laywomen. The history of Buddhism in China was therefore constructed by both monastics and lay people. Lay Buddhism had, of course, existed in China long before the Sung. Jacques Gernet (1995) tells us that traces of many lay associations, called *i* or *she*, were found at Tun-huang spanning the time from the Period of Disunity to the Sui and T'ang. The activities of these associations were extremely varied: the sculpting and the casting of statues, the decoration of caves, the construction of sanctuaries, organization of festivals and feast days, and the copying and recitation of sūtras. Acting as donors, members of these associations hoped to create blessing through the performance of pious deeds. The most distinctive feature of these early associations is the leadership role played by monks. "Not only were the Buddhist *i* and *she* generally founded on the clergy's initiative, but there was also scarcely an association that did not have its Buddhist master" (Gernet 1995:274).

During the Sung, lay associations became increasingly popular in Buddhist circles, particularly under the leadership of Buddhist masters such as Chih-li (Getz 1994). Such associations have been traced back to Hui-yüan's White Lotus Society (Pai-lien She), which, according to the *Fo-tsu t'ung chi*, was founded in 416 on Mt. Lu for the recitation of the Buddha's name. It had 123 religious and lay members (T 49:343a). Like their presumed prototype, these Sung associations were primarily "societies for reciting the Buddha's name" (*nien-fo hui*). During their periodic meetings members recited the name of the Amitābha Buddha together and transferred the merits thus accrued to their speedy rebirth in the Western Paradise. The members also engaged in philanthropic activities, but invocation of the Buddha was the main purpose. In this regard, they represented a departure from the earlier associations. However, like the latter, monks still played leading roles and lay people looked to them for guidance.

In contrast, the White Lotus movement, which began in the twelfth century, opened a new chapter in the history of lay Buddhism. Thanks to new research carried out by Chikusa Masaaki (1982, 1987) and Barend ter Haar (1992), we now have a much better understanding of the early phase of this movement. Because some later groups that carried out rebellions also used this name to refer to themselves, the entire movement has been condemned as heretical and subversive, a result of what ter Haar terms "labeling" and "stereotyping" by government officials and orthodox monks. But in the early period of the movement, during the Sung and throughout the Yüan, it was very respectable and enjoyed the support of political, religious, and educated elites.

The White Lotus movement was founded by Mao Tzu-yüan (c. 1086/8–1166) who styled himself the White Lotus Mentor (Pai-lien Tao-shih). He preached to lay people like himself. He wrote a number of religious manuals for collective worship and ritual. He founded a White Lotus Penance Hall near Lake Tien-shan in Kiangsu, near the P'u-kuang-wang Monastery, which was the center for the cult of Seng-chieh, the monk-incarnate of the Eleven-headed Kuan-yin discussed in chapter 5. The use of the religious affiliation characters *p'u* (universal) and *chüeh* (enlightenment) as a part of one's name among the followers of the movement can be linked to his preaching. For just before he died, he instructed his followers to use the four characters in their names to indicate their religious affiliations. Aside from the two characters mentioned, they were *miao* and *tao* (way).

These new style lay Buddhists, whom ter Haar calls "activist" lay Buddhists, used many different "autonyms" to identify themselves. As ter Haar explains, autonyms were used both by themselves as an important part of their self-image as well as by outsiders as a means of recognizing them as one distinct group of lay Buddhist believers. Among these autonyms, one finds: "People of the Way" (*tao-min*), "Man of the Way" (*tao-jen*), "Friends of the Way" (*tao-che*), "Lord of the Way" (*tao-kung*), "Lady of the Way" (*tao-ku*), "Woman of the Way" (*tao-nü*), and more significantly, "White-clad Followers of the Way" (*pai-i tao-che*) (ter Haar 1992:31–32; Chikusa 1982:262–92). In many ways they were similar to other conventional lay Buddhists. For instance, they kept a vegetarian diet, chanted sūtras and the Buddha's name, and dedicated themselves to good works such as printing sūtras, constructing roads and bridges and distributing tea and drinking water to travelers and pilgrims. But in one very significant way, they were very different. Unlike earlier lay Buddhists' dependence on the monks' leadership, these men and women practiced Buddhism independent of monastic authority and supervision. They took on the religious functions and roles of monks, such as conducting Buddhist services for fellow members, while retaining their married status and their ordinary place in society. Most distinctively, well-to-do adherents founded small, private cloisters (*an*) or halls (*t'ang*) for their bases of activity. Unlike temples and monasteries, which were controlled by government through a system of bestowal of plaques, such privately established shrines were regarded with suspicion by the authorities. Chu Hsi, for instance, made priestesses return to lay life and cautioned against people living in shrines when he was serving in Chang-chou in 1190. But despite governmental prohibitions, local gazetteers noted their increase from the Southern Sung on, reaching a climax in the Yüan, clearly reflecting the energy of the White Lotus movement. It was only in the early Ming that these shrines were incorporated into temples (Chikusa 1982: 274–75, 1987:1–28).[6]

Because of these characteristics, ter Haar suggests that "The People of the Way are best conceived as a new phenomenon, rather than as a development stemming from the recitation gatherings. People of the Way flourished unhampered throughout the Song and were clearly a socially well-accepted group"

(1992:43). Some of the cloisters were erected specifically for the spiritual welfare of the ancestors and in this way continued the tradition of merit cloisters, which had already appeared by the T'ang. Others, known as grave temples (*fen-ssu* or *fen-an*), were built near the tombs of the founders' ancestors and constituted a new development (Chikusa 1982:111–43). Monks were sometimes asked to take care of these cloisters, but lay people retained their control. Kuan-yin worship was a prominent feature in the religious lives of these lay Buddhists, who either built the cloisters and halls, donated land to them, or patronized them. Most of the examples provided by ter Haar (1992) date to the Yüan, although the custom had already begun in the Sung, as the first case illustrates.

The literatus Ch'en Cho (1214–1297) was acquainted with the monk-keeper of a local temple. He was told that it had originally been the private house of the widow Chang. She had been a devout believer who recited the *Lotus Sūtra* daily. Once she dreamed that seven monks were born from a lotus flower in the place where she lived. So in 949 she donated her house and a considerable amount of land to a monk to have it converted into a small cloister for Kuan-yin worship. Later, other people also donated land to it (ter Haar 1992:23). Another literatus named Jen Shih-lin (1253–1309) cited a Tsao family consisting of three generations to show how piety led to good fortune. They would often go to a local temple of the White-robed Kuan-yin and consult the divination sticks kept there. From before 1294 until after 1308 they were continuously blessed with favorable outcomes by the sticks. The father also worshiped a small statue of Kuan-yin, who once visited him in a dream. The family donated hundreds of *mu* of land to the temple in the years 1301 to 1304. Another man named K'ung Yu-fu and his wife Ms. Ch'en Miao-ching also donated land, to show themselves good believers (ter Haar 1992:25). The lay Buddhist named Sun founded a grave-cloister (*fen-an*) in She (in present-day Anhui) for his mother. He invited Friends of the Way and had someone paint a picture of Kuan-yin (ter Haar 1992:42).

Also in Hui-chou, Anhui, there was a Kuan-yin Hall, which was originally an ordinary home, but it was used by the Man of the Way Jen P'u-cheng and his pupil Sun P'u-ho during 1290 and 1307. Regular meetings were held in it on the fifteenth day of every month, when believers would gather to recite the *Diamond Sūtra*. They worshiped Kuan-yin and Amitābha and distributed tea. This group was supported by local officials and leading monks (ter Haar 1992:84). Eight of the halls in Hsiu-ning, Hui-chou can be identified with the White Lotus movement on the basis of their founders' names because they used the affiliation characters *chüeh* (twice), *p'u* (seven times), and *tao* (twice). They were founded during the Yüan and conformed to the common pattern of family involvement, the support of local officials and the worship of Kuan-yin (ter

Haar 1992:85). A certain Ch'en Chüeh-chien in Fukien founded one cloister, but later decided that his own house was more suitable. So he enlarged his house by adding a Buddha Hall and a Kuan-yin Pavilion and had his family live next to it in 1289. All his descendants had the affiliation character *chüeh* and continued to carry out his religious ideals for themselves and for the visitors to the cloister. They had a monk in the cloister, but he was simply a caretaker and did not really run the place (ter Haar 1992:82). Hsieh Ying-fang (1296–1392) was a local literatus of Wu-hsi, Kiangsu. He built Kuan-yin halls and held meetings to recite the *Lotus Sūtra* (ter Haar 1992:92).

Aside from founding cloisters that promoted Kuan-yin worship, followers of the White Lotus movement were also engaged in erecting stūpas or sūtra printing projects. For instance, they contributed to the construction of a stūpa erected in Chiang-hsia county (present-day Han-yang, Hupei) in 1307. Among the names of the contributors published in the inscription, many women had the affiliation character *miao* (ter Haar 1992:86). They also contributed to the 1315 reprinting of the Buddhist canon from the Yen-sheng Chi-sha Monastery. Slightly over half of the lay contributors mentioned by name carried an affiliation character, either *chüeh* (nineteen, of which one was a woman) or *miao* (six, of which four were women, 78). Ter Haar concludes that from the twelfth century and throughout the Yüan dynasty the White Lotus movement was a well-accepted and respected social phenomenon. Famous Neo-Confucians and literati such as Ou-yang Hsüan (1283–1357), Wu Ch'eng (1249–1333) and Chao Meng-fu all showed approval by writing epitaphs or inscriptions for its members (ter Haar 1992:89).

Commenting on the prevalence of the affiliation character *miao* among women, ter Haar makes the suggestion that this must be due to the influence of the Miao-shan legend. "The obvious precedent was of course the name of Guanyin (Miaoshan), in the legend of the female Guanyin with the thousand arms and eyes, where *miao* seems to function in the same way in her name and in the names of her two sisters Miaoyen and Miaoyin. The popularity of Guanyin, as she appears in the Miaoshan legend, among women in general, and female members of religious groups in particular, has been noted before. One suspects some kind of connection between the change from the original male into a female Guanyin, the spread of the use of *miao* as an affiliation character and the popularity of lay Buddhism among women. The custom continued from the Song into at least the early Qing" (1992:40–41). Because most of his sources are dated to the Southern Sung and Yüan, this hypothesis is highly plausible, for by then the legend of Miao-shan was definitely already well known.

However, I have come across not only the character *miao* but also the very name *Miao-shan* among women donors in Szechwan dated to the beginning of the Sung, around the eleventh century. In An-yüeh, Szechwan, there is the Vairocana Cave (Pi-lu Tung), which was constructed to commemorate the Tantric patriarch Liu Pen-tsun (844–907) in which a tableau depicting his ten acts of self-mutilation, called "Pictures of the Ten Smeltings" still stands. Some scholars estimate that the cave was constructed at the beginning of the Sung. Because of the fame of the cave, the site has generally been known as Pi-lu Tung. A number of other caves were constructed. Among the donors listed in inscriptions found in Cave no. 4, we find five women having names containing the character *miao*, and three having Miao-shan as their names (*Ta-tsu shih-k'e yen-chiu* 173).[7] In this case, it would be difficult to argue that this resulted from the influence of the legend, for it predates the latter by at least a hundred years. It is more reasonable to hypothesize that their choice of the name, like the epithet applied to the dead empress or the name Sung T'ai-tsung bestowed on a nun mentioned earlier, or indeed the name of the princess-heroine of our legend, all reflected familiarity with a name that had good Buddhist connotations. This also explains why the author of the legend used the name Miao-shan instead of the canonical Miao-yin for his heroine. As evidenced by women donors in Szechwan, Miao-shan might have been a favorite religious name for women believers long before the birth of the legend. It would be tactical for the author of the story, then, to adopt a name which was familiar to his audience. On the other hand, once the legend took hold in people's imaginations, it was only natural that pious women would prefer to use the same name for themselves. This is similar to the popularity of the names Maria or Mary among Catholic and Christian women in honor of the Virgin Mary.[8]

My reason for bringing the "activist" lay Buddhist movement into the discussion, as I indicated before, is to draw attention to the similarities between their lifestyle and that of Miao-shan. Miao-shan, like those lay women, was a pious religious practitioner. But she was assuredly not a nun. She did not shave off her hair or become ordained in a temple. Yet, like these new style lay Buddhists, she imitated conventional Buddhist monastics in many ways, by taking on the socioreligious roles of priests, monks, and nuns, and acting like them. A major difference between Miao-shan and these lay women, however, was her adamant refusal to get married. Indeed, celibacy was the main reason why she got into so much trouble with her father.

In this respect, she bears a resemblance to Wang Feng-hsien and the other twenty-six Taoist women saints whose lives were compiled by Tu Kuang-t'ing for the first time in the tenth century. Suzanne Cahill summarized the lives of these women saints: Tu Kuang-t'ing's lives begin with information about the saint's family and place of origin, followed by an account of her childhood including any special religious tendencies or practices. Her childhood ends with the crisis of marriage: she must marry or remain celibate. If she marries, she will not be able to give full attention to her Taoist religious practice; if she remains single, she will not be doing her filial duty to her family. After resolution of the marriage dilemma, she carries on with her mature religious practice and may obtain special gifts such as youth as a result. Finally, she departs from this world, leaving evidence of her sanctity, and ascends to heaven where she takes up an office in the celestial bureaucracy (Cahill forthcoming).

The specific religious practices pursued might differ depending on whether these were Buddhist or Taoist believers. Thus, for instance, while Miao-shan followed a strict vegetarian diet, Wang Feng-hsien refrained from eating completely. But as women trying to follow a religious calling, they shared the same problem and faced the same obstacle. Like Miao-shan, Wang Feng-hsien and other Taoist women saints also refused to get married. We cannot say if Tu Kuang-t'ing's work was known to the author of the Miao-shan legend, and if so, if it influenced him. But I think we cannot exclude this as a possibility. The later versions of the story found in the *Precious Scroll of Hsiang-shan* and the *True Scripture of Kuan-yin's Original Vow of Universal Salvation* show clear traces of Taoist influence.

The origin of the Miao-shan legend might be a complex one. While Buddhist sources are obviously primary, non-Buddhist ones may also be present. What Anna Seidel said about the give-and-take relationship between Chinese Buddhism and Taoism some years ago is very much worth bearing in mind: "the abundance of canonical Buddhist sources does not illuminate but rather obscures much of Chinese Buddhism and has led Zürcher and Strickmann (1) to look for those materials that were rejected by the clerical elite, i.e. the original Chinese Buddhist scriptural (*wei-ching*) literature, and (2) to look outside of Buddhism in order to discover, especially in Taoist sources influenced by Buddhism, the parts of the Buddhist message that spoke so strongly to the Chinese mind that they were adopted even by non-Buddhists" (1989–1990:288–89). Just as the Taoist deity Celestial Worthy Savior from Suffering (Chiu-k'u T'ien-tsun), who appeared in the T'ang, was modeled upon Ta-pei Kuan-yin (as shown by Franciscus Verellen 1992:234), could Miao-shan also have a Taoist antecedent? Indeed, as presented by the *True Scripture of Kuan-yin's Original Vow of Universal Salvation*, Miao-shan is the incarnation of Compassionate Sailing Worthy (Tz'u-hang Tsun-che), the Taoist name for Kuan-yin. In fact, there exists a Taoist scripture entitled the *Sūtra of the Lotus Boat of the Great Being Kuan-yin* (Kuan-yin Ta-shih Lien-ch'uan ching) in the Taoist canon. Kuan-yin, who is called the "Great Being Kuan-yin of the South Sea, the Compassionate Sailing Universal Savior Celestial Worthy" (Nan-hai Kuan-yin Ta-shih Tz'u-hang P'u-tu T'ien-tsun), is made to give instructions on Taoist interior alchemy in this text (*Tao-tsang chi-yao* 7:2899–2911). Although the scripture is not dated and neither the preface nor the postscript provides any indication about the time of its composition, it is safe to assume that the author was probably a Ming follower of the Ch'uan-chen (Complete Realization) School, founded by Wang Che (1123–1170). The author repeatedly refers to the Great Way of the Golden Cinnabar (Chin-tan Ta-tao), meaning the interior alchemy, but refers to Kuan-yin as the Great Being of the South Sea, a favorite appellation of the bodhisattva used by writers during and after the Ming period.

The Theme of "Gift of the Body"

The highlight of the Miao-shan legend is undoubtedly her willing sacrifice of her eyes and hands to save her father from dying of an incurable disease. It is precisely as a result of this supreme act of self-sacrifice that Miao-shan was transformed into the Thousand-eyed and Thousand-handed Kuan-yin. As I have indicated, since the T'ang, this particular esoteric form of Kuan-yin has been very popular. Dudbridge (1978:11) explains very convincingly that this is the reason why eyes and hands, instead of some other body parts, feature in this story, for an image of the Thousand-eyed and Thousand-handed Kuan-yin once stood in the Hsiang-shan Monastery (see also Kobayashi 1954: 21:89b,99b; 22:5b-6b). We can imagine that such an exotic image of the bodhisattva must have caused considerable bewilderment to an uninitiated Chinese viewer. The story of Miao-shan offered a reasonable explanation for the bizarre iconography and helped to domesticate the bodhisattva.

I would like to examine in this section the relationship between the Buddhist theme of "gift of the body" and the Chinese tradition of filial piety as illustrated by Miao-shan's action. This is a good example of how Buddhist messages become transformed by Chinese culture and in the process Miao-shan's dilemma becomes resolved. In the Buddhist tradition, giving is one of the six perfections carried out by a bodhisattva. Among different forms of giving and gifts, the gift of one's own body is considered to be the best. This is a central theme in Indian Buddhist narrative literature and Reiko Ohnuma (1997) wrote a dissertation on this topic.[9] There is, however, a major difference between Miao-shan and her bodhisattva counterparts in Buddhist scriptures. While bodhisattvas give their bodies or body parts in order to feed or save sentient beings and only rarely their parents, Miao-shan did it solely for her father. Let us take a closer look at the Buddhist formulations of this important theme.

The classic discussion on the perfection of giving is found in the *Ta chih-tu lun* (The Treatise on the Great Perfection of Wisdom), traditionally believed to have been written by Nāgārjuna and translated into Chinese by Kumārajīva. This received tradition has been challenged by some Western Buddhologists because no Sanskrit or Tibetan versions of this text still exist. Although E. Lamotte, A. K. Wader, and more recently, Christian Lindtner question the traditional attribution of Nāgārjuna as its author, David Seyfort Ruegg suggests that it might be a Central Asian (or Serindian) work that Kumārajīva and his Chinese collaborators translated (Lamotte 1949–80; Warder 1970; Lindtner 1982; Ruegg 1981; Robinson 1978; Ramanan 1966). There is so far no scholarly consensus on this issue. Be that as it may, this is clearly a topic of much interest to the author of the *Ta chih-tu lun* (Ohnuma 1997:99–101). In a long passage on the six perfections in fascicle 11, the perfection of giving is differentiated between external (*wai*) and internal (*nei*), the latter being more excellent. It explains:

> What is called internal giving? It is to give one's own body and life to sentient beings without any regret or stinginess, as is recounted in the *jātakas* and *avadānas.* For instance, when Śākyamuni Buddha was practicing the bodhisattva way in his past life as a king, there were no Buddha, Dharma, or Saṃgha. He went around seeking for the Buddha Dharma and could not find any. At that time a Brahmin said to him, "I know one gāthā taught by the Buddha. If you serve me by offering me gifts, I shall tell it to you." When the king asked what he wanted for gifts, the Brahmin answered, "If you can cut off flesh from your body, light it and offer it to me as a lamp, I shall give the gāthā to you." The king thought to himself: this body of mine is impure and impermanent. It is destined to suffer from life to life without end. It never had a chance to serve truth until now. So why should I cherish it? So thinking, he asked a butcher to cut the flesh all over his body. He then had the cut flesh wrapped in white wool, soaked it with ghee, and lit up like a torch. He was then given the gāthā. Another time in his past lives, Śākyamuni was born as a pigeon. He saw a man lose his way during a snowstorm, driven to the point of starving to death. The pigeon gathered firewood, made a fire and then threw himself into the fire to become food to feed the dying man. Such stories about offering one's head, eyes, marrow and brain to sentient beings are found extensively in the *jātakas* and *avadānas.* This is called internal giving (T 25:143b-c).

In fascicle 12 of the same text, giving is once more discussed:

> Giving is differentiated into inferior, medium, and superior. To give coarse things such as food and drink with a tender heart is inferior giving. When

one increases the heart of giving and gives clothing and treasures, this changes from inferior to medium giving. When one increases the heart of giving even more and gives one's head, eyes, flesh, blood, kingdoms, riches, wife and children without any regret, this is to change from medium to superior giving. These are the three kinds of giving of a bodhisattva (T 25:150a-b).

Reflecting this orthodox bodhisattva ideal, the gift of the body is a prominent theme celebrated in a number of Buddhist scriptures. The *Karuṇāpuṇḍarīka Sūtra*, a sūtra predicting that Kuan-yin will succeed Amitāyus in the future, which we read of in chapter 2, takes up this theme in several places. In fascicle 6 and 8, a bodhisattva declares his willingness to offer everything he has, including all the items mentioned in *Ta chih-tu lun* just quoted, for the benefit of sentient beings (T 3:205a-b; 219c). Fascicle 9 tells of the bodhisattva's offering of his skin and eyes when he is asked for them (224). But the high drama of the bodhisattva's gift of his body reaches a climax in fascicle 10. In a previous kalpa, Śākyamuni Buddha was born as a cakravartin or wheel-turning monarch:

A Brahmin by the name of Lu-chih came to ask for my two feet. Overjoyed, I took a sharp knife, cut off my feet, and gave them to him while making a wish that I would obtain the superior feet of discipline in my next life. A Brahmin by the name of Jih-ya then came to ask for my two eyes. Overjoyed, I plucked out my two eyes and offered them to him, making a wish that I would obtain the five superior eyes [human, deva, Hānayāna wisdom, bodhisattva truth and Buddha omniscience] in my next life. Soon another Brahmin by the name of Ching-chien-lao came to ask for my two ears. Overjoyed, I cut off my ears and offered them to him, making a wish that I would obtain superior ears of wisdom in my next life. Soon a disciple of Nirgranthajñātiputra came to ask for my penis. Overjoyed, I cut it off and offered to him, making a wish that I would achieve supreme unexcelled enlightenment and obtain the intractable penis of a horse [one of the thirty-two major marks of a buddha] in my next life. Soon another person came and asked for my blood and flesh. Overjoyed, I gave them to him, making a wish that I would obtain a superior golden colored body in my next life. Soon a Brahmin by the name of Mi-wei came to ask for my two hands. Overjoyed, I cut off my left hand with my right hand and asked him to cut off my right hand because I could not cut it myself. I made a wish that I would obtain superior hands in my next life. . . . [After giving away the various body parts] my minister then took me outside the city and left me in

> the desolate charnel ground. Many animals came to feed on me. Before I died, I made a wish that I would not give rise to anger or regret no matter what I was asked to give. If what I wish can come to pass, let my body turn into a huge mountain of flesh so that all sentient beings who must drink blood and eat flesh can come to feed on me. After making the wish, many beings indeed came to feed on me, transformed as I had been into a huge mountain with a height of a thousand and a width of five hundred *yojanas.* For a thousand years I offered my flesh and blood to sentient beings as gifts (T 3:228a-c).

I translate this long passage because I think it represents the Buddhist ideal of self-sacrifice par excellence. Motivated by a pure and indiscriminate compassion for all beings, a bodhisattva cannot help but take this kind of extreme action. At the same time, however, there is also another message: by sacrificing his human feet, eyes, ears, and so on, the bodhisattva may attain superior dharmic feet, eyes, ears, and other parts. As Ohnuma points out, some of the stories of "gifts of the body" indeed involve a test, where what the bodhisattva sacrifices is restored to him through an Act of Truth (1997:51–52). Seen in this light, Miao-shan's giving of her eyes and hands fits both patterns, for not only her eyes and hands are restored to her, but they are now also greatly superior, for they are those of Kuan-yin.

But we must remember that Miao-shan did not sacrifice herself to sentient beings. She offered her hands and eyes to be made into medicine in order to save her own father. Are there precedents in Buddhist sources that could serve as inspirations for our story? Though few, there are in fact stories about filial children who offer their flesh as food to feed their starving parents or offer their body parts as medicine.

The story of a filial son feeding his parents with his flesh is told in two different versions in the *Tsa pao-tsang ching* (Sūtra of Miscellaneous Treasure) and *Ta-fang-pien Fo pao-en ching* (Sūtra of the Buddha's Repaying Kindness with Great Skillful Means). In the first version, evil ministers kill the king and his five sons. The youngest son is warned by the gods and manages to escape with his wife and a young son. But because he only has enough food to last them for seven days and they get lost in the journey, they have exhausted all the food after walking for ten days without reaching their destination. So the father decides to kill the mother in order to keep his son and himself alive (by eating the mother's flesh). The young son asks to die in his mother's place. He further suggests to his father, "Please do not kill me right away. For if you do, the flesh will rot and cannot be eaten. It is better not to kill me, but to cut off a piece of my flesh each day when you need it" (T 4:448a). The second version records the same story, but provides more details. The young son tells his father to cut off three catties of his flesh each day and divide it into three parts: two parts for his parents, and one part for himself to keep him alive (T 3:127b–130b).

The *Ta-fang-pien Fo pao-en ching* contains a large collection of stories about how the Buddha performed various filial acts in his previous lives. It has a story about a prince named Patience (Jen-ju, Kṣānti) who offers his eyes and bone marrow as medicine to save his father. Except for the gender difference, it is very similar to the Miao-shan legend. The king, his father, is dying of a serious disease that can only be cured by a medicine made of the bone marrow and eyes of someone who is free of anger. Prince Patience declares that he has never been angry and agrees to have his two eyes gouged out and bones broken up to take out the marrow. He dies and a stūpa is erected for worship by his grateful father (T 3:138a-b). Prince Patience and Princess Miao-shan are both free from anger, a key requirement of the candidate. Both stories demand a medicine made from human body parts: eyes and bone marrow from the prince, eyes and hands from the princess. Although Miao-shan offers her hands because of the requirements of the Ta-pei iconography, her hands presumably could supply the needed bone marrow. Both stories end with the erection of stūpas for worship.

The two stories from the *Ta-fang-pien Fo pao-en ching* are illustrated together with relevant scriptural passages among the sculpture reliefs on Mt. Pao-ting at Great Buddha Creek, Ta-tsu, Szechwan. This important site was constructed by Chao Chih-feng (1159–1249?) in honor of the Tantric patriarch Liu Pen-tsun in the Southern Sung. The same "Pictures of the Ten Smeltings" glorifying Liu's ten acts of self-mutilation, carved also in the Vairocana Cave in An-yüeh, are recreated there. Niche 15 at the same site contains depictions of the ten ways parents care for the baby and the tortures in hells meted to the unfilial child. These come from a popular indigenous sūtra known as *Pao fu-mu en-chung ching* (The Sūtra [Explaining That] the Kindness of Parents is Profound and Difficult to Repay) dated to the T'ang period. Mt. Pao-ting has remained a famous pilgrimage site over the centuries. Although its construction postdates the Miao-shan stele by about a hundred years, it is not at all impossible that there might be some connection between them. Why was the story of Prince Patience chosen for inclusion in the didactic tableau at Ta-tsu? It shows that this story must be a favorite among Buddhist preachers who found its message of filial piety effective and affecting. Just as the author of the legend of Miao-shan might be familiar with the story of Prince Patience, the pilgrims to Mt. Pao-ting might be reminded of Miao-shan when they gazed upon Prince Patience.

Aside from eyes and bone marrow, human flesh is also used for medicinal purposes in a few stories in Buddhist scriptures. This practice is similar to the

Chinese *ke-ku* (slicing off a piece of flesh from the thigh), a topic I take up later. The use of human flesh as medicine occurs in two sūtras, both introduced into China very early: *Fo shuo Yüeh-ming P'u-sa ching* (Sūtra of Moon-light Bodhisattva Spoken by the Buddha), translated by Chih-ch'ien in the third century, and *Yüeh-teng san-mei ching* (Sūtra of the Moon-lamp Samādhi), translated by Na-lien-ti-yeh-she during the Northern Ch'i in the fifth century. Except for the fact that the protagonist is a boy in the former and a girl in the latter, the story is almost the same: There was once a king who was a pious Buddhist. He was friendly with a monk who became afflicted with a painful sore on his thigh. No doctor in the country could cure him, and the king was very sad. In his dream a heavenly being told the king that the monk could be cured only if he consumed human flesh and blood. The king became even more depressed upon waking, for he knew there was no way to secure the cure. But when the young prince learned about it, he told the king not to worry, for he would take care of everything. The prince then retired to his room, took a knife and cut off flesh from his thigh. He offered the flesh and blood to the monk, who, after consuming them, recovered from his illness (T 3:411c). The second sūtra relates the same story, but with some significant differences. The person who saved the monk was not a prince, but a young princess. The king was told in his dream by his dead relatives that the only way the monk could be saved was to bathe his wound with the fresh blood of a sixteen-year-old virgin and to feed him with a soup made from her flesh, mixed with rice and spices. The young princess met the requirement and willingly supplied her flesh and blood. She prepared the soup and offered it to the monk, who ate it without knowing what it was that he was eating (T 15:600b-c; Des Rotours 1968:46). This last point is very important, for all Chinese stories of *ke-ku* make a point that the act must be carried out secretly without the patient ever suspecting anything.

Precious Scroll of Hsiang-shan

The legend of Miao-shan was popularized through a new genre of prosimetric religious literature known as *pao-chüan* (precious scroll), which first appeared in the sixteenth century, during the Ming (Overmyer 1976:113).[10] Thanks to research by scholars such as Li Shih-yü (1959), Sawada Mizuho (1975), Victor Mair (1988), and Daniel Overmyer (1976, 1985, 1999), this type of popular literature is now regularly utilized by students of Chinese religion as yet another important and informative window through which we can get a glimpse into the religious lives of common men and women in late imperial times. Precious scrolls were designed for a lay audience, which was often predominantly made up of women. In a description of the late Ming that is equally applicable to later times, Richard Shek states that *pao-chüan* recitals "often took place at nunneries and temples, but more frequently in the homes of the devout. Surrounded by the women and the children of the household, the principal reciter would, with the help of partner[s] and acolytes, recite and enact various [*pao-chüan*] upon request, with appropriate intermissions for rest and refreshment" (Shek 1980:161). Known as *hsüan-chüan* (recitation of precious scrolls), it is still done today in parts of China, especially in Chekiang and Kiangsu (Chü 1992:341).

The earliest surviving copy of *Hsiang-shan pao-chüan* is in the collection of Yoshioka Yoshitoyo, who has published it in reduced facsimile (1971:129–94). It bears a publication date of 1773 and lists Chao-ch'ing Monastery in Hangchow as the place of publication.[11] The title of the text is given on the first page as *Kuan-shih-yin P'u-sa pen-hsing ching* (Sūtra of the Original Deeds of Kuan-shih-yin Bodhisattva), but on the fold of each folio the more familiar title, *Hsiang-shan chüan*, is printed. Although the eighteenth-century date of the oldest surviving version of the text is rather late, it does not mean that the work itself has such a late origin. Indeed, as Dudbridge's careful research has shown, there is abundant evidence that the legend as first formulated by Chiang Chih-ch'i in the Hsiang-shan stele was well known in the Sung and Yüan in both monastic and lay circles (1976:20–38). I would further suggest that, by the sixteenth century, a work known as *Hsiang-shan chüan* was already circulating, which might have been an earlier, if not identical, version of the one dated 1773. For instance, in a collection of his essays called *Cheng-e chi* (Corrections of Errors), Chu-hung (1535–1635) singles out a work by the name of *Kuan-yin Hsiang-shan chüan* (Scroll on Kuan-yin at Hsiang-shan) for criticism:

> In the book Kuan-yin is identified as the daughter of King Miao-chuang. It says that she left home, became enlightened, and was called Kuan-yin. This is an error. Kuan-yin is an ancient Buddha. He manifests in thirty-two forms in order to save sentient beings responding to their needs. He can sometimes appear as a woman, but did not become enlightened in the body of a woman. King Miao-chuang is neither identified as a king of a specific dynasty nor a specific country. Although this work has some merit in teaching and guiding women, it is going too far when some vulgar monks have faith in it and regard it as a wonderful sūtra for spiritual cultivation. (YCFH 27, 4:10a-b)

The 1773 edition of the text gives the names of four monks as having been responsible for its composition, transmission, revision, and transcription. None of them can be identified. Ch'an master P'u-ming of Ti'en-chu Monastery of Hangchow is given as the compiler and Ch'an Master Pao-feng of

Mt. Lu in Kiangsi as the transmitter of the text. Since Chiang Chih-ch'i served as the prefect of Hangchow between November 23, 1102, and October 31, 1103, and the legend of Miao-shan was inscribed on a stele at the Upper T'ien-chu Monastery, the choice of the same monastery in Hangchow as the site of this revelation might not have been fortuitous (Dudbridge 1976:47).

The book opens with this introductory preface: P'u-ming is said to be sitting alone on the fifteenth day of the eighth month (September 17) in 1103 in Upper T'ien-chu Monastery, having just finished a three-month meditation session. Suddenly an old monk appeared to him and said, "You only practice the correct and true way of the unexcelled vehicle and reach only those who are endowed with superior roots. But how can you save all sentient beings? You should preach all three vehicles on behalf of the Buddha and practice both the sudden and gradual paths. Only by so doing can you help those of medium and inferior capacities and thus repay the kindness of the Buddha." When P'u-ming asks with what teaching he should save the people, the monk answers, "People of this land have long had an affinity with Kuan-shih-yin Bodhisattva. I will tell you briefly the Bodhisattva's life and deeds so that they can be circulated in the world. Those who make offerings and keep and call her name will have unfailing merit." The monk then tells the story in detail and upon finishing it, disappears. P'u-ming remembered everything and wrote this volume. Suddenly Kuan-shih-yin Bodhisattva appeared riding on the clouds, manifesting the purplish golden visage, and holding a pure bottle and a green willow. The vision lasted a long time. Many people witnessed this and none came away without feeling admiration and respect. This was how the book came to be circulated in the world. Those who attained the way through it are numerous (Yoshioka 1971:130–31).

While some copies of later editions begin with this introductory preface only,[12] others, such as the 1773 edition, also provide another origin myth of the text connected with the monk Pao-feng. Pao-feng lived in retirement on Mt. Lu for a long time. One day, a great female being (*nü ta-shih*) by the name of Miao-k'ai came to him with this text. She told him how P'u-ming came to compile it and asked Pao-feng to propagate it in this world. He was at first reluctant, showing a typically Ch'an contempt for words. But the great female being gave him a lecture on the need to help all people, likening them to children. She said, "If you can make one, two, three, or many persons turn to goodness, it is more excellent than building a seven-storied pagoda. If you make people copy, lecture, preserve, and worship this text, buddhas, patriarchs, dragons, and heaven will be delighted, and your ancestors will be delivered from transmigration. When you transform people universally, you are a bodhisattva in this life, and a buddha in the next." When Pao-feng heard this, he immediately made a wish to circulate the text, saying, "If anyone decides to act this way, even if the person does not sacrifice eyes and hands, he/she will assuredly achieve supreme enlightenment. If this does not come to pass, let my own eyes become blind in my present life." He then made ten copies of the text. He prostrated three times after copying down each word. He then distributed the ten copies to different places (Yoshioka 1971:130).

Like P'u-ming, Pao-feng cannot be identified as a historical person. However, Mt. Lu is famous in Chinese Buddhism and has a special significance for followers of the White Lotus Teachings. The choice of this site might not have been without a reason. It is also significant that the "female great being" who revealed this text to Pao-feng was given the name Miao-k'ai, *miao* being a favorite affiliation character used by the lay activist Buddhists since the Sung. Both the old monk and the great female being, understood to be Kuan-yin, criticized Ch'an as being elitist and emphasized the need of making Buddhist teachings accessible to the common people. In the text itself there is also strong anti-clerical language.[13] Although the composition and transmission of this work are attributed to monks, could a lay Buddhist have been its real author? Lay Buddhists have certainly played a major part in its preservation and circulation down the ages.

Hsiang-shan pao-chüan presents Miao-shan as a buddha. The Queen has a dream before conception. When the soothsayer is asked to interpret the dream, he says that she will become "the mother of the buddha." Throughout her pregnancy, she often sees *utpala* (blue lotus) flowers surrounding her, hears heavenly music, and smells strange fragrances, while emitting light from her own body and tasting nectar in her throat. When Miao-shan is born, she has the thirty-two major marks and eighty minor ones of a buddha. Her hands have the mark of the thousand-spoked wheel. Her eyes are like *maṇi* pearls. Her fingernails are like white jade (Yoshioka 1971:132–33). Another major departure from the earlier legend as recorded in the stele is Miao-shan's tour of hell and her salvation of beings there. As we recall, the stele text tells the king's burning the nunnery and executing the nuns. Although we cannot be absolutely sure because of missing words, one gets the impression that Miao-shan is not killed, but is rescued and hidden away by the sympathetic mountain god. In any event, the stele definitely does not speak of her going to hell. I will first discuss the significance of this new theme, and then the theme of marriage resistance, which receives even more emphasis in this text.

Miao-shan/Kuan-yin as Savior of Beings in Hell

Buddhism has a rich mythology concerning hells and hungry ghosts. At the same time, it also provides many saviors for these miserable beings. The logic of compassion calls for the co-existence of suffering sinners and compassionate buddhas and bodhisattvas. The sufferings of the former call forth the salvific energies of the latter. As long as there is suffering in the unhappy realms of rebirth, buddhas and bodhisattvas will continue to carry out their work of salvation, for the former constitutes the object of their compassion. In fact, without the former there will not, and cannot, be the latter.

Among the saviors, Kuan-yin takes pride of place. Although the earlier version of the Miao-shan legend recorded on the stele does not contain any passages about her journey through hell, in the *Hsiang-shan pao-chüan*, emerging as a written text sometime in the Ming—the same time when the ritual of feeding hungry ghosts reached its greatest popularity—her journey through hell was inserted in a long passage (Yoshioka 1971:164–69) between Miao-shan's execution and her retreat to Fragrant Mountain. The addition reflected an intense concern for the welfare of the dead in the afterlife and contemporary knowledge regarding the underworld in late imperial China.

Stephen Teiser has shown how Buddhism contributed to the indigenous Chinese family religion of ancestor worship by providing new resources for assisting one's dead relatives in their postmortem state (1988, 1994). One could make offerings to the Saṃgha during the Ghost Festival every year on the fifteenth day of the seventh month and have the merit from this transferred to one's ancestors. One could also observe the ten feast days after the death of a loved one by holding memorial rites and making offerings to the ten kings of the underworld: on the "seven-seven" (the seventh day of each seven-day period) during the first forty-nine days, on the hundredth day, at the start of the first month after one year had passed and in the third year after their death.

Through frequent copying, chanting, viewing, and lecturing on *The Scripture on the Ten Kings* (Shih-wang ching), the idea of purgatory became very pervasive in Chinese society from the tenth century on. At the same time, with this increased knowledge, there was also more anxiety over the fate of both one's ancestors as well as oneself. This is the reason why the journey through hell looms so large in the *Precious Scroll of Hsiang-shan*. The interest in hell is, of course, not limited only to this *pao-chüan*. As Beata Grant shows in her study on the story-cycle of Woman Huang, popular in various media since the Ming, the heroine's untimely death and her journey to hell is also the highlight of the story (1989). This is also the reason why various mortuary and memorial rites began to be formulated by the Buddhist establishment after the tenth century. In this section, I discuss the depiction of the underworld in this and related *pao-chüan* texts, Kuan-yin as savior of hellish beings in Buddhist scriptures, and the ritual of feeding the hungry ghosts.

The soul of Miao-shan is met by a lad in green (the souls of evil-doers would be met by a yakṣa), and they go through the Gate of Hell and tour Avīci Hell, the Red-hot Iron Bed and Bronze Pillar Hell, the Hell of Knife Mountains and Sword Forests, the Hell of Boiling Cauldron and Red-cindered Stove, and the Hell of Icy Coldness and Dismembering Saws. She next comes in front of the Mirror of Karma Terrace, the Mountain of Torn Paper Money, and reaches the City of the Wrongfully Dead. At this time, the princess invokes Ti-tsang (Kṣitigarbha, "Earth Matrix") who, by sending a dazzling bright light, breaks through the gates of hell and leads the monks and nuns imprisoned in the city to the Pure Land. Feng-tu, the City of the Dead, is transformed into paradise, and hell is changed into happy land. After she accepts three cups of tea from Old Lady Meng, which refresh her, Miao-shan arrives at the Bridge of No Recourse, and she makes a great vow that immediately releases all the ghosts imprisoned in the various hells and enables them to realize enlightenment. Accompanied by the consorts of the ten kings, the princess then takes a sight-seeing tour of Feng-tu. In the meantime, all the yakṣas turn into immortal boys and jade maidens. Overjoyed by the transformation of hell into heaven, the ten kings make offerings to her and request her to chant sūtras and give the five precepts to everyone. The happy occasion is brought to a close suddenly when the officials of the three realms of bad rebirth and jailers of the eighteen hells memorialize the ten kings saying, "Since the arrival of the princess, all tools of torture have turned into lotus flowers, and all sinful ghosts have achieved good rebirth. Our subterranean government has come to a grinding halt. From ancient times there have always been heaven and hell. Because of this system of reward and punishment, people know how to behave. If hell no longer existed, then who would want to do good? We humble subject officials must memorialize you. Please quickly send the soul of the princess back to her body." Lord Yama agrees.

In the *Hsiang-shan pao-chüan*, although the ten kings make their appearances, except for Yama, they are not identified by their names. The organization of the underworld as reflected in the text is a combination of diverse beliefs and cannot be traced to *The Scripture on the Ten Kings*. The author is familiar with the Avīci and other hells derived from Buddhist scriptures. But he also mentions the Green Lad, the titles of underworld bureaucrats, and Feng-tu, none of which is found in the Buddhist sources. On the other hand, they, as well as the names of the hells, are found in Taoist scriptures of the T'ang and Sung, showing the influence of indigenous Taoist beliefs about the afterlife since the Han (Hsiao 1989:611–47). Like the Ming *Precious Scroll on the Three Lives of Mu-lien*, our text is more familiar with King Yama than the fully developed belief in the ten kings. Another similarity between these two precious scrolls is the role played by Ti-tsang: just like Ti-tsang helps Mu-lien in saving his mother, he also helps Miao-shan in saving beings in hell.

Like Kuan-yin, Bodhisattva Ti-tsang has been regarded by the Chinese as the savior of beings in hell. There are several sūtras valued by Ti-tsang's cult: the *Ta fang-kuang shih-lun ching* (Great Extended Sūtra on the Ten Wheels), which is an indigenous Chinese sūtra, although it claims to have been translated anonymously about 412–439, *Ta-sheng ta-chi Ti-tsang shih-lun ching* (Sūtra of the Great Collection of the Greater Vehicle on Ti-tsang's Ten Wheels), translated by Hsüan-tsang (602–664), and especially, the *Ti-tsang P'u-sa pen-yüan ching* (Sūtra on the Former Vows of Ti-tsang Bodhisattva), translated by Śikṣānanda (652–710). They tell the story of Ti-tsang's commitment to save all beings from suffering. According to the last of the three texts, in one previous life he was born a woman and, like Mu-lien, descended to hell to save her mother (T 13:778b–779a). During the T'ang, the cult of Ti-tsang was aided by the vernacular *Mu-lien chiu-mu pien-wen* (Transformation Text on Mu-lien Saving His Mother), written around the eighth century (Teiser 1988:186–87).

Because of the similar savior role played by these two bodhisattvas, Ti-tsang and Kuan-yin began to be linked together in ritual and art in the late T'ang, around the early tenth century. A silk banner from Tun-huang dated to the tenth century and located at the Musée Guimet, Paris, shows the eleven-headed and six-armed Kuan-yin sitting side-by-side with Ti-tsang, who wears a monastic robe and holds a monk's staff (figure 8.2). This motif was even more pronounced among the sculptures in Ta-tsu, Szechwan, where some have been dated to the ninth century (Howard 1990).[14] Illustrated copies of *The Scripture on the Ten Kings* recovered from Tun-huang also feature the pair.[15] At the same time, Kuan-yin and Ti-tsang were evoked together in Buddhist mortuary rituals for the benefit of the dead ancestors. These ritual texts were formulated from the Sung to the Ming, from the eleventh to the seventeenth centuries, roughly paralleling the evolution of the legend of Miao-shan (Dudbridge 1978:115). For instance, in the ritual text *Tz'u-pei Liang-huang pao-ch'an* (Compassionate Precious Penance formulated by Emperor Wu of Liang, preface dated 1138), the presiding priest asks Ti-tsang and Kuan-yin to descend to the consecrated space three times.

The role of Kuan-yin as savior of all beings is firmly grounded in the Buddhist scriptures. As we read in chapter 2, Kuan-yin as deliverer from pain and savior from suffering is very much emphasized in esoteric scriptures that promote the keeping and chanting of dhāraṇīs. One of the earliest such scriptures centering upon Kuan-yin as the universal savior is the *Ch'ing Kuan-shih-yin ching*, which underscores the importance of the dhāraṇī *Oṃ maṇi padme hūṃ*, made familiar to modern Americans through Tibetan Buddhism. The chanting of this dhāraṇī will save a person from all manner of disasters. If one is faithful and dedicated in chanting the dhāraṇī, he or she will be able to have a vision

Figure 8.2. Ti-tsang and Kuan-yin, tenth century. *Courtesy of Musée Guimet.*

of Kuan-yin while alive and, having been freed from all sins, will not suffer rebirth in the four woeful realms of hell, hungry ghosts, animals, and asuras. Because Kuan-yin playfully travels (*yu-hsi*) in all realms of rebirth, even if a person is so unfortunate as to be born in hell or as a hungry ghost, Kuan-yin is right there to help him. The bodhisattva is said to suffer in hell in place of the sinner, and by bestowing sweet milk, which issues forth from his fingertips, the hunger and thirst of hungry ghosts are also satisfied.

The *Karaṇḍavyūha Sūtra*, translated by T'ien-hsi-tsai in 1000, represents the height of Kuan-yin glorification. The eleven-headed and thousand-armed Kuan-yin enters Avīci Hell and transforms it into a realm of coolness and clarity (*ch'ing-liang*). The sūtra does not dwell on the gruesome details of hells except to describe the Avīci Hell as being encircled by rings of iron walls that are constantly heated by a blazing fire. There is also a hell, which consists of an enormous cauldron in which sinners constantly bob up and down in the scalding water in the manner of boiled beans. But when Kuan-yin enters, the fire is immediately extinguished and the cauldron is smashed to pieces. Moreover, the fire pit is changed into a precious pond filled with large lotus flowers as big as cartwheels. As hell becomes paradise, dazzlingly bright light shines forth. Kuan-yin next enters the great Citadel of the Hungry Ghosts and saves them as well. Consumed by the fire of evil karma, these miserable creatures suffer endlessly from hunger and thirst. Kuan-yin also brings them coolness and clarity. Motivated by the heart of great compassion, the bodhisattva issues forth streams of pure water from his fingertips, toenails, and every pore of his body. When the hungry ghosts drink the water, their throats, which formerly were constricted like needles, become enlarged and their bodies, which formerly were disfigured by protruding bellies, also become perfect. Satisfied with delicious food of different flavors, their defilements become cleansed and they achieve rebirth in the Pure Land of Bliss (T 20:48b-c).

Although Kuan-yin is presented as the savior of sinners in many Buddhist scriptures, it is my contention that this knowledge was imparted to people mainly through rituals. Together with the ghost festival (*yü-lan p'en*) and plenary mass (*shui-lu*), the ritual of feeding hungry ghosts (*shih-shih*) is one of three major Buddhist mortuary rituals performed for the benefit of one's relatives as well as all sentient beings. The canonical source for the ritual of feeding hungry ghosts is a Tantric sūtra translated into Chinese by Amoghavajra: the *Yü-chia chi-yao ch'iu A-nan t'o-lo-ni yen-k'ou kuei-i ching* (Sūtra on the Ritual Directions Summarizing the Yoga Dhāraṇīs for Saving Ānanda from the Burning Mouth). Ānanda is visited by a hungry ghost named Burning Face (Mien-jan), a wrathful manifestation of Kuan-yin, who tells Ānanda that three days hence he will die and be reborn as a hungry ghost. Greatly alarmed, Ānanda goes to the Buddha the next morning and is taught the method of feeding hungry ghosts. The food being thus ritually offered becomes a magical nectar, which will transform the partakers into buddhas. The ritual is believed to be the most effective means of delivering one's dead relatives from hell. During the late imperial period, this ritual enjoyed great popularity in Chinese society until the Ming monk Chu-hung wrote a definitive manual for its performance: *Yü-chia chi-yao shih-shih i-kuei* (Ritual Directions Summarizing the Yoga of Bestowing Food to Feed Hungry Ghosts). Less than a hundred years later, in 1693, the Ch'ing monk I-yü Ting-an of Mt. Pao-hua revised it and wrote a more simplified version. It is this text, called *Yü-chia yen-k'ou shih-shih yao-chi* (Essentials for the Yoga of Bestowing Food to Feed Hungry Ghosts) that is still being used by monks in China today. The ostensible reason for the revision was to make the ritual shorter, so that it could be completed within three hours, from seven P.M. to ten P.M., for hungry ghosts can only take food between sunset and midnight. Kuan-yin's role is even more enhanced in this text.

Yü-chia is a transcription of the Sanskrit word "yoga," which means union:

union of the body, speech, and mind as represented by mudrās (signs formed by the hands and fingers), mantras, and visualization that the chief ritual master engages in while performing this ritual. The Ch'ing ritual manual says:

> Yoga practice means that the hands and fingers should form mysterious gestures, the mouth recite true words (*cheng-yen*, mantras) and the mind engages in discernment (*kuan*, vipaśyanā). The body communes with the mouth, the mouth with the mind and mind with the body. The three actions [of body, speech and mind] must be in perfect correspondence.

During the first part of the ritual, the monks and lay donors invoke the help of the Three Treasures. In the second half they break through the gates of hell, open the throats of the sufferers, and feed them various kinds of food and drink. With the help of the power derived from the union of mantra, mudrā, and visualization, they purge the hungry ghosts' sins, have them take refuge in the Three Treasures, and arouse their aspiration for enlightenment. If all these ritual procedures are properly performed, the hungry ghosts will be released from hell to be reborn as human beings or in the Pure Land. Kuan-yin's role is conspicuously prominent throughout the entire ritual.

A picture of the hungry ghost Burning Face, the putative originator of the ritual, is placed on the altar facing the assembled monks. When the ritual begins, the Great Compassion Dhāraṇī and a hymn praising Kuan-yin are chanted before the altar enshrining the Burning Face. A hymn called "Pure Willow and Water" is then chanted to purify the ritual space. Echoing the words found in the scriptures, it says:

> *Pure water is sprinkled in the three thousand worlds.*
> *Eight virtues with the intrinsic nature of emptiness benefit men and gods.*
> *May the sins of the hungry ghosts be eradicated, and may*
> *Flames be transformed into red lotuses.*

After three invocations of Vairocana Buddha, the presiding monk ascends to the platform and puts on a red and golden "Vairocana hat" in the shape of a five-pointed crown. He chants the following verse while all participants repeat it after him:

> *This assembly is being held for the most supreme yoga ritual.*
> *The Buddha transmitted it to benefit men and gods.*
> *He proclaimed in the esoteric texts the way to release suffering beings,*
> *And taught the truth to save those hanging upside down [hungry ghosts].*

When the honorable Ānanda was meditating,
Kuan-yin Bodhisattva, who always saves beings from suffering, manifested himself as a hungry ghost.
His saving compassion and Ānanda's samādhi
Cause efficacious effects which last forever.

After "fixing the area of the five directions," accompanied by an invocation to five different Buddhas, Kuan-yin is invoked directly. The presiding monk makes a mudrā called "Kuan-yin meditation mudrā," through which the celebrant enters into the samādhi of Kuan-yin. Thus identified with Kuan-yin, the main action of the ritual is performed by Kuan-yin in the person of the celebrant.

After a series of other activities, the celebrant recites the following verse attributed to Su Tung-p'o (1037–1101):

If one wishes to know
All the buddhas of the past, present, and future,
One should contemplate the nature of the Dharma Realm (fa-chieh, Dharmadhātu).
Everything without exception is created by the mind.

Then comes the highlight of the ritual when the priest, as Kuan-yin, makes the mudrā of "opening up the gate of hell." He visualizes three red rays emitting from his mouth, hands, and chest, which open up the gates of hell. The three rays represent three powers that can destroy the three categories of sins of the body, speech, and mind committed by beings in hell.

Because Ti-tsang Bodhisattva has made a vow not to fully attain Buddhahood before the hells are emptied, he is also closely associated with the dead and the hells. At this point in the ritual, he is invoked to lead and help the dead to come forth to accept the offerings. The chief celebrant calls upon the dead, including spirits of deceased kings, ministers, officials, soldiers, Buddhist monks and nuns, Taoist priests and priestesses, merchants, barbarians, beggars, prisoners, the disabled, the deserted, those who died by fire, poison, or drowning, and all orphaned souls, to come forward and receive offerings. This is accomplished by several mudrās: "the mudrā to summon the hungry ghosts," "the mudrā to summon up their non-virtues," "the mudrā to destroy their non-virtues." He finally claps his hands to symbolize the demolishment of their offenses piled as high as a mountain. After the invited ghosts are helped to repent by the "mudrā of repentance," the presiding monk transforms water into nectar by performing the "mudrā of sweet dew." He then enables them to drink it by performing the "mudrā of opening up the throat." He visualizes a green lotus held in his left hand, from which "sweet dew" flows out for the ghosts to drink, just as Kuan-yin is described as doing in the *Karaṇḍavyūha Sūtra*.

This ritual of feeding hungry ghosts was developed and elaborated after the tenth century, when the cult of the ten kings reached its maturity. It is interesting to note that while the belief system and the vocabulary contained in the scriptures alluded to above (e.g., sweet dew and lotuses) are fully reflected in the ritual, there is no trace of the ten kings in the ritual manuals for the performance of the ritual of feeding hungry ghosts compiled by Chu-hung and Ting-an. Chu-hung, being a very orthodox monk, was highly critical of divergences from the Buddhist tradition as he defined it. Just as he disapproved of the popular *Precious Scroll of Hsiang-shan*, it would have been natural for him to disapprove of the extra-canonical *Scripture on the Ten Kings*. In this regard, he would have followed the precedent of Chih-sheng who, as Teiser points out, was negative about sūtras concerning hell and excluded the latter text from the canon (1994:82–84). The case is very different, however, with the sectarian text, *The True Scripture of Kuan-yin's Original Vow of Universal Salvation*, in which Miao-shan, accompanied by the Taoist Yellow Dragon True Man (Huang-lung Chen-jen), tours each of the ten hells. She is welcomed by each of the ten kings, who host her visit and then send her off to the next king. Ti-tsang, on the other hand, does not appear in this text. The ritual texts and popular *pao-chüan* seem to represent two different belief systems concerning Ti-tsang and the ten kings. This is not so surprising, for, as suggested by Teiser, the cosmology and soteriology of the Pure Land "may have competed, in theory and in fact, with rites addressed to the ten kings. There appears to be a conflict between the symbolism of the bureaucratic passage characterizing purgatorial rites and that of final deliverance to an unstained realm typical of Pure Land forms" (Teiser 1994:13). *The Scripture on the Ten Kings* and the religious practices recommended by it might constitute a different, and competing, ritual system from the ritual of feeding the hungry ghosts, which is very much based on Pure Land and Tantric traditions.

Two later *pao-chüan*, both derived from the *Hsiang-shan pao-chüan*, neither of which can be dated with any accuracy (my copy was hand-copied in 1906) offer some interesting contrasts. One is entitled *Hsiang-shan shuo-yao* (Synopsis of Hsiang-shan) and the other is simply called *Yu ti-yü* (Tour of Hell). They provide some new details. After the soul of the princess separates from her body, she is met by the same green-clad lad who shows her two paths, a white path to the left for good people and a black path to the right for bad people. The good people are specifically identified as those who have kept a vegetarian diet when they were alive. She first goes to the Palace of Yama, where all newcomers must report for roll call. When she next goes to the Gate of Ghosts, she is told that unless a person has practiced Buddha-invocation while alive, there is no way that he or she can leave there again. The next stop is Avīci Hell, which, interestingly, is identified as the nineteenth hell, created especially for the punishment of Mu-lien's mother, Mrs. Mu (Mu T'ai-t'ai), reflecting the popularity of the story of Mu-lien saving his mother in late imperial China. The second text, *Journey through Hell*, takes special delight in depicting the downfall of Mu-lien's mother. Stretching over six pages, it catalogues her sins.[16]

Both texts add two more places of torment after the Bridge of No Recourse: the Pond of Blood and the Village of Vicious Dogs. The former is for women who die in childbirth, and the latter is for people who like to eat dog meat and appropriately now must be eaten by the snarling dogs they killed. While Miao-shan remains aloof in earlier hells, she shows special compassion for the women languishing in the blood pond. She chants gāthās on their behalf and, scattering red lotuses into the pond, she releases them.

The ten kings have a more prominent place in these later texts. The texts not only identify the kings by their proper names but also match specific hells with each king. This is an innovation, for we do not see this in *The Scripture on the Ten Kings*. For instance, the first king, King Kuang of Ch'in, rules over the Pavilion of Old Lady Meng and the Hell of Icy Coldness (a place reserved for unfilial sons who let their parents suffer from the cold while they and their wives wear warm clothing). The second king, the King of the First River, rules over the Avīci Hell, the nineteenth of the hells, reserved for Mu-lien's mother. The third king, King Ti of the Sung, rules over the third court, which weighs the severity of one's sins. Sinners weigh more than good people. The fourth king, King of the Five Offices, rules over the Knife Mountain Hell. This hell, interestingly, is reserved for people who kill frogs, since frogs are praised for their diligence in watching over the rice plants both day and night. The fifth king, King Yama Rāja, rules over the Hell of Dismembering Saws, which is reserved for people who like to create rumors and gossip. The sixth king, the King of Transformations, rules over the Hell of Bronze Pillars, which is reserved for people who make money by lending at exorbitant interest. The seventh king, the King of Mount T'ai, rules over the Red-hot Iron Bed Hell, which is reserved for sinners who cheat and scheme. The eighth king, the Impartial King, rules over the Hell of Torn Paper Money. This receives special attention, for the evil consequence of stirring the ashes of paper money before the fire is entirely extinguished probably is not universally understood. The ninth king, the King of the

Capital, rules over the Hell of Millstones, which is reserved for sinners who abduct boys and girls and sell them for profit. The last and tenth king, the King Who Turns the Wheel of Rebirth in the Five Paths, decides the destination for the sinner's rebirth.

Like hells in canonical Buddhist scriptures, the Chinese hells mentioned in these texts are not systematized. Their names often differ and the punishments meted out in each one also vary. The storyteller probably could exercise his or her ingenuity and imagination to a considerable degree. Local beliefs could also be inserted in the appropriate places, such as the revulsion for killing and eating watchdogs and frogs.

The compassionate bodhisattva celebrated in the elite Mahāyāna scriptures, the awesome and awful "Burning Face" invoked in the rituals of Feeding Hungry Ghosts, and the pitiful yet pitying young princess Miao-shan immortalized in popular stories appear to be contradictory at first glance. Yet these images resonate with each other. Through sūtra recitation, ritual performance, storytelling, and dramatic performances, I believe the faith in Kuan-yin as the universal savior was deepened and spread throughout the entire society. Because of the lack of contextual data and the limitation of space, I do not discuss the presentation of the legend in dramatic form. But we must bear in mind that in pre-modern China, popular entertainment such as the opera and *t'an-tz'u* ("plucked rhymes"), just as television and movies in modern times, were powerful media for transmitting values.

The story of Miao-shan was turned into both Peking opera and *t'an-tz'u*, with the latter particularly popular among women. Called *Ta Hsiang-shan* (The Great Hsiang-shan) and *Ta Hsiang-shan ch'üan-pen* (The Complete Version of the Great Hsiang-shan) respectively, the texts of both have been preserved (Grant 1989:267). According to the editor of *Hsi k'ao* (On Plays), *Ta Hsiang-shan* is also called by three other names: *Miao-shan ch'u-chia* (Miao-shan Leaving Home), *Huo-shao Pai-ch'üeh Ssu* (Burning White Sparrow Monastery), and *Kuan-yin you shih-tien* (Kuan-yin Touring the Ten Palaces). It was very popular in the Ch'ing and was performed very often. Empress Dowager Tz'u-hsi liked to watch plays in her palace and she would often ask to have this play performed for her. That was why among the attending eunuchs and actors in Peking, quite a few were experts in performing it. But during the Republican period, only troupes in Kiangsu, Chekiang, and Anhui sometimes performed it. Even so, rarely was the entire play performed; only the segments about the White Sparrow Monastery and the tour of hell would be chosen (*Hsi k'ao* 1923, 36:1). People could also learn the role of Kuan-yin as savior of beings in hell by watching plays about Mu-lien. In the *Ch'üan-shan chin-ke* (Golden Lessons for Inculcating Goodness), a play consisting of 240 scenes in ten fascicles written by Chang Chao (1691–1745) and others, which was presented to the Ch'ien-lung Emperor, Kuan-yin appears in Scene 12 (fascicle 2) as Burning Face and utters words very similar to those used in the ritual of feeding hungry ghosts (*Ch'üan-shan-chin-ke* 1923, 2:57a). Not only was the myth of Miao-shan as Kuan-yin disseminated in different media, but in this case, there was a convergence between the media of drama and of ritual.

It has been suggested that after the Sung, with the decline of institutional Buddhism, people had more options to offer help to their loved ones after death. Professional monks with their specialized rituals did not command a monopoly. *The Scripture on Ten Kings* and its rituals provided another choice. As readers of the late Ming novel *Golden Lotus* know, chanting *pao-chüan* was yet another popular way of generating merit. These were definitely different ways of perceiving the underworld and aiding the suffering sinners being tormented there. But should we go so far as to claim that the popular rituals replaced the Buddhist rituals? Judging from a fifteenth-century testimonial left by a man who died and was then restored to life, even the ten kings apparently wanted to forge a relationship with Buddhist orthodoxy. Let me conclude this section with the following amusing story that was appended to the end of a Ming edition of *T'ai-shan shih-wang pao-chüan* (The Precious Scroll of the Ten Kings of Mt. T'ai):

> Formerly, in Ling-ch'ing county, Chi-nan prefecture, Shantung, there lived a student named Li Ch'ing. On the third day of the eighth month in the sixth year of Ching-t'ai (1455), he died. When he appeared in front of Lord Yama, he was asked by the latter what good deeds he had done while living on the face of the earth. Li answered that on the birthday of Śākyamuni Buddha, the eighth day of the fourth month, he would always keep the vegetarian diet for the whole day and call the buddha's name 10,000 times. When Yama heard this, he got up and praised Li saying that this was really good and Li had accumulated a lot of merit. Then Yama asked, "How come no one keeps to a vegetarian diet and calls the name of the buddha on the birthdays of we ten kings?" Li answered that people in the world of the living did not know those dates. So Lord Yama told Li that he would return Li's soul to life if Li would broadcast the ten kings' birthdays and teach people to observe these dates by eating vegetables and invoking buddha's name. If they did so, they would live a happy life and achieve a good rebirth when they died. Yama then ordered a ghost messenger to send the soul of Li back to the earth. When Li revived, he wrote down the dates on a piece of paper and started telling people to observe these birthdays. On these days, if they burned incense, candles, and paper money as offerings to the ten kings, they

would never go to hell but be reborn in heaven. These then are the holy birthdays of the ten kings:

The eighth day of the first month is the birthday of the fourth king, whose surname is Shih. Recite the name of Ti-tsang one thousand times, and you will not go to the Hell of Torn Tongues.

The first day of the second month is the birthday of the first king, whose surname is Hsiao. Recite the name of Buddha of Samādhi Light one thousand times, and you will not go to the Mountain of Knives Hell.

The twenty-seventh day [of the same month] is the birthday of the sixth king, whose surname is Pi. Recite the name of Bodhisattva Ta-shih-chih one thousand times, and you will not go to the Hell of Poisonous Snakes.

The twenty-eighth day is the birthday of the third king, whose surname is Yü. Recite the names of the thousand buddhas of the Bhadra [good] kalpa one thousand times, and you will not go to the Hell of Icy Coldness.

The first day of the third month is the birthday of the second king, whose surname is Ma. Recite the name of the Healing Buddha one thousand times, and you will not go to the Hell of Boiling Cauldron.

The seventh day is the birthday of the seventh king, whose surname is Tung. Recite the name of Kuan-yin one thousand times, and you will not go to the Hell of Pounding Mortar.

The eighth day is the birthday of the fifth king, whose surname is Han. Recite the name of Amitābha Buddha one thousand times, and you will not go to the Hell of Sword Forests.

The first day of the fourth month is the birthday of the eighth king, whose name is Huang. Recite the name of Vairocana Buddha one thousand times, and you will not go to the Hell of Dismembering Saws.

The seventh day is the birthday of the ninth king, whose surname is Hsüeh. Recite the name of Medicine King Bodhisattva one thousand times, and you will not go to the Red-hot Iron Bed Hell.

The twenty-second day is the birthday of the tenth king, whose name is Hsüeh [the same as that of the ninth king]. Recite the name of Śākyamuni Buddha one thousand times, and you will not go to the Hell of Darkness.

Here, not only were the ten kings provided with good Chinese surnames, but they were also made into promoters of orthodox Pure Land practice. Although the dates differ, the schedule does bear a remote resemblance to the ten Buddhist lay feast days.[17] Moreover, by making people chant the name of a specific buddha or bodhisattva on the birthday of each of the ten kings, this text promotes a Chinese version of the Japanese *honji suijaku* (original ground and subsequent manifestation). Like the Japanese text *The Scripture on Jizō and the*

Ten Kings (Jizō jūō kyō), written by anonymous Japanese authors between 1000 and 1300 c.e., in which the ten kings are paired with the first ten of the thirteen Buddhist deities, this text also does something similar, though the identities of the Buddhist deities differ in the Chinese and Japanese versions (Teiser 1994:60, 237). The tendency of *pao-chüan* writers to combine divergent elements into an integrated whole, a point that I have made before, here finds a most persuasive example.

The Theme of Marriage Resistance

Miao-shan's refusal to get married was her major crime, for which she had to suffer many hardships and even death. Later in the story, her selfless sacrifice of her hands and eyes to save her father made possible their reconciliation and her eventual transfiguration. Why was marriage refused and virginity glorified? Why was the supreme act of filial piety conceived of as the offering of parts of one's own body to be consumed and incorporated by one's parent? These were bold and provocative messages that challenged the Confucian value system. The Confucian ideal of filial piety was grounded firmly on the continuance of the family and, as made clear by the *Classic of Filial Piety* (Hsiao ching), ideologically opposed to extreme acts of self-mutilation, as exemplified by the behavior of Miao-shan. In the myth of Miao-shan, the central themes are clearly Buddhist: the heroine opted for a life of austerity and renunciation instead of carrying out her familial obligations as a wife and mother. Even though she did not remain a nun in a convent but carried out her religious cultivation by herself, she followed the Buddhist ascetic ideal.

The rejection of marriage was based on two powerful arguments. The first had to do with a negative attitude toward sexuality and desire and the second was a negative evaluation of the married condition itself. Both reflected the values of Buddhism, which always regarded the monastic and celibate life as more preferable to that of a householder. When Miao-shan is challenged by her father to explain her disobedience, she reminds him of the brevity of human life and the pains of transmigration. She dwells particularly on the horrors of hell. Even if loyal subjects, filial sons, virtuous men and great heroes would be willing to suffer them on behalf of their king, such torments could not be endured by anyone else. "Love of life is the cause and sexual desire is the consequence. When cause and consequence are intertwined, one undergoes ten thousand births and ten thousand deaths. Changing one's heads and faces, one wanders in the six realms of rebirth and sees no beginning for deliverance" (Yoshioka 1971:139). Marriage is explicitly linked to hell, for "when man and woman get married, they plant a tree of bitterness and cast seeds broadly which take roots only in hell" (140). When her father becomes angry and threatens to kill her, she offers to marry a doctor if he can fulfill her ten wishes, which echo the Thousand-handed Kuan-yin's ten great vows, found in the *Ch'ien-shou ching*.[18]

The *True Scripture of Kuan-yin's Original Vow of Universal Salvation* expands on the same theme but goes into greater detail. Miao-shan sets forth the bitterness of a woman's fate in a memorial that she presents to her father.

> Due to the sins I committed in my previous lives, I am now born with a woman's body. How sad!
>
> I have to listen to my father before I get married. If I get married, I must obey my husband and can have no opinion of my own.
>
> Should the husband die an early death from illness, I must then guard my chastity and listen to my son. . . .
>
> The "three obediences" and "four virtues" are serious matters, for hell awaits the woman who dares to ignore them. In this world, only women have to suffer so much for their sins. Killing animals after giving birth is very sinful. Coming to the kitchen before a full month's confinement is over pollutes the stove. Going to the front hall with an impure body offends the family altar.
>
> Washing and pounding bloodstained clothing in the river is a great sin against the gods of the watery region.
>
> Exposing dirty garments under the sun angers deities who pass by. Pouring bloody water in open space pollutes heaven, earth, and the three bodies of light [the sun, moon and stars]. Who keeps track of all these offenses? Lord Yama examines me most carefully after my death (27 a-b).

Such lament over the subservient position of women was not new—it was in fact a leitmotif found in the literature of the time. What is of interest are the specific taboos affecting women after childbirth, as emphasized by popular religion. Although sexual desire is declared to be the driving force behind rebirth and therefore to be avoided (a teaching much stressed in Buddhism), the revulsion against marriage expressed in such popular religious literature is not only an indictment of sexuality per se, but also (and maybe even more) linked with the fear of a difficult married life involving overbearing in-laws, the pain and danger of childbirth, and the folk belief that women who have given birth to children are punished in the underworld for having produced polluting substances (Ahern 1975:214).[19]

This popular belief originates in a Chinese indigenous sūtra, the *Blood Bowl Sūtra* (Hsüeh-p'en ching). According to Michel Soymié (1965), the first literary reference to the "blood pool" is found in an almanac of rites from 1194. The sūtra is included in the Buddhist canon printed by the imperial command in 1437. Several novels written in the Ming mention it. Thus, it is clear that by the Ming period, there was a well-known belief that there was a hell specially reserved for women who would be made to drink the blood from the pool three times a day to expiate their sins of polluting the earth with their menstrual and childbirth blood. Such belief was not only propagated by Buddhists, for there was also a Taoist scripture datable to the thirteenth century that advocated the same idea and was often used in funerals. It is therefore not at all surprising that the author of the *True Scripture* used this fear to argue against marriage, for this was a commonly shared belief in the late imperial times.

As Dudbridge argues, Miao-shan's example indeed provides a charter for female celibacy (1978:85). Some women expressed their resistance to marriage by taking this concrete action. Marjorie Topley studied women living in a rural area of the Canton delta who from the early nineteenth to the early twentieth century "either refused to marry or, having married, refused to live with their husbands. Their resistance to marriage took regular forms. Typically they organized themselves into sisterhoods. The women remaining spinsters took vows before a deity [Old Mother Kuan-yin], in front of witnesses, never to wed" (Topley 1975:67). Andrea Sankar, who studied women living in *chai t'angs* (vegetarian houses) in Hong Kong in the 1970s, also commented on their attraction to Kuan-yin. "One concrete appeal for the spinsters who have chosen to live in chai t'angs . . . is the strong identification many women have with the Goddess [sic] Kuan Yin. Next to discussions on the different categories of chai, stories about the lives of Kuan Yin were a popular topic of conversation" (Sankar 1978:307). Later, she again observes, "For my informants, Kuan Yin is an apotheosized woman. The myths they relate depict her more as a folk heroine than as a saint. . . . Kuan Yin provides a charter for their celibate lives. Her life as a strong, independent, successful woman who lived in the secular world sanctifies and legitimizes their own choice of life style. Now some of their motivations for turning to the religious life as they grow old and retreat from the secular world can be attributed to the kinship they feel with Kuan Yin" (310).

In 1987 when I did field work in Hangchow, I often encountered similar sentiments against marriage expressed by women pilgrims I interviewed. These village women would sing songs glorifying Kuan-yin that were called "Kuan-yin sūtras." They expressed their admiration for Kuan-yin/Miao-shan's determination and courage in refusing marriage. They envied her determination and freedom. I include some of these songs in appendix B. The following is one example:

There is a truly chaste woman in the household of King Miao-chuang.
First, she does not have to bear the ill humor of her parents-in-law.
Second, she does not have to eat the rice of her husband.
Third, she does not have to carry a child in her womb or in her arms.
Fourth, she does not need a maid to serve her.
Every day she enjoys peace and quiet in her fragrant room.
Turning over the cotton coverlet, she sleeps on the bed alone.
Stretching out her legs, she goes into the Buddha Hall.
Tucking in her feet, she withdraws into the back garden.
For the sake of cultivation she suffered punishments from her father.
But now, sitting on the lotus throne, she enjoys blessings.

Was Miao-shan's example followed by women in Ming-Ch'ing China? When we examine the cult of Kuan-yin in late imperial times as represented by the religious lives of women and men, there is clear evidence that Miao-shan's messages received very mixed responses. Although a woman could become a nun and, with the increasing emphasis on the cult of chaste widowhood, she could remain single with great social prestige, there was no large-scale movement of marriage resistance. On the contrary, we can speak of the rise of a kind of "domesticated religiosity" in late imperial times. In a study of seventeenth-century gentry women in the Chiang-nan area, Dorothy Ko uses the term "domestic religion" to describe the "religious rituals and sentiments which were embedded in everyday life in the inner chambers and were integral to the women's worldviews and self-identities" (Ko 1994:198). While devotion to Kuan-yin was very common among these gentry women Ko studied, they were not exclusively Buddhists but syncretic in their religious practices. Furthermore, as expressed through poetry writing, painting, and the appreciation of drama, these sentiments and rituals were often secular in nature. Prayers to Taoist deities, participation in seances, immersion in dream interpretations, and even intense emotional attachments to Tu Li-niang, the heroine of *The Peony Pavilion* (Mu-tan ting) all constituted elements of the domestic religion and the cult of *ch'ing*. *Ch'ing* refers primarily to romantic love between men and women, represented ideally by the death-defying love between the hero and heroine of *The Peony Pavilion*. But as Dorothy Ko and Wai-yee Li (1993) argued, *ch'ing* can also mean the love and sentimental attachment between family members and friends, both of the same and different sexes. In the seventeenth century, many writers celebrated the true love and emotional attachment between human beings. In their view, this ability to love selflessly is what makes human beings unique. *Ch'ing* thus has a religious dimension.

I use the term "domesticated religiosity," however, in a somewhat different yet more definable sense. What I mean by this term can be illustrated by two distinct but related phenomena. In the first instance, the home was literally the physical arena where one performed one's religious activities. One did not have to leave home and join a monastery. This could be seen as a natural extension of the lay Buddhist ideal. But unlike the literati Buddhist laymen who followed the leading Buddhist masters such as Chu-hung and Te-ch'ing in the late Ming, many women did not become affiliated with a particular monk or monastery. A case in point is provided by the short biographies of some 140 women practitioners of Buddhism found in the *Shan nü-jen chuan* (Biographies of Good Women) compiled by P'eng Shao-sheng (1740–1796) in the eighteenth century.[20] Sixty-six, or about half, of the women lived in the Ming and Ch'ing, with the last of the biographies being that of T'ao Shan, the daughter-in-law of the author's own brother. These women were wives and mothers who recited the Buddha's name, worshiped Kuan-yin, kept a vegetarian diet, chanted sūtras, or practiced meditation. All of them carried out their primarily Pure Land practices at home. They were not disciples of monks. Some of them, however, could be said to have led lives similar to those of nuns, as when they did not have sex with their husbands. Even though they were laywomen, they often exhibited the spiritual authority of a Buddhist master. For instance, they could predict the times of their deaths, and they often passed away in full control of their faculties without any sign of pain or distress. As I point out earlier, Miao-shan herself was more a lay Buddhist woman than a nun. Except for a short time when she worked as a menial laborer at the White Sparrow Nunnery, she practiced meditation by herself. She did not seek instruction from any monk, nor did she join any religious establishment. The lifestyles of these women, like Miao-shan, showed the same characteristics of the "activist lay Buddhists" of the Sung and Yüan. For example, as we noted before, they carried out their Buddhist activities parallel to, but not subordinated under, the organized Saṃgha. They performed good deeds for society as well as ritual activities such as chanting sūtras for the benefit of people in need, a specialty normally reserved for monks. They identified themselves as a distinct group by adopting affiliation names which included, among others, the character *miao*.

Another example of what I call "domesticated religiosity" is the case of the woman visionary T'an-yang-tzu (b. 1558) whom Ann Waltner has been studying. We know her primarily through the biography written by Wang Shih-chen (1526–1590) who regarded her as his master. Aside from Wang and his brother, who knew her family well, her own father Wang Hsi-chüeh (who became a Grand Secretary after her death) and her brother were also fervent followers. She claimed four other literati who obtained their *chin-shih* degrees in 1577 as her disciples as well. She had visions of Kuan-yin and the Queen Mother of the

West, who taught her meditational techniques to attain immortality. Although she did not want to get married, she did not refuse the marriage arranged by her father with the son of a fellow townsman who had received the *chin-shih* degree the same year as her father, 1558, the year she was born. But the young man died before the wedding could take place. She mourned him grievously as a wife and served him as his widow. After she finished her meditational regimen, she retired to the grave of her dead husband where she lived and then died (or "cast off the corpse") in a shrine next to it.

Her religious pursuits were carried out completely in a domestic setting. She was said to do embroidery and care for her parents (including curing her father by giving him pure water over which she cast spells), living the life of a dutiful daughter before her betrothal and that of a chaste widow after her fiancé's untimely death. When she went spirit wandering, she asked her father to guard her inert body. Before she left the world as an immortal, there was a farewell scene between parents and daughter full of pathos (Waltner 1987:105–27). Her religious calling was fulfilled through familial obligations. The home, not a Taoist convent, provided the setting for her religious career. There were other examples of "domestic goddesses," talented women who died tragically young and, as a result of being promoted by their male kinsmen like in the case of T'an-yang-tzu, also became immortalized. The gifted seventeenth-century poet Yeh Hsiao-luan was such an example (Ko 1994:200–202).

The second meaning of "domesticated religiosity" is represented by the phenomenon whereby in Ming-Ch'ing times one could achieve religious sanctification by performing one's domestic obligations to the fullest degree. The cult of chaste widowhood is an obvious example. But *ke-ku* (slicing off a piece of flesh from one's thigh) should be viewed in the same light. Through rendering extreme acts of fidelity and filial piety to one's husband, parents or parents-in-law who were in this process transformed into religious absolutes, a woman attained a kind of sainthood.[21] Miao-shan's offering of her eyes and hands resonates strongly in the practice of *ke-ku*.

Ke-ku and Kuan-yin

The highlight of the Miao-shan legend is assuredly the offering of her eyes and hands to save her dying father. This extraordinary act of self-sacrifice not only cancels her crime of unfiliality but triggers her miraculous metamorphosis into a "goddess." Let us look at this image of Miao-shan and the cult of filial piety, as exemplified by *ke-ku* in Ming-Ch'ing times. As we saw in an earlier section, there are many stories about the self-sacrifice of bodhisattvas and, especially, of the Buddha in his previous lives, recorded in Buddhist scriptures. They offered parts of their bodies either as food or medicine to save sentient beings in dire straits. But in most cases, the recipients were not their parents. Among the cases that I discovered, the one most closely resembling that of Miao-shan is the story of Prince Patience, one of the previous incarnations of the Buddha, who offered his eyes and bone marrow to cure his dying father. This story was undoubtedly familiar to the Chinese of the Sung period, for it is not only recorded in a popular Buddhist scripture, the *Ta-fang-pien Fo pao-en ching*, the scene was also carved on the cliff of Mt. Pao-ting in Ta-tsu, Szechwan, by Chao Chih-feng, the founder and architect of this flourishing pilgrimage center. It may not be coincidental that Chao chose to carve this particular scene to illustrate the highest deed of filial piety, for by the Sung, the ideal of *ke-ku* probably had already become well known to Chao, the unknown author of *Hsiang-shan pao-chüan*, as well as ordinary men and women.

The origin of *ke-ku* lies with Chinese medical lore. Chinese historical sources generally identify Ch'en Tsang-ch'i as the legitimator of this belief, for he claimed that human flesh could cure diseases in his medical text, *Ts'ao-mu shih-i* (Corrected Pharmacopoeia), written in 739. Among the dynastic histories, the *Hsin T'ang shu* (New History of the T'ang) is the first to contain three accounts, and subsequently, more cases are recorded in the *Sung shih* (Sung History), and *Yüan shih* (Yüan History). By the Ming, such acts were reported not only in historical sources, but found their way into literature. Both men and women chose to show the utmost filial piety toward their parents by resorting to this drastic action. Typically, the filial child was usually a commoner from an obscure background. But their actions attracted the attention of local officials and literati who wrote commemorative essays and poems to glorify the deed and requested commendation from the government. The literati themselves, however, were ideologically opposed to such behavior, for according to the dictum of the Confucian *Classic of Filial Piety*, the body was a gift from one's parents and one must never do any damage to it. An early condemnation came from Han Yü (768–824) in the T'ang. He strongly argued that filial action consisted of securing medicine for the sick parents but should not involve any harm to one's body. If self-mutilation were really permissible, he asked ironically, then why was it not done by former sages and worthies? Moreover, if such acts resulted in death, it could lead to the extinction of the family line—a most unforgivable sin (*Hsin T'ang shu* 195:2a-b). With rare exceptions, notably Chen Te-hsiu (1178–1235)[22] most neo-Confucian thinkers echoed this sentiment. For instance, Wang Ken (1483?–1540), in his essay "Clear Wisdom and Self-preservation," argued:

> If I only know how to love others and do not know how to love myself, then it will come down to my body being cooked alive or the flesh being sliced off my own thighs, or to throwing away my life and killing myself; and then my self cannot be preserved. And if my self cannot be preserved, with what shall I preserve my prince and father? (*I-chi* 1:12b-13a, quoted in deBary 1970:165)

Li Shih-chen, the Ming medical specialist, was another typical example of the literati. In the *Pen-ts'ao kang-mu* (Classified Materia Medica), he at first mentioned that *ke-ku* and the related practice of *ke-kan* (slicing off a piece of the liver)[23] already existed before the T'ang, so they did not really originate with Ch'en Tsang-ch'i. But he still blamed Ch'en, for the latter gave it credence by writing it down in his book instead of exposing it as a fallacy. Li then took it upon himself to educate his readers, "Alas, we receive our hair, skin, and body from our parents and do not dare to harm or damage them. Even when the parent is seriously ill, how can one allow the children to injure their bodies, not to mention eating the flesh of one's own flesh and blood? This is truly the opinion of foolish people" (Li Shih-chen 1968, vol. 52:110).

Partly because of literati ambivalence, this practice, though widely known in China, has so far received little scholarly attention.[24] The only recent substantive studies treating this topic are the article by Jonathan Chaves, who translated poems written by Wu Chia-chi (1618–1684) glorifying his contemporaries, including his own niece, who practiced *ke-ku* (1986),[25] and a long article analyzing the sociohistorical aspects of this practice by Ch'iu Chung-lin (1996). Literati ambivalence was also responsible for the government's sporadic attempts to discourage such practices among the common people by legislation. Both the Yüan and the Ming issued prohibitions to this effect.[26] But judging from the increasing number of cases mentioned in local gazetteers, popular literature, and collections of miracle tales compiled in the Ming and Ch'ing, such governmental attempts were apparently not effective.

The use of human body parts as medicine to cure illness is well documented in the West as well. Pliny (first century C.E.), for instance, recorded that almost all parts of the human anatomy had been fed to patients for a range of illnesses. Human bones, skins, brains, internal organs, fluids, and excretions have all been tried at one time or another (Chen and Chen 1998:23). The case in China is different, however, for the donor and the recipient must be close relatives. It was believed that when a parent (or parent-in-law) was critically ill and all known medical treatments had failed to yield any cure, the flesh (from the thigh or the arm) or a piece of the liver cut from the body of a filial son, daughter, or daughter-in-law could unfailingly gain the patient's miraculous recovery. I had at first thought of calling this "filial cannibalism" (or "cannibalistic filiality"), for the cure is effected specifically by the consumption of the flesh of the child. But upon further consideration, the use of the term "cannibalism" would not be appropriate here. For in societies where cannibalism is practiced, the central focus is on the "consumer" who sets about consciously and deliberately to capture, prepare, and eat the flesh of his or her victim, which is usually carried out in a ritual setting. The reason for eating the flesh is to incorporate the life force or spiritual power of the victim. Except in cases of famine, the act does not serve a utilitarian purpose (Sunday 1986; Brown and Tuzin 1983). But in the Chinese case, although the beneficiary was the receiving parent, the central focus is always on the "victim," the filial child. The parent invariably did not know that he or she was eating human flesh, for it was always prepared with other ingredients and served in disguise as a soup or gruel. It was the child who received the exclusive attention from the chronicler and eulogist. Detailed description was sometimes lavished on the painful and elaborate ritual of cutting off the flesh, hasty preparation of the life-saving soup, and the return from near death caused by the mortal wound effected by divine help. And finally, it was the child who became sanctified by having part of him or herself reincorporated by the parent. One became spiritually strong by feeding the other and not, as in cannibalism, by consuming the victim.

The relationship between Miao-shan's offering her eyes and hands and the Chinese cult of *ke-ku* is obviously a very close one. But it is difficult to establish either causality or priority. The rationale for Miao-shan's action has a logic that is less discernible in the many cases of *ke-ku* found in dynastic histories and local gazetteers. By refusing to get married and produce an heir, Miao-shan committed the most unfilial action imaginable in Confucian society. The breach in familial and cosmic harmony could only be mended by having herself reincorporated by her father through the latter's eating of her flesh. This is an act of redemption. Her rebellion did not lead to a real separation, but ended with her "reincorporation," into the family. The legend of Miao-shan, in the final analysis, did not challenge the hegemony of Confucian ethical discourse. Moreover, although in most cases it was Heaven or the Kitchen God who was moved by this act of utmost sincerity and came to the filial child's rescue, in some stories of *ke-ku* during the Ming and Ch'ing, it was Kuan-yin who acted as the inspiration and guide for filial children who had difficulty in carrying out or completing this act. She was at other times the savior who protected them from sure death.

Let us look at a few such cases. The first two are from the Ming. Weng Ch'iang-chiang was the niece of a military commander, rank 3b, and, unlike most protagonists of this type of story, she was not a lowly commoner. When she was nine, her father was mortally ill. She prayed to Kuan-yin behind closed doors and sliced her left thigh to get a piece of flesh, which she immediately gave to her mother, née Huang, to make into a soup for her father. He soon recovered. The local people wanted to report this event but she refused to allow them to do so. After her father died, she married a man named Hsi Chia-jui. Her mother became ill within six months of her wedding and she again sliced her thigh as before to save her (*Ku-chin t'u-shu chi-ch'eng* 1934, vol. 397:42a). The next story is about a man, and it is described in gruesome detail:

> The filial son P'eng Yü-yüan of the Ming was a native of I-yang, Hu-kuang. He had the habit of chanting scriptures concerning Kuan-yin, the Three Officials, and other deities in the hope of prolonging his parents' lives. Once his father was very ill and he cut off a piece of flesh from his arm to cure him. The father recovered and lived for more than ten years after that. In the autumn of 1636 his mother became too ill to get up from her bed. Yüan was worried day and night. One night he dreamt of Kuan-yin telling him that the mother's lifespan had come to an end, but if she ate human liver she could survive. When he woke up the next morning, the mother told him that she would like to have some sheep's liver. Realizing the significance of his dream, he knelt down and thanked Kuan-yin tearfully. In the night he saw Kuan-yin come to him surrounded by many saints carrying banners. He woke up with a start and was drenched all over with perspiration. After bathing and worshiping, he took up the knife and aimed at the place where his liver and lung were located. Blood gushed out after one cut. The rib cage was exposed after the second cut. After the third and fourth cuts, there was a resounding sound and after the sixth cut, the heart leapt out. Following the heart he groped for the lung and after the lung he found the liver. By then he had nearly fainted because of the extreme pain. After a moment's rest, he called his wife and told her to quickly cook the liver [the text is not clear if it is the whole liver or a piece of liver] to serve his mother. Not knowing what it really was, the mother ate it happily and soon became well. People from near and far came to know the story and were all greatly moved. Because his wounds did not heal and his lung could still be seen, some people prayed to the gods for help. They dreamt of Kuan-yin, who told them, "It is not difficult to heal the wound, but because few people are filial in this degenerate age, I let the lung hang out for a hundred days so that everyone could view it." The above was recorded by Wang Wen-nan, who holds the second-degree (HTC 134:981a-b).

This story conforms to a general pattern: the filial son was a poor commoner and the one who recorded and broadcast the story was a local gentryman. Kuan-yin played an active role from beginning to end. It was she who gave him the idea in the first place. It was she who guided him in the "operation." And it was she who allowed the wound to remain unhealed for a hundred days as an object lesson for the masses.

Three stories about filial daughters and daughters-in-law in which Kuan-yin appears took place in the Ch'ing.

> The filial daughter-in-law Liu was a native of Hsün county, Hupei. Her husband was not at home. When her mother-in-law was ill and no medicine could cure her, she cut flesh from her thigh and made a congee with it to feed her. The mother-in-law recovered after eating it, but became ill again ten days later. Liu cut more flesh from her thigh and prepared meat balls to feed her and she became well, but then had a relapse several weeks later. Liu prayed to Kuan-yin and wished to offer herself in place of her mother-in-law. The doctor, moved by her sincerity, took pity on her and told her that ordinary pills could not help the patient, whose illness could only be cured by eating a piece of human liver. Liu believed him deeply and, secretly cutting open her underarm with a sharp knife, she got hold of the livers, which had become exposed, and cut off a few inches. She then fainted. In semi-consciousness, she seemed to see Kuan-yin come to her. Caressing her body, Kuan-yin said, "My child, you have suffered much!" and put medicine on her wound. Liu woke up and immediately cooked the liver. After eating it, the mother-in-law recovered and the illness never returned. This happened in the sixth month of the *i-hai* year of Ch'ien-lung (1779) (*Kuan-shih-yin P'u-sa ling-kan lu*, 3a-b).

This woman was a believer in Kuan-yin. Therefore, when she saw that her mother-in-law was still sick even after she tried to cure her by performing *ke-ku* twice, she prayed to Kuan-yin and offered herself as a substitute. For her, Kuan-yin was the supreme authority who had control over life and death. It is also interesting that in this story, it was the doctor who told her that the human liver was the miracle drug. Apparently, despite Li Shih-chen's condemnation, some doctors in the Ch'ing shared the same belief as their less educated countrymen. In this miracle tale, Kuan-yin was not merely an inspiration and guide, but also a savior, for she applied medicine to the wound and saved the filial woman's life.

Another Ch'ing case also presents Kuan-yin as a controller of the human lifespan.

> Sun Fu-chu's wife had the surname of Chin. She was a native of Wu-chin, Kiangsu, and filial by nature. . . . Her husband died when she was twenty-

> four and she kept her integrity. When her father-in-law became ill, she served him day and night for sixty days without sleeping. She prayed to Kuan-yin and cut off flesh from her thighs in the hope of curing him. It just so happened that the patient wanted to eat rice dumplings, so she mixed the flesh with rice flour and served him with broth. After he ate five dumplings, he went to sleep. The next morning, after waking up, he said to her, "I am not going to die. Just now I saw the White-robed Kuan-yin who told me that your sincerity had moved Heaven and I was given another *chi* [300 days] to live." He soon recovered and lived to be seventy-seven, dying exactly three hundred days after this happened. (*Kuan-shih-yin P'u-sa ling-kan lu*, 3b)

The last story is about a little girl of ten years old who received inspiration and courage from Kuan-yin.

> Fang Fu-chu was the daughter of Fang Yü-ch'ing by his concubine. In the thirty-third year of K'ang-hsi's reign [1694] when she was only ten, her mother, née Feng, became ill and did not respond to medical treatment. She cried day and night and tried to think of all possible ways to save her mother. At night she dreamt of a woman in white carrying a barber's knife. She woke up with a start. The next morning, when she saw the mother had become worse, she went upstairs, lighted incense and a lamp, prayed, and sliced her left arm. She cooked a soup with the flesh and served the mother who, upon eating, immediately improved. Officials bestowed on her silver and cloth as a reward .(*Ku-chin t'u-shu chi-ch'eng* 1934, vol. 398:5a-b)

The practice of *ke-ku* had apparently become so widespread that contemporary popular literature often contains it as part of the plot. One *pao-chüan* written probably in the Ch'ing, the *Kuan-yin shih-erh yüan-chüeh ch'üan-chuan* (Complete Biographies of Kuan-yin's Twelve Completely Enlightened Ones) is about how Kuan-yin took different disguises and helped twelve people to become enlightened. One of them, a filial daughter-in-law named Chou was about to perform *ke-ku* in order to save her ailing mother-in-law. Her sincerity moved Kuan-yin who decided to protect her:

> Kuan-yin sighed saying, "Wonderful, wonderful! Such a daughter-in-law is very rare in this world. I fear, though, that she will die if she opens her stomach and cuts her liver." She ordered Wei-t'o, the patron deity of monasteries, to cover her with a copy of the *Scripture of Salvation from Suffering* (Chiu-k'u ching) so that her life might be protected. (*Kuan-yin shih-erh yüan-chüeh ch'üan-chuan* 1938:43a-b)

Contemporary records include anecdotes about Kuan-yin appearing as a real person to filial children and giving them a certain miraculous pill that could save them from death should they one day slice their thighs. We read, for instance, in the *Record of Living as A Hermit* (Ch'ien-ch'u lu), the following:

> Hsieh Fen-lan was extremely filial by nature and she had worshiped Kuan-yin all her life. One day an old nun took out some pills from her sleeve and gave them to her, saying, "These pills can cure injuries resulting from a knife." Fen-lan took them and forgot about it. The following year her mother-in-law became seriously ill and no doctor could help her. She prayed to heaven and asked for help. She then secretly stole into her room and cut flesh from the thigh in order to cook a soup for her mother-in-law. The wound became unbearably painful and she suddenly remembered the pills from before. So she asked her maid to get them and apply them to her wound. As soon as they were applied, new flesh began to grow and it looked as if the thigh had never been cut. The old nun must have been the "Great Being" [Kuan-yin] and filial piety can indeed move the divinity. (*Ku-chin t'u-shu chi-ch'eng* 1934, vol. 398:10b)

Although in these stories, Miao-shan's name does not appear and Kuan-yin is always referred to as *Ta-shih* (Great Being), in view of the fact that the legend of Miao-shan had become widely disseminated throughout society by means of plays and popular texts in the Ming, it is safe to assume that the practitioners of *ke-ku* were aware of the model set by her. The image of Miao-shan as the chaste and filial daughter might not have directly given rise to the cult of filial piety as exemplified by *ke-ku*, but it most likely helped to sustain its attraction. If not only Kuan-yin herself practiced it, but she showed her approval by protecting the filial sons and daughters in their ordeal, surely *ke-ku* was a religious act that would please Kuan-yin and Heaven as well, in addition to saving one's parent. By lending legitimacy to this practice, Kuan-yin was made to uphold the central value system of Confucianism instead of challenging it by offering an alternative.

The religiosity of *ke-ku* in late imperial China turned the parent into the highest object of devotion. The child achieved religious sanctification by worshiping the parent to the point of sacrificing his or her body. The parent, symbolically representing the entire Confucian family system, became the unquestionable moral absolute. Although men also participated in this, women seemed to favor this mode of filial behavior even more (T'ien 1988:159–61). Seen together with the parallel cult of female chastity, which turned widowhood into a religious calling, *ke-ku* possessed an inner logic despite its fanaticism and bizarreness at first sight. Female religiosity became domesticated.

Miao-shan's self-sacrifice and the cult of *ke-ku* are both connected with the ideology of filial piety. The specific form this filiality took in China must, however, be attributed to Buddhist idealization of the "gift of the body" and the related glorification of physical suffering. In this regard, we must examine them together with the tradition of self-immolation and mutilation eulogized in the biographies of eminent monks. As described in chapter 7, famous monks in the Sung period, such as Chih-li and Tsun-shih, frequently practiced self-immolation and mutilation, and *ke-ku* must have given this tradition a boost. Miao-shan and other women performers of *ke-ku*, though lay, coopted this originally monastic and primarily male prerogative and used it to secure the well being of their fathers and family elders.

The stress on filial piety was not the sole concern of Confucians. Alan Cole argues that Buddhist "propaganda" since the fifth century had focused on the need of sons to repay the debt of kindness to their mothers and Buddhist monasteries serve as the indispensable mechanism to enact the dramas of salvation by performing requisite rites. Mothers, sons, and monastics were thus the three main actors in the perpetuation of the Buddhist establishment in China (Cole 1998). He based his analysis on a group of indigenous sūtras all promoting the central importance of repaying the kindness of parents. Although I do not agree with his methodology or conclusion, I agree with him that these texts had enormous influence on the religious lives of the Chinese people.

The earliest such sūtra, *The Sūtra on the Difficulty of Repaying the Kindness of Parents* (Fu-mu en nan-pao ching), attributed to An Shih-kao, is found in Seng-yu's catalogue of 518, noting that this is a work extracted from the *Madhyamāgama*. It states that "If a son carries his father on his right shoulder and his mother on his left shoulder for a thousand years and even when they shit and piss on his back without his showing any grudge, he still would not have repaid their kindness" (T 16:779a). A seventh-century indigenous sūtra, *The Sūtra on the Profound Kindness of Parents* (Fu-mu en-chung ching) advances the argument by describing the pains the mother endures during the ten months of pregnancy and the cares she shows in caring the baby. Scenes from this text were depicted in Tun-huang, for instance, Caves 112 and 156 (Mair 1986:4). Finally, a third text, commonly known as *The Sūtra on the Difficulty of Repaying the Profound Kindness of Parents* (Fu-mu en-chung nan-pao ching), represents the culmination of this development. Hand-written copies of this text have been found in Tun-huang, printed copies dated no earlier than the twelfth century have been discovered in Khara Khoto, and forty-one printed copies of the same text dated from 1443 to 1806 have been found in Korea. This shows that this text must have been very popular. In fact, even today, one can easily find copies donated by the faithful in Taiwan.

According to Ma Shih-chang (1998), this last scripture (which he refers to as *Pao fu-mu en-chung ching*) was probably composed in the middle of the T'ang, but more additions were made during the Sung to the Yüan periods. It contains a section describing ten kinds of kindness a baby receives from his parents. These were the scenes depicted at Mt. Pao-ting, Ta-tsu, Szechwan. Missing there but depicted on the frontispieces of the copies of the text found in Khara Khoto and Korea were the eight scenes of the son showing filial piety: carrying his parents on his two shoulders, cutting off a piece of flesh, gouging out his eyes, slicing off his liver, piercing his body with knife, hanging lighted lamp on his body, drilling marrow from his bone, and swallowing heated iron balls. He performs all these acts because, according to the text, even if a filial son performs all these self-mutilations to repay his debt to the parents' kindness, he still would not have been able to exhaust his debt.

Printed copies of this text with such depictions have not survived in China. It is reasonable to suppose, however, that such works must have once existed so that they could have been exported to other countries. Seen from the perspective of this text, Miao-shan's gouging of her eyes and cutting off her hands as well as those who performed *ke-ku* and chose to cut off a piece of flesh or liver were simply following the textual stipulations faithfully. Once mythical and real women began to carry out such extreme acts of filial piety into action, doctrinal precept became transformed into religious practice and served to reinforce it. Indigenous sūtras, myths, and reports of miracles support each other. Pilgrimage and iconography that broadcast the myths and miracles served as media facilitating this process.

Myth, Pilgrimage, and Iconography

Although the myth of Miao-shan was in the beginning intimately connected with Hsiang-shan Monastery as a pilgrimage center, it did not stay that way. It was imported to Hangchow and took deep root at the Upper T'ien-chu Monastery. Hsiang-shan declined after K'ai-feng fell to the Chin and Hangchow became the capital of the Southern Sung in 1138. The Upper T'ien-chu Monastery in Hangchow then became the undisputed national pilgrimage center for Kuan-yin worship until P'u-t'o emerged as a serious competitor in later centuries.

As P'u-t'o became firmly identified as the scriptural Potalaka, the "home" of the bodhisattva, in the Ming, it completely supplanted Hsiang-shan. The *Pre-*

cious Scroll of Hsiang-shan reveals that P'u-t'o is in fact Hsiang-shan when it declares at the end, "Hiding in retirement on P'u-t'o for a very long time and unknown to men, her name began to appear only in the T'ang dynasty." It goes on to say that if a person wishes to have a vision of the bodhisattva, it is necessary to go to P'u-t'o on a pilgrimage. Once there, Kuan-yin may appear in one of several forms made familiar by paintings and statues representing different iconographies.

> Hidden from the world, the bodhisattva lives on P'u-t'o. She is omniscient, and knows all the things in all the worlds. She is like the moon in the sky that is being reflected in thousand bodies of water everywhere. So when prayers are offered to her in ten thousand locations, they will all be answered without fail. She has vowed to save beings universally and help them to attain Buddhahood. If you do not believe me, just go to P'u-t'o and pray with sincerity. She will appear to you as you imagine her to be. She may appear wearing a jeweled crown and covered with necklaces all over her body. Her face may look like an eighteen-year-old. She may appear wearing a white robe and exhibiting the thirty-two excellent marks. She may appear very big or very small. She may appear in full view or half view. She may resemble purplish gold or white jade. She may appear together with the bird and the pure vase, or with purple bamboo and green willow, or with Sudhana and Dragon Princess. She may appear in an ocean full of lotuses or on a mountaintop bathed in brilliant light. There are many variations to her manifestations, which cannot be fully enumerated (Yoshioka 1971:193).

When Hsiang-shan was merged with P'u-t'o, Miao-shan was also absorbed back into Kuan-yin, who now became feminized and sinicized as the Nan-hai Kuan-yin (Kuan-yin of the South Sea), a form of Kuan-yin popular in the Ming (to be discussed in chapter 10). As I stated in the beginning of this chapter, the myth of Miao-shan as first formulated in the stele was mainly designed to domesticate the esoteric Thousand-handed Kuan-yin. But by the time we get to the later version, this is no longer the main concern for the author. In the *Precious Scroll of Hsiang-shan*, when Miao-shan reveals her true form, she is described as wearing a crown of pearls on her head and necklaces around her body while holding a vase of pure water and willow branches in her hands and standing on a golden thousand-petaled lotus (Yoshioka 1971:188). This contrasts sharply with her form during the earlier theophany as described in the stele inscription, when she appears as the Thousand-eyed and Thousand-handed Ta-pei Kuan-yin.

The myth, then, was modified by pilgrimage and iconography, the subjects to be treated in the next three chapters. In closing this chapter, I want to offer two further observations. The first concerns the dialectical relationship between the fame of the Miao-shan myth and the continued popularity of the Thousand-handed Kuan-yin as an icon in China. Although the initial cult of Ta-pei in the T'ang and the Sung led to the creation of the Miao-shan legend, the latter was responsible for the enduring veneration of this esoteric form of Kuan-yin down the ages by the Chinese people. As we read in earlier chapters, several other esoteric forms of Kuan-yin were introduced into China and the Eleven-headed Kuan-yin enjoyed equal, if not more, popularity in pre-T'ang and T'ang times. Whereas very few Eleven-headed Kuan-yins have survived,[27] however, a number of Thousand-handed Kuan-yin images remain as main icons in Buddhist monasteries today. Two such images dated to the Sung stand in the Lung-hsing Monastery in Ting County, Hopei, and the number 8 Niche on Mt. Pao-ting, Ta-tsu, Szechwan.[28]

More images from the Ming survive, such as the central icon in the Ta-pei Hall of the Ch'ung-shan Monastery in Tai-yüan, Shansi, and the one in the Bodhisattva Hall of the Shuang-lin Monastery in Ping-yao, also in Shansi. I suggest that one of the reasons the Ta-pei icons continue to fascinate and inspire the Chinese is their association with the story of Miao-shan. I cite one example to show what I mean. All the Ta-pei images created in the Ming are attended by a pair consisting of a man and woman on either side. In 1986 when I visited the famous Golden Pavilion Monastery (Chin-ke Ssu) on Mt Wu-t'ai, I was told by the resident monk there that they were the parents of Princess Miao-shan.[29] People see the esoteric Kuan-yin through the lens of Miao-shan.

The second observation is that more than any other media, the legend of Miao-shan contributed to the feminization of Kuan-yin. Not only could the Chinese people hear, read, and watch the story in *pao-chüan*, novels and plays, they could also view it depicted on temple walls. Just as the life of the Buddha had earlier provided rich material for the frescoes in Tun-huang, scenes from the life of Miao-shan were also immortalized on frescoes from at least the Ming on. I have evidence from two temples with such wall paintings that date to the Ming. The Pao-en Ssu in Ping-wu, Szechwan, was founded by Wang Hsi and his son Wang Chien in 1440–1460. The main icon is the Thousand-handed Kuan-yin, measuring over nine meters. It is attended by two wooden statues, one of a man dressed in official garb and one of a woman, who are identified as the "parents" of Kuan-yin. Frescoes and clay bas-reliefs depicting the life of Miao-shan cover the east, west, and north (directly behind the main image) walls of the hall, measuring 3.2 meters in length, 2.85 meters in width, and with a total size of 91.2 square meters (Hsiang 1991:7–9).

The Ta-hui Monastery, familiarly known as Great Buddha Monastery (Ta-

Fo Ssu) in Peking, was constructed in 1513 by the eunuch Chang Hsün. Like the Pao-en Ssu, the Thousand-handed Kuan-yin is also enshrined as the main icon. On the east and west walls, ten scenes from the life of Miao-shan are depicted in frescoes. Cartouches inscribed on the side identify the scenes as: (1) King Miao-chuang announces that he will marry off his daughters; (2) Princess Miao-shan asks to practice Buddhism; (3) King Miao-chuang tries to move Miao-shan to change her mind; (4) Princess Miao-shan is imprisoned in White Sparrow Monastery; (5) King Miao-chuang harms Princess Miao-shan; (6) Princess Miao-shan tours hell in her dream (figure 8.3); (7) Princess Miao-shan attains the Way at Hsiang-shan; (8) King Miao-chuang's life depends on the loyal and filial daughter; (9) Princess Miao-shan sacrifices her body to save the father; and (10) King Miao-chuang takes refuge in the Buddha Dharma (Wang 1994:104–21).

For years I was puzzled by the fact that despite the great fame of the legend of Miao-shan, no particular image or painting of Kuan-yin is identified as Miao-shan. The popular set of thirty-three forms of Kuan-yin, for instance, also does not include it. The reason is now obvious. Miao-shan does not need a specific iconography. She is no different from the Ta-pei Kuan-yin. Whenever one sees the Thousand-handed Kuan-yin, one sees Miao-shan. Through this legend, Kuan-yin was domesticated and feminized. Moreover, not only as Kuan-yin, but she was also presented as the equivalent of the Buddha in *pao-chüan* literature and temple art. The way was thus prepared for some sectarian religions of late imperial China to elevate Kuan-yin to a supreme position as the creator and ruler of the universe, as we shall read in chapter 11, echoing the same claim made by the esoteric scriptures discussed in chapter 2.

Figure 8.3. "Miao-shan Tours Hell," wall painting from the Ta-Fo Ssu, Peking, dated 1513 (from Wang 1994:113).

9

P'u-t'o Shan: Pilgrimage and the Creation of the Chinese Potalaka

The sacred geography of Buddhist China was marked by sites where great bodhisattvas manifested themselves in human form. By journeying to these holy mountains, pious pilgrims hoped to receive blessings and, if they were lucky, obtain a divine vision of the deity. The most famous group of these mountains was called either the *san-ta tao-ch'ang* ("The Three Great Seats of Enlightenment"), or the *ssu-ta ming-shan* ("The Four Famous Mountains" and, alternatively, "The Famous Mountains Representing the Four Great Elements"). The former refers to Mt. Wu-t'ai in Shansi, the home of Wen-shu (Mañjuśrī), Mt. Omei in Szechwan, the home of P'u-hsien (Samantabhadra), and Mt. P'u-t'o in Chekiang, the home of Kuan-yin (Avalokiteśvara). These three bodhisattvas, traditionally called *San Ta-shih* (Three Great Beings), were celestial bodhisattvas who enjoyed veneration throughout Buddhist Asia. The *Ssu-ta ming-shan* include the same three places as well as a fourth one: Mt. Chiu-hua in Anhui, the home of Ti-tsang (Kṣitigarbha). Both expressions came into use quite late. As far as I can ascertain, they were used only after the Sung. An early fourteenth-century gazetteer of Ningpo uses the first expression. But by the late Ming, both expressions become widely used by the writers of the *Gazetteer of P'u-t'o* (*PTSC*).

Ch'iu Lien, the compiler of the 1698 edition of the gazetteer of P'u-t'o, offered an explanation for the number four. "The four sites symbolized the four great elements. Just as the world was constituted by the four great elements, these elements were in turn represented by the four great mountains, with Wu-t'ai representing wind, Omei fire, Chiu-hua earth, and P'u-t'o water." He went on to comment,

> Chiu-hua is situated right by the [Yangtze] river. Although Wu-t'ai and Omei are quite far, they are nevertheless in the interior of the country and can be reached in reasonable time. P'u-t'o alone is totally isolated, hanging by itself in the middle of the ocean. It is truly both far away and difficult to reach. Yet during the past several dynasties, faithful men and women of both high status and low birth, Buddhist monks and Taoist priests have been coming here from nearby and far away. Carrying incense and holding scriptures, they walked until their feet became callous and they knocked their foreheads on the ground until they became bloody. Scaling the mountains and braving the ocean waves, like the gathering of clouds and the roaring of thunders, they came to worship the Great Being. Compared with Omei, Wu-t'ai and Chiu-hua, more pilgrims have come to P'u-t'o. (PTSC 1698, 2:4; Saeki 1961:372–73)

The emergence of P'u-t'o as a national and international pilgrimage center for the worship of Kuan-yin was a slow and late one, beginning in the tenth century, picking up momentum in the sixteenth, and reaching a peak only after the eighteenth century. By contrast, the other "famous mountains," particularly Wu-t'ai and Omei, were already well known during the T'ang, the same time when the cult of Kuan-yin also became popular. This led to the establishment of a number of cultic centers for Kuan-yin worship on the mainland. Although there did not seem to be strong local cultic centers for Mañjuśrī and Samantabhadra against which Wu-t'ai and Omei had to compete, the case was far different for P'u-t'o. The eventual triumph of P'u-t'o as the most important pilgrimage site for the cult of Kuan-yin was the reason it became linked with the other great pilgrimage centers in later periods.

P'u-t'o was able to supersede mainland cultic centers because it claimed to be the Potalaka, the island home of Kuan-yin mentioned in the *Hua-yen ching*, the same scripture that provided legitimacy for Mt. Wu-t'ai and Mt. Omei. The forty-*chüan* version of the sūtra translated by Prajñā between 795 and 810 is particularly important. It describes the pilgrimage of the youth Sudhana (Shan-ts'ai) in search of truth. Kuan-yin is presented in it as the twenty-eighth "good friend" visited by the young pilgrim. Kuan-yin's home is Mt. Potalaka, which is situated in the ocean. Sitting on a diamond boulder in a clearing amid a luxuriant wooded area, Kuan-yin preaches the Dharma to Sudhana. Mt. Potalaka was also the setting for one of the most important esoteric scriptures, the *Sūtra of the Thousand-Handed and Thousand-Eyed Kuan-yin Great Compassionate-Heart Dhāraṇī* (Ch'ien-shou-ch'ien-yen Kuan-shih-yin P'u-sa Ta-pei-hsin t'o-lo-ni ching), or the *Ch'ien-shou ching* for short (discussed in chapters

2 and 7). In this sūtra, Kuan-yin reveals the all-powerful saving dhāraṇī to the great assembly of bodhisattvas and other beings gathered around Śākyamuni Buddha in Kuan-yin's palace on this sacred island.

While connecting the island to these influential scriptures, the builders of the Chinese Potalaka also incorporated mythical and iconographical elements of Kuan-yin developed by local pilgrimage centers on the mainland. Miracles attributed to Kuan-yin gave rise to such centers and to the local traditions connected with them. I would argue that it was only when Kuan-yin became associated with certain sites and people began to make pilgrimages to these places that the cult of Kuan-yin really took root in China. Another reason for the proliferation of pilgrimage sites for Kuan-yin was due to the extensive acculturation that the bodhisattva experienced in China. Of all the great Buddhist deities, Kuan-yin alone underwent a sexual transformation, and in doing so succeeded in becoming completely Chinese. Because of her great popularity in China, many cultic centers devoted to her worship appeared in different localities. Miracles firmly anchored Kuan-yin to these sites, and in the process, provided Kuan-yin with indigenous life stories and iconographies.

As discussed previously, miracles and pilgrimage sites played important roles in the Chinese cult of Kuan-yin. They contributed to the domestication and sinicization of Kuan-yin. Miracle tales, local lore, literature, and art were the media through which information about pilgrimage sites was made known. They created the potential pilgrims' expectations and probably shaped their experiences during the pilgrimage. Pilgrims, both monastic and lay, were the agents who transmitted local traditions to other parts of the country. These traditions were also carefully collected and preserved by the compilers of mountain gazetteers, which, as I argue later in this chapter, constitute a powerful source for the legitimation of each site.

The relationships between the various pilgrimage centers devoted to the same deity deserve careful study. Can we talk about local, regional, national, and even international pilgrimage sites in China? Do they always compete with each other for prestige and patronage? Or do some draw the greater fame of older and better established sites to confirm their newly acknowledged *ling* (efficacy)? The cult of Kuan-yin with its multiple pilgrimage sites provides an ideal case for our study. Although this chapter concentrates on the mechanisms and processes through which P'u-t'o became the Chinese Potalaka, I examine these developments in the light of other pilgrimage sites on the mainland. As Bernard Faure's 1992 study of Ch'an pilgrimage sites shows, the study of the birth and decline of pilgrimage centers can provide us with much needed information about the social history of Chinese religion.

Establishment of Pilgrimage Sites

The founding myths recounting the establishment of most Kuan-yin pilgrimage sites contain two basic motifs: either Kuan-yin appeared in person and performed miracles for the benefit of the people, or the site became known through its possession of a miracle-working image of Kuan-yin. Usually, the image either came into being spontaneously (*tzu-tso*) or had been made by Kuan-yin himself/herself. References to such miraculously formed images can be found in standard collections such as *Fa-yüan chu-lin* and *T'ai-p'ing kuang-chi*. Similar phenomena are reported in Hinduism and Catholicism.

Some stories about such images were never included in any collections but are circulated locally. For instance, among the stelae housed in the Lung-yin Yen (Cliff of the Hidden Dragon) in Kuei-lin, Kwangsi, there is one with a portrait of Kuan-yin on the upper half and an inscription about its origin on the lower half. The portrait shows Kuan-yin wearing three Buddha heads on his crown instead of the usual one. It ends abruptly at the upper chest. The inscription provides an explanation for the unfinished state of the portrait. During the T'ai-ho era (827–835) of the T'ang, a pious layman by the name of Wang Jen of Ch'ang-an worshiped Kuan-yin. One day a monk came to his home and offered to paint him a portrait of Kuan-yin. He made a strict stipulation, however, that he had to be housed in a quiet room and no one should disturb him for seven days. Three days later, when the children of the household out of curiosity made a hole in the paper window pane and took a peek inside, the monk suddenly disappeared, leaving behind the unfinished painting. Wang then realized that the monk had been a manifestation of Kuan-yin. Copies of the painting survived. In 1665 when the monk Hsin-hsiao made a pilgrimage to Kuei-lin, he saw a copy and decided to have it incised on stone for posterity. With the support and donations of the local officials and gentry, this was done.

According to another stele erected in 1914 and containing eighty-eight donors' names, The Cliff of the Hidden Dragon was a pilgrimage center for Kuan-yin worship. Pilgrims came during the second, sixth, and ninth months to celebrate the three holy days of Kuan-yin. The local guide told me in June 1987 that this was the reason why there were three heads on Kuan-yin's crown. Even though the image on the stele has a moustache, local people apparently see Kuan-yin through the legend of Miao-shan. The founding myths of pilgrimage sites reflect the prevailing view of the miraculous. Sometimes, both motifs are found in the founding myths of the same site.

I discussed the establishment of Hsiang-shan Monastery as a pilgrimage site in the previous chapter. Here I discuss the establishment of two more sites located on the mainland. Each represents one motif. I then examine the case of P'u-t'o, where it was primarily the possibility of having a vision of Kuan-yin that first attracted pilgrims and, to some extent, continued to do so, throughout the succeeding centuries.

Nan Wu-t'ai Shan (Southern Mt. Wu-t'ai)

Yin-kuang (1861–1940), a Pure Land master and a great devotee of Kuan-yin, sponsored a new edition of the gazetteer of P'u-t'o during 1930s. In the preface, he wrote, "The bodhisattva is all-merciful and compassionate and thus beloved among people of the entire country. Therefore, there is a common saying that Kuan-yin is found in every household. The places where Kuan-yin carries out the work of enlightening beings are not limited to one. For instance, the Southern Mt. Wu-t'ai, the Great Hsiang-shan, and the Upper T'ien-chu are all well-known. However, Mt. P'u-t'o in the South Sea is the foremost in terms of its efficaciousness and the number of pilgrims going there" (*PTSC* 1924:16).

Nan Wu-t'ai Shan, a five-peaked mountain, was situated at the southern side of Mt. Chung-nan, some fifty *li* to the south of Ch'ang-an (present-day Sian). In the same preface Yin-kuang appended an account about the creation of the Southern Mt. Wu-t'ai, using material recorded on a stele written by a Yüan monk and erected in 1271. The following is a partial translation:

> During the Jen-shou era (601–604) of the Sui, a poisonous dragon lived in the mountain. Relying upon his paranormal powers, he assumed the form of an immortal and came to Ch'ang-an to sell drugs made of cinnabar. He fooled the ignorant by saying that whoever took his drug would be able to ascend to heaven in broad daylight right away. Many people took his bait. They all ended up in the dragon's lair and became his food. But the people were deluded and did not wake up to the truth. The Great Being used the power of the compassionate vow and appeared in the form of a monk. Gathering grasses and building a hut on the top of the mountain, he tamed the evil power with his wondrous wisdom. The wind of purity swept away heated vexation. Wherever the thought of compassion spread, poisonous ether disappeared. The dragon obtained release in clarity and coolness (*ch'ing-liang*) and stayed in his cave peacefully. The residents were no longer endangered.
>
> The news of the monk's efficacy reached the court, which decreed that a monastery should be built for him in gratitude for his benefiting to the

country and the people. The local gentry admired him and some managed to extricate themselves from the net of attachment and, shaving off their hair, entered the Way. The Great Being liked to stay among the rocks. Monkeys and wild animals would sit around him. Birds in the forests would not cry out, as though they were listening to his Dharma talk. They would disperse only after a very long time. Unfortunately, the very next year after the monastery was erected, on the nineteenth day of the sixth month, he suddenly entered nirvāṇa. A strange fragrance filled the room. The sky became overcast. Birds and animals cried piteously and the mountain forests changed color. Members of the Saṃgha reported the sad news to the court and eunuchs were dispatched to offer incense.

At the time of his cremation, heaven and earth darkened. But suddenly, in one instant, the whole area turned into a silvery realm. Music resounded in the sky; the mountain shook; auspicious clouds blew over; and the air was filled with strange fragrance. A golden bridge suddenly appeared above the Eastern Peak. A host of heavenly beings stood on the bridge, carrying banners and scattering golden flowers that did not touch the ground. Finally, on top of the Southern Terrace, brilliant jewels of a hundred varieties filled a space the breadth and height could not be measured. A glimmer of a dignified form in royal ease could be discerned. His compassionate face was grave and beautiful. Wearing a suit studded with coins and covered with necklaces, he moved in the wind and looked at everyone with bright illumination. At that time, there were more than a thousand people, both monks and lay people, who witnessed the true form of the bodhisattva. They were overwhelmed with emotion and realized that the monk was a manifestation of Kuan-yin. The fragrance lingered for several months.

Mr. Kao, the Left Executive Assistant of the Department of Ministries, wrote a memorial about this to the emperor, who read it and offered praise. The bones of the monk were gathered together and housed in a stūpa. The emperor bestowed a plaque naming it Kuan-yin-t'ai Ssu (Monastery of Kuan-yin Terrace) and gave the monks a hundred square *li* of land for their sustenance. Every year the emperor sent messengers who came as pilgrims to make offerings and celebrate the ordination of new monks. The Dharma was greatly promoted.

The monastery was renamed Nan Wu-t'ai Shan Sheng-shou Ssu (Monastery of Holy Longevity on Mt. Southern Wu-t'ai) in the sixth year of the Ta-li (771) of the T'ang dynasty. During the Five Dynasties, it was burned down in a war. In the summer of the third year of T'ai-p'ing hsing-kuo era of the Sung (978), auspicious signs of five-colored circles and clouds appeared six times consecutively. The monk Huai-wei reported these marvels

> to the governor, who memorialized the court. A gold plaque was bestowed on the monastery renaming it Wu-t'ai Shan Yüan-kuang Ssu (Monastery of Circled Light of the Five-Terraced Mountain). The halls were rebuilt and a painting of the true appearance of the bodhisattva was installed. Incense has been offered there ever since, without interruption. Whenever there was drought, supplicants would come here to pray for rain. The prayers were always answered without fail. Such happenings have been recorded in the documents kept by the county and provincial offices. Pilgrims come in the month of the festival of Clear and Bright (Ch'ing-ming) as well as the death anniversary of the monk in the summer. Holding the young and helping the old, pilgrims come from hundreds of miles away. Defying danger and carrying offerings, they crowd the roads leading to the monastery for more than a month without a break (*PTSC* 1924:18–20).

I quote the account at length because the case of Southern Mt. Wu-t'ai can serve as a prototypical example of the establishment of a Kuan-yin pilgrimage center. It began with the manifestation of Kuan-yin and the miracle he performed for the benefit of the community. Kuan-yin appeared as a monk who was a savior figure, a common guise for the bodhisattva recorded in miracle tales collected in the Six Dynasties, as discussed in chapter 4.[1] Moreover, although the holy monk in this case did not have a name, he nevertheless fitted perfectly the model of wonder-working monks as incarnations of Kuan-yin, described in chapter 5. It is also interesting to note that the date of his death was said to be the nineteenth day of the sixth month. As mentioned in the previous chapter, as a result of the popularity of the legend of Miao-shan, Kuan-yin is worshipped on three holy days: the nineteenth day of the second, sixth, and ninth months. These days were chosen because Miao-shan/Kuan-yin was born on the first date, became enlightened on the second date and left the home on the third date. Was the choice of the nineteenth day of the sixth month as the date for the monk's nirvāṇa a pure coincidence? Or could it reflect a possible influence from the myth of Miao-shan, for by the thirteenth century, when this stele was erected, the legend of Miao-shan had already become known. The site was most likely originally Taoist and the Buddhist takeover was implied by the myth about the deceitful immortal who was in fact a man-eating dragon. The rivalry is similar to situations at other holy sites important to both Buddhists and Taoists as discussed by Faure (1987, 1992). Southern Mt. Wu-t'ai developed, furthermore, with imperial recognition and patronage, and was perpetuated through the promotion of its monks. It was revived by reports of new miracles, and finally, it was maintained by the enthusiasm of pilgrims who came with regularity and in large numbers.

The Upper T'ien-chu Monastery in Hangchow

The fame of the Upper T'ien-chu was connected with a miraculous image of Kuan-yin that was "spontaneously formed." The monastery underwent a major revival in 939 under the monk Tao-i, who was responsible for the discovery of this image (HCLAC 80/6b-13b; HHYLC 11). In this year the monk Tao-i came from Mt. Chung-nan, a famous mountain north of Southern Mt. Wu-t'ai, and a numinous place frequented by Tao-hsüan and the mysterious monk who had provided information about Princess Miao-shan. One night while Tao-i was meditating he saw a bright light coming from the stream. When he looked in the water, he found a piece of marvelous wood several feet in length, giving off a strange fragrance, with a radically unusual color and grain. He asked a local artisan, K'ung, to make an image of Kuan-yin with it. When K'ung cut the wood open, he found a ready-made "naturally formed image" of Kuan-yin. The crown and draperies were gorgeous and the bodhisattva's face was compassionate and beautiful. K'ung decided to keep the image for himself and replace it with another one made of ordinary wood. But Kuan-yin warned Tao-i of this in a dream. When the substitution was revealed, K'ung then had to turn over the self-formed image. Some years later, during the Ch'ien-yu era (948–950), Tao-i had another dream in which a "white-robed person" (*pai-i jen*) told him that a monk named Tsung-hsün would arrive from Loyang the next day and that he should ask for an ancient relic of the Buddha that was among the latter's possessions. When Tsung-hsün arrived and saw the image of Kuan-yin, he was greatly moved and offered the relic to be installed on its crown (STCC 1980:29, 86, 227).

Although the chronicle of the Upper T'ien-chu does not describe the appearance of the original Kuan-yin image, it was most likely that of the White-robed feminine Kuan-yin. This becomes clear when we examine another group of founding myths concerning the establishment of the monastery that centered around Ch'ien Liu (851–932), the founder of the Wu Yüeh Kingdom. Before he came to the throne, he dreamt of a woman in white who promised to protect him and his descendants if he was compassionate. She told him that he could find her on Mt. T'ien-chu in Hangchow twenty years thereafter. After he became the king, he dreamt of the same woman who asked for a place to stay and in return, agreed to be the patron deity of his kingdom. When Ch'ien made inquiries, he discovered that the only White-robed Kuan-yin image was found in T'ien-chu. So he established the T'ien-chu k'an-ching Yüan (Cloister for Reading Scriptures at T'ien-chu), which was the earlier name for what became the Upper T'ien-chu Monastery (STCC 31).

From this account, the image housed in T'ien-chu had been the feminine

White-robed Kuan-yin. It was described as seated, 2'4" in height, and accompanied by Shan-ts'ai (Sudhana) and Lung-nü (Dragon Princess) by a pilgrim who saw it during the Wan-li era (1573–1615) (STCC 1980:228). As we read in chapter 6, the White-robed Kuan-yin, one of several feminine forms of Kuan-yin that emerged in the late T'ang, enjoyed widespread popularity from the tenth century on. Paintings, statues, miracle tales, and the founding myths of Kuan-yin temples dated from the Northern Sung, the same time when P'u-t'o became slowly established, all attest to this fact.

The Kuan-yin of the Upper T'ien-chu became known for her efficacy in averting natural disasters and her oracles transmitted to pilgrims in dreams. Based on the reports of miracles recorded by the prefect, Emperor Jen-tsung bestowed the plaque Ling-kan Kuan-yin Yüan (Cloister of Kuan-yin of Efficacious Responses) in 1062, and reclassified it as a Ch'an temple. The friendship between Su Shih (Su Tung-p'o) and the abbot of the temple, the Ch'an master Pien-ts'ai (d. 1091) promoted the fame of Upper T'ien-chu among the literati and officials. Just as the devotion to Kuan-yin prevalent among Ch'an monks and literati officials helped her cult generally, the same classes of people were responsible for the Upper T'ien-chu becoming a center for Kuan-yin worship. Su Shih wrote a poem entitled, "Visiting T'ien-chu Ling-kan Kuan-yin Yüan in the Rain," which again provides us with proof that it was the White-robed Kuan-yin who was enshrined there:

The silkworms are about to mature and the wheat stalks are yellowing,
Rain is swelling like waves in front of the mountain and behind the mountain.
Farmers stop their work and women put down their baskets,
*The White-robed True Person (*Pai-i chen-jen*) sits in the great hall. (*Hangchow sheng-chi tsa-lu *5:56)*

When Hangchow became the capital of the Southern Sung (1127–1279), the temple received frequent visits and favors from the emperors. Hsiao-tsung (r. 1163–1188) bestowed the title "T'ien-chu Kuang-ta Ling-kan Ta-shih" (T'ien-chu's Great Being of Broad and Extensive Efficacious Responses) on Kuan-yin, treating the bodhisattva as a Chinese deity. Emperors in succeeding dynasties continued their patronage. The gazetteer of the monastery records Kuan-yin's success in granting rain in 998, 1000, 1135, 1374, 1455, 1477, 1503, 1539, 1542, 1545, and 1626; in saving the people of Hangchow from flood in 1065, 1580, and 1608; from locusts in 1016; and from plague in 1588. When there was no rain for five months in 998, the reviewing policy adviser moved the image to Fan-t'ien Monastery (Monastery of Brahmā Heaven) in the city and prayed for rain with all the officials. This set the pattern for subsequent requests for Kuan-yin's miracles. Her image was welcomed into the city and invoked by officials (STTC 1980:3–40).

Sometimes additional effort had to be made to call forth her intervention. In the summer of 1135, for instance, Hangchow saw another great drought. The prefect of Hangchow moved the image to Hai-hui (Ocean of Wisdom) Monastery and prayed for rain, but to no effect. In the sixth month, an ascetic by the name of Pan Fa-hui burned out his right eye with a heated iron ball. Rain came in abundance. Three days later he dreamt of a woman in white asking to borrow a pearl from him. He refused but the two monks who were also present in his dream persuaded him to lend it to her, saying that "after six and six" she would give it back. On the twenty-first day of the seventh month he again dreamt of the same three. The two monks invited him to attend a feast and the woman in white led the way. They came to a place where all kinds of ripe fruit fell from the trees. He picked one up and ate it. His mind immediately became cool and clear. Suddenly the white-robed woman threw a billiard ball at him and it lodged in his sunken eye. He cried out loud and woke up. He felt that there was something like a pearl in his eye and gradually regained his sight. This was thirty-six days after his first dream. He then understood the meaning of "six and six" (STCC 1980:36–38).

Pilgrims went to the Upper T'ien-chu to seek dream oracles. This was particularly popular among the literati. For instance, in 1132, candidates from Chekiang for the *chin-shih* degree were to be tested in Hangchow. Tan I, a native of Hu-chou, made a pilgrimage with six friends to the Upper T'ien-chu to seek oracles through dream incubation. That night Tan dreamt of eating an eggplant and his friend Hsü Yang dreamt of eating a huge crab. The next day they asked a specialist in dream interpretation who was attached to the temple for an explanation. They were told that according to a colloquial expression, eggplant meant defeat and crabs victory. Later, Hsü was indeed successful in the examination (STCC 1980:36).

The efficacy of the Kuan-yin of Upper T'ien-chu was attested to by other miracles. Some, like this one, contain a cautionary warning against those pilgrims who go back on their promises. A man named Wang was a native of Hangchow. He suffered from boils and prayed to Kuan-yin, promising to offer lamp oil and broomsticks to the monastery if he recovered. When he went to Upper T'ien-chu to fulfill the vow, a thief stole the offerings from him and sold them cheaply. Wang caught the thief and was about to hand him over to the magistrate. Frightened, the thief offered to repay for his loss doubly. So Wang let him go. Wang had a daughter. When he came home, the daughter was sleeping, but she suddenly said to her father in her sleep, "Today you went to fulfill your vow, yet you allowed someone to give you money for food and wine. The P'u-sa [Kuan-yin] is kind, but the protector of the temple insists on taking me as a substitute. Please prepare the offerings you promised before and go to the temple to ask for forgiveness and thank the protector of the temple." The father did as he was told. When the girl woke up, she did not remember what had happened (STCC 1980:41).

During the Ming dynasty, the nineteenth day of the second month was known as Kuan-yin's birthday. It was the most important day for all sorts of pilgrims. They came from nearby and far away. They would fast and then come to the monastery the day before the observance. Because there were hundreds of thousands of pilgrims, they could not be accommodated in the monastery but had to stay outdoors and wait for daybreak. This was called "spending the night in the mountains" (*su-shan*). In 1554 on the eve of Kuan-yin's birthday, the moon and stars shone brightly. Suddenly a white parrot flew out from the main hall and soared up into the sky.[2] Ten thousand people saw this with their own eyes. Voices calling on buddha's name shook the mountain and echoed in the valley. Such miracles happened four times in a row (STCC 1980:41).

The annual arrival of huge crowds gave rise to the creation of the Pilgrims' Fair of The West Lake (*Hsi-hu hsiang-shih*), also known as Pilgrims' Fair of T'ien-chu. The economic aspect of pilgrimage is a subject worthy of study by itself. Just as political patronage could influence the changing fortunes of pilgrimage sites, economic activities that went on as a byproduct of pilgrimage might very well have been one of the determining factors in the longevity of a site. We are fortunate in having some eyewitness accounts about the Upper T'ien-chu Pilgrims' Fair. The Ming writer Chang Tai, an avid traveler, described the fair as he saw it in the seventeenth century this way:

> It began on the twelfth day of the second month and ended on the fifth day of the fifth month. During these three months, Shantung pilgrims on their return trip from P'u-t'o and Chia-hsing, and Hu-chou pilgrims on their way to offer incense at T'ien-chu, arrived daily. Men and women, old and young, their numbers reached several million. Once they came to Hangchow, they traded with the locals. That was why it was called the Pilgrims' Fair. Trading went on at the three T'ien-chu monasteries, the Temple of Yüeh Fei and the Pavilion in the middle of the West Lake, but particularly at the Chao-ch'ing Monastery. From local products such as scissors, and religious implements such as scriptures and wooden fish, all the way to antiques and imported rare goods, everything could be found among the stalls inside the temples or at the open air markets set up temporarily for the occasion. It was truly a sight! (HCFC 1924, 2:14a–15a)

Fan Tsu-shu, writing in the first half of the nineteenth century, told a similar story. He said that pilgrims came primarily from the Soochow area in Kiangsu and the three prefectures of Hangchow, Chia-hsing, and Hu-chou in Chekiang. But pilgrims also came from Shantung, Anhui, Fukien, Kwangtung, and Kwangsi. There were two routes pilgrims took in coming to Hangchow: the northern route ran by the Grand Canal, disembarking at Sung-mu-ch'ang, and the southern route lay by the Yangtze River, disembarking at the banks of the Ch'ien-t'ang River. He put the figure of daily arrivals at several tens of thousands. Among all the commodities on sale, candles, incense, rosaries, and spirit money decorated with tinfoil headed the list. Hangchow and Shao-hsing were the two main places where these were produced.

According to the same witness, pilgrims from Shao-hsing had a custom of offering huge candles to the Upper T'ien-chu. These candles weighed several tens of catties (one catty is 1 1/3 pounds). Fastened to a scaffold, each was carried by two men and, accompanied by pilgrims who beat on drums and gongs, it was delivered to the monastery. The candles were extinguished soon after they were lighted. Pilgrims then carried the candles back home and used them to light the rooms where the silkworms were kept. Pilgrims would wind together several rolls or even several tens of rolls of white and yellow cloth and make this into a long rope. They would walk to T'ien-chu holding on to the rope and offer it to the monks. This was called "offering banners" (*she-fan*). The incense offered by pilgrims was of two kinds: powdered sandalwood incense (*t'an-hsiang*) and incense sticks (*hsien-hsiang*). The former could weigh several hundred catties, and the latter might consist of several thousand sticks. Having barely been lighted, they would be put out and turned over to the monks. Thus, during the pilgrimage season, the candles and incense that ended up in the temple's storehouse would amount to tens of thousands catties. That is why monks of the Upper T'ien-chu did not give the tonsure to strangers but kept the lineages within their own temple. Merchants who came to the fair from outside of Hangchow accounted for only 10 percent of those present. What the local merchants of Hangchow made in the spring pilgrimage season was better than their combined income from the other three seasons (HCFC 2:15 a-b).

The memory of Pilgrims' Fair was still very much alive for the monks, temple workers, innkeepers, and pilgrims that I interviewed during the pilgrimage season of 1987, which began in mid-February (soon after the Chinese New Year) and ended in mid-April (not long after the Ch'ing-ming festival).[3] By early May it was estimated that two million pilgrims had come to Hangchow. By 10:30 A.M. on March 18, the day before Kuan-yin's birthday, the ticket office of the Upper T'ien-chu sold 40,000 tickets (at 0.50 *yüan* each, the official exchange rate being $1 to 3 *yüan*). There were 3,000 people who "spent the night on the mountain" that evening. The abbot of the Upper T'ien-chu estimated that the income from the season was 600,000 *yüan.* A cadre who worked at the traffic control office overseeing the Grand Canal and Ch'ien-t'ang River transportation estimated that by March 6, 100,000 pilgrims were arriving every day. But because of Hangchow's limited capacity to accommodate them, only 30,000 were allowed to come into the city.

The Hangchow pilgrims came from southern Jiangsu and northern Chekiang, a pattern similar to that noted by earlier writers. In Jiangsu Province, while Soochow, Chang-shu, Wu-hsi, I-hsing and Hu-chou—all bordering Lake T'ai—supplied most pilgrims, a sizable number also came from K'un-shan, Chia-ting, and Chia-shan. In Chekiang Province, Chia-hsing, P'ing-hu, and Hai-yen—all situated in the northeast of Hangchow—supplied the greatest number of pilgrims. Jiangsu pilgrims came by chartered boats, spending two nights on the boat, one coming and one returning, and two nights at an inn in Hangchow. Chekiang pilgrims came by chartered buses and spent about three days and two nights in Hangchow.

The pilgrimage business had become so good in recent years that inns as well as steamship and bus companies were cooperating to serve the need for transportation and housing for Hangchow pilgrims. These people identified themselves as working for the "religious tourism enterprise" (*tsung-chiao lü-yu shih-yeh*). Soochow Steamship Company maintains a business office (*ying-yeh ch'u*) in Ch'ang-shu and a business station (*ying-yeh chan*), smaller in scale, in K'un-shan. From the record kept by the Ch'ang-shu office, one can trace the rapid increase in pilgrimage business since 1979.[4] Pilgrims from the same region would stay in the same inn season after season. The business station at K'un-shan had dispatched two persons to the Jade Spring Hotel near the West Lake since 1980. They would spend the two months of the season every year there in order to take care of pilgrims coming exclusively from K'un-shan. The hotel registry shows that during the two months starting from March 9, twenty-seven groups of pilgrims totaling 5,504 persons had stayed there. About 80 percent were women, and 50 percent were between fifty and sixty-five; 20 percent were over sixty-six years old.

This was similar to the data provided by the Mt. T'ien-mu Hotel, an inn catering exclusively to pilgrims from Ch'ang-shu. From February 6 to April 16, 11,592 pilgrims stayed there. They came to Hangchow on 138 boats. Fifty percent were between fifty and sixty-five; 30 percent were above sixty-five; and only 20 percent were under forty-nine. Since most of the pilgrims were farmers and silkworm raisers with a retirement age of fifty for women and sixty for men, this accounted for the overwhelming majority being over fifty. The cost of the trip for most pilgrims was borne by themselves, along with contributions made by their children. But some communes, like those in Wu-hsi, actually encouraged the retired farmers to go on pilgrimage, for they could have their "tour" expenses reimbursed upon return.

Pilgrims would come to Hangchow in groups (*hsiang-t'ui*) led by group leaders (*hsiang-t'ou*) who took care of practical matters. In addition, some groups also had spiritual leaders, called a *fo-t'ou* (Buddhist leader), who knew how to chant scriptures, sing pilgrims' songs, and go into a trance, becoming a spokesperson for Kuan-yin (*huo p'u-sa*, "living bodhisattva") and practicing healing among her pilgrim group.[5] There were four kinds of group leaders, depending on the size of the groups: chief group leader (*tsung hsiang-t'ou*) leading a group consisting of pilgrims coming from several villages; district group leader (*hsiang hsiang-t'ou*) leading pilgrims coming from the same district; village group leader (*ts'un hsiang-t'ou*) leading pilgrims coming from the same village, and finally, brigade group leader (*tui hsiang-t'ou*) leading pilgrims coming from the same work brigade. A large group could consist of as many as 250 to 300 pilgrims, and a small group about 10 to 20. The average group was about forty to sixty people.

The group leaders worked closely with the steamship companies and innkeepers. They were the ones who visited the homes of villagers to recruit potential pilgrims. Informants provided differing information concerning the economic benefits of being a group leader. According to the representatives from the K'un-shan business station of the Soochow Steamship Company, group leaders would buy incense from dealers in Wu-hsi and spirit money decorated with tinfoil from dealers in Hangchow in bulk and then sell them to pilgrims for a profit. For instance, they would charge .30 *fen* (about a dime) instead of .20 for a packet of incense. Since most pilgrims would spend four or five *yüan* on incense, this could add up. The manager of Jade Spring Hotel said that the group leader would get .05 *fen* each from the steamship company and the inn for every pilgrim she signed up. On the other hand, group leaders from P'ing-hu would receive two *yüan* from each pilgrim. This was referred to as the processing fee (*shou-hsü-fei*). For every 100 tickets she bought from the steamship company, she would receive four free tickets which could be sold for a profit. Thus, for organizing pilgrim groups of 500 people, the leader could get 1000 *yüan*, equivalent to an ordinary farmer's annual income. There were apparently considerable regional variations on this form of enterprise.

Pilgrims wore pieces of red cloth with their group names written in ink on their left arms. Women pilgrims also wore distinctive head coverings that announced their regional identities. Those from Soochow and K'un-shan covered their heads with towels. Those from elsewhere wore square kerchiefs of either green or deep blue. The colored yarn that bound their hair had symbolic meanings as well: red indicated that the husband was alive, white that he died recently, black that he died two years previously, and blue that he had died three years previously. It was desirable for a pilgrim to come to Hangchow for either three years or five years in a row—the first year for the benefit of her father, the second year for her mother, the third year for her husband, the fourth year for herself, and the fifth year for her children. They kept a vegetarian diet, starting with the evening meal before they left home and lasting until their return. If they came with their husbands, they had to sleep in separate quarters. Even their married children back home had to observe the taboo against eating meat and having sex, otherwise some untoward accident would happen to their traveling parents or mothers. They could resume their normal way of life only upon the safe return of the pilgrims.

When asked why they came to Hangchow, the usual answer was because this was the custom. They felt "at peace" only after they had offered incense at Upper T'ien-chu, knowing that the crops would yield a good harvest, the silkworms would be safe, and domestic animals and members of the household would be healthy and prosperous. The majority of informants did not mention *hsü-yüan* (vow-making) or *huan-yüan* (vow-fulfilling). In fact, coming to Hangchow was as much for fun as for religious reasons. They used the term *chieh Fo yu-ch'un* (enjoying a spring outing on the pretext of [worshiping] the Buddha) to describe their trip. But the sightseeing and shopping were reserved for the second day. The first thing they did after embarking from the boat or the bus would be to head for Upper T'ien-chu. The pilgrims' way leading to the temple from Ling-yin Ssu was about three *li* (one *li* is 0.576 mile) and it had to be covered on foot. Once in the Upper T'ien-chu, they busied themselves with lighting candles and incense, burning the spirit money, having their yellow incense bags and incense belts stamped with the seals of the monastery (one *yüan* per stamp), and having their own names and the names of their loved ones entered in the temple's subscription book (*yüan-pu*, the minimum being also one *yüan*). They usually spent half an hour to an hour doing these activities, depending on the size of the group. Even though the temple ground was filled with pilgrims, they always stayed with their own group and never mingled with others. The sense of *communitas* stressed so much by Victor Turner (1969, 1973, 1974) could be found among members of the same group, but was strikingly absent between groups. If it was a large group, composed of people from different villages, new friendships were often formed after spending four days together. The sense of camaraderie and fellowship was especially strong when I visited them at night in the inn. After they returned to the inn around four in the afternoon, they would relax in the evening by visiting each other, sharing gossip and laughter, exchanging stories about Kuan-yin, and singing pilgrims' songs together.

The stories they told about Kuan-yin all came from the *Precious Scroll of Hsiang-shan*, but with strong local coloring. For instance, they referred to the three Kuan-yin images enshrined in the three T'ien-chu temples as the "three sisters," with Princess Miao-shan identified as the Kuan-yin of the Upper T'ien-chu. They also mentioned that there were four manifestations of Kuan-yin, each identified with one month. The Kuan-yin of the second month was called Lotus-stepping Kuan-yin, that of the sixth month was Fish-stepping Kuan-yin,[6] that of the eighth month was the Thousand-armed Kuan-yin and that of the twelfth month was the Bare-footed Kuan-yin. The last one was so named because Kuan-yin, who originally had bound feet, had to practice religion for seven lives and only then succeeded in gaining the freedom to have natural, unbound feet. A song known as the "Great Kuan-yin Sūtra" ("Ta Kuan-yin ching") went like this:

Bodhisattva Kuan-yin has entered my body.
On the nineteenth day of the second month Mother gave birth to me.
On the nineteenth day of the sixth month I went up to Heaven.
Having arrived in Heaven, I turned around,
And sat in the main hall wearing a crown of pearls on my head.
Beating on the wooden fish I go everywhere.
Without a home and without any worries I worship the Third Sister.
The Third Sister does not want food to eat.
The Third Sister does not want clothes to wear.
The Third Sister wants to go to the Ninth Cloud beyond the empyrean to become a living immortal.
First, I want to cultivate an affinity with a thousand people.
Second, I want to cultivate an affinity with ten thousand people.
Immortals are originally born as ordinary mortals.
Yet ultimately ordinary mortals' hearts are not firm.

It is characteristic of all the pilgrims' songs, which are called *Kuan-yin ching* (Kuan-yin Sūtras), that the singer shifts in identity between that of a worshiper and that of Kuan-yin herself (see appendix B for more examples). This is perhaps because the songs were originally created by the living *p'u-sa* who became transformed into Kuan-yin in their trances.

Pilgrims come to Hangchow primarily because of Upper T'ien-chu. This has been the case for the last one thousand years. From all the evidence, the Upper T'ien-chu was the national pilgrimage center for Kuan-yin worship during the Southern Sung. Although it continued to be visited by pilgrims in the Ming and Ch'ing, P'u-t'o eventually took it over and succeeded in becoming the only true home of Kuan-yin in this period. How this came to pass will be the substance of the rest of this chapter.

I examine the processes and mechanisms of the creation of P'u-t'o as Mt. Potalaka. On one level, there is the mythical and ideological construction of the island in order to fit the model provided by the scriptures—thus the transfiguration of the landscape. Specific spots became singled out and identified as places of numinosity and efficacy. The foremost of these places was the Ch'ao-yin Tung (Cave of Tidal Sounds) where Kuan-yin appeared to vision-seeking pilgrims. Other places, with time, were also added to the list: the Diamond Boulder and the Purple Bamboo Grove both signified one of Kuan-yin's places of preaching; the Dragon Princess' Cave, Sudhana's Rock, and the Parrot Stone, all located near the Cave of Tidal Sounds, provided additional places for pilgrims to make divine contact, when the three attendants of Kuan-yin began to appear with the Bodhisattva in pilgrims' visions.

On another level, I examine how P'u-t'o became physically established, was built up, destroyed, and then rebuilt again in several cycles. Each time P'u-t'o rose up from the ruins, new monasteries became established under new leaderships. New spots of efficacy were discovered and promoted. For instance, the Fan-yin Tung (Cave of Brahmā's Voice), situated near the Northern Monastery, became known as a place where Kuan-yin appeared to pilgrims late in the sixteenth century, during a major cycle of rebuilding. It lent prestige to the Northern Monastery, and with the rising fame of the latter, more pilgrims came to this cave instead of the earlier and more famous Cave of Tidal Sounds for visions of Kuan-yin. The physical building and rebuilding of the site tell us much about the dynamics between the pilgrims, within whose ranks we count all the founders of the monasteries and the island itself.

P'u-t'o Shan

While P'u-t'o Shan literally means Mt. P'u-t'o, it is actually the name given to one of the many small islands forming the Chou-shan Archipelago. It is long and narrow, 8.6 miles from north to south and 3.5 miles from east to west, and the total size is 12.76 square miles. Ningpo is 70 miles due west. The development of P'u-t'o was very much connected with the emergence of Ningpo as an international and national trading center. During the Sui and T'ang, two changes contributed to causing the new events. The construction of the Grand Canal extended the main overland trading route to the east coast. By linking the producing south with the consuming north, this also stimulated the economic development of the Lower Yangtze delta. In the meantime, as a result of improvements in navigation following the invention of the steering compass, the maritime trade that connected the Yangtze delta with ports along the Chinese coast, in East Asia, and on the Indian Ocean became very active.

Ningpo reaped the benefits of both changes. Through waterways linking it with Hangchow, Ningpo became in effect the southern terminus of the Grand Canal. Because of shallows and tidal currents in the Hangchow Bay, ocean-going junks from southeastern China had to transfer their cargoes at Ningpo for smaller boats sailing for Hangchow and other inland ports. For the same reason, products from the Lower Yangtze regions had to be shipped to Ningpo for overseas trade. Because of its important location, the Office of Overseas Trade (Shih-po ssu), which supervised the coastal trade and controlled the maritime tribute from Korea and Japan, was located in Ningpo almost continuously from 992 to 1523. By the Southern Sung, shipping flourished and both international and domestic markets had expanded. Ningpo and the region near it, including P'u-t'o, were greatly stimulated by these developments. Among the commodities traded, incense was mentioned with frequency and Ningpo artisans were famous for making Buddhist altar-fittings (Shiba 1977:392–410).

The island, though small, was thus strategically placed in the crossroads of sea traffic between north and south China as well as between China and Japan. In the early T'ang, Japanese ships came to China by the northern route, arriving in Shantung via the Korean peninsula. But after the mid-T'ang, when Silla united the three kingdoms, Japanese ships began to use the southern route, arriving at Ningpo and Yüeh-chou (present-day Yang-chou) via Okinawa. The latter route would take them, if they sailed under northeast winds, five days and five nights to arrive at Shen-chia-men, the harbor next to P'u-t'o. They then had to wait there to be inspected by the Chinese customs before they could proceed. On their return trip to Japan, they also waited at P'u-t'o for good sailing conditions. Thus, during the Ming and Ch'ing, the time when P'u-t'o became a national Kuan-yin pilgrimage site, it was also an important international maritime trading port (Hsü 1987:135–37).

The island is hilly, dotted with many low-lying mountains and natural rock formations. To highlight the mountain-like features of the island, writers of the P'u-t'o gazetteers painstakingly differentiated the various types of elevations of the natural landscape. The most recent (1924) edition of the gazetteer provides the following categories: sixteen hills (*shan*), eighteen peaks (*feng*), twelve hillocks (*ling*), fifteen rocks (*yen*), and thirty stones (*shih*).

Before its founding as a Buddhist holy site in the T'ang, the island seems to have enjoyed the reputation of being a Taoist haven. The most well-known mountain on the island was Mei-ch'en Feng, the highest peak on the southern part of the island. It was named after Mei Fu, who lived at the end of the first century B.C.E. during the reign of Emperor Cheng of the Han dynasty and was reported to have sought refuge on the island and practiced alchemy near the mountain. The monk Ju-chung built Mei-fu Shrine to commemorate him in the late Ming. In fact, the whole island was called Mei-ch'en in pre-Sung sources before it became known exclusively as P'u-t'o. Aside from Mei Fu, other Taoist luminaries were also connected with the island. An Chi-sheng escaped from the chaos on the mainland at the end of the Ch'in (249–209 C.E.) and went there to practice alchemy. Once when he was drunk, he is supposed to have painted peach blossoms by splattering ink on the rocks. This legend accounts for the name Mt. Peach Blossoms (T'ao-hua Shan), situated southwest of the Southern Monastery. Tradition claims that if one looks carefully, one can still discern the faint outlines of the peach blossoms. Ko Hung Well, on the other hand, was named after the famous Taoist (253–333? C.E.).[7]

Gazetteer compilers acknowledged the island's connection with Taoism. Not only did they accept the island's pre-Buddhist past, they actually seem to have taken some delight in exploiting this reputation. Like the fabulous isles of the blessed, P'eng-lai and Fang-chang, P'u-t'o was seen as hallowed ground. But unlike the former, which are impossible to locate, one can travel to P'u-t'o. Sheng Hsi-ming, the compiler of the earliest gazetteer of P'u-t'o (1361) expressed this sentiment when he declared:

> P'eng-lai and Fang-chang are reported to lie in the mythical waters, but they can be reached only by flying immortals. In the past, both the First Emperor of Chin and Emperor Wu of the Han tried to find them for many years. They sent expeditionary parties far and wide. But with so much toiling of the spirit and laboring with the body, the project was like chasing after a shadow and trying to capture the wind. The legendary islands could never be located. Now Mt. Small White Flowers [P'u-t'o] is not far from Ssu-ming [Ningpo]. It is a place where sages and worthies hid their traces. Although it is situated amidst terrifying waves and frightening tides, if one sails with the wind, one can reach it within a few days (T 51:1136a-b).

The Buddhist "takeover" of the island, if indeed one may use such a term, was, however, apparently a peaceful one. There is no evidence of a struggle with any previously existing Taoist religious authority. The difficulty was, therefore, not how to subdue or supplant an earlier cult, but how to legitimize new claims once made. During the eleventh and twelfth centuries, the identity drawn between P'u-t'o and Potalaka was already taken for granted by a number of educated people, both monks and literati, and this led to its legitimatization. Nanhu Tao-yin, who wrote *The Record of A Grass Hut* (Ts'ao-an lu) during 1165–

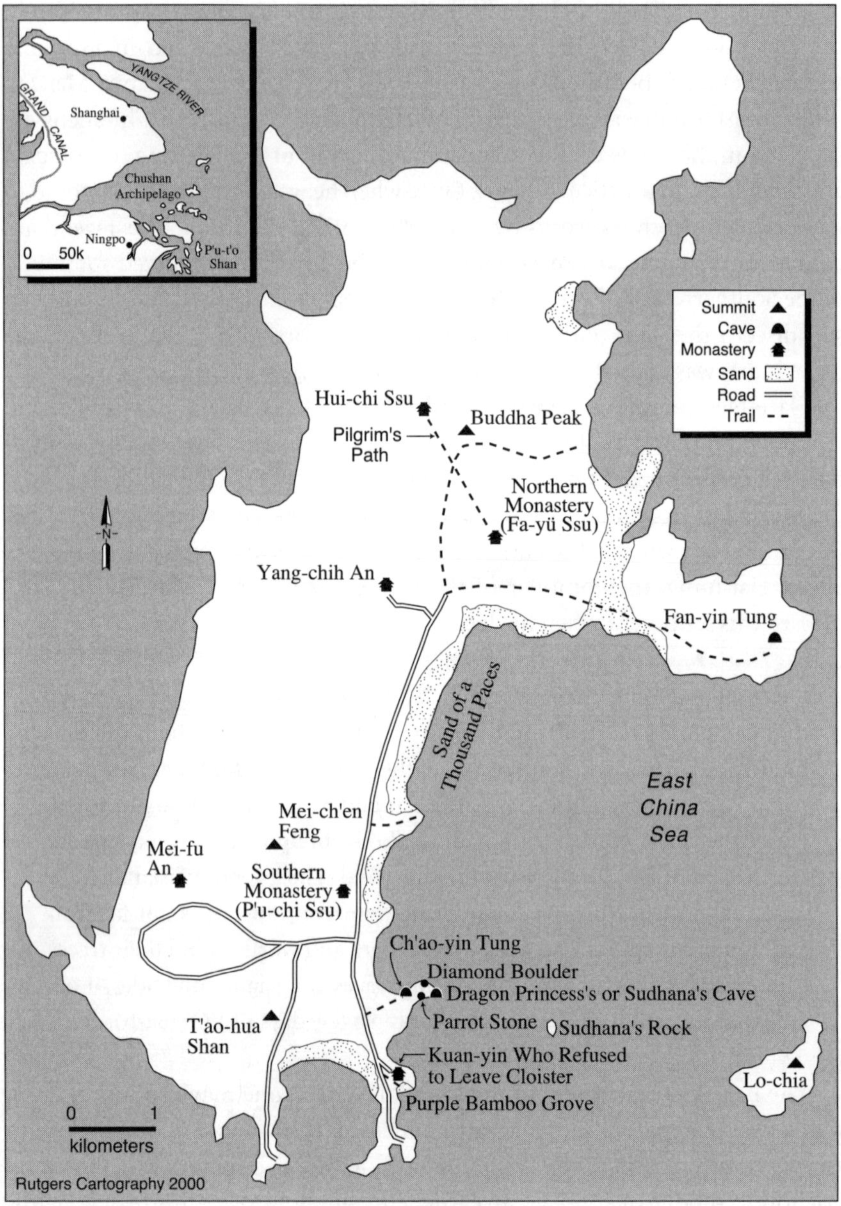
YANGTZE RIVER
GRAND CANAL
Shanghai
Chushan Archipelago
Ningpo
P'u-t'o Shan
0 50k
Summit
Cave
Monastery
Sand
Road
Trail
Hui-chi Ssu
Buddha Peak
Pilgrim's Path
Northern Monastery (Fa-yü Ssu)
Yang-chih An
Fan-yin Tung
Sand of a Thousand Paces
East China Sea
Mei-ch'en Feng
Mei-fu An
Southern Monastery (P'u-chi Ssu)
Ch'ao-yin Tung
Diamond Boulder
Dragon Princess's or Sudhana's Cave
Parrot Stone
Sudhana's Rock
T'ao-hua Shan
Kuan-yin Who Refused to Leave Cloister
Purple Bamboo Grove
Lo-chia
0 1
kilometers
Rutgers Cartography 2000

Map 3. P'u-t'o Shan.

1173, made such an identification. *Fo-tsu t'ung-chi* quoted the following passage from it:

> Mt. P'u-t'o is in the great ocean. It is situated southeast of Chin [Ningpo], about six hundred miles by the water route. It is no other than the mountain called Potalaka which is declared by the *Hua-yen ching* to be the "isolated place at the end of the ocean" where "Kuan-yin Bodhisattva lives". It is also no other than Mt. Potalaka, which is declared by the *Ta-pei ching* to be the place where the palace of Kuan-yin, in which Śākyamuni Buddha reveals the heart-seal of the Mantra of Great Compassion, is located. The Cave of Tidal Sounds is located on the island. Ocean tides pound in and rush out day and night, making deafening noises. In front of the cave there is a stone bridge on which pilgrims stand facing the cave to pray. If they are sincere, they can sometimes see the Great Being sitting there leisurely. Or they will see Sudhana come forward as if to welcome them. Other times one will only see a pure vase of green jade, or the *kalavinka* bird flying as if performing a dance. Some six or seven *li* from the cave there is a large monastery. Merchants, diplomats, and tribute bearers sailing to and from the various countries in the Eastern Sea come here to pray for safety. Those who are reverential and sincere all receive protection without fail (T 49:388b-c).

Like in most early accounts of the island, the Cave of Tidal Sounds was singled out for emphasis, for this was the place where Kuan-yin appeared to pilgrims. Merchants and diplomats receive special mention, for they were the ones responsible for building the island into a pilgrimage site and who continued to serve as its chief patrons through the ages.

From the Sung on, P'u-t'o also began to be written about by important officials, famous literati, and well-known personages who personally came to the island. A large body of poems and commemorative essays left by these pilgrim-visitors to the island are collected in the island gazetteers. Wang An-shih (1021–1086), the Sung political reformer, Chao Meng-fu (1254–1322), the celebrated Yüan painter, and Ch'en Hsien-chang (1428–1500), the Ming Neo-Confucian thinker, are just three notable examples culled from a long roster of writers who recorded their impressions about the island. While their writings undoubtedly contributed to the fame of the island (and for this reason were carefully preserved by the gazetteer compilers), most of the poems are about the natural setting and give impressionistic and formulaic descriptions of the scenery. Very frequently, a set of poems would be composed to celebrate the ten or twelve "views" (*ching*) of the island. Such literary exercises follow an established convention and rarely reveal the writer's inner feelings. Wang An-shih's poem entitled "On Visiting Mt. Lo-chia" is a typical example of this genre.

> *The layout of the mountain overpowers the ocean,*
> *The Ch'an palace is established at this place.*
> *Odors of fish and dragons do not reach here.*
> *But the sun and the moon shine on the island before anywhere else.*
> *The colors of the trees reveal the coming of autumn,*
> *The sound of bells is answered by that of waves.*
> *I never expected that I could use the convenience of my tour of duty*
> *To momentarily brush away the stains of red dust. (PTSC 1607, 5:389)*

Although monks, merchants, diplomats, and officials began to come to P'u-t'o in the Sung and some of them even celebrated it in their writings, the first history of P'u-t'o was not written until 1361. Its author, Sheng Hsi-ming, was the grandson of an immigrant from Kashmir. Sheng traveled widely and was particularly interested in the cult of Kuan-yin. He knew some of the noted Kuan-yin cultic centers on the mainland, including Southern Mt. Wu-t'ai and Upper T'ien-chu, but even he was initially skeptical about P'u-t'o's claim to be Mt. Potalaka until he was converted by a miraculous dream. Sheng then wrote a short history of the island, providing scriptural bases and founding myths for the identification.

As mentioned previously, Sheng's is the first of eight gazetteers of the island. Together these might form one of the most persuasive means of transforming the island into Mt. Potalaka and serve as one of the most influential media proclaiming and broadcasting this fact. Even though the gazetteers range across some six hundred years, they form a self-contained cumulative tradition. Later ones refer to and quote from earlier ones, while each, of course, omits old materials and adds new, just as the island underwent changes and evolved into a national and international pilgrimage center. Since they constitute one of the most useful primary sources for this chapter, I would like to discuss the general characteristics and contents of these documents.[8]

Mountain Gazetteers

As Timothy Brook has pointed out, mountain gazetteers, like the institutional and topographical gazetteers into which broader categories they fall, were written in large number during the Ming and Ch'ing.

> They have antecedents from the Song, which is when the term *zhi* comes into use for identifying gazetteers generally, though it is not until the six-

> teenth century that topographical and institutional gazetteers become common. . . . In the sixteenth century, the production of topographical and institutional gazetteers becomes regular, increasing steadily through the Jiajing and Wanli eras, and rising markedly during the opening decades of the seventeenth century. A second peak of greater magnitude is reached at the end of that century. Smaller rises occur during the middle of the eighteenth century and again at the beginning of the nineteenth, though the most striking peak comes in the closing decades of that century. (Brook 1988:52)

While the compilation of P'u-t'o gazetteers follows the same general pattern, the specific dates coincide with the cycles of building and rebuilding of the island center. Gazetteers of P'u-t'o were written by pilgrims and were about pilgrims. Among the compilers, we find local magistrates, naval commanders, and men of letters who either wrote on their own account or at the request of resident abbots. With the exception of Sheng, the first gazetteer writer, all of them had gone to P'u-t'o as pilgrims. I think this is a point that needs stressing, for it demonstrates most dramatically the dynamics between pilgrims and sites. Sites attracted pilgrims who in turn promoted the sites and thereby attracted more pilgrims. Gazetteer writers, through the printed word, might reach a broader audience (mostly monks and members of the elite). Other ordinary pilgrims, even those who were illiterate, might also promote the fame of a site through word of mouth by repeating stories they heard or marvels they themselves witnessed while there.

Like most works of this genre, the monastic gazetteers of P'u-t'o provide a description of the topographical layout of the land, a history of the monasteries, a record of royal patronages and important donations, biographies of abbots and other famous residents, flora and fauna, and poems and essays about the island written by pilgrim-visitors. These are not entirely impersonal, objective, and factual descriptions. On the contrary, there is, one might say, an almost confessional air about them. Like the collections of miracle tales about Kuan-yin discussed earlier in this book, the gazetteers of P'u-t'o can be regarded as a type of testimonial literature. Because their aim was not only to inform but to convince, they contained extensive collections of miracles wrought by Kuan-yin both in founding the island and in reviving it after successive cycles of decline and recovery. Even nature was miraculously transformed. For instance, the gazetteers inform us that there were no tigers present on the island. Although one or two might occasionally land after swimming across the ocean from the mainland, they usually never stayed long. Snakes, on the other hand, were plentiful but never harmed people (PTSC 1832, 12:4b-5a).

P'u-t'o gazetteers contain another type of invaluable material that provides further evidence of pilgrims' effort to transfigure the landscape and create a sacred place out of natural space: the collection of epigraphical records left by pilgrims describing their visions of Kuan-yin or miraculous deeds performed by Kuan-yin for the benefit of themselves or others whom they knew. Since the buildings on the island were damaged by wars and piracy many times in the last thousand years, all of the stone stelae on which these testimonies had originally been carved were destroyed. The transcriptions kept in the gazetteers furnish the only clue to a possibly extensive body of devotional literature. In this regard, P'u-t'o gazetteers definitely do not fit Brook's observation that "monastic gazetteers, though intended in part to be reading matter for the faithful, were not devotional publications" (1988:55).

The long history of the creation, establishment, and development of P'u-t'o as the Chinese Mt. Potalaka was not only reflected in the successive compiling of gazetteers, but was first proclaimed and then promoted by the compilers. Indeed, when Sheng came to write the first account of the island in 1361, he had to overcome his own doubt about the identity of P'u-t'o as Mt. Potalaka. The difficulty for him, as no doubt for others, was the discrepancy between the mythical grandeur of the sacred island home and the prosaic reality represented by the remote and desolate P'u-t'o.

Sheng wrote that when he made a pilgrimage to Mt. Wu-t'ai, he heard from a Tibetan master the description of Mt. Potalaka found in a "barbarian" (*fan*) book, *An Account of Travel to Mt. Potalaka* (Pu-t'o-lo-chia shan hsing-ch'eng chi). Sheng then briefly summarized what he remembered from the book. This fantastic journey must begin in India. One should first go to the country called Ke-ts'u-to-chia-lo and circumambulate the stūpa there day and night. Eventually one would be told the direction and duration of the journey. The pilgrim would travel through a country inhabited by yakṣas who would entice him with food, drink, music, and sights. He should resolutely refuse these temptations. After this he would encounter other types of demonic obstructions, but the pilgrim should be of good courage and not give up. He would then come to a jeweled pond from which he could drink sweet dew and become strengthened. During the rest of the journey he would encounter marvelous experiences. He should not linger and become attached to these, but must push on. When he approaches the holy land, he will be met by a horse-headed Vajrapāṇi who will lead him to the entrance to a grotto. There he will be comforted and encouraged by holy Tārās. Finally he goes inside the grotto. Purple bamboo and sandalwood trees grow in abundance, clear streams flow, and tender grasses cover the ground like soft cushions. Many bodhisattvas keep company with Kuan-yin who, surrounded by heavenly dragons, lives here all the time. When the pilgrim arrives here, he will receive the teaching of the wonderful Dharma from Kuan-yin and become enlightened. Whatever he desires, it will also come true.[9]

This account is clearly mythical. The actual location of Potalaka has fascinated people over the ages. Hsüan-tsang described it as being east of the Malaya mountains in south India (Watters 1905, vol. 2:229; Beal 1884, vol. 2:233).[10] However, the account given to Sheng does not mention this. It fact, it does not specify the location of Potalaka at all. Still, Sheng was much impressed by this account and felt that Mt. Potalaka was definitely not an ordinary realm that could be reached by anyone easily. Later he came to Ningpo and several times friends invited him to go to P'u-t'o on pilgrimage. But because he doubted that the island could be Potalaka, he never made the trip. One evening he dreamt of a person who said to him,

> Have you forgotten what the scriptures say? Bodhisattvas are skillful in manifesting in many places, for wherever people seek them propelled by their faith, that will be the place where bodhisattvas manifest themselves. This is like when one digs a well for water and finds water, but water is actually present everywhere. Furthermore, this cave [the Cave of Tidal Sounds] has been noted for miraculous happenings for a very long time. Spirit-like, transformative, free and comforting, it is indeed not able to be fathomed by an ordinary intelligence.

After Sheng woke up, he realized that bodhisattvas could indeed be present anywhere. He then gathered information about P'u-t'o and wrote a history of the place, appending stories to it about other cultic centers of Kuan-yin worship located on the mainland (PTSC 1361, T. 51:1138c–1139a).

Sheng mentioned Upper T'ien-chu and related a miracle that had happened there. In 1360 Hangchow suffered from the ravages of war and all the monasteries on the Western Hill were destroyed. No one knew what happened to the image of Kuan-yin housed in Upper T'ien-chu. K'ang Li, the grand councillor, offered gold as a reward and someone found the image among some wild grasses. After a propitious date was determined through divination, K'ang fasted, and followed by officials, soldiers and townspeople, he went outside the north gate of the city on foot to welcome the image and installed it in Western Heaven Monastery (Hsi-t'ien Ssu) on Mt. Ch'ing-ping, a temple he established himself. On that day, the holy image issued forth a bright light, which, piercing through clouds, became separated into three beams. One pointed far to the east, indicating the direction of P'u-t'o. The second beam pointed toward Upper T'ien-chu, and the third beam rested on Hsi-t'ien Ssu. The main point of this tale was of course to establish a connection between these two important centers of Kuan-yin worship.[11] It is highly significant that Sheng chose to write an account of P'u-t'o one year after this miracle took place and that he used this story to link P'u-t'o with Upper T'ien-chu, perhaps the most famous Kuan-yin cultic center on the mainland.[12]

Two gazetteers were compiled during the Wan-li period of the late Ming, a time of major revival for P'u-t'o. The first was compiled by Hou Chi-kao, Regional Commander of Ting-hai, in 1589, some two hundred and thirty years later than the one by Sheng. Even though it bore Hou's name, it was actually written by T'u Lung (1542–1605, DMB:1324–1327), poet, dramatist, and lay Buddhist. It was first published in 1598, some nine years after its completion, but apparently did not receive wide circulation. It consists of six fascicles: the first two contain imperial edicts, maps, scriptural references, miracles, and histories of the monasteries, while the last four are devoted exclusively to literary works about the island. The second, similar in format but named "newly-amended" (*ch'ung-hsiu*), was compiled by Chou Ying-pin, who was a vice minister of personnel in 1607. The justification for compiling this gazetteer so soon was that "whereas the earlier gazetteer emphasizes the mountain in order to make known the efficacy of the Buddha, this gazetteer emphasizes the monastery in order to glorify the imperial gift" (5–6). Chang Sui, a eunuch serving as the director of one of the twelve directorates for imperial accoutrements, wanted to celebrate the completion of the imperially sponsored rebuilding of the Southern Monastery.

A quick summary of the fortunes of P'u-t'o in the previous centuries and a closer examination into the causes for Emperor Wan-li's interest in the island are in order. The strategic location of P'u-t'o in the open seas, which had stood her in good stead in earlier times, created problems for her security in the Ming. In 1387, at the suggestion of T'ang Ho, the Duke of Hsin (1326–1395; DMB:1248–1251), Emperor T'ai-tsu ordered that the entire population of the island be moved inland in order to strengthen the coastal defenses against the Japanese pirates. The image of Kuan-yin was also transported to a temple in Ningpo. During the reign of Shih-tsung (1522–1566) the coastal regions again suffered from the disturbances of Japanese pirates and their Chinese collaborators who, under the leadership of Wang Chih, totally destroyed P'u-t'o. More than three hundred temples on the island fell into ruins. During this long period of darkness in the first half of the sixteenth century, only one temple managed to remain standing, where one monk and one servant stayed to keep the incense burning. The situation did not change for the better until the pirate chief was captured in 1557.

In his preface to the 1589 gazetteer, Hou Chi-kao credited their success in capturing Wang to Kuan-yin's help. As if to signify the return to peace and prosperity, on the seventh day of the seventh month in 1586 auspicious lotuses had appeared in bloom in Empress Dowager Li's palace in Peking. Two days later, on the ninth day, another unusual type of lotus again bloomed in the palace. Emperor Wan-li was greatly pleased and instructed the eunuchs to invite officials to view the flowers and write poems about them. His mother, Empress Dowager Li, dispatched eunuchs twice to sail for P'u-t'o, carrying with them images of Kuan-yin, who was the chief deity of the lotus clan in the Womb-treasury Maṇḍala of Esoteric Buddhism, forty-two cases of the newly printed additions to the Tripiṭaka, and 637 cases of scriptures from the Buddhist canon, printed under imperial sponsorship earlier that same year. The pilgrimage was made in order to thank Kuan-yin for the favors received and to pray for her continued protection.

The connection between the miraculous appearances of rare lotuses in the palace and imperial patronage of P'u-t'o was clear and direct. The lotuses were taken as an auspicious sign from Kuan-yin. They might also have served as the religious basis for the cult of the "Nine-lotus Bodhisattva" (Chiu-lien P'u-sa), which was vigorously promoted by Emperor Wan-li and his mother. As we read in chapter 3, stelae with inscribed images of this bodhisattva, modeled closely after Kuan-yin, have survived.

Emperor Wan-li and his mother, while being benefactors of Buddhism and popular religion in general, continued to shower favors on P'u-t'o for the next three decades. Twice in 1599 P'u-t'o was chosen to receive two more sets of the Tripiṭaka. Among the collection of scriptures contained in the forty-two cases forming the "continuation of the Tripiṭaka" (*hsü-tsang*), which were printed under their sponsorship, pride of place was occupied by a Ming indigenous scripture glorifying Kuan-yin. This is the *Sūtra of the Great Merit of Foremost Rarity Spoken by the Buddha which the Jen-hsiao Empress of the Great Ming Received in a Dream*, which I discussed in chapter 3. Recall that this text had a very unusual origin, for it claimed to have been transcribed by Empress Hsü (1362–1407), wife of Emperor Yung-lo, as a result of a revelation she received from Kuan-yin in her dream.

Indigenous sūtras glorifying Kuan-yin had a long history in China. This tradition seems to have enjoyed a major renaissance in the Ming. Perhaps inspired by the example of Empress Hsü, Emperor Wan-li and his mother also created and promoted a scripture devoted to the Nine-lotus Bodhisattva, an emanation of Kuan-yin. It was not introduced into the Tripiṭaka, and therefore was not as widely known. One extant copy of this sūtra, entitled *Fo-shuo Ta-tz'u Chih-sheng Chiu-lien P'u-sa hua-shen tu-shih chen-ching* (The True Scripture of the Great Compassionate and Utmost Holy Nine-lotus Bodhisattva's Transforming the Body in order to Save the World as Spoken by the Buddha), was printed in 1616 by the order of Emperor Wan-li. This has also been discussed in chapter 3. Advertisements of the miraculous lotus flowers, the carving of stelae and printing of new sūtras promoting the cult of the Nine Lotus Bodhisattva, and the energetic patronage of P'u-t'o under the Wan-li emperor and his mother can be seen as interconnected parts of a grand plan. Religious faith and the desire for self-aggrandizement were probably inextricably entwined within their motives.

Before I turn to the four gazetteers compiled during the Ch'ing, I would like to comment on an account of a trip to P'u- t'o that Hou Chi-kao made in the spring of 1587, written down the following year, one year before he compiled the gazetteer. The confessional tone makes this account resemble that of Chang Shang-yin's trips to Mt. Wu-t'ai, as discussed by Robert Gimello (1992). It differs radically from other travel accounts written by the literati, who usually took a detached and even ironical stance toward pilgrimage sites (discussed later in this chapter and by Wu Pei-yi 1992). For this reason, it is understandable that these other travel accounts were not collected by the gazetteer compilers.

Hou starts out by identifying the island as the place where Kuan-yin preached the Dharma. Since the T'ang, people had vied with each other in coming here to pay homage to the bodhisattva. Hou's own family had lived by the ocean for many generations and since he was little he had heard about the sacred island from his elders and admired it from the bottom of his heart. But not until the spring of 1587 when he was appointed governor of Chekiang did he finally have a chance to make a pilgrimage to P'u-t'o and thereby fulfill his life-long dream. He catalogued the famous spots of the island, singling out the Cave of Tidal Sounds and Sudhana's Cave, both identified in the gazetteer, as the places where Kuan-yin would appear to pilgrims who prayed with sincerity. Displaying his familiarity with the *Lotus Sūtra*, he wrote, "Feeling ashamed on account of my military status, I did not dare to look inside the caves because I have not left the 'burning house.'" Hou mentioned the names of two important abbots, Chen-sung and Ta-chih, who were responsible for reviving Pao-t'o (the former name for the Southern Monastery) and establishing Hai-ch'ao (the former name for the Northern Monastery). He then related his interest in collecting portraits of Kuan-yin. He had earlier obtained a portrait done by the famous T'ang painter Wu Tao-tzu and later, another one by Yen Li-pen, another famous T'ang painter. He characterized the former as simple and elegant, and the latter as splendid and beautiful. He had both portraits inscribed on stone stelae for future generations (PTSC 1598, 3:5a-11a). Even though these have not survived, the stele with Yen Li-pen's drawing of Kuan-yin apparently served as the basis for another stele carved in 1608 by Liu Pen-wen, an Assistant Regional Commander, which he gave as offering of thanks to Willow Branch Shrine (Yang-chih An), a temple he established after his prayer for an heir was answered (PTSC 1924:572). Popularly known as Willow Branch Kuan-yin, it is one of the few treasures remaining on P'u-t'o today and its reproductions are offered to present-day pilgrims as souvenirs.

Interest in the images and portraits of Kuan-yin and efforts to preserve and disseminate them were important mechanisms of linking Kuan-yin with P'u-t'o. As we shall see in later sections of this chapter, wonder-working images of Kuan-yin first brought the island to notice. Miraculous visions of her attracted pilgrims and the eventual emergence of P'u-t'o as Mt. Potalaka was concretely symbolized by a new iconography known as Nan-hai Kuan-yin (Kuan-yin of the South Sea).

All four gazetteers compiled during the Ch'ing were entitled *Nan-hai P'u-t'o Shan chih* (Gazetteer of Potalaka of the South Sea), for by this time the identity between P'u-t'o and Potalaka had become an accepted reality. At the end of the Ming, P'u-t'o had suffered from the havoc wrought by pirates, forces resisting the Southern Ming regime, and "Red Barbarians" (Dutch traders), who all regarded the island as a desirable headquarters. The government carried out the so-called "sea prohibition" as a defense measure and, in 1671 again moved the population inland. But in 1684 Taiwan and P'eng-hu were recaptured and five years later, Emperor K'ang-hsi granted the request to restore P'u-t'o submitted by Huang Ta-lai, the regional commander of Ting-hai.[13] The next year, Lan Li, Huang's successor, installed Ch'ao-yin, a very able monk, as the abbot of the Southern Monastery. K'ang-hsi renewed his support by giving more gold and bestowing the new name P'u-chi (Universal Salvation) on the monastery in 1699. One hundred years later, Hsing-t'ung, a monk originally from Mt. Omei, became the abbot. He discovered a broken stele of Ta-chih's tomb inscription on the abandoned site of Fa-yü Ssu or the Northern Monastery. He was also told about Ta-chih's prediction that the temple would be revived one hundred years after his death. Hsing-t'ung took all of these signs as omens of better days. He sent his disciple Ming-i to Fukien for donations of timber. General Shih Shih-piao dispatched battleships to transport the more than thousand pieces of timber back to P'u-t'o to rebuild Fa-yü (PTSC 1924, 375–377). P'u-t'o continued to receive imperial patronage under emperors Yung-cheng and Ch'ien-lung and eventually became more famous than before. Hui-chi Ssu, commonly known as Buddha Peak Monastery, the third largest monastery on the island, was erected in 1793, the fifty-eighth year of Ch'ien-lung. P'u-t'o had reached the zenith of its fame.

At the time when P'u-t'o had to compete with mainland pilgrimage centers and strive to establish her identity as Potalaka, there was only one major monastery on the island. During the late Ming and particularly in the Ch'ing, a second major monastery became increasingly important. To differentiate between the two, P'u-chi became known as the Southern Monastery and Fa-yü, the latecomer, was called the Northern Monastery. When P'u-t'o reached the height of its development and achieved public recognition as Potalaka, competition between these two major monasteries also began to emerge. The compilation of the four gazetteers in the Ch'ing reflected this rivalry. The first two, both in fifteen fascicles, were compiled in 1698 and 1705, during the reign of K'ang-hsi, and the next two, both in twenty fascicles, were compiled in 1739, during the reign of Ch'ien-lung, and in 1832, during the reign of Tao-kuang, just twenty years before the upheavals brought about by the T'ai-ping Rebellion in the 1850s to the 1860s.

The 1698 gazetteer was compiled at the request of two successive regional commanders of Ting-hai, who campaigned for the rebuilding of P'u-t'o. Kao Shih-ch'i, the vice-minister of the Ministry of Rites and a devout Buddhist believer, also requested the compilation. Although this gazetteer was jointly sponsored by the two monasteries, Fa-yü Monastery published it immediately, while the abbot of P'u-chi sponsored a second, revised edition in 1705.

The 1739 gazetteer was compiled by a Han-lin academician, at the request of the abbot of Fa-yü Monastery. The last Ch'ing gazetteer, compiled in 1832, was written at the request of P'u-chi. Each had a partisan editorial stance and gave more emphasis to the sponsoring monastery.[14] On the other hand, because the two monasteries competed, they served as watchdogs for each other. In the process, materials blatantly damaging to either one would be screened out. Therefore, an article originally contained in the 1598 gazetteer that gave a very biased and uncritical depiction of the abbot of the Southern Monastery was deleted from all Ch'ing editions.[15]

Gazetteers preserved valuable information about the process through which P'u-t'o island became transformed into Mt. Potalaka. They constitute an important mechanism to legitimize this claim, for they also served as an influential medium to broadcast the island's fame and attract more pilgrims. Many actors appear in their pages: emperors and empresses, officials and writers, monks and ascetics, ordinary men and women. But looming above all of them is Kuan-yin him/herself. For it was with the miraculous manifestation of Kuan-yin's efficacy that the island first entered the stage of history. In the rest of this chapter, let us look at a few key elements in the successful creation of P'u-t'o as Potalaka: the founding myths of P'u-t'o, pilgrims' visions of Kuan-yin, pilgrims' testimony regarding Kuan-yin's miracles, and the promotional activities of resident monks and ascetics.

Founding Myths

All gazetteers of P'u-t'o have a section called "efficacious wonders" (*ling-i*) that reported miracles performed by Kuan-yin to indicate the special status of the island. These myths were transmitted through oral traditions by pilgrims or had earlier been gathered in collections of miracle tales. For these reasons, even ordinary pilgrims who usually had no access to mountain gazetteers might be familiar with these stories. The founding myths of P'u-t'o invariably head this section of P'u-t'o gazetteers. They, like many of the miracles found here, are about Kuan-yin's theophanies. In this sense, the promoters of P'u-t'o would agree with Mircea Eliade when he said, "Every sacred space implies a hierophany, an irruption of the sacred that results in detaching a territory from the surrounding cosmic milieu and making it qualitatively different" (1959: 26). Moreover, they would also, again like Eliade, stress that it was Kuan-yin who revealed him/herself and the island to pilgrims, not the pilgrims who discovered the deity on the island and thereafter built it into a sacred site. But perhaps to see things in such dichotomistic terms is to miss the complexity of the real situation. Just as one cannot declare dogmatically that either the site was intrinsically efficacious, or that efficacy was imposed from outside, a more fruitful way of proceeding might be found in examining the mutuality of both claims.

The founding myths of P'u-t'o, like those we have seen in relationship with Upper T'ien-chu, contain Kuan-yin's epiphanies or miraculous images. One traces the founding of P'u-t'o to Emperor Wen-tsung of the T'ang (r. 827–939). Although this story had more to do with the spread of the cult of Kuan-yin in T'ang China, it was nevertheless linked with the special destiny of the island. This is the miracle about the Clam-dwelling Kuan-yin discussed in chapter 4. The 1739 gazetteer concludes, "The founding of Lo-chia [P'u-t'o] began with this" (5:1).[16]

Two other founding myths point to the second half of the ninth century as the time when P'u-t'o began to be associated with Kuan-yin. Both are connected with foreign monks, the first possibly Indian and the second Japanese. Considering the need to affirm the island's identity as the mythical Mt. Potalaka, the gazetteers' special interest in highlighting its "foreign connection" might not be fortuitous. For if P'u-t'o was indeed the Potalaka of scriptural renown, this fact had to be recognized not only by the Chinese, but also by foreign devotees. The 1361 gazetteer states, "In the first year of Ta-chung (848) of Emperor Hsüan-tsung, a foreign monk (*fan-seng*) came to the Cave of Tidal Sounds. He burned his ten fingers in front of the cave. When the fingers were burned off, he saw the Great Being, who preached Dharma to him and gave him a seven-hued precious stone. This was the first of many miracles of P'u-t'o. The monk built a hut and stayed." This monk, whose name is not identified, clearly came to P'u-t'o (and specifically to the Cave of Tidal Sounds) as a pilgrim. How and when the reputation of the cave as a place for pilgrims wishing to obtain a vision of Kuan-yin became known was unclear. However, the monk-pilgrim must have been aware of the fact that the island was a holy site, for his behavior, burning off his fingers, clearly indicates that he came with determination and in expectation of these events.

The second miracle happened to another foreigner, this time the Japanese monk-pilgrim Egaku. While Egaku was on a pilgrimage to Mt. Wu-t'ai, he obtained an image of Kuan-yin that he intended to take back to Japan. But when the boat came near P'u-t'o, it got stuck. Water lilies covered the ocean. Egaku prayed, saying, "If my countrymen have no affinity with the Buddha and are destined not to see you, I will follow your direction and build a temple for you." After a while, the boat started to move and finally came to a spot under the Cave of Tidal Sounds. A man surnamed Chang saw this and marveled. He converted his home into a shrine to house the image, which became known as the 'Kuan-yin Who Refused to Leave' (Pu-k'en-ch'ü Kuan-yin). All later editions of P'u-t'o gazetteers give the year 916 as the date for this miracle.[17] The area in the ocean where Egaku's boat got stuck came to be known as the Water-lily Ocean (Lien-hua Yang), situated to the west of the island.

This image from Wu-t'ai did not stay on P'u-t'o but supposedly was taken to the mainland and installed at K'ai-yüan Ssu in Ningpo by its abbot. The compilers of P'u-t'o gazetteers acknowledged this fact, but counter with evidence that the image that was later enshrined in the same spot on the island was equally miraculous. After the old image left the island, a monk-pilgrim (*yu-seng*) arrived on P'u-t'o. He obtained a piece of rare wood, and shut himself indoors to carve an image of Kuan-yin. Within a month the image was finished, and the monk disappeared. In the early thirteenth century, one finger of the image was lost. The monks felt very unhappy. But later, something resembling a flower was seen floating among the waves in front of the Cave of Tidal Sounds. When it was inspected closely, it turned out to be the lost finger. It was put back on the image, which, according to tradition, has been the one worshiped on P'u-t'o down the ages (PTSC 1924:177).

Over the centuries, it was not only P'u-t'o's reputation as Potalaka, but as a place where Kuan-yin appeared to pilgrims that contributed to its growing popularity. There were a great number of sightings of Kuan-yin at the Cave of Tidal Sounds. Reports about these visions led to royal patronage of the island. They also motivated pilgrims in the centuries after to go to P'u-t'o, hoping to obtain a vision of Kuan-yin.

Visions of Kuan-yin

The earliest recorded sightings of Kuan-yin were not the deliberate results of pilgrims' "vision quests." Rather, Kuan-yin appeared to royal emissaries caught in life-endangering situations and saved them from sure death in the open sea. All editions of P'u-t'o gazetteers, aimed at elite audiences, related the following in the opening paragraphs of their chapters on miracles.

In 1080, Wang Shun-feng was sent from Hangchow as an emissary to the three states of Korea. When the party reached P'u-t'o they suddenly ran into a fierce storm. A big turtle lodged itself underneath the boat and made it impossible to move. The situation was extremely dangerous. Shun-feng became greatly frightened and, kneeling down and facing the Cave of Tidal Sounds, prayed to Kuan-yin. All of a sudden he saw a brilliant golden light. Kuan-yin emerged from the Cave wearing glittering pearl necklaces, and manifested the form of the full moon. The turtle disappeared and the boat could sail again. After he returned from the mission, Wang reported this miracle to the court and the emperor bestowed the plaque Pao-t'o Kuan-yin Ssu (Monastery of Kuan-yin of Precious P'u-t'o) on the temple, later known as the Southern Monastery. This was the first time that it received imperial recognition, and royal patronage continued. The monastery was given land and grain. Each year one monk was allowed to be ordained. According to the gazetteers, whenever sailors ran into storms or pirates, as soon as they took refuge facing the island, dangers would disappear.

Another miracle attested to the same fact. During the Ch'ung-ning era (1102–1106), Liu Ta and Wu Shih were emissaries to Koryŏ (present-day Korea). Upon their return, when they came to the islands near P'u-t'o, the moon became dark and the sky was overcast for four days and nights. No one knew where the boat was headed. The sailors were much frightened and, facing P'u-t'o in the distance, they knelt down and prayed. After a while, wondrous light filled the ocean. Everywhere one looked, it was as bright as daylight. Mt. Chao-pao could be seen clearly. They thus succeeded in making a safe landing at Ningpo (PTSC 1361, T 51:1137a).

While early reports emphasized Kuan-yin's saving grace as symbolized by brilliant light, accounts from the twelfth century on provided more detailed descriptions about pilgrims' encounters with the bodhisattva. These people can properly be called pilgrims, for, though well-educated, they deliberately came to P'u-t'o in order to obtain a vision of Kuan-yin. By this time, reports about Kuan-yin's epiphanies must have spread to the mainland, for these pilgrims knew where to go once they reached the island. Without exception, they all went to the Cave of Tidal Sounds, the focal point of their vision quest. These were not ordinary pilgrims, for they were men of fame and status. Moreover, they wrote about their experiences and advertised P'u-t'o among people of their own class. The gentry-officials' contribution to the creation of the site cannot be underestimated. The first official who came to the island in the early years of Shao-hsing (1131–1162) as an unabashed pilgrim was Huang Kuei-nien, a supervising secretary. The growing interest of the gentry in P'u-t'o was very likely linked to the fact that famous monks started to establish it as a Ch'an center around this time.

In 1131 the famous Ch'an master Chen-hsieh Ch'ing-liao arrived at the island from the mainland. He was a native of Szechwan. After going on a pilgrimage to Mt. Wu-t'ai, he decided to come to P'u-t'o. Quoting a phrase from the *Hua-yen Sūtra*, he called the hut he stayed in "An Isolated Place by the Seashore" (*hai-an ku-chüeh ch'u*). He attracted many brilliant students of the Ch'an tradition. The prefect petitioned to the court and had P'u-t'o's registry changed to Ch'an, a more prestigious school in the Sung, from the original Vinaya classification. At that time there were some seven hundred fishing families living on the island. But tradition says that as soon as they heard the Dharma from the master, they all changed their profession [or left the island and moved elsewhere]. Chen-hsieh was regarded as the first patriarch of the Ch'an lineage of the Ts'ao-tung branch on the island. He later went back to the mainland and served as abbot for several famous monasteries in Chekiang, such as Aśoka Monastery, and Kuo-ch'ing Ssu on Mt. T'ien-t'ai. In 1137 another Ch'an master, Tzu-te Hui-hui (d. 1183), came to P'u-t'o. Prior to this, he had been the abbot of Ching-tz'u Ssu, a well-known Ch'an monastery in Hangchow. Largely due to his teaching activities, P'u-t'o was said to have reached the same level of reputation as T'ien-t'ung Ssu, the training center of the Ts'ao-tung lineage, situated in Ningpo (PTSC 1924:341–42). As P'u-t'o became linked with important mainland Buddhist communities, it began to attract more pilgrims, both monastic and lay. One powerful factor in its favor was doubtlessly its reputation as the place where Kuan-yin appeared to sincere pilgrims.

Huang Kuei-nien's pilgrimage to P'u-t'o, his vision of Kuan-yin and the eulogy he wrote to commemorate the miraculous event, "Pao-t'o Shan Kuan-yin tsan" (Eulogy to Kuan-yin of Precious P'u-t'o) are found in the local gazetteers of Ssu-ming (Ningpo) compiled in 1167 and quoted in some later P'u-t'o gazetteers (CTSMTC 7:2 a-b; 9:26 a-b). *Tsan* (eulogy), *sung* (hymn), and *chieh* (metrical chant, gāthā) are some of the favorite literary genres used by Buddhists to sing the praise of the object of their adoration. They are shorter and more succinct than works of prose. They also tend to be more personal and emotional. In the tribute, Huang described how he prayed in front of the cave together with his companions with respect and trepidation. They chanted the name of Kuan-yin and dhāraṇīs (*mi-yü*). They first saw a brilliant light, and suddenly Kuan-yin appeared in a pose of royal ease, sitting leisurely on the rock outcropping above the cave, her body the color of purple gold (*tzu-chin*).[18] Overwhelmed with feelings of gratitude, Huang knelt down and vowed that from now on he would devote himself to the study of Buddhist scriptures, refrain from killing, and take up a vegetarian diet. He also emphasized the fact that this was not a private vision, but that everyone present, both old and young, had witnessed the same miracle.

In 1148, not long after Huang's pilgrimage to P'u-t'o, another member of the gentry-official class came as a pilgrim and also left a record of his vision. Shih Hao (1106–1194), a native of Ningpo, and a scion of the illustrious and powerful Shih clan, was a *chin-shih* degree holder.[19] When Shih served as the supervisor of salt, following a common pattern of using an official tour of duty as an opportunity for a private side trip, he visited P'u-t'o with a friend in the third month of 1148. When they first went to the Cave of Tidal Sounds, they could not see anything. So they burned incense and prepared tea. Tea leaves floated to the top of the cup, which they took as a sign intimating that something wondrous was about to happen. After they returned to the temple, they talked with the abbot Lan, who told them stories from the *Hua-yen Sūtra*. After the noon meal they went back to the cave. They looked around and only saw wild rocks heaped upon each other. They were disappointed and decided to leave. But a monk told them that there was an opening on top of the cliff and that they should look down from there. Dutifully they climbed to the top on all fours and suddenly saw an auspicious form giving off a brilliant golden color. The whole cave was illuminated by the brilliance. They could definitely see Kuan-yin's eyes and eyebrows. Shih Hao clearly thought what he saw was the form of a woman, for he described her teeth being "as white as jade." They were filled with happiness and gratitude. After paying homage to Kuan-yin, they sailed back to Ningpo. Fearing that this event might be forgotten with the passing of time, Shih wrote it down and had it inscribed on the wall of the cave.[20]

Like Chang Shang-yin's pilgrimage to Mt. Wu-t'ai, discussed by Gimello (1992), the experiences of Shih were very much facilitated and shaped by the guidance of resident monk guides. Like Chang, Shih also wrote the account for posterity. There was, however, no trace of any ambivalence in Shih's attitude, a characteristic that was generally quite noticeable among the literati of the late Ming, as described by Pei-yi Wu (1992). What might account for the difference in their attitudes? One might be tempted to say that the people of the Sung perhaps lived more comfortably with a sense of mystery and awe. But I am not convinced that people living in the late Ming had lost this sense. I think the answer may lie in the medium in which these tales were expressed. Both Chang and Shih wrote for fellow believers or potential believers. Their writings were collected by gazetteers, which constitute, after all, a very different genre from novels and travel accounts. Mountain gazetteers have a more limited, but at the same time, more definite, audience. I suspect that if we comb through more gazetteers, we may find other writings that express the writers' religious feelings with equal openness and honesty.

Probably due to Shih's promotion, the Cave of Tidal Sounds became even better known. In 1209 the monk Te-chao, a dharma heir of the Ch'an master Fo-chao, became the abbot. Because it was very difficult for pilgrims to worship Kuan-yin at the cave, he had a bridge built among the rocks so that pilgrims could stand on the bridge facing the cave. The project took six years. When it was finished, Emperor Ning-tsung personally wrote a plaque naming it Ta-shih Ch'iao (Bridge of the Great Being). One hundred thousand pine trees were planted. In the meantime, Te-chao had earlier, in 1210, started the project of building the great hall. Shih Mi-yüan, son of Shih Hao, had become the prime minister. He followed his father's example and was a devotee of Kuan-yin. He made donations to the project, providing money to build halls, rooms, corridors, and provided for lamps and ritual implements. When the emperor learned about this, he also lent his support. The emperor bestowed golden robes, silver bowls, rosaries made of agate and brocaded banners. At that time, 567 *mu* of arable land and 1670 *mu* of forest land were granted to the monastery (PTSC 1361, T 51:1137c–1138a).

Iconography and Literature

Mountain gazetteers, miracle tales, and testimonials written by elite pilgrims all helped to legitimize P'u-t'o's claim. Other media also played important roles in promoting the attractiveness of the site among people in society at large. Art and literature were two powerful means of communicating this new message. Imagination was superimposed on memory. Fantasy was built upon reality. The Potalaka in art and fiction might have little to do with the actual island in the ocean. No matter. Just as myths about Shangri-La stimulated and molded the Western fantasy about Tibet (Bishop 1989), similarly, depictions of P'u-t'o as Potalaka in art and literature fueled the Chinese pilgrims' longing for the sacred realm. These media drew the pilgrims to the island. They also taught them where to look, and what to see.

The changing iconography of Kuan-yin was closely influenced by how pilgrims saw the deity. From the twelfth century on, Kuan-yin appeared to pilgrims on P'u-t'o increasingly as Our Lady in White, just as she did at Upper

T'ien-chu.[21] But there was a difference: Kuan-yin on P'u-t'o began to be accompanied first by Shan-ts'ai, the boy pilgrim Sudhana, and later, by both the boy and Lung-nü, the Dragon Princess.[22] With the appearance of Kuan-yin's attendants, another cave called Sudhana's Cave, situated to the right of the Cave of Tidal Sounds, began to attract pilgrims. (Some gazetteers identified it as the Dragon Princess' Cave, and named a rock nearby Sudhana's Rock.) For instance, in 1266 Grand Marshall Fan, who suffered from an eye disease, sent his son to pray in front of the Cave of Tidal Sounds. When Fan washed his eyes with the spring water the son had gathered from the cave and brought home, he recovered. The son was once more sent by the father to offer thanks to Kuan-yin. Kuan-yin appeared to him on the left side of the cave. She wore a cape visible as a light haze and seemed to be standing behind a curtain of azure gauze. After that he went to worship at Sudhana's Cave, where first Sudhana and then Kuan-yin appeared. Kuan-yin wore a white robe with long tassels and many strands of pearl necklaces.

In 1276, during the Yüan, Prime Minister Po-yen captured southern China and General Ha-la-tai came to worship at the Cave. When he did not see anything, he took out his bow and shot an arrow into the Cave. When he boarded the boat to go back, suddenly the ocean became filled with water lilies. He was much frightened and regretted his behavior. He went back to the cave in repentance. After a while he saw White-robed Kuan-yin who, accompanied by the boy, walked gracefully by. As a result of this vision, he had an image made (doubtless according to what he saw) and erected a hall for Kuan-yin above the cave. In the fourth month of 1328, executive censor Ts'ao Li came with imperial order to offer incense and donations. He prayed for a vision at the Cave. Kuan-yin appeared wearing a white robe and covered with necklaces. He next went to Sudhana's Cave and saw the boy, who looked like a living person (PTSC 1361, T 51:1137a-b).

Sometimes a direct reference to contemporary art was made. For instance, we are told that on the sixth day of the tenth month in 1355, Liu Jen-pen of T'ien-t'ai was returning from his duty as the supervisor of transport for the circuit granary. He came to P'u-t'o and saw Kuan-yin at the Cave of Tidal Sounds. The appearance of Kuan-yin was "the same as that painted in pictures" (PTSC 1739, 5:4b). But what kind of pictures? Was it White-robed Kuan-yin painted by artists since the Sung? What the pilgrim saw in his vision of Kuan-yin and how Kuan-yin was depicted in religious and secular art became closely connected. For as Kuan-yin was increasingly sighted together with Shan-ts'ai and Lung-nü, a new iconography of the Nan-hai Kuan-yin (Kuan-yin of the South Sea) began to be identified with P'u-t'o from the Yüan on (figure 9.1).

Kuan-yin is called Nan-hai Kuan-yin in the Chinese novel *Hsi-yu chi* (Jour-

Figure 9.1. Kuan-yin, by Chao I, dated 1313 . *Courtesy of the National Palace Museum, Taiwan.*

ney to the West). It has been suggested that Wu Ch'eng-en, the author, probably visited P'u-t'o, for he provided detailed descriptions of the island in no less than nine places in the novel.[23] Kuan-yin appears here as a compassionate and omnipotent savior. There is no doubt about Kuan-yin's gender, for as Potalaka Kuan-yin, she is the beautiful goddess from P'u-t'o.

A mind perfected in the four virtues,
A gold body filled with wisdom,
Fringes of dangling pearls and jade,
Scented bracelets set with lustrous treasures,
Dark hair piled smoothly in a coiled-dragon bun,
And elegant sashes lightly fluttering as phoenix quills,
Her green jade buttons
And white silk robe
Bathed in holy light;
. . . .
With brows of new moon shape
And eyes like two bright stars,
Her jadelike face beams natural joy,
And her ruddy lips seem a flash of red.
Her immaculate vase overflows with nectar from year to year,
Holding sprigs of weeping willow green from age to age.
. . . .
Thus she rules the Mount T'ai,
And lives in the South Seas.
. . . .
She is the merciful ruler of Potalaka Mountain,
The Living Kuan-yin from the Cave of Tidal Sound. (Yu 1977:185)

In this hymn to Kuan-yin, the author connects her with golden light, white robe, willow branch, pure vase, the South Seas, Potalaka Mountain, and, finally, the Cave of Tidal Sounds. Wu Ch'eng-en was not being original here, for by the late Ming, Kuan-yin had come to be seen in this way by society at large. Painters were drawing these epithets in creating a new iconography of Nan-hai Kuan-yin. The same cluster of almost stock phrases was, of course, also used in pilgrims' accounts of their visions of Kuan-yin. Similar depictions of Kuan-yin in different media were most likely due to mutual influence. But once this iconography became established, this mutual reinforcement through different media undoubtedly helped this iconography to gain universal acceptance.

Nan-hai Kuan-yin was clearly a composite image, combining both scriptural elements that had been subjected to indigenous modifications and iconographical elements drawn from diverse sources. The emergence of this iconography coincided with the resurgence of P'u-t'o in the sixteenth century, under the patronage of the Wan-li emperor and his mother, after the island had suffered long periods of neglect. Its triumph over other forms of Kuan-yin probably happened during the seventeenth and eighteenth centuries, when P'u-t'o enjoyed successive patronages under the Ch'ing emperors Kang-hsi, Yung-cheng, and Ch'ien-lung. In this reestablishment of the sacred site, local officials and able abbots collaborated closely.

Along with this new iconography, an extensive corpus of new literature in the form of *pao-chüan* (precious scrolls) also appeared to explain and advertise it. These texts identify P'u-t'o as Hsiang-shan, thus linking Kuan-yin with Princess Miao-shan. Her attendants, Shan-ts'ai and Lung-nü also underwent full sinicization. The texts do not refer to their origins in Buddhist scriptures, but provided them with Chinese life stories. Stylistically, Nan-hai Kuan-yin had come to resemble White-robed Kuan-yin, the deity worshiped primarily at Upper T'ien-chu. As P'u-t'o became Potalaka, it superseded Hsiang-shan and Hangchow by absorbing the myths and images of Kuan-yin connected with these two mainland pilgrimage sites.

Popular texts such as *pao-chüan* not only informed ordinary pilgrims about the Kuan-yin lore connected with P'u-t'o, but more importantly, they also served as effective means to generate financial donations to build temples on the island. *P'u-t'o pao-chüan*, a well-known work published probably in the late nineteenth century, presents Nan-hai Kuan-yin as responsible for the rebuilding of P'u-t'o. By providing expected rewards and retributions appropriate to the protagonists, this *pao-chüan* clearly teaches the virtue of making donations to monks from P'u-t'o who may indeed be manifestations of Kuan-yin herself. Even though the extant editions of this text are late, they could be based on oral traditions or even an earlier written version (now lost) dating back to the two periods of intensive temple rebuilding on P'u-t'o.

The story is supposed to have taken place during the reign of Chen-tsung (r. 997–1021) of the Sung, the time of P'u-t'o's founding days. Assuming the form of a poor monk accompanied by two other monks who were Shan-ts'ai and Lung-nü in disguise, Kuan-yin went to a family named Wang to seek donations to build the Kuan-yin Hall. The old couple were pious Buddhists. They divided their property between their two sons: Yu-chin ("Having Gold"), and Yu-yin ("Having Silver") and devoted their lives to worshiping the Buddha. The parents soon passed away. Yu-chin remembered Father's instruction and loved to do good deeds and believed in Buddhism. Yu-yin, on the other hand, was just the opposite. Influenced by his wife who was greedy, hated monks, and delighted in killing animals, he was only interested in enriching himself by exploiting others. When Kuan-yin came for donations, Yu-chin agreed to assume the entire cost of the building project, to the derision of his younger brother. The total cost of building the temple was 100,000 ounces of silver. In order to fulfill this pledge, he had to sell not only his jewelry, grains, land, and house, which came to 99,600 ounces, but also his thirteen-year old son and ten-year old daughter for 200 each in order to make up the shortfall of 400 ounces. The parents were reduced to utter poverty and supported themselves by selling bamboo. But eventually the daughter was chosen to be the new empress and the son became a *chin-shih*. The parents were reunited with the children and invited to live in the palace by the new emperor. They converted everyone to Buddhism. Upon their deaths they went to the Western Paradise. The emperor had a Ch'an monastery specially built in which an image of Yu-chin made of sandalwood was enshrined to receive people's worship (46b).

The fate of the younger brother and his wife was, alas, very different. Because Yu-yin did good deeds in his past life, but indulged in evil ways in this life, Kuan-yin decided to save him. She assumed the appearance of Yu-yin and took up residence in his house while the real Yu-yin was out. She instructed the servants not to allow anyone in. When the real Yu-yin came back, he was driven out and had to spend the night at the Earth God's temple. He went to court and lodged a complaint. But the judge decided that the one staying at home was the real Wang Yu-yin and sentenced him to forty strokes with a heavy board (36). He remembered his older brother's devotion and turned his heart to Buddhism. He decided to go to P'u-t'o on pilgrimage. Kuan-yin had Shan-ts'ai turn into a woodcutter and direct him to P'u-t'o. He suffered many trials and tribulations on the way. After Kuan-yin left the wife at home instructing her to keep a vegetarian diet and chant Buddha's name, she appeared as an old lady and aided Yu-yin on his pilgrimage (48b). In the meantime, the wife also underwent a change of heart and decided to go on a pilgrimage to P'u-t'o. She sold everything and was on her way. She endured a very perilous passage on the boat, during which she prayed all the time. Once on the island, she met her husband, who repudiated her. Heartbroken, she jumped into the ocean intending to kill herself. She was saved by Lung-nü who took the disguise of a fisherman, and woke up in her own bed. She now realized that the whole thing was arranged by Kuan-yin and became her devotee. Yu-yin, on the other hand, remained on P'u-t'o and became a monk (53a).

In the final analysis, the island and her advertisers had a dialectical relationship of mutual dependency. The fame of P'u-t'o inspired people to write about it. But at the same time, novels, plays, travel accounts, gazetteers, and popular texts also served to bolster the new-found fame of the island. A similar relationship existed between the island and its pilgrims, many of whom were illiterate common people. The reported efficacy of Potalaka Kuan-yin drew many people to the island. But the island achieved new fame through the continuous discovery of new places of efficacy by these pilgrims.

Ordinary Pilgrims

Many ordinary pilgrims (among whom we should count the rank and file monks and nuns) went to P'u-t'o down through the centuries. Being uneducated, they could not write about their experiences or paint a picture of Kuan-yin as they saw her in their visions. But they assuredly made as much of a contribution to the creation of the Chinese Potalaka as their more articulate fellow pilgrims. They did so by going to P'u-t'o en masse, and thereby existentially confirming the ideological transformation of the island into Potalaka effected by the abbots and the elites. They also participated in the physical construction of the island by making financial contributions. We can catch a glimpse of these devout, but mute, humble pilgrims in the pages of travel accounts about P'u-t'o left behind by their more educated contemporaries.

Like other pilgrims, they also congregated around the Cave of Tidal Sounds because Kuan-yin was believed to appear there. This remained the most popular place on the island before the Cave of Brahmā's Voice became a serious contender in the seventeenth century. Hou's gazetteer described the height of the former's fame in the late Ming. Every spring monks from all over the country would come to the island carrying images of Kuan-yin cast in silver and gold. They would welcome Kuan-yin by throwing these images into the water as offerings to her in front of the Cave of Tidal Sounds. They would also offer brocade banners, and bells and tripods cast in gold or bronze to Kuan-yin in the monastic halls. Some monk-pilgrims who came from thousands of miles away would kneel and kowtow all the way until they were covered with blood. Some pilgrims, overcome with religious enthusiasm, would jump into the water to seek deliverance from this world. More pilgrims would burn their arms and fingers to show their sincerity and induce Kuan-yin to appear to them (PTSC 1598:3:27a).

Two late Ming writers left accounts of their travel/pilgrimage to P'u-t'o that confirm the descriptions of the religious zeal shown by pilgrims provided by the gazetteers. The first was "A P'u-t'o Travel Account" (P'u-t'o yu-chi) written by Hsieh Kuo-chen (d. 1632). He said that aside from the two large monasteries, there were over 500 small shrines (*an*) scattered all over the island. Although the island was very beautiful, people looked upon sailing across the ocean with dread, so even natives of Ningpo did not come to the island often. "Western monks," however, regarded coming to the South Sea on pilgrimage as highly desirable. For pilgrims, walking across a narrow stone bridge (located in front of the Cave of Tidal Sounds) was deemed especially meritorious. He describes it this way:

> The bridge is about ten *chang* [a hundred Chinese feet] in length and two to three feet in width. It faces a sheer cliff on the north side, on which a small temple dedicated to Kuan-yin sits. I sat by the window of Shang-fang-kuang Ssu and saw with my own eyes that some twenty monks walked on the bridge as if it were level ground. But one monk walked only a few steps before he started to quake and stood stock still. After a few minutes, he moved again and finally managed to walk to the other side. Everyone's eyes were focused on him, and some people were muttering words that I could not hear. When I asked the local monk in the temple, he said, "He almost did not succeed in achieving a rebirth as a human being in his next incarnation."

It seems that aside from hoping to obtain a vision of Kuan-yin, pilgrims also tried to predict their chances of being reborn as human beings in their next lives by performing this daredevil act of walking on the stone bridge in front of the cave.

Hsieh also provided some information about pilgrims' economic contributions to P'u-t'o. Since the island did not produce any grain, and about seven to eight thousand *shih* of rice were needed per year, this had to be supplied by donors. Most of the rice was donated by women. Pilgrims from Fukien and Kwangtung provided other daily necessities (Hsieh Kuo-chen 1985, vol. 2:242–43).

Chang Tai, in his inimitable style, gave an account of his trip to P'u-t'o. He went to P'u-t'o for the holy day celebration on the nineteenth of the second month, the festival of Kuan-yin's birthday, in 1638.[24] Like pilgrims to the Upper T'ien-chu Monastery in Hangchow, P'u-t'o pilgrims also observed the all-night vigil known as *su-shan* ("spending the night on the mountain"). It was quite a sight!

> The Great Hall is filled with incense smoke, which is as thick as a heavy fog spreading over five *li*. Thousands of men and women are sitting in rows like packed fish. From under the Buddha images all the way to the outside corridors, not one inch of space is not occupied. During the night many nuns burn incense on their heads, or burn their arms and fingers. Women from

> good families also imitate them. They recite scriptures and try not to show signs of pain. If they can refrain from even knitting their eyebrows, this is considered as having faith and very meritorious. I wonder if the compassionate bodisattva would be pleased by the offering of burnt human flesh. The sound of heads knocking against the ground reverberates throughout the valley. Monks of the temple also do not sleep that night. With a hundred candles burning, they sit facing the Buddha. In a state of sleepiness, some see Buddha [Kuan-yin] moving, while others see her sending out brilliant light. Each regards what he or she sees as miraculous. They disperse only at the daybreak. (Chang Tai 1957:208)

Chang went to the Cave of Tidal Sounds, noting that Sudhana's Rock and the Dragon Princess' Cave were nearby.[25] Chang Tai asked the attending monk if he had ever had a vision of Kuan-yin as described in the gazetteers, and the monk answered, "The Bodhisattva used to live here, but during the Wan-li period [1573–1615], because the dragon wind was very strong, it blew away the stone bridge. Since then Kuan-yin has moved to the Cave of Brahmā's Voice." Chang was only able to refrain with difficulty from bursting out laughing at what the monk said, so he bade the monk a hasty farewell (Chang Tai 1957:209). This accords well with the time when Fan-yin Tung emerged as the new place to seek a vision of Kuan-yin following the establishment of Fa-yü Monastery.

Although Chang Tai was skeptical of reported miracles and openly critical of the credulous and fanatical pilgrims he saw on the island, he nevertheless regarded himself as a pilgrim. He seemed to disapprove of vulgar pilgrims, but not of pilgrimage itself. This same ambivalent attitude was present during his trip to Mt. T'ai, as is made clear in Wu's study (1992). Here also, Chang was unabashedly condescending to the uneducated pilgrims. Although he came to P'u-t'o without bringing any offering to the bodhisattva, he saw his act of writing about the island as no different from making religious offerings. In fact, it might be even more valuable:

> Master Chang [referring to himself] says: P'u-t'o is renowned because of the bodhisattva, yet it is neither truly nor exhaustively known because of her. . . . If there is no bodhisattva, then who would bother to come sailing through the ocean? For if there is no bodhisattva, there would be no pilgrim. Although this is the case, those who come here in order to worship her leave as soon as their purpose is fulfilled. While here, they either bow once every three steps or fold their palms once every five steps. Some would also make full prostrations while shouting the name of the bodhisattva at

> the top of their voices. However, not one out of one hundred pilgrims who come to P'u-t'o can tell you much about the place. . . . Arriving on the island, I have nothing to offer the bodhisattva, but I know how to describe the natural scenery [*shan-shui*, literally "mountains and waters"]. So I will perform a Buddhist service [*tso Fo-shih*] by writing about the scenery of P'u-t'o. Perhaps I am the first person among the literati from ancient times until today who, while unable to worship the Buddha by offering money or rice, yet manages to do so through pen and ink. (Chang Tai 1957:205)

Literati writers such as Chang, while disdaining the vulgar beliefs and practices of ordinary pilgrims, nevertheless were fascinated by them. Like modern day ethnographers, they were very much interested in noting down what they observed and discovered. For instance, Chang tells us, "Village men and women would believe that as soon as they went on pilgrimage to P'u-t'o, Kuan-yin would accompany them all the way. Therefore, if they stumbled, they believed it was because Kuan-yin had pushed them, but if they should fall flat on the ground, then it was because she lent them a hand [so that they would not be hurt]. On board the ship, if the punting pole or the rudder should get lost, and in fact, when any little thing should happen, it would be interpreted as either a good or bad omen from the bodhisattva" (Chang Tai 1957:213).

A later writer, making the trip to P'u-t'o in 1822, reported taboos observed by similar types of pilgrims who sailed for P'u-t'o.

> Banisters in the rear part of the boat are reserved for gods and buddhas. One can lean on them or step over them, but one must never sit on them. There is a special place in the back of the boat where one may dump the night soil or perform one's personal hygiene. One may not do so in any other place carelessly. When sitting on the gangplank, one should never wrap one's arms around one's knees, for this will bring stormy weather. When one sits, one must never dangle one's legs in mid-air, for this will cause a delay in the trip. When one finishes eating, one should never lay chopsticks across the rice bowl, for this will also cause further delays. When anyone commits these mistakes, he/she will make the boatmen really angry. (Cheng Kuang-tsu 1845:38a-b)

It is also possible to get a sense of the involvement and dedication of this vast number of ordinary pilgrims by combing through the miracle tales contained in the gazetteers. All of the stories are ostensibly about the efficacious responses of Kuan-yin to the pilgrims' devotion. At the same time, they do provide some interesting data, albeit of an anecdotal nature, about the kind of simple pilgrims who, through their faith and devotion, sustained the pilgrimage tradition.

I have selected a few examples from a large body of material. All the events described happened during the sixteenth and seventeenth centuries, one of the major cycles of P'u-t'o's revival. The first is about the mother of a P'u-t'o monk named T'ien-jan who came originally from Hangchow. The mother kept a vegetarian diet back at home and worshiped the Buddha. She often sought donations from people and would turn whatever she got over to her son and ask him to donate it to temples on the island. One day she was given an image of Kuan-yin whose neck was cast in gold. When she gave it to her son, he became greedy for the gold. He asked a worker to scrape off the gold. The worker died as soon as he did so. A while later, the mother came over from the mainland. Even before she arrived on P'u-t'o, T'ien-jan already knew of her coming. He called out in a loud voice and cursed her, "The enemy who will harm me is now coming." When he saw his mother, he struck her on the cheeks and then, grabbing a knife, he cut his own neck. He ran around the island and called out, "Do not imitate my example. If you act like me, hell is right in front of your eyes." After saying this, he died. The gazetteer reported matter-of-factly that this happened in 1586, the fourteenth year of Wan-li (PTSC 1607:155–56). This story is about a pious mother's unstinting effort to find donations, and a cautionary tale about greedy monks who pocketed pilgrims' offerings, but, above all, it is about Kuan-yin's unfailing efficacy.

Other stories provide some information about the geographical spread and occupational diversity of the pilgrims. For instance, a shopkeeper from Anhui desired to go on a pilgrimage to P'u-t'o. He kept a vegetarian diet for three years to prepare himself for the momentous endeavor. He also moved to K'un-shan (in Chekiang) to be closer to the island. On the New Year's Day of a certain year at the end of the Ming, he was finally all set to depart. Just then someone rushed to the docks and told him that he should turn back because a fire had broken out next door to his shop. He refused to give up his trip, saying that even if the shop should burn to the ground, he would not turn back because he had been waiting for this too long. But after he returned from P'u-t'o, he discovered that all the houses around his shop had been burned to the ground and only his shop remained intact (PTSC 1924:188).

There are two stories about merchants: one was a cloth dealer from Kiangsi and the other a Cantonese overseas trader. We do not know the date of the story, but it is most likely the late Ming. The first man went to P'u-t'o to offer incense as a side trip on one of his business ventures. He saw a decrepit statue of the Heavenly King. Remembering a folk saying that dust from images of famous monasteries could cure illnesses when mixed with medicine, he took a handful. But as soon as he got back to his boat, he became dizzy and suffered tremendous headaches. A very angry Heavenly King of enormous height appeared and scolded him for cutting flesh from the god's leg. The cloth merchant was very frightened and repented for his behavior. He asked a monk traveling with him to take the dust back to P'u-t'o, promising to make a brand new statue of the god.

As for the Cantonese trader, the story went a little differently. On his way home from Japan, he dreamed of a giant asking to borrow his ship to carry a huge bone. He woke up in a fright. It was midnight. Suddenly the ship was about to sink because of a weird storm. Everyone on board started to cry. Then, just as suddenly, the wind changed and they could land safely at P'u-t'o at daybreak. Overcome with relief, he went to a temple to worship Kuan-yin. There he saw the statue of a Heavenly King whose leg had become detached and was lying in front of him. He looked exactly like the giant who had appeared to him in the dream. He marveled at the miracle and donated money right away in order to make a new statue (PTSC 1698, 10:12a-b).

The last story I cite happened in the spring of 1898. A group of pilgrims from San-chia, Huang-yen county, T'ai prefecture (in present-day Jiangsu) went to P'u-t'o to offer incense. On their way back, when they had sailed no more than several hundred *li*, the boat was enveloped in thick fog and could not go any further. When the boatman asked if anyone among the pilgrim group had done anything impure while on the island, an old woman hastily opened her bag and threw a yellow tile into the ocean. As soon as she did so, the fog cleared and they sailed safely home. When asked, she explained that she did not intend to steal anything. It was just that she loved the smoothness and coolness of the yellow tile and wanted to use it as a pillow to keep cool in summer. However, even such a trivial deed was not overlooked. Everyone in the group was struck anew by Kuan-yin's efficacy (PTSC 1924:200).

Ascetics and Abbots

The fame of the Cave of Tidal Sounds also attracted ascetics and serious religious practitioners who came as pilgrims and then chose to stay. The 1607 gazetteer contains an account of two such persons written by the monk Chen-i. Entitled "Biography of Two Great Beings," he describes his encounter with two ascetics, one female and one male, whom he regarded as manifestations of Kuan-yin. The woman came to P'u-t'o in the sixth month of 1605 and the man four months later, after he made a pilgrimage to Mt. Chiu-hua. They had dark faces and matted hair. They lived in two separate thatched huts sitting on top of the hill south of the cave. The huts were no higher than three feet, leaky at the top and damp underneath. They sat inside meditating all day. When people gave them food and money, they would accept but then give the goods to mendicant monks. Sometimes they would go without eating for several days yet suffer no ill effect. Ordinary people took them for beggars. Chen-i paid them a visit one night with a lay devotee. They sat in silence for a long time. The hosts did not show any surprise, but neither did they address the guests. When Chen-i made conversation with them, the man only smiled without speaking, but the woman was sharp-witted and quick on the uptake. In true Ch'an fashion, when asked about her name, she answered, "What name?" When asked about her age, she answered, "What age?" She answered the question about her native place the same way. She did say, however, that she had lived on Mt. Chung-nan, a holy mountain not far from Mt. Wu-t'ai, for a number of years. When asked about her realization, she said, "My eyes see the great ocean, and my ears hear the sounds of the wind, rain, tide and birds." When asked about her method of cultivation, she answered, "Sometimes when I think of Kuan-yin, I will chant the name a few times. But the rest of the time, I merely sit. There is no particular method in my sitting." Chen-i was greatly impressed by her straightforwardness. She seemed to harbor not a thought in her mind. The following spring, when many pilgrims came to the cave during the second month, the height of the pilgrimage season, the two ascetics left (PTSC 1607, 3:268–270).

Ascetics like these two might have added an aura of mystery and sanctity to the island, but it was mainly through the energetic promotion of able monks that old places of renown became revived and new places of efficacy became discovered on P'u-t'o. The activities of Ta-chih Chen-jung (1523–1592), founding abbot of Fa-yü, can serve as one example of the large part monks played in the creation of Potalaka.[26] Ta-chih was an intrepid pilgrim, having spent many years going on pilgrimages to Wu-t'ai, Omei and Chiu-hua. In 1580 he came to P'u-t'o. After praying at the Cave of Tidal Sounds and the Cave of Brahmā's Voice and asking Kuan-yin for a sign, one evening he saw a large piece of bamboo flow in with the tide and came to rest on a beach known as the Sand of A Thousand Paces (Ch'ien-pu Sha), to the left of Southern Monastery. Taking this as the sign from Kuan-yin, he built a hut there and named it Hai-ch'ao An (Shrine of the Ocean Tide), the forerunner of Northern Monastery. Soon many of the faithful began to donate money, which enabled him to expand the originally modest temple. At that time, Ch'an practice was in a depressed state. He insisted on strict discipline and was as well known as Yün-ch'i Chu-hung (1535–1615), Tzu-po Chen-k'e (1543–1603) and Han-shan Te-ch'ing (1546–1623), the other three great masters of the late Ming (PTSC 1598, 3:27a-32a).

The preceding biographical account of Ta-chih was written by someone who called himself Layman Ku-lo Fa-seng Yang-ti. He came to P'u-t'o as a pilgrim and sought out Ta-chih for an interview. After their conversation, Ta-chih gave the writer a document that chronicled his austerities and religious activities during the previous sixty years. Ta-chih chose him as his biographer because Ta-chih had received a dream from Kuan-yin the night before. In the dream, Kuan-yin told him that a layman by the name of Fa-seng ("Monk with hair") would visit him and this person had a predestined relationship with him. When Ta-chih saw the writer, he immediately realized that this was the person predicted in his dream. Ta-chih was an unflagging pilgrim, and an energetic temple builder, but he was also an unabashed promoter of P'u-t'o and himself. Ta-chih, like many of his contemporaries, carried out this promotion through recourse to the miraculous. Citing the dream of Kuan-yin to legitimize his request for a favorable biography is one example. Another example, to which I alluded earlier, was Ta-chih's prediction that P'u-t'o would be revived one hundred years after his death. He further had this prediction inscribed on his funerary stele. The rediscovery of this stele by Hsing-t'ung in 1691 provided the needed impetus to bring about the restoration of Fa-yü in 1692, exactly one hundred years later (PTSC 1698, 12:55a-57b).

Ta-chih was one of several able monks who helped to build P'u-t'o into a great pilgrimage site. Like others, he was himself a pilgrim, having visited Mt. Wu-t'ai and Mt. Omei before coming to P'u-t'o. His relationships with pilgrims and officials were probably also typical of other abbots. The revival of the island always happened as a result of the concerted efforts of pilgrims, officials and abbots. As the Northern Monastery was established, the Cave of Brahmā's Voice also became more famous. In 1626 an Indian pilgrim from Benares came to the cave and, impressed by the topography, offered relics of the Buddha, enshrining them in a stūpa built on top of the cave.[27]

The 1705 gazetteer refers to the two caves as the two eyes of the sacred island (2:13b). Like the Cave of Tidal Sounds, the Cave of Brahmā's Voice also attracted fanatic pilgrims who sometimes chose to commit religious suicide to show their devotion to Kuan-yin. Mui Sui, the prefect, was so disturbed by this that he wrote an impassioned plea, "She-shen chieh" (Prohibition against Sacrificing One's Body) and inscribed it on a stele erected near the cave (12:35a-38a). This was apparently not effective. Robert F. Fitch, who made six trips to P'u-t'o between 1922 and 1928, described the cave this way:

> Into the depths below, in even recent times, pilgrims would throw themselves and commit suicide with the hope that they could not only quickly end their earthly miseries but also become immediately transformed into Buddhas and awaken in the Western Paradise. Hence, such acts are now

> most strictly forbidden. In former years, it was the custom for a priest to be let down in a basket to gather up the remains for cremation (Fitch 1929: 70–71).

He was much impressed by the Cave of Tidal Sounds. "At high tide, when the wind is blowing inward towards the shore, the waves will enter the cave with great violence. At the inner end of the cave is a small exit upward and the writer has seen, in a typhoon, the water emerging like a geyser to a height of over twenty feet" (Fitch 1929:50–51).[28]

Competition between the two caves did not diminish the attraction of either one for pilgrims. On the contrary, reports of Kuan-yin's appearances at both caves highlighted their efficacy and made a visit to both obligatory. The relationship between the Southern and Northern Monasteries was of a similar nature. Although there was a sense of rivalry between them, they actually reinforced each other's reputations. As the island became increasingly developed, all the holy places contributed to the aura of sanctity of the pilgrimage site. At the same time, each individual place derived its attraction from the site as a whole.

Since the Ch'ing dynasty, the two major monasteries have managed the smaller temples and hermitages on the island jointly. The 1924 gazetteer of P'u-t'o listed 88 small cloisters (*an*) and 128 hermitages (literally, "thatched huts," *mao-p'eng*, simple dwellings for monks engaged in solitary meditation) under the jurisdiction of the Southern and Northern Monasteries (77 hermitages belonging to the former and 51 to the latter). Similar figures were cited by missionaries, foreign tourists, and Chinese pilgrims around the turn of the century.[29] A system was worked out by which pilgrims, especially those who came from the northern provinces, were assigned to the two monasteries equitably. The 1739 gazetteer provides an interesting glimpse of how this system worked.

> Pilgrims who come from Northern Chili, Shansi, Shensi, Shantung, Honan, and other provinces north of the Yangtze River are called northern pilgrims (*pei-k'e*). They should be hosted by Southern and Northern Monasteries equally. This system was already in use in former times. Moreover, rules stipulating how the two monasteries should receive the pilgrims were inscribed on stelae: the arrival of each pilgrim boat is registered in a book and the monasteries take turns in receiving the pilgrims. In the case of northern pilgrims, if there are fewer than two in the group, it does not count. But if there are more than three, the group will be counted as one boat no matter whether there are many or few in the group. The two monasteries must

> receive pilgrim groups in turn. Regardless if the pilgrim group is large or small, or if it arrives early or late, the monasteries should not pick and choose. If within a pilgrim group there is someone known to one of the monasteries, or if the pilgrim is a donor to that monastery, this rule can be overlooked. But in that case, another similar group must be substituted to make up the difference. (PTSC 1739:10:13)

In March 1987 I spent a week on P'u-t'o observing the celebration of Kuan-yin's birthday on the nineteenth of the second month. Pilgrims started coming back to P'u-t'o in 1979, when the island became open to the public after the Cultural Revolution. The three large monasteries, P'u-chi (the Southern Monastery), Fa-yü (the Northern Monastery), and Hui-chi (Buddha Peak), had been restored, together with some eight smaller temples. This was but a pale reflection of the past, but in terms of the number of pilgrims and tourists who have visited P'u-t'o, it is definitely one of the most popular places in China today. Abbot Miao-shan told me that there were 920,000 people who visited the island in 1986, and the figure for 1987 would exceed one million. He expected that 100,000 alone would come during the spring pilgrimage season. Like in Hangchow, pilgrims arrived the night before the nineteenth day of the second month and kept all-night vigil in the three monasteries. For the holy day in 1987, some 5,000 pilgrims kept the vigil at P'u-chi, and about 3,000 each at the Fa-yü and Hui-chi.

Among the pilgrims, overseas Chinese from Singapore, Hong Kong, the Philippines, Japan, and the United States were well represented. They tended to be the ones who sponsored rituals of *shui-lu* plenary masses for the benefit of dead relatives. They stood out in the crowd on account of their fashionable clothing and jewelry. Pilgrims from large cities such as Shanghai, Hangchow, Fuchow, and Canton also asked monks to perform religious services. Most pilgrims keeping the vigil came from Kiangsu, Chekiang, Fukien, with fewer from Kiangsi and the interior provinces. People who lived on the islands of the Chushan Archipelago tended to come just for the day.

Aside from the international and cosmopolitan composition of the pilgrims, there were some other striking differences between the pilgrims who came to P'u-t'o and those who went to Hangchow. Although religious tourism professionals had also begun to organize tour packages from Shanghai, pilgrims predominantly came with family members, friends, or by themselves. Pilgrimage groups with their distinctive clothing, head-coverings, and the red tags worn on their left arms, such as those observed in Hangchow, were conspicuously absent on P'u-t'o. Pilgrims came less out of habit than for the sake of fulfilling vows, or in the hope of having a vision of Kuan-yin. Nowadays, the pilgrimage circuit begins with a three-hour boat ride to Lo-chia, a small island lying further east of P'u-t'o. Kuan-yin is believed to have been born there. So it is appropriate that one should begin one's visit with Kuan-yin's native place (*lao-chia*). Upon returning, one should immediately go to offer incense at the huge boulder called Kuan-yin T'iao (Kuan-yin's Jump), for when Kuan-yin jumped from Lo-chia to P'u-t'o in one step, she landed on the rock and actually left two foot-prints on it. The boulder is in the vicinity of the small temple called "Kuan-yin Who Refused to Go Away" (the first temple on the island founded by Egaku), the Purple Bamboo Grove (no bamboo is left, but there is an abandoned temple by this name that serves as a restaurant), and the Cave of Tidal Sounds. Pilgrims would visit all of these sites one by one. From there they would offer incense at the three monasteries, make donations, and collect seals of the three monasteries by having them stamped on their incense bags. The road leading from the Northern Monastery to Buddha Peak was the Pilgrim's Way (*hsiang-lu*) proper. Devout pilgrims or those who were either making vows or fulfilling vows would either kneel down and prostrate themselves every other three steps (*san-pu i-kuei*), or simply bow with folded hands (*san-pu i-pai*). Near the Northern Monastery, pilgrims would line up in front of the Cave of Brahmā's Voice to seek visions of Kuan-yin. Although this cave became popular only in the Ming, it now enjoys equal, if not more, fame among pilgrims as the Cave of Tidal Sounds.

The transformation of P'u-t'o into the Chinese Potalaka took many centuries. Many different kinds of people contributed to this effort, and many different types of media were used to bolster and broadcast the claim. All these were intimately connected with pilgrimage. Because of pilgrimage activities, an isolated island in the ocean came to be identified as the sacred home of Kuan-yin by Chinese as well as foreign pilgrims.

Buddhist leaders in the late Ming were not always happy about the overemphasis on making pilgrimages. Indeed, from the enlightened perspective of *śūnyatā*, Potalaka is nowhere as well as everywhere. Chu-hung criticized the zeal of pilgrims in risking their lives by sailing the stormy ocean. He asked rhetorically:

> Did not the sūtras say that bodhisattvas appear everywhere? Then there is no need to go very far. If you always maintain the heart of compassion and practice deeds of compassion like the bodhisattva, even if you do not leave your own home, you are already looking at Potalaka; and even if you do not see Kuan-yin's golden visage, you are already with the bodhisattva from moment to moment. (YCFH 26:48a)

In true Ch'an fashion, in order to prevent people from forming attachments, Chu-hung deconstructed the myth of Potalaka and denied that Kuan-yin was only found there. But the very reason that he launched this criticism was precisely because of the great popularity of the P'u-t'o pilgrimage in his time. Even though Kuan-yin might not only be found on P'u-t'o, many people, especially pilgrims, found it comforting to believe that she was always there. In order to anchor Kuan-yin to P'u-t'o, a constant effort toward constructing the island (both physically and metaphorically) was needed. The identity between the island P'u-t'o and the scriptural Potalaka therefore had to be repeatedly claimed. As the 1698 gazetteer put it:

> P'u-t'o is the bodhimaṇḍa (*tao-ch'ang*) of Kuan-yin. This is mentioned clearly in the Buddhist scriptures. An obscure place in China thus became known in the world because of secret texts hidden in the dragon's palace and Sanskrit scriptures from the Western Regions. Thus we know that the perfect and bright ones of the ten directions are all manifestations of the Buddha. They are not restricted to the golden ground of Jetavana or the Indian palace of Śrāvastī. Take a look at P'u-t'o today: Is there any difference between it and the description found in the Buddhist scriptures? Does the bodhimaṇḍa today differ from that of yore when the great bodhisattva preached the Dharma surrounded by the holy assembly? Someone may object saying that auspicious gatherings do not occur often and the Dharma feast can no longer be repeated. Therefore there is a difference between the present and the past. But can we really deny that the flowers, fruit, trees, streams, and ponds that we see now are not the realms of the bright and perfect? The Ch'an master Fo-yin Liao-yüan once said, "Green hills filling your eyes are there for you to see." Master Ch'eng Ming-tao [Ch'eng Hao, 1032–1085] was said to have immediately achieved enlightenment when he heard this. Travelers who come to P'u-t'o today must view everything with attention. Ordinary mortals are attached to phenomena. That is why some of them may have doubts. Recalling that the bodhisattva is said to have sat on a precious diamond throne, they think that the rocks on the island are crude and strange. But they fail to realize that mountains, rivers, grasses and trees are originally formed by people's deluded thoughts. Because the Buddha's mind ground is wondrously bright, all that the Buddha sees are gold and jewels. One should study well the *Hua-yen (Avataṃsaka)*, *Śūraṅgama*, *Lotus* and *Nirvāṇa* sūtras. Only then will one know that all the famous mountain bodhimaṇḍas are indeed the places where Buddha lives. (PTSC 1698, 4:2b-3b)

Construction and deconstruction, founding and decline, building and rebuilding—these are some of the cycles P'u-t'o has experienced. Through all these changing fortunes, pilgrims were always in the midst of everything. What we see in the case of P'u-t'o is one example of how the Chinese created a Buddhist sacred landscape on their own land, and by providing Kuan-yin with a Chinese home, domesticated the bodhisattva.

10

Feminine Forms of Kuan-yin in Late Imperial China

The story of Princess Miao-shan, discussed in chapter 8, though most famous, was not the only one circulating in late imperial China. Since the Sung period, another feminine incarnation of Kuan-yin known either as the Fish-basket Kuan-yin (Yü-lan Kuan-yin) or the Wife of Mr. Ma (Ma-lang-fu) have been celebrated in gāthās or poems written by Ch'an monks. She also appeared in drama and precious scrolls as well as paintings. As discussed in the last chapter, with the creation of the island of P'u-t'o as a major pilgrimage site for Kuan-yin, a new iconography, Kuan-yin of the South Sea, also came into being. In this chapter I examine the legends and iconographies of these two feminine forms of Kuan-yin. A final feminine manifestation of Kuan-yin as the Old Mother will be the subject of chapter 11.

Since the sexual transformation of Avalokiteśvara happened only in China, it is natural for scholars to search for the reasons within Chinese religion and culture. What could have facilitated the transformation? Could the feminine Kuan-yin be traced to a native Chinese goddess? And once Kuan-yin appeared as a goddess, did this empower real Chinese women? I first examine the connection between Kuan-yin and native Chinese goddesses and then the relationship between Kuan-yin and gender before we turn to the Fish-basket Kuan-yin and Kuan-yin of the South Sea.

Kuan-yin and Chinese Goddesses

In an article written in 1950 and published in a special issue on Kuan-yin of the journal *Ars Buddhica* (Bukkyō geijutsu), Kobayashi Taichirō (1950:3, 44) stated that the transformation to a feminine Kuan-yin was a result of the mixture between Buddhism and indigenous Chinese goddess worship and that it took place between the T'ang and the Sung. He made the statement without elaboration. Perhaps he assumed that his reader was familiar with his thesis, stated in another long article he wrote two years earlier entitled "Nü-wa and Kuan-yin."

Although the title leads one to expect it to be a comparative study on the goddess Nü-wa and Kuan-yin, it is in fact only about the former. He probably intended this to be a prolegomenon to a future study. Kobayashi's main thesis is that in the spread of religion, certain elements of the new, incoming religion must connect with corresponding elements of the host culture, so as to be absorbed by the latter. In the process, the former will gradually undergo changes. He cites the spread of Christianity in Europe as one example. The introduction of Buddhism into China and the cult of Kuan-yin is another (Kobayashi 1948:5). Through a study of Nü-wa, whom he considers to be the most ancient as well as the most prototypical Chinese goddess, and other important goddesses, he hopes to unravel their relationships to Kuan-yin. According to Kobayashi, the origin of all Chinese goddesses is the wish for fertility in nature and humankind, and their functions all have to do with promoting procreativeness and, especially, the birth of sons. The sites where goddesses are worshiped would usually be mountaintops, waterfalls, springs, riverbanks—places where yin and yang meet (77). Using the locations of Nü-wa's cultic sites as a basis, he traces the origin of the cult to Shantung, the lower reaches of the Yellow River, from where it spread to Hopei, Shansi, Shensi, and Kansu, reaching the upper reaches of the Wei River (78–116). Kobayashi believes that faith in Nü-wa was most prevalent during the transition from the T'ang to the Sung. Although Nü-wa was also worshiped in the Yangtze River region, the cult never took root there and that was why Kuan-yin could replace her in this area (88). Although he mentions Kuan-yin rarely and almost as a digression,[1] he concludes the long and erudite article by claiming that he has provided "the history of the first half of Kuan-yin's life in the Yellow River region" (116), implying that Kuan-yin is a later incarnation of Nü-wa.

Some of Kobayashi's ideas are intriguing and highly ideosyncratic. For example, he does not explain why he leaves out the Queen Mother of the West in his discussion of Chinese goddesses, although she is surely the most famous and best known among all the goddesses. It is helpful to map the catchment area of Nü-wa's cult as he did, but his explanation about Kuan-yin's flourishing in the Yangtze River region as the result of Nü-wa's relative obscurity is not convincing. Indeed, as I described in chapters 3 and 4, during the Six Dynasties (or the fourth to sixth centuries), when the faith in Kuan-yin first appeared, it was the north, the Yellow River region, and not the south, the Yangtze River region, which provided the locale.

Although I am disappointed in not finding in the study any hard evidences linking Kuan-yin to Nü-wa, I am sympathetic to his call that we should see Kuan-yin as a transformation of Chinese goddesses and try to find her origin in the Chinese indigenous tradition. For indeed Kuan-yin has not remained simply the Chinese transplant of an Indian Buddhist deity, if he was ever one. The practical difficulty in pursuing this line of inquiry is one of methodology. Clearly, the presence and even prominence of goddesses in China is beyond doubt. The problem for students of Chinese religion is the lack of data concerning the cultic and social contexts in connection with these goddesses. Although there are literary references and, in recent decades, increasingly abundant archaeological artifacts relating to goddesses, with the exception of the Queen Mother of the West, it is still extremely difficult to know if indeed there was an active cult dedicated to any of the goddesses and if so, what the devotees believed in and what rituals they performed.[2] But even without knowing the whole picture, whatever glimpses we can catch of the ancient Chinese goddesses are tantalizing. The missing link is their relationship with the feminine Kuan-yin.

One of the most exciting finds made by Chinese archaeologists within the last twenty years are the sites located in Inner Mongolia and Liaoning Province, particularly the Neolithic Hung-shan culture (c. 3500–2500 B.C.E.). Clay figurines of pregnant women, jade pig-dragons, and the foundation of what has been called the "Temple of a Goddess" found in these sites have led some scholars to suggest that a fertility cult involving the worship of goddesses and a religion centering on shamanic communication with spirits and deities might be the defining features of this north Chinese culture.[3] Based on burial and ancestor worship practices, mainland Chinese scholars recently have also hypothesized the existence of a "matriarchal society" in the Shang. The tomb of Fu Hao, consort of the late Shang king Wu Ting, who died in 1200 B.C.E., contained a large number of ritual bronze vessels inscribed with her name, which she probably used during her lifetime. But some of the vessels were also inscribed with another posthumous name for her and would indicate that the vessels were cast specifically for the occasion of her burial and for her use in the afterlife. "References to females are also evident in oracle bone inscriptions of the Shang period. Mentions of a deceased mother (*bi*) are more numerous than those of a father or male ruler, and it has been suggested that the predominance of female names points to a matriarchal society. This situation appears to have changed during the Zhou period, by the end of which no special sacrifices seem to have been directed at female ancestors" (Chen 1996:271).

Of the goddesses whose names are known to us from historical times, the Queen Mother of the West is the most famous and also the best studied. Michael Loewe, who wrote about the famous silk painting found in the No. 1 tomb of Ma-wang-tui, Hunan, dated 168 B.C.E. and also Han mirrors, both of which feature the goddess, summarized some key characteristics about her. First mentioned in the *Chuang Tzu*, the Queen Mother of the West became very popular beginning with the Common Era. She is a timeless being who has attained the Tao. A hybrid, semi-human figure, she is believed to possess power to control some of the constellations. She confers the gift of deathlessness. Her home is Mt K'un-lun, although she is sometimes said to reside within a cave. She attracts rulers who seek her out for blessing (Loewe 1979:89). Although she was a favorite subject in Han art, it is not at all clear who worshiped her and how. Loewe commented that "As yet there is nothing to show that the cult of the Queen Mother had affected formal aspects of Han religious practice, or that she was being regularly invoked as a means of procuring immortality on behalf of a dear deceased relative" (101).

She was worshiped by the masses in a short-lived religious movement that took place in February to March of the third year B.C.E. There was a severe drought. People exchanged manikins of straw or hemp with one another as emblems for the Queen Mother of the West, saying that they were preparing for her arrival. Large numbers of persons met on the roadsides, some with disheveled hair or going barefoot. They passed through twenty-six commanderies and kingdoms until they reached the capital city. They sometimes carried fire to the roof-tops by night, beating drums, shouting, and frightening one another. In the village settlements they held services and set up gaming boards for a lucky throw and they sang and danced in worship of the Queen Mother of the West.[4] Loewe commented on the significance of the time of the year when the movement occurred, the advent processions as preparation for the progress of an emperor, the elements of religious enthusiasm, for example, the beating of drums, the raising of fire, song, and dance, and the possible association between the carrying of manikins and seasonal festivals (100). Since the Queen Mother of the West was the personification of yin, perhaps she was invoked in order to overcome the drought that was the catalyst for the movement. Despite her early prominence in Chinese religion and her continuing honored position among Taoist practitioners, the Queen Mother of the West cannot be said to have been a popular goddess for the common people in the succeeding centuries. It was not until the sixteenth century that she reappeared with a new name and identity as the supreme deity worshiped by the sectarians. Known as Wu-sheng Lao-mu (Eternal Mother, Venerable Mother, or literally, the "Unborn Mother") who is also known as Golden Mother of the Jade Pool

(Yao-ch'ih Chin-mu), and Granny Queen Mother (Wang-mu Niang-niang), she was worshiped as the creator and savior of mankind. Daniel Overmyer and Susan Naquin both suggest that this goddess should be traced to the Queen Mother of the West because she, just as the latter, inspired mass movements which contained millennial expectations (Overmyer 1976:139–40; Naquin 1976:9). She continues to be worshiped under this name as one of the central deities by members of spirit-writing religious groups in Taiwan (Jordon and Overmyer 1986).

Recently Jean James has summarized previous scholarship on the goddess and offers a comprehensive iconographic study of her images on Han mirrors, money trees, and offering shrines in different parts of China. She concludes that the Queen Mother of the West was "essentially a personal deity, a benevolent goddess to whom one could pray for wealth, a long life, and who could assist *hun* souls. After the influx of Buddhism following the fall of the Han in A.D. 220, she left her home on Kunlun and its paradisiacal ambiance to the Buddha Amitābha and his Western Paradise, and became a Daoist deity, popular among Tang poets and common folk" (James 1995:39). She further suggests that this goddess was "the very first deity to appear in Chinese religion outside the state cult devoted to sky gods like Tai Yi" (40). It is significant that the first Chinese personal deity is a goddess. It is thus not surprising that some attributes connected with her were adopted by Kuan-yin after the latter became a "goddess." I refer to the role occupied by birds as their attendants or companions. According to the *Shan-hai ching* (Classic of Mountains and Seas) and *Huai-nan Tzu*, the Queen Mother of the West is attended by three blue birds; at the very top of a fine intact money tree excavated in Szechwan stands a phoenix with its wings fully spread, a good omen symbolizing peace and prosperity (James 1995:21;38). As we shall read later in this chapter, when Kuan-yin appears as Nan-hai Kuan-yin (Kuan-yin of the South Sea), the bodhisattva is always depicted as being accompanied by a white parrot who hovers above her in paintings and sculptures in late imperial times. There is absolutely no basis for the presence of the bird in Buddhist scriptural or iconographical traditions. We can understand its presence only when we take into consideration the prior existence of other birds in the iconography of the Queen Mother of the West.

The Queen of the West is described as a beautiful woman of thirty years old in the *Han Wu-ti nei-ch'uan* (Intimate Biography of Emperor Wu of the Han), attributed to Pan Ku since the Sung but written by an anonymous Taoist author in the latter part of the Six Dynasties. It tells the story of the Queen Mother's invitation of the emperor on the seventh day of the seventh month in 110 B.C.E. to her palace and her revelations of a list of magical drugs and esoteric texts, including the "true form of the five mountains" where divine beings dwell. It reflects strongly the Mao Shan Taoist tradition (Nienhauser 1986:396–97; Schipper 1965). Since the goddess is clearly identified as a beautiful matron, it might have served as the inspiration for conceiving the White-robed Kuan-yin in a similar fashion.[5]

In her survey of Buddhist sculpture in China, Angela F. Howard points out that the earliest images of Buddha, what she calls "proto-Buddhist," were either modeled upon or grafted onto existing iconography of the Queen Mother of the West. Since the goddess was the first deity to be represented by the Chinese and the Buddha was regarded as a god similar to the deified Lao Tzu and Yellow Emperor by the people in the Han dynasty, it is not surprising that the early artisans used the goddess as the model in creating the new deity (Howard et al. forthcoming). As Buddhism took hold in China and the creation of independent Buddhist icons became firmly established, images of Buddhas and bodhisattvas dominated the Chinese religious landscape. Although Buddhist iconography eventually liberated itself from its initial dependency on indigenous models, however, I wonder if some of the latter's symbolism might still serve as resources from which new Chinese feminine forms of Kuan-yin might draw.

I have searched for possible antecedents for the feminine Kuan-yin among indigenous Chinese goddesses, but there are few conclusive findings to report. The simple reason is, as I mentioned before, the lack of any data about any of the goddesses' cults. The rise of the Chou dynasty with its emphasis on the Mandate of Heaven and patriarchal lineage clearly had a profound effect on the ancient religion in which female goddesses and female shamans (the word shaman or *wu* originally refers to a female shaman) might have played important roles. With the establishment of Confucianism as the state religion in the Han, goddesses and real women became increasingly marginalized. The state cult consisted primarily of male deities, and the king and his official representatives served as priests. The empire was ruled by the imperial bureaucracy, and the supernatural realm of gods was also conceived in the same way. Thus, the Jade Emperor would be the counterpart of the human emperor, the city god the equivalent of the local magistrate, and in both realms a male bureaucracy reigned supreme. Gods, like human officials, were very much tied to their assigned territories. The triumphant dominance of male gods left many human needs unmet.

The decline of Chinese goddesses left a religious vacuum. I would argue that Kuan-yin filled the empty space. So if indeed there were any relationship between Kuan-yin and native Chinese goddesses, I would say the relationship was a negative one. In other words, precisely because there were no strong goddesses around, Kuan-yin could undergo a sexual transformation. If there had been powerful and popular goddesses in China, Avalokiteśvara probably would not have become a goddess in China, just as he did not become a legitimizing symbol for Chinese emperors. This might explain why Avalokiteśvara did not undergo a sexual transformation in India and Tibet where powerful and popular goddess, such as Durgā and Tārā, are present. Kuan-yin could survive as a goddess because he already enjoyed a strong cult as a male bodhisattva derived from the spiritual authority of Buddhism. Even after the transformation, Kuan-yin was never part of the imperial state cult. While she was the savior of all, she was not controlled by any authority and owed no allegiance to anyone. Although she was not derived directly from any indigenous goddess, her relationship to Chinese culture was still undeniable. She clearly came under the influence of Chinese euhemerization. Although Kuan-yin is originally an ahistorical mythical figure, Chinese myths about her, particularly that of Princess Miao-shan, changed her into a historical person with a biography. Just like all Chinese gods receive the utmost homage on their birthdays, Kuan-yin is also provided with a "birthday" (the nineteenth day of the second month), which is celebrated by both monks and common people since at least the Yüan period.

Another very important point is that the rise of the cult of the feminine Kuan-yin seems to have rekindled the goddess tradition in China. The worship of important goddesses such as Ma-tsu (familiarly known as "Granny"), Pi-hsia Yüan-chün (Niang-niang or "Nanny"), and the Unborn Mother flourished after Kuan-yin became feminine during the Sung and came to serve some of the needs of Chinese people that had gone unfulfilled by the territorial and bureaucratic male gods. This is the issue discussed by P. Steven Sangren in a very thought-provoking article he wrote in 1983, "Female Gender in Chinese Religious Symbols: Kuan Yin, Ma Tsu and the 'Eternal Mother.'"

Kuan-yin and Gender

Sangren begins his article by pointing out that although "[f]emale deities occupy prominent positions in the Chinese religious pantheon and in Chinese ritual," most anthropological studies on Chinese popular religion instead focus on male deities, the "celestial bureaucrats." Many of these male gods are worshiped in territorial cults and, being based on the imperial model, they are hierarchical. In contrast, female deities such as Kuan-yin, Ma-tsu, and the Unborn Mother, are the opposite. They are not tied to a territory. They are not bureaucrats and they are not hierarchical. He suggests that the female Chinese deities are closely connected with the cultural significance of the female gender in China.

Specifically, there are two points connected with the Chinese cultural understanding of femininity that may help us to understand female Chinese deities. One is the belief, shared by both men and women, that women are polluting. Second, women in Chinese domestic groups function as divisive as well as unifying forces. While femininity in China has both positive and negative qualities, female deities have only positive ones. Real women are polluting in their sexual activities and by giving birth to children. "As idealizations of womanhood, then, female deities must overcome the stigma of pollution associated with menstruation, sexual intercourse, death, and childbirth" (Sangren 1983:11). A female deity as a symbol of purity "involves the negation of woman as wife and affirmation of her role as mother (if not childbearer)" (14). For, "[A]s mothers and sisters, Chinese women act to soften the competition for authority between brothers and to mediate between authoritarian fathers and occasionally rebellious sons. As daughters-in-law and wives, Chinese women tend to exacerbate domestic tensions, often agitating for early division of extended families" (15). As mothers, female deities serve as unifying symbols. Their relations to their devotees who are their children have three salient dimensions: inclusivity, mediation, and alliance. Inclusivity explains why "female deities, unlike their male counterparts, do not favor the wealthy and influential over the poor, insiders over outsiders, or men over women" (15). Kuan-yin is worshiped particularly by women in their later years when they undergo the trauma of "postparenthood," and also by prostitutes, social outcasts and other marginalized groups because of her inclusivity (Sangren 1983:15–22). Kuan-yin is the mother figure par excellence, who loves all people as her children without discrimination.

In fact, this image of Kuan-yin as the universal mother has been used as the explanation for the bodhisattva's sexual transformation in China. The most common explanation as to why Kuan-yin became a goddess in China offered by Chinese scholars is that the quality of compassion is a maternal virtue in the Chinese cultural context. The common expression "Father is strict, but mother is compassionate" (*fu-yen mu-tz'u*) would be an apt example for such a tautological interpretation. However, the Buddhist tradition does not share this view. As Cabezón (1992) tells us in "Mother Wisdom, Father Love: Gender-Based Imagery in Mahāyāna Buddhist Thought," although Buddhism uses gender-based imagery for wisdom and compassion, the two most important Mahāyāna concepts and primary virtues of a bodhisattva, it identifies wisdom as feminine and compassion as masculine. "We find in the scriptures of the Mahāyāna several instances in which wisdom is identified as female, and more specifically as mother, whereas the less analytic and more emotive states that constitute 'method,' namely love, compassion, altruism, and so forth, are identified with the male or 'father.'" (1992:183). Since one becomes enlightened as a result of realizing the true nature of everything, wisdom is therefore that which gives birth to a buddha. Prajñāpāramitā (Perfection of Wisdom) is called the "Mother of all the buddhas" and became hypostasized as a goddess as early as the beginning of the Common Era. She is eulogized in one of the oldest Mahāyāna texts:

If a mother with many sons had fallen ill,
They all, sad in mind, would busy themselves about her:
Just so also, the Buddhas in the world-systems in the ten directions
Bring to mind this perfection of wisdom as their mother.
The saviors of the world who were in the past, and also those that are [just now] in the ten directions,
Have issued from her, and so will the future ones be. She is the one who shows the world [for what it is], she the genetrix, the mother of the Jinas,
And she reveals the thoughts and actions of other beings. (Conze 1973:31)

Some feminist scholars interested in positive religious symbols of the feminine have naturally been very excited about this (Macy 1977). In contrast to the West, which defines intellect and reason as masculine traits and emotion and feeling as feminine ones, the Buddhist case is the opposite. The example shows clearly how arbitrary and culturally constructed gender characteristics are. Moreover, taken in isolation, "the use of woman (and more specifically of motherhood) as the symbol of a positive spiritual quality (wisdom) in the Mahāyāna is a great leap forward in the religious thought of India" (Cabezón 1992:188).

But as Cabezón reminds us, it is necessary to contextualize feminine symbols (and we should add, goddesses) historically and sociologically. The presence of goddesses or feminine symbols in a religion does not translate into a respect of real women in that culture. There is no necessary correlation between the veneration of goddesses and the status of women in societies that venerate goddesses. Kālī and Durgā are powerful goddesses of India, yet it has been primarily men who worship them. Similarly, although the Tao is conceived as having feminine characteristics, real Chinese women seldom hold leadership roles in religious Taoism. In her study of Indian women, Leigh Mintum wonders why a culture with powerful goddesses should subordinate women and concludes, "Goddesses did not empower the women I knew in any practical or secular sense, but they did, in my opinion, contribute to the fortitude and pride that are so much a part of their character" (Mintum 1993:183). Eva Cantarella reaches the same conclusion in the case of ancient Greek and Roman religions

(1987). The same can be said about the cult of the Virgin Mary in Christianity and, as I have tried to show in this book, Kuan-yin in Chinese Buddhism.

Coming back to the symbol of the "mother" for wisdom, I am in full agreement with what Cabezón says about Buddhism, "It is naive to think that the mere presence of a symbol of the feminine in a tradition is derived from a conception of gender that is affirming of the status of women or that the presence of such a symbol is sufficient to guarantee that a positive attitude toward the feminine is going to be conveyed to women, or more generally to society through that symbol" (1992:188). This is also the point Sangren makes in regard to gender and feminine symbols. For what appears to an outsider to the Buddhist tradition to be an exaltation of women as symbols of wisdom turns out, upon analysis, both a downgrading of wisdom as well as a denigration of real women.

As Cabezón explains, the Buddhist symbols of motherly wisdom and fatherly love are derived from the Indian and Tibetan notions of parentage. Because Buddhists of all three traditions, be they followers of Hīnayāna, Mahāyāna, or Vajrayāna must realize the nature of reality, which is wisdom, to become enlightened, wisdom is the common cause, like the water and soil, which is compared to the mother. But the mother does not give the child identity, which comes entirely from the father. Depending on the "seed" or ethnicity of the father, the child is similarly identified. The altruistic mind giving rise to compassion and method is a unique Mahāyāna seed that gives birth to a Mahāyāna bodhisattva. Although Hīnayāna Buddhists have the same "mother," because they do not have compassion as their "father," they are thus inferior. Therefore "wisdom is not represented as female because women were considered to be more wise than men or more analytically capable. Indeed, a great deal of literature within the tradition is dedicated to showing that this is not the case. . . . Wisdom is characterized as feminine (1) because of wisdom's inferiority in determining Mahāyānic ethnicity and (2) due to the Mahāyāna's preoccupation with the centrality of emotional states as *the* distinguishing characteristic (its uniqueness) as a tradition, therefore considering them as more important to Mahāyanic identity, and hence characterizing them as masculine. Clearly, neither of these two reasons for using gender-based symbols adds to the status either of wisdom or women" (Cabezón 1992:190).

On the other hand, in developing the essential *bodhicitta* of a bodhisattva, the Tibetan tradition also makes use of one's real mother as the starting point and then concentrates on expanding the love felt towards her to both one's friends and enemies. A bodhisattva regards everyone as his own mother. Gendun Gyatso, the second Dalai Lama (1475–1542) and the first to be recognized as an incarnation of the Dalai Lama line, writes about the practice of "giving and taking," the basis of the *lojong* ("mind training") brought to Tibet by Atiśa (980/90–1055):

> The object of the ingeniously direct and nearly infallible giving-and-taking practice is arousing genuine compassion. It happens in several phases, each of which may only last a few minutes, or as long as it takes to complete. First one meditates briefly on one's aspiration to attain enlightenment. Then, following the cue of the *Metta Sutta,* which presents the attitude of a mother as a paragon, one visualizes and contemplates one's own mother in a particular way, powerfully described in our text. Then one resolves to take responsibility for her welfare, and the practice of taking and giving begins. Taking happens with the in-breath. Giving happens with the out-breath. With each in-breath and out-breath the practitioner does what he or she can to fulfill the attitude and action described. One realizes then that in the course of incalculably many rebirths, everyone has been everyone's mother in one life or another. This enables one to extend whatever compassion one has aroused toward one's own mother to other people. And then the same taking and giving proceeds in relation to others in several successive phases: in relation to a person you dislike, a friend, and a stranger. Next, the level is expanded to include not just one individual but many—all beings. Finally one does the practice in relation to many enemies. (Bercholz and Kohn 1993:158)

Although bodhisattvas love everyone, even the enemy, as they would their own mothers, they, like the Buddha, their spiritual "father," are masters of a skillful method that is conceived as masculine. Chinese monks who are learned in the Buddhist tradition invoke Kuan-yin as the "compassionate father" (*tz'u-fu*) for this reason. For example, both Ta-hui Tsung-kao (1089–1163) and Ch'u-shih Fan-chi (1296–1370), two renowned Ch'an masters, eulogized Kuan-yin as such in their gāthās dedicated to him (T 48:1018b; HTC 124:106b). Being a bodhisattva, Kuan-yin is a masculine and heroic personage (*yung-meng chang-fu*), and a "great being" (*ta-shih*). Compassion did not have to be expressed only as motherly love.

Does this mean that because monks and elite Buddhist laymen faithfully adhered to traditional Buddhist views of Avalokiteśvara, the feminine Kuan-yin is then either a corruption or vulgarization effected by popular religion or, in a recent feminist reconstruction, a tradition created by women? Scholars trying to explain the bodhisattva's sexual transformation in China tend to fall into a dualistic two-tiered model, either elite versus popular or men versus women. We may take Kenneth Ch'en as representing the former and Barbara Reed the latter. In chapter 6 I discussed Ch'en's thesis that the feminine White-robed Kuan-yin resulted from the "appropriation" of Buddhism by Chinese popular religion.

I also question Barbara Reed's suggestion that the female Kuan-yin was primarily created and promoted by women artists in the Ming and that they consciously chose to surround the female Kuan-yin with "female" symbols such as lotuses, vases, willow branches, water, and the moon (Reed 1992: 163). It is very true that Kuan-yin was beloved by women in late imperial China, who showed their devotion through their artistic creations. Some of them became known to us because they painted or embroidered her images, but many remain anonymous. Susan Mann tells us that in the eighteenth-century Kuan-yin iconography was "vivid in women's minds, fills dreams, portraits, and embroidered designs." She relates how the poet Ch'ien Hui once embroidered the bodhisattva's image using her own hair instead of silk thread in a style "not inferior to the inkline style of the Song painter Li Gonglin" (Mann 1997:182). But surely, men also participated in the same construction. In fact, the iconography of the female Kuan-yin was created long before the Ming by male artists, some of whom were Ch'an monks. The celebrated painting of the White-robed Kuan-yin by Mu-ch'i (ca. 1210–1275) preserved in the Daitokuji, Kyoto, is a prominent example. As for the "female" symbols surrounding Kuan-yin, while lotuses and vases were already established as typical attributes for Avalokiteśvara in India, willow branches, water, and the moon, as I have shown in chapters 2 and 6, are based on Buddhist scriptures and connected to healing ritual and philosophy. There is nothing intrinsically "female" about them. We can and should say that Chinese women contributed to the construction of the female Kuan-yin. But it would be going too far to attribute this primarily to them. In fact, I would argue that no single group, class, or segment of Chinese society should be so privileged. Kuan-yin is worshiped by all classes and by both genders. She is gracious to all and, in turn, possessed by none. This is the real reason and the real secret for her success in China.

If the sexual transformation of Kuan-yin was not engineered by popular religion or feminist women, once the female Kuan-yin became popular, she did offer options to real Chinese women and was also welcomed into the popular pantheon. Since the Sung when the female Kuan-yin first made her indisputable appearance, other popular goddesses also emerged and most of them claimed a family connection with her. There seems to be a strong link between the female Kuan-yin and the births of new goddesses such as Ma-tsu, P'i-hsia Yüan-chün, and the Eternal Mother.

Although some scholars have made these arguments, I have not been able to discover any evidence that there was a direct link between Kuan-yin and an earlier indigenous goddess such as Nü-wa or the Queen Mother of the West, despite the latter's sharing some similarities with Kuan-yin. The search for the "origin" of the female Kuan-yin may be a futile one. However, it is possible to talk about the processes, the media, and the consequences of the transformation. Furthermore, I think a more fruitful path to understanding is to view the sexual transformation of Avalokiteśvara in the larger context of the Chinese domestication of the bodhisattva. In previous chapters, I have addressed this process of domestication. As discussed in chapter 5, long before the appearance of the legend of Princess Miao-shan as the manifestation of Kuan-yin in 1100, two wonder-working monks who lived several centuries earlier had already been known as incarnations of the bodhisattva. Why was Kuan-yin believed to appear in China first in the guise of these monks and only later as a woman? How was the change related to new iconography, miracle tales, and the social and institutional settings of religious practice? It was in attempting to answer these questions that I became convinced that we have to examine Kuan-yin's feminization in the larger context of the bodhisattva's domestication in China. In the rest of this chapter, I discuss two more feminine forms of Kuan-yin, which serve as additional examples of this process.

The Fish-basket Kuan-yin

If Princess Miao-shan is a symbol of virginal chastity, Yü-lan Kuan-yin (Kuan-yin with the Fish Basket) is a feminine image of Kuan-yin of far greater complexity. She is often known by another name: Mr. Ma's Wife (Ma-lang-fu). Both images are included in the thirty-three images of Sino-Japanese art: the Fish-basket is number 10 and Mr. Ma's Wife is number 28.

I have already mentioned her story in chapter 4. It can be briefly summarized here. During the T'ang dynasty, when Buddhism enjoyed great popularity, people living in the eastern part of Shensi loved to hunt and had no interest in Buddhism. In 809 (or 817) a beautiful young woman came and told people that she would marry any man who could memorize the "Universal Gateway" chapter (of the *Lotus Sūtra*) in one night. On the next morning, twenty men passed the test. Saying that she could not marry them all, she asked them to memorize the *Diamond Sūtra* (or the *Prajñāpāramitā Sūtra*). More than ten could recite it in the morning. Then she asked them to spend three days memorizing the *Lotus Sūtra*. This time, only Mr. Ma succeeded. So he made wedding preparations and invited her to come to his house. Upon her arrival, she claimed to feel ill and asked to be allowed to rest in another room. Before the wedding guests had departed, she suddenly died. In a short while, the body rotted and had to be buried in a hurry. Several days later, an old monk wearing a purple robe came and asked Ma to show him the tomb. The monk opened it and touched the corpse with his staff. The flesh had already disintegrated, exposing bones that were linked together by a gold chain. The monk told the assembled onlookers that the woman was a manifestation of a great sage who came in order to save them from their evil karma. After washing the bones in the water, he carried them on his staff and ascended into the sky. Many people living in that region became converted to Buddhism.[6] Like śarīras, bones linked by a golden chain were visible signs of a holy person. She was therefore also called Bodhisattva with Chained Bones (*So-ku p'u-sa).*

In the early versions of the story, the woman was not explicitly identified as a manifestation of Kuan-yin. There was also no mention of the fish basket. Neither was the region where the miracle occurred given a name. All these details were added in the succeeding centuries, and as her cult developed, these became common knowledge and were represented by stock expressions. For instance, when the Ch'an master Feng-hsüeh Yen-chao (887–973) of Ju-chou (Shensi) was asked by a monk, "What is the pure Body of Dharma?," he answered, "Mr. Ma's Wife of the Golden Sand Beach (Chin-sha-t'an)" (Sawada 1959:40; Stein 1986:54). Huang T'ing-chien (1045–1105) also used the phrase "Chained bones on Golden Sand Beach" in his poem written in 1088. During the Sung and Yüan, from the twelfth to the fourteenth centuries, many Ch'an masters used this figure in their poems. The woman was now firmly identified as Kuan-yin. She was called either Mr. Ma's Wife or Kuan-yin with the Fish Basket. She was called Yü-lan Kuan-yin, for she came to the Golden Sand Beach as a fish-monger, carrying a basket of fish on her arm. The Sung Ch'an master, Wu-ch'un Shih-fan (1174–1249), for instance, wrote a poem entitled, "Kuan-yin, The Woman Fish Seller (Yü-fu Kuan-yin)":

> *Though covered with a fishy smell and dirty, she is totally oblivious.*
> *Arriving at the fish market, she looks for a bargain.*
> *Among them, not many are alive.*
> *Lifting the basket to the wind, Who is willing to buy?*
> *Fish inside the basket, pearls inside the clothes,*
> *One should buy and sell right away,*
> *For many are false and few genuine. (*Fo-chien Ch'an-shih yü-lu 5, Sawada *1959:41)*

During the same period, she also became a favorite subject of paintings. Many paintings entitled either Mr. Ma's Wife or Fish-basket Kuan-yin have survived. An anecdote reported by Hung Mai attests to the subject's popularity in the Sung. There once was a man named Ho who lived in Chü-shan, Hai-chou (present-day Tai-tung, Kiangsu). His family had specialized in painting Kuan-yin for generations. The entire household kept a vegetarian diet. Each painting would cost 50 to 60,000 strings of cash and take a year to finish, for the work demanded great skill and patience. One day when he was about to paint, a beggar came to the door. He was covered with sores and scabs on his body. Blood and puss oozed out and the smell was unbearable. He offered a basket of carps to Ho and asked for a painting. Ho, offended, told him that the family had given up meat for generations and that the beggar should not insult him with the gift of fish. The beggar said to Ho, "Your paintings are not realistic enough. Although I am a beggar because of my poverty, I have a good painting of Kuan-yin. Would you like to have it?" Ho was overjoyed. He prepared a clean room and asked the beggar to come in. But as soon as he got in the room, the beggar locked the door from inside. After a long time, he called for Ho who, upon opening the door, discovered that the beggar had turned into a true likeness of Kuan-yin. The room was illuminated by a golden light and a strange fragrance lingered for several months. Ho called his students together and offered incense to the painting. After that, Ho's fame as a painter became even greater (*I-chien chih* 4:1772). Although we are not told if the painting was a Yü-lan Kuan-yin, the beggar in the story was definitely intended to be a manifestation of her, as the basket of carp made abundantly clear.

Among paintings with the title of Yü-lan Kuan-yin, the one attributed to Chao Meng-fu and kept at the National Palace Museum in Taipei is one of the better known examples (figure 10.1). Paintings of Ma-lang-fu, on the other hand, are harder to identify, for she is usually depicted as being no different from a Chinese woman. Judging by an inscription appended to it by a monk, however, the subject of a Sung painting of a lady holding a rolled up scroll, from the Metropolitan Museum of Art in New York, might be her (figure 10.2).[7] Sung Lien (1310–1381) wrote an eulogy to a portrait of Yü-lan Kuan-yin entitled, "Yü-lan Kuan-yin hsiang-tsan" (*Sung Hsüeh-shih wen-chi*, fascicle 51), in which he gave her "biography" its mature form.

Both in the paintings and in the Ch'an poems, she was shown as young, beautiful, and sexually alluring. Unlike Miao-shan, she promised marriage and sex. But like Miao-shan, she remained a virgin. She would first offer sexual favors, but then deny their gratification. She would use sexual desire as a skillful means, a teaching device to help people to reach goodness. However, there is strong evidence that she did not simply remain a sexual tease, but in fact she, or rather another woman like her, engaged in sexual activities in order to carry out the mission of salvation. Known simply as the "Woman of Yen-chou," she lived in eastern Shensi during the Ta-li era (766–779), several decades earlier than the

Figure 10.1. Fish-basket Kuan-yin, attributed to Chao Meng-fu (1254–1322). *Courtesy of the National Palace Museum, Taiwan.*

Figure 10.2. "Lady with Scroll," about 1040–1106 in the style of Li Kung-lin. *Courtesy of the Metropolitan Museum of Art, New York (Bequest of Mrs. H. O. Havemeyer,* 1929; The H.O. Havemeyer Collection).

time of Mr. Ma's Wife. She had sex with any man who asked for it. But whoever had sex with her was said to be free from sexual desire forever.[8] She died at the age of twenty-four as a dissolute woman of ill repute. She was buried without ceremony in a common grave by the roadside. A foreign monk from the Western Regions later came and, offering incense, paid respect to her at her grave. When asked by disgusted villagers why he should bother with this husbandless woman of loose virtue, he told them that she acted out of compassion. He predicted that her bones were chained together, for that was one of the signs possessed by a bodhisattva. When her grave was opened, the bones of her entire body were indeed linked together like a chain. The woman was a prostitute and seductress. In the *Ch'ing-ni lien-hua chi* (Lotuses in Black Mud), a Ming work containing biographies of prostitutes, both the stories of Mr. Ma's Wife and the Woman of Yen-chou are listed side by side (Mei Ting-tso 1988:32–34). Indeed, during the Ming and Ch'ing, not only courtesans, but male actors who played female roles were praised by admirers for being as "beautiful as Kuan-yin."[9] The two stories are clearly variations on the same theme: sexuality, either offered outright or first promised and then later withheld, can serve as a powerful tool of spiritual transformation. A bodhisattva uses sex as a skillful means (*fang-pien*, upāya). This is of course not a novel idea, but is documented in many Mahāyāna scriptures, both exoteric and esoteric.

A bodhisattva in his enlightened state, which is characterized by the realization of nonduality, can engage in all kinds of "evil" activities while remaining in samādhi. This is why Vimalakīrti entered the brothels and cabarets and indeed enacted the five deadly sins yet was not tainted by them (Thurman 1976:21, 64). In fact, "the Marās who play the devil in the innumerable universes of the ten directions are all bodhisattvas dwelling in the inconceivable liberation, who are playing the devil in order to develop living beings through their skill in liberative technique" (54).[10] It declares that a bodhisattva "may appear in the form of a prostitute in order to attract those who are full of sexual desire. They are first caught by the bait of desire, and later led to the wisdom of the Buddha" (T 14:519). Vasumitra, the beautiful goddess, may be regarded as such a clever seducer. In the thirty-ninth chapter of the *Avataṃsaka Sūtra*, "Entering the Realm of Reality," she tells the young pilgrim Sudhana that she teaches all men who come to her full of passion in such a way that they become free of passion. Without discrimination, she will offer whatever they want in order to satisfy their desires and in doing so, enable them to become dispassionate. Thus, some reach dispassion as soon as they see her, others do so by merely talking with her, or holding her hand, or staying with her, or gazing at her, or embracing her, or kissing her (Cleary 1986, vol. 3:148).[11]

In her study on the theme of the "gift of the body," Reiko Ohnuma points out the parallelism between the prostitute and the bodhisattva: "Because both eschew the particular love of spouse and family, they are free to bestow their gifts equally upon all. The crucial difference, of course, is that the prostitute is driven by greed and bestows her gifts through exchange, whereas the bodhisattva is driven by compassion and bestows his gifts through pure generosity. Nevertheless, both the prostitute and the bodhisattva are singularly driven to seduce and satisfy their customers, and effectively employ a wide variety of different skills aimed at pleasing all types of beings. In the *Upāyakauśalya Sūtra*, in fact, the bodhisattva's teaching of the Dharma through skillful means is explicitly compared to the diverse methods by which prostitutes fleece their customers" (1997:210). The sūtra is included in the *Ta pao-chi ching* (Mahāratnakūṭa Sūtra). The bodhisattva, who is a master of skillful means, is compared to a prostitute and a fisherman, among others:

> Good man, as an illustration, consider a prostitute. She has sixty-four seductive wiles; for example, to obtain wealth and treasures, she may coax a man into generously giving her his valuables by pretending that she is going to marry him, and then she drives him away without regret when she has obtained precious objects. Similarly, good man, a Bodhisattva who practices ingenuity (*fang-pien*) can use his skill according to [particular] circumstances; he teaches and converts all sentient beings by manifesting himself in forms they like and by freely giving them everything they need, even his body. . . .
>
> Good man, as an illustration, consider a fisherman. He rubs his net with bait and casts it into a deep river; when his wishes are fulfilled, he hauls it out. In the same way, good man, a Bodhisattva who practices ingenuity cultivates his mind with the wisdom of emptiness, signlessness, nonaction, and noself. He knits a net of this wisdom, rubs it with the bait of aspiration for all-knowing wisdom, and casts it into the filthy mire of the five desires. When his wishes are fulfilled, he hauls it out of the Realm of Desire. (Chang 1983: 434, 435)

The bodhisattva shares another similarity with a prostitute, namely, both are nondiscriminatory. That is why the prostitute Bindumati in the *Milindapañha* can perform the Act of Truth, just as King Śivi, for "both use their bodies to please all solicitors equally regardless of their social status." In answer to King Aśoka, she declares, "Whoever gives me money, Great King, whether he be a Kṣatriya, a Brahmin, a Vaiśya, a Śūdra, or anyone else, I serve each of them in the same manner. There is no special distinction in one who is called a Kśatriya, and there is nothing despicable in one who is called a Śūdra. I amuse myself with whomever has money, free of fawning and repugnance alike. This was my Act of Truth, Lord, by which I made this great Ganges River flow backwards" (Ohnuma 1997:211–12). The Woman of Yen-chou found her scriptural ancestress in Bindumati.

The transiency of physical beauty and the emptiness of desire could be most powerfully illustrated by the sexual act. It is to teach these lessons that the *Ta-chuang-yen ching-lun* (Sūtralaṅkārā-śāstra), translated in 405 by Kumārajīva, tells the following two parables. In order to convert a prostitute, a preacher of the Dharma used his magical power to turn the woman into a skeleton of white bones with her interior organs all exposed. He then told the people that everything in the world was as illusory as bubbles and counterfeit gold. Instead of being enamored by the woman's beauty, they should see her as no more than a pile of bones and thereby achieve realization by meditating on impurity. In the second example, a magician changed a log of wood into a woman and had intercourse with her in front of many people. Afterwards he turned her back into wood (Sawada 1959:46).

The theme of submission and the conquest of evil through sex, like the one found in the story of the Woman of Yen-chou, is also firmly anchored in Tantric scriptures, rituals, and art. They concern the rite of Vināyaka, which traces its origin to Avalokiteśvara's conquest of Vināyaka, one form of Ganeśa, through sexual union. In the texts translated in the seventh to eighth centuries we find this story: Maheśvara had three thousand children by his wife. Half of them, headed by Vināyaka, were evil and the other half, headed by Senayaka, were good. The latter was an incarnation of the Eleven-headed Kuan-yin who tamed the former by uniting with him as "oldest brother-youngest brother, husband and wife." In another version, it was as the Thousand-handed Kuan-yin that he subdued Vināyaka. This story became the basis for the Tantric rite known as *Ssu-pu P'i-na-yeh-chia fa* (Fourfold *sādhana* of Vināyaka). A king known as the King of Pleasure (Huan-hsi-wang) had strong desires and did not believe in Buddhism. Kuan-yin, through great compassion, appeared as a beautiful woman and excited him. By using his sexual desire she succeeded in making him take refuge in the Buddha and become a protector of Buddhism. They were depicted as smilingly embracing each other, like the Tibetan *yab-yum* image. The male, Vināyaka, was called "Obstacle" (Chang-ai) and the female, Ganapati, was called "Joy" (Huan-hsi). A twelfth-century Japanese text, the *Kakuzenshō*, provides the origin and rules for this rite (Stein 1986:38; Sawada 1959:47).

The legends of Mr. Ma's Wife, Kuan-yin with the Fish Basket, and the Woman of Yen-chou bear many traces from Buddhist sources. Ordinary Chinese people, however, have come to know these stories primarily through folk literature, which has produced several *pao-chüan* centering on this figure. During my research in mainland China, I came across five texts dealing with this theme: *Yü-lan pao-chüan* (The Precious Scroll of the Fish Basket), printed in 1919 by Yi-hua-t'ang shu-fang, Shanghai, and kept in Chekiang Provincial Library, Hangchow; *T'i-lan chüan* (Lifting the Basket Scroll), hand-copied in the year *hsin-ch'ou* (1891?) and kept in the Beijing University Library; *Mai-yü pao-chüan* (The Precious Scroll of Fish Selling), hand-copied, without a date, and kept in Nan-k'ai University Library, Tientsin; *Hsi-kua pao-chüan* (The Precious Scroll of Watermelon), hand-copied in 1887 and kept in Chekiang Provincial Library, Hangchow; and *Kuan-yin Miao-shan pao-chüan* (The Precious Scroll of Kuan-yin Miao-shan), hand-copied in 1916, in the private collection of the late Professor Wu Hsiao-ling of Beijing. Their times of composition must postdate that of the *Hsiang-shan pao-chüan*, for some important biographical details of the heroine (e.g. her birthday, age, and the status as the third daughter) were based on those of Miao-shan. It is interesting to note that despite considerable variations in detail, all five present the heroine as offering marriage as a bait, but not its consummation nor her participation in sexual activities. Clearly, while the story of Mr. Ma's Wife/Yü-lan Kuan-yin is retained, that of the Woman of Yen-chou has been dropped. This is undoubtedly due to the latter's overly Tantric flavor. With the decline of Tantrism in China after the T'ang and the strong emphasis on sexual propriety by the Neo-Confucians beginning in the Sung, it is not surprising that this story, with its explicit mention of sex and the unconventional transposition of values (prostitute = bodhisattva) proved to be too shocking for general consumption.

Yü-lan pao-chüan bears a long subtitle, *Yü-lan Kuan-yin erh-tz'u ling-fan tu Chin-sha-t'an ch'üan-shih hsiu-hsing* (Yü-lan Kuan-yin Twice Descends to the Earth to Save Golden Sand Beach and Calls the World to Cultivate Virtue). It is so named because it presents both the heroine and the monk as manifestations of Kuan-yin. The story was set in the Sung, correctly reflecting the time when this cult first gained popularity. The place where Golden Sand Beach was located, however, was changed from Shensi to Kiangsu, namely, Hai-men county (east of present-day Nan-tung), renowned for its wealth in salt and fish. The change of place is significant, for it clearly indicates that it was in Kiangsu and Chekiang that this *pao-chüan*, like many others, had its origin. It also indicates that it was in this coastal region that this cult eventually took root. The village of Golden Sand Beach had several thousand households who made their livings by hunting, fishing, butchering, and thieving. The people were very evil, for they did not believe in gods and spirits, nor did they respect their parents. They robbed, killed, and wasted the five grains. Their sins were reported to the Taoist deity the Jade Emperor who became so enraged that he ordered the Dragon King of the Eastern Sea to cover the village with waves and send all the people to hell where they would languish forever. When Kuan-yin, referred to here as Nan-yang Chiao-chu (Religious Leader of the Southern Ocean), learned about this, she felt pity for the people and asked the Jade Emperor to postpone the sentence for a few months. Calling herself a "subject official" (*ch'en*), she volunteered to go to Golden Sand Beach to lead the residents to goodness. If she failed, she would be willing to suffer punishment together with them. The Jade Emperor commended her compassion and agreed to let her descend to earth to carry out the work of salvation.

Kuan-yin first appeared as an old woman fish-monger (*mai-yü p'in-p'o*). The characterization of Kuan-yin as being old and poor began after the Sung. The tendency toward age increase was also noticeable among the bodhisattva figures found in Tun-huang. Shih Wei-hsiang explains, "Among the bodhisattva figures of the Mo-kao Grottoes in Tun-huang dated from the Sixteen Kingdoms to the Yüan dynasty, there is found an outstanding characteristic: namely, the gradual increase of their ages. During the period from the Northern Wei to the Northern Chou, the innocence and guilelessness of the bodhisattvas was usually represented by pure and youthful virginal maidens. During the Sui and T'ang, they gradually became more mature and were depicted as graceful, voluptuous and beautiful young women. Thus the term 'Kuan-yin P'u-sa' could serve as a substitute for a teenage girl of marriageable age in society. But when we reach the Sung and Yüan, the image eventually evolves into that of a staid and experienced matron. Especially when she appears as Kuan-yin with a cape and hood (*p'ei-mao*), she is literally transformed into an old woman" (Shih 1989:12).

In miracle tales and *pi-chi* literature since the Sung, Kuan-yin very often appeared as an old woman. The *Kuan-yin Shih-erh yüan-chüeh ch'üan chuan* (Complete Biographies of the Twelve Perfectedly Enlightened Ones of Khan-yin), a text of uncertain date[12] is vaguely modeled on the *Yüan-chüeh ching* (Sūtra of Complete Enlightenment), which features twelve bodhisattvas or the "Completely Enlightened Ones" as protagonists. It tells the story of how Kuan-yin led twelve persons, both men and women, some good and some bad, into enlightenment. Kuan-yin took the disguises of a monk, a beautiful young woman, but also a poor old beggar woman. Both in popular literature and sectarian precious scrolls, Kuan-yin began to be called Kuan-yin Lao-mu (Venerable Mother Kuan-yin) from the Ming on. This was probably in response to the new sectarian religions, for the patron deity of these religions was Wu-sheng Lao-mu (literally, Unbegotten Old Mother or Eternal Mother). I discuss further the possible origins of the "Mother" as the supreme deity in the new sectarian religions and the intimate relationship between Wu-sheng Lao-mu and Kuan-yin Lao-mu in the next chapter.

To continue with the *Yü-lan pao-chüan*. Failing to attract anyone's attention as an old woman, Kuan-yin then changed into a beautiful young girl. She walked in the marketplace selling fish and immediately attracted a large crowd. Among the onlookers, there was a local ruffian named Ma who was more wealthy and also more ruthless than anyone else. He was nicknamed King Wasp (Ma-wang) for this reason. He was attracted by the fish-monger. Feigning interest in buying fish, he asked her background. She replied that her father was surnamed Chuang, and they lived in the Southern Sea. She was the third daughter, having been born on the nineteenth day of the second month, and was now eighteen years old. All these biographical details of course are based on Miao-shan's life. The major departure from the *Hsiang-shan pao-chüan* is at the same time the connecting link with the legend of Mr. Ma's Wife: namely the emphasis placed on the *Lotus Sūtra*.

She said that the reason why she was not yet married was because she had vowed to marry only someone who could memorize the *Lotus Scripture* (Lien ching) while keeping a vegetarian diet. Hearing this, Ma became very intrigued and asked where one could find this scripture and why it was so important. She answered that this scripture was a priceless treasure, for it contained knowledge about myriad things in the world. Equipped with this scripture, one can obtain the happiness of heaven and escape the punishment of hell under Lord Yama. The *pao-chüan* not only sings the praises of the sūtra in a general way, but uncharacteristically gives some specifics that indicate the writer's technical familiarity with this great Buddhist text. She told him that the scripture *Fa-hua* consisted of seven sections that were broken into twenty-eight chapters and ran more than 60,000 words long. As to where one could find it, the heroine pointed to the fish basket. It turned out that she had put fish on the surface of the basket and hidden the sūtra underneath the fish. She reaffirmed her promise of marriage and asked Ma and many others who had gathered to go home and offer incense to the gods and their ancestors. She prayed for their assistance and informed them of their determination to study Buddhism. At the crack of dawn, she said, they should come to Ch'ing-t'ien Ssu (Temple of Bright Day) and she would teach them how to chant the sūtra.

The prospect of marrying this beautiful fish-monger made butchers give up killing, hunters misfire, and fishermen change their profession. She taught them for a month and fearing that the people would lose faith, decided to choose Ma, the most vicious of them all, as the successful candidate to fulfill her promise. She blew a mouthful of air at Ma who immediately gained clarity in his "stomach" and could recite the *Lien Ching* loudly and without hesitation. Everyone congratulated him on his great success. Overjoyed, Ma asked her how much bridal money was required. She replied that she would demand none but that the entire Ma household should become vegetarians and, on the wedding day, he should prepare a vegetarian feast for the wedding guests. He should also invite the local Taoist priests to thank them for putting up with the disturbances.

As expected, during the wedding ceremony, the bride suddenly took ill. Only at this point did she reveal her true identity as Kuan-yin to Ma. She told him why she had come down to earth, and that for disobeying the Jade Emperor's decree of turning Golden Sand Beach into an ocean, she must remain on earth for three years. After she gave a farewell speech to the assembled audience advising them to chant the sūtra, keep a vegetarian diet, and do good deeds, she died. Ma was inconsolable and sang a dirge called "Crying through the five watches of the night" ("K'u wu-keng") in which he retold the story of his meeting and losing her. He had a painter draw an image of her and enshrined it in his home, and chanted sūtras during the day and did devotions at night in front of the painting. Ma was a changed man, serving as an exemplar for the community. Before three years were over, thanks to Ma's evangelical zeal, the entire village turned into a land of goodness (*shan-ti*).

One day Ma was wondering if the girl would ascend to heaven now that the three-year limit was almost up. His thought alerted Kuan-yin on high and prompted her to appear on earth a second time. This time she came to Golden Sand Beach as a monk and asked for the whereabouts of his long lost cousin who sounded like Ma's wife. Ma's sorrow was renewed and he told the monk that the girl, who had been a manifestation of Kuan-yin, had died. The monk wanted to see the body in order to make sure that it was his cousin. He also told Ma that if she actually was Kuan-yin, the body would be golden in color and undecayed. When the tomb was opened, it was indeed so. Miraculously, the girl revived and, carrying the fish basket in her hand, she ascended to the sky. To the amazement of all, the monk also levitated and stood by her side holding hands with her. The two forms of Kuan-yin merged and, sitting on top of the clouds, Kuan-yin preached a sermon to the people below. She told them that the only reason she descended to earth twice was in order to save them. All repented and promised to obey her instructions. Ma had among his possessions a rare piece of sandalwood that had been handed down in his family. He had it carved in accordance with the portrait, but added a fish basket. This was known as "Kuan-yin with the Fish Basket." He told all the people to make a similar image and worship it in their homes. This was the origin of the image of Yü-lan Kuan-yin, which has been handed down to the present. Ma went out to preach each month on the days containing the numbers two, six and nine. Eventually, accompanied by the Golden Boy and Jade Girl, Ma was summoned by the Jade Emperor who granted him the reward of going to the Western Paradise.

Typical of many *pao-chüan* of late imperial China, Buddhist and Taoist beliefs are indiscriminately mixed in the folk religious consciousness. If anything, it was the Taoist Jade Emperor who was the supreme head of the pantheon, for at the end of the story he bestows on Kuan-yin the formal title "Yü-lan Kuan-yin" and appoints her to rule over the Southern Ocean (Nan-yang). The role of Ma is considerably enlarged and emphasized. He is made into a hero and presented as an admirable example of how an evil man could, through conversion, attain paradise and find salvation. Another interesting feature of the text is the emphasis it places on the image of Yü-lan Kuan-yin. The creation of this image is mentioned twice. One feels as if a primary purpose of writing and chanting this *pao-chüan* was to explain this particular iconography of Kuan-yin.

The *T'i-lan chüan* and the *Mai-yü pao-chüan* are similar in plot to the preceding, but much shorter and different in some important aspects. First, Kuan-yin at first appears as an ugly fishmonger who hawks two smelly salty fishes in the marketplace. When three days have passed and no one has shown any interest in her or her wares, only then does she change into a beautiful woman. Second, the hero is not named Ma, but is called Black Tiger Chang (Chang Hei-hu), so nicknamed on account of his violent temper and rapaciousness. He already has seven wives but, like many other men who are attracted to the young fishmonger, he also wants to marry her. The heroine preaches a sermon, asking the men to take the five precepts, and promises to marry the one who can memorize the *Lotus Sūtra* by the end of one month. She also carries the scripture in her fish basket, but in order to make memorization easier, she leads the people to her boat and distributes copies of the scripture to everyone. Chang puts up money to build a large tent so that they can study with her. At the end of the month, Chang succeeds in the contest. But on the wedding day, when the bridal sedan chair arrives at his house, there was sudden thunder and lightening. The chair is empty and he can not find the bride. Taking the girl for a monster in disguise, he curses his bad luck. Kuan-yin then appears in the sky and tells the assembly why she came to Golden Sand Beach. The *pao-chüan* also ends with the creation and worship of her image. Moreover, because of Chang's good deeds, he receives veneration after death as well and the local people worship him as Great Lord Chang (Chang Ta-ti).

It is clear that even though these three texts used the same story as their main theme, they showed considerable freedom in changing some details to reflect local traditions. A common concern in all of them was to supply a reasonable explanation for the iconography of Yü-lan Kuan-yin and account for its great popularity in the area in which the texts circulated. Rolf A. Stein discussed the sexual themes of nets, fish, the odor of fish etc. in Indian myths and linked them to the Chinese myth of Yü-lan Kuan-yin (Stein 1986:57–61). There were perhaps two other reasons why fish and fish-baskets became connected with Kuan-yin. Commenting on a red terra-cotta figure depicting a goddess holding a pair of fish dated 100 B.C.E., Pratapaditya Pal says, "The fish is an ancient Indian symbol of abundance and fertility, and a pair is considered an auspicious emblem of conjugal bliss" (Pal 1987:40).[13] Similarly, fish (particularly carp—the fish Kuan-yin was most often said to be selling) also connotes good luck to the Chinese. A favorite theme of New Year pictures is a fat boy riding on a big carp. Carp symbolize virility and transformability, for by swimming upstream in the Yangtze River they are believed to become dragons. The image of Kuan-yin with fish could reflect these two similar attitudes toward fish as a symbol of auspiciousness and fertility. Another reason Kuan-yin was provided with a fish basket might be explained by the similarity in sound between *yü-lan* and *yü-lan-p'en* (*ullambana*, "ghost festival"). Indeed, some scholars suggest that "the shortened sound 'yü-lan' represents either 'yü-lan', meaning 'fish basket,' or 'yü-lan,' referring to nectar and a basket of doughnuts." (Teiser 1988:22). As the ghost festival became increasingly popular in medieval China, and as Kuan-yin gradually assumed the role of the savior of beings in hell, similar to Mu-lien, it is possible that the name of the ghost festival could have been represented by a transliteration meaning "fish basket," which then became attached to Kuan-yin.

During the Ming, aside from the *Hsi-yu chi* and one *ch'uan-ch'i*, three *tsa-chü* plays also featured Yü-lan Kuan-yin in their plots and this must have helped her increasing popularity. In chapter 49 of *Hsi-yu chi* Kuan-yin saves Tripiṭaka by capturing the demonic gold fish and putting him in the bamboo basket. The goldfish had been living in the goldfish pond on P'u-t'o. Because he had listened to Kuan-yin's sermons every day, he eventually gained the power to change into a monster and set out to harm Tripiṭaka. After Kuan-yin captured him in the basket, she allowed people to come together to worship her. The novel stated that this was the origin of the Yü-lan Kuan-yin iconography. A gold carp, called a monster fish (*yao-yü*), appears in a *ch'uan-ch'i* play entitled *Kuan-yin yü-lan chi*. It contains thirty-two *ch'u* (scenes) and was printed in Nanking by the Wen-lin-ko, a publishing company that was owned by a father and son named T'ang during the Wan-li (1573–1615) period (included in *Ku-pen hsi-ch'ü ts'ung-k'an*, 2nd collection).

A young scholar by the name of Liu Chen from Yang-chou came to the capital to take the exams in 1052 and stayed in a monastery while he was there. Since he was good at calligraphy done in the "grass" script, he was befriended by Prime Minister Chin, who invited him to tutor his daughter, Golden Peony. Liu and Miss Chin immediately fell in love. But a golden carp living in the pond of the Chin estate assumed the form of the heroine, seduced Liu, and the two ran off secretly to Yang-chou. A servant from the Chin household ran into the pair and came back to warn the father. The real Golden Peony in the meantime had fallen sick. This strange case was brought to the famous Judge Pao, who asked the City God to help him. Soldiers were dispatched by the Dragon King to capture the fish. The carp escaped to P'u-t'o in the South Sea and hid under a lotus leaf. Kuan-yin subdued her and put the carp in a fish basket. In the meantime a Mr. Cheng, who was devoted to a monochrome (*shui-mo*, "water-ink") painting of Kuan-yin (most likely the White-robed Kuan-yin) had a dream in which Kuan-yin told him that the next morning he would meet a middle-aged woman carrying a bamboo basket. He did meet such a woman and the two went to Judge Pao. The woman received fifty strings of cash as her reward for capturing the carp. She gave the money to Cheng, who hired an artisan to paint a monochrome Kuan-yin carrying a fish basket. This then was the origin of the Fish-basket Kuan-yin. Judge Pao served as the go between, marrying Golden Peony to Liu Chen. Liu successfully passed the exam the following year.

A *tsa-chü* play, *Kuan-yin P'u-sa yü-lan chi* (included in *Ku-pen Yüan Ming tsa-chü*, 4th collection), which, like the previous one, was written by an anonymous author in the Ming, differs very much in its plot. Kuan-yin appeared as a beautiful fish-monger in order to convert the hero Chang Wu-chin, who had originally been destined to be one of thirteen lohans (sinicized versions of arhats), but has fallen into a life of sensuality. In the play, Śākyamuni Buddha sends Kuan-yin to earth. She is assisted by her two brothers, Han-shan and Shih-te, who are actually the two bodhisattvas Mañjuśrī and Samanthabhadra in disguise. She promises to marry Chang if he will recite Buddhist scriptures, keep a vegetarian diet, and do good deeds. He pretends to agree, but after the wedding ceremony, reverts to his old evil ways, and Kuan-yin refuses to consummate the marriage. He imprisons her in the back garden and imposes various difficult physical chores on her, just like the punishment Miao-shan had to undergo at the hands of her father. In the end of the play Maitreya, the Future Buddha, appears as Pu-tai Ho-shang (Cloth-bag Monk) to enlighten Chang.

Chang is a historical person. Better known by his formal name, Chang Shang-ying (1043–1122), he was a very famous lay Buddhist of the Sung.[14] Han-shan and Shih-te were a pair of eccentric monks who were active in the eighth century on Mt. T'ien-t'ai, Pu-tai was another unconventional monk from Ningpo living at the end of the tenth century who was regarded as an incarnation of Maitreya. That the three appear in the play are interesting. For although they were near-mythical figures in Ch'an Buddhism, they were also frequently represented by Te-hua porcelain figures that were produced by folk kilns, private enterprises that catered to the market of the common people. Ho Shao-tsung, for instance, made all three figures (Fong 1990:43, 46–47). There was, therefore, a convergence between popular art and literature in that they both showed similar interest in these personages. Mary Fong sees this as the revival of Ch'an Buddhism in the Ming. While this could be the case, we should also keep in mind another important factor. In many sectarian *pao-chüan*, some of which I will discuss in the next chapter, Maitreya is a very central character. Bodhidharma, the putative First Patriarch of Ch'an, was regarded by some sectarian religions to be one of their patriarchs as well. The Ch'an teachings that everyone is endowed with Buddha nature and that enlightenment is not dependent on book learning are democratic and have universal appeal. It was no wonder that the new religions favored Ch'an. The appearance of Ch'an figures in these dramas and Bodhidharma's cameo appearance in the *Precious Scroll of the Parrot* (discussed later) can be seen as a reflection of the contemporary religious atmosphere. At the same time, might the founders of the new religions have chosen these figures for veneration because they had been influenced by their ubiquitousness in folk art and popular literature?

There were two more *tsa-chü* plays on the Fish-basket Kuan-yin. One was called *So-ku P'u-sa* (Bodhisattva with Chained Bones), written by Yü Ch'iao, who was a good friend of the famous playwright T'ang Hsien-tsu (1550–1617). Judging from the title, it was about Mr. Ma's Wife, but it has not survived.[15] The last play, entitled *Yü Erh Fo* (Fish Buddha), was written by a Ch'an monk at the end of the Ming (included in *Sheng Ming tsa-chü*, 2nd collection). His name is Ch'an-jen Tan-ch'eng. The main protagonist is a fisherman named Chin Ying from K'uai-chi in present-day Chekiang. His evil karma, which has resulted from taking the lives of fish, should predestine him for hell. But his wife is a devout worshiper of Kuan-yin. She keeps a vegetarian diet and chants the name of the Buddha. She tries to convert her husband. Kuan-yin is sent by the Buddha to enlighten the couple. She appears in the guise of a fish-seller carrying a fish-basket. Her mission is successful and both husband and wife achieve deliverance.

Let us now resume the survey of precious scrolls. The themes of fish and fish basket were not always present in all the precious scrolls dealing with this image of Kuan-yin as a seductress. The *Kuan-yin Miao-shan pao-chüan* and the *Watermelon pao-chüan*, for instance, do not present the heroine as a fishmonger. On the other hand, both texts emphasize the fact that she is a young widow wearing white—the color of mourning, and also the color of the White-robed (Pai-i) Kuan-yin whose cult, as shown in chapter 6, becomes very important after the tenth century. In these texts, the myths and images of Pai-i Kuan-yin are superimposed on those of Ma-lang-fu/Yü-lan. This is a good example of the composite nature of religious precious scrolls written in more recent times. The author exercised great freedom in combining the different traditions available to him.

Both texts consist of prose and rhymed seven-character verses. The *Watermelon pao-chüan* is shorter than the *Kuan-yin Miao-shan pao-chüan* and also lacks the passages based on Miao-shan's life found in the latter. The main character of the story is Black-hearted Li (Li Hei-hsin) of Chiang-ning (in present-day Kiangsu), who has thirteen wives and thirteen storehouses of silver and gold. But everyone in the Li household, with the exception of the gatekeeper Li An, is evil. Li charges double for the interest on the grain and money that he would lend to people. He hates Buddhist monks and Taoist priests who come to his door to seek donations. If anyone dares to come, he would invariably insult and beat him. In the story Kuan-yin asks permission from the Jade Emperor to convert Li. She appears as a beautiful young widow in white. The text goes into great detail in describing the articles of clothing, all white, that she is wearing. For instance, she wears a white silk blouse tied by a white silk sash, and a white silk skirt over a pair of white silk pants. Her shoes are also made of white silk. And finally, she is carrying a white silk handkerchief in her hand. When she walks down the street, she attracts men from all walks of life (a list of professions is supplied with sarcastic caricatures). In their excitement they would drop whatever they are doing and follow her.

She walks up to Li's door and asks for money to buy a coffin for her dead husband. The servant Li An asks her in and when Black-hearted Li sees her, he immediately wants to marry her. She first takes him to pay their respects to the corpse of her recently deceased husband (her attendant, Shan-ts'ai, pretending to be the dead husband). She then makes one condition after another, each more difficult and outrageous than the previous one: for example, Li has to use rare wood and precious metals to have the coffin made according to her specific design; the corpse has to be laid out in the main hall; Li has to invite thirty-six Taoist priests and seventy-two Buddhist monks to perform "Emperor Liang's Confessional" (*Liang-huang ch'an*) for three days and nights, feed the hungry ghosts for seven days and nights, and after finishing the forty-nine day mourning ritual, place water lanterns in all the rivers and lakes near the region; and he must send steamed bread weighing two catties each as wedding gifts to all the families in the four counties of the province in which Chiang-ning is located. Li is torn between his stinginess and his lust. When he finally agrees to these demands, she makes more new ones. They must first bury her husband. To humiliate him, she demands that Li serve as the chief mourner for the funeral procession, thus making him the laughing stock of the town.

After this, she demands that Li ask the Jade Emperor to serve as the matchmaker, the Big Dipper to give her away, the five hundred lohans to serve as lantern carriers, the Three Officials (San-kuan) to accompany the bridal sedan chair, the patriarchs and bodhisattvas to walk in front while the Weaving Maiden follows behind, and lastly, the Old Mother of Mt. Li (Li-shan Lao-mu) to serve as the maiden of honor. Li agrees to all these conditions. But the heroine changes her mind after all and refuses to marry him, saying that if she should ever marry, she would, like Miao-shan, marry a doctor who could help the suffering humanity. Greatly angered, Li confines her to the back garden and orders her to do hard labor. Like Miao-shan, she takes this punishment calmly and joyously. (This part is missing from the *Watermelon pao-chüan*). After thirty days, Li forces her to marry him. But on their wedding day, she suddenly disappears. Li has already exhausted his thirteen storehouses of silver and gold. Li blames his servant Li An for the back luck and sends for the latter in order to punish him. But Li An is no longer poor but has become very rich. He tells Li the miraculous story of how he was made rich by a watermelon seed given to him by a medicant monk.

The story of the miraculous watermelon is the subplot of these two precious scrolls and is a new element not found in the Ma-lang-fu–Yü-lan Kuan-yin family of legends. Impressed by Li An's kindness, Kuan-yin had earlier appeared as a mendicant monk who came to his home to beg for food in order to test the couple's sincerity further. The monk was warmly welcomed and fed a good dinner. Before leaving, he gave them a watermelon seed and told them to plant it in the backyard. It turned out to be no ordinary seed, for "after it was planted in the first watch, it sprouted in the second watch. When it was watered in the third watch, it began to flower in the fourth watch and produced a melon in the fifth watch." When the watermelon was cut open, silver and gold kept coming out until there was enough to fill thirteen rooms. After Li An tells Black-hearted Li, the latter, of course, wants to imitate his example. So, disregarding his erstwhile hatred for monks, he announces his willingness to offer hospitality to all mendicants. Kuan-yin comes as a begging monk and gives him a watermelon seed. Li eagerly plants it, but after waiting for three months, nothing happens. He thinks that he was tricked by Li An. So he hangs Li An upside down and starts to beat him. Kuan-yin sends down a watermelon from heaven. But when it is cut open, a raging fire breaks out, for Kuan-yin has ordered the god of fire and his entourage to hide inside the melon to destroy Li. The fire burns seven days and nights and reduces Black-hearted Li's home to ashes. He hides in the latrine and turns into a worm. His entire household, due to their evil karma, all receive appropriate punishments. His wives turn into flies or gnats. His servants become ants, and his maids butterflies and praying mantises.

Although the theme of marriage and sex, first promised and then withheld, is present in these two texts, it is no longer the central one as in the other texts. Instead, Kuan-yin takes on the role of an omnipotent god as well as that of a trickster. There is also a lot of folksy humor. Since the text was used in oral recitation, *hsüan-chüan*, it is understandable that there is much repetition and embellishment of details for dramatic effect. They were intended as much for entertainment as for edification.

Although the Fish-basket Kuan-yin is painted by artists and eulogized by poets and Ch'an monks, there is no evidence that any temple was dedicated to her with her image as the main icon in China. However, such a temple exists in Japan. Called Gyoran Kannon Temple, it is located in Mita, a commercial section of Tokyo. The main image is the Fish-basket Kuan-yin (Gyoran Kannon), a statue of a young woman dressed in Chinese style clothing. According to the founding myths, the image was originally made in China during the T'ang dynasty and was carried to Nagasaki by no other than Mr. Ma's descendants. They offered it to the Japanese monk Hōryō who erected a small temple to enshrine it in 1630, and in 1652, his disciple Shōryō built the present temple. Many miracles effected by her have been preserved and published by the temple. The first miracle reads very much like the story of *King Kao's Kuan-yin Sūtra*:

> The first case of the holy figure serving as a surrogate in disaster by sword was in the second year of Kambun (1662). Yamada Naokiyo who worked as the stable hand for Lord Hosokawa of Etchu, committed a crime and was sentenced to be beheaded. But when the sentence was to be carried out, he prayed to the Fish-basket Kannon whom he had worshiped for many years, with all his heart, and the executioner's sword shattered into three pieces. The same thing happened three times. The executioner and witnesses were filled with awe. When the magistrate informed the Lord of it, Naokiyo was summoned and explained exactly what had happened. To this, the Lord replied, "Your faith in Kannon surpasses mine. Go and pray for the prosperity of the entire fiefdom," and with these words, the Lord pardoned him. Filled with gratitude, Naokiyo piously had a statue of Kannon made, based on the Fish-basket Kannon, and worshiped it faithfully for the rest of his life. He is buried in a corner of the temple. From that time on, on account of the efficacy of that Kannon, the statue came to be called the "Surrogate in Disaster by Sword" Kannon. In addition to Naokiyo's testimony, Mr. Kikuchi and Mr. Sakagamin have also added their own testimonies about the benefits of this Kannon. These testimonies describing in detail the benefits they received still hang in front of the statue. In the back of the plaque, it is stated, "I have received benefits in the event of calamity by the sword in

this life. There should be no doubt whatsoever about my future salvation through Kannon. I, Naokiyo, hereby testify to this."[16]

Kuan-yin of the South Sea

As Mt. P'u-t'o became established as the Chinese Potalaka, a new iconography known as Nan-hai Kuan-yin (Kuan-yin of the South Sea) came into being. This is different from the traditional Potalaka Kuan-yin, of which a large number of wooden sculptures have survived and are now shown as prized exhibits in many museums, like the one dated to the twelfth century held at the Rijksmuseum in Amsterdam (figure 10.3). The latter depicts Kuan-yin as a masculine and heroic being. He often has a moustache, with an exposed chest. The Nan-hai Kuan-yin, on the other hand, is feminine and usually indistinguishable from the Water-moon and the White-robed Kuan-yin icons discussed earlier. She sits on a rock before a stand of bamboo, encircled by a full moon. She either carries a vase with willow branches in her hand or such a vase is placed by her side. She is attended by a boy and a girl. She can also be depicted as riding on waves or standing on top of a big fish. Finally, a white parrot is invariably seen hovering on her upper right hand side, carrying a rosary in its beak. Although Nan-hai Kuan-yin is not included in the thirty-three popular forms of Kuan-yin, clearly she incorporates elements from the Water-moon, White-robe, and the Yang-liu (Willow Branch), as well as the Ao-yü (Huge Fish) Kuan-yins, the four forms of which are included in the thirty-three. The painting by the Yüan artist Chao I dated 1313 (figure 9.1) represents her well. The Chinese opera "Heavenly Maiden Sprinkles Flowers" (*T'ien-nü san-hua*) conveniently summarizes this iconography of Kuan-yin when the Heavenly Maiden sings:

P'u-t'o Palace
Full-mooned face of Kuan-yin
Shan-ts'ai and Lung-nü stand on either side
White parrot
Pure vase
Water of sweet dew and willow
Universally saving mankind from suffering.

How early does this iconography appear in China? And are there texts that shed light on the significance of the different elements in the tableau? As I suggested in the previous chapter, I believe that the establishment of P'u-t'o Island

Figure 10.3. Potala Kuan-yin, twelfth century. *Courtesy of the Rijksmuseum, Amsterdam.*

as the pilgrimage center of Kuan-yin worship contributed to the appearance of this iconography and then, later, texts appeared to explain and justify it. An important text in popularizing P'u-t'o as well as the new manifestation known as Kuan-yin of the South Sea is *Nan-hai Kuan-yin ch'üan-chuan* (Complete Biography of Kuan-yin of the South Sea), a sixteenth-century reworked version of the *Hsiang-shan pao-chüan*. It makes an explicit identification between Hsiang-shan and P'u-t'o.

After her tour of hell, Miao-shan was told by Śākyamuni to go to Hsiang-shan to practice. He further informed her that Hsiang-shan was situated in the South Sea beyond the Kingdom of Yüeh (referring probably to the Wu Yüeh Kingdom). It was an ancient temple where immortals had lived in retirement in former times (possibly a reference to Mei Fu who was supposed to have carried out alchemical experiments in the Han dynasty at the Mei-fu An according to the P'u-t'o gazetteers). She was further instructed to practice cultivation on the P'u-t'o Rock (*Nan-hai Kuan-yin ch'uan-chüan* 18b). It also provides a folk explanation (in place of a canonical one) for the triad of Kuan-yin and her two attendants, Shan-ts'ai and Lung-nü, who began to be represented in art from the twelfth century on.[17] In Buddhist scriptures, Kuan-yin has a relationship with either Shan-ts'ai or Lung-nü but not with both at the same time. Shan-ts'ai or Sudhana is the young pilgrim who visits fifty-three teachers in order to learn the Buddha Dharma in the *Hua-yen* (*Avataṃsaka*) *Sūtra* and Kuan-yin is the twenty-eighth holy teacher who instructs him. The canonical sources for Lung-nü, on the other hand, may be traced to the esoteric sūtras glorifying the Thousand-handed and Amoghapāśa forms of Kuan-yin, which relate that the bodhisattva went to the Dragon King's Palace to reveal the dhāraṇī. In gratitude, the Dragon King's daughter presents Kuan-yin with a precious jewel of unparalleled worth. Moreover, because of the great popularity of the *Lotus Sūtra*, she may also be traced to this scripture, although she does not have anything directly to do with Kuan-yin in the text itself.[18] The tradition of providing a deity with a pair of male and female attendants, symbolizing yang and yin, started with Taoism. I believe that these two attendants are the Buddhist counterparts of the Taoist Golden Boy (Chin-t'ung) and Jade Girl (Yü-nü), who have been depicted as the attendants of the Jade Emperor since the T'ang.

The *Biography* tells the story of how the two came to be Kuan-yin's attendants. Shan-ts'ai was now an orphan, living the life of an ascetic on Ta-hua Shan. In order to test his sincerity, Miao-shan asked the Earth God to cause various immortals to assume the disguises of robbers and ruffians. She then had them force her to jump down the face of a cliff. Without hesitation, Shan-ts'ai also jumped down to join her. Kuan-yin then asked him to look down, where he saw his corpse lying there, while he ascended in broad daylight, freed from the constraints of his former mortal body (221–24a). After this, the writer tells the story of Lung-nü. Kuan-yin once saved the third prince of the Dragon King, who had taken the form of a carp and been caught by a fisherman. Kuan-yin sent Shan-ts'ai down to redeem the carp from the fisherman with one string of cash, winning his release back into the ocean. In gratitude, the Dragon King wanted to present Kuan-yin with a night-illuminating pearl, so that she could read sūtras at night. The daughter of the third prince, the granddaughter of the Dragon King, offered to take the pearl to Kuan-yin thereupon asking to become the latter's disciple. Kuan-yin agreed and told her to treat Shan-ts'ai as her older brother (24b–25b).

The author of the *Complete Biography* shows equal freedom in treating other Buddhist materials in the last part of the work where the entire royal family undergoes apotheosis. After Miao-shan completes her cultivation on the nineteenth day of the second month, Ti-tsang Bodhisattva and the Earth God decide to ask her to ascend the high seat to become the Jen-t'ien P'u-men Chiao-chu (Teaching Master of the Universal Gateway for Gods and Humankind), for now not only will she be in charge of all the bodhisattvas in all the universes, she will in fact be the master of all the universes. The Jade Emperor bestows titles on the three princesses. Miao-shan is named "The Efficacious Kuan-yin of Great Loving Kindness and Compassion Who Saves People from Suffering and Hardships" and is appointed to be the mistress of the P'u-t'o Rock of the South Sea in perpetuity. The older two sisters are named Wenchu P'u-sa (Mañjuśrī) and P'u-hsien P'u-sa (Samantabhadra) and given dominion over Mount Wu-t'ai. They are given two beasts as mounts, the Green Lion and the White Elephant, for these two beasts have earlier escaped from their posts as guardians of Śākyamuni's palace and tried to ravish the two sisters, who are saved by Miao-shan/Kuan-yin in the nick of time. This strange addition may represent an attempt to explain a new grouping of the three bodhisattvas that became increasingly popular starting from the Sung. The late T'ang sculpture at the site known as Ying-pan-p'o at Ta-tsu, Szechwan, seems to provide the earliest example with Kuan-yin (of the Thousand-hands and Thousand-eyes) standing in the middle, flanked by Mañjuśrī and Samantabhadra (a more common grouping has Vairocana Buddha in the middle instead of Kuan-yin, the so-called "Three Holy Ones of Hua-yen").[19] But from the Ming on, the icons of the "Three Great Beings" seemed to have been enshrined more and more in temples together. When this triad became popular, Kuan-yin was also accompanied by an animal mount. Called *hou*, the animal resembles a cross between a tiger and a lion (figure 2.9).[20] The animal in the painting of the Child-giving Kuan-yin from the Metropolitan Museum, for instance, looks similar to a lion (figure 10.4).

As Hsiang-shan increasingly became identified with the pilgrimage center of P'u-t'o, Kuan-yin of the South Sea began to be perceived as completely feminine, like Princess Miao-shan. Kuan-yin is called Nan-hai Kuan-yin in *Hsi-yu chi*. As we read in the previous chapter, in the sixteenth century, after a long period of neglect, P'u-t'o reemerged as a major pilgrimage center under the patronage of the Ming emperor Wan-li and his mother, Empress-dowager Li. The island continued to enjoy royal patronage in the seventeenth and eighteenth centuries under the Ch'ing emperors K'ang-hsi, Yung-cheng, and Ch'ien-lung. It is therefore not by accident that the iconography of Nan-hai Kuan-yin appeared and eventually triumphed over other forms of Kuan-yin during the same centuries. In the reestablishment of the sacred site, local officials and able

Figure 10.4. "Kuan-yin Bestowing a Son," late sixteenth century. *Courtesy of the Metropolitan Museum of Art, New York (Purchase, Friends of Asian Art Gifts,* 1989).

abbots collaborated closely. New texts of the "precious scrolls" genre appeared during this time. They might have been created in order to popularize P'u-t'o, like the creation of the new iconography. But popular texts can also serve as an index of the new-found fame of the island in this period. Among these, two are devoted to stories of Kuan-yin's attendants: the *Shan-ts'ai Lung-nü pao-chüan* is about the boy and the girl. The white parrot, on the other hand, is the protagonist of the *Ying-ke pao-chüan*. I have read one edition of the former and two—one printed and the other hand-copied—of the *Ying-ke pao-chüan* while conducting research in mainland China. Neither is dated.

The *Shan-ts'ai Lung-nü pao-chüan* tells the story about how Kuan-yin recruited her two attendants and the white parrot. In the story, Shan-ts'ai is the son of a prime minister named Ch'en during the ninth century. Ch'en is already fifty but still has no son. So he and his wife go to P'u-t'o to ask Nan-hai Ta-shih for a son. Knowing that he is not destined to have one, Kuan-yin grants him "The Boy Who Attracts Wealth" (Chao-ts'ai T'ung-tzu), an attending fairy serving under the Heavenly Official Who Bestows Blessings (Tz'u-fu T'ien-kuan), so that the father can benefit from the future enlightenment of the boy. The child shows his spiritual leaning early on and the father allows him to study under an immortal who is no other than Huang-lung Chen-jen (The True Man of the Yellow Dragon), a "close friend" of Miao-shan and a major character in the *True Scripture of Kuan-yin's Original Vow to Save and Transform Men* (Kuan-yin chi-tu pen-yüan chen-ching), the seventeenth-century sectarian scripture connected with the Way of the Former Heaven (Hsien-t'ien Tao) (Dudbridge 1978:69–73).

In the present *pao-chüan*, it is Kuan-yin who asks the Immortal to appear at the cave near the boy's home and become his master, giving the boy the dharma name Shan-ts'ai. Three years pass and the boy does well, studying uninterruptedly, without going home even once. In order to test him, the master tells him to take care of the cave while he goes away, on a visit to some friends. Since this is the eve of the father's sixtieth birthday, Shan-ts'ai, who is feeling very lonely, decides to go home for a visit. But even before he has left the mountain, he is trapped by a snake demon who cries for help in a girl's voice. After Shan-ts'ai releases her, she reverts to the form of a huge python and decides to eat him, having been starved for eighteen years. After much discussion as to whether people should return favors with favors or with ingratitude, during which Chuang Tzu, among others, is called as a witness, Kuan-yin saves Shan-ts'ai and tricks the snake demon into crawling back into the small bottle that had originally imprisoned her. She then puts the snake in the Cave of Tidal Sounds and tells her to purge herself of the poison in her heart. This she does in seven years and transforms herself into Lung-nü, while her poisonous heart is transformed into the night-illuminating pearl, which she offers to Kuan-yin. In the meantime, Kuan-yin has also recruited the white parrot.[21]

What are the sources for the white parrot? Birds as attendants of deities or residents of paradises are not uncommon. The Queen Mother of the West, for instance, used the blue bird as her messenger, as I mentioned earlier in the chapter. The *O-mi-t'o ching* (Shorter Pure Land Sūtra) states that parrots, *kalavinka,* and other rare birds live in the Pure Land for the benefit of those who achieve rebirth in that happy land. Parrots and *kalavinka* birds were prized novelties in the T'ang period. Edward Schafer believes that the *kalavinka* bird is comparable to the *drongo,* for like the latter, it has metallic plumage, but is indigo blue instead of black like the latter (Schafer 1963:103–4). He suggests that the "white parrots" are white cockatoos from Indonesia. The bird was reputed to be "refined in understanding, discriminating in intelligence, and excellent at answering questions," impressing Emperor T'ai-tsung so much that he returned it to its native forest out of pity. The T'ang painter Yen Li-pen painted this bird together with the five-colored one that accompanied it. Another painter, Chou Fang, painted the famous white cockatoo called the "Snow-Garbed Maiden," who was the pet of Yang Kuei-fei, Emperor Hsüan-tsung's favorite consort (Schafer 1959, 1963:101). Moreover, parrots were subjects of versification by poets as well (Graham 1979).

Parrots are also protagonists in Buddhist scriptures. Among the tableau of didactic sculptures at the Great Buddha Creek at Pao-ting Shan, Ta-tsu, Szechwan, under the scene depicting Prince Patience gouging out his eyes in order to cure his father's illness, there is a scene showing a parrot carrying a grain of rice in its mouth. The inscription next to it quotes from the *Tsa-pao-tsang ching* (T 4:449a) and makes it clear that this is one of the *Jātaka* tales. The future Buddha was once a filial parrot who used to carry grains of rice from a farmer's field. The farmer made the vow of sharing his harvest with all sentient beings. When the farmer saw the parrot doing this he got angry and captured him. Thereupon the parrot reminded him of his own vow, making him relent and let the parrot go (*Ta-tsu shih-k'e yen-chiu* 272). In another *Jātaka* tale (the 62nd item in the *Liu-tu chi ching*, T 4:34a), the parrot escaped from his captor by feigning death, recalling the advice given by Bodhidharma in the *pao-chüan* discussed later. Such examples show that these stories found in the Buddhist scriptures might have served as sources for the *pao-chüan* of folk traditions.

A more plausible source for the parrot, however, comes from popular literature. The clever and filial white parrot was the hero in a Ming *tz'u-hua*, prosimetric ballads, discovered by chance inside a Ming tomb excavated in 1967 in Chia-ting, outside of Shanghai. There were sixteen texts printed during the Ch'eng-hua era of the Ming, five with colophons giving years from 1471 to 1478, which were buried with the deceased who we can imagine to have been a fan of popular stories and plays (Wang 1973). These texts were printed in Peking from woodblocks and were profusely illustrated.

Our text carries the title *Hsin-k'an ch'üan-hsiang Ying-ke hsiao-i chuan* (Newly Printed and Completely Illustrated Tale of the Filial and Righteous Parrot). The story is very intricate and detailed. It undoubtedly served as the basis for the *pao-chüan* composed later. The story happened in the T'ang dynasty, a time described as peaceful and prosperous. Buddhism was practiced in the land. Ministers and officials chanted the name of Amitābha. Soldiers delighted in reading sūtras and doing good deeds. There was a *sāha* tree covered with evergreen leaves in the county of Hsi-lung of Lung-chou (in present-day Kansu).

A parrot family lived in a nest on top of the tree. The parents and the young chick were all pure white. The young parrot was exceedingly intelligent. He could not only read sūtras and chant the name of the Buddha, but also compose poetry. One day, when the father parrot went to the South Garden to gather fruits, he was shot and killed by two hunters, the Wang brothers elder and younger. When the mother parrot went to find out what had happened to her husband, she was then blinded. The young parrot comforted his mother and volunteered to fly to the Western Garden to gather lichi nuts for the mother. When he found them, he thanked his good fortune by first reciting one volume of the *O-mi-t'o ching*. He gathered seven lichi nuts, one for himself, and six for his mother, hoping her wound would heal. Unfortunately, before he could fly home, he was captured by the elder and younger Wang. They sold him for thirty strings of cash to a gentry official, who appreciated the parrot's ability to compose poems on the spot. When they returned home, the master asked the parrot to chant a poem using the white cranes painted on the screen as the theme. The parrot answered:

Cranes are born like balls of snow.
Yet now they are stuck on the surface of the screen.
Although they have wings, they nevertheless cannot fly.
It seems that you and I are in the same boat.

Greatly pleased, the master sent for his wife, who took an immediate liking to the parrot. She also asked him for a poem and said that if she liked it, she would have him released. The parrot straightaway composed a poem comparing her to Kuan-yin:

With hair as fine as black silk flowing down your waist,
Walking, you sway with the wind.
If only there were three bamboos behind you,
You would be an unpainted Kuan-yin.

The mistress rewarded him with a bowl of cherries. The fame of the parrot began to spread. When the governor learned the news, he got hold of this parrot and presented him to the emperor as a tribute, reporting how the Wang brothers had captured this rare bird. So the parrot was taken to the court. In order to avenge the death of his father at the hands of the hunters, the parrot pretended not to be able to compose poetry when he was ordered to do so by the emperor. Enraged, the emperor sent for the two hunters and had them executed. The parrot, now satisfied, began to show his poetic talent in front of the emperor. He was rewarded again with bowls of cherries. Finally the parrot asked to go home, for two months had gone by since he was separated from his mother. But by the time he arrived home, he found that his mother had died. He carried out his duty as a filial son by performing an elaborate funeral conducted by both Buddhist monks and Taoist priests under the personal direction of the Jade Emperor and attended by many species of birds. Afterwards, still grief-stricken, he was directed by the Earth God to go and worship Kuan-yin. Kuan-yin was moved by his filial piety and enabled his parents to achieve rebirth in the Pure Land. She also agreed to take him to the South Sea to be forever by her side.[22]

The *pao-chüan* devoted to the parrot shows strong indebtedness to the story, which was already popular in the fifteenth century. It does not mention the parrot's talent as a poet. But his devotion and filial piety to his mother receive the same emphasis as before. The *Ying-ke (or Ying-erh) pao-chüan* (Precious Scroll of the Parrot [or the Parrot's Son]) was obviously known to the author of the *Shan-ts'ai Lung-nü pao-chüan.* In this version, the father of the parrot dies and his mother is also deadly ill. She wants to eat the cherries that only grow in the Eastern Land (China). Having been warned of the evil disposition of the people in that land, the filial parrot nevertheless flies there to get the cherries. He is captured by hunters who, upon discovering that he can speak human language, sells him to a rich landlord.

The parrot proceeds to give sermons and as a result, the hunters who caught him give up their profession, and many people convert to Buddhism. But the rich man is hard-hearted and refuses to release him. One day, Bodhidharma comes and suggests a way of escape. The parrot is to pretend to have died, and when the rich man sees him, he throws the parrot on the ground. The parrot flies home to his mother, who has in the meantime died. When the parrot discovers this fact, he faints away in grief. Kuan-yin, moved by his filial piety, comes and, with the willow branch, sprinkles him with the pure water she keeps in her vase. This revives the parrot. Kuan-yin also helps his parents achieve a good rebirth. In gratitude, the parrot asks to accompany Kuan-yin ever after. The *Shan-ts'ai Lung-nü pao-chüan* condenses the *Ying-ke pao-chüan* into a couple of pages and concludes, "The bodhisattva stands on the head of the big fish and Shan-ts'ai stands on lotuses. They sail slowly toward the Purple Bamboo Grove. One also sees the white parrot carrying the rosary in its beak flying forward to meet the bodhisattva. This picture has been handed down even to this day." It is indeed possible that the author might have been looking at such a picture as he wrote this. With the increasing fame of P'u-t'o after the sixteenth century, Nai-hai Kuan-yin, represented by this particular iconography, becomes even more popular. So much so that pilgrims to P'u-t'o, as we read in the last chapter, began to have visions of Kuan-yin accompanied by the trio: Shan-ts'ai, Lung-nü, and the parrot, identical to the contemporary paintings of Nan-hai Kuan-yin.

I have devoted much space in this chapter to describing the contents of several precious scrolls because I believe that they offer some important clues to a reading of the feminine forms of Kuan-yin in later Chinese paintings. These popular texts show some familiarity with Buddhist scriptural sources, but they rarely adhere to the original allusions faithfully. They boldly combine different elements in creating an indigenous version of the story. For instance, as I indicated previously, Shan-ts'ai, Lung-nü, and the white parrot, the three companions of Kuan-yin of the South Sea, can be traced to the *Hua-yen* (*Avataṃsaka*) and *Lotus* sūtras, the esoteric sūtras glorifying the Thousand-handed and Thousand-eyed Kuan-yin, and the *Shorter Pure Land Sūtra*, among others. Like the precious scrolls, some of the later paintings also combine originally totally unrelated subjects, such as pairing Kuan-yin with lohan. Precious scrolls, moreover, form a self-contained tradition. Later compositions show familiarity with earlier ones. They repeat, embellish, and combine salient features of the latter. We can also detect this in the hybrid iconographies of Kuan-yin. For instance, a blanc de Chine shrine dated to the seventeenth century shows the White-robed Fish-basket Kuan-yin resembling the Nai-hai Kuan-yin (figure 10.5).

How did the various feminine forms of Kuan-yin come about? Miracles and pilgrimage traditions probably provided the initial impetus. Art and literature then promoted and popularized them. I would suggest that each major form of the feminine Kuan-yin was originally grounded in one specific location, connected with one life story, and depicted with one type of iconography. For instance, Princess Miao-shan was originally worshiped in Honan, Mr. Ma's Wife/Fish-basket Kuan-yin in Shensi, White-robed Kuan-yin in Hangchow, and Kuan-yin of the South Sea on P'u-t'o Island. In this way, Kuan-yin, an originally foreign, male deity was transformed into a female savior with a set of distinctive Chinese identities. While each one might originally have had her own cult, not all of them survived. Princess Miao-shan and Mr. Ma's Wife do not have separate cults, but White-robed Kuan-yin and Kuan-yin of the South Sea do. Moreover, as P'u-t'o developed into the Chinese Potalaka and emerged as the national and international center for Kuan-yin worship in the Ming, Kuan-yin of the South Sea also absorbed the images of Kuan-yin as Miao-shan, the fishmonger, and the White-robed one. When we examine the miracle tales connected with P'u-t'o, it is possible to detect the simultaneous appearances of these different images of Kuan-yin. Similarly, when we examine the iconogra-

Figure 10.5. The White-robed Fish-basket Kuan-yin, seventeenth century. *Courtesy of the Rijksmuseum, Amsterdam.*

phy of the Kuan-yin of the South Sea, traces of the other images of Kuan-yin can also be found in juxtaposition. One image does not obliterate the other images, but through the process of "superscription" (Duara 1988:778–95) Kuan-yin of the Southern Sea succeeds in maintaining her identity yet is at the same time enriched by the mythical lore permeating the other images. All of these views of Kuan-yin, traceable to the different images, though different and even contradictory taken by themselves, mutually authenticate each other and reinforce Kuan-yin's efficacy (*ling*) in the eyes of her devotees.[23]

11

Venerable Mother: Kuan-yin and Sectarian Religions in Late Imperial China

Kuan-yin has not only been worshiped by Buddhist monks and lay people and celebrated by artists, novelists, and playwrights, but has also been invoked by believers of various sectarian religions in China. Describing how a sectarian religion known as Ch'ang-sheng Chiao (Eternal Life Teaching) revived itself in 1766 when its temple was burned down, the governor of Chekiang wrote in a memorial presented to the Ch'ien-lung Emperor, which Overmyer summarizes: "Each contributed a substantial sum of money, while another member went all through the surrounding area seeking donations. By their combined efforts they succeeded in building a new center on the old site. One of the members contributed a porcelain image of Kuan-yin which was worshiped in the new edifice. At one side of the altar they placed an empty chair to represent the deceased founder" (1976:8–9). The installation of a Kuan-yin image, most likely a blanc de Chine White-robed Kuan-yin like the ones discussed in chapter 6, made the new building a cultic site. Kuan-yin, frequently referred to as Lao-mu (Venerable or Old Mother), was indeed a major deity worshiped by the sectarians since the late Ming. Her presence in sectarian religions is neither limited to this particular sect, nor to that time and place.

Several religions still practiced today in Taiwan and elsewhere draw inspiration from the sectarian religions that first appeared in the sixteenth century. The latter, in turn, were spiritual heirs to the White Lotus tradition going all the way back to the eleventh century, whose early history is discussed in chapter 8. I have had personal contacts with three: The I-kuan Tao (Way of Pervading Unity), Li (or Tsai-li) Chiao (Principle [or Abiding Principle] Teaching), and Hsien-t'ien Tao (Way of the Former Heaven). Kuan-yin is worshiped in all three. In 1967, while doing dissertation research in Taiwan, an acquaintance of mine introduced me to his uncle, who was a teacher of I-kuan Tao in charge of a local hall in Hsin-chu, outside of Taipei. Because the religion was not then recognized by the government, I was constantly asked to be discreet and keep everything I learned to myself. I visited the hall, observed their religious rituals, and was given a general introduction to their religion.

I-kuan Tao is a syncretic religion. It incorporates tenets from Confucianism, Taoism, and Buddhism, affirming that the five religions (including Christianity and Islam) contain aspects of the same basic truth. However, because the institutionalized religions had distorted this truth over time, it had to be reestablished by I-kuan Tao, which was founded by Wang Chüeh-i (1821?–1884), also known as Ancient Buddha Wang. For followers in Taiwan, the patriarch Chang T'ien-jan (1887–1947) is even more respected. The supreme deity of this religion, like all sectarian religions since the Ming, is the Eternal Mother, or literally, the Unborn Venerable Mother (Wu-sheng Lao-mu), who is also called the Golden Mother of the Jasper Pool (Yao-ch'ih Chin-mu), the creator and ancestress of all humankind. They believe in three epochs (*chi*) or kalpas (*chieh*), which are understood in a historical and an eschatological sense. The first epoch was called Green Yang and was ruled by the Lamp-lighting Ancient Buddha (Jan-teng Ku-fo, Dīpaṁkara Buddha). It lasted 1500 years and was destroyed by water. The second epoch, in which we are living, is the Red Yang, when Śākyamuni Buddha is the spiritual ruler. It lasts for 3,000 years and will be destroyed by fire. The third epoch to come is the epoch of the White Yang. It is ruled by Maitreya Buddha and will be destroyed by wind in the end. In order to save us who are her children from the disasters at the end of each kalpa, the Mother sends teachers to enlighten humankind: the Duke of Chou, Confucius, Lao Tzu, Śākyamuni Buddha, Bodhidharma, and Chi-kung, who is historically known as Tao-chi (d. 1209) or Chi-tien (Crazy Chi) but revered by many people as a Living Buddha (*huo-fo*) since the sixteenth century (Shahar 1992, 1994, 1999). She also communicates with her devotees by giving instructions through these teachers, most frequently Chi-kung, during spirit-writing or the "flying phoenix" (*luan*) sessions. The goal of the religion is to return to our true home by being reunited with the Mother.

Because of their belief in the Maitreya Buddha and the strong millenarian expectations, I-kuan Tao, like the White Lotus Teaching throughout late imperial times, was suppressed by the government and criticized by the Buddhist clergy until the late 1980s (Sung 1983). One can understand why the Buddhist establishment would show disapproval. The religion has no professional clergy. Its leaders, like the members in general, are lay people. Aside from keeping a vegetarian diet, there are no special rules and rituals to observe. When one joins the religion, he/she undergoes a simple initiation during which the "Three Treasures" are transmitted. Although the term is the same as the Buddhist one, they mean completely different things. Instead of the Buddha, Dharma, and Saṃgha, the Three Treasures in I-kuan Tao refer to having one's secret aperture between the eyebrows opened and being instructed to assume the correct hand gestures and to chant a secret spell known as the "mantra [true word] of five characters" (*wu-tzu chen-yen*) by the teacher.[1]

I-kuan Tao recognizes many deities who come from different religions. Aside from the Mother, there are five main deities: Kuan-yin, Maitreya, Chi-kung, Lü Tung-pin, and Kuan-kung. In many I-kuan Tao halls, however, the image of the feminine Kuan-yin in the form of Nan-hai Kuan-yin is prominently enshrined in the center of the altar. For the Mother, the supreme deity, being unborn and thus formless, is impossible to visualize or depict.

In 1986 when I was doing research on this book in Beijing, I met Li Shi-yü, the authority on *pao-chüan* literature and modern sectarian religions (1948). Li had studied a religion known as Li Chiao for many years. The headquarter of the religion is Tientsin, Li's hometown, and he could thus conveniently carry out fieldwork and gather material on its history and operations over the years. According to the hagiographies of its patriarchs compiled by the religion, Li Chiao was founded by Yang Lai-ju (1621–1753), a native of Shantung. He obtained the *chin-shih* degree in 1641, near the end of the Ming, but instead of seeking an official career, he chose to take care of his mother. After her death, he changed his name and lived like a hermit. He carried out a daily routine of chanting scriptures while kneeling. Imitating the example of Sudhana's adoration of Kuan-yin, he instituted a regimen called "fifty-three presentations" (*wu-shih-san tsan*), doing fifty-three full prostrations every day.[2] His piety moved Kuan-yin, who appeared to instruct him six times during his lifetime. The unique feature of this religion is its emphasis on clean living, as evidenced by its commandments forbidding smoking and drinking.

During the Ch'ing, when opium smoking became a national scourge, members of Li Chiao were credited as helping to halt its devastation and won social approbation. Unlike other new religions, the supreme deity of Li Chiao is not the Mother, but Kuan-yin, who is called the Ancient Buddha of the Holy Teaching (Sheng-tsung Ku-fo). An image in the form of Nan-hai Kuan-yin is enshrined in the main altar of each meeting hall. Not only Kuan-yin herself, but Sudhana and Dragon Princess, her attendants, and the parrot, who is respectfully referred to as Kuan-yin's "prime minister," are worshiped by members as well. The secret spell of the "five characters," in fact, is no other than "Nan-wu Kuan-shih-yin" (Adoration to Kuan-shih-yin).[3] In their liturgical text, *Wu-shan pao-chüan* (Precious Scroll of the Five Mountains), the titles of the indigenous scriptures glorifying Kuan-yin (*Fo-ting hsin t'o-lo-ni ching* and *Pai-i Ta-pei wu-yin-hsin t'o-lo-ni ching*), discussed in chapter 3, are listed for veneration. According to Li, members of the sect in Tientsin used to wear white clothes, shoes, and even belts in order to show their respect for the White-robed Kuan-yin. Their religion was thus also known as Pai-i Tao (White-clothed Teaching; Li 1996:198).

It was also while in China that I discovered several precious scrolls written in the late Ming, in which Kuan-yin appears as the Venerable or Old Mother.[4] This image of Kuan-yin as the Mother was entirely new when it appeared, and without any scriptural basis. The obvious explanation for why it came into being after the sixteenth century is that it was due to the fame of the sectarians' Eternal Mother. But this does not actually answer the question. For what were the sources for the Eternal Mother? Why did the Eternal Mother suddenly emerge as the supreme deity of the sectarians in the sixteenth century? Could she have appeared so suddenly and triumphantly if Kuan-yin were not already a feminine deity commanding great respect and affection? Furthermore, why is it that some sectarian scriptures either claim that their Mother became incarnated as Kuan-yin or Kuan-yin became incarnated as the founder of their religion? It is easy to understand why the sectarians would want to appropriate Kuan-yin, for by the late imperial period, Kuan-yin had become one of the most well-known and popular deities in China. Images of Kuan-yin were enshrined not only in Buddhist monasteries, but also in temples belonging to the so-called popular religion. But unlike popular religion, which does not formulate a conscious theology concerning Kuan-yin and the other gods it venerates, the scriptures of sectarian religions take pains to explain the complicated relationships between their Goddess and their patriarchs and Kuan-yin.

The appropriation of Kuan-yin by the sectarians contributed to the final transformation of the bodhisattva: Venerable or Old Mother Kuan-yin. At the same time, the adoption of Kuan-yin as the central deity or as one of the main deities by many sectarian religions also helped to promote faith in her even more among other segments of the population. The sectarian *pao-chüan* about Kuan-yin thus served as yet another important medium in the spread of her cult and, in the process, created yet another new face for this already multifaceted deity.

In this chapter, I first discuss the Eternal Mother as depicted in some famous sectarian scriptures and the understanding about the relationship between the Goddess, the religions' founders, and Kuan-yin that emerge in these texts. I next look at one clear example of the sectarian appropriation of Kuan-yin. This is the case of the *True Scripture of Kuan-yin's Original Vow of Universal Salvation*, a precious scroll written by a patriarch of the Way of the Former

Heaven (Hsien-t'ien Tao) in the seventeenth century (Dudbridge 1978:69).[5] I-kuan Tao is clearly related to this religion, for it accepts the latter's list of patriarchs as its own. In fact, its original founder, Chang T'ien-jan, is now identified as the eighteenth patriarch of the Hsien-t'ien Tao (Lin 1984:129). This is not surprising, for both derive ultimately from the late Ming White Lotus sectarian tradition. As I mentioned in chapter 8, the *True Scripture* is a sectarian rewrite of the legend of Miao-shan. Kuan-yin does not appear as the Mother in this text.

I then examine three *pao-chüan* written in the late Ming in which Kuan-yin appears as the Mother. As we shall see, in these cases, it is very difficult if not impossible to differentiate Mother Kuan-yin from the sectarian Eternal Mother. Similar if not identical ideas and even words are used to describe both. Did these sectarian *pao-chüan* use Kuan-yin to bolster the prestige of the writer's own religion, as was the case of the *True Scripture*? In two cases, perhaps, for specific names of sectarian religions are mentioned, but it is not possible to be sure in the third one. Just as sectarians might appropriate Kuan-yin, devotees of Kuan-yin might also appropriate the sectarian Eternal Mother to add to the glory of their own deity. Without knowing anything about their authors (who unfortunately remain anonymous), or the circumstances of their production, one can only speculate. Finally, I offer some suggestions as to the possible sources for the Eternal Mother as well as Mother Kuan-yin.

The Venerable Mother in Sectarian Religions

Thirty years ago, C. K. Yang wrote that aside from Buddhism and Taoism, the third form of institutional religion in China "was that of the syncretic religious societies" (1961:301). Daniel Overmyer compared them to religious reform movements such as the Protestant sects in Europe and Jōdo Shinshū in Japan (1976). While they incorporated elements from Maitreyan, Pure Land, Ch'an Buddhism, and Inner Alchemy Taoism, among others, the religions can still properly be regarded as new. Most, including the Way of the Former Heaven and the Way of Pervading Unity, were influenced by or claimed descent from Lo Ch'ing (1443–1527), known as Patriarch Lo.

These new religions shared some important characteristics that set them apart: belief in a mother goddess who is the creator and savior of humankind, an eschatology marked by three stages, and universal salvation unmediated by any religious professionals. All these ideas were emphasized in the new religion called Lo or Non-action Teaching (Wu-wei Chiao), founded by Lo.[6] Like the others that appeared later, it was lay in its organization and millenarian in orientation. He wrote five precious scrolls known as the "five books in six volumes" (*wu-pu liu-ts'e*), which were published in 1509. Although the exact words, Wu-sheng Lao-mu, do not appear in these texts, the central ideas that inspire all sectarian religions are already present: namely, that "true emptiness" (*chen-k'ung*) is our "original home" (*chia-hsiang*), that our "ancestor" (*tsu*) is the "mother" (*mu*), and that the home and the mother are our true destination and nature.[7]

The religion was called "non-action" (*wu-wei*) because, according to Lo, there was no specific thing one needed to do purposively in order to be saved. Reading sūtras, doing meditation, calling the name of the Buddha, or performing religious rituals are all artificial activities (*yu-wei*) regarded by Lo as foolish and misguided. In his writings, he relates incidents from his life. His mother died when he was a child and he experienced keenly the pain of the impermanence of life. When his neighbor's old mother (*lao-mu*) died, monks were invited to chant the *Chin-kang k'e-i*, a popular liturgical text containing commentaries on the *Diamond Sūtra*, dated to the thirteenth century. He was touched to the quick when he heard, "If people want to believe and accept, just let them pick up the sūtra and read for themselves." He got hold of a copy of the text and studied it for three years. At the end of his search, he reached a breakthrough:

Not returning to nonbeing nor being,
I am the true emptiness.
Mother (mu) *is me and I am Mother,*
There is originally no duality.

The realization of nonduality is, of course, the existential verification of the Mahāyāna Buddhist insight of *śūnyatā*. Throughout his writings, he never tired of stressing that one must transcend the conventional distinction of gender and class and that salvation is independent of external work: "neither monk nor lay, neither men nor women, neither precepts nor commandments." He was therefore unrelenting in his criticism against organized Buddhism and believed that enlightenment and salvation were available to men and women in secular society.

It is no wonder that the Buddhist establishment looked upon him with alarm and disapproval. When Te-ch'ing went to Shantung in 1586, he was distressed to find that Lo Chiao had many followers and that they did not know anything about Buddhism (Ma and Han 1992:184). In the code Chu-hung created for his monastery Yün-ch'i Ssu, he specifically forbade any monk to study the "five books in six volumes," and if anyone was caught doing it, he would be expelled (Yü 1981:203). He also called upon all Buddhists to condemn him:

> A man named Lo has written a book . . . called the *Wu-wei chüan* [Book of nonaction]. The ignorant followed him in great numbers, but [the book's] teachings are false. . . . He talks about purity and emptiness, but in fact in his heart he is plotting for his own advantage. In name he is nonactive, but in fact he was active. When people see him quoting from many Buddhist sūtras, they suppose him to be orthodox, not realizing that he falsely uses orthodox texts to support [his own] heresy. . . . All Buddhists should firmly reject him. (YCFH 27:19a-b; Overmyer 1976:37)

Lo referred to Kuan-yin often in his writings. He was familiar with the legend of Princess Miao-shan. This is not surprising, for the reference is found in the liturgical text, *Chin-kang k'e-i*, which exerted so much influence on him and from which he quoted more than seventy times (Ma and Han 1992:192). It states, "Miao-shan refused to take a husband, and most certainly achieved Buddhahood" (*Hsiao-shih chin-kang k'e-i hui-yao chu-chieh,* HTC 93:235). In the precious scroll that Lo wrote, *Ta-ch'eng t'an-shih wu-wei pao-chüan* (Precious Scroll of Great Vehicle of Non-action Which Takes Pity on the World), when he cites earlier exemplary figures for emulation, he mentions Miao-shan going to Hsiang-shan with approval. In the same text, he describes how rare the "true body" (another term for "true emptiness," or the Mother) becomes incarnated in the world as a man or a woman. But when it does, it can manifest itself as a man, with a full moon face, who is "superior to Śākyamuni Buddha." Or, when it manifest itself as a woman, "carrying a fish-basket, it is superior to Kuan-yin." But at the end of the paragraph, he declares, "The true body is the bodhisattva who is no other than Kuan-yin." Such statements as these already imply that the new deity, the Eternal Mother, is closely connected with core Buddhist ideas such as emptiness and the bodhisattva ideals or the cultic figure of Kuan-yin. Still, it is significant that Lo Ch'ing himself does not mention the Eternal Mother as the supreme deity in his writings.

Since Lo did not use the term, when did the Eternal Mother first appear and become the central figure in the sectarian belief system? In his earlier work, Overmyer believes that Kung Ch'ang, the founder of the Huan-yüan Chiao (Return to the Origin), who first wrote about the Eternal Mother in 1588, followed by P'iao Kao, the founder of the Vast Yang Chiao, in 1594 (1976:143). He arrives at this conclusion through his reliance on the writings of Huang Yü-p'ien (fl. 1830–1840), a dedicated Hopei magistrate who, in the course of his official duties, investigated some sixty-eight sectarian texts and wrote four books between 1834 and 1841 intended to refute the "heretical" teachings of the texts. Because Huang often quoted large chunks from the original texts before offering his rebuttals, his writings are very valuable to scholars, for some of the texts have since disappeared.

While it is true that Huang connected the belief in the Eternal Mother with these two religious founders, he also states categorically that the term "Lao-mu" appears only after the end of the Wan-li era (1573–1615). At this time a long list of sectarian religious leaders, including not only the above-mentioned two, but also "P'u-ming, P'u-ching, Bodhisattva Lü, and Bodhisattva Mi" worshiped the "Eternal Mother as the sect master (*chiao-chu*)," and this is how the term came into popular use. "So there is no question that she appeared only at the end of the Ming" (*Hsü-k'e p'o-hsieh hsiang-pien* 71). According to Li Shi-yü and Susan Naquin, most of these individuals were influenced by Lo Ch'ing and his "Five Books in Six Volumes," or else claimed descent from him. However, their research has indicated that the term Lao-mu appeared at least fifty years earlier, in a text entitled *Huang-chi chin-tan chiu-lien cheng-hsin kuei-chen huan-hsiang pao-chüan* (Precious Scroll of the Golden Elixir and Nine Lotuses of the Imperial Ultimate [Which Leads to] Rectifying Belief, Taking Refuge in the True and Returning Home), which was reprinted in 1523. Overmyer now concludes that it is indeed in this text that "the Venerable Mother for the first time has a central role" (1999:139). It is also the text that provided the religious rationale for the cult of the Nine-Lotus Bodhisattva promoted by the Empress Dowager Li, the mother of Emperor Wan-li, discussed in chapters 3 and 9. The text speaks of "the Venerable Mother [*Lao-mu*], chief deity of this religion, the three great kalpas that mark historical time and their attendant buddhas, the dragon flower assembly at which believers would be saved and the dispatch of a patriarch (Wu-wei tsu) to preach his formula for salvation (here, the Golden Elixir method of meditation)" (Li and Naquin 1988:151).[8] The scripture does not refer to Kuan-yin as the Venerable Mother, but instead as the Nine-lotus Kuan-yin, the Founder of the Perfect and Penetrating Teaching (Yüan-t'ung Chiao-chu, Chiu-lien Kuan-yin). She plays an important role in helping the Venerable Mother to carry out her work of salvation.

In the scriptures of the Vast Yang Chiao, the Venerable Mother is invoked together with Kuan-yin and Ta-pei who are also called "mother." All three are called "compassionate sailors" (*tz'u-hang*). Kuan-yin is described as sailing the Dharma Boat (*fa-chuan*), ferrying the saved beings back to the eternal home.[9] Like the previous scripture, this is also full of inner alchemy terminology. For instance, it says,

When you have distilled the priceless treasure of the golden elixir,
The Child (ying-erh) *and the Maiden* (ch'a-nü) *will escape from imprisonment.*
Our patriarch, fortunate in having the affinity to meet Mother Kuan-yin (Kuan-yin Mu),

> *Is now broadly saving sentient beings after receiving the true transmission.*
> (Hung-yang hou-hsü Jan-teng t'ien-hua pao-chüan)

P'u-ming was the founder of Huang-t'ien Chiao (Yellow Heaven Teaching). Li Shi-yü studied this in the 1940s, when it was still in existence some four hundred years after its founding (1948:10–31). The religion was centered in Wan-ch'uan, northeast of Peking. The founder's real name was Li Pin but he was called Ancient Buddha P'u-ming, the incarnation of Maitreya. In the 1550s he wrote the *P'u-ming ju-la wu-wei liao-i pao-chüan* (Tathāgata Pu-ming's Precious Scroll on Complete Revelation through Non-Action), which teaches a similar cosmology and eschatology of salvation by the Eternal Mother (Li and Naquin 1988:152). Yellow Heaven is the name of the "home of true emptiness," the residence of the Eternal Mother. The sect regarded Bodhidharma as its first patriarch and Hui-neng to be the sixth patriarch. P'u-ming was actually the seventh patriarch. After he died in either 1562 or 1563, his wife became the next head. After her death, the leadership then went to his two daughters, P'u-ching and P'u-ch'ao, both married into a K'ang family. After them, the leadership went to P'u-hsien, the daughter of P'u-ch'ao and a granddaughter of P'u-ming (Ma and Han 1992:409–16). She in turn married a man named Mi.[10] The leadership then reverted to the male heirs of P'u-ming's older brother after P'u-hsien. The religion emphasized joint practice by both the husband and the wife.

It is tempting to speculate that the *Kuan-yin shih-erh yüan-chüeh ch'üan-chuan* (Complete Biographies of the Twelve Perfectly Enlightened Ones of Kuan-yin), a text written in the late Ch'ing and mentioned in chapter 8, might have been inspired by this religion. Although it does not mention Huang-t'ien Chiao by name in the text, it tells the story of how Kuan-yin leads twelve persons, some good and some bad, although they are all couples, into enlightenment. Kuan-yin takes the disguises of a monk and a beautiful young woman, but also of a poor old beggar woman. Although the example of Miao-shan is cited with admiration, Kuan-yin does not advise against marriage per se, but only its consummation. The husbands and wives in this scripture end up practicing inner alchemy meditation in the same temple, probably very much like the followers of Huang-t'ien Chiao.

Like the *Hsiang-shan pao-chüan* and the *True Scriptures*, this scripture also has harsh words to say about monks and nuns. Gentry Li, one of the twelve potential converts, has this to say:

> Most Buddhist monks and Taoist priests are lazy and self-indulgent. They pocket the money offered to them by the faithful and secretly use it to gamble and visit prostitutes. Although they are supposed to be compassionate

> and should not wear clothing made of animal fur or silkworms, they nevertheless insist on wearing fur coats and silk shoes and strut about putting on airs. The nuns, on the other hand, are women who either do not get along with their mothers-in-law or who detest the poverty of their husbands. That is why they escape from their homes and enter the temple hoping to enjoy an easy life. If a nun such as this has a disciple, she will let the disciple do all the work. She will not read sūtras, chant the name of the Buddha, or sit in meditation. She will go to the homes of donors every day and incite women to come to the temple to offer incense or pray for a son or a daughter. Some will even use this as an excuse to corrupt their morals and arrange secret trysts for the women at night. Such people are truly evil. This is the reason why I have vowed to kill one hundred monks, nuns, and priests. I have dug a big pit in the yard, into which I dump those I have killed. So far I have killed more than sixty. (*Kuan-yin shih-erh yüan-chüeh ch'uan-chuan* 1938:60)

During the Wan-li period a woman known as Patriarch Mi, whom Huang Yü-p'ien identified as Bodhisattva Mi founded yet another religion called Lung-t'ien Chiao (the Dragon Heaven Teaching), which is also known as Pai-yang Chiao (the White Yang Teaching). She was married to a man surnamed Liu. By 1816 there had been twelve patriarchs, who were all daughters-in-law of the Liu family. The ancestors must be women and not men because only women could be incarnations of Bodhisattva Mi (Ma and Han 1992:695). As we shall soon see, it is most likely that the Yellow Heaven and Dragon Heaven religions produced two of the three precious scrolls glorifying Mother Kuan-yin.

During the late Ming, as new religions developed, the founders were sometimes regarded as incarnations of buddhas or of Kuan-yin. The Venerable Mother herself also was believed to come down to earth, appearing as an actual poor old woman (*p'in-p'o*), like Kuan-yin in the precious scroll just cited, to instruct potential teachers. For instance, Ming-k'ung, the seventh patriarch of Lo Chiao, described in detail his religious experiences in his writings. He related how on the night of the eighth day of the fourth month in the thirty-ninth year of Wan-li (1611) he had a dream in which a poor old woman was begging in the street. When she told him that his voice reminded her of her son, he realized that she was no other than the Venerable Mother (Lao-mu). He knelt down in front of her, feeling completely overwhelmed. She then told him to keep a vegetarian diet. In 1624 he had another dream in which she told him to write scriptures. Upon waking he was troubled, because he did not know how to write a scripture. However, he did not despair. Four years later, he received the revelation of a precious scroll from the Venerable Mother on the first day of the second month, and he completed the writing on the fifth day of the third month. The text was personally examined by the Mother, who gave her approval. She revealed to him another precious scroll in the second month of 1629, which he completed writing down on the fifth day of the fifth month. In the precious scrolls he wrote, however, he describes his two encounters with the Venerable Mother as happening not in his dreams, but in broad daylight. The Mother appeared to him as a kind old woman. The first time she took the guise of a beggar and instructed him to practice religion. The second time she appeared as a white-haired blind woman, walking alone in the street. Feeling sorry for her, he took her home and licked her two eyes. Like a Ch'an master, she enlightened him by performing shocking acts. She asked him to examine her body all over. When he hesitated to touch the lower part of her body, she insisted and he discovered to his great amazement that it was a lotus flower (Ma and Han 1992:232–34).

An explicit identification between the Mother and Kuan-yin as well as between Kuan-yin and the female founders of a sectarian religion occurred with the Hsi-ta-sheng Chiao (Western Great Vehicle Teaching), based in the Pao-Ming Ssu (Protection of the Ming Monastery) outside of Peking. The religion traces its founding to a charismatic nun named Lü, the Bodhisattva Lü mentioned by Huang Yü-p'ien. Li Shi-yü and Susan Naquin tell the fascinating history of this temple in a long article (1988). Pao-Ming Ssu was founded in 1457 by the order of Emperor Ying-tsung for a nun named Lü who was reputed to have warned the emperor before his disastrous campaign against the Mongols in 1449 and appeared to him offering food and water during his captivity and later house arrest. The nunnery received royal patronage under successive emperors and attracted able women, who joined the monastic community. The nun Kuei-yüan, who was active in the temple in the 1570s and 1580s, founded a new religion known as Ta-sheng, for its adherents called themselves "the children of Ta-sheng" (*Ta-sheng tzu*). It was subsequently known as Hsi-ta-sheng (Western Great Vehicle) to differentiate it from another religion with the same name founded by Wang Sen, which was known as Tung-ta-sheng (Eastern Great Vehicle).

Kuei-yüan was extremely precocious and wrote her own "five books in six volumes" during 1571–1573 when she was about twelve. All of the sūtras were printed in the winter of 1584–1585 with the sponsorship of three titled individuals. The scriptures celebrate three nuns, Lü, a nun with the surname of Yang who came before Kuei-yüan, and Kuei-yüan herself. "These books presented these three women as different incarnations of the divine being. This deity is explicitly identified as Kuan-yin, the main god of the temple, but believers understand Kuan-yin to be herself a reincarnation of their special deity, the Eternal and Venerable Mother" (Li and Naquin 1988:156). This trinitarian formulation is a revolutionary idea that had not been encountered previously. Several precious scrolls of this religion emphasize this idea. The *P'u-tu hsin-sheng chiu-*

k'u pao-chüan (Precious Scroll of the New Gospel of Universal Salvation), for instance, declares, "Of the various patriarchs, sages, and gods who fill the heaven, the Eternal Venerable Mother is the most revered. The Bodhisattva is the Venerable Mother, the Venerable Mother is the Bodhisattva" and "The Venerable Patriarch [Nun Lü] is originally the reincarnation of the Bodhisattva Kuan-yin. The Bodhisattva has come down to our world in order to transform mortals. Kuan-yin is no other than Wu-sheng [Eternal Mother]" (Ma and Han 1992:656).[11] The scripture also mentions the "twelve enlightened ones" (Li and Naquin 1988:158). In the "second generation" precious scrolls such as the *Ch'ing-yüan miao-tao hsien-sheng Chen-chün Erh-lang pao-chüan* (Precious Scroll of the True Lord Erh-lang of the Pure Origin, Mysterious Way and Many Manifestations), we read,

> *Mother Kuan-yin came down to this earth and appeared as Patriarch Lü.*
> *Under all heaven, men and women came to see the Eternal [One]*
> *The first time [as Nun Lü], she saved men and women but did not complete the task.*
> *She came a second time [as Kuan-yin] reincarnated again in Zhili Kaiping.*
> *(Li and Naquin 1988:157)*

The same idea is put forward in the *T'ai-shan shih-wang pao-chüan* (Precious Scroll of the Ten Kings of Mt T'ai), reprinted in 1636. It praises Patriarch Lü for having a deep spiritual foundation and declares that she is originally Kuan-yin of the South Sea. The *Hsiao-shih chieh-hsü lien-tsung pao-chüan* (Precious Scroll Explaining the Continuation of the Lotus School), a scripture written by a follower of the Eastern Great Vehicle Teaching and reprinted in 1659, says that 'Venerable Mother Kuan-yin came into this world [as] Imperial Lü, Holy Patriarch whose appellation was Yüan-t'ung" (Li and Naquin 1988:170). He begins the scripture by invoking the Venerable Mother, Venerable Mother Kuan-yin Who Saves One from Suffering (*chiu-k'u*) as well as Ti-tsang, P'u-hsien, and Medicine King who are all addressed as "venerable mother." Later scriptures such as this not only present the supreme deity as a goddess, but also feminize all famous bodhisattvas. This vision of the heavenly realm is an all-inclusive one. Taoist and Buddhist deities co-exist peacefully and all defer to the Eternal Mother, who seems to act mainly through Mother Kuan-yin. Kuan-yin in turn either comes down to earth as the founders of the religions, or in the disguise of a poor beggar woman.

The close parity between Kuan-yin and Nun Lü is evident from the temple layout that Li and Naquin reconstucted from available sources (1988:144). The Venerable Mother herself was not represented. The main hall was dedicated to

Kuan-yin and the rear hall was "for the worship of the founder, now called Bodhisattva Lü. Here offerings were made to her image (or mummified body), which looked like 'an old woman seated cross-legged with furrowed brow.'" Just as Kuan-yin was accompanied by Sudhana and Dragon Princess, the founder was also provided with her own attendants corresponding to the pair. "On either side of Nun Lü were statues of her attendants, Golden Boy and Jade Girl" (147).

One noticeable characteristic of the sectarian religions was their attraction to women. During the Ch'ing period, sectarian religions not only attracted many women followers, but often were led by women. Hung Mei-hua found that in mid-Ch'ing as many as twenty-seven leaders of various sects were women. Among them, nineteen were widows, amounting to 70.4 percent (Hung 1992:233). During the Chia-ch'ing era (1796–1820), for instance, when the Vast Yang Teaching was proscribed in Hopei, all the members were women (Hung 1995:280).

The Appropriation of Kuan-yin by the Way of Former Heaven

The Way of the Former Heaven (Hsien-t'ien Tao) or the Great Way of the Former Heaven (Hsien-t'ien Ta-tao) is a sectarian religion still existing in Taiwan, Hong Kong, and Singapore. Marjorie Topley is the only Western anthropologist who has studied this religion (1954, 1958, 1963). She came across it while studying the vegetarian halls in Singapore, many of the residents of which were vegetarian and celibate followers of this religion. The term *hsien-t'ien* is contrasted with *hou-t'ien*. These are Taoist terms. They have both a cosmic and an individual meaning. According to the *Tao Te Ching*, the classic of Taoism, nonbeing (*wu*) gives rise to being (*yu*), which in turn gives rise to everything including humankind. The former or prior heaven refers to the state of nonbeing, while latter or posterior heaven refers to the state of being. At the same time, they also refer to the states before and after one's birth, thus "prenatal" and "postnatal." It is believed that while the former is characterized by full potentiality and vitality, the latter is fated to decline and depletion.

As I discussed in chapter 1, during the Sung, new religious movements arose within Taoism to offer new methods of finding immortality and salvation. Most important among these was the Taoism of Inner Alchemy (*nei-tan*). The origins and history of the movement are vague and complicated (Robinet 1997:215–29). But it became associated with masters of the Ch'üan-chen (Complete Realization) school, which was founded by Wang Che (1123–1170) in the north. He was supposed to have met Lü Tung-pin, the legendary ninth-century figure and one of the Eight Immortals, who taught him the secret method orally. He had seven disciples, Ma Tuan-yang (1123–1183) being regarded as the second patriarch of his school. Po Yü-ch'an (fl. 1209–1224), on the other hand, was one of the most famous teachers of inner alchemy belonging to the school in the south. The goal of the discipline is to create a true or immortal body called the "golden elixir" (*chin-tan*) or "holy fetus" (*sheng-t'ai*) within the mortal body through a unique method of self-cultivation. The adept must carry out a complicated series of alchemical experiments within his/her own body, using it as an alchemical stove and cauldron. For the body is a microcosm, a duplicate of the macrocosmic universe.

When human beings emerge from the void, each is endowed with nature (*hsing*) and life force (*ming*), which are united. A person is also possessed of the three treasures: spirit (*shen*), breath (*ch'i*), and essence (*ching*). As one grows and matures, nature and the life force become separated and the three treasures gradually become weakened as a result of one's becoming entangled with the external world through confused thinking and sexual indulgence. When they are exhausted, one dies. The way to prevent this from happening is to reverse the process by following the course of "backward flow" and undertaking a strict regimen of psycho-physiological meditational exercise. Instead of using lead and mercury as alchemical agents, as in exterior alchemy, the inner alchemist transmutes essence, breath and spirit, thus creating an elixir or fetus within him/herself.

The life force is yin, water, lead, wood mother, breath, dragon and "beautiful maiden" (*ch'a-nü*), while nature is yang, fire, mercury, metal father, spirit, tiger and "child" (*ying-erh*). When the two are brought together, a holy fetus is created that then has to be matured through fetal breathing (*t'ai-hsi*). In the end, life is reunited with nature, and essence is transmuted back to breath. Breath is then transmuted back to spirit and spirit is refined and transmuted back to void (*hsü*).[12] This is no other than the original nonbeing, the true source of everything. One has then returned to the prenatal state, which is also known as the "former heaven." When this is accomplished, not only does one know the Tao, but also attains eternal life or immortality. Known as the dual cultivation of nature and the life force (*hsing-ming shuang-hsiu*), Taoist inner alchemy differentiates itself from the Ch'an approach, which it criticized as being interested only in knowing one's true nature, while neglecting the life force (Berling 1980:94–102).

The Way of the Former Heaven is heavily indebted to Inner Alchemy Taoism, although it also incorporates Buddhist ideas and practices. For instance, it regards Hui-neng (d. 713), the Sixth Patriarch of the Ch'an school, as its own sixth patriarch. But according to the Way of the Former Heaven, "After the

Sixth Patriarch, the Great Way passed to those dwelling in the fire (*huo-chü*, clergy living in their own houses)" (Topley 1963:367). Po Yü-ch'an is regarded as one of the two seventh patriarchs, the other being Ma Tuan-yang, who reorganized the Great Way. At this time the membership consisted of individuals living in their own homes and meeting for worship either in each other's houses or in nonresidential halls. The religion was entirely vegetarian. They regarded a certain Lo Wei-ch'ün (b. 1488), not to be confused with the far more famous Lo Ch'ing discussed before, to be their eighth patriarch. Their records state that many sects appeared after him, which accords well with the historical facts. Many new sectarian religions indeed flourished during the sixteenth and seventeenth centuries.[13] The ninth patriarch, Huang Te-hui (1624–1690), is said to have named the religion "The Great Way of the Former Heaven." Only sects descended from him are considered to be "true" Great Way sects. The gap between the dates for the eighth and ninth patriarchs is explained in terms of Lo's immortality. When he left the earth, he is said to have made frequent visits and continued to head the religion from above until a suitable successor was found (Topley 1963:368).

The Way of the Former Heaven, like the I-kuan Tao, also refers to the Venerable Mother as the Golden Mother of the Jasper Pool. The Mother and Kuan-yin are closely connected in the minds of the believers. Writing about the vegetarian halls in Hong Kong she visited in 1968, Topley mentions that the Mother was seen as a goddess of great compassion and power and most ordinary members, particularly female members, identify her with Kuan-yin. The relationship between the Mother and Kuan-yin is shown in the placing of the images as well. Because the Mother is the highest deity, she must be placed higher than any other deity and should occupy a room to herself. This means that halls of the sect had whenever possible to be built with two stories, and with "Mother's" Room in the upper story. But she occasionally shares a room with Kuan-yin, with whom she is sometimes identified (Topley 1968:146–47).

The *True Scripture* bears two prefaces. The first and "original" preface is written by the Ancient Buddha Kuan-yin (Kuan-yin Ku-fo) and carries a date of the fourteenth year of Yung-le (1416). The second preface is written by the Mountain Man of the Broad Wilderness (Kuang-yeh Shan-jen) and is dated the fifth year of K'ang-hsi (1666). It also contains eulogies written by Bodhidharma and Lü Tung-pin. The second preface states that the writer was fortunate in meeting a teacher named P'u-tu, who instructed him in the Great Way of the Former Heaven. One day he decided to go to P'u-t'o on a pilgrimage. But before the boat reached the shore, there was a sudden storm and a number of boats were shipwrecked. He was lucky enough to receive divine protection and arrive at the island safely. When he came ashore, he took a walk along the beach and saw a stone door outside a cave with the inscription, Ch'ao-yüan Tung (Cave of Reverting to the Origin), a common name for the residences of immortals and gods. A few miles further he arrived at a cloister, where he was greeted by an unusual-looking youth of the Way. The latter gave him a volume entitled *True Scripture of Kuan-yin's Original Vow of Universal Salvation* (Kuan-yin chi-tu pen-yüan chen-ching), telling him to promote it. But because the scripture was written in Sanskrit and could not be understood by people living in the Land of the East, he hurried home, and after translating it, he had it published so that it could be disseminated in the world.

Kuan-yin is called Tz'u-hang Tsun-che (The Worthy One Who is the Compassionate Sailor), the Taoist title for the bodhisattva. The text begins with Kuan-yin's decision to be born as Princess Miao-shan in order to enlighten humankind. She has decided to do so especially for the benefit of women: "I have observed that men of the world are more or less aware of the principles of the Three Teachings. However, women do not understand the heavenly principle and they are totally ignorant of prohibitions. That is why they have fallen so pitifully. I feel sorry for them and had better go to the world below, take on a woman's body and undo the calamity of the five stages of impurity as an example to future generations, so that women will know their sins and reform. They will avoid the suffering of rebirth, escape the punishments of Hell, the retribution of the Bloody Pool, and set out together on the road to enlightenment, enjoying the beautiful scenes of paradise. Only this will fulfill my vow" (*Kuan-yin chi-tu pen-yüan chen-ching* 7). She asks the Golden Mother of the Jasper Pool and the Heavenly Worthy of the Non-ultimate (Wu-chi T'ien-tsun) for permission. They agree and tell the Buddha about it.

The Buddha then sends Bodhidharma down to earth in order to test the sincerity of Miao-shan/Kuan-yin by appearing as a novice and proposing marriage to her. When Miao-shan rebukes him, and thus passes the test, he instructs her in the Way of the Former Heaven. Compared with the *Hsiang-shan pao-chüan*, the sectarian slant shows most clearly in its emphasis on inner alchemy, which is absent in the latter. Miao-shan uses technical terms from inner alchemy to describe her religious practice. "I hold fast with the child on the left and the beautiful maiden on the right" (17). When Miao-shan goes to the White Sparrow Nunnery, she meets Patriarch Huang who resides in the Hall of Three Pure Ones. The patriarch teaches her the "method of the heart seal" (*hsin-yin fa*): "People who study the Way do not know that mercury and lead are already contained within themselves. They search for the ninety-six elixirs outside but fail to know that they themselves already possess the marvelous drug. Know that essence, breath and spirit are the foundations. They are not minerals or herbs. Neither are they gold, silver, bronze, iron, or lead. But you must seek for an enlightened teacher who can instruct you personally. You will then be able to subdue the red dragon and green tiger. When you can discover the yang within the yin, you will return to your origin" (21–22). Miao-shan is converted to Inner Alchemy Taoism and studies with him. Mistaking the cultivation of a holy embryo to be literally conceiving an illegitimate child, people start to spread rumors about the two. When a children's song satirizing the pair reaches the king, he is so enraged that he orders the nunnery burned down.

The text shares two more themes with other sectarian scriptures: anticlerical sentiments and sympathy toward women. Even more than the *Hsiang-shan pao-chüan*, the text presents the clergy in a poor and sarcastic light. The nuns of the White Sparrow Nunnery are made to say this about themselves:

> We monastics are all people of bad luck. Some of us were born under evil stars and others have unlucky horoscopes. We were poor at birth and that is why we became nuns. Every day we have to beg for donations and address people as "grandfathers" or "grandmothers." We have to hide our pride while walking on big boulevards or narrow lanes, suffering the insults of passersby. When a donor comes to the temple, we must revere him/her as a deity. If there is the slightest neglect, we will be scolded without end. To obtain two meals a day, even if they are only plain rice without oil and washed down with diluted tea, is extremely difficult. When we see other people warmly clothed and well fed, enjoying the conjugal bliss and surrounded by children, we cannot help but cry copious tears over our own sad fate. (19–20)

There are a number of passages in the text, however, in which the author clearly shows sympathy toward women. For instance, in a memorial presented by Miao-shan to her father, she vividly describes the sad condition of women: "I was born a woman because of the evil karma I created in my previous life. I must obey my father before marriage, and after marriage, I must obey my husband. If my husband dies, then I have to remain chaste and obey my son. A woman must also be diligent in work, honest in speech, proper in appearance and pure in character. These are the famous dicta of 'three obediences' and 'four womanly virtues' that must be carefully observed. Otherwise there is no way to avoid of going to hell" (25). The author also condemns female infanticide (43).

Studying other precious scrolls, scholars have commented on the sympathy toward women reflected in them (Grant 1989; Overmyer 1992). The misfortunes of women who are subjected to ritual pollution and the pains of pregnancy and childbirth are eloquently lamented by texts celebrating Woman

Huang, Liu Hsiang-nü, and Hsiu-nü, for instance. Overmyer praises these books for being "egalitarian and non-sexist" and treating the women as "religious heroines of great strength of conviction and powers of persuasion" (1992:109, 111). While I agree that women are indeed the main actors in these precious scrolls, it is not easy for me to read them as "feminist" documents. Like the *True Scripture*, these precious scrolls devote much space to the descriptions of the ten courts of hell. They are didactic texts directed to a predominately female audience. This might be one of the reasons why they feature women as the protagonists in delivering the message of doing good in order to avoid the sufferings in hell after death. The morality advocated by the precious scrolls is not revolutionary, but perfectly conventional and Confucian. In the *True Scripture*, for instance, after Miao-shan tours the seventh court and witnesses the punishment of the Bloody Pool, she specifically cites four crimes that would lead a woman there if she committed them: "When a woman does not listen to the teachings of elders but insults the numinous spirits by blaming heaven and earth or cursing wind and rain, when she does not agree to her husband's taking a concubine in order to obtain an heir, when she disrupts the peace of the family through quarrels caused by her jealousy, or when she mistreats and abuses maids or servants willfully, she has committed four crimes noted clearly in the law book of the underworld. She will be dragged in front of Lord Yama and examined most minutely. After her trial, she will be sentenced to suffer unspeakable pain in the Tongue-plucking Prison" (43). Unlike the *Hsiang-shan pao-chüan*, which provides a consistent argument for a woman's right to seek salvation, the *True Scripture* is ambivalent because it upholds the conservative and traditional societal expectations of women.

Here is another example. Kuan-yin's authority is used to uphold all the traditional Confucian values in a text entitled *Women's Scripture* (Nü-jen ching). It contains instructions from Kuan-yin transmitted through spirit writing and published in Canton in 1904. According to the preface, the planchette sessions were originally held in P'u-t'o Ssu on Mt. Heng, Hunan. The book has two parts and contains sections on how to serve one's parents-in-law, one's husband, his brothers and their wives, one's own children, daughters-in-law, servants and maids; the necessity of remaining chaste in widowhood is also discussed and guidelines on clothing are given as well as personal appearance, comportment, household management, and so on. It shows clear influence from traditional didactic texts directed toward women such as Pan Chao's (?–116) *Instructions for Women* (Nü-chieh) and the *Instructions for the Inner Quarters* (Nü-hsün) by Empress Hsü of the Ming. It places filial piety on the top of its list of womanly virtues. If a woman is filial, she does not have to perform Buddhist rituals or practice Taoist cultivation in order to be spiritually strong. "Know that the room of a filial wife is no different from a Buddhist place of truth (*tao-ch'ang*). Although there are neither wooden fish nor bells and cymbals, the Buddha will listen to the prayer of a filial woman. Ordinary people may chant the *Diamond Sūtra* or the *Great Compassion Dhāraṇī*, but they cannot be compared to the filial wife in her ability to call forth efficacious responses" (*Nü-jen ching* 2:6a). And, "if you serve your parents and parents-in-law sincerely, this is far superior to cultivating the elixir in vain" (1:21b). While Miao-shan has served as a source of empowerment, texts such as these kept women in their place. The relationship between Kuan-yin and Chinese women has never been a simple one.

Three Precious Scrolls Glorifying Mother Kuan-yin

I have come across three scriptures in which Kuan-yin is referred to exclusively as Venerable Mother Kuan-yin (Kuan-yin Lao-mu). Sectarian themes such as the original home, the impending disasters at the end of the kalpa, the need for salvation, and cultivation based on inner alchemy are all present. They do not mention Wu-sheng Lao-mu, nor Kuan-yin being her incarnation. Instead, Kuan-yin is called the Venerable Mother. Two of the texts were probably written by what we might call second-generation religions derived from Lo Chiao. They were characterized by female leaders who were regarded to be incarnations of Mother Kuan-yin herself. Indeed, they mention the Yellow Heaven and Dragon Heaven religions by name. But let me summarize what they say first.

All three precious scrolls were printed in the Wan-li era during the Ming. The first scripture, *Hsiao-shih Pai-i Kuan-yin P'u-sa sung ying-erh hsia-sheng pao-chüan* (Explanatory Precious Scroll of White-robed Kuan-yin Who Comes into the World Bringing Children), is mentioned by Huang Yü-p'ien and Sawada Mizuno. Both regard it as a text created by the Yüan-tun Chiao (Perfect and Sudden Teaching),[14] which, according to Huang, was a branch of the Vast Yang Teaching. Huang further identified the author as Liu Tou-hsüan, whose father, Liu Hsiang-shan, also wrote scriptures on the Queen Mother of the West and the Venerable Mother of Mt. Li, both important goddesses in sectarian religion (Huang 1982:115; Sawada 1975:118–19). This same father and son pair, however, are identified as Taoists belonging to the Complete Realization school and were connected with the Pao-Ming Ssu, thus followers of the Western Great Vehicle Teaching (Li and Naquin 1988:173). To make it more complicated, the text itself recommends the reader to practice the Way of the Yellow Heaven (1994:305, 363).

The story itself is quite straightforward. The frontispiece shows the White-robed Kuan-yin holding a baby and attended by Shan-ts'ai and Lung-nü. On the opposite side, a couple kneel in front of an altar table with candles and an incense burner. The scripture begins with a verse:

Let everyone be full of piety and burn incense together.
May the White-robed Bodhisattva descend from the heavenly palace.
May she give us children, render help to the multitude,
and enable us to obtain eternal life and returning home, find our original source. (159)

Here in this passage, the key tropes of sectarian theology, eternal life (*ch'ang-sheng*), and home, are skillfully combined with the more traditional hope of getting an heir. The White-robed Child-giving Kuan-yin is presented as the Eternal Mother. She is called Lao-mu, Venerable Mother, throughout the scripture. While emphasizing the benefit and importance of chanting the present precious scroll, the author also refers to the presence of the white caul as a sure sign of the baby's being a divine gift, the sign that is mentioned so frequently in the miracle stories. Together with the novels and miracle stories, the precious scrolls share the same popular religious beliefs of the time. The reader is told, "Turn your heart to goodness, keep a vegetarian diet, and call the name of the Buddha. When you chant the precious scroll once yourself, your blessing will be increased many times. Your sons and daughters will live long. When you ask someone else to chant it, you will be protected from disasters and your sins will be reduced. Members of your present household will be safe and sound, and your dead ancestors will be delivered from suffering and go to heaven. If you do not have any children, then you ought to beg the White-robed Bodhisattva. You may build temples for her, or cast images of her, or chant the precious scroll. As long as you are sincere in your prayer, the Bodhisattva will show her compassion and send you a child (*ying-erh*) and maiden (*ch'a-nü*). They will continue your line and bring glory to you. In case people may have doubts, there will be the evidence of the white caul (*pai-i pao*). Everyone will then know for sure that it is true that the child is indeed sent to you by the Venerable Mother. Merciful, merciful, truly merciful!" (164–66).

The story is about a couple who live in Honan. The husband, Ch'ang Chin-li, is fifty-three years old and his wife, née Sui, is forty-eight. They are very wealthy, but have no children. Feeling deeply depressed over this, they pray to the White-robed Mother (Pai-i Mu), addressing her intimately as the "White-robed Granny" (*Pai-i Niang-niang*), for a child. They vow to keep a life-long vegetarian diet, chant the name of the Buddha, build temples, and make pilgrimage to P'u-t'o if their wish is fulfilled. Their prayers reach Kuan-yin who is deep in samādhi. Her ears become hot and her eyes begin to flutter,[15] making her very uneasy. She sends Shan-ts'ai and Lung-nü to find out what is going on. When they come back with the report, Kuan-yin feels obligated to respond, for "Everyone in the world says that I rescue people from suffering and disasters. If I do not respond, people will conclude that I do not have a heart of compassion" (191). After deliberating for a while, she decides to send the two, who are referred to by the Inner Alchemy terms "child" and "maiden," to be born as the couple's children. But neither wants to be parted from her whom they call mother. They embrace each other and all begin to cry.

Mother and children, all three, feel great sadness and utter lamentations.
Children cling to Mother, Mother embraces the children and all start to cry aloud.
Mortals do not understand the Venerable Mother's suffering.
It is truly hard for the Mother to send a child to you.
For after two, three, or five years, the child will forget the Mother.
Who appreciates the Mother's sacrifice in giving up her own children who are as dear to her as her bone marrow to become the child of another? (201–2)

But she has to answer the couple's prayer. She swallows Shan-ts'ai and Lung-nü, changes the boy and girl into two magical peaches and tells Madame Ch'ang in her dream that she has now brought her two children. Madame Ch'ang eats the peaches, wakes up and finds that she is pregnant. The text has a long passage describing her discomfort during the ten months of pregnancy, showing the same sympathy toward women as the *True Scripture* and other precious scrolls. When the twins are born, both are covered with the white caul, and the parents thank the Venerable Mother for her gifts. Three days pass and Kuan-yin starts to miss Shan-ts'ai and Lung-nü already. So she assumes the disguise of a beggar woman and comes to offer her service as a wet nurse to the infants. Prior to her arrival, the parents have hired several wet nurses but the infants, inspired by Kuan-yin, refuse to take any milk from them. But as soon as they see the new wet nurse, they take milk from her. The mother stays for nine years to bring them up and then goes back to P'u-t'o. Three years later, when the children are twelve, they are also taken back to P'u-t'o. This is done in order to teach the couple a lesson. For although they have fulfilled their vows of keeping a life-long vegetarian diet, building a temple to honor Kuan-yin and casting an image for her, they have not gone on a pilgrimage to P'u-t'o as promised. When the children disappear, they are shocked into recollection. They send away all the servants, and give away all their wealth in preparation for the pilgrimage. Helped by various deities, they successfully make the trip to

P'u-t'o, where they are reunited with their children and see Kuan-yin face to face.

At various points throughout the text, the author advises the reader to study the "Great Way," which is another name for three sects identified by name: the Way of Yellow Heaven, the Way of Non-action (304) and the Vast Yang Teaching (352). The Venerable Mother is said to be "seated in meditation on a lotus with nine petals (*chiu-yeh lien*, 231). There are also references to the "Dharma Boat" (*fa-ch'uan*) that carries believers back to their "home." Both expressions, as we recall, are found in texts created by the Vast Yang Teaching. Near the end of the scripture, in describing the pilgrimage to P'u-t'o, the physical trip is seen as a mystical one. Just as Kuan-yin is identified as the Venerable Mother earlier in the text, the earthly P'u-t'o is transformed into the heavenly home. Not only Kuan-yin, but the other three great bodhisattvas are also recruited to serve as shipmates on board in the boat.

> *A boat appeared in the beginning when chaos was first divided.*
> *It sailed east and west in order to ferry across those who were chosen.*
> *Awakened [now], men and women come aboard and go to P'u-t'o quickly.*
> *The golden crow plays with the water at the head of the boat.*
> *The jade rabbit brightens the tail of the boat.*
> *The White-robed Mother stands on the fore deck directing the boat.*
> *Mother Ti-tsang steers the rudder.*
> *Wen-shu and P'u-hsien sit inside the hull of the boat. (515)*

The second scripture is entitled *Chiu-k'u chiu-nan ling-kan Kuan-shih-yin pao-chüan* (Precious Scroll of Kuan-shih-yin of the Efficacious Responses Who Saves One from Suffering and Disasters). As we read in chapter 6, this title has been connected with Kuan-yin since the T'ang. Cartouches attached to images of the bodhisattva recovered from Tun-huang often carry this epithet and Emperor Jen-tsung of the Northern Sung bestowed this title on Kuan-yin of the Upper T'ien-chu Monastery in the early eleventh century. The frontispiece of the scripture shows Kuan-yin saving people from various disasters, similar to the illustrations found in many woodblock copies of the "Universal Gateway" chapter of the *Lotus Sūtra* printed since the Sung. The precious scroll is a conscious attempt to popularize and imitate the sūtra text.

The scripture states that it has a very ancient lineage: "This *Kuan-yin pao-chüan* has been transmitted from one patriarch to the next from ancient times. Like the light of one lamp passes to that of another, one patriarch enlightens another patriarch. It has now come down to us" (6). The merit arising from veneration of the precious scroll is impressive: "Those who listen to the recitation of the scroll will be spared the birth from a womb, those who chant it will be spared the birth from moisture, and those who copy it will be born from a lotus. . . . If one worships the scroll with true sincerity for nine years, one will attain buddhahood" (8–9). After invoking Kuan-yin, Wen-shu, P'u-hsien, and Maitreya, the text begins with the description of the perils from which one is rescued.

Like the previous scripture, Kuan-yin is also called Venerable Mother throughout this text. It describes how she saves specific individuals from twenty-four, instead of the canonical twelve kinds of peril listed in the gāthā section of Kumārajīva's translation of the *Lotus Sūtra* (Watson 1993:304–5). The first twelve perils are

1. falling into a pit of fire,
2. being carried away in a current,
3. robbers,
4. being pushed over the precipice by an evil man,
5. meeting an old enemy,
6. the executioner's blade,
7. imprisonment,
8. poison,
9. rākṣasa,
10. vicious animals,
11. snakes and scorpions, and
12. hailstorms.

They constitute the first volume of the scripture. After stating each peril, the author copies Kumārajīva's gāthā verses verbatim. The second volume describes twelve additional perils not found in the *Lotus Sūtra*, which are the author's own invention:

13. difficult childbirth,
14. facing an enemy in the battlefield,
15. a collapsed house,
16. being caught in a landslide,
17. committing suicide by hanging,
18. being trampled by horses,

19. being run over by carriages,
20. committing suicide by jumping into the river,
21. committing suicide by jumping into a well,
22. encountering a pack of wolves,
23. hell, and
24. miscellaneous dangers not mentioned above.

This list serves as a window into the social and psychic anxieties of people in late imperial China. The dangers Kuan-yin could avert were realistic and ever-present, such as difficult childbirths, the disasters that awaited one while traveling on the streets (such as being trampled by horses and carriages), or the temptations of suicide. The specific forms of suicide mentioned here, moreover, were indeed the favorite choices of the people living at that time.

The writer gives tantalizing clues about the text and himself. One quarter into the text we are told that the scripture was revealed to a "gentleman of bright virtue" (*te-ming chün*) in the eleventh year of Wan-li (1583). The "true person" (*chen-jen*), moreover, is a teacher of Lung-t'ien Tao (Way of the Dragon Heaven, 43). "Bright virtue" and "true person" are both contained in the title applied to P'iao Kao, the patriarch of the Vast Yang religion. He was honored as the "True Person of the Orthodox Medicine of Bright Virtue" (Cheng te-ming i chen-jen), because he was reputed to be a divine doctor (Ma and Han 1992:517). Could this be a reference to him? If so, what was the connection between P'iao Kao and Patriarch Mi, the founder of Lung-t'ien Chiao? And why was the year 1583 so significant if, according to scholars, it was not until 1594 that P'iao Kao founded the Vast Yang religion? Unfortunately, the text does not answer any of these questions.

Characteristic sectarian ideologies and practices, on the other hand, are more easily detected. Kuan-yin is said to "go every day to each door in the four continents to take care of her children, for sentient beings are all within her care" (54). The image of the Eternal Mother in the disguise of a beggar woman going from door to door, not to beg for food, but to seek out her children, comes vividly to mind. She is described as sitting on a "lotus with nine petals" (55) and living in "the palace of nine lotuses" (86). She is attended by the golden boy and jade girl (50), not Sudhana and Dragon Princess, although the parrot still serves as her messenger and she rides on the animal earlier identified as *hou* (121). Perhaps the most telling signature is the elaborate word play on the three characters making up *Kuan-yin Ssu* (Kuan-yin Temple). The text first states:

Everyone carries within himself a Kuan-yin Temple.
The mind is the Buddha, and the Buddha is the mind.
Where is the Kuan-yin Temple erected?
The temple is found within the sun (26).

In the next two lines, the three characters are broken up into their component parts. While the constituent characters do not make sense by themselves, they form *Kuan-yin Ssu* when combined together. "Kuan-yin Temple," like "spiritual mountain" (*ling-shan*),[16] an expression frequently used by Lo Ch'ing and other sectarians, symbolizes our innate Buddha nature for this writer. The predilection for word play is shown in another instance. Under peril number 23—hell—it states that Kuan-yin rescued a good man from the knife-mountain hell whose last name was *Kung Ch'ang*, a veiled reference to Chang (128). At first perhaps as a way of keeping secret to avoid official detection, sectarians liked to refer to certain favorite surnames by the component elements of the written characters. For instance, instead of Li, they would write Mu-tzu or Shih-pa-tzu (Naquin 1976:15). To refer to a man with a surname of Chang as Kung Ch'ang, therefore, is a typical sectarian practice. In fact, an important Yüan-tun Chiao scripture, *Ku-fo T'ien-chen k'ao-cheng lung-hua pao-ching* (Precious Scripture of the Dragon Flower Verified by the Ancient Buddha T'ien-chen) was written by a man identified as Kung Ch'ang and published by his disciple (identified as Mu-tzu) in the seventeenth century (Ma and Han 1992:865). This sectarian predilection of separating a surname into its component parts can be ultimately traced to the Confucian apocryphal texts created in the Later Han. Liu, the surname of the ruling house of the Han, for instance, is referred in these texts as "*mou*" and "*chin*," the two parts making up the character "*liu*". In fact, one of the charges against the prognosticatory literature made by Han critics was that it "vulgarly split up characters" (Dull 1966:198). The lasting influence of Han apocrypha can be seen in the sectarian scriptures of late imperial times.

There is another reason why someone belonging to the Dragon Heaven Teaching might be a good candidate for the author of the text. We know that the religion was particularly obsessed with the disasters happening before the end of the kalpa. Some scriptures of this sect depict these disasters with great relish and imagination. At the same time, according to reports prepared by the governor of Shantung, who confiscated their scriptures in 1742, the scriptures had titles such as *Fa-hua ching* (Lotus Sūtra) and *Fa-hua ch'an* (Lotus Penance) (Ma and Han 1992:695, 711). It makes perfect sense for someone following this religion to have written a scripture modeled upon the canonical *Lotus Sūtra*, with an emphasis on the perils facing humankind. Might not this very text, which is also called a "Kuan-yin Scroll" (106), be the same as the confiscated *Lotus Sūtra*?

While it is possible to argue for a sectarian origin of the two precious scrolls just discussed, it is much more difficult to do the same for the third and last one. This is the *Kuan-yin shih-tsung jih-pei t'ou-nan ching* (Scripture of Kuan-yin Explaining the Truth from North of the Sun to South of the Dipper). Huang Yü-p'ien refers to it as a "heretical" text but without identifying its sectarian affiliation. There is no reference to any specific religion, as in the previous two texts. Nor are there any characteristic sectarian beliefs or expressions. It is in fact unlike any text that I have read, be it a Buddhist sūtra or a sectarian precious scroll. The language is archaic and obscure and the ideas esoteric and strange. If anything, it reminds me of a Taoist liturgical manual. However, I would like to suggest that this might have been written by a Buddhist evangelist. Just as the two previous texts are attempts to coopt Kuan-yin to support a sectarian agenda, this can be seen as a strategy coming from an opposite direction. In other words, here we may have a text that uses Mother Kuan-yin, made familiar to sectarians through their scriptures, to present a cosmology and eschatology based on orthodox Buddhist beliefs. A text is rarely what it appears to be at first glance, particularly if it was written in the late Ming, when so many religions were contending and competing with each other for converts.

The frontispiece shows the White-robed Kuan-yin receiving veneration from a man in official garb identified as T'ai-pai Star, or Venus. Four martial-looking figures are carrying placards that say "hour," "day," "month," and "year." Thirty-seven figures, some with animal faces, appear throughout the text as illustrations, occupying full pages. They symbolize the entire astral assembly: the sun, moon, the stars named after the five phases, Rāhu and Hetu, and the twenty-eight constellations (*erh-shih-pa hsing-su*). The title of the scripture "north of the sun and south of the dipper" refers to the universe,[17] which is created and ruled by Venerable Mother Kuan-yin, who regularly descends to earth to save sentient beings. Kuan-yin is the lord of the heavenly bodies, and so each of them is invoked and their feast days are identified. The twenty-eight constellations are also provided with human names. As we read in chapter 2, Mahāyāna sūtras such as the *Karaṇḍavyūha* present Kuan-yin in exactly the same light: the creator of the universe. In order to be saved by her, humans are advised to set up altars (*t'an*) to worship Kuan-yin, at which sūtras should be chanted and confessions made. Except for the astral worship, the emphasis on the ritual of confession is reminiscent of the ritual of Great Compassion Repentance discussed in chapter 7. The text tells the reader to call the name of Kuan-yin whenever he or she meets with difficulties, a perfectly orthodox Buddhist practice since the Six Dynasties.

The three disasters and eight crises are most painful.
Call the name of Kuan-yin whenever you run into difficulties.
Kuan-yin will come to save you.
When faced with the suffering before the end of the kalpa,
All your household should call upon Kuan-yin,
Both the old and the young must pray together in the inner quarters and outside.
When you call her name, your mind becomes correct,
And the correct thought will dissolve dangers. (30a)

Kuan-yin is said to manifest as a man in order to save men and a woman in order to save women (61a). This idea is of course based on the "Universal Gateway" chapter of the *Lotus Sūtra.* The cultic form such devotion to Kuan-yin takes, moreover, is very traditional and orthodox.

Calling on Kuan-yin day and night without cease,
I invoke Mother Kuan-yin who saves me from pain.
I promise that if my prayer is answered,
I will donate my wealth to build an altar and cast an image of her made of gold.
I will keep a vegetarian diet for life
And worship her until I am old without lapsing. (39b-40a)

What makes me suspect that this is a Buddhist text written in the form of a sectarian scripture are the enigmatic expressions "Kuan-yin Chiao" (Kuan-yin Teaching) and "Mo-ni tzu" (children of Muni) scattered throughout the text and the call for "monks of Tathāgata Muni to subdue demons and stay far away from heterodox paths" (66a). Muni clearly means Śākyamuni. Are "children of Muni" the same as "monks of Tathāgata Muni"? Or more generally, Buddhist believers? There are also more specific Buddhist ideas that stand out. For instance, it declares that "monks are superior," and that "Muni dispatches commandments which are transmitted in the ten directions" (70b). Such procleric language is never attested in sectarian texts. The text mentions the *Lotus* and *Hua-yen* sūtras (72a, 77b). Could we take this as a hint that the author might be a monk specializing in these traditions? It also says the "myriad dharmas all come from the One Mind" (66b). But this is less significant than the former examples, for such Buddhist ideas and expressions seem to have become a common vocabulary that could be freely drawn upon by sectarian scriptures.

Because the three precious scrolls glorifying Mother Kuan-yin were written by anonymous authors and we have little information about the circumstances under which they were produced and printed, it is obvious that what I say about them has to be hypothetical. Nevertheless, it is possible to suggest that while the first two texts were written by disciples connected with religions such as the Yellow Heaven and Dragon Heaven sects, the last one might have been written by a Buddhist monk or layperson. However, they share one aim in common: to elevate Kuan-yin to the position of a supreme deity. Moreover, they do so by utilizing an identical method: making Kuan-yin into Wu-sheng Lao-mu, who is not mentioned separately. This tactic is somewhat different from turning Kuan-yin into the incarnation of the Eternal Mother who, in that case, would occupy a more superior position in the divine hierarchy. It is perhaps also significant that the sects connected with the first two precious scrolls were known for having female patriarchs who were regarded as bodhisattvas. Several of the new religions used the affiliation name *miao* for women members.[18] Clearly, the sectarians in the late Ming were carrying on the tradition of the White Lotus Teaching, which had started in the Sung. As I argued in chapter 8, the legend of Princess Miao-shan might have been a reflection of this lay practice, which, in turn, was further inspired and empowered by it. As we have seen, similar anticlerical sentiments are found in the *Hsiang-shan pao-chüan* and sectarian scriptures. They also exhibit the same sympathy toward women, whose need for enlightenment and salvation are recognized and honored. But Miao-shan is a "daughter" and we are now talking about the Venerable Mother.

What can we make of the relationship between Kuan-yin and sectarian religions since the late Ming? To start with, I would suggest that there definitely exists a two-way dialectic relationship similar to the one I just mentioned. The emergence of Mother Kuan-yin could be inspired by the sectarian worship of the Eternal Mother, but once she was appropriated, she lent the prestige and augmented the attraction of the Mother. In this case, the assumption is that the sectarian Eternal Mother appeared first and Mother Kuan-yin was created afterwards. But what if it were the other way around? What if Kuan-yin Lao-mu appeared first, and then, some sectarians came up with Wu-sheng Lao-mu, modeling her on the former deity? As I mentioned before, Lo Ch'ing, the putative "founder" of late Ming sectarian religions, spoke of "wu-sheng," and "mu," but not "lao-mu" in his writings. Again, as I have already indicated, according to Huang Yü-p'ien and other modern scholars, the term did not appear until the last quarter of the sixteenth century, during the Wan-li period. It is true that the earliest datable precious scroll (1523) speaks of Lao-mu, but she could be either "Kuan-yin Lao-mu" or "Wu-sheng Lao-mu." After all, as the three precious scrolls on Mother Kuan-yin show, she is referred to there simply as "Lao-mu." These texts, which promoted the cult of Mother Kuan-yin and were believed to have been printed in the Wan-li period, hypothetically could have initiated the cult of the Eternal Mother, instead of imitating it.

Precious scrolls are not the only sources that depict Kuan-yin as the Mother. She is sometimes identified as such in the *Hsi-yu chi*, a famous novel written in the sixteenth century by Wu Cheng-en (c. 1500–1582). As I indicated in the previous chapter, Kuan-yin is a prominent character in this novel. Although Kuan-yin generally appears in the novel as Kuan-yin of the South Sea, accompanied by her divine entourage of Sudhana and Dragon Princess, she also assumes the guise of an old woman referred to as "Lao-mu" in chapters 14, 55, and 84, Lao-mu is always rendering help to Tripiṭaka, the monk pilgrim, and providing his party with critical and timely assistance. Writers of precious scrolls, as well as their audience, were familiar with *Hsi-yu chi* and often alluded to it. The fact that the novel presents Kuan-yin in this way may not be insignificant.

Sources for the Image of Mother Kuan-yin

While academics may be interested in knowing whether Mother Kuan-yin gave rise to the Eternal Mother or vice versa, a far more fascinating question is why Kuan-yin in late imperial times assumed the form of the old mother and some Chinese during the same era came to see their supreme deity in that light. This image is that of a powerful matriarchal figure of authority, wisdom and strength, kind, nurturing and sad, yet totally devoid of sexuality.

Unlike the other forms of feminine Kuan-yin discussed in chapter 10, there are very few visual representations of Mother Kuan-yin in art. The only image of Kuan-yin as an unmistakably old woman is found among a group of Buddhist sculpture in Chien-ch'uan, north of Ta-li, Yünan, which were created during the ninth century by Nan-chao artists (Howard, Li, and Qiu 1992:53). She looks emaciated and rather sad. This image may be connected with local myths about Kuan-yin among the Pai people. According to the *Pai-kuo yin-yu* (Origins of the Pai People), a text written in the seventeenth century but containing material dating from much earlier and handed down orally, Kuan-yin, who is the patron deity of the Pai people, has manifested eighteen times to help the people. According to the story of one of the miracles, Kuan-yin appeared as an old woman (Yü 1991:38).[19] We may also consider the last of the five forms of Kuan-yin by Ting Yün-p'eng (1547-ca. 1621) showing a rather severe woman totally enveloped in a white robe receiving homage from the dragon king (figure 2.8d), or the demure matron seated in a grotto on a round fan entitled "Kuan-yin and the Sixteen Lohans," painted by an anonymous artist some time during the sixteenth to the seventeenth century (figure 11.1). Porcelain figures made in the Ch'ing, on the other hand, often depict her as a stately matriarch, like the one displayed at the Rijksmuseum (figure 11.2). There is only one example, so far as I know, showing Kuan-yin as a poor beggar woman. This is the unusual painting entitled, "Kuan-yin in Tattered Robe," painted during the Yen-yu era (1314–1320) of the Yüan.[20]

Where can we find the sources for Mother Kuan-yin, or for that matter, the Eternal Mother? Buddhist scriptures do not provide models for her, just as with feminine images of Kuan-yin in general. Old age symbolizes impermanence and suffering, and was one of the four signs the young Gautama encountered and which were said to have awakened in him the desire to abandon the comfortable life of a prince. Indian Buddhist literature portrays old women as weak and lonely. Some poems written by old nuns describing their spiritual achievements are found in the *Therigāthā*, a collection of seventy-three poems by Bud-

Figure 11.1. Kuan-yin and the Sixteen Lohans, sixteenth or seventeenth century. *Courtesy of the Metropolitan Museum of Art, New York (John Stewart Kennedy Fund, 1913).*

Figure 11.2. Kuan-yin, eighteenth century. *Courtesy of the Rijksmuseum, Amsterdam.*

dhist women of the sixth century B.C.E. Even such enlightened women looked upon the coming of old age with regret and sorrow (Murcott 1991:113–18).

The Chinese indigenous traditions, on the other hand, contain rich resources for the veneration of a deity as the mother. Lao Tzu compares the Tao, the origin and source of everything in the world, to the "mother" (*mu*) in three chapters of the *Tao Te Ching* (1, 25, 52). Lo Ch'ing quotes from this often in his writings. The feminine and maternal was not simply celebrated in philosophy, but also revered as mythological goddesses. When Lao Tzu became the god Lord Lao (Lao-chün) in the Han period, his mother was also deified. In fact, the first official inscription recording Lord Lao was named after his mother, the "Stele of the Holy Mother" ("Sheng-mu pei") dated 153 C.E. Tu Kuang-t'ing (850–933) provided a mythical account of Lord Lao's receiving Taoist teachings from his mother, who was called Holy Mother Goddess (Sheng-mu Yüan-chün), in his *Record of the Assembled Immortals in the Heavenly Walled City*. After giving the teaching, she ascended to heaven and became honored as the Great Queen of the Former Heaven (Hsien-t'ien T'ai-hou). Livia Kohn comments that this follows the pattern of divine females serving "as practical teachers for inspired sages, mythical rulers, and immortals. The tradition is exemplified in the story of the Yellow Emperor receiving sexual techniques from the Pure Woman (Su-nü) and the Mystery Woman (Hsüan-nü)" (1998:242).

The Queen Mother of the West, as we read in the last chapter, was worshiped by both the elite and the masses by the beginning of the Common Era. She was clearly the most famous Chinese goddess until the appearance of the feminine Kuan-yin. She was the goddess of immortality and the revealer of the secret knowledge of eternal life. According to the oldest dictionary, the Han dynasty *Erh Ya*, "Queen Mother" (*wang-mu*) means one's father's deceased mother, an honorific posthumous title conferred on female ancestors in the father's line and used in ancestral cults. Her hagiographies rarely mention her actual age, and when they describe her physical appearance, they say that she looks to be a matron of thirty years old. But because she is believed to be the mother of all, she is also sometimes referred to as the old crone with white hair. According to Susan Cahill, she was a favorite subject in T'ang poetry. "Many [T'ang] poets refer to her by the intimate expression Amah (wetnurse or nanny). This familiar usage occurs especially in contexts in which the goddess is portrayed as a mother figure or a teacher" (1993:69). The poets call her heavenly palace located on top of Mt. Kun-lun, the cosmic pillar, "Amah's household" (205). The Goddess is a protector of young women who choose to live alone and also, particularly, older, widowed women. "One strong tradition depicts the Queen Mother herself as a white-haired crone. Old women are often widowed. By choice or by accident, they may find themselves unprotected and alone, outside the bounds of traditional family circle within which most medieval Chinese women lived and found the meaning of their lives. If they are childless, older women are especially vulnerable in traditional Chinese society, which defines a mature woman's worth in terms of her motherhood. Herself immeasurably old and yet possessed of great dignity and authority, childless and yet the mother of all, the Queen Mother brought respect to the position of the older women" (229).

It seems that the Queen Mother's fame began to be eclipsed by Kuan-yin and other female deities after the T'ang. Like the Golden Mother of the Jasper Pool, she is sometimes also known by a more intimate title, "Wang-mu Niang-niang" (Granny Queen Mother) in later periods. Under different names, she has nevertheless continued to be worshiped by the Chinese down through the ages until today. It is noteworthy that by the Ming dynasty female deities of less renown than the Queen Mother played dominant roles in popular vernacular novels such as *The Water Margin* (Shui-hu chuan) by Shih Nai-an (c. 1290–1365) and *Investiture of the Gods* (Feng-shen yen-i) by Lu Hsi-hsing (c. 1520–1601). These novels undoubtedly drew inspiration from the rich tradition of female deities in popular religion. By the sixteenth century, as we have seen, another powerful new goddess, the Eternal Mother, made her first appearance in the writings of the White Lotus sectarians. The theme of powerful goddesses in such popular novels might have played some role in the birth of the Venerable Mother Kuan-yin, for sectarians were firm believers in the novels. "Those in the northern provinces all firmly believe in the novel *Investiture of the Gods* and all those in the southern provinces venerate *The Water Margin*" (Overmyer 1976:140). These feminine goddesses are understood to be post-menopausal women. They are of course free from the messiness of childbirth and the problems of sexual desire. They represent motherliness, pure and simple. They retain all that is attractive about femininity, but are devoid of anything negative which true womanhood entails.

Another inspiration for Venerable Mother Kuan-yin might have come from stories about real or mythological old Chinese women who practiced Buddhism. Because women were seldom writers of their own histories, we are faced with the perennial problem of sources. There is only one biography of Chinese nuns, for instance. Compiled by the monk Pao-ch'ang in 516, *Lives of the Nuns* (Pi-chiu-ni chuan) contains short biographies of 65 nuns who lived during the fourth to the sixth centuries. Coming from primarily aristocratic backgrounds, they moved easily among the elites and at court. They maintained a high rate of literacy, for only twelve of the sixty-five could not read or write. Noted for their strict observance of the Vinaya (Buddhist discipline), vegetarianism, and meditation, many of them were also devotees of Kuan-yin (Tsai 1994).

Recently, Ding-hwa E. Hsieh has combed through the voluminous body of biographical sources about Ch'an masters known as the "lamp record" (*teng-lu*) compiled in the Sung, and come up with some encouraging discoveries (1999). First of all, she finds that "Ch'an Buddhist texts of the Sung contain many anecdotes of formidable old women of humble background. Unlike the old women portrayed in early Indian Buddhist texts, these old women are not just spiritually enlightened but also physically energetic. Moreover, they are depicted as spiritual guides rather than material benefactresses. . . . In their encounter with Ch'an monks, these women are always depicted as being in the dominant position" (Hsieh 1999:167–68). They are usually called simply "old woman" (*p'o-tzu, lao-p'o, lao-t'ai-p'o*), indicating their humble social status. They are not identified by names or birthplaces. But like the Eternal Mother who appears to her devotee and guides him in his search in later sectarian scriptures, these women of obscure background played an influential role in many monks' religious experiences; they often appeared on the scene to deliver a timely message and served as catalysts to a monk's awakening. There is a possibility that these old women are literary creations instead of real persons and that they serve more to demonstrate the Ch'an rhetoric of equality and non-discrimination instead of reflecting social realities. Since gender and class, like everything else, are human constructs based on ignorance, Ch'an discourse is designed to deconstruct them through transgressive language. Enlightened female Ch'an masters are therefore called *ta chang-fu* (heroically masculine man; Levering 1992) and kind-hearted male Ch'an masters "old women." In order to show that the ability to see into reality is not confined to the educated elite, simple rustic old crones could thus be chosen to serve as the spiritual teachers of conceited monks. However, the presence of these old women in the records is still an important precedent for the investing of old women with spiritual power in Chinese religious literature. Their stories, moreover, are not buried in the Ch'an texts of the Sung but were apparently well known enough to be included in later anthologies of Buddhist female practitioners.

In the mid-eighteenth century, P'eng Shao-sheng (1740–1796), a pious Pure Land lay Buddhist, compiled the only surviving collection of Chinese Buddhist laywomen's biographies, entitled *Biographies of Good Women* (Shan nü-jen chuan). He used the same Ch'an records as his primary sources. From a total of 148 biographies, 18 or a little more than 10 percent are stories about old women. Thirteen of these old women were Ch'an practitioners, while the rest were Pure Land devotees. They were either identified by their place of residence or profession, and if their last names were known, they were simply called "Granny So-and-So." Of the thirteen female Ch'an practitioners, though their birthplaces and family backgrounds are often left blank, we can surmise that they lived probably in the T'ang and Sung, the so-called golden age of Ch'an. They were depicted as enlightened, though some were clearly rustic and uneducated, while others could recite passages from Buddhist scriptures by heart. They often served as catalysts for Ch'an monks on their way to enlightenment. Let us read about a few of these women.

Biography 14: The Old Woman Who Sold Cakes

Regarding the old woman who sold cakes, no one knew her provenance. When Ch'an Master Chien of Te-shan (782–865) lectured on the *Diamond Sūtra*, he wrote a commentary called the *Blue Dragon Commentary*. When he heard that the Ch'an schools in the South were gaining considerable popularity, he felt jealous. Thereupon he decided to go south to spread his teaching. Carrying his commentary on a shoulder pole, he left the Shu region [present-day Szechwan province].

On his way he passed Li-yang, where he saw the old woman who sold cakes. As he stopped to buy some pastries from her, the old woman asked him what books he was carrying on his shoulder pole. The Ch'an Master said:

"*Blue Dragon Commentary*."

"What sūtra does it elaborate?"

"The *Diamond Sūtra*."

"I have a question for you," the old woman said, "If you can answer it, I shall donate these pastries to you. But if you can't answer it, please go elsewhere for your pastries. Now, the sūtra says: 'The mind of the past cannot be acquired; the mind of the present cannot be acquired; and the mind of the future cannot be acquired.' May I know which mind the Master would like to touch [a pun on the Chinese term, *tien-hsin*, for 'pastry' which literally means 'touching the heart or mind']?"

The Master was speechless. Thereupon he went to Lung-tan to seek instructions from Ch'an Master Hsin. There he attained sudden awakening to the essentials of the mind, and subsequently he burned his *Blue Dragon Commentary*.[21]

Biography 35: Old Woman Who Lived in Shan-hua

Biography 35 is also about another old woman and does not even give her last name. She is identified as the "Old Woman Who Lived in Shan-hua." Like the previous woman, she was fond of the *Diamond Sūtra* and chanted it all the time. Although she lived her life as a lowly beggar, she died a peaceful and auspicious death, a sure sign of her saintliness. The entry reads:

> Regarding the Old Woman Who Lived in Shan-hua, no one knew her provenance, but she resided in the Shan-hua county of Tan-chou [present-day Ch'ang-sha, Hunan]. Every day she would chant the *Diamond Sūtra* and beg for food in the street. At nightfall, she would return to rest underneath a cliff.
>
> Then for several days, she was not seen begging on the street, and people in the marketplace began to get curious. Thereupon they tracked her down at her lodging, where a flock of crows was cawing noisily. They saw the old woman leaning against the cliff, and she had transformed herself. In her bosom lay a sūtra that was none other than the *Diamond Sūtra*. Later, the crows carried pieces of earth to bury her.

Biography 21: The Old Woman Who Burned a Lodge

Some old women, such as are described in biographies 15, 16, and 17, exchanged quick and sharp Ch'an repartee with famous Ch'an masters and proved to be their equals and even betters. In the following episode, an old woman acted as a true Ch'an master. She had sheltered a monk for twenty years, but when she tested the level of his achievement and found him wanting, she threw him out:

> The Old Woman Who Burned a Lodge, whose native origin was unclear, had been giving offerings to the abbot whom she hosted in a lodge for about twenty years, during which time she sent a maid to deliver food to the abbot regularly. One day she asked her maid to approach the abbot, give him a pinch, and say, "Right at this moment, what do you do?"
>
> "A withered tree is leaning against a cold cliff," said the monk; "for three winters it has had no warmth in it."
>
> When the maid reported to the old woman, the old woman said, "for the past twenty years, I have been giving my offerings to a monk of the ordinary stock." Thereupon she kicked the monk out and burned the lodge.

Biography 19: Old Woman Yao

Biography 19, which tells the story of "Old Woman Yao," on the other hand, is a good example of Pure Land devotion, another Buddhist path much favored by Chinese women:

> Old Woman Yao, a native of Shang-tang [present-day Ching-chi, Shansi], was a good friend of old woman Fan. Fan once urged Yao to chant the name of Amitābha Buddha, and Yao took the advice. Thereafter she cut herself off from domestic affairs and devoted all her time to the chanting of the name of the Buddha.

> On her deathbed she saw Amitābha Buddha descending from the sky with two bodhisattvas on either side. Old woman Yao said to the Buddha, "Had I not met Fan, how could I have seen the Buddha? I would like to request the Buddha to stay here for a few days, so that I can bid farewell to her."
>
> By the time Fan came, the Buddha was still as vivid as ever, appearing before her eyes. Thus, old woman Yao transformed herself while she was still standing.

The biographies of these old women are interesting on several accounts. First of all, all these women, whether they followed the Ch'an or the Pure Land path, were ordinary women living at home. They were not nuns. Yet they were presented as fully enlightened and sometimes exhibited a higher level of spiritual attainment than monks. Secondly, they were figures of self-confidence and authority. Not only were they not dependent on anyone, they were in charge of the situation and could even make the Buddha do as they wanted. Thirdly, they might appear as poor beggars, yet in reality they were true practitioners of Buddhism. Finally, they were compassionate and ready to teach others. All these make them possible models for the image of Mother Kuan-yin.

A final source for Mother Kuan-yin could be the roles of old women in traditional Chinese society. According to the Confucian ideal for a woman, she must practice the "three obediences," namely, she should obey her father at youth, her husband after marriage, and her son after her husband dies. But although she was theoretically dependent on her son, when a woman reached middle age and became matriarch of the household, her status in actual life could be very impressive. Matriarch Chia ruled her large family as an empress dowager in the famous Ch'ing novel *Dream of the Red Chamber*. Though fictional, it must also have reflected a certain social reality. For even in contemporary Taiwan, "older women have ways of wielding power and influence that are not open to younger women. If they have gained the loyalty of their sons, they can exert considerable control over them, even after they are grown men with wives and children of their own. In many cases too, older women take a strong hand in decisions about household management, investment, or social affairs . . . as a woman's menstrual flow ends in her forties or fifties, she gains increasing power over the people around her" (Ahern 1975:201–2). Old women also enjoyed more freedom of movement, for they were considered both by themselves and society to be free from sexual desire. They could travel in public alone without causing censure. Certain professions belonged exclusively to older women, for instance, midwifery and matchmaking. In traditional China, no proper marriage could be contracted without the service of the matchmakers (Ebrey 1993:73–74). Matchmakers were always older women. Old women also often served as go-betweens between lovers in Chinese drama and novels. So, in assuming the disguise of a matriarchal figure, Kuan-yin absorbed all these nested cultural characteristics associated with old women in China: motherly, powerful, wise, a mediator for spiritual enlightenment but also for worldly happiness.

12

Conclusion

When I decided to study the cult of Kuan-yin in China more than a decade ago, I was mainly interested in knowing why an imported Buddhist savior succeeded in becoming one of the most important Chinese deities, and also in how he was domesticated and transformed into the "Goddess of Mercy" in the process. The questions were daunting and the subject was vast. Initially, it was very difficult for me to know where to begin. Although Avalokiteśvara is a major bodhisattva mentioned in a great many Buddhist scriptures, I knew early on that a textual study of these sūtras would not give me the answer. Similarly, although Kuan-yin has been a favorite subject for Chinese sculpture, painting, and literature, I realized that to study the depictions of Kuan-yin in these works alone would not explain why the cult took such a deep root in China. One should of course study the monks and lay believers who were the devotees of Kuan-yin to find out the social, historical, and geographical distributions of the cult. Miracles, pilgrimages and rituals can also yield important information. Yet to concentrate on any one of these also provides only a partial picture. Although none of these avenues by itself can provide an answer to the mystery, when combined and examined in relation to each other, it is possible to say something meaningful about the topic.

This, then, is what I have done in the book. I have concentrated on the various media and mechanisms through which the cult of Kuan-yin was created and transmitted in China from the Six Dynasties to late imperial times. The preceding chapters look at different facets of the cult from different angles. I have examined how Kuan-yin is presented in canonical and indigenous scriptures, depicted in art and literature, celebrated in rituals and devotional practices, remembered in miracle stories, and embodied by real monks, the founders of new religions, and also a legendary princess. While each medium promoted Kuan-yin, it transformed the bodhisattva at the same time. Thus, while Kuan-yin was represented and perceived as a monk prior to and during the T'ang, the bodhisattva was increasingly feminized and eventually turned into Venerable Mother Kuan-yin. These media, moreover, never existed and functioned in isolation, but constantly interacted and influenced each other. I have been much impressed, for instance, by the fact that visions of devotees and pilgrims were both reflected in and also inspired by the contemporary iconography. And it is interesting to see how closely indigenous scriptures, miracle accounts, ritual practices, and popular precious scrolls reinforced each other. I now believe that the development and evolution of the cult was fueled by such dialectical interactions among these media.

Although I did not set out to create an interdisciplinary study, it became so by necessity. Because of the nature of my question and the impossibility of solving it by traditional methodology, I was compelled to combine in this study several different disciplines and utilize very diverse data. This approach has enabled me to look at the cult of Kuan-yin in a comprehensive and synthetic way. Each aspect of the cult is an integral and organic part of the whole. They cannot and should not be artificially isolated by the researcher, for the consequence of doing so has often been obscuration if not downright misinformation.

I will give just one concrete example. In several places, I pointed out that the White-robed Kuan-yin should be seen as an indigenous creation, just as with the Water-moon and Child-giving Kuan-yin. However, instead of treating them as separate and discrete cultic icons for Ch'an monks, literati, and common folks respectively, I suggested that it would be more fruitful as well as more accurate to regard them as different, yet interconnected, aspects of the same deity. The iconography of the White-robed Kuan-yin was derived from that of the Water-moon and it in turn evolved into that of the Child-giving Kuan-yin. I could not have arrived at this conclusion on the basis of artistic style, for each manifestation is very different. Rather, I did so on the basis of evidence drawn from miracle tales, indigenous scriptures, and descriptions of ritual practices.

I also suggested that it would be more useful to uncover the rich complexity of associations represented by any one image, story or text to diverse audiences, instead of assigning either one monolithic meaning to it or confining it to one single constituency. It is of course true that Kuan-yin was seen and understood differently by different people. It is also the case that different people sought different things from the deity. Thus, when a Ch'an monk contemplated a painting of White-robed Kuan-yin, he would not see her the same way as would a Ming literatus who desperately desired to have a son. Similarly, a woman listening to the story of Princess Miao-shan would not have the same reaction as a Confucian official or a Buddhist abbot. The same could be said about the different readings of the Great Compassion Repentance ritual, depending on whether the participant was a Buddhist exegete or an ordinary lay person. It is precisely the diversity and multivocality that make the cult fascinating. Surely it is more rewarding to know as much as possible the different types of understandings and expectations that the faithful had about Kuan-yin than to put on them the worn out labels of elite and popular, or monastic and lay, thus imposing an artificial neatness that was never there. Such multiple and divergent views about Kuan-yin, furthermore, might even have been known and shared by them. For men and women from different classes and backgrounds went on pilgrimages to the same sacred sites, and attended the same rituals and festivals. They had access to the same stories about Kuan-yin.

I would like to think that what I have said about the cult of Kuan-yin is applicable to the study of Chinese Buddhism and religion in general. I hope the methodology I have used in this book can be applied to other case studies as well. I would like to emphasize here the necessity of not only using different disciplines and materials as I have just suggested, but also the importance of always examining the relationship between Buddhism and indigenous cultural and religious traditions. When we consider Kuan-yin in the Chinese cultural, religious, historical and social contexts, we can understand why Avalokiteśvara could and did become a goddess in China.

As I mentioned in chapter 1, Avalokiteśvara was and is a legitimizing symbol for rulers in South and Southeast Asia as well as Tibet. We need only think of the Dalai Lama who, even in today's secularized world, is still believed by vast numbers of the faithful to be the incarnation of Avalokiteśvara. Kuan-yin, however, did not take on this royal symbolism in China. This did not happen, as I suggested, because it was preempted in China by the Confucian belief in the Mandate of Heaven, which was firmly in place long before the introduction of Buddhism.

On the other hand, prior to the translation of the *Lotus Sūtra* in the third century, there was no Chinese deity to compare with Kuan-yin, who was not only a universal and compassionate savior, but also easily accessible. The gospel of the "Universal Gateway" preached a new and democratic way of salvation. There was no specific thing a person had to do to be saved. One did not need to become a scholar learned in scripture, or a paragon of virtue, or a master proficient in meditation. One did not have to follow a special way of life, take up a strange diet, or practice any ritual. The only requirement was to call his name with a sincere and believing heart. Kuan-yin was the new foreign god who would help anyone in any difficulty. There was no discrimination on the basis of status or gender. And the benefits of worshiping him were both spiritual and worldly. It is no wonder that such a message received an immediate and eager response in the chaotic and turbulent early centuries of the Common Era. Despite Avalokiteśvara's intrinsic attractiveness, his quick "conquest" of China certainly was also due to the fact that there was a vacuum in the native religious tradition that he could easily fill. He did not have to compete for believers. But once he became accepted by the Chinese, new gods like him emerged in Taoism and, later, in sectarian religions. These gods, such as the Chiu-k'u T'ien-tsun and Eternal Mother, also presented themselves as universal saviors just like Kuan-yin. The requirement for salvation was likewise not the fulfillment of any religious command or special discipline, but only sincerity (*ch'eng*), a virtue celebrated by Confucian classics and well known, if not always exemplified, by every Chinese.

The influence, however, was never one way. The Chinese believed that certain individuals were incarnations of Kuan-yin. Chapter 5 discusses two such famous "transformation bodies" (*hua-shen*) of the bodhisattva, two divine monks who lived in the fifth and seventh centuries, while chapter 8 follows the career of a mythical princess. Where did such ideas come from and what were the models for them? The new belief in rebirth (saṃsāra) introduced to the Chinese people by Buddhism must of course be mentioned. Not only human beings, compelled by their karma, are reborn after they die, but bodhisattvas also can choose to appear as human beings out of their compassion. The *Lotus Sūtra* mentions that Kuan-yin appears in many forms in order to carry out his work of salvation. The Hindu tradition, with which Buddhism had enjoyed a relationship of mutual appropriation until the latter disappeared from India in the twelfth century, also speaks of the "down coming" of gods. Thus, for instance, Kṛṣṇa is the avatar of Viṣṇu. But I think the inspiration for Kuan-yin's Chinese manifestation might be closer to home—indigenous beliefs about gods and holy persons. Since the Chinese religion does not posit a sharp distinction between the transcendent and the immanent, human beings can become gods and gods can also appear on earth as human beings. Lao Tzu, for instance, was already deified in the second century and believed to have transformed (*hua*) himself many times to teach people about the Tao. Stories about the Taoist immortals, those fabulous beings who straddle the boundary between the human and the divine, serve as another rich resource for such imagination. Indeed, as we have seen in the cases of Pao-chih and Seng-chieh, many traits exhibited by these Buddhist thaumaturges could equally qualify them as Taoist saints.

In this book I have concentrated on showing the reader how Kuan-yin became popular in China and what being "popular" meant in Chinese Buddhism and religion. But since Avalokiteśvara became a feminine deity only in China and, furthermore, this happened only after the T'ang, it is necessary to offer some hypothetical explanations. Instead of seeking the clues in native goddesses, which, as shown in chapter 10, is at best inconclusive, I think it has to be examined in the context of new developments in Chinese religions including Buddhism since the Sung. The emergence of the feminine Kuan-yin must also be studied in the context of new cults of other goddesses, which, not coincidentally, also happened since the Sung. These are the cults of the Queen of Heaven (T'ien-hou, more familiarly known as Ma-tsu), the Goddess of Azure Cloud (Pi-hsia Yüan-chün), and later, the Eternal Mother. As we have discussed in various chapters in the book, the appearance of the feminine Kuan-yin in indigenous sūtras, art, miracle stories, and the legend of Miao-shan occurred in the tenth to twelfth centuries. Around the same time, lay Buddhist movements known as the White Lotus Teachings, new schools in Taoism, and most importantly, the Confucian revival known as Neo-Confucianism also took place. When Neo-Confucianism was established as the official ideology functioning very much like a state religion in the Ming and Ch'ing, Kuan-yin was also completely transformed into a goddess. I do not think these events happened by coincidence or independent of each other.

I would venture to say that the reason the feminine Kuan-yin and other new goddesses appeared at this particular time might be connected with the antifeminist stance of established religions, chief of which was undoubtedly Neo-Confucianism. This was the hegemonic discourse and ruling ideology of China during the last one thousand years. Neo-Confucianism was a philosophy and a system of political thought, but it was also an ideology sustaining the lineage and family system. In one sense, then, the new goddess's cults can be seen as similar responses to this totalistic system of belief and praxis, but in another way, as I have suggested earlier in the book, the feminine Kuan-yin might be viewed as the model and inspiration for the other goddesses. Organized Buddhism and Taoism do not fare much better. Despite the Ch'an rhetoric of nonduality and the Taoist elevation of the feminine principle, these did not translate into actual institutional support for women. We cannot name any woman who became a prominent Ch'an master or Cheng-i (Correct Unity) Taoist priestess. No wonder women were attracted to new Taoist schools such as the Ch'uan-chen (Complete Realization) or the many sectarian religions flourishing since the Ming.

Having said that the birth of goddesses might have been in response to the overwhelmingly masculine character of the three religions, I must also point out that some of these new goddesses did reflect the belief in universal sagehood and enlightenment espoused by Neo-Confucianism, Buddhism, and Taoism. It is striking to compare the differences between Miao-shan and the earlier manifestations of Kuan-yin. Albeit a princess, Miao-shan was a woman. Yet she was believed to have achieved Buddhahood even though she was not even a nun. When we consider the earthly career of Ma-tsu, it is even more astonishing. For she was the daughter of a humble fisherman. In fact, many new deities who became prominent in late imperial China had once been ordinary men and women. Just as the emperors Yao and Shun were not born sages, but became so, this was apparently also the case for gods and goddesses. Wang Ken (1483–1540) could salute everyone he met as sages because they were potential sages, if not actual ones. Can we also say that the street was full of bodhisattvas and goddesses?

Finally, I would like to revisit the question of Kuan-yin and gender raised in the last chapter. Did the female Kuan-yin offer more options to Chinese women? It is often assumed that when a religion provides goddesses to worship, it can empower women. In my analysis of the legend of Miao-shan, I suggest that she challenges both the Confucian family ideology and the Buddhist monastic ideal. Inspired by her model, some women in late imperial times resisted marriage and practiced lay Buddhism in "vegetarian houses." When Avalokiteśvara was transformed into Kuan-yin, the "Goddess of Mercy," new forms and expressions of religiosity became available to women and men in China. But as long as the traditional stereotypical views about women's pollution or inferiority remained unchallenged, the feminine images of Kuan-yin had to be either more or less than real women. They were not and could not be endowed with a real woman's characteristics. It is for this reason that the White-robed Kuan-yin, though a fertility goddess, is devoid of sexuality. Like the Great Goddess in the Hindu tradition, she is "both a virgin and a mother" (Erndl 1993:144), a condition that no real woman can attain. Real women, in the meantime, together with their male countrymen, worshiped Kuan-yin as the "child-giving" Kuan-yin who saw to it that the family religion would never be disrupted by lack of a male heir. Or, they would call upon her for help when they performed *ke-ku* and carried out this most fanatical ritual according to the dictates of the domestic religion of filial piety. Chinese women, like Miao-shan, never really left the patriarchal home.

But, on further reflection, one may ask, what kind of home was it? Clearly, something close to a sea change occurred after the Sung in both Chinese religion and the Chinese family system. Patricia Ebrey has pointed out an increasing emphasis from the Southern Sung period and following on the lineage ideal, particularly on genealogies and generation markers (1986:32–39, 44–50). By the mid-Ming, around the fifteenth century, with fierce competitiveness in the examinations on the rise, lineages became even more important, for they supported individuals in surviving as successful degree candidates (ter Haar 1992:113). The desperate need to secure a male heir, the frantic effort to keep the head of the household alive, and the fanatical adherence to the ideal of chaste widowhood—all the disparate elements of a "domesticated religiosity" mentioned in chapter 8—began to take on a new significance. The cult of Kuan-yin did indeed serve Confucian family values, and in this sense we can speak of a Confucianization of Buddhism. While it is true that because of the "diffused" character of Chinese religion, the family was never a completely secular institution, separated from the transcendent and devoid of religious status, it was still primarily Confucian in its orientations (Yang 1961:28–57, 294–340). In the end, the influence went both ways. As a common saying familiar to many Chinese people goes, "Kuan-yin is enshrined in every household" (*chia-chia feng Kuan-yin*); thus, it was ultimately a home where Kuan-yin was very much present. Kuan-yin had indeed found a home in China.

Casting a backward look at the long road along which this study has taken me, I realize now that there are still many questions that remain to be explored. It would have been good to be able to say more about the relationship between the media of transmission and the audiences of the cult. For instance, who made the willow-holding gilt bronze images of Kuan-yin? For whom? For what purposes were they used and on what occasions, and where were they installed? Or when was a particular precious scroll written, and by whom, and who read it? I would like to know more than I do about the social context of the media which disseminated the cult. Of course, due to the lack of documentation in some cases, some of the questions may never be answered. I suspect that more attention to the ritual uses of art and scripture might have yielded some important information.

I would also like to know more about the religious lives of Chinese women after the Sung, when the feminine forms of Kuan-yin began to become dominant. We know, for instance, that many cloisters (*an*) were built in the Sung and Yüan. Some were built by men of means for their female kin. Others were built by women themselves. The majority of them were dedicated to Kuan-yin, for they had names such as "White Robe," "Great Compassion," or "Purple Bamboo Grove." Who were those women and what kind of religious practices did they pursue? What kinds of Kuan-yin images were enshrined in the cloisters? Were they the same as those enshrined in the public Ch'an monasteries, or did the more recently created images, showing obviously feminine features, find homes there? Did the women become nuns or did they remain in lay status, like their sisters in the *chai-t'ang* or vegetarian houses of more recent times?

I plan to explore some of these questions in the future. I hope that other scholars may become interested in joining me. The academic study of Chinese religions is still young and many important case studies wait to be written.

Appendix A

. . . .

Stele Text of the "Life of the Great Compassionate One"

The missing words are indicated by ellipses, while a possible reconstruction based on related sources is indicated by brackets.

[Lü Master Tao-hsüan's] pure conduct moved the divine spirit who came to attend him. One day the Master asked the divine spirit, "I have heard that the Mahāsattva Kuan-yin has a special affinity with this land. Of all the places where the Bodhisattva's efficacious traces are manifested, which is the most excellent?" The divine spirit answered, "Kuan-yin's appearances follow no fixed rule, but Hsiang-shan is most excellent because the Bodhisattva left the trace of her flesh-body there." The Master asked, "Where is this Hsiang-shan?" The spirit replied:

Two hundred *li* south of Mt. Sung there stand three hills. The middle one is Hsiang-shan where the Bodhisattva achieved enlightenment. To the northeast of the hill, there was in the past a king whose name was Chuang. His lady was named Pao-te. The king followed heterodox ways and did not respect the Three Treasures. He had no crown prince, only three daughters: the eldest Miao-yen, the second Miao-yin and the youngest Miao-shan. Of these three daughters, two were already married. Only the third [was not married].

[At her birth, fragrance filled the air and light] shone both inside and outside the palace. People throughout the country were astounded, saying that a fire had broken out in the palace. She was born that very evening. At birth she was already clean, without having been washed. Her holy marks were noble and majestic, her body was covered by five-colored auspicious clouds. The people all wondered, saying "Could it be that a holy person has appeared in the world?" The king marveled at this and named her "Miao-shan."

When she grew up, her conduct and appearance far transcended the ordinary. [She always wore dirty clothes and did not adorn herself. She would eat only once a day.] When it was not the proper time (i.e., past noontime), she would not eat. In her conversations she always gave people good advice. She would talk about cause and effect, and about everything being impermanent and illusory. In the palace she was called, "Buddha's Heart." All those who listened to her turned to the good. They fasted and practiced the Way without faltering in their resolve. When the king heard this, he said to his wife, "Our young daughter Miao-shan is teaching my ladies-in-waiting to practice the Way in the palace. They have given up adornment and cosmetics." [The king] said to his daughter, "You have now grown up and should obey my instructions. Do not delude and confuse the ladies in the inner palace. Your father has a country to rule and does not like what you are doing. Your mother and I will find a husband for you. From now on you should follow the correct path and do not practice the heterodox way thus corrupting the custom of our country."

When Miao-shan heard what the king said, she smiled and replied, "Royal Father . . . I would never, for the sake of one lifetime of glory, plunge into aeons of misery. I have pondered long on this matter and deeply detest it [marriage]. I want to leave home to practice the Way in order to realize Buddhahood and attain enlightenment. I can then repay the kindness of my parents and save sentient beings from suffering. If you order me to marry, I dare not obey. Father, please understand and pity me." The king told his wife, "Our daughter does not [want to marry. Please talk to her and make her change her mind. The mother then tried to persuade Miao-shan, who answered,] "I will obey Mother's command only if it will prevent three misfortunes." The mother asked, "What are the three misfortunes?" She answered, "The first is this: when people are young, their face is as fair as the jade-like moon, but when they grow old, their hair turns white and their faces are wrinkled; whether walking, resting, sitting, or lying down, they are in every way worse off than when they were young. The second is this: one's limbs are strong and vigorous, one may walk as briskly as if flying through the air, but when one suddenly becomes sick, one lies in bed [without a single pleasure in life. The third is this: a person may have a large group of relatives and be] surrounded by his flesh and blood, but when death comes, even with such close kin as father and son, they cannot take the person's place. If a husband can prevent these three misfortunes, I will marry him. But if he cannot do so, I vow never to marry. People of the world are all mired in these kinds of suffering. If one desires to be free from these sufferings, one must leave the secular world and enter the gate of Buddhism. Only when one practices religion and obtains its fruit, can one deliver all people from suffering. This is why I have given rise to the thought [for enlightenment. . . .]" [The king became] ever more angry and exiled her to the garden in the back of the palace. Cutting off her food and drink, he ordered everyone in the palace not to go near her. The mother was sad and missed her. She secretly asked a palace maid to take food and drink to Miao-shan. The king said to the queen, "I exiled her to the back garden but she does not seem to fear death. Nor does she eat. Why don't you go with Miao-yen and Miao-yin and persuade her to change her mind? If she does, father and child will meet again. Otherwise. (. . .)"

When they came to the back garden, they saw Miao-shan seated in deep meditation, not paying attention to her mother. The lady embraced her and cried aloud, "Ever since you left the palace, my two eyes are almost dried up and my liver and innards are breaking into pieces. How can you be at peace seeing your mother thus? Your father is so troubled by you that he cannot hold audience in the palace, nor take care of state affairs. So he told me to come with Miao-yen and Miao-yin to talk to you. Please think of your father. (. . .)" Miao-shan said, "I am not suffering here. Why are Father and Mother so unhappy? In all the emotional entanglements of this world there is no term of spiritual release. If close kin are united, they must inevitably be sundered and scattered. Even if one stays with one's parents for a hundred years, when death arrives, we still must be parted. Rest at ease, Mother. Luckily you have my two sisters to care for you and there is no need for me. Please go back and tell them that I have no desire to go back on my resolve." Then Miao-yen and Miao-yin said to Miao-shan, "(. . .) Look at those who have left home and become nuns. Who among them is able to shine light, shake the earth, attain Buddhahood, or become a patriarch so that she can repay the kindness above and save all beings below? Isn't it better to get married in accordance with the rites? Why do you worry our parents so?" Miao-shan replied to her two sisters, "You are attached to glory, luxury and conjugal love. You are bound by the pleasures of the moment. But you do not know that pleasure is the cause of pain. (. . .) As daughters, we cannot be excused from attending parents. But can your husbands do it for you? Sisters, each of us has to live her life. Please think it over and take care of yourselves, but do not keep advising me what to do. Realization is right in front of you. There is no use in empty regret. Please persuade Mother to go back to the palace and tell Father that the empty space may have a limit, but my vow is limitless. Whether I live or die is up to Father to decide." Miao-yen and Miao-yin returned to tell. (. . .) The queen further reported to the king, who then became even more enraged.

There was a nun by the name of Hui-chen. The king sent for her and told her, "My youngest daughter Miao-shan does not follow righteousness and propriety but insists on leaving home. There is no way to dissuade her. You people must try to devise a way to persuade her. I will allow my youngest daughter to stay in your convent for seven days to be instructed by you. If she listens to me, I will decorate your [nunnery]. (. . .)" A messenger was dispatched to go with the nun to the back garden. She invited Miao-shan to go to the nunnery. Five hundred nuns came out to welcome her and accompany her to the main hall to burn incense. The next day, the nuns said to Miao-shan, "You were born in the palace and grew up there. Why do you seek loneliness? You had better go back to the palace, which is so much superior to a temple." Miao-shan heard what they said and replied with a smile, "(. . .) [I want to] save all sentient beings. What you have shown me about the depth of your knowledge is truly pitiable and despicable. If even Buddhist disciples such as yourselves say things like this, no wonder worldly people blame me for what I do. My father, the King, is angry and hateful toward you people and does not allow me to leave the householder's life. Doesn't he have a reason? Don't you know the reason for having a shaved head and wearing a square robe? One who has left the householder's life detests vainglory, luxury (. . .) and sexual love (. . .) [Your behavior, on the other hand,] accords very little with what is demanded of a monastic. The Buddha has left clear instructions: a monastic should give up make-up and adornment, wear rag robes, carry a begging bowl, and sustain herself by begging. How come you people are all interested in luxury, wearing beautiful clothes and behaving in such a bewitching and seductive manner? You entered the gate of Buddhism wantonly, corrupted the pure rules and accepted offerings from the faithful undeservedly. You are monastics in name only and your hearts are not in accordance with the Way!" The nuns had nothing to say when Miao-shan rebuked them thus.

At that time, Hui-chen became worried and told Miao-shan, "The reason why the nuns tried to persuade you just now [to give up the idea of renouncing the world] was because they were following the king's order." She then told Miao-shan about the king's decree as mentioned before and asked her to change her mind so that the nuns could be spared and the nunnery would be safe from disaster. Miao-shan said, "Don't you know [the stories] about Prince Mahāsattva's realization of no-birth as a result of plunging himself off the cliff in order to feed the hungry tigers, and King Śivi's attaining the other shore as a result of cutting his flesh to save a dove? Since you have already left the life of a householder, you should regard this illusory body as impermanent and detestable, and the four great elements as having temporarily come into being but originally non-existent. You should want to be delivered from transmigration in your every thought and seek for release in every moment of consciousness.

Why do you fear death and love life? Don't you know that attachment to this dirty and smelly leather bag [body] is an obstacle? (. . .) You want to escape death by obeying the king's wishes. But be at ease. When I achieve enlightenment, I will save you from transmigration. Do not worry."

When the nuns heard this, they discussed among themselves, saying that because Miao-shan grew up in the palace, she did not know the difficulties of ordinary life outside the palace but thought leaving the world was a happy thing. So now she should be made to feel the pain and humiliation of hard manual labor so that she would know fear and thus repent. They told Miao-shan, "If you want to be a monastic, you (. . .) [should] labor earlier than everyone else and work in the kitchen. You must work at chores no one else is capable of doing. There are no vegetables in the vegetable garden, but you must serve food in a timely fashion without fail." Miao-shan went to the vegetable garden and seeing how few vegetables there were, she became worried about the next day, not knowing how to get food to serve the nuns. But just when she was thinking thus, the dragon spirit of the temple came to her help and with divine assistance (. . .) She served the nuns without a problem. (. . .) Obtaining water was very difficult and Miao-shan was troubled. But a spring appeared miraculously on the left side of the kitchen. The water from the spring was very sweet. Hui-chen then knew that Miao-shan was not an ordinary person, for she could move the dragon spirit to help her. So she reported this to the king who became greatly angered and said to his attendants, "My youngest daughter has practiced the heterodox way for a long time. I put her in a nunnery but she used magic to delude the people and insult me (. . .)"

[When the envoy arrived,] Miao-shan obeyed the royal command and said to the community of nuns, "Retire at once, all of you. I am to suffer execution." Miao-shan then came out [to meet] her death. At the moment when she was about to receive the blade, the mountain-god of Lung-shan (Dragon Mountain), who knew that Miao-shan, the bodhisattva of great power, was on the point of fulfilling her spiritual destiny and delivering the multitude of living beings, realized that her evil royal father was wrongly about to behead her, and used his divine powers to produce (. . .) dark, violent wind, thunder and lightening. He snatched away Miao-shan and set her down at the foot of the mountain. The envoy, no longer knowing where Miao-shan was, rushed in haste to report to the king.

The king, again shocked and enraged, sent off five hundred soldiers to behead the entire community of nuns and burn all their buildings. His lady and the royal family all wept bitterly, saying that Miao-shan was already dead and beyond hope of rescue. The king said to his lady, "(. . .) Do not grieve. This young girl was no kin of mine. She must have been some demon who was born into my family. I have managed to get rid of the demon: that is cause for great delight!"

Now that she had been snatched away by divine power to the foot of Lung-shan, Miao-shan looked around and found no one there. Then with slow steps she climbed the mountain. Suddenly she noticed a foul, reeking smell, and thought to herself: "The mountain forests are secluded and quiet: where does this smell come from?" The mountain god took the form of an old man and met Miao-shan with the words, "Kind one, where do you want to go?" Miao-shan said, "I wish to go up into this mountain to practice religion." The old man said, "This mountain is the abode of creatures with scales and shells, feathers and fur. It is no place for you to practice your cultivation, kind one." Miao-shan asked, "What is the name of this mountain?" He said, "It is Lung-shan. Dragons live on this mountain, hence it is named after them." "What about the range to the west of here?" He answered, "That too is an abode of dragons, and for that reason it is called Lesser Lung-shan. Only between the two mountains there is a small ridge named Hsiang-shan. That place is pure and clean, a fit place for you to pursue your cultivation, kind one." Miao-shan said, "Who are you, that you are showing me the place to live?" The old man answered, "Your disciple is not a man, but the god of this mountain. You, kind one, are going to fulfill your spiritual destiny, and I, your disciple, have sworn to protect and keep you." With these words he vanished.

Miao-shan went to Hsiang-shan, climbed to the summit, and looked around. It was peaceful, without any trace of man, and she said to herself, "This is the place where I shall transform my karma." So she went to the summit and built a shelter for practicing her religious cultivation. She dressed in grasses, ate from trees, and no one knew (. . .) for three whole years.

Meanwhile her father the king sickened with *kāmalā* [jaundice] on account of his sinful karma. It spread all over his skin and body, and he found no rest in sleep. The best doctors throughout the land were unable to heal him. His lady and the royal family were in anxiety morning and night about him.

One day a strange monk stood in front of the inner palace, saying, "I have a divine remedy that can heal the king's sickness." When the king's attendants heard these words they hastily reported them to the king, and he on hearing them summoned the monk into the inner palace. The monk addressed him, "I, poor man of religion, have medicine to cure the king's sickness." The king said, "What medicine do you have that can cure my disease?" The monk said, "I have a prescription that requires the use of two major medical ingredients." The king asked what, and the monk replied, "This medicine can be made by obtaining the arms and eyes of one without anger." The king said, " . . . do not speak so frivolously. If I take someone's arms and eyes, will they not be angry?" The monk said, "Such a one does exist in your land." The king asked where the person was now, and the monk replied, "In the southwest of your dominion is a mountain named Hsiang-shan. On its summit is a hermit practicing religious cultivation with signal merit, though none knows of it. This person has no anger." The king said, "How can I get her arms and eyes?" The monk said, "No-one else can seek them: they are available only to you, the king. In the past the hermit had a close affinity with you. If you obtain her arms and eyes, this sickness of yours can be cured instantly, without any doubt."

When the king heard this, he burned incense and offered this prayer: "If my terrible sickness can really be cured, may I receive this hermit's own arms and eyes bestowed without stint or grudge." His prayer completed, he commanded an envoy to go, bearing incense, up into the mountain. When the envoy arrived he saw, inside a thatched hermitage, a hermit whose body was stately and impressive, sitting there cross-legged. He burned fine incense and announced the royal command: "The king of the land has suffered the *kāmalā* sickness for three years up until now. The great physicians, the wonder drugs of all the land are all unable to cure him. A monk has presented a [remedy]: by using the arms and eyes of one without anger a medicine can be made up. And now, with our deepest respects, we have heard that you, holy hermit, practice religion with signal merit, and so we believe that you must also be without anger. We venture to beg you for your arms and eyes to cure the king's sickness."

The envoy bowed twice, and Miao-shan reflected: "My father the king showed disrespect to the Three Treasures, he persecuted and suppressed Buddhism, he burned monastic buildings, he executed a community [of nuns]. He invited the retribution of this sickness. With my arms and eyes I shall save the king in his distress." Having conceived this idea she said to the envoy, "It must be your king's refusal to believe in the Three Treasures that has caused him to suffer this evil malady. I shall give my arms and eyes to provide medicine for him. My one desire is that the remedy will be a match for the ailment and will drive out the king's disease. The king must direct his mind towards enlightenment and commit himself to the Three Treasures: then he will achieve recovery."

With these words she gouged out both her eyes with a knife, then told the envoy to sever her two arms. At that moment the whole mountain shook, and from the sky came a voice commending her: "Rare, how rare! She is able to save all living beings, to do things impossible in this world!"

The envoy was terrified, but the hermit said, "Have no fear. Take my arms and eyes back to the king, and remember what I have said." The envoy accepted them and returned to report to the king.

When the king received the arms and eyes he felt a deep shame. He told the monk to blend the medicine, then he [took] it. Before ten days were out he recovered completely from his sickness. The king and his lady, his kin, his officials, and all down to the very subjects of his realm, began to rejoice. The king sent for the monk to give him offerings of thanks, saying: "No one but you, [Master], could save us from that terrible sickness." The monk said, "It was not my power. How could you have recovered without the hermit's arms and eyes? You should go up the mountain to offer thanks to the hermit." With these words he vanished.

The king was astounded. He brought his palms together and said, "So slight a condition as mine has moved a holy monk to come and save me!" And then he commanded his attendants: "Tomorrow I shall go to visit Hsiang-shan and make offerings of thanks to the hermit."

The next day the king with his lady, his two daughters and the palace retinue, had carriages prepared, set out from the walled city and reached Hsiang-shan. [Reaching] the hermitage, they lavishly laid out the finest offerings. The king burned incense and offered thanks with the words: "When I suffered that foul disease I could not possibly have recovered without your arms and eyes, hermit. Today, therefore, I have personally come with my closest kin to visit the mountains and offer thanks to you."

When the king with his lady and palace maidens all moved forward to gaze upon the hermit who was without arms or eyes, they were moved to sorrowful thoughts, because the hermit's physical impairment was brought about by [the king]. His lady made a minute examination, gazed at the hermit's physical characteristics, and said to the king, "When I look at the hermit's shape and appearance, she seems very like our daughter." And with these words she found herself choking back tears and lamentations.

The hermit suddenly spoke, "My lady mother! Do not cast your mind back to Miao-shan: I am she. When the king my father suffered his foul disease, your child offered up her arms and eyes to repay the king's love."

Hearing these words, the king and his lady embraced her with loud weeping, stirring heaven and earth with their grief. He said, "My evil ways have caused my daughter to lose her arms and eyes and [endure] this suffering. I am going to lick my child's two eyes with my tongue and join on her two arms, and desire the gods and spirits of heaven and earth to make my child's withered eyes to grow again, her severed arms once more to be whole!"

As soon as the king had expressed this resolve, but before his mouth had touched her eyes, Miao-shan was suddenly not to be found. At that moment heaven and earth shook, radiance blazed forth, auspicious clouds enclosed all around, divine musicians began to play. [And then] the All-Compassionate

Kuan-yin of the Thousand Arms and Thousand Eyes appeared, solemn and majestic in form, radiant with dazzling light, lofty and magnificent, like the moon amid the stars.

When the king with his lady and palace maidens beheld the form of the Bodhisattva, they rose and struck themselves, beat their breasts with loud lament, and raised their voices in repentance: "We your disciples, with our mortal sight, failed to recognize the Holy One. Evil karma has obstructed our minds. We pray you to extend your saving protection to absolve our earlier misdeeds. From this time on we shall turn towards the Three Treasures, we shall rebuild Buddhist monasteries. We pray you, Bodhisattva, in your great compassion, to return to your original body and permit us to make offerings."

In a moment the hermit returned to her original person, with her arms and eyes quite intact. She sat cross-legged, brought her palms together, and with great solemnity passed away, as though entering into meditation.

The king and his lady burned incense and made a vow: "We your disciples will [provide] an offering of fragrant wood, will commit your holy body to the funeral pyre, and, when we return to the palace, will raise a stūpa and make offerings to it in perpetuity." Having made his vow, the king surrounded the transcendent body with all kinds of pure incense, cast flames upon it and burned it. When the fragrant fuel was consumed the transcendent body loomed there still, and could not be moved. The king made another vow: "It must be that the Bodhisattva will not depart [from] this place, and wishes to cause all living beings to see and hear, and make offerings." Having said these words, the king and his lady together lifted the body and immediately [at their touch] it rose lightly.

The king then reverently erected a precious shrine with the Bodhisattva's true body inside, and outside he built a precious stūpa. In all solemnity he buried her on the summit of the mountain, beneath the site of her hermitage. And there on the mountain, with court and kin, he watched and protected her day and night without sleeping.

At length he returned to his capital. He rebuilt Buddhist monasteries, increased the ordination of monks and nuns, and paid reverence to the Three Treasures. He drew resources from his private treasury and built a pagoda with thirteen stages up on Hsiang-shan, to cover the true body of the Bodhisattva.

[The divine spirit said]: "Master, you have asked me, your disciple, about the holy traces of the Bodhisaatva, and I have given a brief account of the broad essentials. As for the Bodhisattva's secret incarnations, these are not known to me."

The Vinaya Master again asked, "What is the present state of the precious stūpa on Hsiang-shan?"

The divine spirit said, "The stūpa has long been abandoned. Now [there remains only] the pagoda, and few know of it. The traces left on earth by a holy one prosper and decay in their due time. Only after three hundred years will a revival occur."

Now that his questions were finished the Vinaya Master brought his palms together and uttered these words of praise: "How great is the spiritual power of the Mahāsattva Kuan-yin! Were it not for the fullness of the Bodhisattva's vow, these signs could not have been revealed. If the living beings of that land had not brought their karmic conditions to maturity, they could not have attracted this response. How mighty, this merit without measure! It cannot be conceived!"

He told his disciple I-ch'ang to set this story down in writing on the fifteenth day of the second summer month in the second year of Sheng-li [April 20, 699].

Written in the third month of the third year of Yüan-fu [May, 1100].

Set up in the seventh month of the first year of Chih-ta [August, 1308] by monks of the Public Ch'an Monastery of the Great Universal Gateway on Hsiang-shan.

Appendix B

. . . .

Chinese Women Pilgrims' Songs Glorifying Kuan-yin

I was in Hangchow during the spring pilgrimage season in 1987. As described in chapter 9, large groups of women pilgrims arrived daily to pay their respects to Kuan-yin at the Upper T'ien-chu Monastery. They were led by women who could sing songs about Kuan-yin. These songs were called "Kuan-yin ching" (Kuan-yin Sūtra). I recorded some of the songs, transcribed them and now provide their translation in the following.

1. "Small Kuan-yin Sūtra" (*Hsiao Kuan-yin ching*)

Sung by a fifty-year-old woman pilgrim from T'ung-hsiang, Kiangsu.

South Sea Temple, Purple Bamboo Grove.
Kuan-yin emerges from Purple Bamboo Grove.
A daughter-in-law from the ends of the earth worships Kuan-yin.
Having been worshiped, Kuan-yin appears in front of my eyes.
A thousand good roads lead to Rocky Mountain.
Adoration of Kuan-shih-yin, the Great Compassionate One.

2. "Seven-fold Kuan-yin Sūtra" (*Ch'i-p'in Kuan-yin ching*)

Sung by a forty-five-year-old "living bodhisattva" from T'ung-hsiang, Kiangsu.

Bodhisattva Kuan-yin has entered my body.
On the nineteenth day of the second month Mother gave birth to me.
On the nineteenth day of the sixth month I went up to Heaven.
Having arrived in Heaven, I turned around.
And sat in the main hall wearing a crown of pearls on my head.
Beating on the wooden fish I go everywhere.
Without a home and without any worries I worship the Third Sister.
The Third Sister does not want food to eat.
The Third Sister does not want clothes to wear.
The Third Sister wants to go to the Ninth Cloud beyond the empyrean to become a living immortal.
First, I want to cultivate an affinity with a thousand people.
Second, I want to cultivate an affinity with ten thousand people.
Immortals are originally made of ordinary mortals.
Yet ultimately ordinary mortals' hearts are not firm.
Green grasses by the roadside serve as the Buddha Hall.
An immortal's boat lands by the sea shore.
Breadfruit trees grow on all four sides.
Three thousand buddhas fell into the lotus pond.
The Four Heavenly Kings came in two pairs.
Someone taught me the Kuan-yin Sūtra.
Every morning I rinse my mouth and chant seven times.
Having chanted seven times, I see Kuan-yin.
Adoration of the Buddha, Amitābha.

3. "Kuan-yin Sūtra" (*Kuan-yin ching*)

Sung by a fifty-nine-year-old woman pilgrim from Chiang-yin, Kiangsu.

Wearing a crown of pearls and striking
A hand-held wooden fish, I go everywhere to proselytize.
I ask buddhas of the ten directions:
Which road leads to spiritual cultivation?
In the west, there is no other than King Miao-chuang.
There is a truly chaste woman in the household of King Miao-chuang.
First, she does not have to bear the ill humor of her parents-in-law.
Second, she does not have to eat the food of her husband.
Third, she does not have to carry a child in her womb or on her arms.

Fourth, she does not need a maid to serve her.
Everyday she enjoys peace and quiet in her fragrant room.
Turning over the cotton coverlet, she sleeps on the bed alone.
Stretching out her legs, she went into the Buddha Hall.
Pulling in her feet, she withdrew into the back garden.
For the sake of cultivation, she suffered punishments by her parents.
But now, sitting on the lotus throne, she enjoys blessing.
Over and over again, I chant the Kuan-yin *Sūtra*
On the first and fifteenth, I receive the offering of incense.
Adoration to the Buddha, Amitābha.

4. "Sūtra Honoring Kuan-yin" (*Tzun-chung Kuan-yin ching*)

Sung by a fifty-eight-year-old woman pilgrim from Soochow, Kiangsu.

When the spring breeze blows and the water is clear.
I must go to Hangchow to worship Kuan-yin.
Look at the high mountain with a thousand buddhas,
Look at the West Lake with limpid water.
The West Lake has bridges spanning fifteen and sixteen li.
The West Lake faces the Ling-yin Temple.
And the Ling-yin Temple faces the Fragrant Water Bridge.
Willow trees alternate with peach trees.
Granny Kuan-yin lives in the mountain creek of nine winding paths.
I come bearing incense from another county, from another province.
Adoration to the Buddha, Amitābha.

5. "Sūtra of the Thousand-handed Kuan-yin" (*Ch'ien-shou Kuan-yin ching*)

Sung by a fifty-eight-year-old woman pilgrim from Soochow, Kiangsu.

Adoration to the Thousand-handed Kuan-yin who comes from the South Sea.
Shan-ts'ai and Lung-nü stand on either side.
I repay Kuan-yin's kindness with my whole life, with my whole life.
I smell the incense rising from the incense burners standing in front of me.

On the nineteenth day of the second month Mother gave birth to me.
On the nineteenth day of the sixth month I went up to Heaven.
Having ascended to Heaven I return to earth.
My sisters obeyed orders and burned the nunnery.
Father and Mother wanted her to accept a royal consort.
But the Princess vowed never to get married.
Carrying a water vessel and willow branches, she went up to Heaven.
She went to the Western Paradise riding on azure clouds.
Returning to the lotus throne, she accepts the offering of incense smoke.
Adoration to the Buddha, Amitābha.

6. "The Sūtra of Fragrant Mountain" (*Hsiang-shan ching*)

Sung by a seventy-year-old woman pilgrim from Chia-hsing, Kiangsu.

Picking up the wooden fish, I begin to chant the sūtra.
Three sisters together engaged in spiritual cultivation.
The Eldest Princess wanted to achieve Tathāgata Buddhahood.
The Second Princess wanted to attain a blessing-enjoyment body.
The Third Princess is young in age.
And wanted to become Kuan-shih-yin of the Purple Bamboo Grove, the Spirit Mountain.
The Cave of Tidal Sounds and the Purple Bamboo Grove.
Holding incense in my hand, I invite Kuan-yin to descend.
I want to invite the three Kuan-yins to take south-facing seats.
With sincerity in my heart I worship Kuan-yin.
The First Kuan-yin comes from the South Sea.
She smiles a broad smile upon hearing my invocation of Buddha's name.
Uninterested in making embroidered shoes for her feet,
She now sits on the lotus throne with her exposed natural big feet.
The Second Kuan-yin sits up on high.
Mt. T'ai can never be as high as Mt. Buddha.
Three sticks of incense made of sandalwood are burning in a golden incense burner.
The smoke rises across from the Immortal-Making-Bridge.
The Third Kuan-yin is very imposing.
Holding the wooden fish she travels everywhere.
Vulgar people of the world say that I am an alms-begging maiden.
My father is no other than King Miao-chuang.

Three images of Kuan-yin have been installed royally.
Carrying the wooden fish I go up to Heaven.
The sound of the wooden fish is heard in Heaven.
The Ninety-nine scriptures flash brilliant light.
Adoration to the Buddha, Amitābha.

Notes

1. Introduction

1. Two examples are Gerda Lerner's *The Creation of Patriarchy* (1986) and Marija Gimbutas's *The Language of the Goddess* (1989). The problems and hidden agendas of both books are well discussed by Katherine K. Young in "Goddesses, Feminists, and Scholars" (1991).

2. Paintings of Kuan-yin with a moustache can be found in Matsumoto, *Tonkōga no kenkyū,* for instance, plate 216 (a painting dating to 864 C.E.), plate 98b (dating to 943 C.E.), and plate 222 (which dates to 968 C.E.).

3. Peter Gregory used sinification in the title of his 1991 book on Tsung-mi: *Tsung-mi and the Sinification of Buddhism.* Robert Sharf (1991) also used this same expression in the title of his study on a Chinese text: "The *Treasure Store Treatise* (Pao-tsang Lun) and the Sinification of Buddhism in Eighth-Century China."

4. Todd Lewis uses this concept in his study of the cult of Avalokiteśvara (known locally as Karuṇāmāyā) in Newar Buddhism. He defines domestication "as the dialectical process by which a religious tradition is adapted to a region's or ethnic group's socio-economic and cultural life. While 'Great Traditions' supply a clear spiritual direction to followers who are close to the charismatic founders, including norms of orthodox adaptation and missionizing, religious traditions' historical survival is related—often paradoxically—to their being 'multivocalic.' So that later devotees have a large spectrum of doctrines, situational instructions, and exemplary folktales to draw on. The study of 'religious domestication' seeks to demonstrate the underlying reasons for selectivity from the whole as the tradition evolves in specific places and times to the 'logic of the locality'" (Lewis 1993:150).

5. Paul Harrison (1996) calls into question the traditional use of "celestial bodhisattvas" by Snellgrove (1986), who follows the tradition of Har Dayal (1932), Ling

(1976), Bashan (1981), and Robinson and Johnson (1982) in an unpublished article, "Mañjuśrī and the Cult of the Celestial Bodhisattvas," presented at a conference held at University of Texas, Austin, in October 1996. His main objection is that it is ahistorical, for it imposes the later situation on the earlier: what the bodhisattva ideal became is taken to be its original impulse. He also thinks "mahāsattva" is simply an alternative designation or stock epithet for bodhisattva, but not an adjective for a special group of bodhisattvas designated as celestial. He grants that Buddhists believed in the existence of great bodhisattvas and in a continuum or differential scale of spiritual attainments. "But such beliefs reflect purely quantitative distinctions, of degree rather than kind, and not a qualitative distinction between two discrete categories of bodhisattva, the mundane and celestial, between which a clear line can be drawn" (Harrison 1996:11).

6. Chutiwongs regards this discrepancy in dating as a misidentification of the images in some cases. During the early centuries of Buddhist image making, the Buddha was the most favorite subject, and next to him, Maitreya, the Buddha to Come. However, because some sūtra texts, such as the *Amitāyusdhyāna* (Visualization Sūtra, translated into Chinese in 430) describe Avalokiteśvara as carrying a miniature buddha on his crown, Mallmann and other art historians regard this as the defining trait of Avalokiteśvara, and they would identify images without such feature Maitreya or simply "bodhisattva" and came to the conclusion that the presentation of this bodhisattva prior to the fifth century was scarce (Mallmann 1948:119–27). Chutiwongs argues, however, that because rules of image making at the early stage were still being formulated, the miniature buddha on the crown did not appear in the very beginning. Statues of the bodhisattva without the miniature buddha in the Kuṣāṇa period (ca. 1st to 3rd century C.E.) could be Avalokiteśvara based on other attributes. On the other hand, although sūtra texts stipulating such characteristics were composed rather late, this does not necessarily mean that the art also appeared late. The texts might in fact reflect an artistic convention instead of the other way around. She challenges the conventional wisdom, which regards sūtra texts as always the inspiration for art. She suggests provocatively, "It seems equally possible, however, that a visual depiction of this theme actually inspired such a textual description of the Bodhisattva" (Chutiwongs 1984:35–36).

As for the reason for confusing Avalokiteśvara with Maitreya, Chutiwongs suggests that it was because the vase containing the nectar of immortality (amṛta-kalasa) was often misidentified as the ascetic's drinking bottle (kamaṇḍalu or kuṇḍikā). During this early period, iconographical markers that were to distinguish the two had not yet been established and Maitreya and Avalokiteśvara looked very much similar in their hand gestures (mudrā) and attributes. "The Matthurā images identifiable as Maitreya and Avalokiteśvara both display the abhaya-mudrā [fear not] with their right hand, while holding in their left hand a small amṭa-flask. In this style of Indian art the two Bodhisattvas can be distinguished from one another only by the inner quality which pervades their physical form. The austere, ascetic, and aloof Buddha nature of Maitreya is apparent in his snail-curls typical of Buddha images, and in the monastic robe he occasionally wears. The active, omnipotent and imperious personality of Avalokiteśvara is revealed in his regal attire and majestic head-dress. Being Bodhisattvas or saviors of the world in our

Buddha-less age, they offer protection to devotees with their raised right hand, and hold in their left hand the supreme blessing for mankind in the form of a vessel containing the nectar of immortality" (Chutiwongs 1984:23). According to Chutiwongs, early artists of India apparently liked to give this emblem of immortality to images of almost every important deity, regardless of their religious affiliations or functions. For instance, Indra, Śiva, Lokapalas [protectors of the world], and the mythical guardians of the nectar of life known as the Nāgarājas [dragon kings], not to mention the unnamed bodhisattvas as well as Maitreya and Avalokiteśvara (1984:25). But because the ambrosia vase was misidentified as the ascetic's drinking vessel, and because Maitreya was believed to represent the ascetic ideal, images holding such a vase who were actually Avalokiteśvara became misidentified as Maitreya. Chutiwongs thus concludes, "The misinterpretation as to the symbolism of the kalasa on the one hand, and the misconception based on the *idee fixe* that Avalokiteśvara could not be depicted without the miniature Buddha on the other hand, seem to have obscured the obvious probability of the images being representations of the only Bodhisattva whose popularity equaled that of Maitreya in the first centuries A.D. That this turbaned personage occupied an important position in the Buddhist art of this time is evident from the fact that his images as an independent deity are not scarce in the Kuṣāṇa art at Matthurā and in the period which immediately followed. . . . We feel justified to regard these turbaned Bodhisattva figures as images of Avalokiteśvara, who was invariably characterized in the early styles of Indian art by his royal appearance, in contrast to the ascetic personality of Maitreya" (1984:27–28).

7. Paul Harrison questions the authenticity of the translation of the *Sukhāvatīvyūha Sūtra* made by Lokakṣema (Chih Lou-chia-ch'en, arriving in Ch'ang-an ca. 167), which is usually taken to be the first historical evidence for the cult of Avalokiteśvara in India, thus putting the text's dating in doubt. Although scholars believe that the *Mahāvastu* was written as early as 200 B.C.E. or as late as 300 C.E., some think that the *Avalokita Sūtra* contained there might be a later interpolation. Because Avalokiteśvara appears only once in the *Cheng-chü kuang-ming ting-i ching* and appears in different order or not at all in some versions of the *Druma-kinnara-rāja-paripṛcchā-sūtra*, similar suspicion of these being later additions has been raised by Harrison (1996:8). Jan Nattier (1992:166) suggests that the *Heart Sūtra* is a Chinese composition written in the fifth century at the earliest and possibly as late as the seventh century. Finally, Gregory Schopen (1978) suggests that the locus classicus for the cult of Avalokiteśvara, the "Universal Gate" chapter of the *Lotus Sūtra*, was a later addition to the Gilgit text, written when the popularity of Avalokiteśvara was already established. Kern (1965:xxi) also believed that the original *Lotus Sūtra* consisted of only twenty-one chapters, the remaining chapters, including this one, were later additions.

8. Hsüan-tsang described the cult of Avalokiteśvara images in several places of his travel account, *Buddhist Records of the Western World*, translated by Samuel Beal (1884), Vol. 1, pp. 60, 127, 160, 212, and Vol. 2, pp. 103, 116, 172–73. The images of Avalokiteśvara were divine and responsive to prayers: the bodhisattva would "come forth from the image, his body of marvelous beauty, and he gives rest and assurance to the travelers" (Beal 1884, vol. 1:60). He would grant anyone's wish to see him in person: "If anyone

vows to fast till he dies unless he beholds this Bodhisattva, immediately from the image it comes forth glorious in appearance" (vol. 1:160). The image also had ability to prophesize and offer advice.

9. I shall base the discussion mainly on the Huntingtons' *The Art of Ancient India* (1985), which is considered to be the most up-to-date comprehensive study on the subject.

10. Chutiwongs makes the interesting suggestion that Avolokiteśvara as Lotus-in-Hand (Padmapāṇi) could have "started his career for the Buddhists in Gandhāra as an independent deity—a venerable person who, because of his importance in his own right, was assimilated into the triad. And, only from that time onwards, did his personality begin to fuse with that of the typical acolyte figures holding offerings of flowers, and continue to develop in that manner. There is ample evidence of Avalokiteśvara being worshipped in Gandhāra as a significant and independent deity. Judging from the abounding number of his images, his cult was apparently not less important than that of Maitreya" (1984:36).

11. I thank Robert Brown of the University of California at Los Angeles for this reference. He showed this image and discussed its significance in his paper, "Soteriological Androgyny: The Gupta Period Sārnāth Buddha Image and Buddhist Doctrine" at the AAS in Boston, March 13, 1999.

12. This particular form of Avalokiteśvara is called Khasarpaṇa Avalokiteśvara, which already appeared in the fifth century. Huntington describes such an image from Sārnāth dated about 475: He is decked with ornaments, has a smiling face, appears to be sixteen years of age, holds lotus stem in his left hand, while the right hand displays the varada (gift-bestowing) mudrā and displays a miniature buddha on his crown. Two preta figures crouch beneath his right hand. "Avalokiteśvara's compassion for all creatures is demonstrated by the nectar that flows from his gift-bestowing hand to feed these ravenous beings" (Huntington 1985:204).

13. Soper discussed several examples in his long article. For instance, "the relatively simple Indian turban was transformed into a more elaborate and specifically religious headdress by the addition of solar and lunar symbols that seem to have been borrowed from the Sasanian royal crown"(vol. 7, no. 3, 1949:264); "It is on a coin of Kaniṣka that the standing Buddha was first presented with an aureole of light about his whole body, like the sun-god. In India proper even as late as the Ajaṇṭā frescoes the aureole is rare; whereas at Haḍḍa the countless seated Buddhas are shown from the Hadda period on with both the solar aureole and the halo" (vol. 8, nos. 1 and 2, 1950:72).

14. Holt summarizes the contents of the two *Avalokita Sūtras* and reviews the problems of dating made by scholars. While Bhattacharyya claims that they date from the third century B.C.E. (1924:143), other scholars believed that they were later interpolations added to the *Mahāvastu* because one of the texts was cited as a separate work by Śāntideva in the *Śikṣāsamuccaya* (Winternitz 1927, vol. 2:245; Holt 1991:31–33, 229).

15. The thirty-three forms are: (1) Willow-branch, (2) Dragon-head, (3) Sūtra-holding, (4) Circle of Light, (5) Royal Ease, (6) White-robe, (7) Lotus-reclining, (8) Waterfall-gazing, (9) Medicine-giving, (10) Fish-basket, (11) Virtuous King (Brahmā), (12)

Water-moon, (13) One Leaf, (14) Blue-necked, (15) Awe-inspiring (heavenly general), (16) Life-lengthening, (17) Many Jewels, (18) Rock-door, (19) Calm and Serene, (20) Anu, (21) Abhetti, (22) Parnasvari, (23) Vaidūrya, (24) Tārā, (25) Clam, (26) Six Periods, (27) Universal Compassion, (28) Wife of Mr. Ma, (29) Añjali, (30) True Suchness, (31) Nondual, (32) Lotus-holding, and (33) Water-sprinkling (Gotō 1958:170–82). He uses the *Butsuzō-zu-i* (Illustrated Dictionary of Buddhist Images), printed in woodblock during the Edo period, as his source. The iconographic drawings of Kuan-yin from the latter were reprinted by Baiei Hemmi (1960:228–32). According to Louis Frédéric, "The different forms of these 33 Kannons are relatively late, and most of them appeared only after the Kamakura period (1333). Some were often represented, usually in painting, while others failed to inspire any artist" (1995:157–62). Although some individual forms of the group are found in medieval Japanese collections of iconographic drawings such as the *Besson zakki* by Shinkaku (fl. 1117–1180), or the *Kakuzenshō* by Kakuzen (b. 1144), the appearance of all thirty-three as a group was definitely much later. The list contains a mixture of allusions to the *Lotus*, esoteric scriptures, and Chinese indigenous legends about Kuan-yin. It is notable that several of the thirty-three Kuan-yin are described as sitting on a rock. Cornelius Chang discusses these forms in chapter 6 of his 1971 dissertation, "A Study of the Paintings of the Water-moon Kuan-yin." See also Marilyn Leidig Gridley, *Chinese Buddhist Sculpture under the Liao* (1993:100).

16. Clam-dwelling Kuan-yin refers to a historical incident that happened during the reign of Emperor Wen-tsung of the T'ang. The emperor delighted in eating clams, but in the first month of 836, the chef could not open a clam. When prayer was offered to it, it showed the form of Kuan-yin. The emperor asked the Ch'an master Nan-shan Wei-cheng about the significance and was moved to give up clam eating. He also ordered all temples to set up Kuan-yin images (*Fo-tsu t'ung-chi, ch'uan* 41. T 49:384b-c). Fish-basket and Wife of Mr. Ma Kuan-yin also allude to legends about a woman living in the ninth century. I discuss the latter in chapter 10.

17. Personal communication from Lowell Skar, March 12, 1999.

18. Robert Campany cites the definitions for the word "cult" in the *Oxford English Dictionary* and then says, "I here propose to revive the term to designate any or all of the ways—ritual, yes, but also verbal, gestural, graphic, plastic, personal, collective, narrative, poetic, musical, mythological, associative, symbolic, theological, and so forth—in which a person or (more properly) group of people imaginatively *construct* and (thus) *render present* a deity, spirit, or saint" (1993:262–63).

2. Scriptural Sources for the Cult of Kuan-yin

1. Eric Zürcher regards this sūtra as one of a small group of earliest Chinese Buddhist scriptures representing the "popularizing sector." They are "characterized by a considerable number of classical admixtures, a very idiosyncratic terminology, and, above all, the fact that the translators have done their utmost to translate everything into Chinese, even including proper names." He believes that this latter peculiarity suggests "an attempt to cater to the taste of a fairly cultured 'nonprofessional' public" (1991:290).

2. Because of the fame of Lokakṣema, spurious attribution to him is a thorny problem. The oldest and most authoritative catalogue, *A Compilation of Notices on the Translation of the Tripiṭaka* (Ch'u-san-tsang chi-chi), compiled by Seng-yu about 515, does not mention this as being translated by Lokakṣema. Some scholars suggest that this is actually the sūtra with the same title but translated by Dharmarakṣa (fl. 265–313) and that Lokakṣema's translation is lost. In this case, the *Longer Sukhāvatīvyūha Sūtra* (Ta O-mi-t'o ching) made by the Scythian layman Chih-ch'ien (fl.220–252) would be the earliest surviving version of the sūtra. *Bukkyō daijiten* 5:4851b.

3. Modern scholarship has also questioned this attribution. "It now seems more likely that the so-called Sanghavarman translation is at least a reworking by members of the translation workshop of the famous Tang [sic] Dynasty translator Buddhabhadra (359–429 C.E.)" (Gómez 1996:126).

4. One is entitled *Kuang-shih-yin Ta-shih-chih shou-chüeh ching,* translated by Dharmarakṣa around 265, and the other *Kuan-shih-yin shou-chi ching,* by Nieh Tao-chen around 300. Although they are no longer extant, their titles are found in *A Compilation of Notices on the Translation of the Tripiṭaka* compiled by Seng-yu about 515.

5. The other five are *Kuan Hsü-k'ung-tsang P'u-sa ching* (Sūtra on Visualizing the Bodhisattva Ākāśagarbha, T no. 409), *Fo-shuo kuan-Fo san-mei hai ching* (Sūtra on the Sea of Mystic Ecstasy by Visualizing the Buddha, T no. 643), *Fo shuo kuan Mi-lo P'u-sa shang-sheng To-shuai-t'ien ching* (Sūtra of Meditation on Maitreya Bodhisattva's Rebirth on High in the Tuṣita Heaven, T no. 452), *Fo shuo kuan P'u-hsien P'u-sa hsing-fa ching* (Sūtra on the Practice of Visualizing the Bodhisattva Samantabhadra, T no. 277), *Fo shuo kuan Yao-wang Yao-shang erh P'u-sa ching* (Sūtra Spoken by the Buddha on Visualizing the Two Bodhisattvas Bhaiṣajyarāja and Bhaiṣajyasamudgata, T no. 1161) (Pas 1995:42–43).

6. Charles Luk comments on this passage: "By discarding the sound to look into the meditator himself, that is into the nature of hearing, he disengages himself from both organs and sense data and thereby realized his all-embracing Buddha nature which contains all living beings. By developing their pure faith in him and by calling his name, or concentrating on him, they achieve singleness of mind that mingles with his Bodhi substance and become one with him; hence their liberation from sufferings which do not exist in the absolute state" (Lu K'uan Yü [Charles Luk]:1966:139).

7. The distinction between these two bodhisattvas became clear when Maitreya was replaced by Kuan-yin in popularity as a bodhisattva and Maitreya's status as a future buddha became emphasized from the sixth century on. Personal communication from Angela Howard, April 7, 1997.

8. Tsukamoto Zenryū translated a similar version of the story from *Fa-yüan chu-lin* 16 (T53:406a-c). According to Tao-shih (d. 683), the compiler, Tai Yung, and his father Tai K'uei were both celebrated carvers. This particular image of Maitreya was formerly in the Lung-hua Temple in K'uai-chi (in present-day Chekiang) and "the style of the images made by the two Tai was unique throughout the ages, their creations being very numerous and scattered throughout various convents, impossible to record in full" (1985:626–27).

9. Based on inscriptions with the identifications of the images, during the Northern Wei (386–534), there were twenty-nine images of Maitreya, twenty Śākyamuni, sixteen Kuan-yin, and twelve Amitābha. The same trend continued during the Eastern Wei (534–550) with twenty-nine images of Śākyamuni, twenty-one Maitreya, sixteen Kuan-yin, and five Amitābha. But after the Sui, with the establishment of the T'ien-t'ai school and the popularity of Pure Land faith, there was a reversal in regard to the two buddhas, with 280+ of Amitābha but only 40+ of Śākyamuni. However, Kuan-yin and Maitreya still remained comparable with 40+ images each (Matsumoto 1937:9).

10. The earliest extant version of the *Lotus*, however, has far less than thirty-three. The *Cheng fa-hua ching*, gives the following list of seventeen: buddha, bodhisattva, pratyeka-buddha, voice-hearer, King Brahmā, gandharva, ghost and spirit, the rich and the powerful, deva, cakravartin, rakṣa, general, monk, vajrapāni, hermit, ṛṣi, and student (T 9:129b-c). It is noteworthy that no feminine forms are mentioned.

11. I follow Hurvitz (1976: 314) in translating these two terms. Watson (1993) translates them as "the heavenly being Freedom" and "the heavenly being Great Freedom," which do not convey much sense to English-speaking readers. The two names of course refer to the Hindu god Śiva, but neither Hurvitz nor Watson identifies them as such.

12. See Nicole Nicolas-Vandier (1976:vol. 2, pp. 51–103).

13. The fourteen fearless powers are

1. Since I myself do not meditate on sound but on the meditator, I cause all suffering beings to look into the sound of their voices in order to obtain liberation.
2. By returning (discriminative) intellect to its (absolute) source, I cause them to avoid being burned when they find themselves in a great fire.
3. By returning hearing to its source, I cause them to avoid drowning when they are adrift on the sea.
4. By stopping wrong thinking and thereby cleansing their minds of harmfulness, I lead them to safety when they wander in the realm of evil ghosts.
5. By sublimating their (wrong) hearing to restore its absolute condition, thereby purifying all six organs and perfecting their functions, I cause them, when in danger, to be immune from sharp weapons which become blunt and useless like water that cannot be cut and daylight that cannot be blown away, because their (underlying) nature does not change.
6. By perfecting the sublimation of their hearing, its bright light pervades the whole Dharma realm to destroy the darkness (of ignorance) thereby dazzling evil beings such as yakṣa, rakṣa, kuṁbhāṇda, piśācī, pūtana, etc., who cannot see them when meeting them.
7. When hearing is reversed so that sound vanishes completely, all illusory objects of sense disappear so that (practitioners) are freed from fetters that can no longer restrain them.

8. The elimination of sound to perfect hearing results in universal compassion so that they can pass through regions infested with robbers and bandits who cannot plunder them.
9. The sublimation of hearing disengages them from the objects of sense and makes them immune from (attractive) forms, thereby enabling lustful beings to get rid of desires and cravings.
10. The sublimation of sound eliminates all sense data and results in the perfect mingling of each organ with its objects and total eradication of subject and object, thereby enabling all vindictive beings to bury anger and hate.
11. After the elimination of sense data and the return to the bright (Reality), both inner body and mind and outer phenomena become crystal clear and free from all hindrances, so that dull and ignorant unbelievers (icchantika) can get rid of the darkness of ignorance.
12. When their bodies are in harmony with the nature of hearing, they can, from their immutable state of enlightenment (bodhimaṇḍala), re-enter the world (to liberate others) without harming the worldly, and can go anywhere to make offerings to Buddha as countless as dust, serving every Tathāgata in the capacity of a son of the King of Law and having the power to give male heirs with blessed virtues and wisdom to childless people who want boys.
13. The perfection of the six organs unifies their divided functions so that they become all-embracing, thus revealing the Great Mirror (Wisdom) and immaterial Tathāgata womb compatible with all Dharma doors taught by Buddhas as unaccountable as dust. They can bestow upright, blessed, gracious, and respect-inspiring girls on childless parents who want daughters.
14. In this great chiliocosm, which contains a hundred lacs of suns and moons, there are now Bodhisattvas countless as sand grains in sixty-two Ganges Rivers. They practice the Dharma to set a good example to all living beings by befriending, teaching and converting them; in their wisdom their expedient methods differ. Because I used one penetrating organ, which led to my realization through the faculty of hearing, my body and mind embrace the whole Dharma-realm in which I teach all living beings to concentrate their minds on calling my name. The merits that follow are the same as those derived from calling on the names of all these Bodhisattvas. World Honored One, my single name does not differ from those uncountable ones, because of my practice and training which led to my true enlightenment. These are the fourteen fearless (powers) which I bestow upon living beings. (Luk 1966:139–41)

14. Robert Sharf, for instance, writes, "But the classification must be used with caution by Western scholars, as it lies in the service of a sectarian polemic interested in establishing the superiority of the later Tantric transmissions brought to Japan by Kūkai and Saichō. In fact, Japanese scholars, following traditional *mikkyō* exegetics, inter-

weave two distinctions when discussing East Asian esotericism: one between exoteric and esoteric teachings (*kengyō* and *mikkyō*), and a second between pure esotericism and mixed esotericism (*junmitsu* and *zōmitsu*). In either case a formal distinction is made contrasting doctrines taught by the *dharmakāya Buddha* (Vairocana), with those taught by the *nirmāṇakāya* or *sambhogakāya* Buddha (Śākyamuni). Kūkai wields the first distinction—that between exoteric and esoteric—as part of a clearly polemic *p'an-chiao*. His interest lies in (1) demonstrating the superiority of the esoteric over the exoteric. At the same time he wants to show that (2) earlier exoteric materials contain esoteric doctrines that go unrecognized by exoteric monks, and that (3) esoteric Buddhism encompasses all exoteric teachings. The desire to maintain all three claims simultaneously created tensions that led to the later distinction between "pure" and "mixed" tantra (Sharf 1991:213–14). Michel Strickmann also warned us not to follow the artificial distinctions created by the sectarian Japanese scholarship, which privileges only the writings, commentaries, and ritual manuals that appeared in China during the eighth century as "pure" esoteric teaching. These texts center around the two mandalas: the feminine Womb-treasure Maṇḍala and the masculine Vajra Maṇḍala, containing 361 and 91 deities respectively. They are regarded as projections or a series of personifications of the multiple powers of Vairocana, the Cosmic Buddha or Dharmakāya. In contrast, the texts translated or composed prior to these are believed to be revealed by Śākyamuni, the Sambhogakāya or "body of realization," a form inferior to and more limited than Vairocana, for he is located in time and space (Strickmann 1996:128–31).

15. Six dhāraṇīs each are contained in fascicle 5 and 10, one each in fascicles 7, 8, and 9, while twenty-two are found in fascicle 6.

16. Ariane MacDonald (1962:36–37). The Chinese version says: "There are bodhisattva mahāsattvas who, using unfathomable means, transform themselves into women in order to guide all beings with worldly methods. They make their minds firm and unswerving from the Way, enable them to obtain vidya-pada and dhāraṇī. They may transform into various birds, yakṣas, rakṣas, maṇi-jewels, human or nonhuman forms so that they could teach and transform all beings and enable them to enter into the bodhisattva path, to practice the method of vidyarāja and achieve enlightenment" (T 20:838b).

Such a bodhisattva who has this marvelous ability to transform himself is given a list of twelve titles, each of which ends with "tzu-tsai" (master) or Īśvara. Among these we find the title Kuan-tzu-tsai or Avalokiteśvara. The other eleven are P'u-pien tzu-tsai (Sammateśvara), Shih-chien tzu-tsai (Lokeśvara), Miao-kuan tzu-tsai (Sulokiteśvara), Sheng-kuan tzu-tsai (Vilokiteśvara), Hsin tzu-tsai (Vidhvasteśvara), Shan tzu-tsai (Someśvara), Hsü-kung tzu-tsai-tsang (Gagana-ganja), Ti tzu-tsai (Kṣiteśvara), Ta tzu-tsai (Maheśvara), Miao-fa tzu-tsai (Dharmiśvara), and Wu-hsing tzu-tsai (Abhaveśvara) (T 20:838c).

17. These eighty-four phrases are accompanied by pictures of Buddhas, Kuan-yin, and other Buddhist figures or mythological beings in modern copies of the text, which is frequently printed by devotees who would distribute them for free in temples in Taiwan and China. I do not know how early this began in China, but I have seen a copy of

the sūtra written by hand with fine drawings dated to the Sung in the Rare Book Collection of the Taipei Palace Museum. It may already begin in the T'ang. These drawings are aids to help the chanter of the dhāraṇī in carrying out visualization.

18. I follow the Sanskrit names of the mudrās given by Lokesh Chandra (n.d.) who published a translation together with the drawings of a hand-copied text dated 1780, which, according to him, was a copy of a twelfth-century original. With some variations in the sequence, they basically agree with the version of Amoghavajra's translation in the Taishō Tripiṭaka. Both have the *amṛta* (sweet-dew) mudrā for providing cool relief to the hungry and thirsty, which is not found in Bhagavadharma's version. The manuscript provides line drawings of all the mudrās. For the meaning of mudrās and some important mudrās as well as the attributes held in the hands of the bodhisattva, see E. Dale Saunders's *Mudrā: A Study of Symbolic Gestures in Japanese Buddhist Sculpture.*

19. The original wording is "*tang yü,*" meaning "ought to be," which I interpret as the practitioner's assuming the mudrās so named for him or herself. The version by Amoghavajra seems to strengthen this possibility because attached to the drawing of the mudrās there are also corresponding mantras one should recite. It can also mean, however, that the practitioner should visualize the Bodhisattva with the specific mudrā. In this case, the surviving images with the forty hands holding the named implements were perhaps originally created for the purpose of aiding the viewer in visualization so that he or she can learn the mudrās. Since the mudrās are many and quite intricate, it is reasonable to hypothesize that the devotee needed help to become familiar with them. Therefore, manuscripts with drawings such as the one found by Lokesh Chandra in Japan as well as statues and paintings of the bodhisattva served an instructional as well as devotional function. I offer one piece of evidence to back up the hypothesis. The *Fo-tsu t'ung-chi* tells a story about the monk Yu-yen, a native of Lin-hai (in present-day Chekiang) who lived in the Sung. His mother suffered from eye illness. "Facing Kuan-yin, the master visualized the mudrā of the sun. In the same night his mother dreamt of a sun shining in front of her. When she woke up, she recovered from her eye illness." We are not told when this miracle took place, but it was probably around 1100 (T 49:218b). The mudrā he visualized was the number 8 *sūryamuni (jih-chin-mo-ni) mudrā.*

20. Bodhiruci's version differs from this by having Avalokiteśvara say that in the past he saw Vipaśyin appearing in the thousand-eyed and thousand-armed form of the subduer of demons and that he himself now assume the same form (T 20:101c).

21. The twenty-five realms of existence are divided into the fourteen realms of the world of desire (hell, hungry ghost, animal, asura, four continents, and six heavens), seven realms of the world of form (the first dhyāna heaven, the second dhyāna heaven, Mahābrahmā's heaven, the third dhyāna heaven, Abhaśvara (sound of thunder) heaven, the fourth dhyāna heaven, Asañjñisattva (without thought) and four realms of the world of formlessness (heavens of infinity of space, infinity of consciousness, nothingness, and neither perception nor non-perception) (T 20:120b-c). The idea that the twenty-five royal samādhis are connected with the twenty-four modes of existence is found in the *Great Nirvāṇa Sūtra* (Ta-pan nieh-p'an ching, T 12:448b-c). The twenty-five emanated Avalokiteśvara are sent to these twenty-five realms in order to destroy

(*p'o*) them and release beings imprisoned there. They have names that are symbolic of the bodhisattva's powers. They are: subsuming suffering, giving wisdom, providing fulfillment, eliminating war, eliminating ignorance, advancing truth, observing correct view, bestowing fearlessness, bestowing light, giving sweet dew, seeing heaven, bestowing wonder, seeing joy, subduing demons, quiet thought, composing literature, entering meditation, obtaining samādhi, harmonization, seeing emptiness, protecting determination, sageness, purity, correct Dharma, leaving desire, and immovability (T 20:121b).

22. Angela Howard saw and photographed such a grouping in Tzu-chung, Szechwan, dated to about the eighth century, making it the earliest Thousand-armed Avalokiteśvara created in China. Why is it found in Szechwan but not Tun-huang is an intriguing question that requires further examination (Howard, personal communication, May 1997).

23. Yen Chüan-yin suggests that the group of sculptures were created for the benefit of Empress Wu. Originally there were eight reliefs guarding the eight corners of the octagonal base of the tower. The Eleven-headed Avalokiteśvara was chosen to be depicted because of the belief that he could eliminate disasters and bring blessings. Earlier, after the war against the Kitans failed, Empress Wu asked Fa-tsang (643–712) for supernatural assistance. Fa-tsang set up a ritual arena dedicated to the Eleven-headed Avalokiteśvara and soon the Kitans were defeated with the assistance from the Turks. The Empress was greatly delighted and named the year 679 as the first year of "Shen-kung" or Divine Feat (1987:45, 57).

24. I am indebted to Jennifer McIntire for drawing my attention to these early esoteric Avalokiteśvara in Tun-huang.

25. This was most likely connected with the cult of the "Three Great Beings" (Avalokiteśvara, Mañjuśri, and Samanthabhadra) that began about the end of the T'ang. Number 10 of the Ying-pan-p'o group of sculptures at Ta-tsu, Szechwan, dated to the late T'ang, seems to provide the earliest example of this grouping where the thousand-handed and thousand-eyed Kuan-yin stands in the middle flanked by Mañjuśri and Samanthabhadra, whereas the more common grouping there has Vairocana Buddha in the middle instead of Kuan-yin (*Ta-tsu shih-k'e yen-chiu*, 432). Once this cult became popular, it would be necessary to provide Kuan-yin with an animal mount in order to match the animal mounts of the other two bodhisattvas. Similar triads are found in many Chinese temples today.

3. Indigenous Chinese Scriptures and the Cult of Kuan-yin

1. The same princess sponsored the printing of a Taoist scripture glorifying Pi-hsia Yüan-chün in the same year (see Chou Shao-liang 1987:vol. 8, 10–11).

2. They are *Kuan-shih-yin's Dhāraṇī Sūtra of Repentance and Elimination of Sins* (Kuan-shih-yin ch'an-hui ch'u-tsui chou-ching), *Sūtra of the Great Compassionate Kuan-shih-yin* (Ta-pei Kuan-shih-yin ching), *Sūtra of Kuan-shih-yin of Marvelous Responses* (Jui-ying Kuan-shih-yin ching), *Sūtra of Kuan-shih-yin's Ten Great Vows* (Kuan-shih-yin shih ta-yüan ching), *Sūtra of Kuan-shih-yin's Bestowing Jewels When Maitreya*

Comes Down to Earth (Mi-le hsia-sheng Kuan-shih-yin shih chu-pao ching), *Sūtra on Rebirth Recited by Kuan-shih-yin* (Kuan-shih-yin yung t'o-sheng ching), *Sūtra on Kuan-shih-yin Becoming A Buddha* (Kuan-shih-yin ch'eng-fo ching), *Sūtra on Ritual Practice as Stipulated by Kuan-shih-yin* (Kuan-shih-yin suo-shuo hsing-fa ching), *On Kuan-yin Having No Fear* (Kuan-yin wu-wei lun), *Sūtra of Kuan-shih-yin Residing in the Sun* (Jih-tsang Kuan-shih-yin ching), *New Kuan-yin Sūtra* (Hsin Kuan-yin ching), *Sūtra of Visualization on Kuan-shih-yin* (Kuan-shih-yin kuan ching) and *Pure Dhāraṇī Sūtra of Kuan-shih-yin and P'u-hsien* (Ch'ing-ching Kuan-shih-yin P'u-hsien t'o-lo-ni ching). Judging from the titles, these lost indigenous scriptures were most likely based on the translated sūtras containing dhāraṇīs and offering worldly as well as spiritual benefits that we have surveyed in chapter 2.

3. I take "two-seven" to mean fourteen days instead of twenty-seven days as Diana Paul did. Buddhists regard every seven days as one unit. For instance, the Buddhist mortuary rites are carried out at each of the seven "seven days," lasting forty-nine days together. They are called "one-seven," "two-seven," up to "seven-seven."

4. Diana Paul emended the text to read "change" instead of translating *pien-tso* literally into "becoming." She did so because she believed that bodhisattvas could assume only forms of sentient beings rather than of inanimate objects and the statement of Kuan-yin becoming mountains, and so on did not make sense to her. She thus interpreted this passage to mean that Kuan-yin would vow to change useless or hostile inanimate objects into useful and harmonious ones (Paul 1985:280). However, as we read in the *Karaṇḍavyūha Sūtra* discussed in chapter 2, it is precisely this ability to change into whatever he chooses that distinguishes Avalokiteśvara. For he is a world creator and everything in the world is evolved from him.

5. For instance, both themes are found in the following works: Chi-tsang's (549–623) *Fa-hua i-shu* (Commentary on the Meaning of the Lotus Sūtra, T no. 1721), Hui-chiao's (650–714) *Shih-i-mien shen-chou hsin-ching i-shu* (Commentary on the Meaning of the Eleven-headed Divine Dhāraṇī Heart Sūtra, T no. 1802), Chih-li's (960–1028) *Kuan-yin hsüan-i chi* (Notes on the Profound Meaning of the Kuan-yin Chapter, T no. 1728), and *Kuan-wu-liang-shou Fo ching shu miao-tsung ch'ao* (Notes on the Mysterious Meanings from the Commentary on the Meditation on Amitāyus Buddha, T no. 1751), and Chih-yüan's *Ch'ing Kuan-yin ching shu ch'an-i ch'ao* (Elucidations of the Commentary on the Sūtra of Inviting Kuan-yin, T no. 1801) written in 1009. All these important commentarial writings were done by clerics who either had a close relationship with Chih-i or belonged to the T'ien-t'ai tradition, of which Chih-i was assuredly the most influential patriarch.

6. The text identifies the five types of people:

> In the world there are five types of people who are not able to become buddhas. The first are kings of remote regions, who always feel anger and succumb to their vices, who subjugate their enemies accompanied by their [military] commanders, whose countries fight each other and kill each other and who think evil day and night and desire to cheat each other. For this reason they are con-

> stantly reborn in a place of difficulties. The second are *caṇḍāla* (outcasts), who always think in their minds of eating human blood, and who roam around a graveyard looking for corpses and have no time to rest. The third are *bhikṣus* and *bhikṣunīs* who have violated the precepts. According to the Buddhist Dharma they are thieves who violate the precepts. They hold jealousy in their minds, bring false charges against other people, wildly bear the right and the wrong, claim that their reputation is good, speak evil of others, are not happy to see wholesomeness, do not speak evil of themselves, and do not think for even a single instant of having a guilty conscience. The fourth are lustful people, who, regardless of intimacy or remoteness, monks or laity, and noble or humble, think of lust day and night, who have no time to cease [desiring], and who do not have even a single thought of numerous wholesome dharmas. The fifth are those who quit the priesthood, who destroy the Buddhist Dharma, who tell people in the world that the Buddha is not a sage, the Buddha has no supernatural power, and that the Buddha is not able to bring people across, and who, because of slandering [the Buddha], fall into evil paths, wander around all evil destinies, and always experience sufferings and distress. If [even among these five types of people] there are those who are able to hold fast to the *Avalokiteśvarasamādhi-sūtra* and amend [their conduct] in the past, cultivate good seeds for the future, hold fast to this sūtra, recite it for seven days and seven nights and understand it thoroughly, then all [their] sins will be extinguished and [they will attain] rewards, as [explained] previously. Furthermore, if they are able to cultivate the path throughout their lives and to recite this sūtra, they will never give up and forget [the teaching of this sūtra] just as they have not. Even if a person forgets it, I will teach it to this person in his dream, and will also cause him to restore it. (Ziegler 1994:121–23)

7. Sylvia Chen-Shangraw, the writer for this entry in the catalogue, *Chinese, Korean, and Japanese Sculpture in the Avery Brundage Collection* (d'Argence and Turner 1974) expresses reserve concerning the date of the stele by saying that it was in the style of Northern Ch'i, but "perhaps executed later." Her main arguments for doubting the early date are that "No standing bejeweled Kuan-yin appears as a central altar or stele group figure in Eastern or Western Wei" and because a Philadelphia stele dated 551 with the same lotus capitals and dragon arch found in the stele bears an 1562 inscription. She thus suggests that this could be either a Ming recarving or reproduction (d'Argence and Turner 1974:146). In view of the dated 548 Szechwan plaque mentioned in chapter 2, I feel that the treatment of Kuan-yin as a central icon, as the case here, could have been practiced in the Northern Ch'i as well.

8. In *Li-tai san-pao chi* compiled in the Sui, under the sūtras translated by Chu Fahu, it is recorded as "*Kuan-shih-yin ching*, one volume: derived from *Cheng fa-hua ching*" (T 49:64c). The T'ien-t'ai master Chih-i (538–597) wrote in his *Kuan-yin hsüan-i*, "Kuan-yin sūtras are many. For instance, there are: *Ch'ing Kuan-shih-yin*, *Kuan-yin shou chi*, *Kuan-yin san-mei*, *Kuan-yin ch'an-hui*, *Ta-pei hsiung-meng Kuan-shih-yin*, etc.

What is being transmitted today is the one chapter consisting 1530 words from the *Lotus Sūtra*. The reason why it became transmitted separately was because of Dharma Master T'an-mo-lo-ch'en [Dharmarakṣa] who was also known as I-po-le Bodhisattva. When he traveled in the Onion Range (the Belaturgh Mountains in Turkestan), he came to Ho-hsi (present-day Kansu). At that time the king of Ho-hsi, Chü-ch'ü Meng-hsün believed in Buddhism and was sick. When he told the master his sickness, the master told him that because Kuan-shih-yin had a special affinity with this land the king should chant it [the name or the sūtra?]. The king soon recovered from the sickness and from this the chapter was transmitted separately" (T 34:891c). It is striking that aside from the *Ch'ing Kuan-yin ching* (the complete title is *Ch'ing Kuan-shih-yin P'u-sa hsiao-fu tu-hai t'o-lo-ni ching* T 1043), translated by Chu-nan-t'i in the Eastern Chin (317–420), all the other scriptures mentioned by Chih-i above were *wei-ching* (Kiriya 1990:20).

9. The last four phrases are similar to some found in a Tun-huang sūtra known as *Chiu-k'u Kuan-shih-yin ching* (S 4456), which is also known as a variant name for *Kao Wang Kuan-shih-yin ching*. It contains the following phrases: "I chant (or think) Kuan-shih-yin in the morning, I chant Kuan-shih-yin in the evening, I chant Kuan-shih-yin while sitting, I chant Kuan-shih-yin while walking, each chanting (or thought) gives rise to another chanting, Buddha-invocation does not depart from the mind." Makita suggested late T'ang or the eighth century as the date this sūtra was composed in *Gikyō kenkyū* (1976:69). The so-called "Kuan-yin Sūtra in Ten Phrases" seems to consist of parts from both *Kao Wang Kuan-shih-yin ching* and *Chiu-k'u Kuan-shih-yin ching*. Kiriya made a careful comparison between the "Kuan-yin Sūtra in Ten Phrases" and existing five recensions of the *Kao Wang Kuan-shih-yin ching* (1990:15–16).

10. P 3916 contains the entire three fascicles, whereas P 3236 contains only part of fascicle 3. The scripture was also carved onto stele in 1143 at Fang-shan. See *Fang-shan shih-ching t'i-chi hui-pien* (1987:617). I thank Kuo Li-ying for sharing this information with me.

11. Copies of the scriptures are found among the twenty hand-copied miscellaneous manuscripts and published as numbers 64 and 65 in *Ying-hsien mu-t'a Liao-tai mi-tsang* (Secret Treasures of the Liao Dynasty Hidden Inside the Wooden Pagoda of Ying county), edited by the Shansi Bureau of Cultural Artifacts and Chinese Historical Museum (1991). Number 64 (pp. 457–459) is in much better shape than 65. Among the thirty-five wood-block printed sūtras found within the Buddha image, there is also a copy of *King Kao's Kuan-shih-yin sūtra*, which bears a postscript saying that the wife of a man by the name of Jen Wei-sheng, née Chou, of Yung-chi-yüan (present-day Tsun-hua, Hopei) had 1,000 copies made and distributed for free (p. 200). All the sūtras were printed in Yen-ching (present-day Beijing) between 990 and 1070 C.E.

12. I take the *hsin* here to mean *hrdaya-dhāraṇī*, meaning the essence of the dhāraṇī. Here I follow the explanation of *hsin* as given by Fukui Fumimasa (1987:213). The reference of five wisdom mudrās derives from Yogācāra and indicates the mystical power of the Buddha symbolized by his *uṣṇīṣa*. I am indebted to Masatoshi Nagatomi for the references.

13. This phenomenon is apparently caused by the membranes staying intact instead

of rupturing when the baby is delivered. I thank Charles B. Jones for consulting his mother, Dr. Mary B. Jones, concerning this and for his sending me the following reference from *Williams Obstetrics* (16th edition): "Spontaneous rupture of the membranes most often occurs sometime during the course of active labor. Typically, rupture of the membranes is manifested by a sudden gush of a variable quantity of normally clear or slightly turbid, nearly colorless fluid. Infrequently, the membranes remain intact until the time of delivery of the infant. If by chance the membranes remain intact until completion of delivery, the fetus is born surrounded by them, and the portion covering his head is sometimes referred to as the *caul*" (386b).

14. I thank Martin Collcutt and Christine Guth, who first brought this painting to my attention.

15. Chou Shao-liang explains the reason why this particular number is called a *tsang* or collection. This is because the *K'ai-yüan shih-chiao lu* (Record of Śākyamuni's Teachings, Compiled during the K'ai-yüan Era), by far the most influential catalogue compiled by Chih-sheng in 730, contains this number of sūtra titles (Chou 1985:37).

16. The surviving copy of the Buddhist sūtra is in the private collection of Chou Shao-liang. The Taoist sūtra whose full title is *T'ai-shang Lao-chün shuo Tzu-tsai T'ien-hsien Chiu-lien Chih-sheng ying-hua tu-shih chen-ching* (The True Scripture of the Heavenly Immortal of Perfect Freedom, Nine-lotus Supreme Sage's Responding to Transformations and Saving the World as Spoken by the Very High Old Lord), is kept in the Rare Book section of the Library of Buddhist Artifacts at Fa-yüan Ssu, Beijing.

17. Recently, Lien Li-ch'ang suggests the text was written in the year 1498 based on internal evidence (1996:116).

4. Miracle Tales and the Domestication of Kuan-yin

1. Chih-i used the water and moon metaphor in the *Mysterious Meaning of Kuan-yin* (Kuan-yin hsüan-i, T no. 1726) in a different sense. He compared the interpretations of "Kuan-shih-yin" from the four perspectives of the *Pitaka* teaching (*tsang-chiao*), common teaching (*t'ung-chiao*), separate teaching (*p'ieh-chiao*), and perfect teaching (*yüan-chiao*). He said, "The perfect teaching correctly illuminates the middle way and stays away from the two extremes. It teaches neither emptiness nor temporariness, neither the inner nor the outer. It views the sentient beings of the ten Dharma Realms as reflections in the mirror, *moon in the water*, neither inside nor outside [the mind]. They cannot be said to exist, nor can they be said not to exist. They are not ultimately real, yet the threefold truth is perfectly contained therein. Neither prior nor posterior, they are found in the One Mind" (T 34:886b, italics mine).

2. Chih-i (538–597) mentions both the collection by Hsieh Fu and that of Lu Kao by name in his *Kuan-yin i-shu* (Commentary on the Kuan-yin Chapter; T 34:923c). He then retells a number of stories from Hsieh Fu's collection as reconstructed by Fu Liang, starting with that of Chu Ch'ang-shu's house being saved from fire as a result of his calling on Kuan-yin. Chi-tsang (549–623) also mentions the collection by Hsieh in his *Fa-hua i-shu* (Commentary on the Lotus Sūtra; T 34:626b) (Makita 1970:7). T'ang Lin, the

seventh-century author of *Ming-pao chi* (Records of miraculous retribution) also refers to these collections by name in his preface (Gjertson 1989:156).

3. As pointed out by Makita, although the idea of the bodisattva's power to save people from difficulties is found in the sūtra, the exact words of this sentence, however, are not found in Dharmarakṣa's translation of the *Lotus Sūtra* (*Cheng fa-hua ching*, T 9:128c). So Fu Liang, the compiler, was taking some liberty here in his eagerness to lend the story with some scriptural justification (Makita 1970:79).

4. Campany translated this story as well as numbers 4 and 7 and numbered them Tale 10, Tale 15, and Tale 8 respectively in his "The Earliest Tales of Bodhisattva Guanshiyin," which is chapter 5 of *Religions of China in Practice*. I consulted his translations in making mine, which differ from his in some places.

5. Another source, the *Precious Mirror of the Lotus School* (Lien-tsung pao-chien, T no. 1973) compiled by P'u-tu in 1305, refers to the bodhisattva specifically as the "White-robed Kuan-yin." By the tenth century, Kuan-yin began to appear in this form, which gradually became feminized and increasingly popular.

6. Jan Min was himself Chinese. He was the son of Jan Chan, the adopted son of Shih Hu, the third emperor of the Latter Chao. After Shih Hu died, Jan Min rebelled against Shih Hu's son, the new emperor, and killed him in 350. He assumed the throne himself and renamed the dynasty the great Wei. Following the advice of a Taoist, he killed all the non-Chinese in the country. This story was an eyewitness account of the massive killing carried out in the capital Yeh (*Chin shu* 107; Makita 1970:81).

7. Stanley Weinsten pointed out that one of the underlying causes for Emperor Wu-tsung's persecution against Buddhism starting in 842 was the fear instilled in him by an obscure apocryphal work called the *K'ung-tzu shu* (Discourses of Confucius), which predicted that after eighteen generations an emperor "in black robes" would take over the country. He, like the populace in general, associated black robes with the Buddhist clergy (Weinstein 1987:125). The emperor was a firm believer in Taoist art of immortality. In the same year, when the seven Taoist priests failed to become immortals after ingesting the elixir on the Terrace for Viewing the Immortals, their explanation to Wu-tsung was "as long as Buddhism continued to be practiced alongside Taoism, the color black, which was associated with Buddhism, would predominate, thus obstructing the path to immortality, presumably by overwhelming the weaker color of yellow which signified the Taoist religion in popular mind" (Weinstein 1987:129). In the *Tao-chiao ling-yen chi* (Efficacious Manifestations in Taoism), a collection of miracle tales compiled by Tu Kuang-t'ing (850–933), "yellow-clad persons" sometimes appeared in visions and dreams just as the Buddhist "white-clad person" did. See, for example, the story in *Cheng-t'ung Tao-tsang* (Taipei: I-wen 1976 reprint edition). Vol. 38, p. 30352.

8. This is not my conjecture, but can be proved by checking the version of the same story as recorded by Wang Yen in the sixth century—*Signs from the Unseen Realm* (Ming-hsiang chi). After Pan is said to see the "true form" of the bodhisattva, the text adds, "just like the popular images seen at present time" (Lu Hsün 1973:599).

9. Sometimes "the person in white" is not explicitly identified as Kuan-yin. But the

implication is so obvious that this is not necessary. I take this as indirect, yet convincing, evidence that Kuan-yin was perceived in this fashion from the fifth century on. Tao-hsüan, for instance, tells this story about a white-clad person saving images, included under the section on miraculous images in his *Chi shen-chou san-pao kan-t'ung lu*: During the K'ai-huang era (581–600) of the Sui, the main Buddha hall of the Hsing-huang Temple in Chiang-chou (in present-day Honan) was burned down. Inside there were statues of the Buddha and two bodhisattvas. They were made from the molds created by Tai Yung, the son of the celebrated artisan Tai K'uei (d. 396). The statues were large, all measuring sixteen *ch'ih*. Although they suffered from the fire, the bodies measuring about five to six *ch'ih* survived and the golden color remained intact. They were moved to the White Horse Temple. In 651 a thief tried to steal the copper by chiseling away the surfaces of the images. He was about to climb out of the window when he was seized by the wrist and could not move. The next morning he was caught by the monks who asked him why he was there. He answered that because a person in white who was inside the room seized his arms, he could not escape (T 52:421a).

10. Wei-cheng was a native of Ping-yüan (in present-day Shansi) and lived in retirement on Mt. Chung-nan in his later years during the reign of Emperor Wu-tsung (840–846), because he foresaw the pending persecution. After he died, forty-nine relics were discovered and a stūpa was constructed to house them. He belonged to the lineage of the Ch'an master P'u-chi (d. 739), who received the transmission from Shen-hsiu (600–706), leader of the Northern Ch'an School (*Shih-shih chi-ku-lüeh;* T49:836c).

11. Emperor Hsiao-tsung (r. 1163–88) had already praised Kuan-yin with the same title. See *Hang-chou Shang-t'ien-chu chih* 1980:33.

12. In the postscript to the collection, there is a brief history about its previous two printings in which two monks were involved. The writer of the postscript is identified only as "Society for the Promotion of Buddhism." It says that in 1911 monk Tsan-chi of Chen-yü Temple in Jen-an, Chekiang, discovered the collection (not compiled). He received donations to have it printed. But because he could not print enough copies, not many people got to read it. Later, Master Hua-chih of the Chieh-chu Temple in Shao-hsing, Chekiang, chanced upon it and, impressed by its broad coverage, decided to have it reissued and carried out a major campaign for funds. So two monks were involved in promoting the work. A third monk, Master Yin-kuang (1861–1940), was identified as the person who verified its contents. Although it received much promotion from monks, the compiler might still be a lay person. Monk authors, in general, do not remain anonymous. The contents of the collection, as I indicate in the text, also seem to reflect more lay concerns.

5. Divine Monks and the Domestication of Kuan-yin

1. For instance, the Ming writer Chou Hui in his *Chin-ling so-shih* (Trivia of Chin-ling [Nanking]) provided a solution to the riddle why Pao-chih carried scissors, a ruler, and a fan. They were intended as symbols for the three successive dynasties: the scissors, which cut things into a uniform height (*ch'i*), stand for the Ch'i dynasty; the ruler,

which measures (*liang*), stands for the Liang dynasty; the fan, which fans away dust (*ch'en*), stands for the Ch'en dynasty. In the Ming, the symbolism of the mirror acquired new significance, for it indicates brightness (*ming*), the same sound as the name of the dynasty. The fact that Pao-chih had the same surname (Chu) as that of the dynasty's founder was of course also seized with enthusiasm (Makita 1984:84).

2. I do not mean obvious examples such as the Cloth-bagged Monk or Crazy Chi mentioned before. I suspect that there might be many less celebrated cases buried in the biographies and chronicles. I have in mind, for example, the brief entry in the *Fo-tsu t'ung-chi*, under the year 1005, of this eccentric figure: Monk Chih-meng was a native of Mao-chou (in present-day Chekiang) and his secular surname was Hsü. He always wore clothes made of brocade and loved to eat pig's head. Whatever he said about people's fortunes, be they good or bad, always came true. He addressed others as "brothers of my wife" (*hsiao-chiu*) and referred to himself as "Brother-in-law Hsü" (*Hsü chieh-fu*). One day he expired while sitting in meditation in Chi-hsiang Ssu of San-ch'ü (in present-day Ch'ü-chou, Chekiang). His last words were that he was the Buddha of Samādhi Light (Ting-kuang Fo). People enshrined his mummified body and prayed to it. Miracles occurred without ceasing. He was called by the people, "Pig-head Monk" (Chu-t'ou Ho-shang, T 50:403a).

3. See vol. 12 of "Sculptures" in *Chung-kuo mei-shu ch'üan-chi*, pl.138, p. 140.

4. The poem is found in his collected poems, *Li T'ai-pai ch'üan-chi* (fascicle 1), compiled with notes by Wang Chi in the Ch'ing (1977:406). However, Chiang Chih-ch'i, the official who wrote the stele setting forth the life of Princess Miao-shan to be discussed in chapter 8 also wrote a biography of Seng-chieh in which he cast doubt on Li Po's being the author of this poem. He cites the "commonness and vulgarity" of the language, and blames the uncritical attitude of compilers for always including it in the poet's collected poems simply because tradition had it so. His stronger evidence, however, is that since Li was born in 702, he was only nine *sui* old when Seng-chieh died in 710. Although Li Po was reputed to be a genius, he doubted that they could have been able to discuss about the "three carts" together. Chiang's biography of Seng-chieh is contained in the *Kuang-chuan shu-pa* (fascicle 10) written by the Sung writer, Tung Chi-ung (*Li T'ai-pai ch'üan chi* 1977, vol. I:408).

5. Kuo Jo-hsü in his *T'u-shu chien-wen chi* (fascicle 2), for instance, records that the painter Hsin Ch'eng who lived in the end of the T'ang painted the image of Seng-chieh in the Ssu-chou Hall of the Ta-pei (Great Compassion) Temple in Ch'eng-tu, Szechwan. Chang Yen-yüan in his *Li-tai ming-hua chi* (fascicle 3), on the other hand, mentions Wu Tao-tzu's paintings decorating the outer walls of the Seng-chieh Hall in the Kan-lu (Sweet Dew) Temple in the western part of Chekiang. In 845 when all the temples in the land were ordered for destruction, only the Kan-lu Temple was spared (Hsü 1995:4).

6. See Vol. 12 of "Sculptures" in *Chung-kuo mei-shu ch'üan-chi*, plate 147, p. 149.

7. They are: a wooden statue in the stūpa of the Jui-kuang Temple in Soochow, built in 1013–1017, a bronze image in the Hsing-chiao Temple in Shanghai, built in 1068–1093, an image made of brick in the Pai-hsiang Pagoda in Wen-chou, Chekiang, built in 1115, a stone image in the T'ien-feng Pagoda in Ningpo, built in 1144, and several gilt bronze

as well as stone images inside the base of the Wan-fo Pagoda in Chin-hua, Chekiang, built in 1062 (Hsü 1995:6–7).

8. As Makita points out, this myth was most likely a reflection of the conflict between Buddhists and Taoists at that time. In 1119, under the influence of Lin Ling-su, Emperor Hui-tsung carried out anti-Buddhist policies by calling the Buddha "Golden Immortal of Great Enlightenment" (Ta-chüeh Chin-hsien), bodhisattvas "Great Being Immortals" (Hsien-jen Ta-shih), and monks "Virtuous Gentleman" (Ta-shih). He called himself "Emperor Teaching Master and Sovereign of the Way" (Chiao-chu Tao-chün Huang-ti). In 1117, the year before the first flooding of the Huai, Lin Ling-su was permitted to have a Taoist temple called "Palace of Divine Empyrean" established in every prefecture. If there was no land to build a new one, then the Taoists could confiscate existing Buddhist temples. The P'u-kuang-wang Temple was seized and turned into a Taoist temple. Hung Mai tells the story of someone named Chao. Inspired by the new zeal, he demolished the huge image of P'u-kuang-wang Buddha standing over a hundred *ch'ih*. Everyone who witnessed it was sad beyond words. Within ten days, his hands began to break out in festers. Gradually his whole body started to break out and he died howling before a hundred days were up (*I-chien chih* 3:1369–1370, quoted by Makita 1984:51). The myth then of how Seng-chieh saved the palace from being flooded two years later could be read as a well placed attack against Lin Ling-su.

9. The water is called "weak" because it cannot support any boat and thus non-navigable. This is either because it is too shallow or the quality of the water is different from that of the ordinary water. The land of the immortals in Taoist lore is often described as being protected by such impassable bodies of water from the profane.

6. Indigenous Iconographies and the Domestication of Kuan-yin

1. I changed Waley's translation in three places: Kuan-yin instead of "Avalokiteśvara," Pure Land (*ching-tu*) instead of "Paradise," and Paradise instead of "Heavenly Hall" (*t'ien-t'ang*).

2. In describing what the natives of Hangchow did in a typical year, the compiler lists their activities in each month. Under the sixth month, he says, "On the sixteenth day the Great Compassionate Kuan-shih-yin Who Saves [One] from Suffering of Mt. P'u-t'o appears. On the seventeenth day the Twelve-headed Kuan-yin of the Ten Oceans in the West (Hsi Shih-yang Hai) appears. On the nineteenth day the White-robed Kuan-yin Who Fulfills Our Wishes (Pai-i Man-yüan), the Occupier of the Pure Throne (Ch'ing-ching Tso-chu) appears. The custom in Hangchow is that women would keep a vegetarian fast for the entire month that is called 'Kuan-yin *chai*.' Sometimes the entire family would keep the fast. On the nineteenth day, they burn incense and worship Kuan-yin. Every family does this. Great officials would offer incense at T'ien-chu. People from neighboring counties would also come to T'ien-chu as pilgrims. This is like what happens in the second month, only slightly reduced in scale."

3. At the end of Pelliot 2055, there is a list of ten titles of scriptures that Chai Feng-ta had copied for the benefit of his wife on each of the 7th day during the forty-nine days, the 100th day, the first anniversary, and the third anniversary of her death (*Tun-*

huang pao-tsang 113:287). Shih Ping-ting mentioned this text in her article, but she did not read the text. Following her reference, I located the text in August 1987 and copied it. It is contained in no. 4532 of Ancient Handwritten Manuscripts held in the Tientsin Art Museum. Despite the name, it does not give any description of the bodhisattva. There is nothing in the text that provides a justification for the iconography of Water-moon Kuan-yin.

4. Liu Ch'ang-chiu states that there are thirty-two frescoes depicting the Water-moon Kuan-yin dated to the Five Dynasties, Sung, and Hsi-hsia in the Mo-kao and Yü-lin Caves in Tun-huang, and other locations in northern Kansu. This does not include the statues of the Water-moon Kuan-yin carved in Szechwan (1995:42).

5. For the various lists of the ten metaphors, see Mochizuki 3:2215b-c.

6. In regard to this relief, I am indebted to Angela Howard, who alerted me to its existence.

7. The boy might be Sudhana instead of the reborn donor. Wang Hui-min interprets a similar boy depicted in number 2 of the Yü-lin Cave. He is similarly riding on the cloud and worships the Water-moon Kuan-yin with folded hands (Wang 1987:35). In view of the fact that this boy is fully clothed and is quite grown if not a teenager, whereas all the other boys in the "Greeting the Soul of the Righteous Man on the Way to the Pure Land of Amitābha" paintings Rudova cited are naked newborns, it is more likely that the boy is Sudhana.

8. Four paintings concentrate on this same theme, which clearly was very popular in Hsi-hsia during that time. See *Lost Empire of the Silk Road* #39, #40, #41, #42 (192–189).

9. See vol. 2 of "Paintings" in *Chung-huo mei-shu ch'üan-chi*, pl. 73 on p. 115.

10. He has two main points of argument. First, White-robed Kuan-yin was first mentioned in a Tantric dhāraṇī sūtra translated in the sixth century (T no. 1336) rather than in the eighth-century texts mentioned by Maspero. Thus this figure was introduced earlier, and not from Tibet, as was the case with White Tārā. As in all Tantric texts that are intended for visualization, the appearance of the deity is clearly described in the sixth-century text. The figure, whose gender is not specified, wears white garments and sits on a lotus, with one hand holding a lotus, and the other grasping a vase. The hair is combed upward. Stein's second, and more important, argument is that in the Tantric scriptures translated in the T'ang dealing with the "mothers" or female counterparts of buddhas (*fo-mu*), Pai-i is mentioned together with Tārā, but is distinct from the latter. She is the mother of the lotus clan who is headed by Avalokiteśvara. She is called White Residence (Pai-chu) because she lives in a white, pure lotus. Pai-i should also be distinguished from the White-bodied One (Pai-shen) who, together with Tārā and others, surrounds Amoghapāśa Avalokiteśvara sitting on Mount Potalaka. In some texts, Pai-i is described as sitting on a lotus, but holding a lasso in her lowered left hand and the *Prajñāpāramitā Sūtra* in her raised right hand, which is very different from the earlier meditating Pai-i holding a lotus and a vase. To make matters even more complicated, in the Womb Matrix (or Treasury) Maṇḍala, three deities—White Residence, White Body, and Great Bright White Body (Ta-ming Pai-shen)—who are located in the court of Kuan-yin, are all clad in white and thus can all be called Pai-i. White is the symbol for the mind of enlighten-

ment, which gives birth to all buddhas and bodhisattvas. That is why the female deities of the lotus clan who are housed in the court of Kuan-yin are mostly white in color, for they are the mothers of buddhas and bodhisattvas (Stein 1986:27–37).

11. This painting was dated to 1211 and is held at the Palace Museum in Beijing. It was reproduced as plate 59 in *Chung-kuo Mei-shu ch'üan-chi: Hui-hua P'ien*. Vol. 4. Beijing: Wen-wu, 1988.

12. Other examples of Pai-i Kuan-yin, all later, are no. 118 niche (dated 1116) and no. 136 niche (dated 1142–46) of Pei-shan. (*Ta-tsu shih-k'e yen-chiu* 174, 395–96, 408). Buddhist sculptures in Szechwan provide very important information on iconographical styles. Because of the good condition of preservation of the many inscriptions, they also serve as excellent sources for our understanding the cultic and devotional aspects of Szechwan Buddhism.

13. The text contains these five mantra-like phrases: Gods in heaven, gods on earth, people depart from disasters, disasters depart from the body, all disasters are reduced to dust (*t'ien lo shen, ti lo shen, jen li nan, nan li shen, i-chieh tsai-yang hua wei ch'en*). The compiler of *Kuan-yin ling-i chi* says, "I once read Wang Kung's (fl. 1048–1104) *Wen-chien chin lu* (Record of Things Heard and Seen Recently), which records this story: 'Chu Tao-Ch'eng's wife, née Wang, daily chanted the 'Heart Spell of Kuan-yin in Ten Sentences' (*Shih-chü Kuan-yin hsin chou* [a variant title for the *Kuan-yin shih-chü ching*]. When she was forty-nine she became very sick. In semi-consciousness, she saw a person in green, who told her that there were nineteen words missing from the sūtra she chanted, and if she added these words she could live long. She then told Wang the five phrases. Wang woke up and recovered from her illness. She lived to be seventy-nine years old. From this episode, we know that these five phrases were already known to people who lived in the Northern Sung,'" p. 14b.

14. The origin of the text has always been traced to a dream, which is the reason why it is also called "Sūtra Transmitted in a Dream." According to the *Fo-tsu t'ung-chi* (ca. 1260), the wife of Lung Hsüeh-mei lost her eyesight during the Chia-yu era (1056–1063) of the Northern Sung. She was advised to go to the Upper T'ien-chu Monastery [in Hangchow] to pray. One evening she dreamt of a person in white (*pai-i jen*) who taught her how to chant the "Kuan-yin Sūtra in Ten Phrases." She did this conscientiously and her two eyes regained their sight. According to *T'ai-ping kuang-chi*, quoted in *Cha-hsiang shih ts'ung ch'ao* (*chüan* 13), Wang Yüan-mo of T'ai-yüan (of T'ang?) disobeyed order when he was on a campaign to the north. He was sentenced to die by military law. He dreamt of a person who told him that if he could chant the "Kuan-yin Sūtra" a thousand times, he would be saved. The person then taught Wang this ten phrases. When Wang was about to be beheaded, the knife suddenly broke into three pieces (*Kuan-shih-yin P'u-sa ling-i chi*, p. 14b–15a).

15. "G. and M. Vovelle, who have catalogued the altars dedicated to the souls in purgatory for Provence as a whole, have outlined the following evolution: between 1650 and 1730, the Virgin as a mediatrix was replaced by the Virgin with the Child, and the intercessors tended to disappear; after 1730 the theme of the Madonna and Child receded, while images of Christ and the eternal Father became more prevalent. From my vantage

point of the very early eighteenth century, I can confirm these changes" (Froeschle-Chopard 1976:167).

16. These are: Miao-ch'ing (1265), Miao-ling (1274), Miao-chen (1342), Miao-an, Miao-kuang (1452), Miao-yü (1436), Miao-yüan (1441), Miao-kuei (1455), Miao-hui (1445), Miao-hui, and Miao-shan (1444), Miao-ching (1457), Miao-lien (1418), Miao-cheng, Ming-hai, Miao-tsung, and Miao-jung (all in the Ming).

7. The Ritual of Great Compassion Repentance and the Domestication of the Thousand-handed and Thousand-eyed Kuan-yin in the Sung

1. The Vinaya master Tu-t'i (1600–1679) simplified Chih-li's text by abolishing the original division of the ritual into ten parts and deleting large portions of the original text. He also gave it a new name, "Great Compassion Repentance" ("Ta-pei ch'an-fa"), which it is called today. Later, another monk by the name of Chi-hsien had both texts printed together in 1795. Then, in 1819, after consulting several available simplified versions that had been in use since the Yüan (1280–1368), he published a new version, which is the one in use today (Reis-Habito 1993:321–22; Kamata 1973:284; Getz 1994:186, note 76). This is why the names of Chih-li, Tu-t'i and Chi-hsien are listed as authors in the present version of the text found in HTC, vol. 129.

2. Although Tsun-shih's repentance ritual based on the *Ch'ing Kuan-yin ching* has not survived in China, its fortune in Japan is the opposite. According to Maria Reis-Habito, the Kannon Zembō (Penitential Rite of Kuan-yin) is not based on Chih-li's manual, but rather that created by Tsun-shih. Not only the Great Compassion Dhāraṇī, but the dhāraṇīs of the "six character phrases" contained in the *Ch'ing Kuan-yin ching* are recited (Reis-Habito 1993:331).

3. Reis-Habito cites the chanting of the Great Compassion Dhāraṇī in death and memorial rites for monks and abbots as stipulated in Te-hui's *Pure Rules of Pai-chang Compiled under Imperial Sponsorship* in 1338. She also used the autobiographical account of Hung-tsan (1610–80) who compiled a collection of miracle stories about Kuan-yin entitled *Kuan-yin tz'u-lin chi* to underscore the themes of ancestor worship and filial piety as strong motivating forces in the performance of the repentance ritual. The account she summarizes appears as a postscript to his work. "Hongzan [Hung-tsan] begins his account with the death of his parents who died when he was twenty-nine years old. As a matter of filial duty towards his parents he tried different methods to help their lot in the other world: renunciation of meat, fish, and vegetables with a strong smell, as well as pious reading of scriptures during the three-year mourning period. Dissatisfied with these efforts, he decided to become a hermit in the wilderness and to carry out daily religious duties 'in order to profit the spirits of the ancestors in hell.' During the Yulanben festival for deceased souls he made all the necessary offerings, but still felt restless and ashamed about his weak efforts. Finally Hongzan invited an artist to paint an image of the thousand-armed Guanyin and ordered a group of monks to perform the repentance ritual for twenty-one days. At the end of that period the following happened: I suddenly noticed that the body of Guanyin emitted a golden light. The red and the blue lotus flower in his hands emitted a white light. Some of the

monks and laypeople present also saw this and testified to this unusual appearance. At the bottom of my heart I felt happy and comforted. I trusted firmly that the compassionate power of Guanyin would save the souls of my ancestors in the other world. We all performed the ritual in front of the statue. The white light continued to flow from it. Everybody who saw it was happy and developed pure faith. According to the *Nilankantha-sūtra* [*Ch'ien-shou ching*], the function of the blue lotus flower is 'for rebirth in the Pure Land.' and the red lotus flower is 'for coming together with all the Buddhas of the ten directions'" (Reis-Habito 1991:49).

4. Around the same time when Bhagavadharma translated the *Ch'ien-shou ching*, Yü-ch'ih I-seng painted an image of "Ta-pei of Thousand-hands and Thousand-eyes" on the tower in front of Tz'u-en Temple in Ch'ang-an. After Bodhiruci made a new translation of the same sūtra, a nun in 713 by the name of Wei-pa of the Miao-chi Temple in Ch'eng-tu often chanted the Great Compassion Dhāraṇī. Liu I-erh, an eleven-year-old girl, became her disciple. She meditated and claimed that the bodhisattva had manifested in the temple. To prove the point, she spread ashes in the courtyard and one evening huge footsteps measuring several feet could be detected. An artisan was hired to make a painting based on what she saw, but nothing satisfactory came out. A monk named Yang Fa-cheng said that he could do it. I-erh would look up with folded hands and instruct the monk how to paint by pointing. It took ten years for them to complete it. Later, around 722, two hundred images of the bodhisattva were carved in Ch'eng-tu, each having forty-two arms. Fifteen scrolls depicting this bodhisattva were also painted. They were circulated in the capital, and were presented to Emperor Hsüan-tsung (r. 713–756) who bestowed them on Kao Li-shih. The famous painter Wu Tao-tzu painted three Ta-pei images between 713 and 755. When Chien-chen went to Japan in 753 he carried with him an image of the Thousand-handed and Thousand-eyed Avalokiteśvara made in white sandalwood as well as a painting of the same deity embroidered on silk, thus introducing the worship of this new deity to Japan (Kobayashi 1983).

5. The ritual was first described in the *Kuo-ch'ing pai-lu*. Both Chih-li and Tsun-shih wrote manuals for the performance of this repentance. Chih-li wrote *Chin kuang-ming tsui-sheng ch'an-i* (T no. 1946) and Tsun-shih wrote *Chin kuang-ming ch'an-fa pu-chu i* (T no. 1945).

6. Aside from the more famous Mt. Pao-ting, where most visitors and pilgrims go, there is also a less well known site located to its left. The former is called Great Pao-ting and the latter Small Pao-ting. Liu's "Pictures of Ten Smeltings" were depicted in both places. Angela Howard has been studying these sites for a long time and has written a monograph (forthcoming). She suggests that the Small Pao-ting functioned as an esoteric maṇḍala and open only to the initiated. It served as a model for the construction of Great Pao-ting. I thank her for sharing her findings with me.

7. Although the cartouches accompanying the scenes explain the various forms of self-mutilation Liu was undertaking, he was nevertheless not depicted as devoid of his left index finger, right eye, left ear, left arm, and so on. Liu remains intact in the artistic depictions. Personal communication from Angela Howard, April 1999.

8. Sources consulted for Chih-li's life include Tsung-hsiao's *Ssu-ming chiao-hsing lu*, vol 1, "Chronological biography" (Nien-p'u), HTC vol. 100, pp. 880–83 and "Veritable

Record of Fa-chih of Ssu-ming (Ssu-ming Fa-chih Tsun-che shih-lu)" by his disciple Tse-ch'uan, included in vol. 7 of *Ssu-ming chiao-hsing lu* (100:1012–1014); Chih-p'an, *Fo-tsu t'ung-chi*, vol 8 (T 49:191c-194b).

9. Chih-li's views on the three kinds of repentance were faithful to the T'ien-t'ai tradition. *Sequential Approach to the Perfection of Dhyāna* (Shih Ch'an-p'o-lo-mi tz'u-ti fa-men, T no. 1916), one of the foundational texts for the T'ien-t'ai penitential rites, regards the ritual activity repentance as supporting discipline (*lü*), the visualization of form repentance as supporting concentration (*ting*), and the unborn repentance as supporting wisdom (*hui*). It classifies the first as Hīnayāna and the last two Mahāyāna (T 46:485c).

10. According to the *Mahāparinirvāṇa Sūtra*, the *icchantikas* are the lowest form of life in the six realms. Two schools of interpretation exist, one asserting that the *icchantikas* are dammed forever and the other insisting that even these wormlike creatures will at last be saved.

11. Chih-li is here referring to the ten kinds of mind that follow the flow of saṃsāra: (1) ignorant and dark, (2) affected by evil companions, (3) not following good companions, (4) creating evil in thought, speech, and deed, (5) allow evil mind take over, (6) allow evil mind to continue its control without ceasing, (7) cover and hide one's mistakes, (8) not afraid of being reborn in evil realms, (9) without shame or remorse, and (10) deny cause and effect. As for the ten kinds of mind that go against the flow of saṃsāra, they are the exact opposite of the above ten: (1) deep faith in cause and effect, (2) sincere shame and remorse, (3) great fear for the evil realms of rebirth, (4) confess with total revelation, (5) cut off the evil mind from continuation, (6) give rise to the thought for enlightenment, (7) cultivate good and cut off evil, (8) keep and protect correct Dharma, (9) remember Buddhas of the ten directions, and (10) realize the empty nature of sin. See *Mo-ho chih-kuan*, Part 1 of chapter 4 (T 46:39c-40b).

12. Tsung-chien. *Shih-men cheng-t'ung*, vol. 5; HTC vol. 130, pp. 834–38; *Lien-tsung pao-chien* T no. 1973.

13. Kuan-yin is again mentioned in question number 34: "Has the Universal Gateway [Kuan-yin] manifested to you?" (Yü 1989:102)

14. In commenting on the thousand eyes and hands of Ta-pei, Wan-sung says, "I have read about one tradition which says that Ta-pei was formerly Princess Miao-shan. This was told to the Lü Master Tao-hsüan who heard it from a heavenly being. However, because the bodhisattva has thirty-two manifestations and myriads of transformation bodies, depending on the person, there can be many differences. Each claim may have its own basis" (T 48:261c).

8. Princess Miao-shan and the Feminization of Kuan-yin

1. In the biographical section of the *Chronicle of Upper T'ien-chu of Hangchow* (Hang-chou Shang T'ien-chu chih), there is an entry on a Vinaya master P'u-ming Ju-ching. He was noted for his power of exorcising ghosts and his uncanny ability to foretell future events. For instance, based on his dream, he predicted that Chin troops

would come to Hangchow in the eleventh month of 1129 (STCC 3:92–93). But there is no mention about his being the compiler of the *Hsiang-shan pao-chüan*. The other P'u-ming, the writer of the text, was actually called a Ch'an, not a Vinaya, master. Yoshioka (1971) made an interesting suggestion that P'u-ming was in fact a name Chiang Chih-ch'i assumed later in his life (Tsukamoto 1955:266–67). Yanagida Seizan (1974), however, suggested that this P'u-ming was no other than Chiang Chih-ch'i. He also identified P'u-ming with the Ch'an monk who created one of the four extant sets of "Ten Ox Herding Pictures" (*Mu-niu t'u*) and wrote poems accompanying them. This set has overtaken the more famous set created by Kuo-an, a Sung monk who lived in the twelfth century, in recent times. Chu-hung wrote a preface to P'u-ming's "Ten Ox Herding Pictures" but said that he could not identify the author (1974:213–17).

2. Dr. Lai Swee-fo provided the transcription of the first half of the text and kindly gave me permission to translate it. The second half, starting with "When the envoy arrived," follows the translation made by Dudbridge (1982:594–606).

3. The story of P'eng Tzu-ch'iao, for example, is included in Lu Kao's *Hsi Kuan-shih-yin ying-yen chi*, no. 40. But in the original version, it does not say explicitly that Kuan-yin appears as a woman. Rather, another man who was imprisoned together with P'eng, in a state of semi-consciousness, saw two white cranes descend and perch on the screen in front of P'eng. Then, one of the two cranes approached P'eng and *changed into a person who had a very pleasing appearance (hsing-jung chih-hao*, italics mine). I do not think that we can take this to mean the form of "a beautiful woman" as the compiler of the *Fa-yüan chu-lin* apparently did.

4. I thank Suzanne E. Cahill for sharing with me her draft translation of the biography with an introduction entitled, "Wang Feng-hsien: A Taoist Woman Saint of Medieval China," to be included in the forthcoming book, *Under Confucian Eyes: Texts on Gender in Chinese History*, edited by Susan Mann and Yu-yin Cheng (Berkeley: University of California Press).

5. The sūtra is no. 37 in the exhibition entitled, *Latter Days of the Law: Images of Chinese Buddhism*, 850–1850. For further information, see the exhibition catalogue with the same title, pp. 303–5 (Weidner 1994).

6. Chikusa provides several tables to illustrate his point. For instance, take the case of Soochow prefecture. 127 *an* were erected during the fifty years of the last part in the Southern Sung (1225–1274), and 207 *an* in the Yüan. In contrast, only ten were built before the Five Dynasties, twenty-six during the Northern Sung, fifty-six during the early part of Southern Sung (1127–1173), and thirty-six during the middle part of Southern Sung (1174–1224) (Chikusa 1987:12–13).

7. Although Liu Ch'ang-chiu believes that this cave, like the main Vairocana Cave, was constructed in the Sung, other scholars date it to the Ch'ing. The dating is still an on-going and unresolved matter. See, for instance, Tsao Tan and Chao Ling (1994, 3:38).

8. I am interested here more narrowly in tracing the use of *miao-shan* as the name for a woman. The use of *miao* as part of the name for nuns must be very widespread. In a register of nuns of Ling-hsiu Ssu in Tun-huang dating from about 895, aside from the nun Miao-fu, who may or may not be the same nun who commissioned the copying

of *The Scripture on the Ten Kings*, ten other nuns have names that also begin with *miao* (Teiser 1994:132, n. 13). The famous Ch'an master Ta-hui had several female disciples. The names of two prominent nuns also contained *miao*—Miao-tsung (1095–1170) and Miao-tao (fl. 1134–1155). The latter was the first person to achieve enlightenment through the use of *kung-an*, and became Ta-hui's dharma successor (Levering 1999).

9. I thank Reiko Ohnuma for sending me her dissertation, which was still not available through the University Microfilms International when I wrote this chapter, though it is available now.

10. Scholars agree that the earliest writings bearing the name of *pao-chüan* were written by Lo Ch'ing (f. 1509–1522), founder of the Non-action Sect. He wrote six books in five fascicles, the so-called *wu-pu liu-ts'e*, all bearing the term *pao-chüan* in their titles. They were printed in the Cheng-te period (1506–1522; see Overmyer 1976:109–29).

11. Yoshioka argues for a Yüan date of his copy, but I agree with Dudbridge (1976:46) that it does not differ in significant ways from later editions of the text. In fact, I have a photocopy of a copy from the Institute of Oriental Studies in St. Petersburg, Russia, printed in 1872 in Shanghai, which is identical to the Yoshioka copy.

12. For instance, the copy I own, which was printed in 1886, contains only the story of P'u-ming but not that of Pao-feng. Unlike the 1773 edition, however, it includes a long passage telling the person who recites the *pao-chüan* what to say, sounding very much like a stage direction. This is because these texts were usually recited aloud. Known as *hsüan-chüan* (recitation of precious scrolls), it is still done today in Chekiang and Kiangsu. Several women I interviewed in 1987 at Hangchow knew other women who did this in their villages. They would be invited to the homes of someone who wanted to create merit for health, wealth, or in celebration of weddings. The session would begin in the evening and lasted all night. *Hsiang-shan pao-chüan* would always be included. The passage is to be announced in the beginning of the recitation session, which is held on Miao-shan's birthday to turn it into a ritual occasion. The person who reads must first bathe, fast, and change into clean clothes to show respect for the Bodhisattva. After offering incense, the reader must "ascend the platform and announce: It is the nineteenth day of the second month of such and such year, the birthday of the All Compassionate Kuan-shih-yin Bodhisattva. I now ascend the platform and recite the *Precious Scroll of Kuan-yin* (Kuan-yin pao-chüan). All of you must gather your minds and sit properly. Show your respect by regulating your bodies. Do not talk or laugh. Loud noises and disorder are not allowed. [The chanter now snaps the ruler.] Listen attentively, for the pure organs of hearing are emphasized by the scriptural passage, 'You should cultivate thought by following hearing. The saintly and the worldly are non-dual.' The sūtra also says, 'Why is Kuan-shih-yin Bodhisattva called Kuan-shih-yin? If sentient beings suffer from various pains and afflictions and upon hearing Kuan-shih-yin Bodhisattva, call the name single-mindedly, Kuan-shih-yin Bodhisattva will deliver them without fail upon hearing their cries. If one keeps the name of Kuan-shih-yin bodhisattva and enters the fire, fire cannot burn him. If he calls the name while being carried away by a flood, he will reach shallow ground. It is because of this reason that the bodhisattva is named Kuan-shih-yin.'" (*Hsiang-shan pao-chüan* 1a-b).

13. When Miao-shan is finally allowed by her father to join the nuns at the White

Sparrow Temple, the abbess and the nuns try to make her give up her resolve under the order of the king. Miao-shan ridicules them for being hypocrites and gives them a lecture, "The reverend abbess has narrow understanding and wrong views. Although you have left the householder's life, your mind has not attained the way at all. Do you know that ancient sages would sacrifice their bodies to feed tigers, slice off flesh to feed an eagle, light their bodies as torches, offer head, eyes, marrow, brains, hands, feet, and even the entire body in order to obtain half a gāthā? They do not hesitate to offer their bodies and hearts in pursuit of the unexcelled supreme enlightenment. You, on the other hand, cherish your body and love your life. If you are attached to greed, how can you cultivate yourself to attain the way? To sacrifice oneself and benefit others is the essence of the Buddhist tradition. But to benefit oneself and harm others is to depart from it" (Yoshioka 1971:151).

14. Niches holding both Kuan-yin and Ti-tsang are found among sculptures in Nan-shan, Ta-tsu. They are dated 896, 897, 995–997, and 1001. See *Ta-tsu shih-k'e yen-chiu*, pp. 376, 378, and 420.

15. For instance, in one illustration held at the British Museum, a six-armed Kuan-yin sits to the right of Ti-tsang (Teiser 1994:plate 1b) and in another held at Bibliothéque Nationale, the two are included in a group of six bodhisattvas who come to pay respect to the Buddha (Teiser 1994:plate 2). Although it is difficult to be absolutely certain because of the crudeness of the drawing, I think Kuan-yin in the second illustration is holding a willow branch, instead of a "fly-whisk" as Teiser states (171), because the image is identified as Kuan-shih-yin Bodhisattva Who Saves from Pain (*chiu-k'u*) in the cartouche and the willow branch is that bodhisattva's traditional attribute.

16. It states that Mu-lien once made eighteen mud images of lohan (arhat). He put them out in the courtyard to dry and asked his mother to take care of them while he was away. It rained and Mrs. Mu forgot to take them inside. By the time she remembered, the muddy images had been much damaged and she, heaping insult upon injury, simply dumped them in a corner of the kitchen. Another time Mu-lien tried to give his mother a chance to create some merit. So he begged Ti-tsang to help. Ti-tsang turned himself into five monks who came to the house for food. The mother posed a puzzling question to the begging monks. She asked, "Do you want to receive a 'long' feast, a 'short' feast, a 'square' feast, or a 'round' feast?" Not knowing exactly what she meant but thinking these terms stand for "noodle," "rice," "New Year cake," and "dumplings made of glutinous rice flour" (*t'ang-t'uan*), they asked for all four. Thereupon Mrs. Mu dealt them a thorough thrashing using a door-bolt, a stick, a brick, and a weight for the scale.

17. The Buddhist ten lay feast days occur each month on the first, eighth, fourteenth, fifteenth, eighteenth, twenty-third, twenty-fourth, twenty-eighth, twenty-ninth, and thirtieth and are dedicated to ten different buddhas and bodhisattvas. See Teiser (1994: Appendix 7, p. 234).

18. As described in Yoshioka (1971:141), The ten great vows of Thousand-handed Kuany-yin are:

1. Never grow old but forever young.
2. Never die.

3. Realize enlightenment with this very body.
4. See one's true nature.
5. Three obstacles [three poisons of ignorance, greed, and hatred] all disap pear.
6. Emotional attachments are cut off from their roots.
7. Wisdom exceeds the sun and moon.
8. Hatred among relatives in the three worlds be dissolved.
9. Be worshiped by humans and devas.
10. Preach the Dharma to save all sentient beings.

19. Postpartum discharges are considered to be extremely polluting. A mother who has thus offended the gods by this unavoidable sin in childbirth, and particularly if she dies while giving birth, has to go to a special region in the underworld called "blood pond" to undergo torment. A filial son can help his mother to lessen or avoid the punishment by performing a religious ritual called "breaking the blood pond" at the time of the mother's death.

20. Yuet-keung Lo of Grinnell College is finishing an annotated translation and study of this work. I am grateful to him for showing me his draft manuscript.

21. One index of the enthusiasm surrounding female chastity is the overwhelming proportion of the section devoted to "female chastity" (*kuei-chieh*) in the *Ku-chin t'u-shu chi-ch'eng,* which covers 206 *chüan*. There are eight *chüan* devoted to "female filiality" (*kuei-hsiao*). They contain short biographical notices, culled from local gazetteers. Women who practiced *ke-ku* became notable only after the Sung. While only 4 out of 61 women in pre-Sung times did this, 14 out of 51 (about one fourth) women in the Sung, 306 out of 632 Ming women (about 1/2), and 226 out of 340 Ch'ing women (2/3) did it.

22. Chen Te-hsiu promoted filial piety among the people of Ch'üan-chou when he became the prefect there in 1217 and asked for names of filial children. Among those reported to him, Huang Chang, a commoner, saved his mother by offering his liver, another commoner, Liu Hsiang, saved his father by doing the same, and Liu Tsung-ch'iang, a low level government official, cured his mother by offering flesh sliced from the thigh. Chen Te-hsiu commented that although such acts were not recommended by holy scriptures, they nevertheless deserved commendation because they issued from real sincerity of filial hearts (*Wen-chi* 40). In 1219 he wrote an inscription for an arch memorializing the filial behavior of an eighteen-year old girl named Lü Liang-tzu. When her father became hopelessly ill, she prayed to her ancestors and asked them to take her instead because her father, being addicted to books, would be of little use to them in the other world. She then sliced flesh from her thigh and cooked a gruel with it. The father, after imbibing it, soon recovered (*Wen-chi* 24). Chu Ronguey, who wrote a dissertation on Chen Te-hsiu, told me that he had come across similar cases of Chen's great admiration of *ke-ku*.

23. Ch'iu Chung-lin rightly points out that *ke-ku* is a generic term referring to this practice. Counting the references in the *Ku-chin tu-shu chi-ch'eng,* he comes up with

2,470 cases of offering different parts of the body to heal the parents. While the majority cases involve *ke-ku* (cutting off flesh from the thigh), 140 are about cutting off flesh from the arm, 85 cutting of liver, 46 cutting off flesh from the chest, armpit, and breast, 10 of fingers, and several cases each of cutting heart, ear, lung, eye, brain, knee, intestine, and so on (Ch'iu 1996:52). He also points out that by the time of Ming and Ch'ing, this was no longer confined to a specific region or among Han Chinese, but also found in border regions such as Yünnan, Kweichow, the Northeast and Northwest and practiced by Muslims, Mongols and Manchus (Ch'iu 1996:91).

24. *Ke-ku* and medical use of human flesh are treated in J.J.M. De Groot, *The Religious System of China* 4:357–406 (Taipei: Ch'eng-wen ch'u-pan-she, 1969, reprint); Robert Des Rotours's main focus in his two articles was on cannibalism (1963, 486–27; 1968, 1–49); T'ien Ju-k'ang discussed this in an appendix to his book, *Male Anxiety and Female Chastity* (1988: 149–61); and finally, Kuwabara Jitsuzō wrote two articles on this subject (1919:121–24) and an extended version (1924:1–61, the section on medical use of human flesh appearing on pp. 51–59). See also Chong Key-Ray, *Cannibalism in China* (1990).

25. I am grateful to Professor Pei-yi Wu who alerted me to Jonathan Chaves' presentation of this article at the Columbia Traditional China Seminar. I also thank Jonathan Chaves for sending me his published article.

26. For instance, under Chih-yüan third year (1266) and seventh year (1270), people were told not to cut pieces of liver or flesh from their thighs or gouge out their eyes (*Yüan tien chang, chüan* 33). In Hung-wu twenty-seventh year (1394), not only was such action discouraged, but those who did it should not receive any government commendation (*Li-pu chih-kao, chüan* 24).

27. One image of the Eleven-headed Kuan-yin enshrined as the main icon in the Kuan-yin Pavilion of Tu-lo Monastery in Chi county, east of Peking, dated to the tenth century is described by Gridley (1993:86–88).

28. See vol. 12 of "Sculptures" in *Chung-kuo mei-shu ch'üan-chi* (1988), plate 175, p. 178.

29. The founding of the Golden Pavilion Monastery (Chin-ke Ssu) is traced to the monk Tao-i's visions in 736 of Mañjuśrī Bodhisattva (appearing as an old man) and the scene of golden mansions approached by a golden bridge. This eventually led in 766 to Emperor Tai-tsung's grant for its establishment. The Ta-pei image was itself constructed in the Ming. For the history of the temple, see Birnbaum (1983:14–16, 25–38), Gimello (1992:133), and Weinstein (1987:77–89). A pair similar to those at the Golden Pavilion Monastery also attend the Ta-pei image in the Shuang-lin Monastery in Ping-yao, Shansi. However, the one on stage right is identified as Śakra and the one on stage left Brahmā, although the latter looks decidedly feminine (see *Shansi fo-chiao ts'ai-su* 1991:332).

9. P'u-t'o Shan: Pilgrimage and the Creation of the Chinese Potalaka

1. Pilgrimages to this sacred site have continued down the ages. In September 1986, I interviewed Hsü Li-kung and Ming-ta , the Chairman and the Secretary of the Shen-

si Buddhist Association. Both were natives of Shensi and were familiar with the local tradition, referring to Kuan-yin as "Dragon-taming Kuan-yin" (Hsiang-lung Kuan-yin). But in their version, Kuan-yin appeared as an old woman, instead of a monk. There used to be a temple called Sheng-shou Ssu situated at the base of the mountain. Inside the temple, there were wall paintings depicting Kuan-yin's act of salvation that Hsü saw in the 1940s. Near the temple there was a cave, at whose entrance, an image representing Kuan-yin's "flesh body" was enshrined. The temple and the image were destroyed during the Cultural Revolution.

From the base of the mountain to the top terrace where the Yüan-kuang Ssu was located, seventy-two small temples called *t'ang-fang miao* ("Soup-house temple") lined the way. Each temple maintained relationships with specific villages. During the pilgrimage season which lasted from lunar twenty-fifth day of the fifth month to the nineteenth day of the sixth month and was called *Ta Kuan-yin miao-hui* (Great Temple Fair of Kuan-yin), pilgrim associations (*hsiang-hui*) from these specific villages would donate soup and water to these temples, which provided lodgings to pilgrims who brought their own food. Ming-ta participated in the pilgrimage activities of 1948. He recalled that the whole area was crowded with people. Pilgrims came with bands of musicians who played music. The tune was always the same, but the lyric varied. The last sentence, however, always ended with "Everyone calls on Buddha's name (*jen-jen nien-fo*)." In the valley, there were also *mao-p'eng* ("thatched huts") where ascetics meditated. Hsü told me that pilgrims once more were returning to Nan Wu-t'ai beginning with the early 1980s, even though only a few of those small temples remained. Monks had also started their efforts to rebuild the two large monasteries.

2. In paintings made in the Ming period, Kuan-yin is always accompanied by a white parrot. The bird is an attendant of Kuan-yin. This is the typical iconography for Kuan-yin of the South Sea, discussed in chapter 10.

3. I talked with members from forty-four pilgrim groups ranging from 8 to 700 people, totally 6,262 pilgrims who came from southern Kiangsu and northern Chekiang. In descending order, they came from Ch'ang-shu, I-hsing, Soochow, P'ing-hu, Wu-hsi, K'un-shan, T'ung-hsiang, and Chia-hsing. I carried out in-depth interviews with seventy people, including pilgrims and workers in the "religious tourism" business. The observations I make here are based on the data I gathered at that time. More information is provided by the videotape *Kuan-yin Pilgrimage* (R.C. Video, 1989) that I directed and produced.

4. In 1979 the company used three boats, which sailed fifteen times in twenty-seven days during the pilgrimage season. It served 1,959 pilgrims, each spending an average of 20 *yüan*; 10.4 percent of the pilgrims were men and 89.6 percent women, with a median age of 55.5. By contrast, in 1987, the company sent out twenty boats, which sailed seventy-eight times in eighty days and served 48,433 pilgrims. The pilgrims spent more money, averaging 60 *yüan*. There were also more men (15%), and more younger people, for the median age was 43.4 years. The sudden burst began in 1981 when the number of pilgrims doubled (14917) from previous year. The upward trend continued after that, with a yearly increment ranging between 5,000 and 9,000. The peak was in 1983 and

1984. According to the informants, this was so because of the implementation of a new policy called *pao-ch'an tao-hu* (return the production to the household) in 1983. It gave peasants more control over production. They had more autonomy over their time.

5. One forty-five year old living *p'u-sa* from Soochow told me her story. She came from a very poor peasant family. She had four children and suffered from bad health. Twenty years ago she suddenly lost her voice. Three years later she could speak again and realized that she was the daughter of the "Great Bodhisattva of Upper T'ien-chu" (Shang T'ien-chu Ta P'u-sa). She had been coming to Upper T'ien-chu as a *fo-t'ou* since 1980. She would go into trance frequently and had to be helped by five women followers. In trance she would speak as Kuan-yin (*p'u-sa k'ai-k'ou*, "Bodhisattva opens her mouth"). She knew what she was saying during the trance, for she remained lucid, but she could not predict when this would happen. On the day I met her, she held several healing sessions after she returned to her normal conscious state.

6. The image of Kuan-yin standing on top of a large fish can often be seen in temples in Kiangsu and Chekiang and seems to be a favorite in this region. A huge image representing this iconography, for instance, was enshrined in the main hall of Ling-yin Ssu, Hangchow, behind the Buddha image. One pilgrim explained it this way: The big fish resembled the shape of Hangchow. By standing on top of the fish, who could keep the wild forces in check, Kuan-yin protected the city from disasters.

7. The 1704 gazetteer mentions all three, but earlier gazetteers only Mei Fu. The 1924 gazetteer shows skepticism about the legend of Ko Hung (PTSC 1924:525).

8. Mountain gazetteers are important sources for studies of Mt. Wu-t'ai, Mt. T'ai, Huang Shan, and Wu-tang Shan, which are discussed in Gimello (1992), Wu (1992), Dudbridge (1978, 1982), Cahill (1992), and Lagerwey (1992) respectively.

9. Such travel accounts to Mt. Potalaka were well known in India and Tibet. Tucci (1958) mentions two Tibetan accounts; one is *Po ta la'i lam yig*, which is contained in the *bsTan-'gyur*. The author, Spyan ras gzigs dban p'yug, is supposed to be Avalokiteśvara himself. The other, an account written by Taranatha (b. 1575) in which the travel of Śantivarman to Potala is narrated, is later than the first. The book mentioned by Sheng could be the *Po ta la'i lam yig*. On the other hand, it could be some earlier book, for "a travel to Potala is already known to Hsüan-tsang, viz, to an author who wrote some centuries before the *Po ta la'i lam yig* of which we are speaking; this, in fact, is certainly late as its contamination with Śaiva ideas (the linga) clearly shows" (Tucci 1958:409–500). In this account known to Hsüan-tsang, Mt. Potalaka is situated east of the Malaya Mountain. One reaches its summit through winding and narrow path over cliffs and gorges. On the top there is a lake from which a river flows that runs twenty times around the mountain. In a stone temple Kuan-tzu-tsai Bodhisattva dwells. Many devotees attempt to reach that place, but very few succeed. The people living at the feet of the mountain who worships him are sometimes blessed by his view: he then appears to them in the aspect of Pāśupata Tīrthika or Maheśvara.

10. Specifically Potiyil in Tamil Nandu. I thank N. Ganesan for this reference.

11. By the late Ming, however, the fame of Upper T'ien-chu was overshadowed by that of P'u-t'o. A new strategy advanced by promoters of Upper T'ien-chu was to make

it substitute for P'u-t'o. Even though most pilgrims hoped to go to both P'u-t'o and Upper T'ien-chu and in some cases they did so, apologists began to argue that if one came to Upper T'ien-chu, he did not have to go to P'u-t'o, but if one went to P'u-t'o, he must then come to Upper T'ien-chu. This was because Kuan-yin of the Upper T'ien-chu and Kuan-yin of P'u-t'o were the same. "But when one comes to Upper T'ien-chu, he does not have to go to P'u-t'o. This is because the small can contain the great, for this accords with the rounded view (*yüan*). However, if one goes to P'u-t'o, he must then come to Upper T'ien-chu. This is because one should not neglect what is nearby in favor of that which is far away, for that would make one fall into the one-sided view of partiality (*p'ien*)" (STCC 66).

12. The existence of other regional Kuan-yin cultic sites, which did not achieve any national stature, was proven by the story about a third pilgrimage site that Sheng mentioned in passing. It was Mt Wu-ling (Misty Efficacy), located near Peking, which was devoted to the cult of White-robed Kuan-yin. Sheng related the custom of yearly pilgrimages made by devotees who came to the mountain to seek visions of Kuan-yin. She sometimes appeared to them clad in white, but seldom showed her face. At night "heavenly lamps" (*t'ien-teng*) flickered mysteriously like stars or torches. Water in the streams flowing in the valley would rise and ebb with the tides, for it was rumored that the streams were connected with the ocean, implying perhaps another connection with P'u-t'o (PTSC 1361/T 2101:1138c). Except for Sheng, Mt. Wu-ling would have remained unknown to us. But there must be other sites like it that are waiting to be discovered. The proliferation of similar regional pilgrimage centers and their possible competitions would be a fascinating topic for research. Which site survives and which site disappears into the crags of history would make an interesting story. Mountain gazetteers surely constitute one powerful mechanism that safeguards a site from possible oblivion.

13. The gazetteer of P'u-t'o attributed this to Kuan-yin's intervention. Kuan-yin was supposed to have appeared to Emperor K'ang-hsi in the form of an old woman while he toured in Chekiang. The two had a conversation and she suddenly disappeared. When Huang Ta-lai came forward to protect the emperor, the emperor asked about his position and then inquired about the conditions of Chushan Archipelago. Huang used this opportunity and made a detailed report about P'u-t'o. This led to the emperor's gift of a thousand ounces of gold to build the monastery. The gazetteers described a similar encounter between Lan Li, the new regional commander, and an old lady carrying a fish basket in front of the Cave of Tidal Sound in 1690. Both Huang and Lan helped in rebuilding P'u-t'o and they received sacrifices from the grateful monks at their "living shrines" (*sheng-tz'u*) (PTSC 1924:190–91, 462–466). Porcelain figures depicting Kuan-yin holding a fish basket and attended by Sudhana and Dragon Princess were made during the K'ang-hsi period. This was the "Fish-basket Kuan-yin." As I discuss in chapters 10 and 11, in *pao-chüan* and popular literature composed during the Ch'ing, Kuan-yin was often described as being an old woman or referred to as "Old Mother," echoing the Venerable or Eternal Mother worshipped by the sectarians. In fact, Kuan-yin was proclaimed by the same people as incarnation of their goddess. The female founder of some sectarian sects, in turn, was believed to be the incarnation of Kuan-yin (Li and

Naquin 1988:180). The relationships between Kuan-yin and other female deities, as well as between her and female devotees are complicated and deserve further study.

14. The most recent gazetteer was compiled in 1924 by Wang Heng-yen, an instructor at the local academy. The project was under the joint sponsorship of the magistrate of Ting-hai and Master Yin-kuang, one of the most eminent monks in modern China, who lived on P'u-t'o for over thirty years. Wang used the materials found in previous gazetteers but also carried out on-site investigations (*ts'ai-fang*). He showed judicious judgment in his selections and took an impartial attitude toward both monasteries (PTSC 1924). To differentiate his gazetteer from those before, he called it *P'u-t'o Lo-chia hsin-chih* (New Gazetteer of Potalaka). It was reprinted in 1980.

15. This was in relation to something that happened in 1590 in which Ta-chih, the abbot of Fa-yü, supposedly played a major role in helping a local official who punished P'u-t'o monks and then suffered from divine retribution as a result. The 1698 gazetteer noted the incident but refrained from either giving praise to Ta-chih or heaping blame on Chen-piao (PTSC 1698:X/10a–10b). T'u Lung, the original writer of the article, was far from being so judicious. He devoted six pages to this story which he called "An Account of Efficacious Response on Mt. Pu-t'o." There were two abbots on P'u-t'o, one being Ta-chih and the other Chen-piao. T'u described Ta-chih as a model of strict discipline and religious austerity. Being humble and patient, he was beloved by everyone. Chen-piao, on the other hand, was described as being arrogant, violent, and obstinate. He did not observe monastic rules, but ate meat and drank wine. Moreover, he would beat novices at the slightest excuse and often injure them. T'u presented a most unflattering portrait of Chen-piao. A very different picture of this abbot was found in later gazetteers. He was said to be honest and straightforward. He was known for his strict observance of discipline. He was friendly to serious practitioners, therefore he was respected and beloved by famous monks. He built fifty-three hermitages on the island. When Ta-chih arrived at the island to build the Northern Monastery, he was said to have received much help from Chen-piao (PTSC 1832:XV/6a-7a, 1924:353).

16. This story was recorded in *Fo-tsu t'ung-chi*, *chüan* 42, under Kai-cheng first year (836). It made no direct reference to P'u-t'o (T 2035:385). The Ch'an master was described as from Mt. Chung-nan, a site holy to both Buddhists and Taoists and near Southern Mt. Wu-t'ai mentioned earlier in the chapter. At the end of the story, the master went back to Mt. Chung-nan. Earlier gazetteers of P'u-t'o would mention this story, but did not date the founding of the island with this event (PTSC 1589:III/20).

17. However, *Fo-tsu t'ung-chi* gives 858 and *Pao-ch'ing Ssu-ming chih* (Gazetteer of Ningpo compiled in 1225–1227) gives 859. The latter provides more details about the history of the image. Under the entry on K'ai-yüan Monastery, one of the monasteries in Ningpo, we read that it was originally built in 740, during the K'ai-yüan era and was destroyed in the Hui-ch'ang persecution. But in the early years of Ta-ch'ung (847–859), at the request of the governor, it was allowed to be rebuilt on the old site of another temple. Among the treasures of K'ai-yüan Ssu, there was the image of the "Kuan-yin Who Refused to Leave." It then explained the origin of the image. In 859 the Japanese monk Egaku made a pilgrimage to Mt. Wu-t'ai. When he came to a temple on the Mid-

Terrace, he saw an image of Kuan-yin that looked elegant, beautiful and joyous. He begged to take this image back to his country. The monks agreed. So he put the image on a sedan chair and carried it all the way to Ningpo to board the boat. But the image became so heavy that it could not be lifted up. He had to ask all the merchants who traveled with him for help before the image could be put on aboard. When they passed P'u-t'o, waves leapt up in anger and there was a great storm. Boatmen became greatly frightened. Egaku had a dream in which a foreign monk said to him, "If you put me safely on this mountain, I will send you off with favorable wind." Egaku wept in gratitude and after waking told the people about his dream. Everyone was much astonished. After building a room and respectfully settling the image there, they left. That is why the image was called the "Kuan-yin Who Refused to Leave."

A while later, monk Tao-tsai of the K'ai-yüan Ssu dreamt that Kuan-yin wanted to come to stay in his temple. So he went to P'u-t'o to welcome the image and had it installed there. Townspeople in Ningpo prayed to the image and always received responses. So the temple came to be known as "Kuan-yin of Auspicious Responses" (Kuan-yin Jui-ying Yüan). During the T'ai-p'ing hsing-kuo era (976–983) of the Sung, the monastery was refurbished and had the name changed to Wu-t'ai Kuan-yin Yüan, indicating that the image originally came from Mt. Wu-t'ai (11/10a-b). Saeki Tomi regarded the date 916 as unreliable, for Egaku, who was a historical person, was reported to have gone to China in 839. It would be difficult to believe that he stayed in China for 77 years, if one were to accept the later date (Saeki 1961: 383–84).

18. The purple gold-hued form is the iconography for Kuan-yin in the *Kuan-shih-yin san-mei ching* (Sūtra of the Samādhi of Kuan-yin), a scripture composed in China during the Six Dynasties and provided one of the textual basis for Kuan-yin worship at that time (discussed in chapter 3). As Makita pointed out, many miracle accounts about Kuan-yin's epiphanies during that period described Kuan-yin's appearance in this way (Makita 1976:111–55).

19. Shih Hao held a series of government posts, starting as an instructor of Imperial University (9A) in 1157 and ended up serving jointly as the Chief Councillor of the Right (1A) and Commissioner at the Bureau of Military Affairs (1B) in 1165. He was a friend of Chang Chiu-ch'eng (1092–1159), a prominent Confucian literatus and lay Buddhist who followed the Ch'an master Ta-hui Tsung-kao (1089–1163). Shih also sponsored the careers of Lu Chiu-yüan (1139–1193), Yeh Shih (1150–1223), and Chu Hsi (1130–1200). Thus by all accounts, he was well connected with the establishment (Davis 1986:53–75).

20. *Pao-ch'ing Su-ming chih*, the local gazetteer compiled during Pao-ch'ing era (1225–1227), recorded Shih's pilgrimage (XX/9b-10a). Another local gazetteer compiled in the Yüan, the *Chang-kuo chou t'u chih* retold the story and provided a verbatim transcription of Shih's essay (VI/7a-8a). It is, of course, also recorded in the gazetteers of P'u-t'o.

21. Among the accounts given in the chapter on "Miracles" in the chronicles, only one refers to Kuan-yin as sitting in the pose of royal ease (PTSC 1924:177). Kuan-yin images created with this iconography are perhaps most familiar to modern visitors to major museums, for many fine specimens have survived from the Sung. In view of the

great popularity of this type of Kuan-yin images at that time, it is strange that not more pilgrims saw Kuan-yin appear in this form.

22. The pair appeared as Kuan-yin's attendants already in the Sung. The stone sculptures in Szechwan provide several examples. Number 8 of Yüan-chüeh Tung (Cave of Complete Enlightenment) grottoes in An-yüeh contains three chambers in which three main images are placed. The central one is Śākyamuni Buddha who is flanked by two images of Kuan-yin in the two chambers. The chamber on his right has an image of Kuan-yin holding a lotus. There is an inscription stating that the carving of this chamber began in 1099 and ended in 1108. In the chamber to the left of Śākyamuni Buddha there is another image of Kuan-yin holding a pure vase and willow branch in his hands. A kneeling Sudhana is on his right and a Lung-nü (damaged in 1983) is on his left. Images of four donors who were a family surnamed Sun stand next to Sudhana. The accompanying inscription states that the mother was born in 1097, her first son in 1139 and her second son in 1140 when the mother was already forty-two years old. The donors' images were set up in 1153, carved after the main images. Scholars estimate that this group of sculptures were made between 1100 and 1150, which makes this site the earliest example for the pairing of Sudhana and Lung-nü. Other examples for the pair are found in Pei Shan (#133 no dated inscription), Shih-men Shan (no. 6, dated 1141), and Miao-kao Shan (dated 1155) of Ta-tsu, Szechwan. However, unlike the Sudhana in An-yüeh, Sudhana in the latter sites looks like an old Brahmin. I thank Angela Howard for sharing this information with me.

23. See chapters 17, 22, 26, 42, 49, 57, and 58 of the novel. See also Kung Lieh-fei and Wang Tao-hsing (50).

24. The account of this trip was called *Hai chih* (Record of a Sea Journey). Chang's description of the pilgrim's boat (*hsiang-ch'uan*) could frighten away any would-be pilgrim: "A pilgrims' boat is a living hell. 'Good men' sit on the top deck and 'good women' the deck below. The boat is enveloped with sails and covers and no air is allowed to circulate. Within the close quarters, several hundred unwashed people urinated and defecated. The persons who take care of pilgrims' food, drink, and all other kinds of need are called *hsiang-t'ou* (pilgrims' leader). They are monks from this or that temple" (Chang Tai 1957:213). Despite his critical attitude, Chang apparently observed the formality of a pilgrim. He kept vegetarian diet for over a month, the entire length of his P'u-t'o trip. When he finally ate herring, his favorite fish, in Ting-hai, he had become so unaccustomed to its taste that he threw up (212). The sea voyage must be very uncomfortable and frightening. Another literatus who made the trip in 1737 in a presumably much better equipped boat than this one remarked wryly that he was tossed up and down like "a grain of rice in a winnowing basket" and vomited throughout the crossing (Chi Chou-hua, 1987:152). I am indebted to Pei-yi Wu who told me of Chang Tai's account of his trip to P'u-t'o.

25. By the seventeenth century, with the appearance of the new iconography of Potalaka Kuan-yin, in order to provide symmetry for the two attendants, the original Sudhana's Cave came to be known as Dragon Princess' Cave and a rock nearby became known as Sudhana's Rock, where the boy was supposed to have worshiped Kuan-yin when he first came to the sacred island.

26. Ta-chih was a native of Ma-ch'eng, Hupei, and received tonsure at fifteen. He went to Mt. Ox-head in Nanking in 1547 and the next year, after he received the full ordination in Peking, he went to Mt. Wu-t'ai and stayed in the mountain for five years. In 1558 he made a pilgrimage to Mt. Omei and stayed on top of the mountain for twelve years without leaving the area. In 1574 he made a pilgrimage to Mt. Chin-hua in the north of Szechwan, a distance of eighty *li* from Mt. Omei . Many pilgrims would travel between these two pilgrimage sites. But because there were no resting places along the way, it was a very arduous journey. Ta-chih established the Golden Lotus Monastery to benefit pilgrims.

27. The 1705 gazetteer contains two stele inscriptions of the stūpa (XI/44a-47a;47a-48a). The relics "did not always present the same appearance to different people. Persons of inferior character saw nothing but a black object; those of higher moral standing saw a white object; to those of moderately good character the relics assumed a red appearance; and saintly people saw the figure of Buddha" (Johnston 1976:315).

28. Johnston was far less impressed by Cave of Tidal Sound and offered a rational explanation for the visions of Kuan-yin. "As a cave the Ch'ao-yin-tung is disappointing, for it is merely a perpendicular rent in the rocks by the sea-shore, and would attract no particular attention but for its sacred associations. At times the tidal waters rush into it with resounding roar and dashing spray, and the waves, says a monkish chronicler, lash the cliff walls like the tossed mane of a wild animal. If the critical Western inquirer insists upon extorting a prosaic explanation of the ghostly appearances of Kuan-yin, he may perhaps find one in the fact that at certain times, when atmospheric and tidal conditions are favorable, a shaft of sunlight streams into the cave through a gap in the roof called the *t'ien-ch'uang* , or 'heaven's window,' and strikes athwart the flying foam. The cave then seems to be filled with a tremulous haze, in which the unbeliever sees nothing but sunlit spray, but which to the devout worshipper is a luminous veil through which the 'Pusa of Love and Pity' becomes visible to the eyes of her faithful suppliants" (Johnston 1976:299).

29. Karl Gätzlaff visited P'u-t'o in order to convert the monks to Christianity in 1883. He noted that there were two large monasteries and some sixty small ones. About 2,000 monks lived on the island (Gätzlaff 1968:443). Boerschmann visited P'u-t'o in 1908 and reported that there were more than seventy small temples and over 100 hermitages. About 1,500 monks lived on the island, with 200 to 300 each in the two large monasteries (Boerschmann 1911:11). A Chinese monk went to P'u-t'o on pilgrimage in 1915 and observed that aside from the three large monasteries, there were more than eighty small temples and 100 hermitages. While the small temples could house thirty to forty monks at best and ten to twenty normally, one hermitage could house several people without any problem. Theoretically 10,000 to 20,000 monks could be accommodated by the various temples. But except during the height of pilgrimage seasons of the second and sixth months, when about 6,000 to 7,000 monks would come to stay on P'u-t'o, only about 2,000 monks would usually be living on the island. He commented that there were more images of Kuan-yin and other deities than monks on P'u-t'o (Hsin-fan 1915:17).

10. Feminine Forms of Kuan-yin in Late Imperial China

1. For instance, Kobayashi mentions that the White-robed Kuan-yin is connected with Plain Maiden (Su-nü), the consort of the Yellow Emperor (1948:51), but he does not say why. In discussing the iconography of Nü-wa, he links the twin carps, symbol of felicity and good fortune, with the Fish-basket Kuan-yin and the myth of twin willow trees sprouting on top of Nü-wa's tomb located in T'ung-kuan in the year 754 with the Willow-branch Kuan-yin (115). Again, he does not offer any evidence for his imaginative observations.

2. To give one example: the goddess Nü-wa is enshrined to the left of the Queen Mother of the West in the halls of the Compassion Society (Tz'u-hui T'ang), a present-day sectarian religion using spirit writing (*luan*) as a distinctive means of communication with the deities. But besides the Queen Mother of the West and Nü-wa, they also worship the Jade Emperor, Kuan-yin, the Earth Mother and the Mysterious Woman of the Nine Heavens (Jordan and Overmyer 1986:xviii). Aside from informing us that Nü-wa is still included in the pantheon of this contemporary religion, we do not know how she is conceived and understood by the believers.

3. One female figurine from the Hung-shan culture, excavated at Tung-shan-tsui in Liaoning, is included in the exhibition "Mysteries of Ancient China" held at the British Museum in 1996 (Rawson 1996). The catalogue description says that the female figurine has slightly enlarged breasts and belly, perhaps indicating pregnancy, and is a part of a fertility cult. Large clay images of women are found in Niu-he-liang, about 50 km away (Rawson 1996:44). Lei Congyun describes an even earlier site in the eastern part of Inner Mongolia at Hsing-lung-wa dated to 6000–5000 B.C.E where a stone figure of "a standing female is well formed with distinctly projecting breasts. It was found half-buried in the middle of the room, not far from the fireplace, with its head turned to face the entrance. The figure has been considered by some to be a goddess of the hearth, provider of food and warmth" (Lei 1996:219–20). Sites of Hung-shan culture were first discovered in May of 1979 at Tung-shan-tsui when a rectangular stone structure flanked on all sides by stone walls was unearthed. At the center was a round altar and there were also three round mounds of stone. The small clay figurines of women including the one on exhibition were found in the area of the rectangular structure. Then in October 1983 another site, Niu-he-liang, was excavated and it is where the foundation of a structure named by the archaeologists "Temple of a Goddess" was found. Fragments of a clay figure including a handsome female head with inlaid eyes are also found there (Lei 1996:220–21).

4. This is a composite description of the event. Loewe (1979:98–101) gives the translation of the three accounts that have been preserved.

5. I thank Mu-chou Poo for suggesting this link.

6. The story, with minor variations, is found in many standard Buddhist historical records. Three are dated to the Sung: Tsu-hsiu, *Lung-hsing pien-nien t'ung-lun* (fascicle 22), and Chih-p'an, *Fo-tsu t'ung-chi* (fascicle 41), and Tsung-hsiao, *Fa-hua ching hsien-ying lu* (fascicle 2). These versions were followed by later compilations. Chüeh-an of the Yüan, *Shih-shih chi-ku lüeh* (fascicle 3), Liao-yüan of the Ming, *Fa-hua ling-yen ch'uan*

(fascicle 2). Chou K'e-fu of the Ch'ing, *Kuan-shih-yin chih-yen chi* (fascicle 1). It is also included in the *T'ai-p'ing kuang-chi* (fascicle 101).

7. The eulogy says: "Coursing playfully in the worlds of the ten directions, you open the wonderful doors of Dharma straight away. Recognize this form as a manifestation: Such is the image of the Great Merciful One!"

8. These are the words used by the Sung writer Yeh Ting-kuei in the *Hai-lu sui-shih chi*, fascicle 13. *T'ai-p'ing kuang-chi*, fascicle 101 gives the same story omitting the last sentence. Echoes of the former sentiment are found in many poems written by Ch'an monks in the Sung. A Sung work *Tsung-lin sheng-shih* says, "The painting called 'Bodhisattva of the Golden Sand Beach' has an Indian monk carrying a staff with a skeleton on his shoulder while looking back at Mr. Ma's Wife behind him. There are many eulogies on this type of painting. But the one that I like best is written by Ssu-ming Tao-ch'uan. It goes like this: She looks at everyone equally with compassion. She entices people and draws them to her with desire. One knocks out a wedge with another wedge and fights one type of poison with another type of poison. While the thirty-two responses are found in completion in the 'P'u-men' chapter, this one is paralleled by none" (HTC 148:89).

9. For instance, Ch'en Wei-sung (1626–1682) made a painting of the actor Hsü Tzu-yün who was also known as Yün-lang in the pose of Kuan-yin and gave it to Hsü as a wedding gift. The two men had been lovers for seventeen years. The painting is included in *Chung-kuo Yen-tu li-yüan shih liao* (Historical Materials of the Theatre in Peking, China), vol. 2. I thank Sophie Volpp for the information.

10. As Stein points out, this is related to the Mahāyāna theme of transformation through reversal that bears the technical term *chuan-i* (āśraya-paravrtti). He cites the examples found in the *Fan-wang ching* (Sūtra of Brahmā's Net, T no. 1484): a bodhisattva using the great power of upāya can "turn a pure country into an evil country and an evil country into a land of wonder and happiness; turn good into evil and vice versa; form into nonform and vice versa; man into woman and vice versa; the six realms of rebirth into no six-realms of rebirth and vice versa; and even turn the four great elements of earth, water, fire and wind into no earth, water, fire and wind" (T 24:1001b-c). Stein also cites the old version of *Śūraṅgama Sūtra* (T 645) in which Māra, the Fisherman who must be tamed, was contrasted with the bodhisattva, he was not "Uncontaminated-by-activity-in-Māra's-domain" (1986:29–30). In all these cases, a bodhisattva deconstructs the ordinary reality held by unenlightened people and by turning everything upside down, shocks them into a new vision. In the words of Thurman, like the great magician Vimalakīrti, Ch'an masters and Tantric mahāsiddas also delighted in using these "liberative techniques."

11. The Chinese translation ends with kissing. But the Sanskrit original, which is retained in the Tibetan translation, goes on to mention sexual intercourse, which would be the logical conclusion of the forgoing progression. The omission was probably due to the translator's consideration for the Chinese Confucian sensibility. I owe this observation to Masatoshi Nagatomi.

12. The version I read belonged to the private collection of Professor Wu Hsiao-ling

and was printed in 1938. Fu Hsi-hua had a copy printed in 1909 by I-hua-t'ang of Shanghai. See Fou Si-Houa, *Catalogue des Pao-kinan* (Universite de Paris, Center D'etudes sinologiques de Pekin, 1951), p. 8.

13. This terra-cotta figure was found in Uttar Pradesh. But Pal pointed out that a female holding a pair of fish was a common motif in terracotta figures of this period and was known from Mathurā, Kanśāmbī, and Chandraketugarh, northwest of Calcutta. He suggested that she represented a goddess of abundance whose cult was popular across a wide area of the north Indian riverine plains (Pal 1987:40).

14. In addition to this play, he was also featured in the *Hsüan-ho i-shih* (Anecdotes of the Hsüan-ho Era) and several other plays, including *Lin-chiang-i Hsiao-hsiang ch'iu yeh-yü tsa-chü* (Autumnal Night Rain Falling on the Station Bordering on Hsiao-hsiang River, included in *Yüan-chü hsüan*, first *ts'e*) and *Sung-shang-huang yü-tuan chin-feng-cha tsa-chü* (Sung Emperor's Personal Judging the Case of Golden Phoenix Hairpin, included in *Yüan-chü hsüan wai-p'ien*, first *ts'e*) as a main character. But he was depicted as a stock-character of an upright official in these works. I thank Robert Gimello for sharing the information concerning the depiction of Chang Shang-ying in these literary works.

15. Ku Sui, a playwright of the twentieth century, wrote a play entitled *Ma-lang-fu tso-hua Chin-sha-tan* (Mr. Ma's Wife Transpires while Sitting on Golden Sand Beach), published in *K'u-shui tso-chü san-chung* (Three *Tsa-chü* Plays by Ku Sui). In a preface dated 1936, he explained that he wrote it based on the story of Ma-lang-fu in the *Lotuses in Black Mud*, the Ming collection of biographies of famous courtesans. I am grateful to Wu Hsiao-ling, who was a student of Ku, for showing me the text of the play in 1986. This is the only play on Ma-lang-fu.

16. Wooden plaques with drawings of the miracles referred to in the founding myths of the temple are hung on the upper walls of the main hall. They were originally commissioned by the grateful beneficiaries of Gyoran Kannon's salvific deeds and donated to the temple as offerings. I visited the temple in May 1995 and saw these votive plaques. Each has an image of the Gyoran Kannon and a summary of the miracle. The full texts of the miracle stories, including the story translated here, were preserved on woodblocks in the temple. Copies printed on rice paper are given to the faithful as souvenirs. I thank Peter Gregory for securing a copy for me in 1993. Since the manuscript was written in cursive Japanese of the Edo period, it is difficult for me to read. I thank Hiroshi Obayashi and Paul Schalow for their aid in rendering it into English.

17. Sudhana and Dragon Princess appear in three dated groups of sculptures that feature Kuan-yin as the main icon located in Ta-tsu, Szechwan: Number 6 at Shih-men-shan dated 1141, Number 8 at Pei-ta, dated 1148, and Number 136 at Pei-shan, dated 1142–1146 (*Ta-tsu shih-k'e yen-chiu* 544, 435, 395). Sudhana appears not as a young boy, but as an old man resembling a foreign ascetic or Brahmin. It is only in the Cave of Perfect Enlightenment (Yüan-chüeh Tung) in An-yüeh dated 1099–1107 that Sudhana appears more like a young man. It is more rare to see the two in other medium. A beautiful set of Kuan-yin figure accompanied by the pair cast in gilt bronze appears as Number 104 in *The Crucible of Compassion and Wisdom* catalogue (1987:200). It is dated

to the thirteenth century. Number 102 in the catalogue shows Kuan-yin sitting on a rock with a vase on the left and a parrot perching on the right. The parrot is another iconographical indicator for the Kuan-yin of the South Sea. This is also dated to the thirteenth century (*The Crucible of Compassion and Wisdom* 1987:198).

18. Lung-nü appears in chapter 12, "Devadatta," of the *Lotus Sūtra*. She was eight years old. Mañjuśrī predicted that she would attain enlightenment, but Bodhisattva Wisdom Accumulation and Śāriputra doubted it. In response, the dragon girl held up a precious gem and offered it to the Buddha. She asked if the offering and accepting of the gem was quick or not, the doubters answered in the affirmative. She then said that she could achieve Buddhahood in even shorter a time than this. "In the space of an instant" she transformed herself into a man and achieved Buddhahood (Hurvitz 1976:199–201).

19. This is Number 10 of the Ying-pan-p'o group of sculptures (*Ta-tsu shih-k'e yen-chin* 432).

20. The animal, so identified, appears in chapter 71 of the *Hsi-yu chi*.

21. The White Parrot appears in chapters 42 and 57 of the *Hsi-yu chi*.

22. The summary of the story is based on the Ming text reprinted in 1979 as vol. 10 in *Ming Ch'eng-hua shuo-ch'ang tz'u-hua tsung-kan* (Collections of the Spoken and Sung *tz'u-hua* of the Ming Ch'eng-hua Era). The original is kept at the Shanghai Museum. I thank Mr. Wang Ch'ing-cheng, the Vice Director of the Museum, for generously sending the material to me.

23. P. Steven Sangren's work on the social construction of *ling* can be consulted for a theoretical analysis of such processes in Chinese religion. See his *History and Magical Power in A Chinese Community*.

11. Venerable Mother: Kuan-yin and Sectarian Religions in Late Imperial China

1. When the teacher points with his fingers at the spot between the initiate's eyes, called *ch'iao* (cavity or aperture), he opens it for the latter. When the initiate dies, the soul will leave the body through this opening and thus escape rebirth. Otherwise, the soul must leave via the normal bodily orifices and is reincarnated in undesirable realms. This is the first treasure. The second treasure refers to the correct hand gestures or mudrās symbolizing the three buddhas of the three epochs. The third treasure is a secret spell invoking Maitreya Buddha, "Wu-t'ai Fo Mi-le" (Oh! Great Buddha Maitreya), which must never be divulged to anyone.

2. This is the only ritual that each member must learn upon joining the religion. More than a way to show respect, it combines meditation and *ch'i-kung* together. First one stands in front of the altar with head slightly bowed, feet close together, and hands touching the thighs. One meditates for a short time with eyes focusing on the tip of the nose. Then, without moving the feet, one quickly kneels on the ground with hands touching the ground and placed as close to the knees as possible. One again meditates for a short time. Finally, after prostrating fully with the top of the head touching the ground, one gets up and resumes the original position and meditates a third time. In the beginning, one is advised to do the prostration twelve times in the morning and

evening. At that time, one silently chants the "five-character true word" (*nan-wu Kuan-shih-yin*) three times during meditation breaks. However, one should advance to the fifty-three prostrations, when one has to chant a text written by Patriarch Yang. It contains fifty-three sentences, each consisting three phrases that have to be chanted during the three meditation breaks. For instance, during the first prostration, one chants, "The first prostration is to worship the Venerable Mother whose compassionate heart is without limit (*Ti-i tsan, tsan Lao-mu, tz'u-hsin wu-liang*)." It is clear that for believers of Li Chiao, Kuan-yin is the Venerable Mother. It is interesting that the South Sea, Potalaka, the Parrot, and Cave of Tidal Sound are objects for worship as well (21, 22, 37, and 52 prostrations respectively), indicating Yang's familiarity of P'u-t'o (Li 1996:193–95).

3. I first learned about Li Chiao from Li Shi-yü, who told me about the founder and his main teachings. The information is confirmed by *Li Chiao hui-pien*, a sourcebook about the religion compiled by Chao Tung-shu and published by the Chung-hua Li Chiao Tsung-hui (Central Association of Chinese Li Chiao), located in Taipei, in 1953. I thank Li Shi-yü for sharing his knowledge about the religion with me and providing me with valuable handwritten copies of their liturgies.

4. The Chinese title *lao-mu* can of course be translated literally as "old mother." However, since this is a title of respect, it should be regarded the same way as the term *lao-shih,* which is rendered as "venerable teacher," instead of literally, "old teacher." It is for this reason that "Venerable Mother" is a better English equivalent. However, when the context makes it clear that the author is stressing her old age and her physical appearance as being old, then "Old Mother" is more appropriate.

5. Yü Sung-ch'ing argued that the *True Scripture* was composed by Yang Shou-i (1796–1828), the thirteenth patriarch of the Way of the Former Heaven, who was believed to be the reincarnation of Kuan-yin, and published by P'eng Te-yüan (1796–1858), who was the fourteenth patriarch and called himself Old Man of the Broad Wilderness (Kuang-yeh Lao-jen), a name very similar to the writer of the second preface. She therefore suggests that despite the earlier date indicated in the preface, the book was actually completed sometime in the early nineteenth century (Yü Sung-ch'ing 1993:116).

6. There is a considerable body of literature on this topic in English and Japanese. See Daniel L. Overmyer (1976:113–29, 1978, 1999), Shek (1980:162–66, chapter 7), Sawada Mizuho (1975:300–42), Ma Hsi-sha and Han Ping-fang (1992:165–241).

7. Lo quotes eight times from chapter 1 of *Tao Te Ching,* which says, "Non-being is the beginning of the universe and being is the mother of myriad things." He states, moreover, that "Mother is the ancestor (*tsu*) and the ancestor is the mother" (Ma and Han 1992:213).

8. Because the scripture mentions a patriarch named Non-action, Ma Hsi-sha and Han Ping-fang concluded that this scripture was written by the followers of Wang Sen (1542–1619), the founder of Ta-sheng Chiao (Great Vehicle Teaching), or Wen-hsiang Chiao (Incense Smelling Teaching), for he regarded himself as a successor to Lo Ch'ing, the founder of the Wu-wei Chiao (Non-action Teaching) and Wang's own religion was also known by the same name in the Ch'ing (Ma and Han 1992:615). However, this can-

not be the case because the date of 1523 is clearly written in the text belonging to the collection of Wu Hsiao-ling, which was used by Li and Naquin (as well as Ma and Han). How could the scripture be written, not to say published, nineteen years before Wang was born? The Patriarch of Non-action must therefore refer to Lo Ch'ing who died in 1527.

9. This is found in the *Hung-yang hou-hsü Jan-teng t'ien-hua pao-chüan* (Precious Scroll of Heavenly Flower of the Vast Yang which Continues [the Work] of the Lamp-lighting Buddha). Similar ideas are found in the *Hun-yüan hung-yang lin-fan P'iao Kao ching* (Scripture of Vast Yang of Undifferentiated Origin, P'iao Kao's Coming down to Earth). I thank Susan Naquin for lending me both texts, which are photocopied versions without pagination.

10. Li Shi-yü was told differently by his interviewees, who said that P'u-ming had three daughters. The oldest daughter was the incarnation of Ancient Buddha P'u-ching, the second daughter was the incarnation of Ancient Buddha P'u-hsien (Samanthabhadra) and the third daughter was the incarnation of Ancient Buddha Perfect Penetration (Yüan-t'ung) which was a well-known title for Kuan-yin (Li 1948:15). I wonder if this modern version might be influenced by the legend of Miao-shan.

11. I take "bodhisattva" to mean Kuan-yin and thus differ from the interpretation of Li and Naquin who take it to mean Lü herself (1988:156). I reached this conclusion after considering the whole sequence of sentences in the text. Since Nun Lü is called in the text "*lao-tsu*" (venerable patriarch), "bodhisattva" should more logically mean Kuan-yin.

12. The terminology of inner alchemy comes from *Ts'an-t'ung ch'i* (Token of the Concordance of the Three) attributed to Wei Po-yang of the mid-second century and *Pao-p'u-tzu* (The Master Who Embraced Unity) by Ko Hung (283–343), the classics of the alchemists, but are reinterpreted. The *Wu-chen p'ien* (On Realizing the True) written by Chang Po-tuan (d. 1082), on the other hand, being written by a master of the school, is a basic reference text for inner alchemy. The understanding of the exact meanings of the terms and the relationships with each other varies depending on the traditions and teachers one consults. My summary is based on the interpretations of Li Yü-chieh, the founder of T'ien-ti Chiao (Teachings of the Lord of the Universe), a syncretic new religion registered with the Taiwan government in 1982 that has drawn large numbers of followers, particularly among intellectuals and scientists. Li who died in 1994 was a life-long practitioner of inner alchemy and emphasized meditation based on the inner alchemy tradition in his teachings. I studied with him and participated in the meditation classes run by the sect from 1993 and 1995. I find his explanation most clear and straightforward because he simplified it for a modern audience. I discussed it more fully in my introduction to the English translation of the sect's basic teachings, *The Ultimate Realm: A New Understanding of Cosmos and Life* (1994:1–18). I have also consulted Berling (1980) and Lu K'uan Yu (1973).

In struggling with the exotic and esoteric terms in inner alchemy, I think it is salutary to bear in mind what Isabelle Robinet says about them. "No term has meaning except insofar as it functions with or in relation to another term or several others, because it is these relationships that are most important and unite the terms, along with the organization and functioning that gives rise to them. . . . This is why no meaning can be given for a term except in a specific context. One must always keep this rule in mind and make it a firm principle, with the goal being to treat all signifiers—words and images used in relation with each other—systematically as tools, seeing them in terms of the meanings they carry without stopping to examine the provisional and contingent nature of their existence. The meaning that they carry in each setting is the important thing, but this tends to destabilize them since meaning is necessarily polyvalent and the system consists of inviting the adept to hold onto this polyvalence and all its ramifications" (1997:231).

13. "In the last century of Ming rule, there had been an explosion of lay preachers of the White Lotus religion, and both the *Lung-hua* and *Lien-tsung* sūtras attempt to systematize the relationships of this formative period. They each give long lists of patriarchs and sect names, usually beginning with religious teachers of centuries before such as Lao-tzu, Buddha, Bodhidharma etc." (Li and Naquin 1988:171).

14. The term "*yüan-tun men*" appears only once in the text and it is at the very end of the scripture. After the final dedicatory "ten repayments" (*shih-pao*) of indebtedness with which all sectarian precious scrolls end, it says, "This precious scroll is left behind to be transmitted to later generations, so that the Perfect and Sudden Door can be restored (*Hisao-shi Pai-i Kuan-yin P'u-sa sung ying-erh hsia-sheng pao-chüan* 1994:543). It does not appear in the main body of the text, which instead refers to Huang-t'ien Tao and Hung-yang Chiao.

15. According to popular belief, when someone is thinking about you or talking about you, these are the signs that this is happening. This belief is still current today.

16. For instance, Lo Ch'ing often quotes the following gāthā, which is originally from the *Chin-kang k'e-i*:

> Do not seek far for the Buddha who is on the spiritual mountain.
> For the spiritual mountain is inside your heart.
> There is a stūpa of spiritual mountain within everyone.
> So just go and cultivate yourself under the stūpa of spiritual mountain.
> (Ma and Han 1992:192)

17. I owe this interpretation to the late Wu Hsiao-ling who told me in 1986. This is supported by statements to this effect in the text itself. For instance, it says, "North of the sun, Kuan-shih-yin saves four groups of people (*ssu-chung*, namely, monks, nuns, laymen, and laywomen). South of the dipper, Kuan-shih-yin protects people everywhere" (39a).

18. The Yüan-tun Chiao, with which the first Kuan-yin precious scroll discussed in this section was connected, used affiliation names for self-identification. Men's names all had the character *p'u*, and women's names *miao* (Ma and Han 992:871). Li and Naquin also note that many of the female donors on the 1670 stele in the Pao-Ming Ssu also had the character *miao* in their names. In the *Lien-tsung pao-chüan* reprinted in

1659 by a follower of the East Ta-sheng Chiao, we read, "Men use the character 'blessing' [*fu*] in their Buddhist names, women use the character 'marvelous' [*miao*] to continue the Lotus palace [Community]" (1988:174).

19. This is the sixteenth miracle. In the time of the Latter Han (947–950), Chinese soldiers invaded Ta-li. When they came to Kan-t'ung Monastery (in the foothills of Mt. Tien-tsang, south of Ta-li), they saw an old woman carrying a large boulder fastened by a grass rope on her back. When asked why she was carrying such a huge boulder, she answered that because she was old she could only carry a small stone. She could no longer compete with younger men who were all much stronger. When the invaders heard this, they became frightened and beat a hasty retreat (*Pai-kuo yin-yu* 25b-26a). The old woman was, of course, a manifestation of Kuan-yin. The large boulder forms the foundation for the Big Stone Shrine (Ta-shih An) that sits below Kan-t'ung Monastery today. When I visited the site in July 1987, I saw the stone stele commemorating the miracle, and an image of Kuan-yin as a matronly figure enshrined in the temple. Although the story postdates the Chien-ch'uan sculpture that Howard studied by about one century, there might still be a connection. Both could refer to the same belief that Kuan-yin appeared as an old woman to save the people. Such folk belief might have existed in oral form before the making of the statue and recording of the miracle.

20. It bears an inscription written by Ch'ien-yen Yüan-chang (1284–1357), a monk who lived on Mt. T'ien-mu in Chekiang province. He wrote that the painting was seen by Chung-feng Ming-pen (1263–1323), a famous Ch'an master also from Mt. T'ien-mu who wrote eulogies on many surviving Kuan-yin portraits. This painting is in the Soshiro Yabumoto Collection, Tokyo, Japan. It was published as number 5 in *Sōgen-ga* (Cahill 1982:9). I thank James Cahill for the reference.

21. All materials from the *Biographies of Good Women* are based on the draft translation made by Yuet-keung Lo, who has prepared the manuscript for publication. I am thankful to him for sharing it with me.

Bibliography

Works in Buddhist Collections (Cited in Text by Canon and Volume Number)

HTC. *Hsin-pien wan-tzu hsü-tsang ching* 新編卍字續藏經 (Newly Compiled Continuation of the Buddhist Canon). 1977. 150 vols. Reprint of *Dainippon zoku zōkyō* 大日本續藏經. Taipei: Hsin-wen-feng.

T. *Taishōshinshū daizōkyō* 大正新修大藏經 (The Buddhist Canon Newly Compiled during the Taishō Era). 1924–1935. Edited by Takakusu Junjirō 高楠順次郎 and Watanabe Kaigyoku 渡辺海旭. 100 vols. Tokyo: Taishō issaikyō kankōkai.

Besson zakki 別尊雜記 (Miscellaneous Notes on Buddhist Images other than the Buddha), by Shinkaku 心覺. T vol. 88, no. 3007.

Ch'an-yüan ch'ing-kuei 禪苑清規 (The Pure Rules for Ch'an Monasteries), by Ch'ang-lu Tsung-tse 長蘆宗賾. HTC vol. 111.

Cheng-chü kuang-ming ting-i ching 成具光明定意經 (Sūtra on the Mental Fixation of Integral Illumination), translated by Chih-yao 支曜. T vol. 15, no. 630.

Cheng fa-hua ching 正法華經 (Sūtra of the Lotus of the Correct Law), translated by Dharmarakṣa. T vol. 9, no. 263.

Cheng-tao ko 證道歌 (Song of Enlightenment), by Yüng-chia Hsüan-chüeh 永嘉玄覺. HTC vol. 111.

Ch'ien-kuang-yen Kuan-tzu-tsai P'u-sa mi-mi-fa ching 千光眼觀自在菩薩祕密法經 (Sūtra of the Secret Method [spoken] by Master Perceiver Bodhisattva Who Has a Thousand Luminous Eyes), translated by Su-p'o-lo 蘇嚩羅. T vol. 20, no. 1065.

Ch'ien-shou chien-yen Kuan-shih-yin P'u-sa kuang-ta yüan-man wụ-ai Ta-pei-hsin t'o-lo-ni ching 千手千眼觀世音菩薩廣大圓滿無礙大悲心陀羅尼經 (The Vast, Perfect, Unobstructed Dhāraṇī Sūtra of Great Compassionate Heart [taught by] the Thousand-Handed and Thousand-Eyed Avalokiteśvara Bodhisattva), translated by Bhagavadharma. T vol. 20, no. 1060.

Ch'ien-shou Ch'ien-yen Ta-pei hsin-chou hsing-fa 千手千眼大悲心呪行法 (Ritual Procedure for Performing the Great Compassionate Heart Dhāraṇī of the Thousand Hands and Thousand Eyes), by Tu-t'i 讀體. HTC vol. 29.

Ch'ien-shou Kuan-yin tsao-tz'u-ti fa i-kuei 千手觀音造次第法儀規 (Rules for the Sequential Setting Up of Thousand-Handed Avalokiteśvara), translated by Śubhakarasiṃha. T vol. 20, no. 1068.

Ch'ien-shou-yen Ta-pei-hsin chou hsing-fa 千手眼大悲心呪行法 (Ritual Procedure for Performing the Great Compassionate Heart Dhāraṇī of the Thousand Hands and Eyes), by Chih-li 知禮. T vol. 46, no. 1950.

Ch'ien-yen ch'ien-pi Kuan-shih-yin P'u-sa t'o-lo-ni shen-chou ching 千眼千臂觀世音菩薩陀羅尼神呪經 (Sūtra of the Divine Dhārāṇī of the Thousand-Eyed and Thousand-Armed Avalokiteśvara), translated by Chih-t'ung 智通. T vol. 20, no. 1057.

Chih-chüeh Ch'an-shih tzu-hsing lu 智覺禪師自行錄 (Record of Self-Cultivation of Ch'an Master Chih-chüeh), by Wen-ch'ung 文沖. HTC vol. 111.

Ch'ih-hsiu Pai-chang ch'ing-kuei 敕修百丈清規 (Pure Rules of Pai-chang Compiled under Imperial Order), by Te-hui 德輝. HTC vol. 111.

Chih-yüeh lu 指月錄 (Record of Pointing at the Moon), by Ch'ü Ju-chi 瞿汝稷 and Yen Tao-ch'e 嚴道徹. HTC vol. 143.

Ch'ing Kuan-shih-yin P'u-sa hsiao-fu tu-hai t'o-lo-ni ching 請觀世音菩薩消伏毒害陀羅尼經 (Dhārāṇī Sūtra of Invoking Avalokiteśvara Bodhisattva to Dissipate Poison and Harm), translated by Nan-t'i 難提. T vol. 20, no. 1043.

Ch'ing Kuan-shih-yin P'u-sa hsiao-fu tu-hai t'o-lo-ni san-mei i. 請觀世音菩薩消伏毒害陀羅尼三昧儀 (Samādhi Rite for the Dhārāṇī Sūtra of Invoking Avalokiteśvara Bodhisattva to Dissipate Poison and Harm), by Tsun-shih 遵式. T vol. 46, no. 1946.

Ching-te ch'uan-teng lu 景德傳燈錄 (Transmission of the Lamp Compiled in the Ching-te era), by Tao-yüan 道原. T vol. 51, no. 2076.

Chin-kuang-ming ching 金光明經 (Sūtra of the Golden Light, *Suvarṇaprabhāsa Sūtra*), translated by Tan-wu-ch'en 曇無讖. T vol. 16, no. 663.

Chi shen-chou san-pao kan-t'ung lu 集神州三寶感通錄 (Record of the Miraculous Responses of the Three Treasures in China), by Tao-hsüan 道宣. T vol. 52, no. 2106.

Chiu mien-jan e-kuei t'o-lo-ni shen-chou ching 救面燃餓鬼陀羅尼神呪經 (Divine Dhārāṇī Sūtra for Saving Hungry Ghosts with Burning Faces), translated by Śikṣānanda. T vol. 21, no. 1314.

Chiu-pa yen-k'ou e-kuei t'o-lo-ni ching 救拔焰口餓鬼陀羅尼經 (Dhāraṇī Sūtra for Saving Ghosts with Burning Mouths), translated by Amoghavajra. T vol. 21, no. 1313.

Chung-ching mu-lu 衆經目錄 (Catalogues of Sūtras), by Fa-ching 法經. T vol. 55, no. 2146.

Chung-ching mu-lu 衆經目錄 (Catalogues of Sūtras), by Yen-ts'ung 彥琮 et al. T vol. 55, no. 2147.

Ch'u san-tsang chi-chi 出三藏記集 (A Compilation of Notices on the Translation of the Tripiṭaka), by Seng-yu 僧祐. T vol. 55, no. 2145.

Fa-hua ching-lun 法華經論 (Treatise on the *Lotus Sūtra*), translated by Bodhiruci. T vol. 26, no. 1520.

Fa-hua chuan-chi 法華傳記 (Record of the *Louts Sūtra*), by Seng-hsiang 僧祥. T vol. 51, no. 2068.

Fa-hua san-mei ch'an-i 法華三昧懺儀 (Rules for the Lotus Samādhi Repentance), by Chih-i 智顗. T vol. 46, no. 1941.

Fa-hua san-mei hsing-shih yün-hsiang pu-chu-i 法華三昧行事運想補助儀 (Supplementary Rite of Meditation in Performing the Lotus Samādhi), by Chan-jan 湛然. T vol. 46, no. 1942.

Fang-kuang po-jo ching 放光般若經 (Sūtra of Illuminating Prajñā), translated by Mokṣala. T vol. 8, no. 221.

Fan-i ming-i chi 翻譯名義集 (Meaning of Buddhist Terms), by Fa-yün 法雲. T vol. 54, no. 2131.

Fa-yüan chu-lin 法苑珠林 (Forest of Gems from the Garden of Buddhism), by Tao-shih 道世. T vol. 53, no. 2122.

Fo-chien Ch'an-shih yü-lu 佛鑑禪師語錄 (Recorded Sayings of Ch'an Master Fo-chien), by Wu-ch'un Shih-fan 無準師範 and recorded by Tsung-hui 宗會 and Chih-che 智折. HTC vol. 121.

Fo-shuo shih-i-mien Kuan-shih-yin shen-chou ching 佛說十一面觀世音神呪經 (Sūtra of the Divine Dhārāṇī on the Eleven-Headed Avalokiteśvara Spoken by the Buddha), translated by Yeh-she ch'üeh-to 耶舍崛多. T vol. 20, no. 1070.

Fo-shuo Wu-liang ch'ing-ching p'ing-teng chüeh ching 佛說無量清淨平等覺經 (Sūtra of the Enlightenment of Measureless Purity and Equality Spoken by the Buddha), translated by Lokakṣema. T vol. 12, no. 261.

Fo-shuo wu liang-shou ching 佛說無量壽經 (Sūtra of the Buddha of Measureless Life Spoken by the Buddha), translated by Sanghavarman. T vol. 12, no. 360.

Fo-shuo Yüeh-ming P'u-sa ching 佛說月明菩薩經 (Sūtra of Moon-light Bodhisattva Spoken by the Buddha), translated by Chih-ch'ien 支謙. T vol. 3, no. 169.

Fo-tsu li-tai t'ung-tsai 佛祖歷代通載 (A Comprehensive Record of the Buddhas and Patriarchs in Successive Generations), by Nien-ch'ang 念常. T vol. 49, no. 2036.

Fo-tsu t'ung-chi 佛祖統記 (Record of the Lineage of the Buddhas and Patriarchs), by Chih-p'an 志磐. T vol. 49, no. 2035.

Hsiao-shih chin-kang k'e-i hui-yao chu-chieh 銷釋金剛科儀會要注解 (Compendium of Commentaries Explaining the Ritual of Reciting the *Diamond Sūtra*, by Tsung-ching 宗鏡 and Chieh-lien 覺璉. HTC vol. 92.

Hsü kao-seng chuan 續高僧傳 (Continuation of the Biographies of Eminent Monks), by Tao-hsüan 道宣. T vol. 50, no. 2060.

Hua-yen ching 華嚴經 (Flower Garland Sūtra, Avataṃsaka Sūtra), translated by Śikṣānanda. T vol. 10, no. 279.

Hung-ming chi 弘明集 (Collection in Propagating and Illuminating Buddhism), by Seng-yu 僧祐. T vol. 52, no. 2102.

Hung-tsan fa-hua chuan 弘贊法華傳 (Biographies of Promoters of the *Lotus Sūtra*), by Hui-hsiang 慧祥. T vol. 51, no. 2067.

Jōgyō oshō shōrai mokuroku 常曉和尚請來目錄 (Record of Items Respectfully Brought Back by Monk Jōgyō), by Jōgyō 常曉. T vol. 55, no. 2163.

Ju-i-lun t'o-lo-ni ching 如意輪陀羅尼經 (Dhāraṇī Sūtra of Cintāmanicakra), translated by Bodhiruci. T vol. 20, no. 1080.

K'ai-yüan shih-chiao lu 開元釋教錄 (Record of Śākyamuni's Teachings, Compiled in the K'ai-yüan Era), by Chih-sheng 智昇. T vol. 55, no. 2154.

Kakuzenshō 覺禪鈔 (Notes Made by Kakuzen), by Kakuzen 覺禪. T vol. 89, no. 3022.

Kao-seng chuan 高僧傳 (Biographies of Eminent Monks), by Hui-chiao 慧皎. T vol. 50, no. 2059.

Kao Wang Kuan-shih-yin ching 高王觀世音經 (King Kao's Kuan-shih-yin Sūtra). T vol. 85, no. 2898.

Kuang hung-ming chi 廣弘明集 (Extended Collection of Propagating and Illuminating Buddhism), by Tao-hsüan 道宣. T vol. 52, no. 2103.

Kuan-shih-yin ching-chou chih-yen chi 觀世音經呪持驗記 (Record of Manifestations [Resulting] from Recitation of Kuan-shih-yin Sūtras and Mantras). compiled by Chou K'e-fu 周克復. HTC vol. 134.

Kuan-shih-yin P'u-sa shou-chi ching 觀世音菩薩授記經 (Sūtra of Avalokiteśvara Bodhisattva's Receiving Prediction), translated by Dharmodgata. T vol. 12, no. 371.

Kuan-shih-yin P'u-sa wang-sheng ching-t'u pen-yüan ching 觀世音菩薩往生淨土本願經 (Sūtra of the Bodhisattva Kuan-shih-yin [Who explains] the Conditions to be Born in the Pure Land). HTC vol. 87.

Kuan-tzu-tsai P'u-sa sui-hsin t'o-lo-ni ching 觀自在菩薩隨心陀羅尼經 (Master Perceiver Bodhisattva's Dhāraṇī Sūtra Which Conforms to One's Wishes), translated by Chih-t'ung 智通. T vol. 20, no. 1103.

Kuan Wu-liang-shou Fo ching 觀無量壽佛經 (Sūtra of Visualization of Amitāyus Buddha), translated by Kalayaśas. T vol. 12, no. 365.

Kuan-yin hsüan-i 觀音玄義 (Profound Meanings of the Kuan-yin Sūtra), by Chih-i 智顗. T vol. 34, no. 1726.

Kuo-ch'ing pai-lu 國清百錄 (One Hundred Items about Kuo-ch'ing [Temple]), by Kuan-ting 灌頂. T vol. 46, no. 1934.

Li-tai san-pao chi 歷代三寶記 (Record of the Three Treasures Throughout Successive Generations), by Fei Ch'ang-fang 費長房. T vol. 49, no. 2034.

Liu-tu chi ching 六度集經 (Sūtra on the Collection of the Six Perfections), translated by K'ang-seng-hui 康僧會. T vol. 3, no. 152.

Lung-hsing pien-nien t'ung-lun 隆興編年通論 (A Year by Year Chronicle of Buddhist History from 64 to 957 C.E.), by Tsu-hsiu 祖琇. HTC vol. 130.

Miao-fa lien-hua ching 妙法蓮華經 (Sūtra of the Lotus Flower of the Wonderful Law), translated by Kumārajīva, T vol. 9, no. 262.

Miao-fa lien-hua ching hsüan-i 妙法蓮華經玄義 (Mysterious Meanings of the *Lotus Sūtra*), by Chih-i 智顗. T vol. 33, no. 1716.
Pan-chou san-mei ching 般舟三昧經 (Samādhi Sūtra of Direct Encounter with the Buddhas of the Present, *Pratyutpanna-Buddha-saṃmukhā-vasthita-samādhi Sūtra*), translated by Lokakṣema. T vol. 13, no. 418.
Pei-hua ching 悲華經 (Sūtra of the Compassionate Lotus, Karuṇāpundarīka Sūtra), translated by T'an-wu-ch'en 曇無讖. T vol. 3, no. 157.
Pi-chiu-ni chuan 比丘尼傳 (Lives of the Nuns), by Pao-ch'ang 寶唱. T vol. 50, no. 2063.
Pi-yen lu 碧巖錄 (Blue Cliff Record), by Hsüeh-t'ou Ch'ung-hsien 雪竇重顯. T vol. 48, no. 2003.
Po-jo hsin-ching yu-tsan 般若心經幽贊 (Profound Eulogy on the *Heart Sūtra*), by K'uei-chi 窺基. HTC vol. 41.
Pu-k'ung-ssu-so chou ching 不空羂索呪經 (Dhāraṇī Sūtra of Amoghapāśa), translated by She-na-ch'üeh-t'o 闍那崛多. T vol. 20, no. 1093.
Reiganji oshō shōrai hōmondōgu tō mokuroku 靈巖寺和尚請來法門道具等目錄 (Record of Ritual Implements and Other Items Respectfully Brought Back by the Monk of the Reigan Temple), by Engyō 圓行. T vol. 55, no. 2164.
Seng-chieh Ho-shang yü ju nieh-pan shuo liu-tu ching 僧伽和尚欲入涅槃說六度經 (Sūtra Spoken by Monk Seng-chieh on the Six Perfections Before His Entering Nirvāṇa). T vol. 85, no. 2920.
Shan nü-jen chuan 善女人傳 (Biographies of Good Women), by P'eng Shao-sheng 彭紹升. HTC vol. 150.
Shih-chia fang-chih 釋迦方志 (Buddhist Gazetteer), by Tao-hsüan 道宣. T vol. 51, no. 2088.
Shih-shih chi-ku lüeh 釋氏稽古略 (Brief Compilation of Buddhist History), by Chüeh-an 覺岸. T vol. 49, no. 2037.
Shih-shih chi-ku lüeh hsü-chi 釋氏稽古略續集 (Continuation of A Brief Compilation of Buddhist History), by Huan-lun 幻輪. T vol. 49, no. 2038.
Shih-shih yao-lan 釋氏要覽 (Essential Readings for Buddhists), by Tao-ch'eng 道誠. T vol. 54, no. 2127.
Shou leng-yen ching 首楞嚴經 (*Śūraṅgama Sūtra*), translated by Paramiti. T vol. 19, no. 945.
Ssu-ming tsun-che chiao-hsing lu 四明尊者教行錄 (Record of the Venerable Master of Ssu-ming's Words and Deeds), by Tsung-hsiao 宗曉. T vol. 46, no. 1937.
Sung kao-seng chuan 宋高僧傳 (Biographies of Eminent Monks Compiled in the Sung), by Tsan-ning 贊寧. T vol. 50, no. 2061.
Ta chih-tu lun 大智度論 (Commentary on the Great *Prajñā-pāramitā Sūtra*), translated by Kumārajīva. T vol. 25, no. 1509.
Ta Chou k'an-ting chung-ching mu-lu 大周刊定眾經目錄 (Catalogue of Sūtras, Authorized in the Great Chou), by Ming-ch'üan 明佺 et al. T vol. 55, no. 2153.
Ta-chuang-yen ching lun 大莊嚴經論 (Treatise on the Splendor of Mahāyāna Sūtras, *Sūtrālaṅkāra-śāstra*), translatedby Kumārajīva. T vol. 4, no. 201.

Ta-fang-kuang p'u-sa tsang Wen-chu-shih-li ken-pen i-kuei 大方廣菩薩藏文殊師利根本儀軌 (Fundamental Ordinance of Mañjuśrī, Mañjuśrīmulakalpa), translated by T'ien-hsi-tsai 天息災. T vol. 20, no. 1191.

Ta-fang-kuang shih-lun ching 大方廣十輪經 (The Great Extended Sūtra on the Ten Wheels, *Daśacakrakṣitigarbha*). T vol. 13, no. 410.

Ta-fang-pien Fo-pao-en ching 大方便佛報恩經 (Sūtra of the Buddha's Repaying Kindness with Great Skillful Means). T vol. 3, no. 156.

Ta-jih ching 大日經 (The Great Sun Sūtra), translated by Śubhakarasiṃha. T vol. 18, no. 848.

Ta Ming Jen-hsiao Huang-hou meng-kan Fo shuo ti-i hsi-yu ta kung-te ching 大明仁孝皇后夢感佛說第一希有大功德經 (The Sūtra of the Great Merit of Foremost Rarity Spoken by the Buddha Received by the Empress Jen-Hsiao of the Great Ming in a Dream). HTC vol. 1.

Tao-hsüan lü-shih kan-t'ung lu 道宣律師感通錄 (Records of Spiritual Resonance of the Vinaya Master Tao-hsüan), by Tao-hsüan 道宣. T vol 52, no. 2107.

Ta O-mi-t'o ching 大阿彌陀經 (The Greater Amitābha Sūtra), by Wang Jih-hsiu 王日休. T vol. 12, no. 364.

Ta-pei ch'i-ch'ing 大悲啟請 (Invocation of the Great Compassionate One). T vol. 85, no. 2843.

Ta po-jo p'o-lo-mi-to ching 大般若波羅密多經 (The Great *Prajñā-pāramitā Sūtra*), translated by Hsüan-tsang 玄奘. T vols. 5–7, no. 220.

Ta-sheng chuang-yen pao-wang ching 大乘莊嚴寶王經 (Sūtra of the Mahāyāna, the Precious King of Adornment, *Karaṇḍavyūha Sūtra*), translated by T'ien-hsi-tsai 天息災. T vol. 20, no. 1050.

Ta-sheng pen-sheng hsin-ti kuan ching 大乘本生心地觀經 (Sūtra on Observing the Mahāyāna Mind Ground of Original Birth), translated by Prajñā Tripiṭaka. T vol. 3, no. 159.

Ta-sheng ta-chi Ti-tsang shih-lun ching 大乘大集地藏十輪經 (Sūtra of the Great Collection of the Great Vehicle on Ti-tsang's Ten Wheels), translated by Hsüan-tsang 玄奘. T vol. 13, no. 411.

Ta-shu-chin-na-lo Wang so-wen ching 大樹緊那羅王所問經 (Sūtra Answering the Questions of king Druma-kinnara, *Druma-kinnararājaparipṛcchā*), translated by Kumārajīva. T vol. 15, no. 625.

Ta T'ang hsi-yü chi 大唐西域記 (Record of the West Regions Compiled in the Great T'ang Dynasty), by Pien-chi 辯機 and Hsüan-tsang 玄奘. T vol. 51, no. 2087.

Ta T'ang nei-tien lu 大唐內典錄 (The Record of Buddhist Scriptures of the Great T'ang), by Tao-hsüan 道宣. T vol. 55, no. 2149.

T'ien-p'in miao-fa lien-hua ching 添品妙法蓮華經 (Sūtra of the Lotus Flower of the Wonderful Law with an Additional Chapter), translated by Jñānaguptā and Dharmagupta. T vol. 9, no. 264.

Ti-tsang P'u-sa pen-yüan ching 地藏菩薩本願經 (Sūtra of the Original Vow of Ti-tsang Bodhisattva), translated by Śikṣānanda. T vol. 13, no. 412.

T'o-lo-ni chi-ching 陀羅尼集經 (Sūtra on the Collection of Dhāraṇīs), translated by Ajikuta 阿地瞿多. T vol. 18, no. 901.

T'o-lo-ni tsa-chi 陀羅尼雜集 (Dhāraṇī Miscellany). T vol. 21, no. 1336.

Tsa pao-tsang ching 雜寶藏經 (Sūtra of Miscellaneous Treasures), translated by Chi-chia-yeh 吉迦夜 and Tan-yao 曇曜. T vol. 4, no. 203.

Tseng-hsiu chiao-yüan ch'ing-kuei 增修教苑清規 (Expanded and Revised Pure Rules for Teaching Cloisters), by Tzu-ch'ing 自慶. HTC vol. 101.

Ts'ung-jung lu 從容錄 (Record of Leisure), by Wan-sung Hsing-hsiu 萬松行秀. T vol. 48, no. 2004.

Wei-mo-chieh ching 維摩詰經 (*Vimalakīrti Sūtra*), translated by Chih-ch'ien 支謙. T vol. 14, no. 474.

Yao-shih liu-li-kuang ch'i-fo pen-yüan kung-te ching 藥師琉璃光七佛本願功德經 (Sūtra of the Merit of the Original Vows Made by the Seven Medicine Buddhas of Lapis-lazuli Light), translated by Hsüan-tsang 玄奘. T vol 14, no. 451.

Yüan-chüeh ching 圓覺經 (Sūtra of Complete Enlightenment, Short for *Ta-fang-kuang yüan-chüeh hsiu-to-lo liao-i ching*), translated by Buddhatrata. T vol. 17, no. 842.

Yü-chia chi-yao chiu A-nan t'o-lo-ni yen-k'ou kuei-i ching 瑜伽集要救阿難陀羅尼焰口軌儀經 (Sūtra on the Ritual Directions Summarizing the Yoga Dhāraṇīs for Saving Ānanda from the Burning Mouth), translated by Amoghavajra. T vol. 21, no. 1318.

Yüeh-teng san-mei ching 月燈三昧經 (Sūtra of Moon-lamp Samādhi), translated by Narendrayaśaṣ. T vol. 15, no. 639.

Zozōshō 圖像抄 (Iconographical Sketches). T vol. 88, no. 3006.

Other Primary and Secondary References

WORKS CITED BY ABBREVIATED TITLE

CKCTC. *Ch'ang-kuo chou t'u-chih* 昌國州圖志 (Gazetteer of Ch'ang-kuo with Maps). Compiled by Feng Fu-ching 馮福京 et al. in 1297–1307. 7 *chüan.*

CKFSC. *Chung-kuo fo-ssu shih-chih hui-k'an* 中國佛寺史志彙刊 (Collections of Temple Gazetteers of Chinese Buddhist Monasteries). 1980. 1st collection, Taipei: Ming-wen.

CLFCC. *Chin-ling fan-ch'a chih* 金陵梵刹志 (Gazetteer of Temples in Nanking). 1980. Compiled by Ko Yin-liang 葛寅亮 in 1607. 5 *chüan.* Reprinted in *Chung-kuo fo-ssu shih-chih hui-k'an*, 1st collection, vol. 3. Taiwan: Ming-wen.

CTSMTC. *Ch'ien-tao Ssu-ming t'u-ching* 乾道四明圖經 (Gazetteer of Ssu-ming Compiled in the Ch'ien-tao Era), compiled by Chang Ching 張津 et al. in 1169. 12 *chüan.*

DMB. *Dictionary of Ming Biography, 1368–1644.* 1976. Edited by L. Carrington Goodrich and Chaoying Fang, 2 vols. New York: Columbia University Press.

HCFC. *Hang-chou fu-chih* 杭州府志 (Gazetteer of Hangchow). 1924. Separate issue on customs and produces. 8 *chüan.*

HCLAC. *Hsiang-ch'un Lin-an chih* 咸淳臨安志 (Gazetteer of Lin-an Compiled in the Hsiang-ch'un Era). Compiled by Ch'ien Shuo-yu 潛說友 in 1268.

HHYLC. *Hsi-hu yu-lan chih* 西湖遊覽志 (Record of Sightseeing of the West Lake). Compiled by T'ien Ju-ch'eng 田汝成 in 1526. 24 *chüan.*

PCSMC. *Pao-ch'ing Ssu-ming chih* 寶慶四明志 (Gazetteer of Ssu-ming Compiled in the Pao-ch'ing Era). Compiled by Lo Chün 羅濬 et al. in 1225–57. 21 *chüan.*

PTSC. *P'u-t'o shan-chih* 普陀山志 (Gazetteer of P'u-t'o), in eight editions:

——. 1. *P'u-t'o-lo-chia Shan chih* 普陀洛迦山志. Compiled by Sheng Hsi-ming 盛熙明 in 1361. 1 *chüan.* T vol. 51, no. 2101.

——. 2. *P'u-t'o-lo-chia shan chih* 普陀洛迦山志. Compiled by Hou Chi-kao 侯繼高 in 1589. 6 *chüan.* Tokyo: Naikaku Bunko.

——. 3. *Ch'ung-hsiu P'u-t'o shan chih* 重修普陀山志. 1980. Compiled by Chou Ying-pin 周應賓 in 1607. 6 *chüan.* Reprinted in *CFSC*, 1st collection, vol. 9. Taiwan: Ming-wen.

——. 4. *Tseng-hsiu Nan-hai P'u-t'o Shan chih* 增修南海普陀山志. Compiled by Ch'iu Lien 裘璉 in 1698. 15 *chüan.*

——. 5. *Tseng-hsiu Nan-hai P'u-t'o Shan chih.* Compiled by Chu Chin 朱瑾 and Ch'en Chün 陳璿 in 1705. 15 *chüan.*

——. 6. *Ch'ung-hsiu Nan-hai P'u-t'o Shan chih* 重修南海普陀山志. Compiled by Hsü Yen 許琰 in 1739. 20 *chüan.*

——. 7. *Ch'ung-hsiu Nan-hai P'u-t'o Shan chih.* 1982. Compiled by Ch'in Yao-tseng 秦耀曾 in 1832. 20 *chüan.* Reprinted in *Chung-kuo ming-shan sheng-chi chih tsung-k'an* 中國名山勝跡志叢刊, edited by Shen Yün-lung 沈雲龍, 6th collection, vols. 50–53. Taiwan: Wen-hai.

——. 8. *P'u-t'o-lo-chia hsin-chih* 普陀洛迦新志. 1980. Compiled by Wang Heng-yen 王亨彥 in 1924. 12 *chüan.* Reprinted in CKFSC, vol. 10. Taiwan: Ming-wen.

STCC. *Hang-chou Shang-t'ien-chu Chiang-ssu chih* 杭州上天竺講寺志 (Gazetteer of Upper T'ien-chu Monastery of Hangchow). 1980. Compiled by Shih Kuang-pin 釋廣賓 [of the Ming]. Reprint of 1897 edition. Reprinted in CKFSC, vol. 26. Taiwan: Ming-wen.

YCFH. *Yün-ch'i fa hui* 雲棲法彙 (Collected Works of Master Yün-ch'i), by Chu-hung 袾宏. 1897. 34 *ts'e.* Nanking: Ching-ling k'e-ching ch'u. Reprinted in Taipei, 1973.

——. *Cheng-e chi* 正訛集 (Refutation of Mistaken Views), 27.

——. *Chu-ch'uang san-pi* 竹窗三筆 (Final Jottings Under a Bamboo Window). 26.

——. *Fa-chieh sheng-fan shui-lu sheng-hui hsiu-chai i-kuei* 法界聖凡水陸勝會修齋儀規 (Ritual Rules for Conducting the Solemn Assembly of Water and Land for Saints and Mortals of the Dharma Realm), 18–19.

——. *Yü-chia chi-yao shih-shih i-kuei* 瑜伽集要施食儀軌 (Ritual Rules for Conducting the Bestowing of Food on Hungry Ghosts). 20.

YYSMC. *Yen-yu Ssu-ming chih* 延祐四明志 (Gazetteeer of Ssu-ming), compiled in the Yen-yu Era (1320) by Yüan Chüeh 袁桷.

OTHER SOURCES

Ahern, Emily M. 1975. "The Power and Pollution of Chinese Women." In *Women in Chinese Society*, edited by Marjorie Wolf and Roxanne Witke, 193–214. Stanford: Stanford University Press.

Baiei Hemmi 逸見梅榮. 1960. *Kannonzō* 觀音像 (Kuan-yin Iconography). Tokyo.

Basham, A. L. 1981. "The Evolution of the Concept of the Bodhisattva." In *The Bodhisattva Doctrine in Buddhism*, edited by Leslie Kawamura, 19–59. Waterloo: Wilfried Laurier University Press.

Beal, Samuel, translator. 1884. *Si-yu-ki: Buddhist Record of the Western World.* 2 vols. New York: Paragon Book Reprint, 1968.

Beijing T'u-shu-kuan tsang Chung-kuo li-tai shih-k'e t'o-pen hui-pien 北京圖書館藏中國歷代石刻拓本匯編 (Collections of Rubbings from Stone Inscriptions through the Dynasties Kept in the Beijing Library). 1991.

Bercholz, Samuel, and Sherab Chodzin Kohn, editors. 1993. *Entering the Stream: An Introduction to the Buddha and His Teachings.* Boston: Shambala.

Berkowitz, Alan J. 1995. "Account of the Buddhist Thaumaturge Baozhi." In *Buddhism in Practice*, edited by Donald S. Lopez, Jr., 578–85. Princeton: Princeton University Press.

Berling, Judith. 1980. *The Syncretic Religion of Lin Chao-en.* New York: Columbia University Press.

Bhattacharyya, Behoytush. 1924. *The Indian Buddhist Iconography.* London: Oxford University Press.

Birnbaum, Raoul. 1983. *Studies on the Mysteries of Mañjuśrī.* Boulder, Colo.: Society for the Study of Chinese Religions.

Bishop, Peter. 1989. *The Myth of Shangri-La. Tibet, Travel Writing and the Western Creation of Sacred Landscape.* Berkeley: University of California Press.

Bodde, Derk. 1961. "Myths of Ancient China." In *Mythologies of the Ancient World*, edited by Samuel N. Kramer, 367–508. Garden City: Doubleday.

Boerschmann, Earnst. 1911. *Die Baukunst und Religiöse Kultur der Chinesen.* vol. 1, *P'u T'o Shan.* Berlin: Druck und Verlag von Georg Reimer.

Boisselier J. 1965. "Precisions sur quelques images Khmeres d'Avalokiteśvara." *Arts Asiatiques* 11(1):75–89.

——. 1970. "Pouvoir royal et symbolisime architectureal: Neak Pean et son importance pour la royaute angkorienne," *Arts Asiatiques* 21:91–108.

Bokenkamp, Stephen R. 1986. "The Peach Flower Font and the Grotto Passage." *Journal of the American Oriental Society.* 106.1:65–78.

——. 1997. *Early Daoist Scriptures.* Berkeley: University of California Press.

Boucher, Daniel J. 1996. "Buddhist Translation Procedures in Third-Century China: A Study of Dharmarakṣa and His Translation Idiom." Ph.D. dissertation, University of Pennsylvania.

Boucher, Sandy. 1999. *Discovering Kwan Yin, Buddhist Goddess of Compassion: A Woman's Book of Ruminations, Meditations, Prayers, and Chants.* Boston: Beacon Press.

Bray, Francesca. 1997. *Technology and Gender: Fabrics of Power in Late Imperial China.* Berkeley: University of California Press.

Brook, Timothy. 1988. *Geographical Sources of Ming-Qing History.* Ann Arbor: University of Michigan, Center for Chinese Studies.

Brough, John. 1982. "Amitābha and Avalokiteśvara in An Inscribed Gandhāran Sculpture." *Indologia Tanrinensia* 10:65–70.

Brown, Paula, and Donald Tuzin, editors. 1983. *The Ethnography of Cannibalism.* Washington, D.C.: Society for Psychological Anthropology.

Bunnag, Jane. 1984. "The Way of the Monk and the Way of the World: Buddhism in Thailand, Laos and Cambodia." In *The World of Buddhisam*, edited by Heinz Bechert and Richard Gombrich, 159–70. London: Thames and Hudson.

Buswell, Robert. 1989. *The Formation of Ch'an Ideology in China and Korea: The Vajrasamādhi Sūtra, A Buddhist Apocryphon.* Princeton: Princeton University Press.

——, editor. 1990. *Chinese Buddhist Apocrypha.* Honolulu: University of Hawaii Press.

Cabezón, Jose Ignacio. 1992. "Mother Wisdom, Father Love" Gender-Based Imagery in Mahāyāna Buddhist Thought." In *Buddhism, Sexuality, and Gender*, edited by Jose Ignacio Cabezón, 181–99. Albany: State of New York University Press.

Cahill, James. 1982. *Sōgen-ga. 12th–14th Century Chinese Painting as Collected and Appreciated in Japan, Catalogue of March 31, 1982–June 27, 1982 Exhibition at University Art Museum.* Berkeley: University Art Museum, University of California.

——. 1992. "Huang-shan Paintings as Pilgrimage Pictures." In *Pilgrims and Sacred Sites in China*, edited by Susan Naquin and Chün-fang Yü, 246–92. Berkeley: University of California Press.

Cahill, Suzanne E. 1993. *Transcendance and Divine Passion: The Queen Mother of the West in Medieval China.* Stanford: Stanford University Press.

——. forthcoming. "Wang Feng-hsien: A Taoist Woman Saint of Medieval China." In *Under Confucian Eyes: Texts on Gender in Chinese History*, edited by Susan Mann and Yu-yin Cheng. Berkeley: University of California Press.

Campany, Robert F. 1991. "Notes on the Devotional Uses and Symbolic Functions of Sūtra Texts as Depicted in Early Chinese Buddhist Miracle Tales and Hagiographies," *Journal of the International Assoication of Buddhist Studies* 14(1):28–72.

——. 1993. "The Real Presence." *History of Religion*, 32:233–72.

——. 1996a. "The Earliest Tales of Bodhisattva Guanshiyin." In *Religions of China in Practice*, edited by Donald S. Lopez, Jr., 82–96. Princeton: Princeton University Press.

——. 1996b. *Strange Writing: Anomaly Accounts in Early Medieval China.* Albany: State of New York University Press.

Cantarella, Eva. 1987. *Pandora's Daughters: The Role and Status of Women in Greek and Roman Antiquity.* Translated by Maureen B. Fant. Baltimore: Johns Hopkins University Press.

Chan, Wing-tsit. 1963. *A Source Book in Chinese Philosophy.* Princeton: Princeton University Press.

Chang, Chia-feng. 1996. "Aspects of Smallpox and Its Significance in Chinese History." Ph.D. dissertation, School of Oriental and African Studies, University of London, London.

Chang, Cornelius. 1971. "A Study of the Paintings of the Water-Moon Kuan-yin." Ph.D. dissertation, Columbia University, New York.

Chang, Garma C.C. 1983. *A Treasury of Mahāyāna Sūtras: Selections from the Mahāratnakūta Sūtra.* University Park: Pennsylvania State University Press.

Chang Hsin-min 張新民. 1978. "Wu-tai Wu Yüeh k'e te yin-shua" 五代吳越刻的印刷 (Printing in Wu-yüeh during the Five Dynasties). *Wen-wu* 12:74–76.

Chang Tai 張岱. 1957. "Hai chih" 海志 (Record of a Sea Journey). In *Lang-hsüan wen-chi* 琅環文記 (Collected Essays from the Blessed Land). Included in *Chin-tai san-wen ch'ao* 近代散文抄, edited by Shen Ch'i-yüan 沈啟元. Hong Kong: T'ien-hung Press.

Chang Yen 張演. 1970. *Hsü Kuang-shih-yin ying-yen chi* 續光世音應驗記 (Continued Records of Kuang-shih-yin's Responsive Manifestations). In *Rikuchō koitsu Kanzeon ōkenki no kenkyū*, edited by Makita Tairyō, 19–24. Kyoto: Hyorakuji shoten.

Chang Yen-yüan 張彥遠. 1963. *Li-tai ming-hua chi* 歷代名畫記 (Record of Famous Paintings in Successive Dynasties) 847. In *Hua-shih ts'ung-shu*, vol. 1. Shanghai: Shanghai jen-min mei-shu ch'u-pan-she.

Chao I 趙翼. *Hai-yü ts'ung-k'ao* 陔餘叢考 (Reading Notes of a Filial Son). 1957. Shanghai. reprint.

Chao Tung-shu 趙東樹, editor. 1953. *Li-chiao hui-pien* 理教彙編 (Compendium on the Li Teaching). Taipei: Chung-hua Li-chiao tsung-hui.

Chapin, Helen B. with revision by A. C. Soper. 1970–71. "A Long Roll of Buddhist Images." *Artibus Asiae* 32(1):5–41, (2/3):157–99, (4):259–306; 33(1/2):75–140.

Chaves, Jonathan. 1986. "Moral Action in the Poetry of Wu Chia-chi (1618–84)," *Harvard Journal of Asiatic Studies* 46(2):387–469.

Ch'en, Kenneth K.S. 1964. *Buddhism in China: A Historical Survey.* Princeton: Princeton University Press.

Chen Lie. 1996. "The Ancestor Cult in Ancient China." In *Mysteries of Ancient China: New Discoveries from the Early Dynasties*, edited by Jessica Rawson, 269–72. New York: George Braziller.

Chen, Thomas S.N., and Peter S.Y. Chen. 1998. "Medical Cannibalism in China: The Case of *Ko-ku.*" *The Pharos* 62(Spring):23–25.

Cheng Chen-t'o 鄭振鐸. 1985. *Chung-kuo ku-tai mu-k'e hsüan-chi* 中國古代木刻選

集 (Selections from Ancient Chinese Woodblock Prints). Beijing: Jen-min mei-shu ch'u-pan-she.

Cheng Kuang-tsu 鄭光祖. 1845. *I-pan-lu tsa-shu* 一斑錄雜述 (Jottings from Glimpsed Records). In *Chou-ch'e suo chih* 舟車所至.

Ch'i Chou-hua 齊周華. 1987. "Yu Nan-hai P'u-t'o shan chi" 遊南海普陀山記 (On A Trip to P'u-t'o in the South Sea). In *Ming-shan tsang fu-p'en* 名山藏副本. Shanghai: Ku-chi.

Chikusa Masaaki 竺沙雅章. 1982. *Chūgoku bukkyō shakaishi kenkyū* 中國佛教社會史研究 (Studies on the Social History of Buddhism during the Sung). Kyoto: Dohosha.

——. 1987. "Sō Gen jidai no okeru ando" 宋元時代の於ける庵堂 (Halls and Cloisters in the Sung and Yüan Periods). *Toyoshi kenkyū* (Studies in Asian History) 46(1):1–28.

Ch'iu Chung-lin 邱仲麟. 1996. "Pu-hsiao chih hsiao—T'ang i-lai ke-ku liao-chin hsien-hsiang te she-hui shih ch'u-t'an" 不孝之孝——唐以來割股療親現象的社會史初探 (A Sociohistorical Study of the Phenomenon of "Cutting Flesh to Heal Parents" from the T'ang Dynasty to Modern China). *Hsin shih-hsüeh* 6(1):49–92.

Chiu-k'u chiu-nan ling-kan Kuan-shih-yin pao-chüan 救苦救難靈感觀世音寶卷 (The Precious Scroll of Kuan-shih-yin of Efficacious Responses Who Saves One from Suffering and Disasters). n.d. Copy held at the Oriental Institute, St. Petersburg, Russia.

Chong Key-Ray. 1990. *Cannibalism in China.* Wakefield, N.H.: Longwood Academic.

Chou Shao-liang (Zhou Shaoliang) 周紹良. 1985. "Lüeh-lun Ming Wan-li nien chien wei Chiu-lien P'u-sa pien-tsao te liang-pu ching" 略論明萬曆年間為九蓮菩薩編造的兩部經 (A Brief Discussion of the Two Scriptures Composed for the Benefit of Nine-Lotus Bodhisattva during the Wan-li Period of the Ming). *Ku-kung Po-wu Yüan yüan-kan* 2:37–40.

——. 1987. "Ming-tai huang-ti, kuei-fei, kung-chu yin-shih te chi-pen fo-ching" 明代皇帝貴妃公主印施的幾本佛經 (Several Buddhist Sūtras Printed by Ming Emperors, Imperial Concubines, and Princesses for Free Distribution). *Wen-wu* 8:8–11.

Chou Yi-liang. 1944–45. "Tantrism in China." *Harvard Journal of Asiatic Studies* 8:241–332.

Chü Hsi-lung 車錫倫. 1992. "Hsüan-chüan yü ming-chien hsin-yang" 宣卷與民間信仰 (Recitation of Precious Scrolls and Popular Beliefs). In *Wu-yüeh min-chien hsin-yang min-su—Wu-yüeh ti-ch'ü min-chien hsin-yang yü min-chien wen-i kuan-hsi te k'ao-ch'a ho yen-chiu,* 吳越民間信仰民俗——吳越地區民間信仰與民間文藝關係的考察和研究 edited by Chiang Pin, 295–341. Shanghai: Shanghai Wen-yi Ch'u-pan-she.

Ch'üan-shan chin-k'e 勸善金科 (Golden Lessons for Inculcating Goodness). Chang Chao 張照 (1691–1745) and others. Reprint in *Ku-pen hsi-ch'ü ts'ung-k'an chiu-chi* 古本戲曲叢刊九集, 5 [series 9, no. 5], vol. 1–10. Beijing: Chung-hua shu-chü, n.d.

Ch'üan T'ang shih 全唐詩 (Complete Collection of Poems of the T'ang). 1960. Compiled by P'eng Ting-ch'iu 彭定求. 12 vols. Beijing: Chung-hua shu-chü.

Ch'üan T'ang wen 全唐文 (Complete Collection of Essays of the T'ang). 1965. By Tung Kao 董誥, 20 vols. Taipei: Ching-wei shu-chü.

Chung-kuo mei-shu ch'üan-chi 中國美術全集 (Complete Collections of Chinese Art). 1988. Vol. 2, "Sui T'ang Wu-tai hui-hua" 隋唐五代繪畫 (Paintings of the Sui, the T'ang and the Five Dynasties). Beijing: Wen-wu ch'u-pan-she.

——. Vol. 12, "Ta-tsu shih-k'e" 大足石刻 (Sculpture of Ta-tsu), by Li Ssu-sheng 李巳生. Beijing: Jen-min Mei-shu ch'u-pan-she.

Chung-kuo shih-k'e Tun-huang Mo-kao-k'u 中國石窟敦煌莫高窟 (Chinese Cave Sculptures: Mo-kao Caves in Tun-huang). 1987. Compiled by Tun-huang Wen-wu Yen-chiu-suo 敦煌文物研究所 (Research Institute of Dunhuang Literary and Artifact Materials), 5 vols. Beijing: Wen-wu.

Chung-kuo shih-k'u Yung-ch'ing Ping-lin Ssu 中國石窟永靖炳靈寺 (Chinese Cave Sculptures: Ping-lin Temple of Yung-chi'ng). 1989. Edited by Cultural Bureau of Gansu Province and Ping-lin Ssu. Beijing: Wen-nen.

Chutiwongs, Nandana. 1984. *The Iconography of Avalokiteśvara in Mainland Southeast Asia.* Ph.D. dissertation, Rijksuniversiteit, Leiden.

Cleary, Thomas, translator. 1986. *The Flower Ornament Scripture, The Avataṁsaka Sūtra.* Boston: Shambala.

Cole, Alan. 1998. *Mothers and Sons in Chinese Buddhism.* Stanford, California: Stanford University Press.

Conze, Edward. translator. 1959. *Buddhist Scriptures.* Penguin Books.

——, translator. 1973. *The Perfection of Wisdom in Eight Thousand Lines and Its Verse Summary.* Berkeley: Four Seasons Foundation.

The Crucible of Compassion and Wisdom, Special Exhibition Catalog of the Buddhist Bronzes from the Nitta Group Collection at the National Palace Museum. 1987. Taipei: National Palace Museum.

D'Argence, Rene-Yvon Lefebre, and Diana Turner, editors. 1974. *Chinese, Korean, and Japanese Sculpture in the Avery Brundage Collection.* San Francisco: Asian Art Museum.

Davidson, Ronald M. 1990. "An Introduction to the Standards of Scriptural Authenticity in Indian Buddhism." In *Chinese Buddhist Apocrypha*, edited by Robert E. Buswell, Jr., 291–325. Honolulu: University of Hawaii Press.

Davis, Richard L. 1986. *Court and Family in Sung China, 960–1279: Bureaucratic Success and Kinship Fortunes for the Shih of Ming-chou.* Durham, N.C.: Duke University Press.

Dayal, Har. 1970. *The Bodhisattva Doctrine in Buddhist Sanskrit Literature.* Delhi: Motilal Banarsidass. Reprint of 1932 edition by Routledge & Kegan Paul, London.

Dean, Kenneth. 1993. *Taoist Ritual and Popular Cults of Southeast China.* Princeton: Princeton University Press.

deBary, Wm. Theodore. 1970. "Individualism and Humanitarianism in Late Ming

Thought," in *Self and Society in Ming Thought*, edited by Wm. Theodore deBary, 175–247. New York: Columbia University Press.

Des Rotours, Robert. 1963. "Quelques notes sur l'anthropophagie en Chine," *T'oung Pao* 50(4–5):486–527.

——. 1968. "Encore quelques notes sur l'anthropophagie en Chine." *T'oung Pao* 54(1–3):1–49.

Donnelly, P. J. 1969. *Blanc de Chine: The Porcelain of Tehua in Fukien*. New York.

Donner, Neal, and Daniel B. Stevenson. 1993. *The Great Calming and Contemplation: A Study and Annotated Translation of the First Chapter of Chih-i's Mo-ho chih-kuan*. Honolulu: University of Hawaii Press.

Duara, Prasenjit. 1988. "Superscribing Symbols: The Myth of Guandi, Chinese God of War." *Journal of Asian Studies* 47(4):778–95.

Dudbridge, Glen. 1978. *The Legend of Miao-shan*. London: Ithaca Press for the Board of the Faculty of Oriental Studies, Oxford University.

——. 1982. "Miao-shan on Stone: Two Early Inscriptions" *Harvard Journal of Asiatic Studies*. 42(2):589–614.

——. 1995. *Religious Experience and Lay Society in T'ang China: A Reading of Tai Fu's Kuang-i chi*. Cambridge: Cambridge University Press.

Dull, Jack L. 1966. "A Historical Introduction to the Apocryphal (*Ch'an-Wei*) Texts of the Han Dynasty." Ph.D. dissertation, University of Washington, Seattle.

Ebrey, Patricia Buckley. 1986. "The Early Stages in the Developemnt of Descent Group Organization." In *Kinship Organization in Late Imperial China*, edited by Patricia Ebrey and James Watson, 16–61. Berkeley: University of California Press.

——. 1993. *The Inner Quarters: Marriage and the Lives of Chinese Women in the Sung Period*. Berkeley: University of California Press.

Edgren, Søren. 1972. "The Printed Dhāraṇī Sūtra of A.D. 956." *The Museum of Far Eastern Antiquites*. 44:141–52.

——. 1989. "Southern Song Printing at Hangzhou." 1989. *Bulletin of the Museum of Far Eastern Antiquities* 61.

Eliade, Mircea. 1959. *The Sacred and the Profane*. New York: Harper & Row.

Erndl, Kathleen M. 1993. *Victory to the Mother: The Hindu Goddess of Northwest India in Myth, Ritual, and Symbol*. New York: Oxford University Press.

Fang Kuang-ch'ang 方廣錩. 1997. "Tun-huang i-shu chung te *Miao-fa lien-hua ching* chi yu-kuan wen-hsien" 敦煌遺書中的妙法蓮華經及有關文獻 (The *Lotus Sūtra* and Related Documents in the Recovered Books from Tun-huang). *Chung-hua fo-hsüeh hsüeh-pao* 10:212–31.

Fang-shan shih-ching t'i-chi hui-pien 房山石經題記匯編 (Collections of Prefaces of Stone Sūtras of Fang-shan). 1987. Compiled by Beijing T'u-shu Kuan Chin-shih-tsu and Chung-kuo Fo-chiao T'u-shu-kuan Shih-ching-tsu. Beijing: Wen-hsien ch'u-pan-she.

Farqhar, David M. 1978. "Emperor As Bodhisattva in the Governance of the Ch'ing Empire." *Harvard Journal of Asiatic Studies* 38:5–34.

Faure, Bernard. 1987. "Space and Place in Chinese Religious Traditions." *History of Religions* 26(4):337–56.

——. 1992. "Relics and Flesh Bodies: The Creation of Ch'an Pilgrimage Sites." In *Pilgrims and Sacred Sites in China*, edited by Susan Naquin and Chün-fang Yü, 150–89. Berkeley: University of California Press.

Fields, Rick. 1986. *How the Swans Came to the Lake: A Narrative History of Buddhism in America.* Boston: Shambhala.

Fitch, Robert F. 1929. *Pootoo Itineraries, Describing the Chief Places of Interest with A Special Trip to Lo-chia Shan.* Shanghai: Kelly & Walsh.

Fo-chiao chao-mu k'e-sung 佛教朝暮課誦 (Buddhist Morning and Evening Devotions). 1978. Taipei.

Fong, Mary H. 1990. "Dehua Figures: A Type of Chinese Popular Sculpture." *Orientations* 21(1):43–8.

Fontein, Jan. 1967. *The Pilgrimage of Sudhana.* The Hague: Mouton.

Forte, Antonino. 1976. *Political Propaganda and Ideology in China at the End of the Seventh Century.* Napoli: Instituto Universitario Orientale.

——. 1990. "The Relativity of the Concept of Orthodoxy in Chinese Buddhism: Chih-sheng's Indictment of Shih-li and the Proscription of the *Dharma Mirror Sūtra.*" In *Chinese Buddhist Apocrypha*, edited by Robert E. Buswell, Jr., 239–49. Hawaii: University of Hawaii Press.

Fo-shuo Ta-tz'u-chih-sheng Chiu-lien P'u-sa hua-shen tu-shih tsun-ching 佛說大慈至聖九蓮菩薩化身度世尊經 (Exalted Sūtra Spoken by the Buddha on the Incarnation of the Great Compassionate and Supreme Holy Nine-Lotus Bodhisattva to Save the World). n.d. Private collection of Chou Shao-liang.

Foulk, T. Griffith. 1993. "Myth, Ritual, and Monastic Practice in Sung Ch'an Buddhism." In *Religion and Society in T'ang and Sung China*, edited by Patricia Buckley Ebrey and Peter N. Gregory, 147–208. Honolulu: University of Hawaii Press.

Frédéric, Louis. 1995. *Buddhism: Flammarion Iconographic Guides.* Paris: Flammarion.

Froeschle-Chopard, M. H. 1979. "The Iconography of the Sacred Universe in the Eighteenth Century: Chapels and Churches in the Dioceses of Vence and Grasse." In *Ritual, Religion and the Sacred, Selections from the Annales, Economies, Societes, Civilisations.* vol. 7, edited by Robert Forster and Orest Ranum and translated by Elborg Forster and Patricia M. Ranum, 146–81. Baltimore: Johns Hopkins University Press.

Fu Liang 傳亮. 1970. *Kuang-shih-yin ying-yen chi* 光世音應驗記 (A Record of Kuang-shih-yin's Responsive Manifestations). In *Rikuchō koitsu Kanzeon ōkenki no kenkyū*, edited by Makita Tairyō, 13–18. Kyoto: Hyorakuji shoten.

Fujita Kōtatsu 藤田宏達. 1970. *Genshi Jōdo-shisō no kenkyū* 原始淨土思想の 研究 (A Study of Early Pure Land Buddhism). Tokyo: Iwanami shoten.

——. 1985. *Kanmuryojukyō koza* 觀無量壽經講座 (Lectures on the *Visualization Sūtra*). Kyoto: Shinshu Otaniha shumushu.

——. 1990. "The Textual Origins of the *Kuan Wu-liang-shou ching*: A Canonical Scripture of Pure Land Buddhism," translated by Kenneth K. Tanaka. In *Chinese Buddhist Apocrypha*, edited by Robert E. Buswell, Jr., 149–73. Honolulu: University of Hawaii Press.

Fukui Fumimasa 福井文雅. 1987. *Hannya shingyō no rekishiteki kenkyū* 般若心經の歷史的研究 (Historical Studies on the *Heart Sūtra*). Tokyo: Shunjusha.

Fukushima Kōsai 福島光哉. 1979. "Chigi no kannoron to sono shiso teki haikei" 智顗の感應論とその思想的背景(Chih-i's Understanding of Efficacious Response and the Background of This Thinking) *Ōtani Gakuhō* 49(4):36–49.

Furth, Charlotte. 1999. *A Flourishing Yin: Gender in China's Medical History, 960–1665*. Berkeley: University of California Press.

Gätzlaff, Karl. 1968. *Journal of Three Voyages Along the Coast of China in 1831, 1832, 1833*. London. Taipei reprint, Originally published 1834.

Gernet, Jacques. 1960. "Les Suicides Par Le Feu chez Les Bouddhistes Chinois du Ve au Xe Siecle." *Melanges publies par l'Institute des Hautes Êtudes Chinoises* 2:527–58.

——. 1995. *Buddhism in Chinese Society: An Economic History from the Fifth to the Tenth Centuries*, translated by Franciscus Verellen. New York: Columbia University Press.

Getz, Dan. 1994. "Siming Zhili and Tiantai Pure Land in the Sung Dynasty." Ph.D. dissertation, Yale University, New Haven.

Gillman, Derek. 1983. "A New Image in Chinese Buddhist Sculpture of the Tenth to Thirteenth Century" *Transactions of the Oriental Ceramic Society*. 47:33–44.

Gimbutas, Marija. 1989. *The Language of the Goddess*. San Francisco: Harper & Row.

Gimello, Robert M. 1992. "Chang Shang-yin on Wu-t'ai Shan." *Pilgrims and Sacred Sites in China*, edited by Susan Naquin and Chün-fang Yü, 89–149. Berkeley: University of California Press.

Gjertson, Donalds E. 1989. *Miraculous Retribution: A Study and Translation of T'ang Lin's Ming-pao chi*. Berkeley: University of California Press.

Gómez, Luis O., tr. 1996. *The Land of Bliss, The Paradise of the Buddha of Measureless Light: Sanskrit and Chinese Versions of the Sukhāvatīvyūha Sūtras*. Honolulu: University of Hawaii Press.

Gotō Daiyō 後藤大用. 1958. *Kanzeon Bosatsu no kenkyū* 観世音菩薩の研究 (The Study of Kuan-shi-yin Bodhisattva). Tokyo.

Graham, William T., Jr. 1979. "Milteng's 'Rhapsody on A Parrot.'" *Harvard Journal of Asiatic Studies* 39(1):39–54.

Grant, Beata. 1989. "The Spiritual Saga of Woman Huang: From Pollution to Purification." In *Ritual Opera, Operatic Ritual: "Mu-lien Rescues His Mother" in Chinese Popular Culture*, edited by David Johnson, 224–311. Berkeley: Chinese Popular Culture Project, University of California.

Gregory, Peter N. 1991. *Tsung-mi and the Sinification of Buddhism*. Princeton: Princeton University Press.

Gregory, Peter N., and Daniel A. Getz, Jr., editors. 1999. *Buddhism in the Sung.* Hoholulu: University of Hawaii Press.

Gridley, Marilyn Leidig. 1993. *Chinese Buddhist Sculpture under the Liao.* New Delhi: International Academy of Indian Culture and Aditya Prakashan.

Gyatso, Janet. 1986. "Signs, Memory and History: A Tantric Buddhist History of Scriptural Transmission." *Journal of the International Association of Buddhist Studies* 9(2):7–35.

——. 1996. "Drawn from the Tibetan Treasury: The *gTer ma* Literature." In *Tibetan Literature*, ed. Jose Cabezón and Roger Jackson, 147–69. Ithaca: Snow Lion.

——. 1998. *Apparitions of the Self: The Secret Autobiographies of a Tibetan Visionary.* Princeton: Princeton University Press.

Hansen, Valerie. 1990. *Changing Gods in Medieval China, 1127–1276.* Princeton: Princeton University Press.

Han Wu-ti nei-chuan 漢武帝內傳 (Intimate Biography of Emperor Wu of the Han), attributed to Pan Ku 班固. *Pai-pu tsung-shu chi-cheng* 百部叢書集成, vol. 4361.

Harrison, Paul. 1987. "Who Gets to Ride in the Great Vehicle? Self-image and Identity Among the Followers of the Early Mahāyāna." *The Journal of the International Association of Buddhist Studies* 10(1):67–89.

——. 1990. *The Samādhi of Direct Encounter with the Buddhas of the Present. An Annotated English Translaton of the Tibetan Version of the Pratyutpanna-Buddha-Sammukhāvasthita-Samādhi-Sūtra.* Studia Philologica Buddhica, Monograph Series V. Tokyo: The International Instutute for Buddhist Studies.

——. 1993. "The Earlist Chinese Translations of Mahāyāna Sūtras: Some Notes on the Works of Lokakṣema." *Buddhist Studies Review* 10(2):135–77.

——. 1995. "Searching for the Origins of the Mahāyāna: What Are We Looking For?" *Eastern Buddhist* (n.s.) 28(1):48–69.

——. 1996. "Mañjuśrī and the Cult of the Celestial Bodhisattvas." Paper presented at the conference on "The Ambiguity of Avalokiteśvara and the Questions of Bodhisattvas in Buddhist Traditions," University of Texas, Austin.

Hayashima Kyōsei 早島鏡正. 1964. "Jōdokyō no seijōgōshokan ni tsuite" 淨土教の清淨業處觀について (On the Meditation on Purity and Karma Taught in the Pure Land School). *Higata Ryūsho Hakushi koki kinen ronbunshu* 干潟龍祥博士古稀紀念論文集.

Hayashiya Tomojiro 林屋友三郎. 1941. *Kyōroku kenkyū* 經錄研究 (Studies on Catalogues of Buddhist Scriptures), vol. 1. Tokyo: Iwanami shoten.

Henderson, Gregory, and Leon Hurvitz. 1956. "The Buddha of Seiryoji: New Finds and New Theory." *Artibus Asiae* 19(1).

Henderson, John B. 1984. *Development and Decline of Chinese Cosmology.* New York: Columbia University Press.

Hevia, James. 1993. "Lamas, Emperors, and Rituals: Political Implications in Qing Imperial Ceremonies." *The Journal of International Association of Buddhist Studies* 16.2.

Hirakawa Akira 平川彰. 1984. "*Kangyō* no seiritsu to seijōgōshokan" 觀經の成立と清淨業處觀 (The Creation of the *Visualization Sūtra* and the Meditation on Purity and Karma). *Tōyō no shisō to shukyo* 東洋の思想と宗教 1.

Holt, John Clifford. 1991. *Buddha in the Crown: Avalokiteśvara in the Buddhist Traditions of Sri Lanka.* New York: Oxford University Press.

Honda Yoshihide 本田義英. 1930. "Kannon yakugo kō" 觀音釋名考 (Investigation on the Translations of the Names of Kuan-yin). *Nara* 13 (Special Issue on the Study of Kannon):15–31.

Horney, Karen. 1967. "The Distrust between the Sexes" In *Feminine Psychology,* edited by Harold Kelman, 327–40. New York: W. W. Norton.

Howard, Angela F. 1985. "Royal Patronage of Buddhist Art in Tenth Century Wu Yueh." *The Museum of Far Eastern Antiquities Bulletin* 57:1–60.

——. 1990. "Tang and Post-Tang Images of Guanyin from Sichuan." *Orientations* 23(1):49–57.

——. 1993. "Highlights of Chinese Buddhist Sculpture in the Freer Collection." *Orientations* 24(5): 93–101.

——. 1996a. "Buddhist Cave Sculpture of the Northern Qi Dynasty: Shaping a New Style, Formulating New Iconographies." *Archives of Asian Art* 49:7–25.

——. 1996b. "Buddhist Monuments of Yunnan: Eclectic Art of a Frontier Kingdom." In *Arts of the Sung and Yüan,* edited by Maxwell K. Hearn and Judith G. Smith, 231–45. New York: Metropolitan Museum of Art.

——. 1999. "The Brilliant Kings of Wisdom of South-West China." *Res* 35(Spring):92–107.

——. Forthcoming. *Summit of Treasures: Buddhist Cliff Sculpture of Dazu, Sichuan.* New York: Weatherhill.

Howard, Angela F., Wu Hung, Li Song, and Yang Hung. Forthcoming. *Three Thousand Years of Chinese Sculpture. Culture and Civilization of China,* vol. 2. New Haven: Yale University Press.

Howard, Angela F., Li Kunshang, and Qiu Xuanchong. 1992. "Nanzhao and Dali Buddhist Sculpture in Yunnan." *Orientations.* 23(February):51–60.

Hsiang Ta-mu 向達木. 1991. "Szechwan Ping-wu Ming Pao-en Ssu kan-cha pao-kao" 四川平武明報恩寺勘察報告 (Investigative Report of the Pao-en Monastery Dated to the Ming in Ping-wu, Szechwan). *Wen-wu.* 4:1–17.

Hsiang-shan pao-chüan 香山寶卷 (Precious Scroll of Hsiang-shan), 1886, 2 vols., woodblock edition.

Hsiang-shan shuo-yao 香山說要 (A Brief Account of Hsiang-shan). n.d. Hand-written copy kept at the Library of the Institute of Literature, Chinese Academy of Social Sciences, Beijing.

Hsiao Teng-fu 蕭登福. 1989. *Han Wei Liu-ch'ao i-chiang te Tao-chiao ssu-hsiang* 漢魏六朝以降的道教思想 (Taoist Thought Since the Han, Wei and Six Dynasties). Taipei: Taiwan Hsüeh-sheng shu-chü.

Hsiao-shih chieh-hsü lien-tseng pao-chüan 銷釋接續蓮宗寶卷 (The Precious Scroll Explaining the Continuation of the Lotus School). n.d.

Hsiao-shih Pai-i Kuan-yin P'u-sa sung ying-erh hsia-sheng pao-chüan 銷釋白衣觀音菩薩送嬰兒下生寶卷 (The Precious Scroll Explaining White-Robed Kuan-Yin's Coming into the World and Bringing Children). 1994. In *Pao-chüan ch'u-chi* 寶卷初集, vol. 12. Shansi: Jen-min ch'u-pan-she.

Hsieh, Ding-hwa E. 1999. "Images of Women in Ch'an Buddhist Literature of the Sung Period." In *Buddhism in the Sung*, edited by Peter N. Gregory and Daniel A. Getz, Jr., 148–87. Honolulu: University of Hawaii Press.

Hsieh Kuo-chen 謝國幀. 1985. "P'u-t'o yu-chi" 普陀遊記 (A P'u-t'o Travel Account). In *Chung-kuo ku-tai yu-chi hsüan* 中國古代遊記選. 2:239–45. Beijing: Chung-kuo lü-yu she.

Hsi k'ao 戲考 (On Plays). 1923. Shanghai: Chung-hua t'u-shu-kuan.

Hsi-kua pao-chüan. 西瓜寶卷 (Precious Scroll of the Watermelon). 1887. Hand-copied and kept at Chekiang Provincial Library, Hangchow.

Hsin-fan 心梵. 1915. "P'u-t'o li-Fo kuei-lai te kan-hsiang" 普陀禮佛歸來的感想 (Thoughts on Returning from Paying Homage to the Buddha at P'u-t'o). *Hai-ch'ao-yin* 11(9):17–24.

Hsin-k'an ch'üan-hsiang ying-ke hsiao-i chuan 新刊全相鸚哥孝義傳 (Newly Printed and Completely Illustrated Tale of the Filial and Righteous Parrot). 1979. In *Ming Cheng-hua shuo-ch'ang tz'u-hua tsung-k'an* 明成化說唱詞話叢刊, vol. 10. Beijing: Wen-wu.

Hsin T'ang shu 新唐書 (New History of the T'ang). 1975. By Ou-yang Hsiu 歐陽修 (1007–1072) and Sung Chi 宋祁 (998–1061). Beijing: Chung-hua shu-chü.

Hsiung Ping-chen 熊秉真. 1995. *Yu-yu: Ch'uan-tung Chung-kuo te pao-chiang chih tao* 幼幼：傳統中國的褓襁之道 (Caring for the Young: Methods of Child-care in Traditional China). Taipei: Lien-ching.

Hsü, Ming-te 徐明德. 1987. "Lun shih-ssu chih shih-chi shi-chi Ning-po-kang tsai Chung-Jih ching-chi wen-hua chiao-liu shih shang te chung-yao ti-wei" 論十四至十七世紀寧波港在中日經濟 文化交流史上的重要地位 (On the Importance of Ningpo Port in the History of Sino-Japanese Economic and Cultural Communications during the Fourteenth to the Seventeenh Centuries). *Tang-tai Shih-chieh Tung-hsin* 當代世界通訊, no. 3, 120–41. Chekiang: Chekiang tang-tai kuo-chi wen-ti yen-chiu-hui.

Hsü Ping-fang (Xu Pingfang) 徐苹芳. 1995. "Seng-chieh tso-hsiang te fa-hsien ho Seng-chieh ch'ung-pai" 僧伽造像的發現和僧伽崇拜 (Recently Discovered Seng-chieh Statues and the Worship of Seng-chieh). Paper presented at the Paris Conference on Cults and Sites organized by Franciscus Verellen.

Hsüan-ho hua-p'u 宣和畫譜 (Catalogues of Paintings Compiled in the Hsüan-ho Period). 1963. In *Hua-shi ts'ung-shu,* 畫史叢書 vol. 1. Shanghai: Shanghai jen-min mei-shu ch'u-pan-she.

Hu Ying-lin 胡應麟, compiler. 1980. *Kuan-yin Ta-shih tz'u-jung wu-shih-san hsien-hsiang tsan* 觀音大士慈容五十三現相贊 (Eulogies to the Fifty-three Compassionate Manifestations of the Great Being Kuan-yin). Taipei: Kuang-wen shu-chü, reprint.

Huang, Chi-chiang 黃啟江. 1990. "Sung-tai te i-ching yün-wen kuan yü fo-chiao" 宋代的譯經潤文官與佛教 (Sung Officials Who Translated Sūtras and Polished Styles and Buddhism). *Ku-kung hsüeh-shu chi-k'an* 7(4):13–32.

——. 1995. "Sung T'ai-tsung yü fo-chiao" 宋太宗與佛教 (Emperor T'ai-tsung of the Sung and Buddhism). *Ku-kung hsüeh-shu chi-k'an* 2(January):107–34.

Huang Hsiu-fu 黃休復. 1963. *I-chou ming-hua lu* 益州名畫錄 (Catalogue of Famous Paintings of I-chou). In *Hua-shih ts'ung-shu*. Shanghai: Shang-hai jen-min mei-shu ch'u-pan-she.

Huang Yung-wu 黃永武, editor. 1981–. *Tun-huang pao-tsang* 敦煌寶藏 (Treasures of Tun-huang). Taipei: Hsin-wen-feng ch'u-pan-she.

Huang Yü-p'ien 黃育鞭. 1982. *P'o-hsieh hsiang-pien* 破邪詳辯 (Detailed Refutations of Heresies) together with the three sequeals *hsü* (continuation), *yu-hsü* (more continuation), and *san-hsü* (third continuation). In *Ch'ing-shih tzu-liao* 清史資料 (Materials on Ch'ing History), vol. 3, edited by Ch'ing History Research Section, 1–131. Institute of History, Chinese Academy of Social Sciences. Beijing: Chung-hua shu-chü.

Huang-chi chin-tan chiu-lien cheng-hsin kuei-chen huan-hsiang pao-chüan 皇極金丹九蓮正信皈真還鄉寶卷 (The Precious Scroll of the Golden Elixir and Nine Lotuses of the Imperial Ultimate [Which Leads to] Rectifying Belief, Taking Refuge in the True and Returning Home). In *Pao-chüan ch'u-chi*, vol. 8.

Hung Mai 洪邁. 1982. *I-chien chih* 夷堅志 (Record of the Listener), 4 vols. Taipei: Ming-wen shu-chü.

Hung Mei-hua. 洪美華. 1992. "Ch'ing-tai min-chien mi-mi tsung-chiao chung te fu-nü" 清代民間祕密宗教中的婦女 (Women in Popular Sectarian Religions in the Ch'ing Period). Master's thesis, Institute of History, Taiwan Normal University.

——. 1995. "Ch'ing-tai chung-chi min-chien mi-mi tsung-chiao chung te fu-nü" 清代中期民間祕密宗教中的婦女 (Women in the Popular Sectarian Religions of the Mid-Ch'ing Period), In *Chung-kuo fu-nü shih lun-chi* 中國婦女史論集, vol. 4, edited by Pao Chia-lin 鮑家麟, 273–316. Taipei: Tao-hsiang.

Hung-tsan 弘贊, compiler. 1980. *Kuan-yin tz'u-lin chi* 觀音慈林集 (Compassionate Grove of Kuan-yin). In *Ssu-ta p'u-sa sheng-te tsung-shu* 四大菩薩聖德叢書 (Collections of the Holy Virtues of the Four Great Bodhisattvas), vol. 1, edited by Hui-men 慧門, 435–99. Taiwan: Mi-le ch'u-pan-she, reprint. Originally compiled 1668.

Huntington, Susan L., with contributions by John C. Huntington. 1985. *The Art of Ancient India: Buddhist, Hindu, Jain*. New York: Weatherhill.

Hurvitz, Leon, translator. 1976. *Scripture of the Lotus Blossom of the Fine Dharma*. New York: Columbia University Press.

Idema, Wilt. 1999. "Guanyin's Parrot, a Chinese Animal Tale and Its International Context." In *India, Tibet, China: Genesis and Aspects of Traditional Narrative*, 103–50. Firenze: Leo S. Olschki Eitore.

James, Jean M. 1995. "An Iconographic Study of Xiwangmu during the Han Dynasty." *Artibus Asiae*, LV, 1/2:17–41.

Jan Yun-hua. 1965. "Buddhist Self-Immolation in Medieval China." *History of Religions.* 4, 4:243–26.

——. 1966–67. "Buddhist Relations between India and China," *History of Religions.* 6(1):24–42; 6(3):135–68.

Jessup, Helen Ibbitson, and Thierry Zephir, editors. 1997. *Sculpture of Angkor and Ancient Cambodia: Millennium of Glory.* National Gallery of Art, Washington, D.C., and Reunion des musees nationaux, Paris.

Johnston, Reginald Fleming. 1976. *Buddhist China.* London: John Murray, 1913. San Francisco: Chinese Materials Center.

Jordan, David K., and Daniel L. Overmyer. 1986. *The Flying Phoenix: Aspects of Chinese Sectarianism in Taiwan.* Princeton: Princeton University Press.

Kajiyama Yuichi 梶山雄一 and Sueki Fumihito 末木文美士. 1992. *Jōdo Bukkyō no shiso* 淨土佛教の 思想 (Thought of Pure Land Buddhism), vol. 2. Tokyo, Kodansha.

Kamata Shigeo 鎌田茂雄. 1973. "Honkon no Bukkyō girei: Daihiseibo ni tsuite 香港の 佛教儀禮：大悲懺法について (Buddhist Rituals in Hong Kong: On Great Compassion Repentence)." *Indogaku Bukkyōgaku Kenkyū* 22(1):281–4.

——. 1986. *Chūgoku no Bukkyō girei* 中國の 佛教儀禮 (Chinese Buddhist Rituals). Tokyo: Kodansha.

Kapstein, Matthew. 1989. "The Purificatory Gem and Its Cleansing: A Late Tibetan Polemical Discussion of Apocryphal Texts." *History of Religions.* 28(3):217–44.

——. 1992. "Remarks on the *Mani bKa'-'bum* and the Cult of Avalokiteśvara in Tibet." In *Tibetan Buddhism: Reason and Revelation*, edited by Steven D. Goodman and Ronald M. Davidson, 57–93. Albany: State University of New York Press.

Karashima Seishi 辛嶋靜志. 1992. *The Textual Study of the Chinese Versions of the Saddharmapuṇḍarīka Sūtra in Light of the Sanskrit and Tibetan Versions.* Tokyo: Sankibo.

Kasugai Shinya 春日井眞也. 1953. "*Kan Muryōjukyō* ni okeru shomondai" 觀無量經に於ける 諸問題 (Various Problems Concerning the *Visualization Sūtra*), *Bukkyō Bunka Kenkyū* 3.

K'e Yü-hsien 柯毓賢. 1983. "Chuan-t'ien-t'u ching kao" 轉天圖經考 (Investigation of the *Sūtra on the Diagram of Turning Heaven*)," *Shih-huo* 13(5–6): 197–203.

——. 1987. "Chuan-t'ien-t'u ching hsü-kao" 轉天圖經續考 (Further Investigation on the *Sūtra on the Diagram of Turning Heaven*)," *Shih-huo* 16(9–10):394–71.

——. 1988. "Wu-kung P'u-sa yüan-liu yü Kuan-yin hsin-yang" 五公菩薩源流與觀音信仰 (The Origins of the Five Masters Bodhisattvas and the Cult of Kuan-yin), *Tung-fang tsung-chiao yen-chiu* 2:119–37.

Kent, Richard K. 1994. "Depictions of the Guardians of the Law: Lohans Painting in

China." In *Latter Days of the Law: Images of Chinese Buddhism, 850–1850*, edited by Marsha Weidner, 183–213. Honolulu: University of Hawaii Press.

Kern, Johan Hendrik. 1963. *The Saddharma-Puṇḍarīka, or the Lotus of the True Law.* New York reprint of 1884 *Sacred Books of the East* 21. New York: Colonial Press.

Kieschnick, John. 1997. *The Eminent Monk: Buddhist Ideals in Medieval Chinese Hagiography*. Honolulu: University of Hawaii Press.

Kiriya Shoichi 桐谷征一. 1990. "Gikyō *Kōō Kanzeon kyō* no tekisuto to shinkō" 偽經高王經のテキストと信仰 (The Text of the Apocryphal Sūtra *King Kao's Kuan-yin Sūtra* and Its Beliefs). *Hokke bunka kenkyū* 法華文化研究 16:1–67.

Kleeman, Terry. 1993. "Expansion of the Wenchang Cult." In *Religion and Society in T'ang and Sung China*, edited by Patricia Buckley Ebrey and Peter N. Gregory, 45–73. Honolulu: University of Hawaii Press.

——. 1994. *A God's Own Tale: The Book of Transformations of the Divine Lord of Zitong*. Albany: State University of New York Press.

Knapp, Keith N. 1996. "Accounts of Filial Sons: *Ru* Ideology in Early Medieval China." Ph.D. dissertation, University of California, Berkeley.

Ko, Dorothy. 1994. *Teachers of the Inner Chambers: Women and Culture in Seventeenth Century China*. Stanford: Stanford University Press.

Kobayashi Taichirō 小林太一郎. 1948. "Nyoka to Kannon" 女媧と觀音 (Nü-wa and Kuan-yin). *Ars Buddhica* (Bukkyō geijitsu) 1:5–30; 2:38–123.

——. 1950. "Shin Tō no Kannon" 晉唐の 觀音 (Kuan-yin of the Chin and T'ang.) *Ars Buddhica* 10:3–73.

——. 1953–54. "Tōdai Daihi Kannon" 唐代大悲觀音 (Ta-pei Kuan-yin of the T'ang Dynasty). *Bukkyō Bijutsu* 20(1953):3–27; 21(1954):89–109; 22(1954):3–28.

——. 1982. "Tōdai no Daihi Kannon" 唐代の 大悲觀音 (Ta-pei Kyan-yin in the T'ang Dynasty). In *Kannon shinkō* 觀音信仰 (Cult of Kuan-yin), edited by Hayami Tasuku 速水侑, 39–136. Tokyo: Yūzankaku Shuppansha.

Kohn, Livia. 1998. *God of the Dao: Lord Lao in History and Myth*. Ann Arbor: Center for Chinese Studies, University of Michigan.

Ku Yen-wu 顧炎武. *Ku-chung sui-pi* 菰中隨筆 (Random Notes Taken Amid the Reeds). 1967. In *Han-shan-hsien-kuan ts'ung-shu*, vol. 61. Taipei. Reprint.

Kuan-shih-yin P'u-sa ling-kan lu 觀世音菩薩靈感錄 (Record of Kuan-shih-yin Bodhisattva's Efficacious Responses). 1929. Shanghai: Chung-hua shu-chu.

Kuan-yin chi-tu pen-yüan chen-ching 觀音濟度本願真經 (True Scripture of Kuan-yin's Original Vow of Universal Salvation). 1991. In *Chiu-ch'üan pao-chüan* 酒泉寶卷 (Precious Scrolls from Chiu-ch'üan), vol. 1, 3–89. Lang-chou: Kansu jen-min ch'u-pan-she.

Kuan-yin Miao-shan pao-chüan 觀音妙善寶卷 (The Precious Scroll of Kuan-yin Miao-shan). Hand-copied in 1916, private collection of Wu Hsiao-ling.

Kuan-yin P'u-sa yü-lan chi 觀音菩薩魚籃記 (Story of the Fish-basket of Kuan-yin Bodhitsattva). In *Ku-pen Yüan Ming tsa-chu* 孤本元明雜劇. 1958. Fourth collection. Beijing: Chung-kuo hsi-chü ch'u-pan-she.

Kuan-yin shih-erh yüan-chüeh ch'üan-chuan 觀音十二圓覺全傳 (Complete Biographies of the Twelve Perfectly Enlightened Ones of Kuan-yin). 1938.

Kuan-yin shih-tsung jih-pei t'ou-nan ching 觀音釋宗日北斗南經 (Scripture of Kuan-yin Explaining Truth North of the Sun and South of the Dipper). n.d. Private collection of Wu Hsiao-ling.

Kuan-yin Ta-shih lien-chuan ching 觀音大士蓮船經 (Scripture of Kuan-yin's Lotus Boat). 1906. In *Tao-tsang chi-yao* 道藏集要 (Selections from the Taoist Canon), 7:2899–901. Taipei: Hsin-wen-feng. Reprint.

Kuan-yin yü-lan chi 觀音魚籃記 (Story of Kuan-yin's Fish Basket). In *Ku-pen hsi-ch'ü ts'ung-k'an* 孤本戲曲叢刊, 2nd collection.

Ku-chin t'u-shu chi-ch'eng 古今圖書集成 (Synthesis of Books and Illustrations of Ancient and Modern Times). 1964. Compiled by Ch'en Meng-lei 陳夢雷 et al, 100 vols. Taipei: Wen-hsing shu-tien. First published 1728.

Kung Li-fei 龔立非 and Wang Tao-hsing 王道行. n.d. *Hai-t'ien fo-kuo P'u-t'o Shan* 海天佛國普陀山 (P'u-t'o Shan, the Buddhist Realm of Ocean and Sky). Chekiang: Chou-Shan tso-chia hsieh-hui.

Kuo Li-ying. 1994a. *Confession et contrition dans le bouddhisme chinois du V au X siecle.* Paris: Publications de l'Ecole francaise d'Extreme-Orient.

———. 1994b. "Divination jeux de hasard et purification dans le bouddhisme chinois: autour d'un Sūtra apocryphe chinois, le Zhanchajing." In *Buddhisme et cultures locales: Qulques cas de reciproques adaptations*, edited by Fukui Fumimasa and Gerard Fussman, 145–67. Paris: Ecole francaise d'Extreme-Orient.

———. 1995. "Le recitationdes noms de buddha en Chine et au Japon." *T'oung Pao* 81:230–68.

———. 1998. "Mandala et rituel de confession a Dunhuang." *Bulletin de l'Ecole francaise d'Extreme-Orient* 85:227–56.

Kuwabara Jitsuzō 桑原騭藏. 1919. "Shina no shokujinniku fūzoku" 支那の食人肉風俗 (The Custom of Eating Human Flesh in China). *Taiyō* 太陽 25(7; June):121–24.

———. 1924. "Shina no shokujinniku fūzoku." *Tōyō gakuhō* 14(1):1–61.

Lagerway, John. 1992. "The Pilgrimage to Wu-tang Shan." In *Pilgrims and Sacred Sites in China*, edited by Susan Naquin and Chün-fang Yü, 293–332. Berkeley: University of California Press.

Lai Swee-fo (Lai Jui-ho) 賴瑞和. 1980. "Miao-shan chuan-shuo te liang-chung hsin tzu-liao" 妙善傳說的兩種新資料 (Two Pieces of New Material on the Legend of Miao-shan). *Chung-wai wen-hsüeh* 9(2; July):116–26.

———. 1993. "Wai-li hsiun-pei chi" 萬里尋碑記 (Looking for the Stele from Ten-thousand Miles Away." *Chung-kuo shih-pao* April 6–8, 1993.

Laing, Ellen Johnston. 1988. "Catalogue Entry on Miss Qiu." In *Views from Jade Terrace: Chinese Women Artists 1300–1912*, edited by Marsha Weidner, 70–72. New York: Indiana Museum of Art and Rizzoli.

Laing, Mary E. D., editor. 1982. *Along the Ancient Silk Routes: Central Asian Art from the West Berlin State Museum.* New York: Metropolitan Museum of Art.

Lawton, Thomas. 1973. "Kuan-yin of the Water Moon." In *Chinese Figure Painting.* 89–90. Washington, D.C.: Smithsonian Institution.

Lee, Sherman E., and Wai-kam Ho. 1959. "A Colossal Eleven-faced Kuan-yin of the T'ang Dynasty." *Artibus Asiae* 22:121–37.

Legge, James, translator. 1965. *A Record of the Buddhist Kingdoms.* New York: Paragon Book Reprint and Dover Publications. Originally published 1886, Clarendon Press, Oxford.

Lei Congyun. 1996. "Neolithic Sites of Religious Significance." In *Mysteries of Ancient China: New Discoveries from the Early Dynasties*, edited by Jessica Rawson, 219–25. New York: George Braziller.

Lerner, Gerda. 1986. *The Creation of Patriarchy.* New York: Oxford University Press.

Leung, Angela 梁其姿. 1987. "Ming-Qing yü-fang t'ien-hua tsuo-shih chih yen-pien" 明清預防天花措施之演變 (The Development of Smallpox Preventive Techniques During the Ming and Ming). In *Huo-shih shih-lun* 國史釋論 (Explanatory Essays in Chinese History), 239–53. Taipei.

Levering, Miriam L. 1992. "Lin-chi (Rinzai) Ch'an and Gender: The Rhetoric of Equality and the Rhetoric of Heroism." In *Buddhism, Sexuality and Gender*, edited by Jose Ignacio Cabezón, 137–56. Albany: State of New York University Press.

——. 1999. "Miao-tao and Her Teacher Ta-hui." In *Buddhism in the Sung*, edited by Peter N. Gregory and Daniel A. Getz, Jr., 188–219. Honolulu: University of Hawaii Press.

Lewis, Todd. 1993. "Newar-Tibetan Trade and the Domestication of *Simhalasarthabahu Avadāna.*" *History of Religions* 33(2):135–60.

Li Chien 李荐. *Hua-p'in* 畫品 (On Paintings). In *Pao-yen-t'ang mi-chi* 寶顏堂祕笈, case 3, vol. 4.

Li Lin-ts'an. 1982. *A Study of the Nan-chao and Ta-li Kingdoms in the Light of Art Materials Found in Various Museums.* Taipei: National Palace Museum.

Li Shih-chen 李時珍. 1968. *Pen-ts'ao kang-mu* 本草綱目 (Classified Materia Medica). In *Kuo-hsüeh chi-pen tsung-shu ssu-pai chung* 國學基本叢書四百種 (Four Hundred Selections of Basic Books in Sinology), vol. 146. Taipei: Shan-wu ch'u-pan-sh.

Li Shih-yü (Li Shiyu) 李世瑜. 1948. *Hsien-tai Hua-pei mi-mi tsung-chiao* 現代華北祕密宗教 (Contemporary Secret Religions in North China). Studia Serica Monographs. Series B, no. 4. Ch'eng-tu.

——. 1959. "Pao-chüan hsin-yen" 寶卷新研 (New Studies on Precious Scrolls) *Wen-hsüeh i-ch'an tseng-k'an* 文學遺產叢刊 4:165–81.

——. 1996. "T'ien-chin Tsai-li chiao tiao-ch'a yen-chiu" 天津在理教調查研究 (Investigative Research on the Tsai-li Teaching in Tientsin). *Ming-chien tsung-chiao* 民間宗教 2:169–210.

Li, Thomas Shiyu, and Susan Naquin. 1988. "The Baoming Temple: Religion and the Throne in Ming and Qing China," *Harvard Journal of Asiatic Studies* 48(1):131–88.

Li, Wai-yee. 1993. *Enchantment and Disenchantment: Love and Illusion in Chinese Literature.* Princeton: University of Princeton Press.

Liang shu 梁書 (History of the Liang Dynasty). 1973. By Yao Cha 姚察 (533–606) and Yao Ssu-lian 姚思廉 (d. 637). Beijing: Chung-hua shu-chü.

Lien Li-ch'ang 連立昌. 1996. "Chiu-lien ching k'ao" 九蓮經考 (On "Nine-lotus Sūtra"). *Ming-chien tsung-chiao* 2:113–20.

Lin Wan-ch'uan 林萬傳. 1984. *Hsien-t'ien ta-tao hsi-t'ung yen-chiu* 先天大道系統研究 (The Study on the Lineage Connections of the Great Way of Prior Heaven). Tainan: Chi-chü shu-chü.

Lindtner, Christian. 1982. *Nāgārjuna: Studies in the Writing and Philosophy of Nāgārjuna.* Copenhagen: Akademisk Forlag.

Ling, Trevor. 1976. *The Buddha.* Harmondsworth: Penguin Books.

Li-tai ming-hua Kuan-yin pao-hsiang 歷代名畫觀音寶相 (Precious Kuan-Yin Images in Famous Paintings of Successive Dynasties). 1981. Nanking: Chin-lin shu-hua ch'u-pan-she.

Li T'ai-pai ch'uan-chi 李太白全集 (Collected Works of Li T'ai-pai). 1977. Compiled by Wang Chi 王琦 (circa 1758). Beijing: Chung-hua shu-chü.

Liu Ch'ang-chiu 劉長久. 1995. "Yeh-lun An-yüeh Pi-lu Tung shih-ku: chien yü Tso Tan, Chao Ling erh chün shang-chueh" 也論安岳毗盧洞石窟：兼與曹丹趙玲二君商権 (Once More on the Stone Sculptures of Vairocana Cave of An-yüeh: Discussion with Two Scholars Tso Tan and Chao Ling). *Szechwan Wen-wu* 四川文物 5:37–43.

Liu, Chen-tzu. 1983. "The Iconography of the White-robed Kuan-yin in the Southern Sung Dynasty (1127–1279)." Master's thesis, University of California, Davis.

Lamotte, Étiene. 1949–1980. *Traite de la Grande Vertu de Sagesse de Nāgārjuna.* Louvain: Institute Orientalise.

Lo Ch'ing 羅清. 1980. *Ta-sheng t'an-shih wu-wei pao-chüan* 大乘嘆世無為寶卷 (The Precious Scroll of Great Vehicle of Non-action which Takes Pity on the World). In *Wu-pu liu-ts'e*, vol. 2. Taichung: Ming-te-t'ang. Reprint.

——. *Wu-pu liu-ts'e* 五部六冊 (Five Books in Six Volumes). Taichung: Ming-te t'ang. Reprint of 1596 *K'ai-hsin fa-yao* 開心法要 edition.

Loewe, Michael. 1979. *Ways to Paradise: The Chinese Quest for Immortality.* London: George Allen & Unwin.

Lokesh, Chandra. n.d. *An Illustrated Japanese Manuscript on Mudras and Mantras.* New Delhi: International Academy of Indian Culture.

Lu Hsün 魯迅. 1973. *Lu Hsün ch'uan-chi* 魯迅全集 (Complete Work of Lu Hsün). Beijing: Jen-min wen-hsueh ch'u-pan she.

Lu Kao 陸杲. 1970. *Hsi Kuan-shih-yin ying-yen chi* 繫觀世音應驗記 (More Records of Kuan-shih-yin's Responsive Manifestations). In *Rikuchō koitsu Kanzeon ōkenki no kenkyū*, edited by Makita Tairyō, 24–61. Kyoto: Hyorakuji Shoten.

Lu K'uan Yü (Charles Luk), translator. 1966. *The Śūraṅgama Sūtra.* London: Rider.

——. 1973. *Taoist Yoga: Alchemy and Immortality.* New York: Samuel Weiser.

Ma Hsi-sha 馬西沙 and Han P'ing-fang 韓秉方. 1992. *Chung-kuo min-chien tsung-chiao shih* 中國民間宗教史 (History of Chinese Popular Religion). Shanghai: Jen-min ch'u-pan-she.

Ma Shih-chang 馬世長. 1998. "*Pao Fu-mu En-chung Ching* hsieh-pen yü yin-pen" 報父母恩重經寫本與印本 (Written and Printed Copies of the *Sūtra of Repaying the Kindness of Parents*). A paper delivered at the Conference on Buddhist Literature and Art, April, Taipei.

MacDonald, Ariane. 1962. *Le mandala du Mañjuśrīmulakalpa.* Paris: Adreien Maisonneuve.

Macy, Joanna. 1977. "Perfection of Wisdom: Mother of All the Buddhas." *Anima* 3:75–80.

Mair, Victor H. 1986. "Records of Transformation Tableaux." *T'oung Pao* 72(1–3):3–43.

——. 1988. *Painting and Performance: Chinese Picture Recitation and Its Indian Genesis.* Honolulu: University of Hawaii Press.

Mai-yü pao-chüan 賣魚寶卷 (The Precious Scroll of Fish Selling). n.d. Handwritten copy, Nan-kai University Library, Tientsin.

Makita Tairyō 牧田諦亮, editor. 1970. *Rikuchō koitsu Kanzeon ōkenki no kenkyū* 六朝古逸觀世音應驗記の 研究 (Studies on the Tales of Kuan-shih-yin's Miraculous Manifestations Surviving from the Six Dynasties). Kyoto: Hyorakuji shoten.

——. 1976. *Gikyō kenkyū* 疑經の 研究 (Studies on Apocryphal Sūtras). Kyoto: Kyoto Daigaku Jinbum Kagaku Kenkyūsho.

——. 1981–84. *Chūgoku Bukkyō shi kenkyū* 中國佛教史研究 (Studies in the History of Chinese Buddhism), vols. 1 and 2. Tokyo: Daito.

Mallmann, Marie-Therese de. 1948. *Introduction a l'Etude d'Avalokiteśvara.* Paris: Annales du Musée Guimet.

Mann, Susan. 1997. *Precious Records: Women in China's Long Eighteenth Century.* Stanford: Stanford University Press.

Matoba Yoshimasa 的場慶雅. 1980. "Zui Tōdai ni okeru Kanzeon Bosatsu no shinkō keitai ni tsuite 隋唐代於ける觀世音菩薩の 信仰形態について (On the Forms of Faith in Kuan-yin Bodhisattva Taken in Sui and T'ang Periods)." *Indogaku Bukkyōgaku Kenkyū* 29:244–46.

——. 1982. "Chūgoku ni okeru Hokekyō no shinkō keitai (1)—Hokke Denki" 中國に於ける法華經の 信仰形態(1)——法華傳記 (The Forms of Faith in the *Lotus Sūtra* as Manifested in China—the *Fa-hua chuan-chi*). *Indogaku Bukkyōgaku Kenkyū* 31(1):275–77.

——. 1984. "Chūgoku ni okeru Hokekyō no shinkō keitai (2)—Hokke Denki to Kosan Hokke-den ni okeru Hokekyō no dokusho to reigen setsuwa ni tsute" 中國に於ける法華經の 信仰形態(2)——法華傳記と弘贊法華傳に於ける法華經の 讀誦と靈驗説話について (The Forms of Faith in the *Lotus Sūtra* as Manifested in China—Recitation of the *Lotus Sūtra* and Miracle Stories in the *Fa-hua chuan-chi* and the *Hung-tsan fa-hua chuan*). *Indogaku Bukkyōgaku Kenkyū* 32(2):375–77.

——. 1986. "Chūgoku ni okeru Hokekyō no shinkō keitai (3)—Shin, Shin, So wo chushin to shite" 中國に於ける法華經の信仰形態(3)——秦晉宋を中心として (The Forms of Faith in the *Lotus Sūtra* as Manifested in China—Centering on Chin, Former Chin and Liu Sung Dynasties) *Indogaku Bukkyōgaku Kenkyū* 34(2):57–59.

Matsubara Saburo 松原三郎. 1995. *Chūgoku Bukkyō chōkoku shiron* 中國佛教雕刻史論 (History of Chinese Sculpture), 4 vols. Tokyo: Yoshikawa Kobunkan Heisei.

Matsumoto, Eiichi 松本榮一. 1926. "Suigetsu Kannon zu kō" 水月觀音圖考 (Investigation on the Paintings of Water-moon Kuan-yin). *Kokka* 36(8):205–13.

——. 1937. *Tonkōga no Kenkyū* 敦煌畫の 研究 (Studies on the Paintings of Tun-huang), 2 vols. Tokyo: Hatsubaijo bunkyūdō shoten.

Matsumoto Fumisaburo 松本文三郎. 1939. "Kannon no gogi to kodai Indo Shina ni okeru sono shinko ni tsuite" 觀音の 語義と古代印度支那に於ける其信仰に就いて (On the Meaning of Kuan-yin and His Cult in India and China), *Nara* 13:1–10.

Matsunaga Yūkei 松長永慶. 1979. "Zōbumikkyō no tokushitsu to sono genryu" 雜部密教の特質と其源流 (The Characteristics of Mixed Esoteric Buddhism and Its Origins). In *Henge Kannon no seiritsu to genryū* 變化觀音の成立と源流. Kyoto: Bukkyōgeijutsu Kenkyū Ueno Kinen Zaidan Josei Kenkyūkai Hohokusho.

Mei Ting-tso, 梅鼎祚 compiler. 1988. *Ch'ing-ni lien-hua chi* 青泥蓮花記 (Lotuses in Black Mud), Ming dynasty. Cheng-chou: Chung-chou ku-chi ch'u-pan-she, reprint.

Miao-shan yu shih-tien 妙善遊十殿 (Miao-shan Tours the Ten Courts). n.d. Hand-copied manuscript, Institute of Literature, Chinese Academy of Social Sciences, Beijing.

Miao-yin pao-chüan 妙英寶卷 (The Precious Scroll of Miao-yin). n.d. Hand-copied, Chekiang Provincial Library, Hangchow.

Ming shih 明史 (History of the Ming). 1974. Compiled by Chang T'ing-yü 張廷玉 (1672–1755). Beijing: Chung-hua shu-chü.

Mintum, Leigh. 1993. *Sita's Daughters: Coming Out of Purdah.* Oxford: Oxford University Press.

Mironov, N. D. 1927. "Buddhist Miscellanea" 241–79. *The Journal of the Royal Asiatic Society of Great Brittain and Ireland* (April, 1927).

Mochizuki Shinkō 望月信亨. 1946. *Bukkyō kyōten seiritsu shiron* 佛教教典成立史論 (On the History of the Establishment of Buddhist Canon). Kyoto: Hōzōkan.

——, editor. 1954–1963. *Bukkyō daijiten* 佛教大辭典 (Great Buddhist Dictionary), 10 vols. Tokyo: Seikai Seiten Kankō Kyōkai.

Monnika Eleanor. 1996. *Angkor Wat: Time, Space and Kingship.* Honolulu: Hawaii University Press.

Murase, Miyeko. 1971. "Kuan-yin as Savior of Men: Illustration of the Twenty-fifth Chapter of the *Lotus Sūtra* in Chinese Painting," *Artibus Asiae* 37(1–2):39–74.

Murcott, Susan. 1991. *The First Buddhist Women: Translations and Commentaries on the Therigāthā*. Berkeley: Parallax Press.

Nakamura Hajime. 1987. *Indian Buddhism: A Survey with Bibliographical Notes*. Delhi: Montilal Banarsidass.

Nan-hai Kuan-yin ch'uan-chuan 南海觀音全傳 (Complete Biography of Kuan-yin of the South Sea). n.d. Shuang-men-ti ku-ching-ko (copy kept in Beijing Library).

Nan-shih 南史 (History of the Southern Dynasties). 1974. By Li Yen-shou 李延壽 (fl. 618–678). Beijing: Chung-hua shu-chü.

Naquin, Susan. 1976. *Millenarian Rebellion in China: The Eight Trigrams Uprising of 1813*. New Haven: Yale University Press.

Naquin, Susan, and Chün-fang Yü, editors. 1992. *Pilgrims and Sacred Sites in China*. Berkeley: University of California Press.

Nattier, Jan. 1992. "The *Heart Sūtra*: A Chinese Apocryphal Text?" *The Journal of the International Association of Buddhist Studies* 15(2):153–223.

Needham, Joseph. 1956. *Science and Civilisation in China*, vol. 2. Cambridge: Cambridge University Press.

Nienhauser, William H., Jr., compiler and editor. 1986. *The Indian Companion to Tradtional Chinese Literature*. Bloomington: Indiana University Press.

Nü-jen ching 女人經 (Scripture on Women). 1982. Anonymous. Taipei: Ta-li ch'u-pan-she.

Ohnuma, Reiko. 1997. "Dehadana: The 'Gift of the Body' in Indian Buddhist Narrative Literature." Ph.D. dissertation, University of Michigan, Ann Arbor.

Omura Seigai 大村西崖. 1918. *Mikkyō hattatsu-shi* 密教發達史 (History of the Development of Esoteric Buddhism). Tokyo.

Overmyer, Daniel L. 1976. *Folk Buddhist Religion: Dissenting Sects in Late Traditional China*. Cambridge: Harvard University Press.

———. 1978. "Boatmen and Buddhas." *History of Religions* 17(3–4):284–302.

———. 1985. "Values in Chinese Sectarian Literature: Ming and Ch'ing *Pao-chüan*." In *Popular Culture in Late Imperial China*, edited by David Johnson, Andrew J. Nathan, and Evelyn S. Rawski, 219–54. Berkeley: University of California Press.

———. 1992. "Women in Chinese Religions: Submission, Struggle, Transcendence." In *From Benares to Beijing: Essays on Buddhism and Chinese Religion in Honor of Prof. Jan Yün-hua*, edited by Koichi Shinohara and Gregory Schopen, 91–120. Oakville, Ontario: Mosaic Press.

———. 1998. "History, Texts and Fieldwork: A Combined Approach to the Study of Chinese Religions." Paper delivered at the Workshop for the Study of Chinese Religions, Sun Moon Lake, Taiwan, July.

———. 1999. *Precious Volumes: An Introduction*. Cambridge, Mass.: Harvard University Press.

Pachow, W. 1987a. "Kuan-yin P'u-sa yü Ya-chou fo-chiao" 觀音菩薩與亞洲佛教 (Kuan-yin Bodhisattva and Asian Buddhism), *Chun-hua fo-hsüeh hsüeh-pao* 1(March):59–79.

——. 1987b. "The Omnipresence of Avalokiteshvara Buddhisattva in East Asia." *Chinese Culture Quarterly* 28(4; December):67–84.

Pai-i cheng-ch'eng pao-chüan 白衣成証寶卷 (The Precious Scroll of the Enlightenment of the White-robed One, or *Pai-i pao-chüan* 白衣寶卷, The Precious Scroll of the White-robed One). n.d. Hand-written copy kept at Chekiang Provincial Library, Hangchow.

Pai-kuo yin-yu 白國因由 (Origins of the Pai People). 1984. Ta-li, Yünnan: Ta-li Pai-tsu Tzu-chih-chou T'u-shu-kuan.

Pal, Pratapaditya. 1987. *Icons of Piety, Images of Whimsy. Asian Terra-cottas from the Walter-Grounds Collection.* Los Angeles: Los Angeles County Museum of Art.

Pan Liang-wen 潘亮文. 1996. "Suigetsu Kannon zu no tsuite no itchi kosatsu" 水月觀音圖の就の一考察 (An Investigation into the Paintings of Water-moon Kuan-yin). *Ars Buddhica* 224 (January):106–16; 225 (March):15–39.

Pao-ning Ssu Ming-tai shui-lu hua 保寧寺明代水陸畫 (Water-Land Paintings of the Pao-ning Temple). 1988. Beijing: Wen-wu ch'u-pan-she.

Pas, Julian. 1977. "The Kuan Wu-liang-shou-Fo Ching: Its Origin and Literary Criticism." In *Buddhist Thought and Asian Civilization*, edited by Leslie Kwamura and Keith Scott, 194–218. Emeryville, California: Dharma Publishing.

——. 1991. "The Human Gods of China: New Perspectives on the Chinese Pantheon." *From Benares to Beijing: Essays on Buddhism and Chinese Religion in Honor of Prof. Jan Yün-hua*, edited by Koichi Shinahara and Gregory Schopen, 129–60. Oakville: Mosaic Press.

——. 1995. *Visions of Sukhāvatī: Shan-tao's Commentary on the Kuan Wu-liang-shou-Fo Ching.* New York: State of New York University Press.

Paul, Diana Y. 1985. *Women in Buddhism: Images of the Feminine in the Mahāyāna Tradition.* Berkeley: University of California Press.

Pei-Ch'i shu 北齊書 (History of the Northern Ch'i). 1972. By Li Te-lin 李德林 (530–590) and Li Pai-yao 李百藥 (565–684). Beijing: Chung-hua shu chü.

Pei shi 北史 (History of the Northern Dynasties). 1974. By Li Yen-shou 李延壽 (fl 618–676). Beijing: Chung-hua shu-chü.

Poo, Mu-chou. 1995. "The Images of Immortals and Eminent Monks: Religious Mentality in Early Medieval China (4th–6th c. A.D.)" *Numen* 42:172–96.

Przyluski, P. 1923. "Les Vidyārāja, contribuion a l'etude de la magie dans les sectes Mahāyānistes." *Bulletin de l'Ecole Francaise d'Extreme Orient* 23:301–18.

P'u-ming ju-lai wu-wei liao-i pao-chüan 普明如來無為了義寶卷 (Tathāgata P'u-ming's Precious Scroll on Complete Revelation Through Non-action). 1994. In *Pao-chüan chü-chi*, vol. 4. Shensi: Jen-min ch'u-pan-she.

P'u-t'o pao-chüan 普陀寶卷 (Precious Scroll of P'u-t'o). 1894 edition. Private collection of Wu Hsiao-ling.

P'u-tu hsin-sheng chiu-k'u pao-chüan 普度新聲救苦寶卷 (The Precious Scroll of the New Gospel of Universal Salvation). Chekiang Provincial Library, Hangchow.

Ramanan, K. Venkata. 1966. *Nāgārjuna's Philosophy: As Presented in the Mahāprajñāpāramitāśāstra.* Delhi: Motilal Banarsidass.

Rawson, Jessica, editor. 1996. *Mysteries of Ancient China: New Discoveries from the Early Dynasties.* New York: George Braziller.

Ray, Reginald A. 1994. *Buddhist Saints in India: A Study in Buddhist Values and Orientations.* Oxford and New York: Oxford University Press.

Reed, Barbara E. 1992. "The Gender Symbolism of Kuan-yin Bodhisattva." In *Buddhism, Sexuality, and Gender,* edited by Jose Ignacio Cabezón, 159–80. Albany: The State University of New York Press.

Reis-Habito, Maria Dorothea. 1993. *Die Dhāraṇī des Großen Erbarmens des Bodhisattva Avalokiteśvara mit tausend Händen und Augen: Übersetzung und Untersuchung ihrer textlichen Grundlage sowie Erforschung ihres Kultes in China.* Nettetal: Steyler Verlag.

——. 1991. "The Repentance Ritual of the Thousand-armed Guanyin," *Studies in Central and East Asian Religions: Journal of the Seminar for Buddhist Studies.* Copenhagen & Aarhus. 4 (Autumn):42–51.

Robinet, Isabelle. 1997. *Taoism: Growth of a Religion,* translated by Phyllis Brooks. Stanford: Stanford University Press.

Robinson, Richard. 1978. *Early Mādhyamika in India and China.* New York: Samuel Weiser.

Robinson, Richard H., and Willard L. Johnson. 1997. *The Buddhist Religion: A Historical Introduction.* Belmont: Wadsworth.

Rudova, Maria L. 1993. "The Chinese Style Paintings from Khara Khoto." In *Lost Empire of the Silk Road: Buddhist Art from Khara Khoto (X–XIII Century),* edited by Mikhail Piotrovsky, 89–99. Electa, Milano: Thyssen-Bornemisza Foundation.

Ruegg, David Seyfort. 1981. *The Literature of the Mādhyamika School of Philosophy in India.* Wiesbaden: Otto Harrassowitz.

Saeki Tomi 佐伯富. 1961. "Kinsei Chūgoku ni okeru Kannon shinkō" 近世中國に於ける觀音信仰 (Kuan-yin Faith in Modern China). In *Tsukamoto Hakase Shoju Kinen Bukkyōshigaku Ronshu* 塚本博士頌寿紀念佛教史論集 372–89. Kyoto: Hozoken.

Said, Edward W. 1978. *Orientalism.* New York: Random House.

Sangren, P. Steven. 1983. "Female Gender in Chinese Religious Symbols: Kuan Yin, Ma Tsu, and the 'Eternal Mother.'" *Signs: Journal of Women in Culture and Society.* 9(11):4–25.

——. 1987. *History and Magical Power in A Chinese Community.* Stanford: Stanford University Press.

——. 1996. "Myths, Gods, and Family Relations." In *Unruly Gods,* edited by Meir Shahar and Robert P. Weller, 150–83. Honolulu: University of Hawaii Press.

Sankar, Andrea. 1978. "The Evolution of Sisterhood in Traditional Chinese Society: From Village Girls' Houses to Chai T'angs." Ph.D. dissertation, University of Michigan, Ann Arbor.

Saunders, E. Dale. 1960. *Mudra: A Study of Symbolic Gestures in Japanese Buddhist Sculpture.* Princeton: Princeton University Press.

Sawada Mizuho 澤田瑞穗. 1959. "Gyoran Kannon" 魚籃寶卷 (Fish-basket Kyan-yin). *Tenri daigaku gakuhō* 30:37–51.

——. 1975. *Zōhu hōkan no kenkyū* 增補寶卷の 研究 (A Study of Precious Scrolls, Revised and Expanded Edition). Tokyo: Kokusho kankokai.

Schafer, Edward H. 1959. "Parrots in Medieval China." In *Studia Serica Bernhard Karlgren Dedicata.* 271–82. Copenhagen.

——. 1963. *The Golden Peaches of Samarkand: A Study of T'ang Exotica.* Berkeley: University of California Press.

——. 1973. *The Divine Woman: Dragon Ladies and Rain Maidens in T'ang Literature.* Berkeley: University of California Press.

Schipper, K. M. 1965. *L'Empereur Wou des Han dans la legende Taoiste: Han Wou-ti nei-tchouen.* Paris.

Schopen, Gregory. 1987. "The Inscription on the Kusan Image of Amitābha and the Character of the Early Mahāyāna in India" *Journal of the International Association of Buddhist Studies* 10:99–138.

——. 1997. *Bones, Stones, and Buddhist Monks: Collected Papers on the Archaeology, Epigraphy, and Texts of Monastic Buddhism in India.* Honolulu: University of Hawaii Press.

Seidel, Anna. 1989–1990. "Chronicle of Taoist Studies in the West 1950–1990" *Cahiers d'Extrême-Asie,* 5:223–347.

Seijin 成尋. *San Tendai Godaisan ki* 參天台五台山記 (Record of Making A Pilgrimage to Mt. T'ien-t'ai and Mt. Wu-t'ai). 1972. In *Dainihon Bukkyō zenshu* 大日本佛教全書, compiled by the Suzuki Research Foundation, vol. 72, 238–302. Tokyo: Kodansha.

Shahar, Meir. 1992. "Fiction and Religion in the Early History of the Chinese God Jigong." Ph.D. dissertation, Harvard University, Cambridge.

——. 1994. "Enlightened Monk or Arch-Magician: The Portrayal of the God Jigong in the Sixteenth-Century Novel *Jidian yulu.*" In *Min-chien Hsin-yang yü Chung-kuo Wen-hua Kuo-chi Yen-t'ao-hui Lun-wen chi* 民間信仰與中國文化國際研討會論文集 (Proceedings of the International Conference on Popular Beliefs and Chinese Culture), 1:251–303. Taipei: Han-hsüeh yen-chiu chung-hsin.

——. 1996. "Vernacular Fiction and the Transmission of Gods' Cults in Late Imperial China." In *Unruly Gods,* edited by Meir Shahar and Robert P. Weller, 184–211. Honolulu: University of Hawaii Press.

——. 1998. *Crazy Ji: Chinese Religion and Popular Literature.* Cambridge, Mass.: Harvard University Press.

Shahar, Meir, and Robert P. Weller, editors. 1996. *Unruly Gods.* Honolulu: University of Hawaii Press.

Shansi Bureau of Cultural Artifacts and Chinese Historical Museum. *Ying-hsien mu-t'a Liao-tai mi-tsang* 應縣木塔遼代密藏 (Secret Treasures of the Liao Dynasty

Hidden Inside the Wooden Pagoda of Ying County). 1991. Beijing: Wen-wu ch'u-pan-she.

Shansi fo-chiao ts'ai-su 山西佛教彩塑 (Buddhist Sculpture of Shanxi Province). 1991. Hong Kong: Buddhist Culture Publishing.

Shan-ts'ai Lung-nü pao-chüan 善財龍女寶卷 (The Precious Scroll of Sudhana and the Dragon Princess). n.d. Hand-written copy, private collection of Wu Hsiao-ling.

Sharf, Robert H. 1991. "The *Treasure Store Treatise* (Pao-tsang Lun) and the Sinification of Buddhism in Eighth-Century China." Ph.D. dissertation, University of Michigan, Ann Arbor.

Shek, Richard. 1980. "Religion and Society in Late Ming: Sectarianism and Popular Thought in Sixteenth and Seventeenth Century China." Ph.D. dissertation University of California, Berkeley.

Shiba, Yoshinobu. 1977. "Ningpo and Its Hinterland." In *The City in Late Imperial China*, edited by G. William Skinner, 396–439. Stanford: Stanford University Press.

Shih P'ing-ting 施萍亭. 1987. "Tun-huang sui-pi chih san—i-chien wan-cheng te she-hui feng-su-shih tzu-liao" 敦煌隨筆之三：一件完整的社會風俗史資料 (The Third Jottings on Tun-huang: A Complete Document about the History of Social Customs). *Tun-huang yen-chiu* 2:34–37.

Shih Wei-hsiang 史葦湘. 1989. "Tsai-lun ch'an-sheng Tun-huang fo-chiao i-shu shen-mei te she-hui yin-su" 再論產生敦煌佛教藝術審美的社會因素 (Further Discussions on the Social Factors Which Produced the Esthetics of Buddhist Art in Tun-huang). *Tun-huang yen-chiu* 1:1–8.

Shioiri Ryōdō 鹽入良道. 1964. "Chūgoku Bukkyō ni okeru raizan to butsumyo kyoten" 中國佛教に於ける禮懺と佛名經典 (Scriptures on Repentance Rituals and Buddha's Names in Chinese Buddhism). In *Yuki kyoju kiju kinen Bukkyō shisoshi ronshu* 由木教授喜壽紀念佛教思想史論叢, 569–90. Tokyo: Daizo Shuppan.

Snellgrove, David. 1986. "Celestial Buddhas and Bodhisattvas." In *The Encyclopedia of Religion*, edited by Mircea Eliade, vol. 3, 134–43. New York: Macmillan.

——. 1987. *Indo-Tibetan Buddhism: Indian Buddhists and Their Tibetan Successors*, 2 vols. Boston: Shambhala.

Soper, Alexander C. 1948. "Hsiang-kuo Ssu: An Imperial Temple of Northern Sung." *Journal of the American Oriental Society* 68(1):19–45.

——. 1949–1950. "Aspects of Light Symbolism in Gandharan Sculpture," *Artibus Asiae* 12(3):252–83; 12(4):314–30; 13(1, 2):63–85.

——. 1960. "A Vacation Glimpse of the T'ang Temples of Ch'ang-an: *Ssu T'a chi* by Tuan Ch'eng-shih." *Artibus Asiae* 23(1):15–40.

Sørenson, Henrik H. 1991–1992. "Typology and Iconography in the Esoteric Buddhist Art of Dunhuang," *Journal of Silk Road Studies* 2:285–349.

Soymié, Michel. 1965. "*Ketsubonkyō* no shiryoteki kenkyū 血盆經の 史料的研究 (A Study on the Historical Sources for the Sūtra of the Blood Bowl)." *Dokyō kenkyū* 1(December):109–66.

Stein, Rolf A. 1986. "Avalokiteśvara/Kouan-yin, un exemple de transformation d'un dieu en deesse," *Cahiers d'Êxtreme-Asie* 2:17–77.

Stevenson, Daniel B. 1986. "The Four Kinds of Samādhi in Early T'ien-t'ai Buddhism." In *Traditions of Meditation in Chinese Buddhism*, edited by Peter N. Gregory, 45–97. Honolulu: University of Hawaii Press.

——. 1987. "The T'ien-t'ai Four Forms of Samādhi and Late North-South Dynasties, Sui, and Early T'ang Buddhist Devotionalsim." Ph.D. dissertation, Columbia University, New York.

Strickmann, Michel. 1977. "The Mao-shan Revelations: Taoism and the Aristocracy." *T'oung Pao* 64:1–64.

——. 1990. "The Consecration Sūtra: A Buddhist Book of Spells." In *Chinese Buddhist Apocrypha*, edited by Robert E. Buswell, Jr., 75–118. Honolulu: University of Hawaii Press.

——. 1996. *Mantras et Mandarins: Le Bouddhism Tantrique en Chine*. Paris: Gallimard.

Sueki Fumihito 末木文美士. 1986a. "*Kan Muryojukyō* no shohon ni tsuite" 觀無量壽經の 諸本について (On the Various Versions of the *Visualization Sūtra*). *Tōyō Bunka* 66.

——. 1986b. "*Kan Muryojukyō* kenkyū" 觀無量壽經研究 (Studies on the *Visualization Sūtra*). *Tōyō Bunka Kenkyūsho Kiyo* 東洋文化研究所記要 101.

Sui shu 隋書 (History of the Sui). 1973. By Wei Cheng 魏徵 (580–643). Beijing: Chung-hua shu-chü.

Sun Chang-wu 孫昌武. 1996. *Chung-kuo wen-hsüeh chung te Wei-mo yü Kuan-yin* 中國文學中的維摩與觀音 (Vimalakīrti and Kuan-yin in Chinese Literature). Beijing: Kao-teng chiao-yü ch'u-pan-che.

Sun Hsiu-shen 孫修身. 1987. "Tun-huang pi-hua chung te *Fa-hua ching Kuan-yin p'u-men p'in* t'an-t'ao" 敦煌壁畫中的法華經觀音 普門品探討 (Investigation of the "Universal Gate of Kuan-yin Bodhisattva" Chapter of the *Lotus Sūtra* among the Frescoes of Tun-huang). *Ssu-lu lun-t'an* 1:61–69.

Sunday, Peggy Reeves. 1986. *Divine Hunger: Cannibalism as A Cultural System.* Cambridge: Cambridge University Press.

Sung Kuang-yü 宋光宇. 1983. *T'ien-tao kou-ch'en* 天道鈎沈 (Fishing for the Sunken Way of Heaven). Taipei: Yuan-yu Ch'u-pan-she.

Sung Lien 宋濂. *Sung Hsüeh-shih wen-chi* 宋學士文集 (Collection of Writings by Scholar Sung). 1968. In *Kuo-hsüeh chi-pen ts'ung-shu* 國學基本叢書, vol 303–4. Taipei.

Sung shih 宋史 (History of the Sung). 1974. By Tuotuo 脱脱 (Toghto, 1313–1355). Beijing: Chung-hua shu-chü.

T'ai-p'ing kuang-chi 太平廣記 (Extended Record Compiled in the Tai-p'ing Era). 1961. Compiled by Li Fang 李昉 (925–996), 5 vols. Beijing: Chung-hua shu-chü.

T'ai-p'ing yü-lan 太平御覽 (Compilation of the T'ai-p'ing Era for Imperial Viewing). 1591. Compiled by Li Fang 李昉 (925–996), 12 vols. Taipei: Wen-hsing shu-chü.

T'ai-shan chih 泰山志 (Gazetteer of Mt. T'ai). 1802.

T'ai-shan shih-wang pao-chüan 泰山十王寶卷 (The Precious Scroll of the Ten Kings of Mt. T'ai). 1921. Peking. reprint.

Takakusu, J., translator. 1969. *The Amitāyur-dhyāna-Sūtra.* In *Buddhist Mahāyāna Texts.* New York: Dover, reprint.

Tambiah, Stanley J. 1982. "Famous Buddha Images and the Legitimating of Kings," *Res* (4):5–19.

Tang Changshou, 1997. "Shiziwan Cliff Tomb No. 1," *Orientations* 9 (September):72–77.

Ta-tsu shih-k'e yen-chiu 大足石刻研究 (Studies on the Stone Sculpture at Ta-tsu). 1985. Edited by Liu Ch'ang-chin 劉長久, Hu Wen-ho 胡文和, and Li Yung-ch'iao 李永翹. Ch'ung-tu: Szechwan Academy of Social Sciences Press.

Tay, C. N. 1976. "Kuan-yin: The Cult of Half Asia," *History of Religions* 16(2):147–77. Reissued separately, 1987, as book with the same title in English and Chinese. Taipei: Wisdom Torch.

Teiser, Stephen F. 1988. *The Ghost Festival in China.* Princeton: Princeton University Press.

——. 1994. *The Scripture on the Ten Kings and the Making of Purgatory in Medieval Chinese Buddhism.* Honolulu: University of Hawaii Press.

Teng Ssu-yü. 1968. *Family Instructions for the Yen Clan.* Leiden: E. J. Brill.

ter Haar, Barend J. 1992. *The White Lotus Teachings in Chinese Religious History.* Leiden: E. J. Brill.

Thurman, Robert A. F., translator. 1976. *The Holy Teaching of Vimalakīrti, A Mahāyāna Scripture.* University Park: Pennsylvania State University Press.

T'ien Ju-k'ang. 1988. *Male Anxiety and Female Chastity.* Leiden: E. J. Brill.

T'i-lan chüan 提籃卷 (Lifting the Basket Scroll). 1891. Hand-written copy, Peking University Library.

Tokuno, Kyoko. 1990. "The Evaluation of Indigenous Scriptures in Chinese Buddhist Bibliographical Catalogues." In *Chinese Buddhist Apocrypha*, edited by Robert E. Buswell, Jr., 31–74. Honolulu: University of Hawaii Press.

Topley, Marjorie. 1954. "Chinese Women's Vegetarian Houses in Singapore." *Journal of the Malayan Branch of the Royal Asiastic Society* 27:51–67.

——. 1958. "The Organization and Social Function of Chinese Women's Chai-t'ang in Singapore." Ph.D. dissertation, University of London, London.

——. 1963. "The Great Way of Former Heaven: A Group of Chinese Secret Religious Sects." *Bulletin of the School of Oriental and African Studies* 26:362–92.

——. 1968. "Notes on Some Vegetarian Halls in Hong Kong Belonging to the Sect of the Hsien-t'ien Tao: The Way of Former Heaven." *Journal of Royal Asiatic Society Hong Kong Branch* 8:135–48.

——. 1975. "Marriage Resistance in Rural Kwantung." In *Women in Chinese Society*, edited by Margery Wolf and Roxane Witke, 67–88. Stanford: Stanford University Press.

Toshio Ebine 海光根敏郎. 1986. "Chinese Avalokiteśvara Paintings of the Song and

Yuan Periods." In *The Art of Bodhisattva Avalokiteśvara—Its Cult-images and Narrative Portrayals.* International Symposium on Art Historical Studies 5:94–100. Osaka: Department of the Science of Arts, Faculty of Letters, Osaka University.

Tsai, Kathryn Ann, translator. 1994. *Lives of the Nuns: Biographies of Chinese Buddhist Nuns from the Fourth to Sixth Centuries.* Honolulu: University of Hawaii Press.

Tsao Shih-p'ang 曹仕邦. 1990. *Chung-kuo fo-chiao i-ching shih lun-chi* 中國佛教譯經史論集 (Collected Essays on the History of Buddhist Sūtra Translation in China) Taipai: Tung-chu ch'u-pan-she.

Tsao Tan 曹丹 and Chao Ling 趙玲. 1994. "An-yüeh Pi-lu Tung shih-ku tiao-ch'a yen-chiu" 安岳毗盧洞石窟調察研究 (Investigative Research on the Stone Sculptures of the Pi-lu Cave of An-yüeh). *Szechwan wen-wu* 3:34–39.

Tsukamoto Zenryū 塚本善隆. 1955. "Kinsei Shina taishū no nyoshin Kannon shinkō" 近世支那大眾の 女身觀音信仰 (Popular Cult of the Feminine Kuan-yin in China During Recent Times). In *Yamaguchi Hakase Kanreki Kinen Indogaku Bukkyōgaku Ronsō* 山崎博士還曆記念印度學 佛教學論叢 (Essays in Indian Studies and Buddhist Studies in Honor of Dr. Yamaguchi's Sixtieth Birthday), 262–80. Kyoto: Hōzōkan.

——. 1985. *A History of Early Chinese Buddhism: From Its Introduction to the Death of Hui-yuan*, vol. 1, translated by Leon Hurvitz. Tokyo: Kodansha International.

Tsukinowa Kenryū 月輪賢隆. 1971. *Butten no hihanteki kenkyū* 佛典の 批判的研究 (Critical Studies on the Buddhist Scriptures). Tokyo: Hyakka-en.

Tu Kuang-ting 杜光庭. 1976a. *Tao-chiao ling-yen chi* 道教靈驗記 (Efficacious Manifestations in Taoism). In *Cheng-t'ung Tao-tsang* 正統道藏. Taipei: I-wen, reprint.

——. 1976b. *Yung-ch'eng chi hsien lu* 墉城集仙錄 (A Record of the Assembled Transcendants of the Fortified and Walled City). In *Cheng-t'ung Tao-tsang*, vol. 38. Taipei: I-wen, reprint.

Tu Wei-ming, 1989. "The Continuity of Being: Chinese Visions of Nature." In *Nature in Asian Traditions of Thought: Essays in Environmental Philosophy*, edited by J. Baird Callicott and Roger T. Ames, 67–68. Albany: State of University of New York Press.

Tucci, G. 1948. "Buddhist Notes, I: Àpropos Avalokiteśvara." *Melanges Chinois et bouddhique* 9:173–219.

——. 1958. *Minor Buddhist Texts*, part II. Rome: Instituto Italiano per il Medio ed Estremo Oriente.

Tulku Thondup Rinpoche. 1986. *Hidden Teachings of Tibet: An Expanation of the Terma Tradition of the Nyingma School of Buddhism*, edited by Harold Talbott. London: Wisdom.

Turner, Victor W. 1969. *The Ritual Process: Structure and Anti-structure.* London: Routledge & Kegan Paul.

——. 1973. "The Center Out There: Pilgrim's Goal." *History of Religions* 12:191–230.

——. 1974. "Pilgrimages as Social Processes." In *Dramas, Fields, and Metaphors*, edited by Victor Turner, 166–230. Ithaca: Cornell University Press.

Vander-Nicholas, Nicole, et al., editors. 1974, 1976. *Banniers et peintures de Touen-houang conservées au Musée Guimet*, vols. 14 and 15. Paris: Mission Paul Pelliot.

Verellen, Franciscus. 1992. "'Evidential Miracles in Support of Taoism': The Inversion of A Buddhist Apologetic Tradition in Late Tang China." *T'oung Pao* 78:218–63.

Waley, Arthur. 1931. *Catalogue of Paintings Recovered from Tun-huang by Sir Aurel Stien.* London: British Museum and Government of India.

Waltner, Ann. 1987. "T'an-yang-tzu and Wang Shih-chen: Visionary and Bureaucrat in the Late Ming." *Late Imperial China* 8(1):105–27.

Wang Ch'ing-cheng 汪慶正. 1973. "Chi wen-hsüeh hsi-chü ho pan-hua shi shang te i-tz'u chung-yao fa-hsien 記文學戲曲和版畫史上的一次重要發現 (On An Important Discovery in the History of Literature, Drama and Woodblock Printing)." *Wen-wu* 11:58–67.

Wang Ch'ung-wen 王重文, et al. 1957. *Tun-huang pien-wen chi* 敦煌變文集 (Collections of Transformation Texts from Tun-huang). 2 vols. Peking.

Wang Hui-min 王惠民. 1987. "Tun-huan Shui-yüeh Kuan-yin hsiang" 敦煌水月觀音像 (Images of Water-moon Kuan-yin in Tun-huang). *Tun-huang yen-chiu* 1:31–38.

Wang Kuang-kao 王光鎬, editor. 1994. *Ming-tai Kuan-yin Tien ts'ai-su* 明代觀音殿彩塑 (Kuan-yin Hall of Ming Dynasty). Taipei: I-shu t'u-shu kung-ssu.

Wang-Toutain, Françoise. 1994. "Une peinture de Dunhuang conservée a la Bibliothéque Nationale de France." *Arts Asiatiques* 49:53–69.

Warder, A. K. 1970. *Indian Buddhism.* New Delhi: Motial Banarsidass.

Watson, Burton, translator. 1993. *The Lotus Sūtra.* New York: Columbia University Press.

Watson, William, editor. 1984. *Chinese Ivories from the Shang to the Qing.* London: Oriental Ceramic Society.

Watters, Thomas, translator. 1905. *On Yuan Chwang's Travels in India*, 2 vols. New York: AMS Press. Reprinted in 1971.

Weidner, Marsha, editor. 1994. *Latter Days of the Law: Images of Chinese Buddhism, 850–1850.* Lawrence: Spencer Museum of Art, University of Kansas, in association with University of Hawaii Press.

Weinstein, Stanley. 1987. *Buddhism Under the T'ang.* Cambridge: Cambridge University Press.

Wei shu 魏書 (History of the Wei). 1974. By Wei Shou 魏收 (506–572). Beijing: Chung-hua shu-chü.

Welch, Holmes. 1967. *The Practice of Chinese Buddhism, 1900–1950.* Cambridge, Mass.: Harvard University Press.

Wen-yüan ying-hua 文苑英華 (The Most Excellent Flowers from the Garden of

Literature). 1967. Compiled by P'eng Shu-hsia 彭叔夏, 20 vols. Taipei: Hua-wen shu-chü.

Whitfield, Roderick, and Anne Farrer. 1990. *Caves of the Thousand Buddhas: Chinese Art from the Silk Route*. London: British Museum.

Winternitz, Maurice. 1927. *History of Indian Literature*, 2 vols. Calcutta: University of Calcutta Press.

Wood, Donald. 1985. "Eleven Faces of the Bodhisattva." Ph.D. disseration, University of Kansas, Lawrence.

Wu Hung. 1986. "Buddhist Elements in Early Chinese Art (2nd & 3rd Centuries A.D.)." *Artibus Asiae* 47(3–4):263–352.

——. 1989. *The Wu Liang Shrine: The Ideology of Early Chinese Pictorial Art*. Stanford: Stanford University Press.

——. 1995. *Monumentality in Early Chinese Art and Architecture*. Stanford: Stanford University Press.

Wu, Pei-yi. 1992. "An Ambivalent Pilgrim to T'ai Shan in the Seventeenth Century." In *Pilgrims and Sacred Sites in China*, edited by Susan Naquin and Chün-fang Yü, 65–88. Berkeley: University of California Press.

Wu-shan pao-chüan 五山寶卷 (The Precious Scroll of the Five Mountains). n.d. Hand-written copy, private collection of Li shih-yü.

Yabuki Keiki 矢吹慶輝. 1927. *Sangaikyō no kenkyū* 三階教の 研究 (Studies on the School of Three Stages). Tokyo: Iwanami shoten.

——. 1930. *Meisha yoin* 鳴沙餘韻 (Echoes of the Singing Sands). Tokyo: Iwanami shoten.

——. 1933. *Meisha yoin kaisetsu* 鳴沙餘韻解説 (Rare and Unknown Chinese Manuscript Remains of Buddhist Literature Discovered in Tun-huang Collected by Sir Aurel Stein and Preserved in the British Museum). Tokyo: Iwanami shoten.

Yamada Meiji 山田明治. 1976. "Kangyō kō: Muryōju-butsu to Amida-butsu" 観經考：無量壽佛と阿彌陀佛 (Investigating the *Visualization Sūtra*: Amitāyus Buddha and the Amitābha Buddha). *Ryūkoku daigaku ronshū* 408:76–95.

Yamamoto Yōko 山本陽子. 1989. "Suigetsu Kannon zu no seiritsu ni kansuru itchi kosa" 水月観音圖の 成立に関する 一考察 (An Investigation about the Formation of the Moon and Water Kuan-yin Image) *Bijutsushi* 38(1):28–37.

Yanagida Seizan 柳田聖山 (with Kajitani Soni 梶谷宗忍 and Tsujimura Koichi 辻村公一). 1974. *Shinjinmei, Shōdoka, Jūgyūzu, Zazengi* 信心銘，証道歌，十牛圖，坐禪儀 (Inscription on the Believing Mind, Song of Realizing the Way, Ten Ox Herding Pictures, and the Rules for Sitting Meditation). Tokyo.

Yang, C. K. 1961. *Religion in Chinese Society*. Berkeley: University of California Press.

Yang Tseng-wen 楊曾文. 1985. "Kuan-shih-yin hsin-yang te ch'uan-ju ho liu-hsing" 觀世音信仰的傳入和流行 (The Introduction and Spread of the Belief in Kuan-shih-yin). *Shih-chieh tsung-chiao yen-chiu* 3:21–33.

Yao, Tao-chung. 1980. "Ch'uan-chen: A New Taoist Sect in North China during the

Twelveth and Thirteenth Centuries." Ph.D. dissertation, University of Arizona, Tucson.

Yen Chüan-yin 顏娟英. 1987. "Wu Tze-t'ien yü T'ang Ch'ang-an Ch'i-pao-t'ai shih-tiao fo-hsiang" 武則天與唐長安七寶台石塑佛像 (Wu Tze-t'ien and the Stone Buddhist Sculptures at the Seven Treasure Terrace of Ch'ang-an in the T'ang). *I-shu hsüeh* 1:41–89.

Ying-ke pao-chüan 鸚哥寶卷 (The Precious Scroll of the Parrot). n.d. Hand-written copy, Beijing University Library, Beijing.

Yoshida, Mayumi. 1998. "Politics and Virtue: The Political and Personal Facets of the *Neixun*." Ph.D. dissertation, University of California, Berkeley.

Yoshioka Yoshitoyo 吉岡義豐. 1971. "Kenryuban Kozan Hōken kaisetsu 乾隆版香山寶卷解說 (The Precious Scroll of Hsiang-shan of the Ch'ien-lung Edition, Explained). *Dokyō kenkyū* 4:115–95.

Young, Katherine K. 1991. "Goddesses, Feminists, and Scholars." *The Annual Review of Women in World Religions.* Albany: State of New York University Press 1:105–79.

Yu, Anthony C., translator and editor. 1977–83. *Journey to the West*, 4 vols. Chicago: University of Chicago Press.

Yü Cheng-hsieh 俞正燮. 1957. *Kuei-ssu lei-kao* 癸巳類稿 (Essays Written in the Year Kuei-ssu [1833]). Shanghai: Shang-wu ch'u-pan-she, reprint.

Yü, Chün-fang 于君方. 1981. *The Renewal of Buddhism in China: Chu-hung and the Late Ming Synthesis.* New York: Columbia University Press.

——. 1989. "Ch'an Education in the Sung: Ideals and Procedures." In *Neo-Confucian Education: The Formative Stage*, edited by Wm. Theodore de Bary and John W. Chaffee, 57–104. New York: Columbia University Press.

——. 1989. "Kuan-yin Pilgvimage" Videotape. New York: R. G. Video.

——. 1991. "Der Guanyin-Kult in Yunnan." In *Der Goldschatz der Drei Pagoden*, edited by Albert Lutz, 28–29. Zurich: Museum Rietberg.

——, editor. 1994. *The Ultimate Realm: A New Understanding of Cosmos and Life.* Taipei: Ti Chiao ch'u-pan-she.

——. 1998. "Buddhism in the Ming." In *Cambridge History of China*, edited by Frederick Mote and Denis Twitchett, 893–952. Cambridge: Cambridge University Press.

Yü Sung-ch'ing 喻松青. 1993. "Ch'ing-tai *Kuan-yin chi-tu pen-yüan chen-ching* yen-chiu" 清代觀音濟度本願真經研究 (Studies on the *True Scripture of Kuan-yin's Original Vow of Universal Salvation* of the Ch'ing). In *Ch'ing-shih lun-ts'ung* 清史論叢, 116–24. Liao-ning: Ku-chi ch'u-pan-she.

Yüan shih 元史 (History of the Yüan). 1976. By Sung Lien 宋濂 (1310–1381). Beijing: Chung-hua shu-chü.

Yüan Shu-kuang 袁曙光. 1991. "Cheng-tu Wan-fo-sse ch'u-tu te Liang tai shih-k'e tsao-hsiang" 成都萬佛寺出土的梁代石刻造像 (Carved Stone Statues of the Liang Dynasty Excavated from the Ten-thousand Buddha Temple of Ch'eng-tu). *Szechwan wen-wu* 3:27–32.

Yü-chia yen-k'ou shih-shih yao-chi 瑜伽焰口施食要集 (Essentials for the Yoga of Bestowing Food to Feed Hungry Ghosts). 1980. Originally compiled by I-yü Ting-yen 一雨定庵 in 1693. Taipei: Fo-chiao ch'u-pan-she. Reprint.

Yü Erh Fo 魚兒佛 (Fish Buddha). In *Sheng Ming tsa-chü* 盛明雜劇, 2nd collection.

Yü-lan pao-chüan 魚籃寶卷 (The Precious Scroll of the Fish Basket). 1919. Shanghai: I-hua-t'ang shu-fang.

Ziegler, Harumi Hirano. 1994. "The *Avalokiteśvarasamādhi-Sūtra Spoken by the Buddha*: An Indigenous Chinese Buddhist Scripture." Master's thesis, University of California, Los Angeles.

Zürcher, Eric. 1959. *The Buddhist Conquest of China: The Spread and Adaptation of Buddhism in Early Medieval China.* Leiden: E. J. Brill. Reprinted 1972. 2 vols.

——. 1977. "Late Han Vernacular Elements in the Earliest Buddhist Translations." *Journal of the Chinese Language Teachers Association* 12(3):177–203.

——. 1980. "Buddhist Influence in Early Taoism." *T'oung Pao.* 66:84–147.

——. 1982. "Prince Moonlight." *T'oung Pao* 68(1–3):1–75.

——. 1991. "A New Look at the Earliest Chinese Buddhist Texts." In *From Benares to Beijing: Essays on Buddhism and Chinese Religion in Honour of Prof. Jan Yün-hua,* edited by Koichi Shinohara and Gregory Schopen, 277–304. Oakville, Canada: Mosaic Press.

Zwalf, W. ed. 1985. *Buddhism: Art and Faith.* London: British Museum.

Index and Glossary

4–5, 6, 9–10, 15–21, 26, 33, 195, 305, 311, 346, 489–92; and Confucianism, 5, 19, 101, 271, 333, 493; cult of the saints in, 198; and divine kingship, 3–4; domestication of, 5–6, 15, 21, 141; early, 2, 16; esoteric, 19, 23, 48–49, 65–67, 379; feminism in, 1, 2; and filial piety, 466–67; gender in, 414–19; goddesses in, 20, 408, 411, 478; of Han period, 4–5; Hīnayāna, 416; and Hinduism, 3, 7, 356; Hua-yen (Kegon), 5, 18, 19, 32, 276; in India, 3, 198, 312; and indigenous religions, 3, 408; and *kan-ying* theory, 155; lay, 25, 305–12, 307–8, 309, 320, 332, 337, 537n17; localization of, 21, 262; Maitreyan, 453; in Ming period, 337, 340, 378; models of, 198; monastic, 20; Newar, 511n4; and pilgrimages, 404; popular *vs.* elite, 22; rituals of, 197, 205, 206, 209; schools of, 5, 18, 19–20, 33; and sectarian religions, 431, 450, 454–55, 460, 462, 474–76; Shingon, 49; of Sui period, 18, 306; of Sung period, 185, 251, 277, 279, 288, 310, 337, 339; of T'ang period, 18, 20, 206, 215, 268, 277, 306, 311; and Taoism, 5, 18, 19, 21, 221, 239, 242, 311, 359, 370, 371, 474, 526n7, 529n8; Theravāda, 100, 198; Tibetan, 100, 143–44, 323, 416–17; Vajrayāna, 2, 4, 198, 416; and visualization, 519n17, 520n19; in the West, 1–2; women in, 20, 21, 25, 309, 481–85; of Yüan period, 143–44, 337. *See also* Ch'an (Zen) Buddhism; Mahāyāna Buddhism; Pure Land (Jōdo) Buddhism; Tantric Buddhism; T'ien-t'ai (Tendai) Buddhism

Burma, 3

Buswell, Robert, 95

Cabezón, Jose Ignacio, 414–15, 416

Cahill, Suzanne, 310, 480

cakravartin (universal monarch), 36, 45, 66, 120

Cambodia, 3–4, 75

Campany, Robert, 23, 24, 155, 158, 193, 515n17, 526n4

Cantarella, Eva, 415

Cave of Brahmā's Voice. *See* Fan-yin Tung

Cave of Reverting to the Origin (Ch'ao-yüan Tung), 464

Cave of Tidal Sounds. *See* Ch'ao-yin Tung

Central Asia, 15, 19, 40, 43, 99

Ceylon, 4

Chai Feng-ta 翟奉達, 233, 529n3

chai-t'ang 齋堂 (vegetarian houses), 335, 494

Champa kingdom (Vietnam), 3

ch'an 懺 (performing penances), 205

ch'an 讖 (prognostication), 101

Ch'an 禪 (Zen) Buddhism, 5, 18, 138, 548n10; forms of Kuan-yin in, 127, 233, 251, 361, 407, 418, 420, 433, 434, 488; gender in, 417, 482; and inner alchemy, 462; modern, 167; monks of, 187–88, 197, 200, 206, 237, 295, 318, 535n1; poems of, 209, 421; and P'u-t'o, 361, 386, 388, 393, 400, 404–5; and repentance rites, 263, 275, 288; schools of, 19, 21, 386, 527n10; and sectarian religions, 453, 459; in Sung period, 185, 251, 277; and sūtras, 32, 143, 185; in T'ang period, 20; teachings of, 279, 319; and women, 482, 483, 484, 485, 491

Ch'an Chiao ho-i 禪教合一 (combining Teaching and Ch'an schools), 19

Ch'an Ching ho-i 禪淨合一 (combining Ch'an and Pure Land schools), 19

Ch'an Hall of Wonderful Enlightenment (Monastery for National Protection), 303

ch'an-chu 懺主 (master of repentance), 263

Chandra, Lokesh, 520nn18,19

Chang, Cornelius, 239, 251

Chang Chao 張照, 331

Chang Chi-ch'ang 張季常, 202

Chang Chiu-ch'eng 張九成, 544n19

Chang Hsün 張珣, 350

Chang Jung 張融, 19, 161

Chang Liang 張良, 160

Chang Seng-yao 張僧繇, 202, 203

Chang Shang-ying 張商英 (Chang Wu-chin), 380, 387, 433, 549n14